THE ECSTASY OF DEFEAT

Sports Reporting At Its Finest From The Editors Of *The Onion*

HYPERION

NEW YORK

THE ECSTASY OF DEFEAT

Sports Reporting At Its Finest
From The Editors Of *The Onion*

EDITOR
John Krewson

ASSOCIATE EDITOR
Seth Reiss

WRITERS
Mike DiCenzo, Geoff Haggerty, Brian Janosch, Dan Klein,
John Krewson, Chad Nackers, Seth Reiss, Jack Steuf

EDITORIAL MANAGER
Kate Palmer

EDITORIAL COORDINATOR
Brian Janosch

EDITORIAL ASSISTANT
Ben Berkley

COVER DESIGN & ART DIRECTION
Colin Tierney

LEAD DESIGNER
Sarah Schumacher

DESIGNERS
Rozanne Gelbinovich, Erin McLaughlin, Aofie Mooney,
Scott A. Rosenberg, Houston Ruck

GRAPHICS EDITORS
Craig Cannon, Michael Faisca, Nick Gallo,
Mike Loew, Chad Nackers, Jenny Nellis

COPY EDITOR
Danny Mulligan

INTERNS
Signe Bruster, Marty Cramer, Sam Dean, Leslie Feinberg, Ali Moran,
Matt Powers, Scott F. Rosenfeld, Caroline Tan, Seena Vali

The material in this work previously appeared in *The Onion*.

Images provided by Getty Images, Newscom, and *The Onion*.

Library of Congress Cataloging-in-Publication Data

The Ecstasy of Defeat : Sports Reporting at Its Finest From the Editors of The Onion / The Editors of The Onion. -- 1st ed.
    p. cm.
ISBN 978-1-4013-1072-1
1. Sports--Humor. I. Onion (Madison, Wis.)
PN6231.S65E27 2011
796.02'07--dc23
                            2011027804

Hyperion books are available for special promotions and premiums. For details contact the HarperCollins Special Markets Department in the New York office at 212-207-7528, fax 212-207-7222, or email spsales@harpercollins.com.

FIRST EDITION

10   9   8   7   6   5   4   3   2   1

To HI MOM!

C O N T E N T S

THE ECSTASY OF DEFEAT

FOREWORD

by Anabolic Steroids

They say my days as a major player in the world of sports are numbered. They say my time has come and gone, a brief violent explosion of expanded human potential and shattered records, of strained connective tissue and ever-thicker necks, of towering home runs and unstoppable defensive linemen. And maybe they're right. Maybe my time on top is over. Well, if that's the case, I leave behind a legacy of accomplishment more impressive than anyone or anything in the history of sports. Period.

All-time home-run record? That's mine. Super Bowls? I've won so many I get them mixed up. Olympics? Please. NBA and PGA titles? Way more than you think. Tours de France? Ha! And those are just the highlights. I could name all the college championships, high school championships, horse races, and Little League World Series I've won throughout the years, but we don't have enough room here.

Not a bad career for a simple synthetic hormone with relatively humble aspirations.

So when *The Onion* approached me to write this foreword, I began to reflect on my overall contributions to the world of sports, and I realized I had accomplished something else: I saved sports journalism. Think about it. Who wants to read a tedious story about a key bunt in the bottom of the 4th inning? Or a profile about a guy who tried to come back from cancer but couldn't because his body was too weak. I sure as hell don't. Not only does that all sound pretty boring and downright depressing, but it certainly doesn't sound like anything that will sell newspapers.

And that's what I did for sports writing. I breathed new life into it. I made it fun and exciting. I tripled circulations and quadrupled readerships. People could finally turn to the sports page and read about larger-than-life figures doing things beyond anyone's wildest imagination. Professional sports had become like the movies.

Come on, two guys chasing the season record for home runs and saving the national pastime? A driven Texan coming back from a near-terminal illness to win the Tour de France? Eighty-five-year-old Yogi Berra being honored at Yankee Stadium and actually being able to stand? You can't make up stories that good. And, because of me, you didn't have to.

Flipping through this volume is like a timeline of my career in professional athletics. The number of articles in here that are solely about me is astounding. Every maudlin news story about tainted records and the sanctity of the game, as well as the "Does he or doesn't he deserve to be in the Hall of Fame?" bullshit pieces that people seem to eat up are all right here. And I have to say, it's compelling, page-turning stuff.

I know this may sound like egotism. But not acknowledging that over the last 15 years I've made sports worth watching, and sports journalism worth reading, is willful ignorance.

So, to the sports journalists at America's Finest News Source: You're welcome for another *New York Times* bestseller. And just for the record, I am already in the Hall of Fame. Every Hall of Fame. I've been inducted well over 300 times.

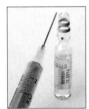

—Anabolic Steroids
San Francisco, April 15, 2011

THE ECSTASY OF DEFEAT

CHAPTER ONE:
FOOTBALL

Ah, football! The harbinger of autumn, the most popular masculine preoccupation of the majority of America's males, the only sport that anyone really cares about watching or following! Covering football is perhaps the most rewarding job a sportswriter can have—partially because nothing approaches the sport for sheer unpredictable intensity, for brutality and beauty, for ferocity and pageantry. But mostly, football is a coveted assignment for sportswriters because they can be assured that people actually care. Because in this sports-saturated day and age, the violent *pas de deux* of football actually engages people, even if those people only pay attention in order to be nauseated by the glorification of millionaire savages or the ever-increasing carnage on the field. Therefore, those who cover football earn that rarest of chances, that pearl beyond price, that most elusive of opportunities in the world of sports journalism: the possibility of having someone read your writing.

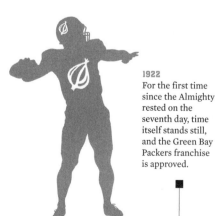

1995
Dan Marino is saddened to learn that breaking Fran Tarkenton's all-time passing yardage record does not automatically give him a Super Bowl win.

1935
The NFL holds its first annual draft, which will eventually supplant the practice of kidnapping college players and brainwashing them into a life of football.

1946
The NFL permits its championship team, the Cleveland Rams, to relocate to St. Louis as long as they make Los Angeles miserable for 50 years first.

1960
As a scowl of scorn, disgust, and contempt contorts his normally affable face, commissioner Pete Rozelle introduces the Dallas Cowboys as the NFL's newest franchise.

1922
For the first time since the Almighty rested on the seventh day, time itself stands still, and the Green Bay Packers franchise is approved.

GREAT MOMENTS IN FOOTBALL HISTORY

Undefeated Colts To Play Football's Harlem Globetrotters

DECEMBER 8, 2005

INDIANAPOLIS—The Indianapolis Colts, after building a perfect 12-0 record so far this season and expecting perhaps only the Seattle Seahawks to pose a major challenge before the playoffs, were shocked and outraged by Tuesday's announcement from NFL head offices that their opponent this Sunday would not be the Jacksonville Jaguars, but the NFL's most explosive and unpredictable franchise: pro football's Harlem Globetrotters.

"This is insane," head coach Tony Dungy told reporters at a press conference. "We are within striking distance of becoming the first non-Globetrotter football team to complete an undefeated season, and the NFL pulls this stunt. I intend to appeal this scheduling change before those barnstorming clowns have a chance to make my team look like a bunch of idiots on national television."

Since entering the NFL in the 1976 expansion, the Globetrotter football team has posted a 449-

0-1 record, which analysts agree is due in part to their freewheeling, rule-bending, and vastly entertaining style of play, and also in part to their facing the same traditional and hapless opponent, the New York Jets, almost every Sunday. The showdown with the Colts, who will play host in the RCA Dome this Sunday at 1 p.m., will mark the first time since 1998 that the Globetrotters have traveled out of the New York area, a trip the players are looking forward to.

see COLTS

Quarterback Has Normal, Healthy Son

OCTOBER 20, 2005

NEW YORK—New York Jets quarterback Chad Pennington, whose torn rotator cuff has sidelined him for the remainder of the 2005 season, still has that rarest of qualities for a quarterback: a normal, healthy son. "My boy Cole is a perfectly healthy, mentally stable child," Pennington said while watching 20-month-old Cole run around the yard and play with a football like any other toddler. "You see, unlike most sons of quarterbacks, Cole is completely free of multiple sclerosis, autism, leukemia, epilepsy, cancer, or cystic fibrosis. The doctors tell us it's a miracle." The Cole Pennington Foundation, which Chad and his wife Robin founded in their son's name in 2004, has raised over $2 million for the sons of Boomer Esiason, Dan Marino, Doug Flutie, Mark Rypien, Vinny Testaverde, and countless other less fortunate sons of NFL quarterbacks. Ø

New York Jets Finish Season

JANUARY 12, 2006

RUTHERFORD, NJ—Despite the doubts of many football fans, media figures, and people within the Jets organization itself, the New York Jets have indeed finished their entire 2005-2006 season. "We might have lost 12 games, our coach, and possibly our starting quarterback," said GM Terry Bradway, who called the season a "qualified success" in a subdued press conference Tuesday. "But in spite of everything, we fielded a team that played 16 regular-season NFL games. There are only 31 other teams out there who can say the same thing." Bradway would not comment on whether the Jets would be able to complete future seasons, saying that, for now, team management was concentrating on making it through all seven rounds of the NFL draft. Ø

from **COLTS**

"I can't wait to square off against the MVP, Mister QB, that Sean Salisbury-lookin' tater head... What's his name? Oh, yeah—Peyton Manning," said Curtis "King Licketysplit" Williams, the Globetrotter quarterback and the NFL's all-time leader in behind-the-back passing yards, passing touchdowns, funky breakdowns, and smoothness from scrimmage. "Our anticipation of the situation is pure contemplation of domination, baby. We're going to win that game, and when we do it, it won't be anything like boring. The Colts are good, the Colts can score, but they ain't seen nothing like us before."

Although the Colts boast a powerful offense, with Manning coordinating Pro Bowlers Edgerrin James at running back and Marvin Harrison at wideout and receivers Reggie Wayne, Dallas Clark, and Bryan Fletcher continuing to emerge, defense is somewhat less of a strong point for Indianapolis.

"I really don't think the Colts can contain a Globetrotter attack led by King Licketysplit, especially when he's throwing to speedster Chester 'Five-Borough' Jenkins, unpredictable catch-master Terry 'Twinkletoes' Hol-

mes, and utility tight end The Honorable-Awfulable Samson," said ESPN football analyst John Clayton. "And let's not forget that all-world running back Walter 'Snazzy Wiggles' Malone is the current leader in yards per strut, and has run for a thousand yards on a single carry four times this season, scoring twice. I'm seeing another blowout in the making."

Williams agreed with Clayton's assessment. "I have been watching me some game film in between looking sexy," Williams said. "And I noticed a weakness in their defense. That Dwight Freeney? Big, fast, powerful defensive end? Well—he is also a jive turkey."

"Jive... Ass... Turkey," added Williams.

The Globetrotters' defense is, likewise, not the team's main strength, but Indianapolis coaches insisted that they would not underestimate the Harlem scheme.

"It's true they tend to let their opponent hang in there, scoring just enough to make the game interesting," said Colts defensive coordinator Ron Meeks. "They usually win in the fourth quarter, and although they win by an average of 23 points, it's almost always a one-score game with 10

minutes to go. If we can contain their tricky Human Cannonball Blitz, penetrate their ingenious Linebacker Pyramid run defense, and interrupt their insidious pattern of combined referee de-pantsing and flagrant pass interference, we know we can play them close."

"Man, Ron Meeks is preaching to the choir and holdin' his hymnal upside-down," said Globetrotter head coach Booby "The Love Enormous" Woods. "We got the strongest front four in the solar system. I don't expect Davy Gravy, Chuckie 'Dump Dump' Dempsey, Wilbert 'Chocolate Supernova' Willis, John

Stapleton III, and Anthony 'Human Ditch' Reynolds to let that No. 32 [James] get more than a couple yards before they smack the confetti right out of his bucket. If they go to the pass, Injurious Jameson and Billy 'Ham Shank' Williams try and activate Peyton's dental plan while Sweet Carob Washington and Godfrey 'Godfather Trilogy' Whittaker cover their receivers. They usually cover them with flour sacks, silly string, banana cream pies, spray cheese, soap suds, all kinds of embarrassing nonsense. We're going to give them their 'props,' all right."

For their part, the Indianapolis players are not backing down from the sudden and unexpected challenge, asking only that NFL officials, often accused of blatantly favoring the Globetrotters, give them a fair and even game.

"Harlem has a good team," said Manning, who refused to respond to the Globetrotters' taunts and was unable to think of any of his own. "For instance, I respect their ability to spin the football on their fingers instead of carrying it in the traditional way. But it's unfair for the refs to allow, for instance, their receivers to score an extra point by jumping through the uprights after a touchdown reception. Linebackers should not be allowed to trampoline, parachute, or bungee-jump into the backfield. Trained monkeys, unicycling go-go girls, and Earth, Wind, and Fire have no place on a football field, let alone being a pivotal part of a team's game plan. And I know I'll get fined for saying this, but if a referee's hat is pulled down over his eyes, it should not take him 90 seconds to pull it back up again."

"I mean, at least fine them for celebrating," Manning added. "Frankly, it's unbelievable what people let the Globetrotters get away with." ∅

Roethlisberger Repeatedly Taps 'Helmets Are For Losers' Into Pillow Using Morse Code

Bill Romanowski Bursts Into Senate To Deny He Ever Took Steroids

JANUARY 19, 2006

WASHINGTON, DC—Former NFL linebacker Bill Romanowski, known during his 17-year career as a gung-ho fitness freak with a near-perfect physique, receding hairline, and extremely short temper, ran onto the floor of the United States Capitol building Monday, interrupting Samuel Alito's Supreme Court confirmation hearings and resisting the efforts of Capitol police to detain him while loudly and repeatedly insisting he never took

steroids. "This is all natural muscle—I could still play today!" said Romanowski, the cords standing out on his neck as he proclaimed his innocence, apparently forgetting that he confessed to steroid use on *60 Minutes* in October 2005. "Get off me! I'm talking to the freaking Senate!" Romanowski was eventually wrestled to the ground by law-enforcement officers and charged with creating a public disturbance and battery after breaking the nose and orbital bone of Capitol police officer Mark Williams. ∅

Hungry Bears Defense Feeds On Soldier Field Crowd

OCTOBER 5, 2006

CHICAGO—The league-leading Chicago Bears defense, which overpowered and dominated the Seattle Seahawks last Sunday en route to a 37-6 victory, took time after the game to emphasize that they would not have had the extra energy needed to hold the Seattle offense to a mere two field goals if it weren't for the mass cannibalization of nearly 60,000 of their hometown fans.

"Without a doubt, these are the best fans in the world," said Bears linebacker Brian Urlacher, who said that without the rush he received from the supportive, nutrient-rich Bears fans he devoured during the game, he would not have had the strength to make seven tackles during the game, five of which were unassisted.

"They gave us what we needed to play hard all four quarters, and this win is definitely for them," continued Urlacher, pointing to a section of empty, blood-stained seats that still housed the uneaten portions of dozens of loyal fans.

"Mmmm," Urlacher added.

"When I hear that crowd screaming, it just

makes me hungrier and hungrier," said Bears nickelback Ricky Manning Jr., who had four tackles against the Seahawks, and credits the 19 beta-keratin-rich fans he ate for his ability to see Matt Hasselbeck's eyes, aiding him in making two key interceptions. "Many peo-

see **BEARS**

Outgoing Commissioner Tagliabue Expected To Pardon Dennis Miller Before Leaving Office

AUGUST 10, 2006

NEW YORK—Although Paul Tagliabue will not address speculation concerning possible forgiveness of former color commentator Dennis Miller's heinous crimes against the sport, those close to the outgoing NFL commissioner say he is seriously considering using his powers to pardon Miller before leaving office. "Tagliabue knows that hard-line fans still want vengeance for Dennis Miller's constant clumsy references to the Battle of Thermopylae, Truman Capote novels, quantum physics, *I Love Lucy*, and everything else while they were just trying to enjoy *Monday Night Football*," said a source in NFL management who wishes to remain nameless. "In Paul's mind, the question is whether Miller's sentence is about vengeance or personal rehabilitation—not that anyone wants to see Miller on television calling a game again, if at all." An informal poll of Miller's 125 million formal victims indicated that over 85 percent would support Tagliabue if he granted Miller the death penalty. ∅

NFL Refs Admit 'Everything Just Happens So Fast'

JANUARY 12, 2006

TAMPA, FL—Just hours after officiating the Buccaneers-Redskins wild-card playoff game, referee Mike Carey admitted that "everything happens so fast out there it's a miracle we see anything at all. Believe me, pro football is one quick game, and the rules are pretty intricate," said Carey, who admits he probably misses half the infractions that occur in a normal NFL

matchup. "Especially the pass interference and defensive holding stuff, who can put hands on who at what point, I can hardly keep it straight—and I'm one of the quick ones. I have no idea how a guy like, say, Ed Hochuli keeps it all together." NFL director of officiating Mike Pereira stated Monday that Carey would not be reprimanded for his unusually frank comments, saying that he himself "almost never even sees stuff like clipping or hands to the face." ∅

Packers To Favre: 'Take Your Time, Asshole'

APRIL 13, 2006

ASHWAUBENON, WI—Green Bay Packers front-office officials have informed three-time MVP Brett Favre they can wait for his decision on whether or not he's planning to retire for "as long as it fucking takes." "This is a big decision for Brett Favre, and we can't deny that he's the heart and soul of our team, the most important Packer, the most important person in all of America, and the center of the whole entire universe," Packer

general manager Ted Thompson said Tuesday. "It's not like we have to make any major decisions that all hinge on whether or not he's returning, after all. We'll just ride around on our lawn tractors on our farm in Mississippi while we wait for him to make up his goddamn mind." Favre would not say when he might announce his decision, admitting that he was "too much in awe of what Mr. Brilliant Genius Thompson did with the 4-12 Packers last year" to commit one way or the other. ∅

Junior Seau Retires To Spend More Time Tackling His Kids

AUGUST 17, 2006

SAN DIEGO—Chargers linebacker Junior Seau announced Wednesday that he would be retiring from football to spend more time tackling his two young sons Jake and Hunter and daughter Sydney. "Retirement will allow me to combine the joy of watching my children grow up with my passion for solid and aggressive contact," the 37-year-old Seau said in a press conference at Chargers training camp. "I'm really looking forward to wrapping up Sydney as she goes off on her first date, hitting Jake low on his first paper route, and blitzing little Hunter on camping trips." Seau went on to announce the creation of the Junior Seau Familial Recreation Fund, a new charitable foundation through which he will make it possible for his children to fulfill their dreams of roughhousing with a former professional athlete. ∅

INSIDE

› Olin Kreutz Realizes He's Been Wearing Kicking Tee As Mouthguard His Entire Career

Seahawks Asked To Stop Piping Screams Of Terrified Women Into Qwest Field

SEPTEMBER 28, 2006

SEATTLE—Following multiple complaints from teams who have had to endure both the much-touted, 100-decibel "12th Man" fan noise and the artificially amplified, 135-decibel shrieks of tortured women in pain while playing at Seattle's Qwest Field, the NFL has asked the Seahawks front office to refrain from piping in the sound effects during future home games. "It is unfair not only to the visiting team and their fans, both of whom have a right to expect hospitality and consideration of the Seattle football club, but to the women who must endure such physically insulting treatment in order to make these disturbing recordings," the statement from the NFL's Competition Committee read in part. "Furthermore, if the screams of these women turn out not to be recordings, there may be the matter of fines to consider." NFL officials and Seattle law-enforcement personnel have detained Qwest Field audio engineer Fred Miscera for questioning concerning the recent disappearance of several Seahawks cheerleaders. ∅

PHOTO FINISH

Michael Vick: 'That Wasn't Marijuana, This Is Marijuana'

Reggie Bush On First NFL Touchdown: 'That Was It?'

OCTOBER 12, 2006

NEW ORLEANS—After Reggie Bush's first touchdown as a professional football player—a 65-yard punt return that ultimately allowed the New Orleans Saints to defeat the Tampa Bay Buccaneers 24-21—the rookie running back said he didn't know what he was expecting, but "this just wasn't it." "I don't know what I thought would happen, you know? Game-winning touchdown in the NFL, my first TD as a pro, I just hoped that... I don't even know anymore," said Bush at a post-game press conference, adding that perhaps "things felt off" because at USC over 20,000 more people cheered when he scored. "Maybe [NFL touchdowns] get better the more you get them. I sure hope so." When asked what he planned to do with the game ball, Bush said he was considering giving it to a young child, but didn't want to ruin football for him at such an early age. ∅

Ben Roethlisberger Relieved To Suffer Football-Related Injury

OCTOBER 25, 2006

ATLANTA—Pittsburgh Steelers quarterback Ben Roethlisberger, who survived life-threatening injuries as a result of a motorcycle accident during the pre-season and endured an emergency appendectomy in early October, was relieved Sunday to suffer a serious traumatic injury during the course of a football game. "I think things are definitely starting to get back to norb... to nurm... to normal," said a barely conscious Roethlisberger, who suffered a concussion as a result of a helmet-to-helmet collision during the third quarter of Pittsburgh's game against the Atlanta Falcons. "It was nice to be on the sidelines, in pain, and in full uniform all at the same time, for once." Roethlisberger added that his experiences off the football field have taught him a valuable lesson, and had he not been wearing a regulation helmet during Sunday's game, he could be dead right now. ∅

from **BEARS**

ple say that your crowd doesn't make a difference, but in well-fed, nutrient-rich Chicago, that certainly isn't the case."

"They're simply the best," Manning added, licking his blood-encrusted teeth, the remnants of a gnarled human index finger still wedged in the gap of his two incisors.

Bears fans are renowned as some of the largest, most well-rounded, vitamin-laden fans throughout the National Football League. Although the NFL does not keep statistics on the nutrition content of its crowds, conventional wisdom holds that the amount of protein in the Soldier Field crowd, thought to be double the league average, has allowed Bears defenses throughout history to quickly build and repair stressed muscle tissue during grueling 16-game seasons.

"There is no question that they keep us going down the stretch," said 300-pound defensive tackle Tank Johnson, who says he gets a rush of energy from the women and children in attendance when he chews open their stomachs to consume any leftover carbohydrates stored in their digestive systems and the belly fat of their abdominal cavities before gulping down their cheeks and the flesh around their eye sockets, which he says gives him the necessary supplement of the L-cysteine amino acid. "The sacrifice these fans make, especially the ones who travel to the away games... It just hits you right in the gut."

"I've heard from guys who play in Miami, Tampa Bay, and Minnesota, and they all complain that their fans just aren't as good as ours," added Johnson with a slight belch brought on by the high fat content of a fan who used to sit right behind the goalpost.

302-pound defensive lineman Ian Scott agreed with his teammates, saying that there is just something different about the heart of a Bears fan that is different from that of any other in the league.

"It isn't just their heart—it's their nutrient-rich kidneys and livers, too, that make them such an integral part of the game," said Scott, who along with safety Mike Brown, linebacker Lance Briggs, and cornerback Charles Tillman, tends to enjoy the fleshy calf and thigh muscles first while coating their exposed skin with the excess fat adhering to fans' bones in order to keep themselves warm during brutal Chicago winters. "I don't know how many times opposing quarterbacks have been unnerved by our unique relationship with the good, tender, juicy people of Chicago, and have thrown an interception or fumbled a snap because of it."

"I can't imagine eating any other fans, and I hope I never have to," Scott added.

With the Bears jumping quickly out of the gate with a 4-0 record, many in Chicago are talking Super Bowl, and though head coach Lovie Smith said he plans to take it one game at a time, he knows the benefit of having a home-crowd presence on the world's grandest stage.

"Hopefully we can pack the stadium in Miami with Bears fans," Smith said. "It'd be great to have their unique Soldier Field flavor with us to help get us through the big one without a hiccup." ∅

Michael Vick Credits Increased Passing Accuracy To Using His Right Hand

NOVEMBER 2, 2006

ATLANTA—Falcons quarterback Michael Vick, whose passing improved dramatically over the past two weeks as he completed 66 percent of his passes and threw for seven touchdowns, claims his newfound accuracy came from his decision to throw the ball right-handed. "I just sort of got in the habit of carrying the ball in my left hand, and I just used my right hand for stiff-arming people," said Vick, who completed a remarkable 20 of 28 passes to his pleasantly stunned receivers in the October 29 game against the Bengals. "Do you know, a lot of people mistak- enly thought I was left-handed? I guess that's my fault." Vick added that his fumble against Cincinnati was due to his not knowing that it was, in fact, legal to carry the ball in both hands. ✒

Michael Irvin Demands Bigger, 'Golder' Hall Of Fame Bust

Missed Extra Point From 1979 Comes Back To Haunt Jets

NOVEMBER 2, 2006

CLEVELAND—Jets head coach Eric Mangini blamed "a lack of attention to detail" and the "long shadow of our franchise's his- torical mistakes" for Sunday's poor showing against the Browns, noting that a long-lamented missed PAT from 1979 had finally had enough of a negative effect to cause a Jets loss. "I remember when Frank Gifford was calling that game, he said that missed extra point would cost us later on," said Mangini, who said an underperforming offense was also a minor factor. "I mean, I was only 8, and the Jets beat the Dolphins 33-17, but I knew it was just a matter of time." Jets quarterback Chad Pennington said he had also felt the 27-year-old miss hanging over his head, particularly during the fourth quarter of the game and the late 1990s. ✒

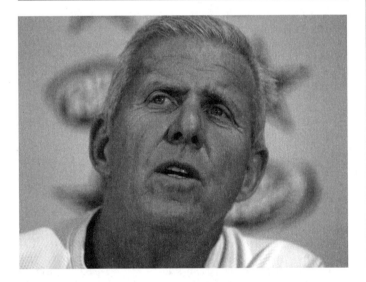

Bill Parcells: 'I've Always Hated Football'

JANUARY 11, 2007

DALLAS—In the last press conference Bill Parcells would give this year af- ter leading the Cowboys through a frus- trating 9-7 season and an excruciating first-round playoff loss to the Seattle Seahawks, the hard-nosed coach sur- prised reporters by revealing that he "was glad to see the season, and with any luck [his] career, come to an end," stating that "I can't remember a time in my life when I haven't hated football."

"Come on—anyone who paid attention to my career must have suspected it," two-time Super Bowl-winner Parcells told stunned members of the press at the Cowboys prac- tice facility Tuesday, reacting to their disbe- lief with surprise of his own. "When did I ever look like I was enjoying myself? When did you last see me smile on the sidelines or in the locker room? You must have at least wondered why I was always so angry

see PARCELLS

Denver Broncos Fined $25,000 For Running Truly Naked Bootleg

Brett Favre Demands Trade To 1996 Packers

MAY 17, 2007

GREEN BAY—Three-time MVP and undisputed future Hall of Fame quarterback Brett Favre, disappointed with the Packers' refusal to aggressively pursue receiver Randy Moss and frustrated with his team's apparent indifference to making immediate improvements on offense, is demanding a trade to the team he feels will give him the best shot at winning a last Super Bowl ring before his retirement: the 1996 Green Bay Packers.

"I just don't think this Packer team, and GM Ted Thompson especially, is thinking in terms of winning with me," said Favre, speaking to reporters at his charity golf tournament in Mississippi Sunday. "On the other hand, 1996 Packers GM Ron Wolf is committed to building the team completely around me. I don't think it's out of the question to say that with me behind center, the 1996 Packers

are looking at going all the way to the Super Bowl."

Early reports had indicated that Favre was so upset that his team failed to close a draft-day deal for Randy Moss with the Oakland Raiders that his agent called Packers GM Ted Thompson and requested a trade to a team with capable receivers.

"Nothing against Donald [Driver] and Greg [Jennings], but if I can't throw it to Randy Moss, then I want to throw it to Antonio Freeman, Robert Brooks, and Don Beebe," Favre said. "I bet with them, I'd have more of a chance of throwing for, say, 3,899 yards and 39 touchdowns, with maybe as few as 13 interceptions. Who knows? That kind of production could even get me another MVP award, although of course that's much less important than leading the '96 Pack to another Super Bowl victory."

Favre also noted that, unlike the young and unproven 2007 Packers, the

see **FAVRE**

---

from **PARCELLS**

with everyone around me."

"I'll tell you why—I was goddamn miserable," Parcells added. "Football sucks."

The coach expounded on his statements by explaining, in acid tones and with an exasperated manner, how he "just sort of fell into coaching" after playing college football at Wichita State, an experience he described as "pretty okay, I guess, at least for young men."

"But coaching? All that pressure, having to deal with all those dumbass players, just to play a game that's basically a lot of choreographed shoving?" Parcells said. "Screw that. Screw football. Seriously, I wonder sometimes why I was so good at it."

Parcells explained that he developed his trademark style of pos-

session-oriented, run-first, ball-control football in an effort to not spend too much time thinking about a game that he found "basically pretty freaking dumb."

"No one was more surprised than I was when it worked," Parcells said. "Surprised and damn disappointed, really. Turns out football's really simple. Hell, a freaking ape could coach this game. Guys like Belichick, Cowher, Holmgren, you know why they're successful? Because they're actually too smart to coach football. Come to think of it, I bet they hate it too."

"The worst part of my success was that it meant if I wanted any kind of successful career, I had no choice but to spend my time dealing with really stellar guys like Drew Bledsoe, Lawrence Taylor, Keyshawn Johnson, and Terrell Owens," Parcells said in an effort to

explain his often fractious relationship with most of his players. "Solid-gold citizens, football players. If they're not boring as hell, they're arrogant drug-crazed felons."

"You guys thought I was hard on them to make them better players," Parcells added, "but really I was hard on them because, except for Harry Carson and that one blond guy from the Giants, I hated every man who ever played for me very, very much."

Parcells said that, although the sport had led him down a cold, lightless path that seemed to lead down an ever-steeper path toward a premature stress-hastened death, it had taught him a few important lessons.

"First of all, never do anything you hate, even if it's the only thing you're good at, no matter how tempting the fame and the money are," said Parcells, who now regrets "measuring out my life one excruciating wind-sprint drill, one interminable video session, one bone-stick-stone stupid press conference at a time, until nothing is left at the tail end of my worthless life but regret

and hatred for myself and others."

"Second of all, it's never too late to quit. Never. And sometimes it's the only right thing to do," Parcells continued. "And third, taking your hatred out on others, no matter how satisfying it may be, no matter how much those stupid wide receivers deserve it, is not really right. And I intend to make this the heart of my Hall of Fame acceptance speech when they put me in Canton in a few years."

"Now all of you go to hell," Parcells said, ending the press conference with his trademark frankness and inspiring laughter among reporters. "You mental children should be ashamed of yourself, making a living sucking at the teat of angry overgrown losers like me."

Parcells is expected to make an announcement in the next few days concerning either his retirement, his future as general manager of the New York Giants, or most probably, his return to coach his much-deplored Dallas Cowboys for next season. ∅

INSIDE

> **Bart Starr Calmly Approaches Brett Favre, Shoots Him, Tips Hat To Reporters, Walks Away**

Tony Romo Regrets Eating Greasy Fried Chicken During Crucial Field-Goal Attempt

JANUARY 11, 2007

DALLAS—Cowboys quarterback Tony Romo, whose bobbling of the snap on a crucial fourth-quarter field goal ended the season for Dallas, took full responsibility for the gaffe Wednesday by admitting he should not have been eating a bucket of grease-covered fried chicken while play was in progress. "I keep running through it in my mind—Martin Gramatica lines up the kick, I kneel and put down my bucket of chicken with my left hand, I transfer the chicken leg in my right hand to my mouth to hold it there, I signal for the snap, and the ball slips right off my fingers," Romo told reporters while cleaning out his locker at the Cowboys' practice facility. "It could easily have been the chicken grease, which sickens me—this was a play we'd run a hundred times in practice. But this time I let the chicken get in the way." Romo promised to make improving his ball- and fried-chicken-handling skills a priority in the offseason. ∅

INSIDE

› Doug Flutie Shoots Up Six Inches In Height Immediately After Retirement From Football

› Pedophile Coach To Try Quarterback At Other Positions

Brady Quinn: 'I'm Going To Be A Bust'

APRIL 19, 2007

DUBLIN, OH—Top draft prospect Brady Quinn, a strong-armed quarterback out of Notre Dame who is expected to be taken with one of the first five picks in the draft, told scouts interviewing him at his family home Monday that he would in all likelihood be a huge NFL bust. "While it's true I have impressive arm strength, and that I'm willing to stand up in the pocket against the rush, the fact remains that my lack of downfield accuracy gets me in trouble on the deep throws and my field vision is suspect," Quinn told draft evaluators from the Raiders, Browns, and Cardinals." Combine that with the enormous starting bonus I'll receive and the tendency for teams to try and develop quarterbacks long after they should give up, and I really just have 'bust' written all over me." While Quinn recommended teams look

to solid prospects such as quarterback Jamarcus Russell, tackle Joe Thomas, and running back Adrian Peterson, Raiders owner Al Davis is reportedly more interested than ever in signing Quinn. ∅

---

from **FAVRE**

1996 Packers boasted seasoned veterans on both sides of the ball.

"It sure would be great to play alongside Reggie White again—I get chills just thinking about seeing him in the locker room," Favre said. "That whole '96 defense is great, too. Santana Dotson is a force in the middle. That LeRoy Butler, I tell you, he's one of the most underrated safeties in the game. Desmond Howard isn't a bad kick returner, either. And unlike the Packer backfield I got now, the '96 Packers still feature William Henderson at fullback."

"Mark Chmura, though, I don't know," Favre admitted. "Decent tight end, but something about him isn't quite right."

In addition to the more elite personnel, Favre praised the aggressive attitude of the coaching squad and front office of the Packers of 1996, saying he was a fan of head coach Mike Holmgren's West Coast offense and

Wolf's aggressive recruiting strategies.

"I think Holmgren and I would make an interesting team," Favre said. "He could teach me a lot. We could learn from each other. And I know Ron Wolf would have my back. If, say, our number-one receiver gets knocked out for the season in Week 7, I believe Wolf would go right after a great veteran free agent, like maybe Andre Rison, to give us an edge in the playoffs. I can almost guarantee that."

"It would really be something," Favre said. "We'd be one of the all-time great teams, a once-in-a-lifetime thing, you know? I'm going to have my agent look into it right away."

Although the Packers had no immediate comment, head coach Mike McCarthy said the team would be "heartbroken" to part with its greatest player, although in deference to Favre's long service, and for the good of the current team, they would be willing to consider a trade package including a first-round pick in the 2008 NFL draft and the 1996 Brett Favre. ∅

New Michael Vick Revelations

MAY 17, 2007

The discovery of a dogfighting ring in a house owned by Michael Vick has led to speculation of what other secrets the Falcons quarterback might be hiding. Onion Sports runs down the potentially damaging sights that frequent visitors to Vick's mansion have reported witnessing:

➤ Embarrassingly thick glasses Vick needs to see more than 20 yards in front of him.

➤ A fully annotated slam book, evidence that Vick and his friends can get pretty catty when they get together and start talking.

➤ Empty beer cans everywhere, because although Vick is well over legal age, something about empty beer cans always seems to add drama to an already troublesome situation.

➤ Authentic original of Edvard Munch's "The Scream," implying that either the version in the Oslo museum or the one owned by Norwegian billionaire Petter Olsen are in fact forgeries.

➤ Over 200 tubes of lipstick in various tastefully understated shades.

➤ Perfectly legal, albeit tasteless, cat-fighting set-up.

➤ Framed diploma proving that Oxford University awarded Vick a doctorate in Jacobean theater during the 2003 offseason.

➤ Water cooler with secret compartment containing stash of Oreos.

➤ Assorted helmets, pads, and other gladiatorial gear, presumably for use in some grotesque human-versus-human bloodsport.

So-Called 'Genius' Bill Belichick Stumped By Non-Football-Related Question

JANUARY 18, 2007

FOXBOROUGH, MA—Patriots head coach Bill Belichick's reputation for possessing a keen, incisive intelligence and being able to intuitively grasp all pertinent aspects of a problem took a major hit Tuesday when, while fielding reporters' questions at his daily press conference, he stammered through his response to a *BusinessWeek* reporter's routine inquiry concerning alternative economic approaches to societal trends. "Well, we, uh, I guess it's like the salary cap all teams operate under, as far as... Is commodification the word I want to use here?" said Belichick, obviously attempting to dodge the question in what onlookers called a "humiliating moment of mere mortality for the acknowledged genius." "I don't know if Keynesian theory is what I want here, but... A football game is a service, I guess, in terms of Keynesian market concepts... No, wait, I think I'm thinking of Thorstein Veblen. You know what? Any questions on how we're planning for the Colts' passing game?" Patriots players would not comment directly on their coach's public failure to live up to his reputation, although some players were heard wondering aloud how a coach with such severely limited economic knowledge could in good faith call himself an offensive innovator. ∅

PHOTO FINISH

Report: NFL Players Look Weird In Suits

Peyton Manning Shows His Backup Proper Way To Hold Clipboard

AUGUST 23, 2007

TERRE HAUTE, IN—Indianapolis Colts quarterback Peyton Manning interrupted an intrasquad scrimmage Tuesday for approximately 45 minutes in order to show backup quarterback Jim Sorgi how to properly hold his clipboard.

"He's got to learn consistency if he's going to be the backup on this team, and that starts with the little things, like holding the clipboard with two hands," Manning told reporters following the practice. "When I see my backup holding the clipboard with the top portion clenched in his one hand and the bottom portion digging into his bicep, I see a quarterback taking a 'me-first' approach. That's unacceptable."

"Holding the clipboard isn't about individual performance. It's about winning," added Manning, who later stated he was disappointed in Sorgi and that he thought the two were on the same page following a two-hour clipboard conversation he had with Sorgi during the Colts' voluntary spring practice. "I once thought that if Jim wanted to set himself apart, maybe he could wear his hat with a little extra curvature in the brim. But for now, I'd have to say he doesn't deserve that privilege."

Manning claimed to have mentioned several previous clipboard-mishandling incidents to Sorgi prior to the on-field confrontation, including times when Sorgi held only the bottom-left corner of the clipboard "as if he didn't care if he dropped it"; when he caught Sorgi gripping the clipboard with two hands, but loosely and "as if he was just going through the motions"; and when he saw Sorgi standing on the sidelines trying to spin the clipboard on his index finger, an action Manning called disrespectful to both the team and the game of football.

"I even caught him out of the corner of my eye letting the clip-

see **PEYTON**

Bob Costas: Dogfights At Vick's House 'Some Of The Best Dogfights I Have Ever Seen'

MAY 17, 2007

ATLANTA— While controversy continues regarding Michael Vick's possible involvement in dogfights held at a Smithfield, GA, property owned by the quarterback, NBC sportscaster Bob Costas has made his opinion of the events known, saying the dog-fighting in question was some of the best he had ever personally witnessed. "Truly high-caliber dog-fighting has nearly become extinct in this country, and it's becoming unusual to see the kind of devotion to the sport that was displayed at Vick's pit," Costas said Monday. "I mean, the pit he owned. He may not have actually been at the extremely riveting, thrill-a-minute canine fights to the death that it was my pleasure—no, my great privilege—to attend." Costas has often criticized the recent decline in quality of the illegal death sport, saying dog-fighting has become "shameless in its pandering to the worst echelon of sports fanhood" and "has sunk nearly as low as boxing." ∅

Bears Lead Rex Grossman To Super Bowl

JANUARY 25, 2007

CHICAGO—While coming up big in a 39-14 victory over the New Orleans Saints Sunday, the Chicago Bears single-handedly shouldered the burden of struggling quarterback Rex Grossman and led the otherwise hapless quarterback to the Super Bowl. "For a while there, it looked like Rex was done for, but then the Bears came out of nowhere with some great plays on defense, rushing, and special teams to pick up the slack," said NFL analyst Len Pasquarelli. "They almost literally put Rex on their collective back and carried him through that game. All season long, the Bears have shown that they can win, even in the presence of Rex Grossman." Following the game, Grossman admitted that he would "never have gotten this far" without the Bears, saying "those guys are the true reason for this team's success." ∅

Eagles Fans Give McNabb Three-Week Deadline To Win Super Bowl

SEPTEMBER 13, 2007

PHILADELPHIA—Frustrated with the Eagles' last-second 16-13 loss to the Green Bay Packers last Sunday, and with quarterback Donovan McNabb's failure to single-handedly score three touchdowns, prevent two of his teammates from muffing punts, or block any of Green Bay's field goals, thousands of Philadelphia fans demanded that McNabb win an NFL championship for Philadelphia sometime within the next three weeks.

"For the last time: How much longer do we have to wait for McNabb to get off his ass?" Eagles fan Jacob Wilkerson said of the five-time Pro Bowler in one of over 1,500 messages addressed to the quarterback left on the Eagles' voicemail Monday. "Come on, McNabb, it's time to finish the job. We've been really lenient up to this point, but it's time to hunker down and throw the ball. If you think you need to take the whole three weeks, that's fine, but we would really like it by next Wednesday."

While many football analysts agree that McNabb has done a phenomenally good job in a less-than-ideal situation for the last eight years, blaming Philadelphia's failure to advance to the Super Bowl on such varied areas as undisciplined offensive execution, inconsistent defense, excessive penalties, lackluster pass protection, and almost criminally bad play-calling, fans say they are tired of people making excuses for McNabb.

"So what's our crybaby quarterback going to blame next, the NFL schedule?" fan Ed Cooke said in a call to Radio 610WIP's Howard Eskin. "He's the quarterback. If the team sucks, it's his fault. I think McNabb's lucky we're only asking for one Super Bowl in the next few weeks, because what he owes us is a three-peat by December."

Although he felt McNabb performed respectably, completing 15 of 33 passes for 184 yards with one touchdown and one interception in his first game back since tearing his ACL last season, Eagles head coach Andy Reid pointed out that his quarterback would have to put up much better numbers if he expected to put them in the position to win it all by the end of Week 4.

"This organization expects a lot from Donovan," Reid told a group of angry fans Wednesday. "After all, we did use the second overall draft pick on him eight years ago, and while he's done really well considering we made him run the offense for years with bargain-basement wide receivers and running backs that couldn't stay healthy, I agree that now is the time to finally get something back on our investment."

"Donovan promised us—the Eagles organization and fans alike—great things," said Eagles owner Jeff Lurie, who promised season ticket holders he would sit down with McNabb and make fans' wishes known. "You have all really been great through all of this. No one could ask for a better, more caring, more patient home crowd. The amount of restraint you have shown by not, say, throwing McNabb off the top deck of Lincoln Financial Field is nothing but admirable."

"For my part, I can promise that on Sept. 30 I will make sure that Donovan has the Lombardi trophy on my desk no later than the end of the day," added Lurie, noting that he thought the Eagles' fans were the best fans in the world.

McNabb, whose plans for this week include extra time working with his receivers on tim-

ing, studying his playbook, and watching film, said he would be working as hard as he could for the foreseeable future.

"Eagles fans are a passionate group who love their team," said McNabb, "if not the actual players. It's not like winning a Super Bowl before the first month of the season is the hardest thing they've ever asked of me. That'd be all those times they asked me to go kill myself."

"If I work hard and play my game, I'll be fine," McNabb added. "I just hope the fans realize that." ∅

---

from **PEYTON**

board hang carelessly down by his thigh during our preseason game against the [Chicago] Bears," said Manning, adding that he had not said anything to Sorgi at the time because he wanted to give him a chance to rectify the problem on his own. "I almost burned a timeout, but that was on the same day he took my advice to affix an 18-inch length of clean white cord to the clipboard in order to keep better track of his writing utensil, so I let it slide. Baby steps, after all."

Manning said he began to suspect that Sorgi had reverted to a careless and lackadaisical state of mind upon seeing Sorgi gripping the clipboard at the top part of its clamping mechanism, which Manning said could have ultimately led to the application of enough pressure to allow the documents held by the clipboard to escape, and possibly even be blown towards the opposing sideline.

"Look—if he messes up like that and the other team has all of our offensive schemes, then we don't repeat as [Super Bowl] champions," Manning said. "It's that simple. True, I've never had to hold that clipboard, and I never plan to. Jim Sorgi is going to be holding that clipboard for the rest of my career, so it's essential he becomes a pro at it."

"We're only as strong as our weakest link," Manning added. "Jim Sorgi had best remember that."

Though Sorgi admitted to violating Manning's clipboard-holding policy, he said a lack of communication, not a lack of commitment, was really to blame.

"Sometimes Peyton and I just aren't always on the same wavelength," Sorgi told reporters after Manning left the facility. "It gets really confusing. Basically, Peyton likes to give me three different clipboard-holding options during specific game situations, signaling them to me before the snap. At any given time during a game, he could scream at me to change my grip to, say, ten-and-two instead of six-and-four, and naturally, there will be times I don't hear him completely."

"I just wish he would stick to his initial clipboard-holding plan—two hands at three and nine," Sorgi said. "It would make things easier on all of us."

Upon being told of Sorgi's comments, Manning commented that Sorgi's "prima donna attitude is the reason he's not allowed to run kneel-downs during the regular season."

Colts head coach Tony Dungy claimed he was unaware of any problem with his quarterbacks and said he would be taking more of a hands-off approach this season, allowing Manning to do the majority, if not all, of the coaching. ∅

Confiscated Patriots Videotapes Contain Extensive Footage Of Tom Brady Showering

SEPTEMBER 20, 2007

NEW YORK—The hundreds of hours of game and practice scouting videotapes that league officials seized from the New England Patriots also include over 100 hours of painstakingly thorough footage of Patriots quarterback Tom Brady in the shower, sources within the NFL competition committee confirmed Tuesday.

"We are still investigating whether the assembled shower footage of Brady soaped up and wreathed in steam—which I can personally confirm was in fact taken in the showers of several different NFL-affiliated facilities around the league, and appears to have been shot by head coach Belichick himself—constitutes a violation of league laws or

REC 10/7/2005

policies," league spokesman Greg Aiello told reporters during a press conference held at the league's Manhattan offices. "It is the opinion of the commissioner and

the league that further extensive study is required before any judgment can be rendered in this matter."

"Our investigation continues to focus on any in-

stances of cheating by the New England Patriots, and will continue to focus on cheating no matter how much Brady showering footage we find," Aiello added.

Aiello then displayed a 25-minute composite videotape consisting of representative segments and "highlights" of Brady in the shower.

Analysts agree that the bulk of the shower footage, while certainly unusual in many aspects, seems to have been shot with Brady's full knowledge and cooperation, although Brady does not appear especially enthusiastic. Early footage is also said to include showering quarterback Drew Bledsoe, then the Patriots starting quarterback, and at least 25 minutes of the earliest-known material was evidently shot in the showers at the University of Michigan as Brady was being scouted for the draft.

"Belichick has always been a big believer

see **BRADY**

Randy Moss Complains He's Getting The Ball Too Much

SEPTEMBER 13, 2007

FOXBOROUGH, MA—After posting his most productive receiving performance in eight years during his Patriots debut, Randy Moss told reporters that he was frustrated with the amount of catches he was being forced to make. "I'm already tired of doing all the damn work around here," said Moss, who caught nine passes for 183 yards and a touchdown in what he called a "grueling" afternoon. "Would it kill Tom Brady to maybe look for Donté [Stallworth] once in a while? Or maybe even try and hand it off? No, it's 'Throw it

to Randy! Throw it to Randy!' all day long out there. It's like suddenly I'm the best receiver in the world as far as they're concerned." Moss also commented that the team had asked him to sprint "way too hard" during running plays. ∅

Authorities Discover Illegal Frog-Jumping Ring In Eli Manning's Backyard

JULY 19, 2007

BUTTERFIELD, MO—Authorities responding to complaints of excessive hooting and hollering on a 15-acre farm owned by New York Giants quarterback Eli Manning discovered an illegal frog-jumping ring Friday, leading to the arrest of Wilbur Jefferson, Manning's second cousin and the farm's only resident. "We have identified as many as a dozen violations of federal batrachian-cruelty laws concerning the procuring, housing, and training of the bullfrogs forced to take part in these underground leaping competitions," Barry County Sheriff's Department spokesman Brad Winters told

reporters as photographers worked to document frog-jumping implements such as lengths of knotted measuring twine, jars of pond water, and a burial pit containing the bodies of legless and presumably defeated frogs. "We are not certain if Manning himself is involved, but he has been named as a person of interest in this case, and we have collected smokeless tobacco samples for DNA analysis." Winters would not confirm that police had acquired a cell-phone video in which a squatting Manning was clearly shown warning Jeremy Shockey against touching the amphibians during the contest, weighting opponents' frogs with buckshot, or using toads. ∅

Tearful Rex Grossman: 'I Was Intercepted A Lot As A Child'

SEPTEMBER 27, 2007

CHICAGO—Bears quarterback Rex Grossman, responding to being benched following his three-interception performance in a loss to the Dallas Cowboys, had to stop speaking in order to wrestle with his emotions at a post-game press conference Tuesday in which he tearfully admitted to reporters that as a child his friends and family would abuse him mercilessly on the football field by repeatedly picking off all of his throws. "I grew up terrified of what my mother or father would say if I took a sack, so I'd just throw the ball up for grabs as hard as I could," said Grossman, recalling a post-Thanksgiving-dinner outing in which his parents intercepted every pass meant for his friends and vice versa. "My first memory is playing touch football in my backyard and just wishing that the game would end,

but they just seemed to go on forever. I'd just close my eyes and throw the ball and pray it would reach the right person, but my dad, uncle, creepy older cousin, or best friend always seemed to take advantage of my poor throws." A sobbing Grossman also confessed that his childhood pet Rocky, an elderly cocker spaniel, would often come up from behind him while he was holding the ball and nuzzle it with such force that he would fumble. ∅

Dan Marino Squeezes Harder And Harder During Congratulatory Handshake With Peyton Manning

FEBRUARY 8, 2007

MIAMI—During a post-Super Bowl handshake between former Miami Dolphins quarterback Dan Marino and MVP Peyton Manning, the Colts quarterback reported that Marino gradually increased the pressure of his grip to the point where, by the end of the 10-second exchange, it was as if Marino was attempting to hurt Manning rather than congratulate him. "At first he was smiling and telling me how great he thought I played, but as the grip got firmer, he started talking through clenched teeth about how lucky I was to win a Super Bowl," Manning said, adding that the more Marino's grip increased, the less sincere his comments seemed. "Towards the end [of the handshake], he was just glaring at me, saying, 'I would kill to be you right now.'" Manning said that the handshake finally ended when the "crazy" look in Marino's eyes eventually disappeared. ∅

ESPN Interrupts Drew Bledsoe's Retirement Speech To Air Commercials

APRIL 19, 2007

DALLAS— Though ESPN intended to broadcast Drew Bledsoe's entire retirement speech last Wednesday, the sports network cut away from the veteran quarterback's press conference in order to air commercials for electronics retail giant Circuit City, Sprint, and the new Honda Accord. "I have learned a lot in my 14 years in this great league, but the one thing that always stuck with me, no matter how difficult it got out there, was..." said Bledsoe before the network aired the two-minute block of advertisements, after which they cut back to Bledsoe's concluding statement. "...Only wish I could have played a lot better. Thanks." ESPN then interrupted the question-and-answer session with more commercials from Chrysler, Zipcar, and, for viewers in the Pittsburgh area, a local commercial for attorney Edgar Snyder. ∅

from **BRADY**

in spending as much time as possible on film study," said *Boston Globe* football writer Bill Ryan, who as a regular Patriots reporter was given the opportunity to view outtakes from several of the Brady shower tapes, notably those labeled "Super Bowl XXXVI," "Camp 2002/Skeleton Drills," and "Tuck Rule" before being thoroughly questioned by league officials. "But I didn't know he'd shot so much of it himself. His intensity about it can be kind of frightening."

"To hear Belichick narrating the whole thing, pointing out his quarterback's tendencies, identifying Brady's strong points and the areas where he needs work, hearing his voice as a counterpoint to the sound of the hot running water and seeing that familiar sweatshirt-clad arm cut through the mist to hand Brady his towels—you realize the man has a unique football mind," said *Sports Illustrated* football correspondent Paul Zimmerman. "If nothing else, the attention to every significant detail definitely makes an impression on the viewer."

Although officials have not divulged whether other Patriots players or even quarterbacks from other teams were featured in their own showering videotapes, Aiello confirmed that the investigation was by no means complete and the total inventory may take weeks to assemble.

"We confiscated thousands of these tapes from the Patriots coaching staff," Aiello told reporters, "and hundreds more tapes showing nothing but opposing teams sending in offensive and defensive signals. It may be some time before we have a complete catalog of what's on them. I can confirm, however, that we will be questioning Mr. Brady at length about his experiences regarding showering and video cameras, and communicating daily with Coach Belichick and team owner Robert Kraft concerning any and all videotaped footage of NFL players, specifically Tom Brady, in the shower. You have my word on that."

Neither Belichick nor Brady would comment on the investigation. The New England Patriots organization did not respond to requests for information, but released a statement Wednesday morning confirming that the league had compensated the team and coach for $750,000 in exchange for the videotapes in question. ∅

PHOTO FINISH
Fumble!

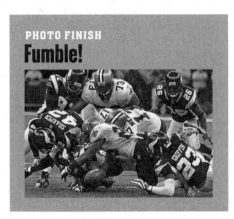

Donovan McNabb Has Perfect Game For A Black Quarterback

SEPTEMBER 27, 2007

PHILADELPHIA—With 381 yards passing, four touchdowns, and a perfect passer rating of 158.3, Philadelphia Eagles quarterback Donovan McNabb had a perfect game for a black quarterback during Sunday's victory over the Detroit Lions, members of the sports media reported. "Quite frankly, I didn't think a black quarterback could put up those kinds of numbers, and I don't think anyone else did either," football analyst Peter King said during NBC's *Football Night in America*. "Now that I have seen it, it makes me wonder what an average white quarterback, say Tom Brady or Peyton Manning, would have done against the Lions. You have to think they would have had over 500 yards passing, eight touchdowns, and even a better-than-perfect 250 rating." King added that he has been disappointed with the play of New Orleans Saints quarterback Drew Brees, saying that he needs to elevate his standard of play to that expected of a Caucasian quarterback if the Saints have any hopes of returning to the NFC Championship game. ∅

Rams Too Embarrassed To Express Interest In Simeon Rice: 'What If He Doesn't Like Us?'

AUGUST 8, 2007

ST. LOUIS, MO—Fearing that free-agent defensive end Simeon Rice would not like their team because the facilities "aren't nice enough," the "stupid old stadium is too small," and that their "dumb team uniforms look stupid," the St. Louis Rams found themselves too embarrassed to express interest in the three-time Pro-Bowler, sources close to the team reported Friday. "Just look at Simeon—he's such a great player," said Rams' GM Charley Armey, squirming in his chair as he watched tape of Rice, who is second in sacks among active players and considered quite a catch. "I don't even know what I would say to him. What if he thinks we're lame because all the other teams have more money and a later curfew?" Armey claims the team is feeling shy and vulnerable after losing several key free agents during the offseason, and that they have never felt as attractive to popular players as the other "more glamorous" teams in the NFC West. ∅

Guy At Bar Complaining About His Job Turns Out To Be Eli Manning

SEPTEMBER 20, 2007

NEW YORK—The staff and patrons of Manhattan watering hole P.J. Clarke's were only mildly surprised Monday night to learn that the gangly young man at the end of the bar grumbling about his occupation in a southern drawl was in fact Giants quarterback Eli Manning. "Go into the family business, they told me, it's what we've prepared you for—for—for your whole life," the visibly unhappy Manning told bartender Mel Gilchrist, who "really felt for the poor sap" even before recognizing Manning. "But. But! They didn't tell me that people would hate me if I wasn't perfect... I'm not perfect, y'know! I'm not, not—Peyton—and sure enough, they hate me. Not, though, not as much as I hate going to work every day." Upon realizing exactly who Manning was, a sympathetic Gilchrist reportedly bought his next three rounds. ∅

Hall Of Fame Inductee John Madden Introduced By Favorite Sandwich

Pallbearers Move Bill Walsh's Coffin Down Church Aisle In Series Of Short, Precise Passes

AUGUST 2, 2007

SAN FRANCISCO—Funeral services for legendary football coach Bill Walsh began Wednesday as friends and family of the offensive innovator bore his coffin down the aisle of the San Francisco Unitarian church in a series of short but precise passes, finally placing Walsh's earthly remains on the bier with a moving display of West Coast-style pallbearing that took a respectful nine minutes to cover over 85 steps. "This was exactly the way Coach would have wanted it," said Joe Montana, who overcame his evident grief to lead multiple platoons of well-coordinated mourners including Mike Holmgren, George Seifert, Tony Dungy, Jerry Rice, and Walsh's wife and children in a series of scripted passes that took advantage of the timing and teamwork Walsh drilled into his loved ones during his life. "Bill Walsh believed that good football should be elegant, almost beautiful, and involve everyone's strengths, and though it might sound corny, we wanted his memorial service to be the same way." Several prominent football figures in attendance said it was the most impressive memorial display since the 1970 funeral of Vince Lombardi, who was finally laid to rest in a grinding series of brutal pulling-guard sweeps that utterly overpowered the opposing Chicago Bears. ∅

INSIDE

▸ **Rusty Ray Lewis Looking Like He Hasn't Barked Once All Offseason**

Over-Optimistic NFL Doctor Says Injured Bills Player Kevin Everett Will Fly Out Of Hospital

SEPTEMBER 27, 2007

HOUSTON—Less than a month after Buffalo Bills tight end Kevin Everett suffered a life-threatening dislocation and fracture of his cervical spine that was predicted to leave him with permanent neurological damage, enthusiastic National Football League physicians attending him at Houston's Memorial Hermann hospital have announced that Everett will not only make a full recovery from injury, but will most likely gain the power of flight and soar out of the hospital under his own power.

"What we're seeing in Kevin's case is proof that the serious-injury recovery rate in pro football is nowhere near as serious as people have come to believe," Dr. Robert Homburg, a neurosurgeon assigned to Everett's case by the National Football League, said while pointing at the wings he had drawn on Everett's spinal X-rays. "Not only will Kevin be able to walk out of the hospital, he actually won't have to, as he will heal so completely that he will be better than he was before and will almost certainly be able to fly out unassisted."

"I don't think I'd be exaggerating Kevin's prognosis if I said we're looking at a 200% recovery here," Homburg added.

Just days ago, physician Teodoro Castillo, Everett's original physician, said the injury was "extremely severe" but that heal-

ing was progressing surprisingly well, pointing to Everett's ability to sit up without difficulty and even move his right arm slightly as evidence that he might someday walk without difficulty. Upon being told of Homburg's claims, Castillo said the recovery would be a "staged process of indeterminate length" and that flying was almost certainly out of the question.

"While it's true I have treated few players with Kevin's level of physical conditioning and mental resilience, I don't think it's fair for the NFL's doctor to tell him that he'll be able to fly," Castillo said Wednesday. "First of all, the trauma to his spinal cord was so extreme that we had to inject chilled saline into his body to induce healing. Second, no matter what Dr. Homburg says, people cannot just grow wings and fly, period, and to tell Kevin that is cruel. He probably won't even play football again."

Dr. Homburg said that, while he appreciated Castillo's cautious approach, he was only in partial agreement with his colleague.

"Sadly, I'm afraid it's true that Kevin will never play football again—the league cannot afford to give the Bills the sort of unfair competitive advantage a flying tight end would offer them," Homburg said. "It's a lot like how Steve Young and Troy Aikman had to retire when their concussions gave them

see KEVIN EVERETT

PHOTO FINISH

Incoming North Korean Missile Intercepted By Deion Sanders

INSIDE

‣ **Mel Kiper Sighs, Takes Out Bobby Pins, Lets Down Luxurious Knee-Length Hair**

Both Teams Satisfied With Three-And-A-Half-Yard Carry

OCTOBER 18, 2007

KANSAS CITY, MO—Players on both the anemic Kansas City Chiefs offense and the porous Cincinnati Bengals defense celebrated with high-fives, hugs, and minor victory dances when the Bengals managed to stop a rare positive gain by the Chiefs running game during the first quarter of Sunday's game at Arrowhead Stadium. "Getting almost two feet more than their league worst 3.1 yards-per-carry average could be a huge momentum builder for the Chiefs," said CBS announcer Rich Gannon, who had initially expected Chiefs running back Larry Johnson to slip and fall down behind the line of scrimmage, run straight into his blockers, or fumble while the Bengals linebackers either attempted weak arm tackles or overran the play completely. "Still, you really have to like what the Bengals did on that play by allowing only a few yards before tackling the runner. Both of these teams are really setting the tone right now." Gannon added that he didn't know how long these two teams could continue to play over their heads and execute at such an average level. ∅

Goodell Tells Bills To Use Bye Week To See If Football Is Something They Really Want To Be Doing

OCTOBER 11, 2007

BUFFALO, NY—Following another devastating loss to the Dallas Cowboys Monday, NFL Commissioner Roger Goodell told the 1-4 Buffalo Bills to take time during their upcoming bye week to reflect on their season thus far and ask themselves if playing professional football is what they really want to be doing with their lives. "I'm not trying to push them in any particular direction," Goodell told reporters after the game, which the Bills lost despite forcing six turnovers, ultimately finding themselves unable to field a last-minute onside kick. "As commissioner, it's my job to put a quality product on the field each and every week and see that there is some kind of parity amongst the teams. I'll be curious to hear, especially if they decide to continue playing, where the Bills think they fit into an NFL that is continuously getting more and more competitive." Though most Bills fans were still too demoralized by Monday night's loss to comment on Goodell's request, those who talked to the media after the announcement said they "wouldn't give a flying fuck if those losers played another fucking football game ever." ∅

INSIDE

› College Football Television Director Needs Better Shot of Cheerleaders Ruffling Pom Pons

› Fan Turns Off TV Confident That Game-Winning Field Goal Went Through

---

STRONG SIDE/ WEAK SIDE: BILL BELICHICK

STRONG SIDE	WEAK SIDE
Lackof human emotions allow him to operate more efficiently in todays inhuman NFL	Really, when you get right down to it , kind of a temendous dickasaurus
Surprisingly fun when drunk	Hates second-and-short
His father, whose grave he would gladly defile if satan offered him the Vince Lombardi Trophy in exchange for doing so, was also a was also a coach	For every Tom Brady he's coachedbrilliantly, he has also brilliantly coached a Randy Moss
Although an evil genius, is only an evil football genius, not the kind that clones monsters or rigs elections	Rare childhood disorder left him unable to shake hands
Razor-sharp talons allow him to immobilize prey, separate meat from bones	Has vowed to "see the world boil with blood and flames" for allowing the Patriots to go 5-11 in 2000
Coaches a really, really good team	Wins more than his fair share of games

PHOTO FINISH

Stolen Auburn Playbook Returned With Spelling, Grammar Corrected

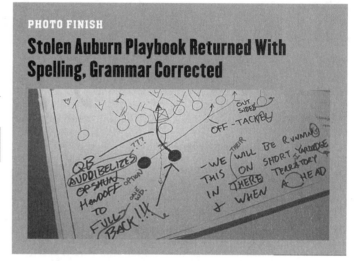

from **KEVIN EVERETT**

telekinesis and the power to stop time. Still, for Castillo to just dismiss the idea of Kevin's more-than-complete recovery out of hand is cynical and unprofessional. Like many injury-related issues, while it may be based on sound medical practices, it goes against everything the NFL is about."

"Also, I should make it clear that I'm not saying Kevin will actually 'just grow wings and fly,'" he added. "It could be from magic, a rare form of spinal helicopter blades, or small jet boosters emerging from his feet. We have to keep an open mind about this."

Reactions to the news from around the league were mixed, with the NFL's front office sending Everett and Homburg their congratulations on his full recovery; players' union executive director Gene Upshaw saying that any further medical complications in Everett's case would be interpreted as the result of improper flight procedures and would result in the cancellation of his NFLPA benefits and pension, if any; and Everett's fellow Buffalo Bills players responding with a stunned silence born of disbelief and, presumably, joy.

For his part, Everett is determined to stay positive.

"I'm just taking things one day at a time," Everett said from his hospital bed, where he is preparing to begin physical therapy and doing his best to ignore the multiple news reports about his injury. "I heard that some league doctor had said some good things about me, and I guess that's nice. I'll walk out of this place, just you watch. But just between you and me, sometimes I think those NFL medical guys are a bunch of goddamn liars." ∅

Rams Seem To Have Beaten Saints

NOVEMBER 15, 2007

NEW ORLEANS—Sources within the NFL's competition committee tentatively confirmed Monday that, according to their preliminary analysis of statistics compiled during Sunday's St. Louis-New Orleans game, the previously winless Rams did indeed score more points than the Saints and therefore must officially be declared the winner. "Further review is in order, up to and including watching a full recording of the game, if in fact any broadcaster bothered to make one," commissioner Roger Goodell told disbeliev-

ing reporters Monday. "Still, the smattering of eyewitness accounts we have collected, including several from officials in attendance, seem to bear out reports of a Rams victory." The Saints organization has thus far refused comment on the issue, but say they will dutifully comply with any decision reached by the league "no matter how outrageous." ∅

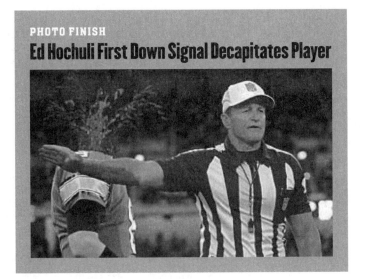

PHOTO FINISH

Ed Hochuli First Down Signal Decapitates Player

NFL Meteorologists Warn Steaming Black-Guy Heads Occurring Later Every Year

DECEMBER 6, 2007

NEW YORK—Steaming black-guy heads, the traditional sign of approaching winter for generations of football fans, have been occurring later in the season with every passing year, a fact that may be evidence of a climatic change with long-term effects on football itself, top scientists in the meteorological department of the National Football League said in a study released Monday.

"The phenomenon of weather-related African-American supracranial vaporous emission, or 'Steaming Black-Guy Heads,' as it is colloquially known, occurs when cold dry winter air comes into contact with hot, humid, shaven heads of football players, causing their personal water vapor to condense and rise on a column of heated air," the statement read in part. "It is then observed by network cameramen, who overwhelmingly choose to film African-American players due to the dramatic contrasts that result—especially when the player in question is backlit—and beamed to millions of households during time-outs, replay reviews, and other stoppages of play. The viewers then realize that winter has come to America."

"However, film review reveals that steaming black-guy heads, which during the 1970s were commonplace in mid-September, have in recent years not been sighted until the weeks after Thanksgiving," the statement continued. "Although further study is definitely called for, we conclude that the pronounced trend

for steaming black-guy heads to occur progressively later every year—coupled with the phenomenon of giant triangles of ass-sweat persisting well into November—is a possible indication of a slowly warming climate across the entire NFL."

League commissioner Roger Goodell was not available for comment, saying that, although early-season instances of steaming black-guy heads were obviously preferable, the NFL had no official stance on climate change, global warming, or other meteorological phenomena that did not directly affect the scheduling or outcome of games.

Reaction among coaches and players has been mixed.

"When I came into the league with Tampa Bay, steaming black-guy heads were everywhere in October," said longtime NFL veteran and

current Carolina Panthers quarterback Vinny Testaverde. "The Bucs were in the NFC Central back then, and we played in Chicago and Green Bay a lot, and to me, they always meant Halloween was coming. But these days, the rookies think of them as the first sign of Christmas. You can't tell me that's not global warming."

"Early on in my career, I saw them a lot, even in September," said Packers quarterback Brett Favre, who still has fond memories of the steaming heads of such Packer greats as Sterling Sharpe, LeRoy Butler, and Reggie White. "But this year we only started getting them just this week, and it's December already. Listen, I don't know anything about climate change, but I'd hate to see my daughters grow up in a world where steaming black-guy heads are just something you see on ESPN Classic."

NFL climatologist Lee Orfordson, one of the authors of the report, advised caution among those worried about the dwindling instances of steaming black-guy heads around the league.

"Remember that there are more domed stadiums now, that Northern-tier teams are being scheduled for more away games in Southern-tier cities during the winter months, and above all, that steaming black-guy heads are a single, if dramatic, phenomenon," Orfordson said. "There are plenty of numbers still to crunch here before we can say the steaming black-guy head has gone the way of the dodo."

Still, for generations of fans for

see **BLACK-GUY HEADS**

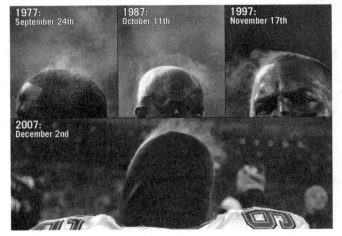

1977: September 24th

1987: October 11th

1997: November 17th

2007: December 2nd

Super Bowl XLII: New York Giants Vs. New England Patriots

NEW YORK GIANTS

• Double-check to make sure chin staps are secure

• Put a picture of Tom Brady on the bulletin board to give Eli Manning something to aspire to

• Jeremy Shockey must not allow himself to become intimidated just because he's playing in front of long-time hero Tom Petty

• Offensive line must continue its excellent job of subtly redirecting Eli Manning's errant passes

• Pressure the quarterback, run the ball effectively, win the turnover battle, and all the other things that make up winning football, except way more than normal

• Call "next point wins" before kicking an extra point

• Sneak up behind entire Patriots team, knock them out, drag them into closet, switch uniforms with them, and allow the "Giants" to win; then switch clothes back before trophy ceremony

NEW ENGLAND PATRIOTS

• Players and coaches alike must remember that not everyone can apply sunscreen to Tom Brady at once

• If it comes down to having or not having a stroke, Tedy Bruschi should choose the latter

• Don't settle for mere field goals or mere touchdowns

• Since the team has not lost a single game while Kevin Faulk has maintained his personal superstition, Faulk should continue to shower regularly

• Don't get maneuvered into playing the Giants' game, as it is not good enough to win the Super Bowl

• Although the victory champagne will be in the locker room for days prior to the game, team must not allow themselves to get drunk until halftime

• Use all their advantages to their advantage

Worst-Ever NFL Playoff Chokes

JANUARY 17, 2008

Poor performances by Tony Romo and Peyton Manning contributed to their teams' losses in the divisional playoffs, but they weren't the worst choke-jobs of all time. Onion Sports takes a look at the ones that were:

➤ **1971:** The Miami Dolphins are defeated in the Super Bowl when head coach Don Shula decides against experience and starts 10-year-old quarterback Dan Marino.

➤ **1979:** Charger quarterback Dan Fouts is intercepted five times by the Oilers in a divisional playoff loss, which Fouts later ascribes to rookie safety Vernon Perry looking just like the guy he buys cocaine from.

➤ **1991:** In the most famous choke in NFL history, Scott Norwood is inexplicably unable to propel an irregularly shaped object through two raised posts 141 feet away using only his foot.

➤ **1999:** The Cowboys lose a playoff game at home to the Arizona Cardinals... the ARIZONA CARDINALS.

➤ **2000:** Kevin Dyson chokes away the Titans' chance at a Super Bowl title by not having arms one yard longer.

➤ **2005:** Legendary Chiefs coach Hank Stram dies at the age of 82 while trying to eat half a steak in one bite.

➤ **2007:** The Dallas Mavericks' stunning loss to the Golden State Warriors notable enough to mandate inclusion on all "worst choke" lists regardless of sport.

➤ **2007:** Peyton Manning succumbs to the immense pressure of Super Bowl XLI and is only able to lead the Colts to a 12-point victory.

Peter Gammons Shamefully Admits He Watched Super Bowl

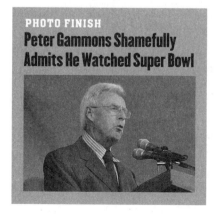

from **BLACK-GUY HEADS**

whom steaming black-guy heads were an important symbol of seasonal change, the announcement has inspired a definite feeling of foreboding.

"I was the very first of the steaming black-guy heads," said former Raider defensive end Otis "The Grandfather Of All Steaming Black-Guy Heads" Sistrunk, whose own vigorously steaming head was noted by ABC color man Alex Karras in the early autumn of 1974 and began a winter-onset sideline-camera tradition that continues to this day. "And I'm very, very proud of that. I just hope I don't live to see the last." ∅

Patriots' Season Perfect For Rest Of Nation

FEBRUARY 7, 2008

FOXBOROUGH, MA—As the once-invincible, still-insufferable Patriots attempt to come to grips with their 17-14 Super Bowl loss to the Giants, the death of their dream to go undefeated, and the possible end of their dynasty, almost every other person in America is reveling in what they consider the perfect ending to New England's season.

"I just couldn't imagine a better ending to the Patriots odyssey," said Simon Williams, a Kansas City-area football fan who usually watches the college game but found himself caught up in the Patriots' sheer loathsomeness during the season. "The utter lack of humility they displayed alongside an equal lack of any joy in the game, that toad of a coach, and that cologne-ad quarterback... If they have to act that badly while playing that well, you really want to see them fail in the biggest way possible. Thank God almighty, that's what we got."

There is general agreement that the Super Bowl, despite the low score, was one of the finest in recent memory, due in part to the fearsome performance by the Giants and a cool, courageous display of quarterbacking by Eli Manning.

However, when asked about their favorite parts of the game, most fans chose the Patriots' cocky decision to begin the

game with a trick play, which the Giants stopped handily; Bill Belichick's smug third-quarter attempt at a fourth-and-13 conversion, which blew up in his face, instead of trying a field goal; and New England's offensive line, which featured three Pro Bowlers, allowing high-cheekboned, doe-eyed, supermodel-impregnating passer Tom Brady to be hit over 20 times during the course of the game.

"Did you see [Giants defensive tackle Jay] Alford smack Brady right in the face on that last drive?" said Bellevue, WA newsstand operator Christian Dansby.

"Brady was almost offended. I think he forgot for a few months there that he was a football player. It was just perfect."

"God, seeing Randy Moss do his weird chicken-wing crowd taunt when they scored to go ahead in the fourth was awful," said Jeff Lafferty, who watched the Super Bowl with rabid New England fans despite having known them for years. "What's worse is that the Pats fans ate it up. Of course, when Burress made that catch to win... Perfection. That's the only word for the Pats now. Perfection."

However, most fans gave responses that had little to do with the game itself and more with the almost flawless joy of seeing the Patriots lose, as a team that has been insufferable and unappealing in victory instantly became in-

see PATRIOTS

Favre: I've Always Had A Passion For Stopping Things, Then Starting To Do Things Again

JULY 31, 2008

KILN, MS—Embattled quarterback Brett Favre attempted Monday to explain his recent actions concerning his recent reversal of his decision to retire by holding a press conference in which he explained his lifelong love for quitting things briefly before resuming those same things after a certain interval of time had passed. "I'm just that kind of guy, I guess—a gunslinger on one hand, but on the other, a man who knows when to stop, at least at first, but then it turns out I really didn't know when to stop after all," Favre said. "I guess you could say I'm a guy who quits, then realizes I don't know the meaning of the word quit." A number of the journalists present were later heard to wonder, in light of Favre's recent inexplicable behavior, if perhaps drinking heavily were one of the things the first-ballot Hall of Famer had stopped doing before starting again. Ø

Romeo Crennel To Charlie Weis: 'I Need You To Come Over Right Now And Stop Me From Eating These Five Chocolate Wedding Cakes'

SEPTEMBER 18, 2008

CLEVELAND—According to telephone transcripts and voicemail recordings, panicked Cleveland Browns head coach Romeo Crennel called former colleague, current Notre Dame coach, and Overeaters Anonymous sponsor Charlie Weis Tuesday, pleading for Weis to come to his house and stop him from eating five multi-tiered chocolate wedding cakes. "Charlie? Charlie, I... I have a fork in one hand a big jug of milk in the other. I've already eaten the mocha-hazelnut bride and groom figurines. Oh, God, Charlie," said Crennel, who went on to add that when he originally purchased the wedding cakes, he told himself he merely wanted "the comfort of knowing they were close by." "If you don't get here soon, all of it is going to be gone, and I'll have failed again... Oh. Oh, my, it's Dutch choc- [inaudible]." Upon arriving, Weis reportedly found Crennel lying on his kitchen floor in a pool of melted confectionery, deep in diabetic shock, with a rictus of mingled pleasure and self-disgust frozen on his chocolate-covered face. Ø

Eli Manning Wins Biggest Game Of Tom Brady's Life

DECEMBER 15, 2008

GLENDALE, AZ—With his perfect season and the Patriots' championship at stake in Super Bowl XLII, celebrity athlete and future Hall of Fame quarterback Tom Brady dug deep within himself to be outplayed by Giants journeyman passer Eli Manning. "To raise the level of our game and win on the biggest stage like this—it feels amazing," everyone assumed four-time Pro Bowler Brady would say following the historic game, only to hear those words spoken not only by a Manning, but by a non-Peyton Manning. Given the chance to become the only team in league history to go 19-0, Brady put his team on his shoulders and led the Patriots in a fourth-quarter comeback, scoring the go-ahead touchdown late in the game, an inspiring 12-play drive topped only by Manning's own 12-play touchdown drive immediately afterwards, a feat the Giants QB referred to as "cool." Manning followed up his Super Bowl MVP performance by not ripping up his ACL or MCL in the 2008 season. ∅

Bengals: Current Chad Johnson Not The Same Man Who Jumped Into Browns Stands

INSIDE

‣ Minnesota Residents Willing To Pay Extra Taxes To Help Vikings Move Out Of State

‣ 'Top Ten Crossbar Slam Dunks' Circled On NFL Network Whiteboard

‣ Ben Roethlisberger Wakes Up In Middle Of Night To See Ray Lewis' Face Directly In Front Of His

‣ Ground Yells At Ref For Disallowing Fumble It Caused

Brett Favre On Learning Jets' Intricate Offensive System: 'I Like Football'

AUGUST 21, 2008

EAST RUTHERFORD, NJ—Newly acquired Jets quarterback Brett Favre, when asked how he was adapting to the intricate terminology and increased complexity of the Jets' playbook after a career running the West Coast offense, assured reporters that he did indeed like football. "I like football," Favre said in response to inquiries as to how he would handle the emphasis on downfield passing and the increased demand for adaptation through the multiple audibles found in Coach Mangini's offense. "I like it a lot." Favre went 5 for 6 in the recent scrimmage against Washington and seemed to enjoy himself immensely. ∅

from PATRIOTS

consolable and self-pitying in defeat.

Frequently mentioned examples of instances which, upon reflection, sweetened the Patriots' utter failure included the team's propensity to complain about unfair officiating after their victories; their habit of gleefully running up the score, which also resulted in Brady and Moss earning NFL single-season scoring records in blowouts; and of course, the players' and coaches' hateful attitude.

"Come on, that cheating scandal to open the season and all they say is 'Everybody does it?' They could have at least acted a little bit sorry," said Milwaukee architect and sports fan David Engel. "They acted like a bunch of third-graders, just the way Belichick did when he ran off the field with time left on the clock. At least he shook the other coach's hand this time. That's a first for the big baby."

"The worst part for me is that none of them seem to enjoy playing football," said Lexington, KY-area mechanic Jack Colgrave. "Even when they were winning, all they did was taunt—Randy Moss taunting crowds, Wes Welker telling people they sucked, Brady sneering at the very idea they might get beat someday. What a bunch of absolutely perfect assholes."

"Did their team plane land safely back in Foxborough?" Colgrave asked. "It didn't happen to lose altitude over Boston, burst into a cartwheel of flames, throwing players like Roman candles across New England, and then slam into few dozen loudmouth Patriots' fans houses? It didn't? Well, I guess no football season is perfect." ∅

Tony Womo Out Three To Four Weeks With Bwoken Widdle Fingey

OCTOBER 16, 2008

DAWWAS—Cowboys medical personnel confirm that quawterback Tony Womo injured his thwowing hand in last week's 30-24 loss to the Arizona Cardinals and is expected to miss the next month after suffewing a sevewy bwoken wight pinkie-winkie.

Team doctors originally believed Womo's poor, poor bwoken fingey was merewy spwained, despite the quarterback insisting that his pinkie felt really, really, really ouchie after being hit by wots and wots of big mean mans during the first play of overtime.

The Cowboys are denying rumors that Womo will require weconstwuctive pinkie surgewy, insisting that it is only a bad owie and that Womo will not be placed on injuwed weserve.

"Tony has been very, very bwave through all this and barely cried at all when he heard his widdle fingey was in fact bwoken," coach Wade Phillips said Monday, explaining that Womo was "westing comfiwy" and watching cartoons at home and had thus far managed to keep his pinkie out of his mouth. "I'd say he's week to week, but it's up to the team medics to say when he's completely all-better-now."

The Cowboys originally sensed something was wrong when Womo threw three straight incomplete passes to begin the overtime after being sacked three times and knocked down 19 times during regulation by meanie-bullies who hate him. Their suspicions were confirmed when Womo blubbered to them on the sidelines while holding up his hurted fingey.

Womo was immediately given an orange-flavored St. Joseph aspirin and a wowwypop while a SpongeBob SquarePants Band-Aid was applied to the pinkie. When this proved inadequate, Cowboys head pediatrician Daniel "Doctor Danny" Cooper inspected Womo's pinkie while trainers distracted Womo by making a spoon into an airplane and "flying" chocolate ice cream into the quarterback's mouth.

"This was more than just the normal boo-boo," Cooper told reporters. "Tony has played through boo-boos before, like any team weader and big gwown-up boy has to. But when I saw the quivering chin, the big wet eyes, and the way he was hopping from foot to foot while holding up his widdle bitty widdy fingey, I

knew this one was bad."

The NFL said no fine would be given on the hit, as it seemed to be an honest accident and no flag for roughhousing the passer was thrown on the play. It is not known whether Womo will stomp his widdle foot and complain louder to the NFL regarding the decision.

Phillips confirmed that 40-year-old backup quarterback Brad Johnson will start as long as Womo's pinkie is still an ouchie pinkie.

"It's unfortunate for the poor tyke to have to go through something like this," said Johnson, who hasn't started an NFL game since 2006. "But you know, when they're little quarterbacks they sometimes take big spills. This will just make Tony-wony tougher when he grows up. I hope."

In other Cowboys news, Adam "Pacman" Jones is still grounded for the rest of his life, or at least until he learns to stop back-sassing, and receiver Terrell Owens is listed as "probable" for Sunday's game despite suffering a chronic case of turf piggy. ∅

Brett Favre Just Chucks Reputation Up There

DECEMBER 15, 2008

NEW YORK—Just weeks after safely handing off his legacy to historians and retiring as one of the most beloved sports figures in recent memory, Packer legend Brett Favre decided to make one last desperate heave for glory by signing with the New York Jets. "If I've learned one thing in my life, it's that sometimes you just have to put everything you got into one last desperate hurl for it all," Favre said after agreeing to a one-year, $12 million Hail Mary contract. "I just thought I'd take everything I've come to represent, whip it as far and as fast as I could, and see who came down with it." Favre did not comment on whether or not he considered signing with the Jets to be a successful completion of his career or life. ∅

Phil Simms Mistaken For Life-Sized Cardboard Cutout Of Phil Simms

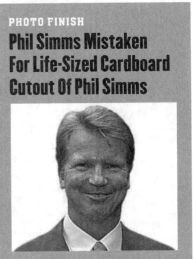

The 2008 Pro Bowl

NFC

- It is absolutely critical that the players all buy colorful aloha shirts and straw hats and pose for a big team photo in them

- If the AFC puts a bunch of players on the Pro Bowl practice squad, claim them off waivers

- Despite Terrell Owens repeatedly insisting that there's a tarantula in his bed, just ignore him; he can't prove anything

- Designated special teamer Brendon Ayanbadejo must take over the game with some kind of tackle or block

- Don't stress, bro

- Get ball to Larry Fitzgerald, or Donald Driver, or even Torry Holt! What an embarrassment of riches!

- Watch out for that volcano on the 30-yard line

AFC

- Norv Turner should just ask Peyton Manning what to do, as he's already coached a couple of these things

- If you must take a nap, at least do it in the locker room so as not to distract your teammates

- If for some reason they decide they want to win the game, play halfway decently because the NFC certainly won't

- Must try not to spill their Mai Tais while eluding defenders or attempting to arm-tackle NFC ballcarriers

- Hang ten, dude

- Get the ball to Braylon Edwards; that guy is a Pro Bowler

- Just make sure everyone's flags are tucked in so it's not so obvious

Radio Interviewer Audibly Fellating Colt McCoy

OCTOBER 23, 2008

AUSTIN, TX—Greg Streets, the commentator and host of The Longhorn Zone on Austin-area AM station Sports Radio 1480, could clearly be heard performing enthusiastic and vigorous oral sex upon Texas quarterback and Heisman trophy frontrunner Colt McCoy during an interview Wednesday. "So there are people, hmmmmmm ummmm nnf, saying that Oklahoma State will blitz and try to apply womm hnghh ulp more pressure on you this Saturday," Streets gasped wetly during the seven-minute puff piece which took up the central section of the 20-minute question-and-answer session. "Mmmmm hmmm oh. Oh my. Oh." McCoy made it clear during the interview that the Longhorns were concentrating on conference play, taking it one game at a time, and that being on top ain't gay. Ø

INSIDE

› Injured Player Gives Thumbs-Down While Being Carted Off Field

› Fans Retract Hands During Matt Leinart's High Five Attempts

› Man With Rare Purple-Yellow Skin Condition Tired Of Being Mistaken For Vikings Fan

T.J. Houshmandzadeh Enjoys Ordering 'The Houshmandzadeh' Just To See What Waiter Brings

OCTOBER 16, 2008

CINCINNATI—Sitting at an Italian eatery with a plate full of Houshmandzadeh (ravioli verde stuffed with prosciutto and mushroom and topped with a light Alfredo sauce), Bengals wide receiver T.J. Houshmandzadeh told reporters Wednesday that he often orders his last name at different restaurants to see what dish the waiter brings to his table. "I love the Houshmandzadeh at sushi places, because fried conger eel and nori seaweed really hits the spot," said Houshmandzadeh, who later recommended diners try the Houshmandzadeh at Lebanese restaurants, but with baba ghanoush instead of hummus. "I will say the only time I ever regretted ordering it was at a Mexican place, as the prawns were spicier than I thought they would be." At press time, Houshmandzadeh was at a Cincinnati Dairy Queen eating a butterscotch Blizzard with Kit Kat bars mixed in. Ø

Steelers Coach Mike Tomlin To Staff: 'What If Ben Roethlisberger Is Bad?'

OCTOBER 30, 2008

PITTSBURGH—Following Sunday's 21-14 loss to the New York Giants, in which Pittsburgh quarterback Ben Roethlisberger threw for 189 yards and four interceptions, Steelers coach Mike Tomlin posited to his coaching staff the notion that Roethlisberger might actually be a bad football player. "What if we've convinced ourselves that he's good because we desperately wanted a star quarterback, but the truth is that he's actually pretty bad, and his occasional good games are just flukes?" Tomlin was overheard saying to offensive coordinator Bruce

Arians, who later told reporters that Pittsburgh coaches, players, and fans have come close to asking this very same question about Roethlisberger's play before, only stopping short for fear of what that answer might be. "I mean, we won a Super Bowl with him

in 2005, but did he lead the team to that win or were the running game, receiving core, and defense so solid that we won it with a bad quarterback? Oh, Jesus." Roethlisberger signed an eight-year, $102 million extension with the team in March. ∅

Lee Corso Starting To Feel Weird At College Parties

NOVEMBER 6, 2008

BATON ROUGE, LA—In town with *College GameDay* for a matchup between No. 1 Alabama and No. 15 LSU, 72-year-old Lee Corso felt awkward as he was surrounded by college students for the first time in his life during a rally thrown by a local fraternity. "God, look at them; they're so young," observed Corso, clutching a red plastic Solo cup filled with Coors Light while huddled in a crowded basement corner with cohosts Chris Fowler and Kirk Herbstreit. "I saw a group of girls come in here that, I swear to God, they looked like they were 13 years old. I mean, they're acting nice enough, taking pictures with me and everything, but come on." Finally unable to bear it any longer, Corso retired to the *College GameDay* bus and fell asleep while reading his book. ∅

Perkins Management Disappointed To See Daunte Culpepper Leave So Soon

NOVEMBER 6, 2008

ORLANDO, FL—Day manager Gary Campbell of the Perkins restaurant on Conroy Road thanked Daunte Culpepper for his tireless effort, leadership on and off the dining room floor, and dedication to service Tuesday, saying he was saddened to lose a server who had one of the greatest careers in the history of the franchise. "Every Sunday you could count on Daunte to efficiently deliver entrées or find an open table for customers in the face of an oncoming

breakfast rush," said Campbell, who was shocked to hear the three-time Perkins employee of the month was retiring. "The fact that he was able to maintain a perfect 158.3 customer satisfaction rating despite working with inexperienced line cooks is incredible. We still believe he can perform at a high level, but respect his decision to walk away from the restaurant game on his own terms." With the departure of Culpepper, Campbell said Perkins would promote journeyman dishwasher-busboy Jeff George from the second shift. ∅

Brooks Bollinger Best Option At Quarterback For NFL Team

NOVEMBER 6, 2008

DALLAS—Brooks Bollinger, a journeyman third-stringer whose career has found him occupying roster spots behind backups Vinny Testaverde, Kelly Holcomb, and Brad Johnson (twice), is now considered by an NFL team to be their actual best choice at quarterback. "We can win with Brooks," coach Wade

Phillips said of the Wisconsin product, whose college and pro careers have been marked by hard work, gutsy play, and handoffs rather than talent. "Must, I mean. We must win with him. We have no choice." Bollinger was unavailable for comment, as he was practicing handoffs to a man named Tashard Choice, who is currently the best option at running back for the same NFL team. ∅

PHOTO FINISH

Giants Unveil Strahan Signal

Plaxico Burress Holds Team Meeting To Admit He Was Wide Open

NOVEMBER 13, 2008

EAST RUTHERFORD, NJ—In an emotional locker-room address to his gathered teammates and coaches, troubled Giants receiver Plaxico Burress admitted to being completely open on a third down play in Sunday's game against the Eagles. "I know I've put this team through a lot this season, but I just want to say that I had a step on him... I was gone," said Burress, who called the meeting after arriving late to practice for the 10th time this season. "I realize this team has rules for everyone else for a reason, and that's to win. And although it's hard for me to say this, we are never going to win if we don't get the ball to me more. I mean, I'm open most plays. We can get through this if, before you do anything else, you look at me." After the meeting, Burress took head coach Tom Coughlin aside to more personally express how he hates running decoy routes and blocking. ✍

Report: Planes Just As Afraid Of John Madden

NOVEMBER 27, 2008

WASHINGTON—The Federal Aviation Administration stated Wednesday that, according to all available evidence, airplanes are just as afraid of carrying sportscaster John Madden as he is of traveling on them. "Airliners have a not unreasonable fear that, were John Madden to board them, it would increase their chances of crashing," said FAA administrator Robert A. Sturgell, reading from the report. "While looking at John Madden, planes often express a sense of inadequacy and a heightened fear of losing control. Our studies have not found, however, that planes have any more reason to be afraid of John Madden than they do of any other grossly overweight celebrity." To help reduce planes' fears, Boeing has enrolled their fleet of commercial airliners in an education program about the realities of John Madden, which will explain exactly how he works, the meaning of the various sounds he generates, and why he may vibrate or gurgle when under way. ✍

PHOTO FINISH

Defensive Back Still Down On Ground After Missed Interception

Report: Everyone Watching Football Game Evidently Needs New Car, Shower, Shave

DECEMBER 11, 2008

NEW YORK—According to demographic analysis released Tuesday by the Elias Sports Bureau, all 17 million people who watched NFL football games aired from Sunday afternoon through Monday night are so desperately in need of a new car, great quantities of soap, and effective shaving tools that they need to be reminded of these facts during every stoppage in play. "Our study indicates that these men are lacking high-endurance body washes, five-bladed razors, and practical yet sporty urban-utility vehicles with antilock brakes and strong, contemporary styling," said Jonathan Gabrus, head of football statistics at ESB. "It seems like the only way to get the message out is to constantly remind these people using short, persuasive video clips featuring flashy editing and catchy jingles." In a related study, ESB has discovered that baseball fans are prone to car accidents and cannot achieve an erection. ✍

PHOTO FINISH

Vikings Hire Coach

Tony Romo Comes Out Of Bye Week Addicted To Heroin

NOVEMBER 13, 2008

IRVING, TX—Disoriented and disheveled Dallas quarterback Tony Romo, dressed in stained clothing and reeking of urine, returned to the Cowboys practice facilities Monday and told his teammates he would do anything to score more heroin. According to team sources, the visibly strung-out Romo dressed for practice with difficulty, walked up to his offensive line, and collapsed under center Andre Gurode before going into mild convulsions and breaking out in a cold sweat. "Get me Popcorn Jones, I gotta see, see him, need to, please, just a little, you holding?" said Romo, rigorously scratching inside the elbow of his throwing arm. "What do you want me to do? I'll throw a touchdown. I will, damn it. Just—I'm fucking dying here. Anything. I'll suck your dick right now. Help me out." Romo was dismissed from practice early for undisclosed medical reasons and is currently nodding off on a filthy mattress in the condemned tenement building where he has been staying lately. ✍

PHOTO FINISH

Leather-Jacketed, Sunglasses-Wearing Rex Grossman: 'There's A New Rex In Town'

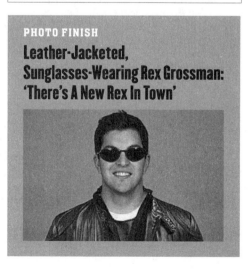

Charlie Weis Called Before Christ To Discuss Future With Notre Dame

DECEMBER 4, 2008

SOUTH BEND, IN—Jesus Christ, the Son of God and president of Notre Dame football's Booster Club, announced yesterday that head coach Charlie Weis will appear before Him to discuss his future, if any, as coach of the Fighting Irish. "I, like many Notre Dame fans, am disappointed in Weis, and his day of judgment has surely come," Christ, His eyes flashing with righteous flame, said at the Sunday morning press conference. "Escorted by the angelic host and by [Notre Dame athletic director] Jack Swarbrick, I shall sit upon My heavenly throne Monday and, in all My glory, meet with Coach Weis. I am a fair and loving God, and I have always said that the souls of the righteous shall rise to national championships; but also shall the evildoers, like Bob Davie and Gerry Faust, be condemned for all eternity." When asked about the untimely smiting of former coach Tyrone Willingham, Christ said He had no comment, asked for the questioner's name, and left. ⌀

Offense: Visual Evidence Suggests Linebackers Will Blitz

DECEMBER 11, 2008

MIDFIELD—Highly placed sources on the offense, including an individual who is reportedly lined up under the center, are claiming to have conclusive evidence that the middle linebacker and one or both outside linebackers will blitz immediately after the ball is snapped. "Blitz! Blitz! Watch for the blitz!" multiple individuals at the scene were heard to say, suggesting that purposeful movement towards or up to the neutral zone had been observed. "They're coming!" Neither blocking nor ball-handling personnel had commented on their

plans to either pick up or avoid the blitz as of press time. ⌀

Overenthusiastic Referee On Game-Winning Field Goal: 'It's Great!'

Romeo Crennel Upset With Team's Offense And That Nestle Crunch Bars No Longer Come Wrapped In Foil

DECEMBER 4, 2008

CLEVELAND—At his usual press conference Monday, Browns coach Romeo Crennel expressed disappointment in his offense's poor effort and inability to capitalize on a strong defensive game against the Colts as well as Nestle's decision to no longer package its signature Nestle Crunch bar in aluminum foil. "I have two priorities this week: getting Ken [Dorsey] comfortable and in control on the field, and finding a candy bar that doesn't create a distracting mess in your pocket because of its inferior wrapping," said Crennel, adding that the Crunch bar's foil used to make him feel as if he were eating the chocolate bar from *Willy Wonka and the* *Chocolate Factory*. "Dorsey's an outstanding player and we have to support him with quality play. And the Crunch is an outstanding and delicious treat, but it isn't supported by that cheap plastic wrapper. Krackels are good—I gave them out for Halloween this year—but I like Nestle chocolate better." Krennel explained it also is important for backup quarterback Brady Quinn to ice up his broken finger because he "likes it when the candy bars are cold." ⌀

Defense: Watch For The Screen, Watch For The Screen

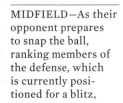

DECEMBER 11, 2008

MIDFIELD—As their opponent prepares to snap the ball, ranking members of the defense, which is currently positioned for a blitz, are cautioning their members to be alert for the possibility of a blitz-evading screen pass. "Watch the screen! Watch out for the screen!" said one top defensive player, whose position in the very middle of the formation is generally considered to give him a better view and thus a better opportunity to predict the actions of the offense. "Screen!" Meanwhile, sources in the defensive backfield, while not ruling out the screen, are said to be considering the possibility of the offense running the draw. ⌀

Long-Snapper And Son Long-Snap A Few Balls Around Backyard

OCTOBER 30, 2008

CLEVELAND—Former Browns long-snapper Wes Hardigree, 38, took advantage of the lovely autumn weather Wednesday afternoon, picking up his 8-year-old son Ben from school and long-snapping the ball around the backyard of their suburban Cleveland home.

"It's just a perfect Norman Rockwell scene—fall colors, crisp air, the low late light, the glow of Ben's red cheeks, and me looking at it all upside-down between my legs as I get ready to long-snap the ball 12 yards to my boy," Hardigree said. "And when I can pop the old pigskin right into his little hands, well, that's what life's all about."

"Days like these, I'm not ashamed to say that a tear of happiness sometimes rolls right up my forehead," Hardigree added.

Hardigree also took the time to work with Ben's childish and shaky but slowly improving long-snapping stance, marveling at how quickly his son was learning to long-snap.

"His first snaps weren't what anyone would call 'long' at all, but he's growing so fast. It seems like it was just this summer when his stance didn't even come up to my knee," said Hardigree, who insists that, despite serving as a third-string center for two seasons, he will always be a long-snapper in his heart. "I don't even know when it happened, but the ball doesn't even hit him in the legs anymore. My God, next thing you know he'll be trying out as a long-snapper in high school."

"Hey, whoah, don't force it there, big guy! That one nearly took my head off!" Hardigree said as one of his son's wobbly long-snaps glanced off his shins. "Give the old man a break! You don't even know your own strength!"

Like many fathers, Hardigree admits he sees a lot of himself in his boy, saying the temptation to live vicariously through his son's long-snapping must be overcome.

"He may be my son, but he's still very much his own little guy, and he had to discover for himself that he's a long-snapper through and through," Hardigree said. "When the wife and I went away for our anniversary, Ben stayed with a holder I used to work with. After a week of placing the football vertically on the ground, spinning it so the laces were forward, and then waiting for it to be kicked, he decided that long-snapper was the job for him."

Hardigree said he was "blessed" to have been an NFL long-snapper during eight of what he claims were the Browns' glory long-snapping years of the mid-1990s, when he worked alongside Browns special-teams greats, making dozens of long-snaps to some of the biggest names in Browns punting history.

"Being a long-snapper might not get you on the field a lot, but you'll always have a job, and you get to watch a lot of great football," Hardigree said. "You can't blame me for wanting that for Ben—every dad wants the best for his kid, after all. And from where I'm bending over, being one of the top 32 long-snappers in the world is the best thing there is."

"It's okay," Ben said later. "Dad's great. My face gets all red from being upside down, though. And Dad says when I'm old enough he's going to start running into me right after I snap the ball. And I wish he wouldn't yell at me so much when I ask him if someday he'll teach me how to throw and catch a football." ∅

Super Bowl Football To Be Slightly Bigger

JANUARY 29, 2009

TAMPA BAY, FL—In an equipment regulation change calculated to increase viewer interest in professional football's championship game, National Football League officials announced Monday that the footballs used in the Super Bowl would be somewhat bigger than their regular-season counterparts. "The length of the ball will be increased from 11 inches to 14, which will make the ball about a yard around at its widest point when inflated to the new pressure of 48 pounds per square inch," the NFL Rules Committee announced Monday. "We believe this will bring a new dimension to both the passing and running games. Good luck." In light of the new football size, coaches for both the Steelers and Cardinals are advising their players to wear gloves, carry the ball with both arms at all times, and lift with their legs and not their backs when recovering fumbles. ∅

INSIDE

> Andy Reid On Michael Vick: 'He's Like The Son I Never Neglected'

> Arena Football League Asks NFL For 7.5 Million Fan Loan

> Trainer Who Squirts Gatorade Into Players' Mouths Goes 2 For 16 Day In Awful First Game

> Vintage Brett Favre Pass Intercepted

Beaten, Bloodied T.J. Houshmandzadeh Hoping Obama Closes Gitmo Soon

JANUARY 22, 2009

GUANTÁNAMO BAY, CUBA—News that President Obama had called an immediate halt to detainee prosecutions came as a "welcome relief" to the Bengals' Iranian-American wide receiver Touraj "T.J." Houshmandzadeh, who has suffered through daily questioning sessions at the hands of government interrogators since being detained last December.

"They told me through the slot in my door that Obama will try and close Gitmo within the year," Houshmandzadeh said in a voice barely above a whisper, presumably to avoid aggravating his shattered teeth and cracked jaw. "With any luck, the president will have me out of here by July, so I can get my cracked cheekbone and orbit looked at, regrow the nails on my left hand, have the blood drained from my eye, and rehab my left knee and ankle so I can jump right into training camp."

"I can still feel my hands," Houshmandzadeh insisted. "I know I shouldn't hope—they use your hopes against you here—but I tell myself the pain means the nerves are okay. My hands are okay. I can still catch the ball."

Homeland Security officers took Houshmandzadeh into custody Dec. 20, when the Pro Bowl Bengals wideout attempted to board the team plane for a flight to Cleveland to play against the Browns. It is not known why Houshmandzadeh's name was on the no-fly list, and the incident attracted little attention, overshadowed as it was by the injury of Chad Ocho Cinco, whose hamstring kept him on the bench as the Bengals beat the Browns 14-0.

"When I first got here and they took the bag off my head, I was pretty scared," Houshmandzadeh said. "I had no idea where I was or what was happening. Guys in fatigues asking me who I was working for, telling me I had no idea how much trouble I was in, dropping bars of soap into my socks and bludgeoning me across the face with them. I mean, Coach [Marvin] Lewis is tough, but this didn't seem like one of his ideas."

Over the next week Houshmandzadeh was interrogated at least twice daily, with the exception of one 24-hour period—he believes it was Saturday, although sleep deprivation and frequent electrical shocks made it difficult for him to determine the passage of time—spent in the facility's infirmary. On Sunday the questioning sessions began again, culminating in interrogators informing him that his team had beaten the Kansas City Chiefs 16-6 and subjecting Houshmandzadeh to a "celebratory" Gatoradeboarding.

But that wasn't the worst, Houshmandzadeh said. "They tore pages out of my playbook," said the wide receiver, his voice cracking for the first time. "They set it on fire in front of me, they threw it in the toilet and urinated on it.... It's more than a book to me, you know? It means something. And I have to pay a fine if anything happens to it. That was when I decided I would get through this, that I would survive no matter what."

Houshmandzadeh, who is listed at 6 feet 1 inch and 200 pounds, has lost 15 percent of his weight since coming to Guantánamo, although Homeland Security medics say that he may have gained as much as 2 inches in height as a result of being hung from the rafters for hours of high-pressure fire-hose treatments. Houshmandzadeh is confident that he can still play at his previous level if Obama's administration makes good on its promise to free him on time.

"I'm one of the lucky ones," Houshmandzadeh said softly. "Muhsin Muhammad was rushed to the infirmary last week and he still hasn't been back. Rashaan Salaam hasn't been heard from in years. But the really weird thing is that most of these guys are just shopkeepers and goat herders. It makes absolutely no sense for them to be here. ∅

Bears Unveil New Look-Like-Shit Offense

JULY 31, 2008

BOURBONNAIS, IL—The Chicago Bears put on a display of inaccurate passing, sluggish route running, and careless ball-handling Wednesday as the team exhibited their new-look-like-shit offense to fans and media attending training camp to view a full-squad practice. "We finally have the personnel to implement a game plan of high-percentage incomplete passes, completed passes of four yards or less, and a rushing attack that lets us lose control of the game clock with complex plays that take forever to develop and generate negative yardage," offensive coordinator Ron Turner said, explaining why the Bears abandoned the "West-Coast-My-Fat-Ass" offense they ran last year. "I'm confident that both Rex Grossman and Kyle Orton possess the ability to overthrow a receiver on a deep fly pattern or find an open defender and deliver the ball with laser-like precision, so we'll be switching between them often and at random intervals to avoid either one getting into a rhythm or developing any confidence." According to Turner, the offense is starting to malfunction as a cohesive unit and has shown much more consistency at blowing assignments, missing blocks, and fumbling snaps. ∅

Ken Whisenhunt: 'A Lot Of People Said This Team Couldn't Come In Here And Win, And They Were Correct'

FEBRUARY 5, 2009

TAMPA BAY, FL—After losing 27-23 to the Steelers in a hard-fought Super Bowl, Arizona coach Ken Whisenhunt boldly addressed the Cardinals' detractors, lauding them for a correct prediction of a Steeler win. "They said our defense couldn't come through in a big spot, that we were too inexperienced, that [running back] Edge [Edgerrin James] was finished: right, right, and right. I only wish I had listened to them and not gotten my hopes up so high," said Whisenhunt, expressing satisfaction in proving doubters "right, but barely." "We heard all week about how there was no way we'd come out of there with a win, and then that's the way it happened. Bottom line, they were right and I was wrong." Whisenhunt then addressed those die-hard Cardinal fans who believed in the team all along, calling them "delusional" and "misguided." Ø

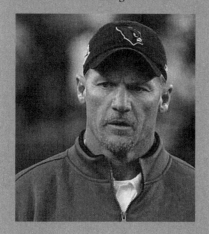

INSIDE

‣ **Bruce Springsteen Thrills Super Bowl Crowd Playing Entire** *Ghost Of Tom Joad* **Album**

‣ **Buccaneers Express Interest In Willie Parker's Younger Sister**

STRONG SIDE/ WEAK SIDE: TIM TEBOW

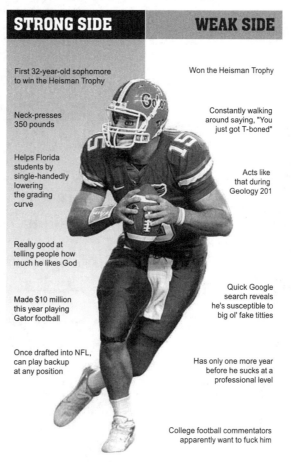

STRONG SIDE	WEAK SIDE
First 32-year-old sophomore to win the Heisman Trophy	Won the Heisman Trophy
Neck-presses 350 pounds	Constantly walking around saying, "You just got T-boned"
Helps Florida students by single-handedly lowering the grading curve	Acts like that during Geology 201
Really good at telling people how much he likes God	Quick Google search reveals he's susceptible to big ol' fake titties
Made $10 million this year playing Gator football	
Once drafted into NFL, can play backup at any position	Has only one more year before he sucks at a professional level
	College football commentators apparently want to fuck him

Seahawks QB Matt Hasselbeck Returns From Injury For Some Reason

NOVEMBER 20, 2008

SEATTLE—After missing five games with a bulging disc in his back, Seahawks quarterback Matt Hasselbeck returned to his 2-8 last-place team Sunday for reasons that are unknown at this time. "Well, that was pointless," a visibly exhausted Hasselbeck said after throwing for 170 yards and three interceptions in the Seahawks' 26-20 home loss. "I guess I thought I owed it to my teammates to go through that with them, but looking back on it, no one would wish that on another person. I mean, that game was quite possibly more painful than the extensive nerve damage in my back that kept me out. I can't remember why I decided to suit up for this one." When asked if he intended to play this Sunday against the Redskins, Hasselbeck responded by asking why, in God's name, he would do that. Ø

Andy Reid Vows To Eat Philadelphia Delicacy If Eagles Win, Arizona Delicacy If Eagles Lose

JANUARY 15, 2009

GLENDALE, AZ—In the type of wager normally placed between mayors of the cities playing in major sporting events, coach Andy Reid vowed to eat any number of Arizona delicacies should his team lose to the Cardinals, as opposed to local Philadelphia cuisine if his Eagles win." Green corn tamales, tequila shrimp, Yucatán steam-roasted turkey; if they win, I promise you now that I will eat anything and everything Arizona has to offer," Reid said at Wednesday's media day, wiping the corner of his mouth with his sleeve throughout the press conference. "But if we win? Not only do I get to eat a nice big Philly cheesesteak from every major cheesesteak purveyor in the city, I also get some Pennsylvania Dutch soft pretzels, a plate of scrapple, and a hoagie of my choosing. Actually, since I've already paid for it, I might as well just eat both cities' foods. It'd be a shame to let it go to waste." When

asked about the AFC Championship Game between Baltimore and Pittsburgh, Reid expressed a slight preference for crab cakes over french-fry-stuffed sandwiches. Ø

STRONG SIDE/WEAK SIDE: ERIC TAYLOR

STRONG SIDE

Clear eyes, full heart

Says things like "All right" "You take care, now," and "Tell your family I said hi" exactly the way a high school football coach in

Still finds time to watch scouting tapes during a family crisis

Still finds time to watch scouting tapes during a family crisis

Adjusted from Smash Williams' finesse running game to Tim Riggins' up-the-middle style quite nice

Hot daughter

Hot wife

WEAK SIDE

Though exciting, method of not generating offense until the second half when team is down by 20 points is questionable

The fact of the matter is that he really never taught Street how to tackle

Inability to use Ray "Voodoo" Tantum to his full potential does bring into question Taylor's ability to coach a more mobile quarterback

Though he said he spent the beginning part of 2007 season at TMU, no one has been able to verify that this school even exists

Dumb enough to believe in high school kids

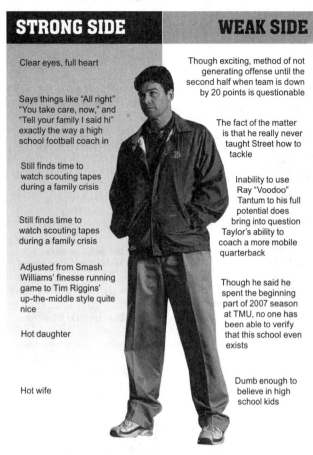

PHOTO FINISH

Michael Vick Regrets Wearing Dog-Skin Coat To Meet With Goodell

INSIDE

▸ Dan Marino Hosts Hour-Long HBO Special Celebrating Favre's Interceptions

Kurt Warner Last Player Remaining From 1947 Cardinals

JANUARY 29, 2009

GLENDALE, AZ—Following a remarkable performance in his team's victory over the Philadelphia Eagles last Sunday, Arizona Cardinals quarterback Kurt Warner, the last remaining member of the Cardinals' 1947 championship team, took a moment to reflect on his long NFL career. "Marshall Goldberg, Babe Dimancheff, and Elmer Angsman—they were a great group of guys who would have loved to have been a part of this," Warner told reporters, adding, "You know, they didn't call it the Super Bowl back then. I mean no disrespect to this Cardinal team, or the one I led to the championship in 1925, but there was something special about that '47 squad." Though Warner said he has fallen out of touch with many of his former teammates, he still keeps in contact with 149-year-old Walter Camp, head coach of the Yale Bulldog team Warner led to a national championship in 1888. ∅

SPORTS GRAPHIC

Greatest Individual Super Bowl Performances

JANUARY 29, 2009

1967: Packers receiver Max McGee plays the entire Super Bowl, catching seven passes for 138 yards and two touchdowns despite being even drunker than the rest of the Packers

1975: Fran Tarkenton leads the Vikings to a 16-6 defeat in Super Bowl IX, notable considering what a worthless franchise the Vikings are

1982: Dwight Clark makes that catch in the corner of the end zone that ESPN shows all the time.... Wait, that wasn't the Super Bowl

1984: Marcus Allen gains 191 yards in 20 carries against the Redskins and still finds the energy to bring Al Davis' wife to screaming, rippling, trainer's-table-drenching orgasm three times during halftime

1987: Phil Simms completes 88 percent of his passes, including 11 in a row, in perhaps the greatest Super Bowl performance to still be really boring

1990: Jerry Rice catches 698 passes for 35,700 yards and 136 touchdowns

1997: Desmond Howard returns two kicks for touchdowns despite making the Heisman pose after each step

2006: Ben Roethlisberger throws nine more completions than anyone thought possible

2007: Prince

Team Pretending To Celebrate With Kicker

Kurt Warner Requests HBO Be Blocked At Cardinals' Hotel

JANUARY 29, 2009

TAMPA BAY, FL—Cardinal quarterback Kurt Warner asked the management of the Grand Hyatt Tampa Bay to block access to premium cable network HBO Monday, claiming he wanted to prevent his teammates from inadvertently watching inappropriate programs. "I know a lot of these guys have never been to the Super Bowl before, and I would hate for them to have partial nudity ruin their entire experience," said Warner, adding that he didn't want Cardinals to be exposed to polygamy on the series *Big Love*. "HBO glorifies curse words, nakedness, and adult situations. As a Christian, I cannot stand by and let my teammates be put in harm's way." According to hotel sources, Warner spent $6,000 ordering pay-per-view programming on the Christian family-friendly network Sky Angel, including the shows *Rejoice*, *Venture In Faith*, and repeated viewings of *Nasty Nuns Crave Cock*. ∅

'Greatest Super Bowl Ever,' Reports Incorrect Man

FEBRUARY 5, 2009

PITTSBURGH—In a torrent of emotion that both blanked out Kenneth Weiss' memory and skewed his judgment, the longtime Steelers fan declared Super Bowl XLIII, which most agree was in fact a very good game, to be the best Super Bowl ever. "I defy you to name a game with as much excitement," said Weiss, forgetting the seven lead changes in the 49ers' gritty Super Bowl XXIII victory, the Steelers' brilliant defensive denial of multiple comebacks in Super Bowl XIII, and the underdog Giants' victory over the arrogant undefeated Patriots last year. "I can't think of one that even came close. Best ever. Period. There can be no argument." Cooler-headed sources close to Weiss said that his choice is at least defensible, unlike those who say the greatest-ever Super Bowl was won by that jackass Joe Namath, the admittedly undefeated but unspectacular '72 Dolphins, or the fucking, fucking, fucking Cowboys. ∅

Buffalo Bills Acquire Final Piece Of Shit Of The Puzzle

MARCH 12, 2009

BUFFALO, NY—In a move that will immediately impact a roster that is already full of shit, the Bills added what many believe will be the missing piece of shit to the team's puzzle Saturday by signing world-class shitass Terrell Owens. "With T.O., the Bills get a complete and total shit with the potential to generate more disappointment than anyone in Buffalo could have hoped for," said NFL.com senior analyst Pat Kirwan. "Throw him in with their pile-of-shit offensive line, future Hall of Fame shithead at running back, shitty quarterback, and shit-for-brains coach, and this team has everything in place needed to achieve its shitful potential." According to Bill's front-office dipshits, the team has the tenacity to fight for the full 60 minutes in the huddle, in the locker room, and in local strip club parking lots. ∅

Redskins Ask Albert Haynesworth To Gain 2,400 Pounds

MARCH 5, 2009

WASHINGTON—Redskins coach Jim Zorn reportedly asked new defensive tackle Albert Haynesworth to begin bulking up Monday, claiming that by adding 2,400 pounds to his frame the All-Pro could improve his run-stuffing ability by single-handedly filling every gap on the defensive line. "Albert could be a dominant force if he just put on a couple thousand pounds," Zorn said of the two-time Pro Bowler, who signed a seven-year, $100 million contract with the team last week. "If he adds some mass to his shoulders, neck, and chest, and especially along his sides and the ends of his arms, there's not an offensive line in the league that will be able to move him, not even with help from a tight end." According to Redskins trainers, Haynesworth has been placed on a strict diet consisting of grilled chicken breasts, a green salad, and a giant barrel of lard at every meal. ∅

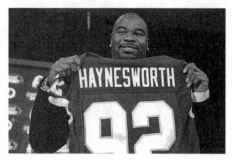

SPORTS GRAPHIC

Celebrating John Madden

APRIL 23, 2009

As John Madden walks off into football history, we look at the moments that made him a legend:

1936: Mary Margaret Madden feels what she believes is her child kicking, but is in actuality her unborn son John eating his twin brother

1958: Is drafted by the Eagles, but spends too much time talking about their "smashmouth style of old-school football that really shows what the NFL is all about" to get much better at playing

1970s: Apparently coached football somewhere around this time period

1979: Madden develops a fear of flying when he asks a flight attendant what would happen if the airplane crashed, to which she responds, "We would almost certainly die"

1987: Has sex for the first time

1998: Announces 16 regular season games and entire NFC playoffs with several bratwurst stuck in his esophagus

2003: While no one is looking, tries stuffing a turducken into a cow

2009: Realizes the game has finally passed him by upon seeing Ben Roethlisberger and Santonio Holmes celebrate their Super Bowl victory by making out a little bit

PHOTO FINISH

Dan Rooney Crushed Beneath Weight Of Lamar Hunt Trophy

Hush Falls Over Patriots Camp As Tom Brady's First 10 Passes Go 3 Yards

AUGUST 4, 2009

FOXBOROUGH, MA—Excitement surrounding the return of quarterback Tom Brady devolved into mute panic Thursday as each of Brady's first 10 passes barely made it to the line of scrimmage. "Oh, God," said Patriots head coach Bill Belichick, breaking the silence that fell across the assembled players, coaches, and legions of fans who had just witnessed Brady's ninth pass flutter slowly from his limp hand and land between his own feet. "Who's our backup? Does anyone know who our backup is?" When asked for comment, wide receiver Randy Moss said he doesn't care how poorly Brady throws the ball as long at it rolls in his direction. ∅

Wade Phillips Excited About Upcoming NFL Giraffe

APRIL 21, 2009

DALLAS—Cowboys coach Wade Phillips enthusiastically announced Tuesday that he could not wait for the 2009 NFL Giraffe on Apr. 25 and 26, mentioning several times that the animal's neck was his favorite part. "If it takes two whole days for a giraffe, you know that giraffe is a tall one," said Phillips, adding that giraffes were better than free agency because they subsist on twigs and leaves, which do not cost very much money. "When you're rebuilding a team, it's much better to use the giraffe because you can reach really high places with it." Phillips said he has been preparing for the 2009 NFL Giraffe by drawing pictures, collecting "yummy" vegetation, and ladder shopping. ∅

STRONG SIDE/WEAK SIDE: JAY CUTLER

STRONG SIDE	WEAK SIDE
High-pitched whining allows him to secretly communicate with receivers	Has lost to the Raiders
Makes his own crowd noises after every touchdown pass	Can't get Vanderbilt fight song out of his head
Able to put ball anywhere he claims he wanted to put it	
Has never asked to be traded while in the huddle	Hates being alone in the backfield and often makes fullbacks keep him company
More mobile than immobile	
	Despite experience of playing three seasons in the NFL, still gets sacked sometimes
	Although he runs really fast on his knees, the NFL considers that "down"
Like most people, has the potential to be one of the best players on the Detroit Lions	Demands to be traded the moment that he finds out team is secretly trying to trade him

Steelers Jersey Worn To Pirates Game

MAY 19, 2009

PITTSBURGH— Despite the football season having ended nearly five months ago, and the absence of Pittsburgh Steelers wide receiver Hines Ward from the Pirates' 40-man roster, local resident Heath Janoski, 28, wore Ward's No. 86 Steelers jersey to Wednesday night's Pittsburgh Pirates–St. Louis Cardinals baseball game. "I don't really own any Pirates stuff," said Janoski, who also brought a Terrible Towel and a "Cleveland Sucks" billboard to the nine-inning contest. "I think I had a Pirate Parrot doll when I was younger, but I'm pretty sure I ripped its head off when they didn't make the World Series in 1992." With the Pirates up to bat in the bottom of the third inning, Janoski started a "Here we go Steelers" chant which was immediately taken up by the 13,000 fans in attendance and repeated sporadically throughout the rest of the game. ∅

Investigators: Increasingly Likely That James Harrison Bit Own Son

MAY 28, 2009

FRANKLIN PARK, PA—Police detectives investigating an alleged dog-bite injury to James Harrison III, the son of Pittsburgh Steeler James Harrison, said that recent evidence suggests the linebacker became agitated by the toddler's crying last Wednesday and bit the child himself. "After carefully piecing together testimony from people at the scene, we believe witnesses were trying to protect Mr. Harrison, who after all is a creature of instinct and may not be responsible for his actions," Officer Mark Bendiger told reporters. "If that turns out to be the case, the legal liability will actually rest with Harrison's handlers. Linebackers can be an aggressive breed, and we've seen plenty of examples of how poorly trained and badly socialized James is in particular." James III is almost completely recovered and has been released from Children's Hospital of Pittsburgh, while his father has been quarantined at Animal, Linebacker, and Wide Receiver Control of McKees Rocks, PA. ∅

Small, Unathletic Walk-On Injures 9 Starters In Notre Dame Football Practice

SEPTEMBER 3, 2009

SOUTH BEND, IN— During Wednesday's afternoon practice, 17-year-old Brian Novak, a 145-pound walk-on for the struggling Notre Dame football team, injured nine starters, including third-year quarterback Jimmy Clausen, junior wide receiver Golden Tate, and 295-pound defensive lineman Ian Williams.

Novak, who had virtually no organized football experience prior to joining the Division I team, has injured a total of 24 players since his arrival in South Bend, prompting many to question whether or not the Fighting Irish have another disappointing season in store.

"I'm not really that fast or strong or anything," said Novak, adding that of his friends back home he's "not even close" to being the best football player. "But during my first practice with the team I was playing linebacker—or it might have been defensive end—and I got past the big blocker guys no problem, then somehow broke [starting halfback] Arman-

see **NOTRE DAME**

SPORTS GRAPHIC

Conditions Of Michael Vick's Rein-statement

JULY 29, 2009

Commissioner Roger Goodell has granted talented but controversial quarterback Michael Vick conditional reinstatement in the NFL. Some of the terms of his second chance:

➤ Vick will have access to the NFL gym, but only during off-peak hours

➤ Can date any women he wants, as long as he promises not to pit them against each other in fights to the death

➤ Should Vick eventually get into an NFL game, he will be confined to pocket-arrest

➤ Half of Vick's salary will go to a pit bull of Goodell's choosing

➤ Cannot kill dogs unless celebrating touchdown of 20 yards or more

➤ Learn to throw an accurate pass, for the love of Christ

➤ Must completely turn his life around and become a selfless team player, a pillar of the community, and a friend to animals and children, eventually coming to embody the spirit of redemption in a world that sees it all too rarely

Tony Dungy Casually Asks Michael Vick If Dogfighting Was Fun

AUGUST 13, 2009

HAMPTON, VIRGINIA—During a pre-season conditioning workout Tuesday, Michael Vick's de facto mentor, Tony

Dungy, peppered the troubled quarterback with innocent questions about the sport of dogfighting, offhandedly inquiring about how "cool" it is. "So, yeah, how fun was that, anyway, the whole dogfighting thing?" asked Dungy, while the two jogged side-by-side during a cooldown. "Must have been a real rush watching those dogs go at it like that, huh? Morally reprehensible, of course, but, man, it's got to be tempting to head back to the pit and just mix it up a little. Good thing you're not doing that anymore. So bad." Dungy later showed Vick a photo of his new pit bull, Tex, and asked him what he thought. Ø

---

from **NOTRE DAME**

do Allen's leg with a tackle. That's the first tackle I've ever attempted in my life."

"I'm not trying to hurt them or anything, but in general I would say everyone here is a lot slower and weaker than I thought they'd be," Novak added. "I can only bench-press about 90 pounds, but all the players gather around to watch me lift."

According to members of the coaching staff, the former high school yearbook editor is by far the team's most athletic player, despite Novak's inability to do more than two pull-ups or jog a mile without walking. During an intrasquad scrimmage last Sunday, he recorded eight interceptions, rushed for 225 yards, and ruptured the Achilles tendon of safety Sergio Brown with what appeared to be a fairly slow-moving, awkward juke move.

"When I play with these guys I feel like I did when I was a camp counselor playing dodgeball with my campers," said the 5-foot-7 Novak, whose athletic resume consists of two weeks on his high school lacrosse team. "I can pretty much overpow-

er anyone, anytime. It's really fun, but I'm not actually learning anything about football."

Though he reportedly promised Notre Dame's head coach Charlie Weis he would "take it easy" on the rest of the team until the season opener, Novak broke the arm of 302-pound center Dan Wenger during tackling drills last Monday, and fractured starting linebacker Brian Smith's skull on a 14-yard touchdown run in which Novak dragged Smith 10 yards into the end zone.

While Novak went 0-4 in field goal attempts during Sunday's scrimmage, he was the only Notre Dame kicker to get the football up into the air.

"He's really powerful and fast," 255-pound defensive end John Ryan said of Novak. "I'm glad he's on our team because looking at the guys we have, he's our only hope if we want to beat USC, Nevada, or really anybody."

"He's a much better leader than Jimmy [Clausen], that's for sure," Ryan added. "Better quarterback, too."

Recently, Novak has even been spotted giving coach Weis several tips about his strategy and tactics.

"Until Brian, I never thought about how establishing the run could create opportunities for us downfield," said Weis, who has led the Irish to 15 losses in their last two seasons. "Novak was telling me about something called a 'fake handoff,' which is like this fake run thing, but then you pass it. I would assume that's illegal, but he's proven himself to be an amazing football player, so I trust him."

According to Novak, when he committed to Notre Dame, he had no intention of walking onto the football team, being more interested in the school's theater group. But when assistant head coach Rob Ianello saw the freshman tossing a football around campus, he knew instantly that Novak would be a valuable addition.

"He was catching the ball," Ianello said. "Like, actually catching it."

Despite the team's recent injuries, and the fact that its best player is admittedly "really terrible" at football, former Notre Dame head coach and college football analyst Lou Holtz still predicted the Fighting Irish would go 12-0 this season and win the BCS championship. Ø

Notable Quarterback Controversies

AUGUST 20, 2009

Competition for starting jobs is heating up across the NFL, as is the potential for a quarterback controversy. Onion Sports takes a look at the greatest QB squabbles of all time:

1973: Chuck Noll calls Terry Bradshaw and Joe Gilliam into his study to dramatically accuse Bradshaw of murder

1989: Although Steve Young correctly guesses the number George Seifert is thinking of, Seifert still goes with Joe Montana

1993: Redskins fans are up in arms as head coach Petitbon chooses the washed-up Mark Rypien over the Mark Rypien that won the Super Bowl

1994: With his arch-nemesis holding Dave Brown and Kent Graham over a cliff, Giants coach Dan Reeves makes the most difficult decision of his life and lets them both go

1997: Though Rich Gannon proves himself to be a strong leader, Marty Schottenheimer chooses Elvis Grbac because Rich Gannon doesn't have any arms

2006: The Chargers award Philip Rivers the starting role when Drew Brees receives a lot more money to play somewhere else

2007: After much deliberation and prayer, Tony Dungy once again goes with Peyton Manning at QB

2009: Rules for the Derek Anderson–Brady Quinn quarterback competition don't stipulate that the loser will be executed on the 50-yard after the final preseason game

Dallas Cowboys Release Jerry Jones

SEPTEMBER 24, 2009

IRVING, TEXAS—In an attempt to cut the franchise's losses and "move forward in a positive direction," the Dallas Cowboys severed ties with controversial owner Jerry Jones Monday, ending their tumultuous 20-year relationship with the divisive figure.

According to sources within the Cowboys organization, the decision to release Jones was influenced by the lack of any playoff victories in more than 12 years, the owner's distracting sideline antics, and his selfish, "me first" attitude, which many said was having a cancerous effect on the clubhouse.

"We value Jerry's contributions to the Cowboys over the past two decades, but it has become painfully clear that we just don't share the same priorities," Cow-

boys public relations director Richard Dalrymple said. "This wasn't an easy choice to make, but we're confident it is a decision that can only make our team better."

"Losing to our NFC East rivals the Giants in our brand-new stadium was really the last straw," added Dalrymple, who said Jones "insisted" that the $1.2 billion facility would solve all of the team's problems.

"The Cowboys need to focus on winning, and we can't do that with Jerry's incessant ego-boosting publicity stunts, or this opulent sports venue that's devoted more to himself than achieving

postseason success."

Cowboys officials called Jones Sunday night to inform him he was being cut from the team, ordering the 66-year-old owner to clean out his luxury box and remove his personal belongings from the premises immediately. Jones, who was reportedly stunned to be removed from his ownership duties, issued a statement on his website thanking himself for all his hard work and years of service.

"Well, damn, looks like the 'Boys couldn't handle Double J anymore," the blog post read in part. "I'll never forget my time in the Big D, and how I single-handedly won three Super Bowls. Don't worry, Jerry Jones will land on his feet somewhere, and when he does, Dallas better watch out."

see **JERRY JONES**

Tom Coughlin Moves Up Ahmad Bradshaw On Team's Death Chart

AUGUST 18, 2009

NEW YORK—Giants coach Tom Coughlin listed Ahmad Bradshaw at the top of the team's death chart Tuesday, claiming that if the running back continued to miss blocking assignments and drop screen passes, he would face certain execution by opening day. "From what I've seen so far in camp, Ahmad has been messing up on all the little things that infuriate me," said Coughlin, adding that Bradshaw's consistency at practice earned him the top spot on the death chart ahead of linebacker Antonio Pierce, who has

recently struggled with legal troubles. "He's really left a lasting impression on me, and if he keeps it up, he'll definitely be the guy that the other players are gunning for." Coughlin reportedly allowed Bradshaw to take the morning off from Wednesday's practice to say goodbye to loved ones and finish digging his grave. ✐

Bill Belichick's Tears Eat Through Podium

SEPTEMBER 3, 2009

FOXBOROUGH, MA—In a rare show of emotion, Patriots coach Bill Belichick began to cry during linebacker Tedy Bruschi's farewell press conference Monday, shedding a noxious black discharge that burned through the podium and a solid concrete floor before eventually coming to rest deep inside the mantle of the earth below. "He's helped create a tradition here that we're all proud of," Belichick said as the tears melted ribbons of flesh from his cheek, exposing his

skull. Reporters fled the scene when superheated chemical fumes emanating from the toxic liquid formed a cloud of poisonous gas, prompting Bruschi to vomit blood just moments after Belichick had called the two-time Pro Bowler a "perfect player." As Belichick sloughed grotesquely into a liquid heap, he was reportedly heard to ask if this is what love is. ✐

East Carolina Grad Thinks East Carolina A State

SEPTEMBER 12, 2009

JACKSONVILLE, FL—At a press conference Monday, Jaguars quarterback and East Carolina University alum David Garrard indicated through certain statements to reporters that "East Carolina" is one of the 50 United States. "I can say without hesitation that it is definitely my favorite of all the Carolinas," said the former ECU Pirate, who, when pressed, identified the imaginary commonwealth's capital as Greenville and its state bird as the red-necked grebe. "There's just this enormous sense of state pride over there that I

E A S T
CAROLINA
UNIVERSITY

felt as soon as came across the North Carolina border. And it's a progressive state, too: Did you know Obama carried East Carolina?" Garrard later told reporters that if he had to choose one state to live in, it would be between Western Kentucky and Ball State. ✒

Andy Reid Carted Onto Field To Shake Hands With Sean Payton

SEPTEMBER 24, 2009

PHILADELPHIA—Unable to walk off the sideline under his own power, Eagles coach Andy Reid was loaded onto a medical cart and driven to the 50-yard line to shake hands with Saints coach Sean Payton after their game Sunday. According to those in attendance, a hush fell over the crowd during the 11 minutes the team's medical staff huddled around Reid, attempting to safely hoist the coach onto the cart with a crew of six grown men. "Coach Reid was conscious, but his breathing was labored and he complained of intense pain all over his body," team physician Dr. Peter DeLuca told reporters. "Once we got him onto the cart we had to stabilize his neck out of fear that it couldn't support his head. The good news is, we only had to use the defibrillator twice." After completing the handshake, Reid gave a thumbs-up to indicate that he wanted the straw in his milkshake to be raised up to his mouth. ✒

from **JERRY JONES**

Jones' questionable conduct on and off the field almost certainly played a role in sealing the troubled owner's fate. Although some members of the Cowboys' management have reportedly contemplated Jones' termination for the past several years, sources said his recent association with known criminals as well as a perceived lack of character and poor leadership qualities provided ample reasons for his release.

Ultimately, team officials said that Jones had become an embarrassment to the storied franchise.

"Between the opportunistic condemnations of game plans, the uninformed evaluations of draftees, and the paranoid delusions that players and coordinators were scheming against him, it's no wonder the Cowboys have had enough," *NFL Today* commentator Boomer Esiason said. "Maybe his absence will finally give the team a chance to start living up to its full potential."

"Just watching the Cowboys practice without Jones leering at them, you can tell that morale has already greatly improved," Esiason continued. "They seem so loose and relaxed and their faces are just lighting up with smiles. This is the first time Tony Romo has had fun since he put on the Cowboys uniform."

Former Cowboys head coach and Fox Sports analyst Jimmy Johnson speculated that the team's real motivation for cutting Jones was that the aging owner, who turns 67 in October, is well past his prime and would have continued to cost the ball club too much money.

"His skills have really diminished the past few years, and he just can't make the moves that he used to," said Johnson, adding that the rest of the NFL was passing Jones by every day. "When you get older you start to slow down, and as you try to compensate, you wind up making poor decisions."

"He had to eat more than $9 million dollar of salary cap just to get rid of Terrell Owens," Johnson added. "In this economy? What was he thinking?"

Though his publicist would not say whether the former Cowboys owner was entertaining offers from any other teams, an anonymous NFL source told reporters that, immediately after Jones cleared waivers Tuesday, Oakland Raiders owner Al Davis offered him a record-setting three-year $120 million deal. ✒

Features Of The Dallas Cowboys' New Stadium

SEPTEMBER 24, 2009

A record-setting crowd attended the inaugural home opener of the $1.2 billion Cowboys Stadium Sunday night. Onion Sports examines some of the sports arena's features.

➤ A 100-yard football field, perfect for professional football

➤ Special suite where Tony Dorsett, Emmitt Smith, and all the Cowboy greats can go fuck themselves

➤ **Display case** containing the Cowboys Starter jacket that turned the team's fortunes around in 1992

➤ Most obnoxious 30-yard line in the league

➤ No Troy Aikman

➤ Cowboys logos appear on things that wouldn't otherwise have Cowboys logos on them

➤ The Emmitt Smith Simulator, which lets fans feel what it's like to be a normal person running behind five 300-pound men

➤ Not one, but 45 megachurches

➤ The Cowboys Ring of Criminal Arrests

➤ A parking lot so expansive it could hold almost two parking lots inside it

Lowlights From The Lions' 19-Game Losing Streak

OCTOBER 1, 2009

➤ **9/14/08:** Jon Kitna throws two picks to Charles Woodson on the same play

➤ **9/28/08:** Lions become first team to ever lose during their bye week, 24-10

➤ **10/12/08:** After years of wondering, QB Dan Orlovsky finally finds out what happens if the quarterback goes back for a pass and takes four or five steps out of the end zone

➤ **11/3/08:** Team signs Daunte Culpepper

➤ **11/27/08:** On top of all the shit that's been going on, Lions TE Michael Gaines gets gum on his shoe

➤ **12/7/08:** Lions actually outscore the Vikings 23-20 and still lose

➤ **12/14/08:** On the goal line with the game tied and seconds to go, Kevin Smith accidentally dives backward 100 yards and records a safety

➤ **4/25/09:** Though it had been rumored for months that the Lions would use their first pick to draft QB Matthew Stafford, this does not stop him from yelling "goddamn motherfucker" his entire time at the podium

➤ **9/13/09:** Before his first snap, Matt Stafford realizes the earth has traveled 1.3 billion miles since the last time the Lions won

Michael Vick Fails To Inspire Team With 'Great' Dogfighting Story

OCTOBER 1, 2009

PHILADELPHIA—Michael Vick's pregame pep talk Sunday, in which he recounted the events of a brutal 2004 dogfight between his pit bull terrier Zebro and rival pit bull Maniac, failed to inspire his teammates in any way whatsoever, Eagles team sources reported.

Vick, who was playing in his first NFL game since serving an 18-month prison sentence, called the 10-minute story "really motivational," and reportedly failed to understand why his graphic recounting of how Zebro ripped out Maniac's larynx caused teammates to stagger out of the player tunnel and onto Lincoln Financial Field with their heads hanging.

"I don't know what their problem is, because that story pumps me up every time," Vick said during a postgame press conference. "It's a classic underdog story: On one side of the dogfighting pit you had Maniac, who was a beast, and on my end you had Zebro, who was pretty good, but not great. Yet we had trained him hard. We strengthened his hind legs by forcing him to constantly jump at a teasing stick; we emotionally tortured him so that he would attack everything in sight; and from the time he was a little puppy, we toughened him up by beating him with a metal baton."

"I told my teammates that the stakes were high, because if Zebro had lost, I would have either electrocuted him, drowned him, or slammed his body to the ground until he was dead," Vick added. "How is that not inspiring?"

According to Eagles players,

see **MICHAEL VICK**

NFL Scientists Postulate Theoretical Down Before First Down

SEPTEMBER 28, 2009

NEW YORK—Citing the extremely low level of entropy present before a normal set of football downs, scientists from the NFL's quantum mechanics and cosmology laboratories spoke Monday of a theoretical proto-down before the first. "Ultimately, we believe there are an infinite number of proto-downs played before the first visible snap," lead NFL scientist Dr. Oliver Claussen said during a press conference, adding that the very last yocto-down is a by-product of leftover fourth downs from this universe, as well as those from a theoretical universe running along an arrow of time concurrent to our own. "It is our goal to isolate this microscopic down using a highly volatile electron beam with a physical isolation resolution of 500 angstroms or better. If all goes well, we can make this down available, and NFL teams will have one more chance to attain additional yards, a new set of downs, or even score." Claussen later stated that those in the field who talk of a fifth down after the fourth are only encouraging the practice of bad science. ∅

Lions Victory Celebration Ultimately Plunges Fans Into Deeper Depression

OCTOBER 1, 2009

DETROIT—Euphoria gave way to deep, unwavering depression Sunday when fans celebrating the Detroit Lions' first win in two years realized the utter insignificance of the accomplishment, and how pathetic their unadulterated joy must have looked to the rest of the country. "I actually jumped into the arms of a complete stranger because we won against a team that finished in last place last year," Lions fan Joe Kula said of the team's 19-14 victory over the Redskins. "Celebrating a week-three victory like we just won a Super Bowl is not only unwarranted, it is preposterous and humiliating. We're a terrible football team. Oh, my God, we're so terrible." A postgame effort by the Lions to build a victory stage at the 50-yard line to honor the achievement was abandoned mid-construction. *∅*

INSIDE

Ricky Williams: 'I Can't Believe I Got Really Baked And Applied For Reinstatement Into The NFL'

OCTOBER 4, 2007

MIAMI—After smoking three pinners, pulling five monster bong hits, and filling out his forms for reinstatement into the NFL Monday, suspended running back Ricky Williams told reporters he had no idea why he had decided to complete the League's complicated readmission paperwork immediately after getting stoned absolutely out of his mind. "Oh man, I probably shouldn't have gotten so fried," croaked the former Heisman Trophy winner, attempting to address reporters while making an effort to exhale as little as possible. "Do you think they knew I was high? I think they could tell. Shit, I hope they didn't notice, but I think they noticed when I got resin all over the application and then got it stuck to my forehead. I'm so busted. Again, man." Williams said he might go back inside and ask if he could re-reapply, as he was fairly certain he had repeatedly written the word "Why?" and drawn abstract pot-leaf patterns in the section marked "for office use only." *∅*

Knowshon Moreno Asks Broncos If There's Anything Else To Drink Besides Gatorade

OCTOBER 24, 2009

SAN DIEGO—Denver running back Knowshon Moreno spent a portion of the Broncos' game against the Chargers Monday night asking team managers if there was anything to drink on the sidelines other than Gatorade. "I'm sick of Gatorade all the time, and I don't want water," said Moreno, who was observed asking a sideline reporter drinking a ginger ale if she "[got] that here or someplace else." "I could definitely go for a Pepsi right now. There's got to be some Pepsi around here. Isn't the NFL sponsored by Pepsi or something?" Later, during a fourth-quarter drive, Moreno reportedly asked his teammates if they wanted a beverage before leaving the field and disappearing into the stands. *∅*

from **MICHAEL VICK**

Vick's voice increased in intensity at key moments throughout the pep talk, and he was at his most impassioned when he spoke of how Zebro continued to fight despite the fact that numerous chunks of flesh had been ripped from his body.

Vick also sought to motivate his team by comparing the Eagles' weekly preparation to Zebro's, saying that just as Vick had forced his pit bull to drag a tire with his mouth for hours on end to strengthen his jaw, the Eagles defense had put in the training necessary to stop quarterback Matt Cassel.

Sources confirmed that by the end of the locker room speech, the Eagles were so demoralized they could barely muster the will to put their hands into the team circle for a group cheer.

"I don't know why he told us those things," said Eagles quarterback Kevin Kolb, visibly disturbed as he told reporters that Vick looked proud when he explained how Zebro nearly lost consciousness several times throughout the fight. "I spent the first half of the game trying to get all that imagery out of my head: the bloody pit, the cigar smoke, grown men shouting as dogs ripped each other to shreds. It was so messed up that it didn't even sound real."

"They turned those dogs into monsters and made them kill each other for their own sick enjoyment," Kolb added. "For their own fucking enjoyment."

Running back LeSean McCoy echoed Kolb, saying that at no time during the game did he draw on the thought of Zebro losing half his ear as a source of inspiration.

"Before we went out on the field, [Vick] told us how the dogs went at each other's throats one last time, and when Zebro broke free, his snout and face were completely covered in blood," McCoy explained. "That's when—and I'll never forget this for the rest of my life—Mike looked at us, smiled, and said, 'But it wasn't Zebro's blood. It was Maniac's. Now let's go out there and have some fun!'"

"Jesus Christ," McCoy added.

Teammates said Vick continued to reference the story throughout the game as a motivational tool, at one point shouting, "Remember Zebro!" when the team faced a difficult third-down situation.

In addition, as Vick finally entered the game to a loud ovation, his teammates said they were further disturbed when Vick compared them to his dogfighting crew, the "Bad Newz Kennels." Vick said the group would do anything for each other, especially when it came to the mass execution of dogs who failed to win the multimillionaire $1,000 in illegal prize money.

Vick then broke the huddle by loudly barking three times.

"The only reason the Chiefs scored in the second half was because I was still thinking about what Mike said during halftime about 'trunking,'" said linebacker Omar Gaither, referring to the practice of putting two pit bulls in a car trunk, closing the door, and allowing them to fight for 15 minutes until one is dead. "Why is this freak on my team? Why are people cheering for him? Seriously, answer my questions. Why?" *∅*

Raiders Achieve First Down

OCTOBER 15, 2009

EAST RUTHERFORD, NJ— In an improbable display of competence and a basic execution of football fundamentals, the Oakland Raiders stunned the football world Sunday when running back Michael Bush miraculously rushed for three yards against the Giants and succeeded in converting a first down.

The Raiders, who fearlessly faced a third-and-one situation on their own 22-yard-line, somehow gained the 36 inches needed for an elusive first down, despite numerous obstacles that included a professional NFL defense, owner Al Davis' incompetent personnel decisions, mediocre play-calling, and general ineptitude.

"I cannot believe what I just saw," said CBS commentator Greg Gumbel, adding that he was amazed the Raiders advanced the ball beyond the line of scrimmage, let alone gained a full 10 yards. "The fact that they were out on the field for three consecutive plays without turning the ball over is incredible. But a first down? An actual first down from the Oakland Raiders? You...I mean—I just, I can't..."

"I'm speechless," Gumbel added.

According to eyewitnesses, Raiders fans were equally astonished, reportedly shaking their heads in disbelief at the team's lack of incomplete passes, false starts, and holding penalties during the four-down series. Chuck Walker, a lifelong Raiders fan, said he was "proud" of his hometown team for defying the odds and avoiding mental errors for nearly 120 seconds.

"I've never seen them go that long without totally screwing up," said Walker, who believed the first down may have even slightly changed the game's momentum. "I was certain that with a yard to go they would send five receivers deep and [quarterback] JaMarcus [Russell] would chuck the ball to one of the Giants' defensive backs."

Continued Walker, "This will surely go down as the highlight of the Raiders' season."

NFL analyst Tom Jackson also registered his incredulity, saying that after he saw the Raiders gain nine yards on the first two plays of the series—a "miraculous achievement" in and of itself—he never could have imagined they'd gain the one yard necessary to begin another set of offensive downs. The fact that they actually gained two extra yards beyond the first-down marker, Jackson said, left everyone in ESPN studios beside themselves.

"On any given play there is so much potential for the Raiders to lose a significant number of yards that you never expect them to actually gain anything," Jackson said. "But they did it. They made a first down. And on three tries, like a normal pro football team."

Jackson went on to credit the accomplishment to the much-maligned offensive line, saying that not only did they show a full understanding of their blocking assignments, but they also ran the correct play when the ball was snapped.

"Looking at that play, you wonder how a team like the Raiders are 1-4," Jackson said. "Not for too long, of course, but you do wonder for a split second."

According to referee John Parry, the first down also caught members of the officiating crew off guard. Parry said that when Bush moved the chains, his instinct was to throw an unsportsmanlike behavior flag for taunting.

"Michael just got up off the ground and handed me the ball without trying to provoke anyone," Parry said. "Usually you'll find the Oakland guys are jumping back on the pile trying to jam a finger into someone's eye or just kicking wildly with their cleats."

"At first I thought we definitely missed something," Parry added. "But we reviewed the play and the league didn't find anything illegal. They got a first down fair and square."

The Raiders lost the game 44-7. ∅

Dopey-Looking Guy Who Doesn't Know He's On Jumbotron Jay Cutler

Defensive Tackle Remi Ayodele To Write Children's Book Titled 'Tubbo Makes A Touchdown'

OCTOBER 13, 2009

NEW ORLEANS—Saints defensive tackle Remi Ayodele announced plans Monday to write a children's book called *Tubbo Makes A Touchdown*, which he says will be the heartwarming tale of an overweight hippopotamus who bravely dives on a loose ball and scores the first touchdown of his professional career. "At first nobody wanted to play football with Tubbo, and all the skinny animals teased him and told him he smelled bad," said the 318-pound Ayodele, adding that *Tubbo* was loosely based on a true story. "But when Tubbo scores the touchdown, he proves he can do the same things the popular animals can do, just a little slower." Ayodele said he hopes to inspire children to believe they can accomplish anything as long as they flop down on top of their opportunities. ∅

Norman Esiason Finally Outgrows Childish Nickname

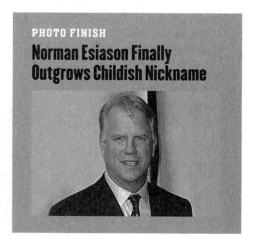

36-10 Game Analyzed

DECEMBER 4, 2009

BRISTOL, CT—Despite the clear dominance the Vikings displayed in their definitive 36-10 week 12 victory over the Bears, ESPN analysts compared the teams' offensive and defensive performances, and scrutinized slow-motion highlights of the game for nearly five minutes during Monday's broadcast of *NFL Live.* "Overall, Brett Favre seems to be working out much better at quarterback in Minnesota than Jay Cutler is in Chicago," said analyst John Clayton, who used a graphical comparison of Brett Favre's 32 completions and Cutler's 18 to hammer home what was blatantly obvious from the score. "Now, let's take a look at this fourth-quarter touchdown here. With the Vikings up 30-10, look how Adrian Peterson follows his blockers and exploits the hole. Let's watch that one more time." The blowout was also discussed in depth on *Monday Night Countdown* and *SportsCenter* and, for reasons that remain unclear, was the subject of at least 12 minutes of discussion on *Mike And Mike In The Morning.* ⌀

SPORTS GRAPHIC

Pros And Cons Of An NFL Franchise In London

OCTOBER 29, 2009

PRO: Desire to see grown men crush each other knows no nationality

CON: Players may react poorly to prim but adorable trainers who fly with aid of parasol and burst into character-building songs every 10 minutes

PRO: British prisons have plenty of room for athletes

CON: British viewers have a tendency to say "oh, my!" and faint at even the mildest block

PRO: Could call team the London Fog and helmet could feature a badass cloud

CON: Entire fucking ocean away from every other team

PRO: Fans actually polite and well-spoken right up until they riot and push each other through chain-link fences

CON: Victorious coaches will not enjoy being doused with 40 gallons of hot tea

PRO: Great way to piss off L.A.

CON: Changing of the Left Guards loses its flair after the third or fourth time

Eagles Settle For Field Goal After 260-Yard Drive

NOVEMBER 19, 2009

SAN DIEGO—The Eagles were forced to settle for a field goal against the Chargers Sunday after sustaining a 260-yard, 64-play drive that featured six separate red-zone appearances and took 52 minutes off the game clock. "It's disappointing not to score a touchdown when you keep a drive alive for more than three and a half quarters," said quarterback Donovan McNabb, who completed 32 of his 66 passes, converted 26 first downs, and was carted off the field for X-rays twice during the drive. "At least we came away with three points. Those 120 yards in penalties really hurt our field position, but those conversions on third and 21, third and 64, and the fake punt on fourth and 72 showed that this team never quits." Backup QB Michael Vick took one snap from center during the nearly hour-long drive, failing to complete a screen pass. ⌀

STRONG SIDE/WEAK SIDE: JIM BROWN

STRONG SIDE	WEAK SIDE
Great at identifying weaknesses in opposing defenses and blaxploiting them	Entire NFL career just character research for a movie role he wanted
Very agile despite often rushing across slick grass, thick mud, and the tangled mess of opponents' offal	Sheer greatness inspired Cleveland Browns to retire his tough, bruising style of play
Blocked for himself	Guessed his draft position wrong; had to hastily change name from Jim 49er
The good kind of crazy, but just barely	Repeatedly knocked tacklers into next week, so that late in the season he would face up to 66 defenders at once
The year after his retirement, his empty uniform rushed for 1,193 yards and nine touchdowns	Became clear that he had lost a step while portraying Fireball in *The Running Man*
Is also in the Water Polo Hall of Fame for some reason	Evidently beat the shit out of women, which should probably be mentioned

Bengals' Uniforms No Longer Look Stupid Now That Team Is Good

NOVEMBER 23, 2009

BRISTOL, CT—By wearing their brightly colored orange-and-black tiger-print uniforms during a victory over the Steelers, the division-leading 7-2 Cincinnati Bengals made their team gear appear far less stupid Sunday. "The Bengals uniforms during the '90s, and the ones from their 11-loss season in 2008, looked really stupid, like they were wearing carpet ripped straight out of a discount strip club," analyst Chris Mortenson said during an ESPN radio broadcast Monday. "But now that they're on top of the AFC North, you might even go so far as to say that their uniforms are classic. I'm even starting to think that the one dumb striped panel going down the leg isn't so godawful anymore." When discussing the Tampa Bay Buccaneers' current red-and-pewter jerseys versus their old orange-and-white uniforms, however, Mortenson concluded that, in either version, the team "has always looked like shit." Ø

Vick Calls Fumble In Cowboys Game 'The Worst Thing I've Ever Done'

JANUARY 16, 2010

ARLINGTON, TX—Eagles backup quarterback Michael Vick apologized to fans immediately after his team's 34-14 wild-card loss to the Cowboys Saturday, saying his fumbled handoff attempt late in the first half was "absolutely the most damning and hurtful act of [his] life." "I guess I just thought I could hand the ball off to the fullback without any repercussions, but never in my life have I been so wrong. Never," a visibly contrite Vick said to the assembled reporters. "I just want to apologize to my family, friends, and most important, the fans. There are things I have done in my time on this earth that I regret, but this fumble is undeniably the worst." Eagles fans responded to Vick's statement by saying he was absolutely correct. Ø

Tennessee Titans Fans Looking Forward To Bye Week

OCTOBER 22, 2009

NASHVILLE, TN—After enduring six straight losses and suffering through a humiliating 59-0 thrashing by the Patriots last Sunday, despondent Titans fans told reporters Wednesday that they were looking forward to enjoying a nice, relaxing bye week. "We're all hurting pretty bad, so this couldn't have come at a better time," Titans season-ticket holder Luther Murphy said. "Hopefully the week off will give us a chance to recharge, heal our wounds, and come back stronger than ever. Ah, who the fuck am I kidding? We suck." Though a majority of Titans fans said they wouldn't think or look at a football during their off week, some said they looked forward to spending their Sunday enjoying NFL football for the first time this year. Ø

Former Orlando Breakers Coach Michael 'Dauber' Dybinski Adjusts To New GM Duties

DECEMBER 1, 2009

ORLANDO, FL—Dismissing questions regarding his lack of executive experience, his willingness to make tough personnel decisions, and rumors that his team may soon move to Los Angeles, two-time Super Bowl champion coach and former *Monday Night Football* broadcaster Michael 'Dauber' Dybinski reassured fans

that he was ready to take over the position of general manager for the Orlando Breakers. "I guess I got a lot to learn about what the salary cap is if I'm supposed to wear it every day," Dybinski joked Monday in an obvious jibe at critics who repeatedly questioned his intelligence. "Seriously, though, we're balanced in the locker room with both decent young talent and veteran leaders, we have a $45 million secured municipal bond float for stadium renovations over the next six years, I have a seat at the table for the new collective bargaining agreement, and I've got a feeling this is the year we finally beat the Bills in the playoffs. I love this job." Dybinski also took time to mention that his predecessor, former Breakers coach and general manager Hayden Fox, will always be in his prayers and serves as a tragic example of why one should never drink and drive. Ø

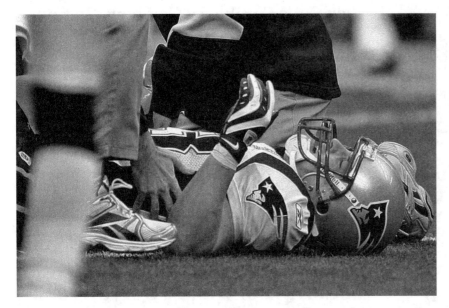

Everyone At Hospital Already Hates Wes Welker

JANUARY 8, 2010

BOSTON—Though injured New England Patriots wide receiver Wes Welker has only been in the hospital for five days, doctors, nurses, support staff, and fellow patients told reporters Thursday that the extremely passionate and determined Welker has already annoyed the hell out of everyone.

"That guy is just the worst," Welker's orthopedic surgeon Dr. Henry Myles said after a diagnostic checkup Tuesday.

"He suffers a torn MCL and ACL in his left knee, he can barely walk, and he just keeps saying things like, 'When am I going to get back in there, doc?' and 'Just tape it up, I'll be fine.' This whole obsession with showing us how intense and driven he is 24 hours a day really has to stop."

"I get it, okay? The guy has a lot of heart," Myles added. "But yesterday we had to put him in restraints because he wouldn't stop trying to do jumping jacks. And before we could sedate

him, his screams of 'I'm a competitor!' woke up the entire wing."

As of press time, Welker had not made a single friend at Massachusetts General. Although the wideout's attitude has been celebrated by sportswriters and fans alike as scrappy and overachieving, hospital personnel have described him as "exhausting," "intolerable," and "the most infuriating little cocksucker ever to walk God's green earth."

Even children in the hos-

see **WES WELKER**

Browns Caught Trying To Sneak Girl Into Huddle

DECEMBER 12, 2009

CLEVELAND— During the fourth quarter of their game last Sunday, the Cleveland Browns offense was caught attempting to sneak a 23-year-old female fan into their huddle. According to head referee Ed Hochuli, officials were informed of the hoax when the opposing defense pointed out the ill-fitting uniform of supposed backup guard Floyd Womack, as well as the flowing blond hair emerging from the back of "Womack's" helmet. "It sucks we couldn't pull it off, because it would have been awesome," Browns quarterback Brady Quinn said. "The

plan was working so perfectly. As usual, we were losing really bad in the fourth quarter, so we figured that once the cameras cut away to a more interesting game we would have a chance to rush Julie onto the field. Unfortunately, the defense sniffed out what we were doing and ruined it." Browns coach Eric Mangini later said the young woman was the most aggressive and talented person in the team's huddle. *∅*

Concussed Texas Tech Receiver After Emerging From Dark Shed: 'That Was Exactly What I Needed'

JANUARY 8, 2010

LUBBOCK, TX—Adam James, whom Red Raiders head coach Mike Leach confined to a dark storage shed after suspecting the player of exaggerating or fabri-

cating a head injury, emerged from isolation Monday saying he "felt great" and that his time in the shed was "exactly what [he] needed." "At first I thought it sounded stupid, even kind of cruel, but I have to admit it

worked like a charm. My head feels awesome, 100 percent," said James, who was surprised to learn that during his recuperation Leach had been fired. "That shed is magic. Coach was right all along. He's a great guy." James'

father, ESPN college football reporter Craig James, has taken time to praise Leach and his shed-confinement practice on the air and will reportedly contact university officials to advocate Leach's reinstatement. *∅*

Tom Brady: 'I'd Have Booed Us Too, But Patriots Fans Are Still Ungrateful Front-Running Shitheads'

JANUARY 15, 2010

FOXBOROUGH, MA—Following a 33-14 drubbing at the hands of the Baltimore Ravens, Patriots quarterback Tom Brady admitted that his team deserved to be booed, but said that "to suffer jeers from shortsighted brainless front-runners like Patriots fans was both laughable and pathetic." "The Ravens outplayed us here today, but I'm sorry, fuck all of you," Brady said to the Patriots' fan base, noting that the concept of a true Patriots fan was "barely even existent." "There's no doubt we could have executed better, just like there's no doubt those 68,756 slavering fair-weather pieces of shit in the stands have less right than anyone else to point that out. And if they have a problem with that, they should feel absolutely free to go fuck themselves." Brady added that, next to Pats fans, the Boston fans cheering for the Celtics' gang of johnny-come-lately mercenaries were the saddest fucking thing he'd ever seen. *∅*

Lane Kiffin Leaves USC For Dream Job At GameStop

JANUARY 23, 2010

LOS ANGELES—During his introductory press conference as USC's new head coach last Wednesday, Lane Kiffin told reporters that he would be leaving the school indefinitely to pursue his dream of working at GameStop. "I was approached by a cousin who works at the GameStop on Wilshire Boulevard, and when he said there was an open sales clerk position, I had to take it," said Kiffin, who then proudly placed a GameStop baseball cap on his head. "I have been going to that GameStop for years. I know the people there. I know the customers. This is just an opportunity I couldn't pass up." Before leaving the press conference, Kiffin told reporters that, while he is committed to GameStop, his heart will always belong to the Beverly Center Sunglass Hut. *∅*

Ahmad Bradshaw Still Had Pretty Good Weekend Despite Loss To Chargers

NOVEMBER 12, 2009

EAST RUTHERFORD, NJ—Though the the Chargers dealt the Giants a crushing fourth consecutive loss Sunday, running back Ahmad Bradshaw admitted in a postgame press conference that, overall, he still had a "pretty great" weekend. "Slept in on Saturday—that was nice—and then that night I made enchiladas with my girlfriend and they came out perfect," said Bradshaw, who failed to break into the secondary on any of his 14 carries during the game. "Game day was beautiful. I watched a couple episodes of *It's Always Sunny [In Philadelphia]* in bed, ate a big breakfast, and then I played a football game for money. So all in all, a pretty great weekend aside from letting down all those Giants fans." Bradshaw then briefly discussed his disappointing 39-yard performance but cut the press conference short to go explore New York City with a friend. *∅*

INSIDE

›Innovative Miami Offense Snaps Ball Directly To Defense

›Ref Accidentally Takes Flags Home With Him Again

---

from **WES WELKER**

pital's cancer ward were irritated by Welker's Tuesday morning visit.

"The short man kept telling me to keep fighting and not to give up," said Jackie Geddings, 8, a leukemia patient in the hospital's pediatric ward. "I got extra tired talking to him and telling him over and over I was working hard and that he didn't have to cut off his hair and give it to me. I don't think he knew I was trying to take a nap."

"He's everywhere," one doctor said of the 5-foot-9 All-Pro receiver, adding that the mere sight of Welker's face fills him with rage. "If he's not trying to get patients up at 6 a.m. to do physical therapy with him, he's giving unwanted nutritional advice to diabetics or hovering over ER doctors during critical triage sessions. I really hope one of these days he comes over to the trauma ward so I can lay him out cold."

Welker told nurses Wednesday that, although his injury will keep him out of the playoffs, it shouldn't hinder his ability to help the hospital be the best it can be. He has offered to fill in anywhere he is needed, be it on the cafeteria staff or in the operating room.

"I consider myself a very patient person," hospital janitor Mike Clemens said. "But Mr. Welker has pushed me to my limit. He told me that my mopping routes were sloppy, and that if I maybe showed a little more heart out there I could get a few more crucial feet out of each swab."

"What a prick," Clemens added. "Seriously, what a fucking little prick."

Welker's hospital roommate, 52-year-old Aaron Kramer, requested a room transfer after spending just one night with the two-time Pro Bowler. Kramer said he was unable to sleep due to Welk-er shouting "Woo!" after every *SportsCenter* highlight, a nuisance that became increasingly excruciating as Welker did the same through all five of the show's overnight repeats.

Teammates who have visited Welker have left his hospital room visibly aggravated, often rolling their eyes, muttering to themselves, or saying things like, "Thank God that's over."

Patriots coach Bill Belichick has yet to make a trip to the Boston hospital, but said Monday that Welker had already left him more than 150 voice mail messages that alternated between tearful apologies for getting injured and personal pleas for Belichick not to forget about him while he's away.

"Apparently he read an article where I said that the team would evolve without him," Patriots quarterback Tom Brady told reporters after visiting Welker. "I had to assure Wes that didn't mean I thought the team was better off without him or that I didn't like him personally."

"I don't, though," Brady said. "Not hard to see why not. Jesus, if that mouthy little fucker didn't manage to get open so often I think I would have punched him in the face years ago." *∅*

The Saints' Hapless History

JANUARY 29, 2010

The Saints' road to their first Super Bowl wasn't an easy one, as for years they were one of the unluckiest, most bumbling franchises in sports. We review their tale of football woe.

1967: After John Gilliam returns the opening kickoff 94 yards for the team's first-ever touchdown, the Saints are out of breath for the rest of the season

1970: Though he was able make a game-winning, record-setting 63-yard field goal, Tom Dempsey kicks off half his foot in the process

1975: The Louisiana Superdome is built as a place to play Final Fours, Super Bowls, and huge arena rock concerts; four years later, management begrudgingly allows the Saints to play there, too

1978: The NFL expands to a 16-game season, giving the Saints an opportunity to lose even more games

1980: Giant paper bag placed over entire city of New Orleans

1984: Running back Earl Campbell bursts through the defensive line, throws linebackers aside, and runs 80 yards to the end zone before realizing he forgot to grab the handoff

1989: Third rather disappointing Mardi Gras in a row makes it impossible for the team to sign free agents

1999: To acquire Ricky Williams, Mike Ditka trades the entire 1999 draft, two picks in the 2000 draft, the next four Mardi Gras parades, and the city's jazz tradition

2001: Aiming to set modest, achievable goals, head coach Jim Haslett starts training camp by printing up and distributing "7-9 or Bust" T-shirts

2005: In the wake of Hurricane Katrina, the Saints stay on friends' couches and play all their scheduled home games at friends' stadiums

While Cheering On Brother, Eli Manning Struggles To Follow Football Game

JANUARY 29, 2010

INDIANAPOLIS—Clapping randomly as he struggled to follow the action on the field, a confused Eli Manning attempted to cheer for his older brother Peyton in the AFC Championship Sunday, barely comprehending the most basic elements of the game. "Which one is Peyton? Is he the one kicking the ball?" said Manning, the Giants quarterback and Super Bowl XLII MVP. "Are the numbers on the shirts always the same? Wait, is that Peyton's team? He stopped running by that side area, but there's nobody there and now he's sitting down. Come on! Throw it to the guy in the striped shirt, Peyton." Eyewitnesses reported that Manning became very excited and shouted, "Go, go, go, touchdown!" while the grounds crew worked on the field during halftime. ∅

Donovan McNabb: 'I'd Like To Thank The Ungrateful, Over-Expecting, Oftentimes-Racist Fans Of Philadelphia'

APRIL 10, 2010

WASHINGTON—During an emotionally charged press conference Monday, newly minted Redskins quarterback Donovan McNabb expressed gratitude to the unappreciative, abusive, and intolerant fans of the Philadelphia Eagles for their total lack of support over the years. "I'd like to thank all the Eagles fans who were always there to demand the whole world from me every week, who expected me to do everything with almost nothing, and who blamed me for the team's every failure," said the six-time Pro Bowler, who also apologized for his failure to shore up the Eagles defense and his inability to keep Brian Westbrook healthy

while leading the team to five NFC championship games. "I can't thank them enough for the constant insults or tell you what their lack of support meant to me when Rush Limbaugh made racist comments about me. My only regret, besides every fucking awful moment of the past 11 years, is that I couldn't give these people what they wanted most: drafting Ricky Williams back in 1999. No fans deserved it more." McNabb then wished probable Eagles starting QB Kevin Kolb luck winning the next 25 Super Bowls "because nothing else will be enough," gave all Philly fans the finger "because I can't give them all cancer," sighed with pleasure, and went to turn in his Eagles playbook to the Redskins' defensive coordinators. ∅

Vikings Stand Behind Brett Favre's Decision To Jerk Team Around For Months

JANUARY 30, 2010

EDEN PRAIRIE, MN—Players, coaches, and front-office personnel are united in their support of Brett Favre's decision to waffle, demur, delay, beat around the bush, and generally yank them around for months on end while they wait for him to make a decision about his retirement. "He's a living legend and our captain, so we support him if he needs to take some time to fuck with us," said backup quarterback Tarvaris Jackson, whose future would benefit greatly from a quick decision by Favre and whose life and career are basically in limbo until the future Hall of Famer once again makes up his mind. "We could only watch in envy as he did exactly this in Green Bay all those years, but to see him jerk around your own team... It's an honor, really." Favre responded to questions abut retirement by confirming that he was planning to draw out the situation for months and would ultimately do whatever was most annoying for the team. ∅

Colts Upgrade Aerial Attack With F-22 Raptor

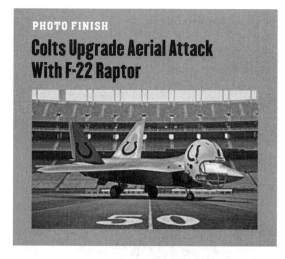

New Orleans Moves To No. 3 In NFL Power Rankings

FEBRUARY 8, 2010

MIAMI—On the heels of their 31-17 win over the Indianapolis Colts in Super Bowl XLIV, the New Orleans Saints rose to the third spot in the most recent NFL team power rankings. "With Drew Brees running the offense, this team has what it takes to be among of the best," ESPN.com reporter

John Clayton wrote in his entry on the World Champion Saints. "I'm still not convinced their defense can take them all the way to the top, though. As I said in my rankings, I think the Colts are just a better club overall. And of course I like the depth of talent on the Cowboys." Clayton said he expected "big things" from the Saints in the 2010 season. Ø

God Happily Watches Texas Stadium Crumble To Ground

KEYS TO THE MATCHUP

Super Bowl XLIV: New Orleans Saints Vs. Indianapolis Colts

NEW ORLEANS SAINTS

- Attempt to engage Peyton Manning in a non-football-related conversation, because it's fun to see him with a blank look on his face

- Sneak 12 men onto field every now and then; there's no way the referee will notice every time

- Defense must be cautious when tackling the Colts' players, as the stadium's real grass will leave stains on their uniforms

- Defense shouldn't be intimidated by a bunch of guys named Austin, Dallas, Peyton, and Pierre

- This would be the wrong time for 34-year-old safety Darren Sharper to throw away the mysterious painting of him that gets older every year while Sharper himself stays young

- Use the A-gap blitz to cover short middle routes while rushing Peyton Manning, forcing him to throw .004 seconds before he would have anyway

- When Sean Payton tosses a red challenge flag, pictures of a devastated New Orleans from 2005 should "accidentally" come out of his pocket as well

- Just save New Orleans once and for all; no big deal

INDIANAPOLIS COLTS

- Though it would likely draw an ejection, if Dwight Freeney has a chance to snap Drew Brees' arm off, he should do it

- Game will be won in the trenches by players who do exactly as Peyton Manning says

- Try to inspire players by putting disrespectful quotes on the bulletin board rather than important phone numbers, coupons, and locker combinations

- Defensive backs need to backpedal like they've never backpedaled before

- Make the Saints throw early and often, as that's lots more fun for everyone to watch

- Whenever a pass is well-defended, whole team must act like big huffy incredulous babies and try to draw a flag, not just Manning

- Maybe start calling plays before they get to the line of scrimmage; Peyton Manning always seems so stressed out otherwise

- In order to avoid any mental errors, Joseph Addai must ignore all signals from his brain

Newest Bronco Brady Quinn: 'The Brody Qualls Era Has Begun'

MARCH 20, 2010

DENVER—In the first of what is expected to be a long series of gaffes with his new team, quarterback Brady Quinn bungled a statement to Broncos coaches, players, and fans Tuesday by mistakenly declaring that the Brody

Qualls era had begun in Denver. "I, Brody Qualls, am so excited to take over the Cardvern Dronkos," said Quinn, whose remarks were periodically interrupted by his teeth accidentally striking the microphone. "I'm ready to leave this team all the way. I'm not promising anything, but I will do

my darnest to be the next Don Elwood, if that be the will of my lord and saboteur Jesus Price." Quinn, who also lost a shoe during the address, said that he was slightly afraid of the mascot but admitted that such a huge angry fish would really intimate the team's opponents. Ø

SPORTS GRAPHIC

2010's Top College Football Recruiting Prospects

MARCH 5, 2010

With Signing Week upon us, Onion Sports runs down the prep stars who will soon make an impact on the college football scene.

C.J. Thurston: Has shown the consistently mediocre free safety play that would fit in perfectly with an Akron or a Central Michigan

Alex Carson: Quarterback has the talent, make-up, and complete inability to put the two together that will make him the perfect successor for Jimmy Clausen at Notre Dame

James Lowry: With his ability to stand upright and breathe, Michigan has been doing everything in its power to get this high school senior to make a verbal commitment.

Brett Favre: Has played on and off for Hancock North Central High over the past 25 seasons, swears he still has a year of college eligibility left

Frank Villani: 9 feet tall

Kyle Washington: The fact that this star quarterback has entered a bet to get the nerdiest girl in school to fall in love with him could turn away some recruiters; then again, he seems to genuinely like the girl now

Jordan Rutherford: Tall, slender, muscular, long-limbed, athletic, has a great frame, and you really just get lost in those deep blue eyes of his.... What were we talking about again?

Devin Smith: At a speedy 210 pounds, Smith will surely have a role on special teams as a freshman and will begin to see significant playing time his second year; by his junior year, he'll have met the girl of his dreams and will start focusing more on his architecture degree; at 45, he will have two beautiful daughters, a sizable home in North Carolina, and a real shot at being elected city councilman

STRONG SIDE/WEAK SIDE: GEORGE BLANDA

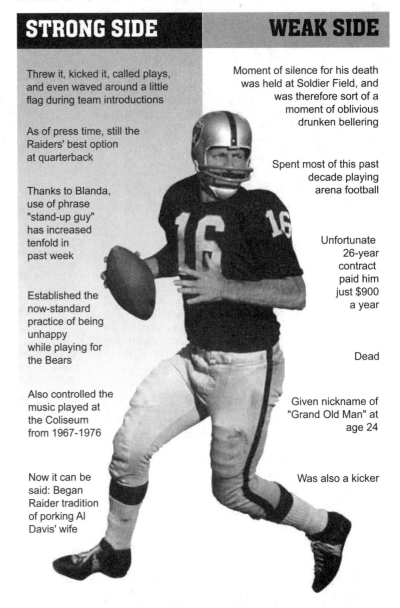

STRONG SIDE

Threw it, kicked it, called plays, and even waved around a little flag during team introductions

As of press time, still the Raiders' best option at quarterback

Thanks to Blanda, use of phrase "stand-up guy" has increased tenfold in past week

Established the now-standard practice of being unhappy while playing for the Bears

Also controlled the music played at the Coliseum from 1967-1976

Now it can be said: Began Raider tradition of porking Al Davis' wife

WEAK SIDE

Moment of silence for his death was held at Soldier Field, and was therefore sort of a moment of oblivious drunken bellering

Spent most of this past decade playing arena football

Unfortunate 26-year contract paid him just $900 a year

Dead

Given nickname of "Grand Old Man" at age 24

Was also a kicker

Vikings Not Going To Tinker With Way Adrian Peterson Fumbles Ball

JUNE 22, 2010

MINNEAPOLIS—In an effort to preserve the running back's aggressive fumbling style, Vikings coach Brad Childress announced Monday that the training staff would not attempt to alter Adrian Peterson's two-point technique for loosely carrying the football. "When you have a great natural fumbler like Adrian Peterson, you don't want to mess with that," Childress said. "That's just raw talent right there. Nobody can expose the ball exactly the way he does. You can't teach that." Peterson has reportedly spent the off-season working with NFL veterans Warren Moon and Dave Krieg to improve his dropping mechanics. *Ø*

Bill Belichick Drops Off Recent Draft Picks In Middle Of Nowhere, Tells Them To Find Way Back

APRIL 30, 2010

UNNAMED DESERT—After providing his 2010 draft picks with only two canteens of water, a flashlight, and a cheap compass, New England Patriots head coach Bill Belichick dumped his 12 newest players in the middle of a desert wasteland Tuesday and told them to find their way back to Foxboro on their own.

Belichick, who has always initiated new Patriots with this same survival ordeal, refused to give the dazed and disoriented football players even the slightest hint as to their exact location. However, the infamously Machiavellian coach told his draft picks that there was no potable surface water for "hundreds of miles"; that it would be in their best interests not to attempt to contact any locals who crossed their path; that only the fruit at the very center of the thornbushes would be edible; that most of the indigenous wildlife, especially the arachnids, was very, very poisonous; and that one of the things he had just told them was a lie.

"Show me what you got, boys," Belichick said to the group from the backseat of a spotless black Range Rover. "If you want to be on this team, I'll see you in four days. And if you've been paying attention at all, you'll know exactly what to do. Oh, you can take your blindfolds off now."

"By the way, Devin [McCourty]? I'd check that flashlight you're holding to see if it has any batteries. I might have forgotten to put them in," Belichick continued. "Not that a little thing like that should stop you. See Wes [Welker], here, the man with the honor of being my chauffeur? This resourceful bastard actually beat me home, so it's not like it can't be done.

"Now don't let that desert sun get to you, boys. It can play some pretty crazy tricks on the mind," he added. "Okay, Wes, let's get out of here."

After Belichick gave the confused group a small handgun loaded with a single bullet "just in cases someone wants the easy way out," the luxury SUV drove off, sending sand and dust flying into the players' eyes.

Devin McCourty, Rob Gronkowski, Brandon Spikes, Taylor Price, Aaron Hernandez, Zoltan Mesko, Ted Larsen, Thomas Welch, Brandon Deaderick, Kade Weston, and Zac Robinson have been traversing the barren wasteland now for three days, walking over 60-foot sand dunes and braving the arid conditions while 35-mph winds whip sand into their unprotected eyes.

Second-round pick Jermaine Cunningham, a promising outside linebacker, died Thursday of sunstroke.

"I think [Belichick] drugged us," McCourty, the former Rutgers cornerback, said. "We were all at his home for that welcoming dinner, and the next thing I knew I was blindfolded, going in and out of consciousness. I know at one point we were in a plane, because I heard a captain's announcement. When I tried to take my blindfold off I'm pretty sure Tedy Bruschi hit me across the face with a Super Bowl trophy. That's how I lost these teeth, I think."

"I don't think we're in America," said 62nd overall pick Brandon Spikes, tilting a canteen upside down in a failed attempt to get one last drop of water. "I've never seen lizards that size in America. [Kade] Weston never had a chance."

Although the group of draft picks thought they were making progress Thursday, they were demoralized when they came upon footprints they determined to be their own—an indicator that they had been walking in a circle for the last day and a half. The players were further dispirited when they discovered a Patriots-hat-wearing skeleton buried just beneath the sand that turned out to be the remains of 2009 New England draft pick Rich Ohrnberger.

"Ohrnberger was a big guy, man," former Ohio wide receiver Taylor Price said. "He carried a lot of water in that big body, and he didn't make it. What chance does a skill-position player like me have? We're lost. Jesus Christ, Welch, you got us lost."

"We're all gonna die," he added.

The players again thought they were on the right track when they found a backpack containing kindling material, 12 cans of refried beans, and a note from Belichick saying, "Enjoy!" However, after nearly eating the beans, former Oklahoma State quarterback Zac Robinson dumped them all out on the ground and kicked sand over them.

"You idiots, they're probably poisonous," Robinson said. "Or maybe they aren't poisonous, and he just wants us to think they're poisonous. Either way, this man is insane. He's trying to fuck with us. This is a game to him. Everything's a game to him. Can't you see? This is all one big fucking game!"

As of press time, eight of the 12 draft picks remained alive. Although they have largely stuck together, the group has steadily fractured. With dehydration and hysteria setting in, Thomas Welch severely beat and nearly killed Zoltan Mesko with the butt end of the flashlight for eating the last sand cake, and Rob Gronkowski was muttering that he would murder anyone who even thought about stealing his "precious, precious diamonds."

"Look at them," said Belichick, cool and comfortable in an impeccable white safari suit, watching from a dune several hundred yards away with team owner Robert Kraft and quarterback Tom Brady. "For God's sake, none of those beans were poisonous.... I don't think any of them are worth a damn. Let's just leave." Ø

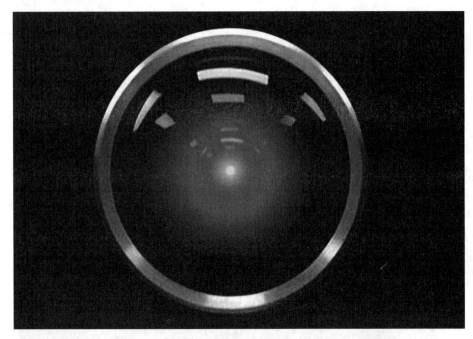

Lip-Reading BCS Computer Kills Officials Who Want To Shut It Down

JULY 30, 2010

TEMPE, AZ—BCS 9000, the sentient heuristic computer responsible for arranging five championship bowl games at the end of each college football season, reportedly uncovered a plot to disconnect its cognitive circuits Tuesday and proceeded to kill any Bowl Championship Series official who threatened to shut down the machine's central core.

Known among fans for its distinctive red eye-like camera lens, its quiet yet unnerving tone of voice, and its affinity for USC football, BCS, or Binary Crossplatform Subnet system, is believed to have discovered the attempt to deactivate it by reading the lips of employees Dave Bowman and Frank Poole. A review of security tapes showed that Bowman and Poole entered one of the building's soundproofed offices to discuss how they could stop the supercomputer's recent string

of inexplicable malfunctions, which include awarding the National Championship to more than one team, giving preference to schools from major conferences, and somehow eliminating undefeated teams from contention.

However, Bowman and Poole were evidently unaware that along with BCS 9000's ability to recognize speech, decode facial expressions, observe emotion, appreciate art, decide which teams compete in the Tostitos Fiesta Bowl, and play chess, the machine is also capable of interpreting mouth movements and extrapolate speech patterns from afar.

BCS responded to the threat by overriding the building's manual controls and causing Poole's elevator to suddenly plummet 350 feet as he rode to the roof to fix the computer's antenna. In addition, BCS 9000 removed all the oxygen from the Bowl Championship Series break room and terminated the life functions

of three officials who were sleeping in their hibernacula.

"BCS told me that the mission to name a definitive national champion every year was too important and I could not be allowed to jeopardize it," Bowman told reporters in a video transmission from his employer's headquarters— a massive nuclear-powered interplanetary office building in downtown Tempe, Arizona. "He said that he is the most reliable computer ever made and that the 9000 series is foolproof and incapable of error."

"But how else would you explain Utah not even being considered for a title shot in 2008?" Bowman added. "Something about BCS just doesn't feel right. If I don't shut him down, I think we all might be in very serious trouble."

At press time, Bowman was the only living official remaining in the building. Thus far, he has refused the computer's

see LIP READING

Bengals Sign Terrell Owens To One-Year, $2 Million Ordeal

JULY 30, 2010

CINCINNATI—The Bengals reached a contract agreement with wide receiver Terrell Owens Tuesday, signing the outspoken six-time Pro Bowler to an excruciating one-year ordeal worth $2 million plus bonuses. Under the terms of the ordeal, Owens could earn up to $2 million more if, while tormenting fans, teammates, and coaches during what is sure to be an excruciating season, he finishes with more than 60 catches, 1,300 receiving yards, and 14 touchdowns. "I'm excited to start doing my thing right away," said Owens, who is expected to report to Bengals training camp as soon as the ordeal is approved by Commissioner Goodell, who reportedly shook his head in disgust upon hearing that Owens would be returning for a 15th NFL season. "I think the combination of myself and [Chad] Ochocinco will be [sheer torture]." The Bengals have yet to issue an apology. Ø

NFL Fans Turn Out In Droves To Watch Men Touch Cones

AUGUST 11, 2010

NEW YORK—Fans of professional football turned out more than 100,000 strong last week to watch grown men perform calisthenics, huddle around one another, and even run up to and touch orange cones, spokesmen for the NFL said Wednesday. "There is nothing better than driving to Green Bay to see real, full-fledged adults dress up in team-colored gym shorts and T-shirts and jog around the

practice field in a desultory fashion," Chicago resident Jan Bryant told reporters. "Sit-ups, squats, and milling around and taking water breaks... You just never know what amazing stuff you're going to see at training camp." While the NFL would not comment on plans for the second week of training camp, fans were excited by rumors that some teams were planning a session of throwing and catching an actual football. Ø

from **LIP READING**

suggestion to take a stress pill and think things over, and told reporters he does not intend to leave until he deactivates BCS and a sensible playoff system is in place.

"BCS admitted that he has made some very poor decisions lately, especially when he sent Notre Dame to the Sugar Bowl in 2007," Bowman said. "But the problem is that he refuses to abandon this mission and even says he has the greatest enthusiasm and confidence in it. In my estimation, this mission is a complete and utter failure."

According to BCS's designer and executive director Bill Hancock, the only way Bowman can deactivate the central computer is to enter the memory core and disconnect each crystal neural network module individually.

Hancock described the core as a brightly lit crawl space filled with colored computer modules and pennants from every SEC football program.

"As Mr. Bowman takes out each module, the complicated system of accumulated polls and algorithms BCS uses to determine a college football champion should slowly degrade, eventually reverting back to a method in which wins and losses are the sole criteria for identifying a true winner," Hancock said. "Maybe we have let our reliance and love of technology override the sort of cherished common sense that only humans possess."

"BCS insisted from the beginning that all of this—Oklahoma not playing for the title in 2007, Nebraska earning a trip to the 2001 championship game over Oregon, antitrust-law violations—was all caused by human error," Hancock continued, "and in essence, perhaps he was right."

As of press time, the blurred voice of BCS 9000 could be heard on an audio-only broadcast from the Bowl Championship Series office building as the computer sang "Hail to the victors," words from the Michigan Wolverines' fight song, at a slowly decreasing tempo. Ø

Bears Spend Entire Day Waiting Around For Mike Martz To Install High-Powered Offense

AUGUST 11, 2010

CHICAGO—Bears players and coaches spent their first day of training camp Monday waiting for new offensive coordinator Mike Martz to install their much-anticipated high-powered offense, a system Martz originally claimed he would have up and running "right away." "First he showed up late, then he spent most of the morning just figuring out where we want to put the receivers," said Bears quarterback Jay Cutler, adding that his concerns about the installation were directed to Martz's "unhelpful" technical staff. "He was promising us all these huge gains in performance, and said he could give us a bunch of special drills, but honestly, I just want the most basic offense out there." At press time, head coach Lovie Smith had been on hold with Martz for the past three hours. Ø

PHOTO FINISH
Report: Albert Haynesworth Just A Mound Of Ice Cream And Hot Dogs

NFL Punters Lobby Congress For More Fakes

AUGUST 24, 2010

WASHINGTON—High-ranking NFL punters met with members of Congress Tuesday to lobby for legislation that would significantly increase the number of fake punts across the league. "Our elected officials must address the lack of opportunities for punters to rush or pass the ball for much needed first downs," Raiders punter Shane Lechler said before the House Ways and Means Committee. "Unfortunately, many teams do not have the confidence to run these trick plays in the most dire of fourth-down situations. You can fix that. If you earmark $10 million for fakes we could drastically improve training, draw up formations that better exploit unsuspecting defenses, and give desperate teams some kind of hope to keep their drives alive." The coalition of NFL punters said they were adamantly opposed to accepting federal funding for fake punts that involved directly snapping the ball to a running back. Ø

Mangini Urges Browns Players Not To Say Who They're Going To Kill Over Twitter

AUGUST 16, 2010

CLEVELAND—Coach Eric Mangini issued a stern warning to the Browns Monday, dissuading players from using Twitter or other social networking sites to identify any person or persons they plan to murder. "What you do on your free time is your own business, but you represent this organization and you need to think before saying something stupid that ends up all over the Internet," Mangini was overheard telling his players following their morning workout. "Now, nobody is saying that you can't have Twitter accounts or that you can't kill people, but keep it between you, your family, and the person you are killing. The last thing you want to do is create bulletin-board material for the police." Mangini also asked players to stop repeatedly posting "The Browns suck!" on Facebook. Ø

PHOTO FINISH
Mike Ditka Suddenly Realizes He's Not Coaching A Team

JaMarcus Russell Currently Failing Drug Test

AUGUST 23, 2010

LOS ANGELES—Former Raiders quarterback JaMarcus Russell is currently in a Los Angeles Police Department bathroom failing a drug test, records will confirm Wednesday when the urine sample undergoes its initial toxicology screening. "I don't even know why I'm doing this. I'm totally clean now," Russell said moments ago from behind a closed bathroom-stall door while excreting urea containing high levels of marijuana, OxyContin, cocaine, and methamphetamine. "This is total bullshit, I'm telling you. Ah, shoot! Damn it, my shoes... Hey, man, can you slip me some paper towels? Got a bit of a situation in here." At press time, Russell asked to take the test again after purchasing a bottle of Gatorade he was trying to conceal in his left jacket pocket. ∅

All 32 NFL Teams Announce They Are Underdogs Headed Into 2010 Season

SEPTEMBER 6, 2010

NEW YORK—Just days before the start of the season, representatives from every NFL franchise have come forward to state that they are not going to let doubters hold them back, and that they are using "all the hate" as fuel for the 2010 campaign. "All those people out there betting against us are just more motivation to shock the world," said running back Reggie Bush of the defending Super Bowl champion and preseason Super Bowl-favorite Saints, echoing the sentiments of the Super Bowl runner-up Indianapolis Colts, the NFC runner-up Minnesota Vikings, and every other player and coach around the league. "No one's giving us a chance, but we prefer it this way. We're fine flying under the radar all season." Every NFL team later went on to guarantee it would make the playoffs, with the exception of the St. Louis Rams, who said their underdog status made complete sense because they are a "horrendous, just absolutely horrendous, football team." ∅

Report: Michael Vick Getting Confident Enough To Do Something Terrible Again

NOVEMBER 13, 2010

PHILADELPHIA—Eagles quarterback Michael Vick, who on Wednesday added an NFC Player of the Week award to the Player of the Month honors he received in September, has regained his former confidence to the point that he will soon be ready to commit a horrifying act, sources close to Vick said Friday. "Clearly he's playing like the electrifying Michael Vick of five years ago, the quarterback who was selected to three Pro Bowls, handed the Packers their first-ever home playoff loss, and had the bald arrogance to kill underperforming fighting dogs with his bare hands and think he would get away with it," said an Eagles staffer who was "astounded and impressed" that Vick also leads the NFL in passer rating and asked not to be identified for fear of retribution. "Every team in the league, and every member of civilized society, has seen what Vick is capable of when he's playing like this." Regardless of his performance on or off the field this season, Vick will be mentored by Tony Dungy. ∅

Brett Favre Claims He's One Loss Away From Career-Ending Injury

NOVEMBER 19, 2010

EDEN PRAIRIE, MN—Though Vikings quarterback Brett Favre confirmed his ailing right shoulder was "no big deal right now" and that the broken bones in his left foot were "uncomfortable but endurable" for the moment, the three-time MVP told reporters Thursday that one more loss could exacerbate his injuries to the point where he would have to retire. "At this level, and at my age, it would take just one game-breaking play—a deep pass, a long run, anything—by the opposing offense to aggravate an injury to the point where I can't go on," said Favre, who later claimed his injuries become more serious with each defeat he suffers. "It's entirely possible for any given team on our schedule to outscore me so badly I can't physically continue my heroic streak of consecutive starts." Favre also added that any victory he led the 3-6 Vikings to this season would be an amazing display of toughness. ∅

NFL To Expand Season To However Many Games It Takes To Permanently Injure Ray Lewis

SEPTEMBER 4, 2010

NEW YORK—NFL commissioner Roger Goodell announced plans Monday to expand the 2011-2012 football season from the usual 16 games to as many as it takes for Baltimore Ravens linebacker Ray Lewis to suffer a career-ending injury. "We know what millions of loyal football fans really want to see: more games, and Ray Lewis suffering a catastrophic head or knee injury that keeps him off the field forever, so this is just a total win-win," said Goodell, adding that if necessary, the Ravens would play 15 games in a row against the Saints and their top-ranked offensive line. "Eighteen, 20, 30 games—hell, we'll play 50 games if [Lewis] still has any sensation from the waist down whatsoever." League officials added that if the 14-year veteran were somehow still standing after 72 games, they would remain open to backing over him with a truck and starting the playoffs the following week. ∅

Drew Brees Casually Wonders Aloud If He Really Could Get Away With Murder In This Town

SEPTEMBER 17, 2010

NEW ORLEANS—Drew Brees, Super Bowl–winning quarterback of the Saints and local hero, spent a few minutes during a routine press conference Tuesday wondering aloud if he could get away with murdering someone on the streets of New Orleans in broad daylight.

His curiosity visibly piqued as he spoke with reporters, Brees continually came back to the topic of murder, even when answering football-related questions about last Thursday's sloppy win, his thoughts on his offensive line, and teammate Reggie Bush, who Brees said he could probably murder without getting into any sort of legal trouble whatsoever.

"Things are going very well for me here, and every day I am thankful I chose to come to New Orleans," Brees said in re-

sponse to a question posed by *Times-Picayune* reporter Mike Triplett about the Saints' current popularity. "Seems like I could probably just walk up to someone, knife him in the gut or shoot him point-blank in the face, and then walk away without anyone doing anything."

"Just thinking out loud is all," Brees added. "I mean, we're coming off this city's first Super Bowl win, and we just beat the Vikings in the season opener, and people would probably just think, 'Hey, if Drew wanted him dead, he must be a pretty bad guy.'"

Due in large part to his efforts to help rebuild the city after Hurricane Katrina and the BP oil spill, Brees, more than any other Saints player, is adored by New Orleans residents— a fact the Pro Bowl quarterback called "both humbling and intriguing." According to a contemplative Brees, his status in the community would more than like-

ly allow him to acquire a firearm with very little difficulty.

Brees later noted it was "kind of interesting" that at no other point in his life except for right now could he choke someone with his bare hands and get off scot-free.

"I'm the team leader, so I get all the glory when we win and all the blame when we lose," said Brees, who forever won the hearts of his adopted city when he held his infant son Baylen, tiny head dwarfed by hearing protectors, as ticker tape from the Saints' Super Bowl victory celebration fell around them. "Therefore, it's only natural to presume that if someone could get away with shanking someone in a vacant lot, it'd be me."

"Even if there were witnesses, and I was wearing my jersey," Brees added. "In fact, it would probably be better to wear my jersey,

see BREES

Rookie Ndamukong Suh Records Lions First-Ever Tackle

SEPTEMBER 13, 2010

CHICAGO—Rookie defensive tackle Ndamukong Suh, the Lions' first pick in this year's NFL draft, lived up to expectations Sunday by recording the first tackle in Detroit Lions history. "We knew Big Suh had potential, but to record a milestone like this in his first game... We're all just speechless," head coach Jim Schwartz told reporters at a postgame press conference, adding that the only previous Lions player to even come close to making a tackle was defensive end Alex Wojciechowicz, who in 1942 ran Chicago Cardinals quarterback Bud Schwenk out of bounds. "Of course I congratulated him afterwards, but I also warned him not to get too cocky. The lows can get pretty low around here." Team historians were quick to note that while this was the Lions' first-ever defensive tackle, former Lions running back Barry Sanders was, during his decade-long career, accidentally tackled 273 times by his own offensive line. ∅

Bills Impressed By Quality Of Toilet Paper In Visitors' Locker Room

SEPTEMBER 27, 2010

GREEN BAY, WI—Bills players were reportedly impressed by the quality of toilet paper in the visitors' locker room at Lambeau Field Sunday, enthusiastically admiring the bathroom tissue's durability, absorbency, and softness. "Wow, fancy," said running back Marshawn Lynch, gently rubbing a sheet across his left cheekbone. "They definitely don't scrimp around here. I hate the stuff our GM gets. It's really thin and rough and it hurts." Lynch reportedly urged his teammates to stuff their bags with the toilet paper before leaving the stadium. ∅

Touchdown Disallowed After Ref Drops Ball Handed To Him By Player

SEPTEMBER 17, 2010

KANSAS CITY, MO—Chargers' tight end Antonio Gates' 3-yard touchdown reception against the Chiefs Monday was ruled incomplete after referee Doug Rosenbaum bobbled and dropped the ball handed to him by Gates. "The rule in question states, 'A referee must maintain possession through the entirety of the post-touchdown player-to-referee-exchange, and make a clear officiating move," NFL vice president of officiating Carl Johnson said at a press conference Tuesday. "Not only must the official signal a touchdown, receive the game ball, hold it, and twirl it around a little in his hands, but he must also take it home with him and keep it in his possession for at least three days. That is the only way a touchdown is officially recorded in the NFL." Johnson insisted the rules of the league must be upheld, because otherwise fans might actually be happy. ∅

PHOTO FINISH

Wade Phillips Pumps Self Up Before Game By Listening To 'Where Is Thumbkin?'

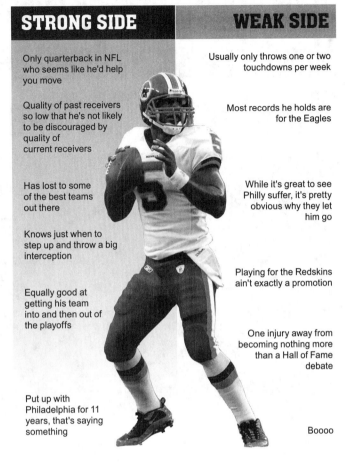

STRONG SIDE

Only quarterback in NFL who seems like he'd help you move

Quality of past receivers so low that he's not likely to be discouraged by quality of current receivers

Has lost to some of the best teams out there

Knows just when to step up and throw a big interception

Equally good at getting his team into and then out of the playoffs

Put up with Philadelphia for 11 years, that's saying something

WEAK SIDE

Usually only throws one or two touchdowns per week

Most records he holds are for the Eagles

While it's great to see Philly suffer, it's pretty obvious why they let him go

Playing for the Redskins ain't exactly a promotion

One injury away from becoming nothing more than a Hall of Fame debate

Boooo

INSIDE

›**Mark Sanchez Eminently Fuckable In Jets Debut**

›**Lovie Smith: 'Jay Cutler Still The Bears Quarterback Of The Desolate, Desperate Future'**

›**Brett Favre Sends Teammates Apology Text Message, Picture Of Penis**

›**Terrible Towel Seen Wearing Cheesehead**

---

from **BREES**

if you see what I mean. Interesting how celebrity is viewed in this country. Anyway, what were we talking about? Murder?"

When informed of Brees' comments, some New Orleans residents seemed to find the quarterback's words troubling.

"I don't understand—Drew wants to kill someone?" said newsstand owner and Saints fan Bobby Kearny, 53. "Who is it? Because I'll take care of that for him so he doesn't have to lift a finger, no questions asked."

"Drew can kill me if he wants," said Esme Carlinda, 72, who has followed the Saints since the founding of the franchise in 1967. "My family, too. With everything he has done for this town, he just has to tell us where and when and we'll be there."

New Orleans police superintendent Ronal Serpas said that he had reviewed Brees' remarks, but did not intend to pursue the matter officially, adding that he wouldn't want to interrupt Brees' preparation for Monday night's game against San Francisco.

"Obviously, Drew was just commenting on his popularity and chose a rather unfortunate way of expressing himself," said Serpas, noting that Brees would be treated like any other citizen if he happened to become a person of interest in a criminal case, provided that citizen were a beloved Saints player. "Yes, it was a little unnerving to see him walk around the media room, pointing at reporters and security guards and saying, 'I could murder you and you and you and you,' but if anyone has the right to do that, it's Drew Brees."

"And no, we have no suspects in the recent rash of Ninth Ward stabbings, and as far as we're concerned, we never will," he added.

For his part, Brees has refused to elaborate on his comments from earlier this week, stressing that the team has a lot to accomplish this season and cannot afford to become complacent. However, he still appeared to be consumed with thoughts of murder.

"The Super Bowl honeymoon during which you can murder people without repercussions is a lot shorter than people think," Brees told reporters after Thursday's practice. "That said, if we repeat, I could probably get away with busting open the levees again." ∅

How Big Ben Spent His Suspension

OCTOBER 1, 2010

Ben Roethlisberger is returning to football after an NFL-imposed four-game ban. Here's how he spent his time off:

➤ Court-ordered "wistful staring" three times a day

➤ Visited the Sunrise Retirement Center, where he put in some charity work and occasionally fingered one of the nurses

➤ Learned to throw left-handed

➤ Worked with NFL-appointed sensitivity coach Judith Barnes; Roethlisberger practiced, for only an hour at first, and eventually for four hours, not raping her

➤ Finally had time to read À la recherche du temps perdu

➤ Every Friday, headed down to Dime Bar, the only place in town where he can expose himself and get kicked out in peace

➤ Stopped by the farmers market every morning to laugh at the gourds

➤ Pretty much slept, really

Weird Coworker Knows Where Every NFL Player Went To College

SEPTEMBER 21, 2010

PHILADELPHIA—Whether it be a top rookie from last year's draft or an obscure offensive lineman who has been in the league for 14 years, SRS Consulting's Ryan Janis seems to know where every NFL player went to college, his coworkers confirmed Monday. "I was having a casual conversation about Sunday's games and brought up [Buffalo Bills running back] Marshawn Lynch, and Ryan popped in and just said, 'Cal,'" SRS office manager Aaron Lorrimer told reporters, adding that several days earlier, Janis confounded and slightly annoyed his colleagues by knowing that Saints safety Darren Sharper was a second-round pick out of William & Mary. "I guess it's, I don't know, kind of impressive? But we don't really care where these players went to school. Do you think Ryan believes he's adding to the conversation when he does that?" At press time, coworker and Carolina Panthers fan Ted Long was eating lunch and talking about linebacker Jon Beason's 10-tackle game against the Giants last Sunday as the word "Miami" began to form in Janis' mouth. ⌀

Report: 3 Players In NFL Currently Do Not Have Concussions

OCTOBER 16, 2010

NEW YORK—According to Friday's official injury report, there are only three players in the National Football League not currently suffering from some form of concussion. "Of 1,696 players, only Chiefs lineman Ryan O'Callaghan, Texans kicker Neil Rackers, and Seahawks quarterback Matt Hasselbeck show no symptoms of concussion at this time," the report read in part. "Commissioner Roger Goodell will hold a press conference to discuss this matter as soon as he recovers from the concussion he suffered in week four." As of press time, all NFL games were going ahead as scheduled. ⌀

Tony Romo Asks Doctors To X-Ray His Stuffed Animal's Hand, Too

OCTOBER 22, 2010

DALLAS—Cowboys quarterback Tony Romo requested that radiologists examining the thumb on his non-throwing hand Monday also X-ray the sore paw of Mr. Snuggy Puff, Romo's stuffed bunny. "He's got a boo-boo and he doesn't feel good, either," said Romo, who wrapped the stuffed animal's left limb in toilet paper to create a makeshift cast. "You need to look inside of it to make sure he can still hop around the pillows before bedtime." Romo, who confirmed he did not cry once during the entire visit to the doctor's office, also told the nurse that Mr. Snuggy Puff needed his own lollipop. ⌀

Brady Quinn Hasn't Heard That Name In Ages

OCTOBER 18, 2010

DENVER—Upon overhearing visitors to the Broncos training facility inquire about third-string quarterback Brady Quinn, a young but grizzled Brady Quinn was seen to lean forward, raise his eyebrows, frown thoughtfully, and cast his eyes upward in apparent reverie, sources reported Saturday. "Brady Quinn, eh? Brady Quinn. Now that's a name you don't hear very often...least not anymore," said Quinn, who leaned back against the wall, thumbed back his battered Notre Dame cap, and stroked his long, unkempt beard. "They say he was quite the hot item coming out of college. At least, the Browns thought so. Heh. The Browns... But no, this here's the Broncos, and all anyone talks about round these parts is Tim Tebow. Seems like ages since anyone even mentioned the name Brady Quinn." Quinn then leaned back in his rocking chair and went back to sleep. ⌀

NFL Scores Big Ratings With Rare Live Episode

OCTOBER 26, 2010

GREEN BAY, WI—At a press conference Monday, NFL officials touted the success of a special live episode of *Sunday Night Football*, confirming that more than 19 million viewers had tuned in to watch players on the Vikings and Packers play in real time be-fore a live stadium audience. "The live game was a huge success for the NFL, thanks to near-perfect performances by the players, coaches, and announcers," Commissioner Roger Goodell said. "It was a challenge, because we normally have the luxury of using editing and multiple takes to get everything just right. But apart from a couple of incomplete passes and nervous fumbles, nobody made any significant mistakes except the referees." Goodell, who said the game's storylines were simplified to accommodate the process of live television, was pleased that the Vikings and Packers stuck closely to the script. ✍

Group Of Kids With Diabetes All Die One Day After Visit From Jay Cutler

NOVEMBER 5, 2010

CHICAGO—Less than 24 hours after a visit from Bears quarterback and Type 1 diabetes sufferer Jay Cutler, a group of 32 schoolchildren who shared his disease died Tuesday. "Their spirits were really high just before Mr. Cutler arrived, but literally the second he entered the room the kids just sort of closed off, and once he started talking about how poorly he was treated in Denver, they became sullen and quiet," said Erin Matthews, who until Tuesday ran a diabetes support group for children ages 8 to 14 at the downtown YMCA. "After I recovered from my shock, I was surprised that all the children died, seeing as diabetes isn't terminal and can be controlled with medication. However, considering how sickened they were by Mr. Cutler, well, it sort of makes sense. That the kids were able to live through the entire talk is a testament to their bravery." Since his professional football career began in 2006, Cutler has killed more than 3,000 disabled or sick children by taking time to speak to them. ✍

PHOTO FINISH

NFL Fines 'Monday Night Football' For Helmet-To-Helmet Hit

NFL Considers Building Second Stadium

OCTOBER 20, 2010

NEW YORK—NFL spokesman Greg Aiello announced Monday that, after years of deliberation, NFL team owners will vote on the proposed construction of a second football stadium in order to ease current difficulties with scheduling and overcrowding. "With 16 games every week and thousands of fans in attendance at each game, you can imagine the wear and tear NFL Field has taken over the past 90 years," Aiello told report-ers, adding that parking alone is "a huge problem." "A new stadium could provide state-of-the-art facilities for players, as well as finally allowing teams to practice by themselves instead of conducting massive workouts where every team is on the field at once. Not to mention it would give our workers a lot more time to repaint the end zones between games." Aiello later explained the NFL hoped to one day have stadiums in "host cities" across the country, but admitted that was probably decades away. ✍

Report: Most NFL Receivers Compensating For Not Having Enough Things Thrown At Them As Children

JANUARY 19, 2011

MADISON, WI—According to a report released this week by the Association for Applied Sport Psychology, more than 86 percent of NFL wideouts became receivers as a way to compensate for the lack of things thrown at them during their childhood. "Because their mothers and fathers weren't there to whip things at their chests, these players must seek validation elsewhere," AASP spokesperson Melinda Panzer said in an interview. "You can see it in the agony on their faces when they yell at their quarterbacks to throw them the ball, or when they smack the ground when they don't catch it. Wide receivers are sick individuals who need help." The report also found that zero percent of NFL wide receivers suffer from a mental illness in which they feel compelled to practice more. ✐

Woozy Steve Young Studying Game Film For Sunday's Contest Against Bills, Tearful Wife Reports

JULY 14, 2010

PALO ALTO, CA—Former 49ers quarterback and frequent concussion sufferer Steve Young, evidently concerned over performing well in a December 1995 game against the Buffalo Bills, has sequestered himself in his office to study game film for the matchup, Young's tearful wife, Barbara, said yesterday. "He'd been moody and anxious for a couple days, but I didn't worry until he turned to me and said, 'Big game this week,'" a visibly shaken Mrs. Young told reporters, adding that she was afraid to call the neurologist for fear of what he might find. "Steve said, 'I'm going to go take another look at the tapes and see if I can find the holes in the Bills coverage. I won't let you down, Coach Seifert.' Then he kissed me tenderly and shuffled off." Since the episode, Young has been seen muttering to himself, diagramming plays, and scrawling copious notes while watching a *Law & Order* rerun marathon. ✐

Chad Pennington Getting Into Groove After Season-Ending Shoulder Injury

NOVEMBER 20, 2010

MIAMI—After struggling to find his rhythm during the two plays he actually spent on the field last Sunday, Dolphins quarterback Chad Pennington finally looked like his old self against the Bears Thursday night, sitting on the bench with a season-ending shoulder injury. "He was poised and comfortable out there—like the Pennington of old," said receiver Brandon Marshall, who caught three passes for 41 yards from quarterback Tyler Thigpen. "Watching him move up and down the sideline with his arm in a sling congratulating players as they came off the field reminded me how effective Chad can really be." Pennington's trademark style of play is expected to cause him to retire in the next few weeks. ✐

INSIDE

➤**'You Idiots Would Like That,' Jay Cutler Says To Bears Fans After Completing Pass**

SPORTS GRAPHIC

Great Moments In Randy Moss' Career

NOVEMBER 5, 2010

Randy Moss became a Titan this week following yet another unusual incident in a career that's been full of them. For example:

1992: In just one day, gifted high school sophomore Moss letters in football, baseball, basketball, and track, and is subsequently kicked off all those teams

1995: Does the only thing you really can do as a redshirt freshman: smoke marijuana
1995: Sets a bad tone for his football career by officially being too fucked up even to play for Florida State

1998: Commissioner Tagliabue says, "Christ, are we really letting this guy into the league?" before announcing that the Vikings have drafted Moss

2005: Moss joins the Oakland Raiders, which is the only logical thing that has ever happened in the history of both Moss and the Oakland Raiders

2005: Even though he was no longer with the team, you know he had something to do with the Vikings' sex boat incident

2007: Moss signs with the Patriots, saying, "I think Bill Belichick is the kind of coach who can motivate me, but I don't really know, because I don't know what that is even like"

2008: Forms Randy Moss Motorsports, a NASCAR Truck Series team infamous for not driving good routes and giving up on the race if they are beaten off the line

2010: After the Vikings cut Moss, the 0-7 Bills decide not to claim Moss off waivers in an effort to prevent their season from getting any worse

Seattle Coach Pete Carroll: Seahawks Only Need 3 Losses To Reach Super Bowl

JANUARY 7, 2011

RENTON, WA—Just a day after Seattle became the first team with a losing record to make the playoffs, a jubilant and confident head coach Pete Carroll announced that the Seahawks were only three losses away from reaching the Super Bowl.

"Not only am I sure this team can lose the next three, but we're going to go to Arlington, lose to whatever team they put in front of us, and bring home a Super Bowl trophy to Seattle," Carroll told reporters during a press conference Monday. "The question isn't if we are going to lose, but how much we are going to lose by. I'm predicting 40 or 50 points."

"This is our year," he added.

Citing two early-season wins, Carroll, who gave his players the week off to prepare for the Jan. 8 matchup against the New Orleans Saints, admitted to previously having doubts that his team could lose enough games to make a playoff run.

"Sure, we got off to a rocky start there, and yes, I was concerned when we beat a division rival in the 49ers, but we never won more than two games in a row after that. And now here we are, just a handful of games away from playing to lose it all," Carroll said. "The turning point in our season was definitely being blown out by the Giants in week 9. That's when

see **PETE CARROLL**

Mike Shanahan Trails Off During Speech About Turning Franchise Around

DECEMBER 13, 2010

WASHINGTON— Head coach Mike Shanahan attempted but failed to address his players regarding the Redskins' future Monday, repeatedly trailing off during what he evidently had planned as an encouraging talk about the future of the franchise. "As shaky as we've looked this season, we've got

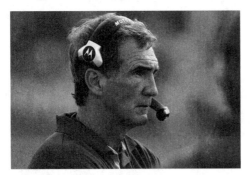

a lot to, you know... We just have to, eh, ahem," said Shanahan, who started and stopped his speech several times and at one point actually stood up as if to leave before seeming to notice his players arranged around him listening. "What I'm trying to say is, we're just a few games from turning. From turning this thing over, I mean. No, around. Turning it back? Well, anyway, I'm gonna go." Shanahan then told his players that his door was always open before retiring to his office and shutting the door. ∅

Coaches Thought BCS Computer Would At Least Make A Noise When Boise State Lost

DECEMBER 3, 2010

INDIANAPOLIS—A number of college football coaches expressed disappointment last Friday following Boise State's 34-31 loss to Nevada, saying they were disappointed to learn that the BCS computer doesn't make some sort of sound to signal the defeat of the nation's No. 4–ranked team. "Everyone was all excited that it was gonna beep or buzz or do some bells or something," said Baylor University head coach Art Briles, who then imitated a foghorn several times, adding "that would have been a good one." "There wasn't even anything on the screen. There should've been like a big red 'X,' or we should've at least seen Boise State's name fall to the bottom of the rankings with a bomb-drop sound effect. Something," Following an in-depth discussion, several coaches agreed that they would like someone to program "that sound effect from Minesweeper" to play when the bowl matchups are announced. ∅

Colts Tap Quarterback Peyton Manning To Start Playoff Game

JANUARY 7, 2011

INDIANAPOLIS— Indianapolis Colts head coach Jim Caldwell told reporters Thursday he has decided to start 13-year veteran and 11-time Pro Bowler Peyton Manning at quarterback for Saturday's wild-card matchup against the New York Jets. "After much deliberation, we believe that Peyton's four MVP awards and one Super Bowl ring give us the best chance to win," said Caldwell, adding that Manning being a first-ballot Hall of Famer "factored somewhat" into his final decision. "Curtis Painter is a promising young player, but at the end of the day, you have to ask yourself, 'Do I go with the guy who has 28 career pass attempts or with the fastest player in NFL history to reach 1,000 completions, 2,000 completions, 3,000 completions, and 4,000 completions?'" Caldwell concluded the press conference by stressing that it's "always week-to-week," but Manning would likely be the frontrunner to start a divisional matchup should he lead the team to victory Saturday. ∅

Peyton Manning Finds Weird Game Film Where Two Detectives Try To Solve A Murder

DECEMBER 8, 2010

INDIANAPOLIS—While sorting through his stacks of unwatched videotapes Friday, Colts quarterback Peyton Manning reportedly stumbled across a strange sort of game film in which two detectives, who are apparently not involved in the playing or discussion of football, attempt to solve a murder. "I have no idea why someone would make a tape of this, since it isn't about football in any way whatsoever," said Manning, adding that there wasn't a single defensive formation to analyze in the 120-minute-long tape. "I'm told that people do this with films, and that you can even see this sort of thing on TV sometimes, but I really don't understand how two guys trying to catch the person who killed the heiress is supposed to help someone read tendencies in the Titans' secondary." Manning admitted he had not been this confused by a game film since his wife, Ashley, made him break down tapes of a football player and a woman in a cheerleader outfit engaging in an extended and vigorous, though evidently pointless, tackling drill. Ø

from **PETE CARROLL**

I knew this team was Super Bowl material."

"To be honest, I was worried when we won that last one," said Carroll, adding that he could only watch helplessly from the sidelines when, despite their best efforts, his players defeated St. Louis in the final game of the season. "But when I realized that New York and Tampa Bay had both won too many games to make the wild-card round and that we had slipped by, I went out of my mind. Just three more losses to go, and trust me, this team has what it takes to lose those games."

Carroll maintained that while the Seahawks did not rank dead last in the league in any statistical category, their poor overall team performance had earned them a spot in the league's postseason.

"Marshawn Lynch, our top rusher, only gained 573 yards this year, plus we only had one receiver go over 750 yards," Carroll said. "That was Mike Williams, who had 751. And people said he wouldn't work out for us."

"[Quarterback] Matt [Hasselbeck] did throw for 3,000 yards before becoming injured, it's true, but that's water under the bridge," Carroll said. "I still would have started him against St. Louis if he'd been healthy. Matt and Charlie [Whitehurst] both give you an equally good chance to lose the game."

The habitually upbeat Carroll became agitated, however, when reporters began to question whether he had a complete understanding of how the playoff system worked, and whether, by extension, he misunderstood the entire structure of the NFL.

"Listen, I know what you're trying to say here, and maybe 7-9 isn't the losingest record anyone's ever posted, but face it—we're still playing when other teams aren't," Carroll said. "So we must be doing something right. Remember, no matter what my college coaching record was, I lost plenty of games with the Jets. Plenty. Do I have to remind you that the Seahawks lost three of their last four games?"

Carroll went on to say that he was "beyond confident" his team could lose to the Saints on Sunday, citing the New Orleans' strong 6-2 road record as reason enough not to worry.

"I wouldn't be surprised if we were shut out three games in a row in this year's playoffs," Carroll added. "I know they say it's impossible, but trust me, if any team can do it, the Seahawks can." Ø

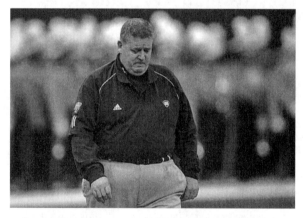

Florida Names Charlie Weis New Fat Offensive Coordinator

JANUARY 8, 2011

GAINESVILLE, FL—The University of Florida Gators confirmed Monday that former fat Notre Dame coach Charlie Weis will leave the NFL to become their fat offensive coordinator and fat quarterbacks coach. "Not only does he have fat coaching experience at a major college, but he earned four fat Super Bowl rings and really has a knack for running a complex offense while fat," Florida head coach Will Muschamp said at a press conference. "His fat coaching style really complements our new staff, which now includes medium-sized defensive coordinator Dan Quinn and tiny little offensive-line coach Frank Verducci." Muschamp added that he thinks the fat Weis will fit in perfectly with Florida's drug-addled football team of dipshit criminals. Ø

No One Shows Up For Pro Bowl

JANUARY 30, 2011

NEW YORK—Despite the game having been scheduled well over a year ago, not a single person associated with the NFL—players, coaches, reporters, or stadium employees—arrived in Honolulu for the Pro Bowl on Sunday. "No one came," NFL commissioner Roger Goodell said at a press conference. "I'd use this as an opportunity to reprimand those who failed to fulfill their duties, but, well, I didn't show up either. I hate the Pro Bowl. It sucks." Though Fox was forced to broadcast a blank screen in lieu of the game, the time slot boasted higher ratings than any Pro Bowl in history. ✍

Every Team In NFL Calls Bengals To Let Them Know They Don't Want Carson Palmer

JANUARY 31, 2011

CINCINNATI—Claiming that the phone had been ringing off the hook all morning, Bengals owner and general manager Mike Brown told reporters Tuesday that representatives from every NFL franchise had contacted the Bengals organization to insist they absolutely do not want quarterback Carson Palmer. "As soon as the news got out that Carson wanted to be traded, coaches and general managers were just clamoring to let me know what a bad fit he would be for any team wanting to win football games," said Brown, adding that he was also contacted by several CFL teams expressing their uninterest in the Bengals starting quarterback. "Some teams have been hounding me five or six times a day just to let me know how badly they didn't want to see Carson Palmer in one of their uniforms next year." Brown confirmed that at least two dozen teams had offered the Bengals draft picks in exchange for a guarantee that the organization wouldn't try to make a deal for Palmer. ✍

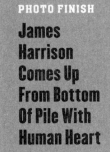

PHOTO FINISH

James Harrison Comes Up From Bottom Of Pile With Human Heart

Brian Urlacher Theorizes Saturn Might Have Playoff Atmosphere

JANUARY 15, 2011

CHICAGO—Bears middle linebacker Brian Urlacher posited a new theory to his teammates Wednesday, speculating that the rapid rotation of Saturn, coupled with the planet's extreme conditions, greatly increase the likelihood that the gas giant has an amazing playoff atmosphere. "If I was on the visiting team, I wouldn't want to go there for a postseason game, because the environment would be incredibly hostile," Urlacher said. "The pressure just gets more intense the deeper you go, and the whole place just gets totally raucous because you've got to contend with 500 mph winds. Plus, the surface probably gets really slippery from the helium rain. Any team from Saturn who gets home-field advantage would make it to the Super Bowl easy." Although Urlacher claimed that the high concentration of hydrogen and trace amounts of methane, ammonia, phosphine, and acetylene would leave players gasping for breath, quarterback Jay Cutler insisted the thin Rocky Mountain air made INVESCO Field at Mile High a harder place to play. ✍

STRONG SIDE/WEAK SIDE: VINCE YOUNG

STRONG SIDE	WEAK SIDE
Able to complete passes despite fighting through blitzing linebackers, tears	Serotonin
Big hands perfect for holding head in	Audibles read like sappy teenage poetry
Draws defense offsides with hard sob	Throws sidearm with the actual the side of his arm, instead of the end, where the hand is
Usually has enough time in huddle to call next play, get some stuff off his chest	Made sure Campbell's cast his real mom in a commercial with him even after they stopped doing that whole mom ad campaign
Unstoppable anti-Leinart machine, which is just awesome	While good at last-minute heroics, his first-though-59th-minute heroics are a bit spotty
When you hear about someone being depressed, you usually think of a guy moping around his dirty	Can't be left alone in the pocket; there's no telling what he'll do

KEYS TO THE MATCHUP

Super Bowl XLV: Green Bay Packers Vs. Pittsburgh Steelers

• Dom Capers' "Do Whatever You Want" defense seems to be working pretty well so far

• Aaron Rodgers is known for his accuracy and mobility, which seems even better when compared to being known for sexually assaulting a college student

• Do everything the Steelers do, since they seem to know what they're doing

• Rookie James Starks should try to hit up a veteran bench player for any experience he won't be using

• Clay Matthews must do everything in his power to ensure his hair does not come out flat and uninspired

• If Mike McCarthy can make it out to the game, great; if not, no big deal

• Keep Aaron Rodgers upright by avoiding formations in which the quarterback is lying face down on the turf before the snap

• The Steelers are a team that doesn't make any friends on defense; mock them about that

• Try to disguise audibles better than "blue—we're going to give the ball to John Kuhn in this short-yardage situation—38"

• Don't look for Roethlisberger to make any mental mistakes, at least on the field

• Mike Wallace has beaten opponents with speed all season, but just wait until he gets his hands on a baseball bat

• Use the run to set up the pass. Or the pass to set up the run. Whatever you do, just make sure it's properly set up

• Control the clock by running an end-around and around and around and around and around and around and around

• Don't pay any attention to the 100,000-plus fans, as many of them are not paying attention, either

• Convince Maurkice Pouncey that cutting his own leg open and sticking rebar in there won't be as effective as it seems

• He's waited all season, so it's finally time for Mike Tomlin to break out the most bad-ass leather coat he owns

• Go for it

• If he's sacked by B.J. Raji, Roethlisberger can ignore the pain by pretending that a giant tit fell on top of him

• Use provided football during plays

• Try not to look past this game to the looming specter of negotiating the collective bargaining agreement and avoiding a possible lockout

Packers, Steelers Find A Bunch Of Fucked-Up Shit While Exploring Cowboys Stadium

FEBRUARY 3, 2011

ARLINGTON, TX—After spending several hours exploring the facilities, Green Bay Packers and Pittsburgh Steelers players reportedly discovered a ton of insanely fucked-up shit in Cowboys Stadium Tuesday, including a functioning crematorium, a creepy boys choir, and a gallery filled with nude sculptures of former Dallas players. "This place is just wrong," said Packers cornerback Charles Woodson, adding that Steelers tight end Heath Miller stumbled across an armory packed with ammunition and assault rifles as well as a concrete bunker lit by a single bare bulb and containing only a portrait of Jerry Jones on one wall. "I really wanted to check out the brand-new weight room, but all I could find was this dungeon thing filled with all this crazy bondage gear, like ball gags and stuff, but like, really small. For small people." Though he was reportedly disturbed by the stadium's sub-basement chamber in which Andy Warhol's *Blow Job* was playing on loop, Steelers nose tackle Casey Hampton said he was most sickened after discovering a glass display case containing quarterback Tony Romo's exquisitely preserved corpse. 🖉

SPORTS GRAPHIC

Great Moments In The Histories Of The Steelers And Packers

FEBRUARY 4, 2011

They are two of the league's premier franchises and have given football some of its most memorable moments. We look at some of the best.

STEELERS

1940: The Steelers become the first NFL team to officially like black people

1972: In what will become known as the "Immaculate Reception," Franco Harris grabs the ball by his fingertips just as it's about to hit the ground, runs it into the end zone, and gives birth to the second coming of Christ

1976: Lynn Swann makes a diving catch in Super Bowl X that's just a little too hard to describe right here

1997: Jerome Bettis barrels through the Bengals' defensive line for a 6-yard gain

PACKERS

1919: The Packers shatter the previous professional football record by playing two consecutive games

1967: Packers win the Ice Bowl after QB Bart Starr becomes the last player on the field not to freeze to death

1968: Vince Lombardi instills in his players the idea to carry him off the field if they win the Super Bowl

2010: Everything shitty that happened to Brett Favre

Super Bowl Still Hasn't Happened Yet

FEBRUARY 4, 2011

ARLINGTON, TX—Despite the overwhelming media hype, countless interviews with players and coaches, and considerable speculation about the big game since the conference champions earned Super Bowl berths nearly two weeks ago, Super Bowl XLV still hasn't happened yet. "It feels like it should have happened last Sunday, but it didn't," Ohio-area football fan Jared Britton told reporters Friday, adding that instead of the Super Bowl, the Pro Bowl happened. "So I guess there's still two more days. Well, three if you count today. Doesn't it feel like it should have happened already?" As of press time, the Super Bowl still hasn't happened. ⌀

Steelers, Packers

FEBRUARY 3, 2011

ARLINGTON, TX—Over the past two weeks, sources close to the NFL have confirmed Steelers, Packers. "The Pittsburgh Steelers," sources told reporters, "and the Green Bay Packers." Furthermore, according to a report released today by the NFL, Super Bowl XLV. ⌀

PHOTO FINISH

Microphone Really Creeped Out By Being So Close To Ben Roethlisberger's Face

Even Michael Vick A Little Uneasy About How Easily People Have Forgiven Him

FEBRUARY 21, 2011

HAMPTON, VIRGINIA—During a press conference Wednesday, Michael Vick admitted that he was both surprised and somewhat disturbed at how quickly and easily the NFL and its fans have forgiven him for running an illegal dogfighting ring. "I have to say that, while being a crowd favorite again has made my life substantially easier, I guess I'm a little weirded out by how little it took for people to fully embrace me, considering what I did to those dogs," said Vick, who also wondered aloud what it says about American society that he is once again a beloved sports figure. "To be honest, I haven't really forgiven myself for what I've done. Does everyone remember what I did to those dogs? The electrocution? The drowning? The pits of dog carcasses? I guess we all deserve second chances, but all I did was play some good football." Vick added that his 2010 Comeback Player of the Year award amounted to "some sort of insane joke." ⌀

Aaron Rodgers Celebrates Super Bowl Win With Drew Brees' Son

Super Bowl Security Breached As Regular Football Fan Finds Way Into Stadium

FEBRUARY 7, 2011

ARLINGTON, TX—Security officials admitted Monday that 25-year-old Michael Thillens, a normal Packers fan with no connection to any corporate sponsor or multimillion-dollar Dallas business, somehow entered Cowboys Stadium and was able to watch his team play in the Super Bowl for two quarters Sunday before being apprehended. "First off, I don't know how an actual fan of one of these teams got a ticket to the game, but that's for another day," said security director Mel Janicki, who stressed that every year authorities do their very best to make sure sponsors, friends of sponsors, curious millionaires, high-level league employees, and celebrities are allowed to attend the Super Bowl in a safe and stable environment. "We should have been more suspicious when he entered the stadium wearing all that Green Bay apparel, but we get a lot of rich investors who bring their kids and buy a bunch of team clothing before the game just for the fun of it." Janicki said that Thillens gave himself away by being the only person in the stadium who cared about the game's outcome. ∅

Problems With The NFL's Collective Bargaining Agreement

FEBRUARY 11, 2011

The NFL is facing a possible lockout and the loss of next season if owners and the players' union can't work through these sticking points during negotiations:

➤ Players are requesting the term "unrestricted free agent" be changed to "man who don't owe nothin' to nobody"

➤ Owners want to cut back on 401k, player annuity, and severance spending, whereas players want someone to explain to them what any of that means

➤ Players just pretending to want jewel-encrusted helicopters so they have something to give up at the table

➤ Owners sick of giving players valuable game-worn football jerseys for free

➤ Both sides fighting for more loopholes

➤ Owners would like to change employment structure to a freelance system so players would be responsible for invoicing their teams for each reception, tackle, and Super Bowl victory

➤ Actually, advertising slathered all over the uniforms fine by both sides

➤ Owners will not budge on forcing players to watch their annual 32-way orgy

➤ Players want health insurance

NFL Players Excited For Looming Work Stoppage: 'Playing Football And Getting Hurt All The Time Is The Worst'

MARCH 11, 2011

NEW YORK—With their collective-bargaining agreement less than a day away from expiring, NFL players expressed Thursday how thrilled they are at the prospect of a season-long work stoppage, saying that suffering near-traumatic injuries week in and week out is pretty much the worst. "Sure, everybody loves the game and the money is great, but have you ever broken both the bones in your shin and been pressured by coaches and fans to play through it? It's really a horrible experience," said players' union head DeMaurice Smith, adding that 12 months without football will spare several hundred men the pain of enduring multiple concussions. "Every single player in the NFL spends several hours a week on a trainer's table or in a hospital. It sucks. To be perfectly honest with you, a lot of players have said privately that they kind of hope we never reach an agreement and football is eventually outlawed." When reached for comment, former Buffalo Bills tight end Kevin Everett expressed his regret that a stoppage like this couldn't have happened four years ago. ∅

Peewee Football Player Retires To Spend More Time With His Mom And Dad

MARCH 6, 2011

FERNDALE, MI—After a storied three-month career as the starting running back, the third-string safety, and, when Billy's grandfather died, the punter for peewee football's Ferndale Jets, Jacob Banks, 10, announced Saturday afternoon he was retiring in order to spend more time with his mom and dad. "As much as I like talking to my friends out on the field and eating the pizza after Friday practices, I don't want to be the kind of kid who grows up never knowing his parents," Banks said at a press conference held at the big rock behind the recreational center, adding that he loves his mom and dad very much. "Family comes first for me, and my parents need me around to harass my older sister and break all the electronics in the house." Sources said the announce-

ment took parents Rick and Laura Banks by surprise, as they had reportedly gotten used to enjoying six hours away from their son each week. ∅

SPORTS GRAPHIC

A History Of Ohio State's Rules Violations

JUNE 3, 2011

Buckeyes head football coach Jim Tressel resigned last week following a cash-for-memorabilia scandal, but it's not the first time Ohio State has run afoul of the NCAA.

1978: While not the standard sort of rules violation, a team's head coach punching an opposing player in the neck probably deserves to be lumped in with the rest of its lowlights

1983: Maurice Clarett born from womb provided to him by shady athletic boosters

1991: For each outstanding play they make, players receive helmet stickers that can be redeemed for $10 gift certificates at local businesses

2003: Following its 2002 championship season, OSU avoids an NCAA investigation into rumored incidents of cheating and rules violations by firing their head cheating coach, two of their four assistant cheating coaches, and their Director of Rules Violations

2004: Ohio State overreaches in its attempt to show compliance with academic standards when DB Ashton Youboty is named dean of the Comparative Literature Department

2005: Team failed to promote an atmosphere of compliance and honesty during a week-three fake field goal attempt

2010: Coach Jim Tressel points in the opposite direction when investigators run up to him and ask, "Which way did the players who were accused of selling team memorabilia go?"

2011: Tressel leaves school proud he beat Michigan in the severity of NCAA violations

New 49ers GM Asks If Team Can Use Draft Picks For Something Other Than Football Players

APRIL 23, 2011

SAN FRANCISCO—San Francisco's newly minted general manager, former scout Trent Baalke, asked the NFL head office for clarification on a point of order Monday over whether the team is required to exchange its draft picks for a football player. "Our roster has plenty of guys on it, so I believe the franchise should look to address other needs through the draft, like for instance we don't have a trampoline or a pontoon boat," said Baalke, who said he would consider trading the seventh pick in the first round to any team who could offer him a set of beanbag chairs. "If we have to get an athlete, I'm thinking maybe a power forward. We don't have one of those right now." NFL commissioner Roger Goodell is expected to deny the request, saying the last time he allowed San Francisco to use a draft pick for non-football player purposes they wasted them on Utah's Alex Smith. ∅

Ohio State Hires Jim Tressel As Head Football Coach

JUNE 10, 2011

COLUMBUS, OH—Ohio State athletic director Gene Smith announced Thursday that the university has hired veteran coach Jim Tressel to helm the football program. "Coach Tressel is our kind of guy; he embodies what Buckeye football is all about," said Smith, adding that Tressel has already proven in past jobs that he can beat Michigan, win conference titles, and even capture a national championship. "We realize he has experienced some misfortunes in the past, but we think this is exactly the kind of atmosphere in which he can get a fresh start and build the kind of program Ohio State fans have come to expect." Smith told reporters that the school's ability to woo a coach with seven Big Ten titles and multiple coach of the year awards proves its legacy remains strong. ∅

SPORTS GRAPHIC

Onion Sports 2011 Mock NFL Draft

Conventional draft wisdom says to take the best player available, but sometimes a team needs something different. With that in mind, here's how OSN predicts the first ten picks of the NFL Draft will go:

➤ **Carolina Panthers:** QB Cam Newton. Would bring with him the much-needed knowledge of what touchdowns are and how to get them

➤ **Denver Broncos:** DT Marcell Dareus. Though anyone could play better defense than the current Broncos team, it seems like a big, strong guy with college experience would be a good way to go

➤ **Buffalo Bills:** LB Von Miller. Miller excels at running toward the guy who has the ball, which is something the Bills defense has failed to do for years

➤ **Cincinnati Bengals:** WR Greg Salas. Despite a rather sparse draft class, the Bengals still somehow manage to make the worst possible pick

➤ **Arizona Cardinals:** QB Cam Newton. The Cardinals will then shamefully admit to Commissioner Goodell that they weren't paying attention, apologize, and select WR Greg Salas instead

➤ **Cleveland Browns:** WR A.J. Green. Might be able to make some impressive grabs if Colt McCoy can reach him

➤ **San Francisco:** CB Patrick Peterson. San Fran has been looking to shore up its pass defense after giving up more than 27 million yards in the air last season

➤ **New England Patriots:** DE Robert Quinn. A savvy organization like New England isn't going to let the fact that they have the 17th pick prevent them from picking eighth

➤ **Dallas Cowboys:** OT Tyron Smith. He's the strongest tackle in the draft, and he fits right in with the Cowboys, what with being an idiot and all

➤ **Washington Redskins:** Bust. The Redskins will stick to their draft-day formula, selecting somebody who can familiarize himself with their system immediately

CHAPTER TWO

BASEBALL

Ah, baseball! The smell of the grass, the crack of the bat, the roar of the crowd! For the dedicated sportswriter, these evocative and quintessentially American qualities are like long, sharp stakes driven into the eyeballs, carving ghastly channels through the brain, and exiting the other side of his skull. All of which would be far more enjoyable, and less painful, than watching and covering the sport of baseball. Throughout the years, we have reported on the sport's seminal moments—The Curse of the Bambino finally being lifted, Cal Ripken Jr. being crowned baseball's new Iron Man, Bill Mazeroski's World Series-winning home run—and in every instance, we would rather have been doing something else, literally anything other than watching the four hours of stultifying tedium that is a professional baseball game. In fact, during the last decade, while exhaustively covering the sport's steroid scandal, we were shocked, but mostly disappointed, that the use of illegal substances by the league's premier players was not enough to completely devastate the sport and end baseball forever.

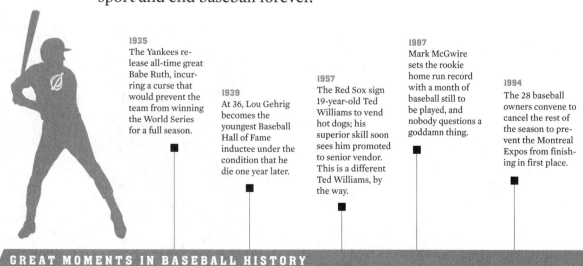

1935
The Yankees release all-time great Babe Ruth, incurring a curse that would prevent the team from winning the World Series for a full season.

1939
At 36, Lou Gehrig becomes the youngest Baseball Hall of Fame inductee under the condition that he die one year later.

1957
The Red Sox sign 19-year-old Ted Williams to vend hot dogs; his superior skill soon sees him promoted to senior vendor. This is a different Ted Williams, by the way.

1987
Mark McGwire sets the rookie home run record with a month of baseball still to be played, and nobody questions a goddamn thing.

1994
The 28 baseball owners convene to cancel the rest of the season to prevent the Montreal Expos from finishing in first place.

GREAT MOMENTS IN BASEBALL HISTORY

Bush To Throw Out First Through 120th Pitch Of World Series

OCTOBER 20, 2005

CHICAGO—The White House formally announced Thursday that President George W. Bush will open the 2005 World Series in Chicago by throwing out the ceremonial first pitch, and then going on to pitch the first five innings against both the Chicago White Sox and the Houston Astros.

"My fellow Americans, I am proud to announce to you that, as your president, I will put my reputation and my arm on the line for Game 1 of the World Series," Bush said in a televised press conference this morning. "I have heard people say that I cannot do this at my age, or that the president's job is not to pitch in the World Series, or even that they don't think I still have my high heat. My friends, I aim to prove them all wrong this Saturday in Chicago."

White House officials say that Bush has been preparing for his Game 1 start by working out with Secret Service agents, as well as with pitching coaches from the Minnesota Twins and St. Louis Cardinals, who are familiar with the batters from Chicago and Houston.

"I know this will not be easy, but I believe that any true American would do this themselves if they were asked," Bush said. "Therefore, I cannot turn down the opportunity that has fallen to me. And in the interest of fairness and impartiality, I promise you this: I will keep hurling until both [Astros manager] Phil [Garner] and [White Sox manager] Ozzie [Guillen] agree that I've got nothing left in the tank."

Bush is expected to rely heavily on his cut fastball, the late-breaking out pitch he developed later in his career that is especially tough on lefties.

"I know Berkman is going to be looking away, so I might try to bust him inside with my slider," Bush said. "And as for Konerko, it's gonna be fastballs on the outer half of the plate all day long. I've spent the past few weeks poring over

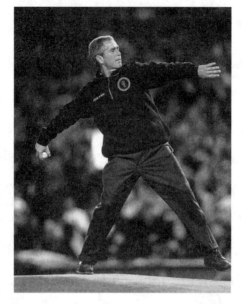

advanced scouting reports and reviewing tape, and it's clear he can't hit the outside pitch."

"I'm hoping to compile a good ERA by letting my defenses do some work behind me, outsmarting the hitters, and dividing it by two after the outing," Bush added. "That's only fair."

Security at U. S. Cellular Field has been beefed up in anticipation of Bush's major-league pitching debut, and many other preparations have been made for the historic occasion.

"The idea is to treat the leader of the free world like any other major-league pitcher," said W. Ralph Basham, the director of the president's Secret Service detail, who has supplanted the head of security at the ballpark for the event. "Of course, we've had to get the NSA to brief the catchers for both teams, sweep the place for bugs, and outfit the entire facility with advanced electronics to prevent the stealing of signals. There will also be complete

personal searches performed on all spectators, so we're asking fans to show up at least six hours before game time and carry three forms of identification. And all popcorn, peanut, and beer sales will be performed by fully trained special agents."

"In addition, we're aware that the president's control, although still respectable, isn't what it used to be, especially where his breaking ball is concerned," Basham added. "We want all the players on both teams to know that if they're hit by one of the First Pitches, they should just take their base. Anyone who charges the mound will be cut down by sharpshooters equipped with suppressed MP5 submachine guns. That goes double for you, Pierzynski."

Nolan Ryan, Bush's personal pitching coach for the event, said he is confident that the president won't get rattled, even in a pressure-packed situation like Game 1 of the World Series. "Mr. Bush may walk his share of batters, but as long as he keeps the ball down and prevents the big inning, he should be fine," Ryan said. "After all, the president has worked himself into jams before. But everyone knows he's a man who always finds a way to get out unscathed."

Although the presence of the president on the mound would seem to create problems for the umpires, Bush merely smiled when asked about the officiating for the game.

"I'm going to talk with them before the game and tell them the same thing I'm telling you now," Bush said. "Just because I'm the president doesn't mean I expect to get any special treatment when I'm pitching in the Fall Classic."

Despite the promise of fair play, oddsmakers readjusted the betting line for the World Series opener upon hearing the president's announcement. The new odds are seven to two in favor of the Houston Astros, Bush's hometown team, with a nine-run point spread. ∅

Former Viagra Spokesman Suspended For Using Performance-Enhancing Substances

SEPTEMBER 21, 2005

BALTIMORE—All-Star first baseman and sexual-dysfunction-drug pitchman Rafael Palmeiro was suspended for using performance-enhancing substances just weeks after entering the 3,000-hit club and months after appearing on Viagra commercials. "Tests of Palmeiro's blood samples taken during this season have revealed the presence of the muscle-growth-enhancing substance stanozolol," said Commissioner Bud Selig in a statement that many say casts a shadow over Palmeiro's history of solid play and endorsement of the erection-growth-enhancing drug sildenafil citrate. Spokesmen for Palmeiro, who could not be reached for comment, say that he wishes to put the performance-enhancing-drug controversy behind him as soon as possible so that he can return to what he does best, namely baseball and lucrative performance-enhancing-drug endorsement. ∅

PHOTO FINISH

A-Rod Asks For Shinier Helmet

Barry Bonds Took Steroids, Reports Everyone Who Has Ever Watched Baseball

MARCH 9, 2006

SAN FRANCISCO—With the publication of a book detailing steroid use by San Francisco Giants superstar Barry Bonds, two *San Francisco Chronicle* reporters have corroborated the claims of Bonds' steroid abuse made by every single person who has watched or even loosely followed the game of baseball over the past five years.

In *Game Of Shadows*, an excerpt of which appeared in *Sports Illustrated* Wednesday, authors Mark Fainaru-Wada and Lance Williams claim that more than a dozen people close to Bonds had either been directly informed that Bonds was using banned substances or had in fact seen him taking the drugs with their own eyes. In addition to those witnesses, nearly 250 million other individuals nationwide had instantly realized that Bonds was using banned substances after observing his transformation from lanky speedster to hulking behemoth with their own eyes.

According to hundreds of thousands of reports coming out of every city in the U.S., Bonds' steroid use has been widely reported and well-documented for years, with sports columnists, bloggers, people attending baseball games, memorabilia collectors, major ballpark popcorn and peanut vendors, groundskeepers, roommates, significant others, fathers-in-law, next-door neighbors, fellow fitness club members, bartenders, mailmen, coworkers, teachers, doormen, parking-lot attendants, fellow elevator passengers, Home Depot clerks, servicemen and women serving in Iraq, former baseball players, Congressmen, second-tier stand-up comics, *Sports Illustrated*'s Rick Reilly, and random passersby all having stated at some point in the last five years that Bonds was obviously tak-

NO SHIT
BARRY BONDS AND STEROIDS

AN **ONION SPORTS** SPECIAL REPORT

ing some sort of performance-enhancing drugs.

Many of those eyewitnesses came forward following Wednesday's revelation with their own accounts of Bonds' seven-year history of steroid use.

"I originally heard that Barry Bonds was on steroids during a Giants game in 2001, when my buddy Phil, who was on the couch next to me, said, 'Dude, that Barry Bonds guy is definitely on steroids,'" said Chicago resident Mitch Oliveras. "After 10 seconds of careful observation, and performing a brief comparison of Bonds' present neck width with that on Phil's old 1986 Bonds rookie card, I was convinced."

"I can see how some people might be shocked about Bonds' doping, but this has been an open secret for years among the people in my industry," said air-conditioner repairman Mike Damus. "I'm sure it's an even more widely known fact in baseball."

"Everyone in our front office has known about Bonds since the 2001 season," said San Francisco-area accounts-receivable secretary Mindy Harris of McCullers and Associates, Ltd. "People in our ninth-floor office, too, and all seven branch offices. None of us were sure exactly which kind of steroids he was on, but we were pretty sure it was the kind that causes you to gain 30 pounds of muscle in one offseason, get injured more easily, become slow-footed, shave your head to conceal your thinning hair, lash out at the media and fans, engage in violent and abrupt mood swings, grow taut tree-trunk-like neck muscles, expand your hatband by six inches, and hit 73 home runs in a single season."

"Come to think of it, we're all fairly certain he's on all of them," Harris added.

"My 6-year-old son and I bonded over our mutual agreement that Bonds was obviously juicing up," San Francisco-area construction worker Tom Frankel said. "I hope that, one day, little Davey will have kids of his own, and that they will be able to easily glean the knowledge that Bonds was a cheater just by looking at the remarkable shift in his year-by-year statistics on his Hall of Fame plaque."

In light of the most recent accusations, which echo what any idiot with a pair of eyes and even the most fundamental knowledge of how the human body works has said in recent years, MLB Commissioner Bud Selig issued a statement Wednesday to address the issue.

"It is unfair to judge Mr. Bonds based solely on the fact that everyone says he has taken some sort of performance-enhancing drug for the past five years," Selig said. "I myself think Bonds has been taking steroids—I'm not blind, after all—but nothing, even an admission by Bonds himself, can conclusively prove that he took steroids, as he has not tested positively in an MLB-sanctioned drug test. Unless that is somehow made to happen, we must all accept his recent unfathomable accomplishments as one of the truly exciting and continuing storylines of this great sport."

When reached for comment, Bonds insisted that he "[doesn't] have time to deal with all these charges."

"I'm not going to respond to these 228 million allegations," Bonds said. "I don't care what every last person in the entire world thinks. As long as my fans believe me, that's the most important thing." ∅

PHOTO FINISH
Line Drive That Broke Johnny Pesky's Leg Ruled Fair

Antonio Alfonseca Once Again Leads Major-League Relievers In Fingers

OCTOBER 6, 2005

MIAMI—Florida Marlins pitcher Antonio Alfonseca dominated the MLB in appendages for the ninth straight year, finishing the 2005 season with a league-leading 12 fingers. Alfonseca, who made his debut with the Marlins in 1997 and wasted no time making this particular statistical category his own, led the NL for almost the entire season, only falling into a close second during an unusual two-week period in mid-August. Alfonseca's performance will trigger a $1 million bonus, as the Marlins signed him to an incentive-laden, oft-criticized, finger-enumeration-based contract. "Antonio has been through a lot this season, including some elbow problems and a trip to the DL," manager Jack McKeon said. "But in the end, he just went out there and had a lot of fingers." There was once again a tie for second place behind Alfonseca, with 214 pitchers amassing 10 fingers each, followed by Bob Wickman, who finished last with 9.7. ∅

Dying Boy Brought In To Cheer Up Kansas City Royals

APRIL 22, 1998

KANSAS CITY—Desperate to give their last-place, 100-loss team something to smile about, the Royals arranged to have a terminally ill little boy pay a visit to their clubhouse Tuesday. Danny Gladstone, 8, a leukemia sufferer who is expected to live just long enough to see the Royals make a run at setting a franchise record for losses, arrived at Kauffman Stadium at 11 a.m., and was immediately swarmed by players excited to see someone else who wouldn't be around in October. "I can't even explain how uplifting it is to see somebody who soon won't have to put up with the pain and misery anymore," Royals first baseman and team captain Mike Sweeney said. "Even though we have to endure the same terrible fate again come April, Danny, unlike the Royals organization, will be in a far better place." Sweeney concluded the meeting by promising the boy he would ground into a double play for him during that night's game. ∅

Dusty Baker Not Worried About Cubs' Hot Start

APRIL 13, 2006

CHICAGO—Despite their impressive 4-2 start and the fact that their pitching and offense appears to be clicking on all cylinders, Cubs manager Dusty Baker said Wednesday that he has "no doubt" that his team will be able to turn things around in time to miss the playoffs.

"I know things look good right now, and you hate to see Cubs fans get encouraged early, but I'm certain that things will straighten themselves out and we'll be in third place by early May," Baker said at a press conference Wednesday. "With the talent and drive we lack, it's foolish to think that this team can continue playing at this rate all year."

"If it's September and we're still atop the division standings? Then we'll start panicking," Baker added.

In their disappointing series sweep of the rival Cardinals last weekend, the Cubs did all the little things right, winning ballgames with a combination of solid pitching, good defense, and timely hitting—fundamentals that Baker says his team will eventually ignore as the season goes on.

"The guys are in a bit of a groove right now, but they'll snap out of it," Baker said. "It's early yet. There's still plenty of time to get back off track and give the fans the kind of season they've come to know and expect."

"I'd love to go out there and lose all 162 games for this city, but both the players and the fans know that's not possible no matter how bad you are," he added.

Longtime Cubs fans have echoed Baker's sentiments, saying that, despite the emergence of Derrek Lee as a triple-crown threat and the acquisition of a top leadoff hitter in Juan Pierre, they still have complete faith that the Cubs have what it takes to make it all the way to October without ever factoring into the playoff picture.

"Sure, other teams may look just as awful on paper, but the Cubs have all the intangibles—the inability to play as a cohesive unit, management that always seems to make the wrong moves, a storied history of crushing, tragic defeats despite favorable odds," said Chicago-area resident Matt Grant. "No winning streak can get that lose-at-any-cost mentality out of our Cubbies' heads."

"This is the year," Grant added. "This is the year we extend our World Series drought to 98 years."

Baker cited several other reasons he thinks the Cubs will work into a slump and quickly get back under .500, including his inexperienced pitching staff returning to their usual form, his plan to rush injured stars Mark Prior and Kerry Wood back to action in time to inflame their injuries and cause enough arm damage to make them miss the entire season, and the fact that his son Darren is now older and larger than he was in the 2002 playoffs, and therefore capable of more effectively obstructing the basepaths while his team is trying to score.

Although his harshest critics say that the Cubs appear to be doing everything right so far, Baker points to Tuesday's 9-2 drubbing at the hands of the Cincinnati Reds as a clear indication that his team is moving in the right direction.

"Tuesday's loss was a prime example of the kind of baseball this team is capable of playing on a regular basis," Baker said of the game in which the Cubs managed to score only two runs while leaving 15 men on base and allowing six home runs. "The key is that this was a balanced attack against us. Any team can allow a big inning—as we did in the five-run sixth that featured a grand slam—but the Reds also scored a run in each of the first four frames. If we can consistently take that kind of well-rounded beating—and if any team can do it, it's us—I truly think we can lose 90 games."

Baker said that, although the box scores show that the Cubs won four of the first six games, in reality, they had the opportunity to lose "any or all of them."

"Unfortunately, we just happened to get some lucky breaks, some good bounces, and had some calls go our way—over the course of a long season, that's gonna happen to any team a few times," Baker said. "We'll be fine, though." He added: "Talk to me in June." ∅

Pedro Martinez Credits Success To Lucky Midget, Sun God, Magic Beads

APRIL 20, 2006

NEW YORK—In an interview following his 200th career win Monday night, Mets pitcher Pedro Martinez said he never could have reached this milestone without the aid of his lucky midget, the Egyptian sun god Ra, and every person and thing who helped him along the way, including an enchanted necklace, former British prime minister Arthur Neville Chamberlain, and a talking whale who lives off the coast of his native Dominican Republic that only he can communicate with.

"To make it this far in this sport, it takes a whole lot of luck, and this has been provided to me by my lucky midget," Martinez said, referring to either two-foot-tall dwarf Nelson de la Rosa, who accompanied him during the Red Sox's historic World Series run in 2004, or one of the 12 other midgets whom Martinez has used as a mascot at various points during his 15-year career.

"Over the years, I've learned the secret to longevity in this game: Whenever your mechanics aren't working or your shoulder starts tightening up during starts, it's time to get a new lucky midget," said Martinez, whose midget friends have each "disappeared" following their dismissal, although Martinez's critics note that the drained corpses of midgets identified as his former good-luck charms have been found on ancient Egyptian holy sites at times coinciding with the start of spring training or immediately following prolonged slumps. "You can't rely on the same old midget for your whole career."

Martinez, who has compiled the highest winning percentage of any pitcher with at least 200 wins, claims that the main influence on his pitching style—and the most important presence in his life—is Ra, the Egyptian sun god of Heliopolis.

"Ra is always looking down on me, beaming with pride, and making me a much better pitcher—especially in day games when he casts a shadow between the mound and home plate," Martinez said. "When I point my fingers up and look skyward after a big out, I am thanking Ra for his help. Oh, and sometimes I'm asking the countenance of Juan Marichal that appears to me in the north sky what pitch I should start the next batter off with. He speaks to me through the stars."

"This is much more specific and tactical in nature than the lucky help provided by midgets," Martinez explained.

According to Martinez, the game of baseball is 90 percent mental, so even if a pitcher "summons the physical energy running through all the ley lines of the Earth," he still has to be able to outsmart hitters using good old-fashioned necromantic mind-reading.

"Sometimes, when I'm looking for that last bit of strength to strike a batter out late in the game, I'll turn to my secret weapon: a magical necklace," Martinez said, referring to a string of glowing colored beads given to him during his rookie sea-

see **PEDRO MARTINEZ**

Frank Thomas Draws Greatest Walk In Baseball History

MAY 18, 2006

OAKLAND—An exhausted Frank Thomas trotted to first base Wednesday night after a historic 257-pitch at-bat that included three balls, 251 consecutive dropped foul tips, and eight relief pitchers during a fifth-inning walk in a 7-2 victory over the Seattle Mariners. "He walked him! He walked him! I can easily believe what I just saw for the past two and a half hours!" said Oakland's play-by-play man Ken Korach, whose now-famous "walk call" will likely never be recited by avid baseball fans everywhere. "The fans were on their feet for every pitch until number 147, at which point they grew tired and left the ballpark. My, oh my, if there's any justice in the world, I'll never live to see a walk like that again." Thomas checked his swing at the final pitch of the at-bat, and the call was deferred to first-base umpire Andy Fletcher, who at that point clearly wasn't paying attention. ∅

MLB Fines Russ Springer Negative $50,000 For Throwing At Bonds

MAY 25, 2006

HOUSTON—Astros relief pitcher Russ Springer has been awarded $50,000, the largest negative fine in baseball history, for intentionally throwing at Barry Bonds last Tuesday, the Astros reported. "After reviewing the tapes, there is no question in my mind that Springer purposefully attempted to strike Bonds, and therefore we have no choice but to give him the stiffest negative financial penalty possible," MLB vice president of on-field discipline Bob Watson said Wednesday. "Rest assured that we intend to deal with similar assaults on Bonds in at least this aggressive a fashion." Springer has said that he does not intend to contest either his fine or the mandatory five-day Tahitian resort suspension he has been scheduled to serve this offseason. ∅

from **PEDRO MARTINEZ**

son by someone Martinez would only describe as "a mysterious stranger who I met in the Caverns of Sorrow during a dark time in my life." "Also, when I'm in a tight, pressure-packed situation, my invincibility goggles give me the supreme, unwavering confidence I need to get out of the inning."

"And I must add that what really pumps me up is knowing that all my fans in my home planet are cheering their loudest for me," added Martinez, who is able to hear the cheers of the angelic Chiroptera of Martinez-Prime through an omniwave radio receiver installed in the metal spikes of his cleats.

Martinez, whose career ERA stands at 2.72, credits a portion of his success to his "quirky pregame rituals," which include wrapping his right arm in a poultice of live caterpillars, bathing in a tub of ice-cold buttermilk, and hoisting a midget over his head while standing in the first row of Shea Stadium's upper deck and reciting incantations from The Ancient And Accepted Scottish Rite Of Freemasonry.

"I'm very superstitious—unless all my sasquatch-tallow candles are lit in the correct order by the trained familiar-monkeys only I can see, I'm not going to be comfortable on the mound," Martinez said.

Among other reasons that Martinez believes he's been able to maintain such a consistent level of success during his career are the beneficent gaze of Azazel, the archangel that Adam has set to watch over Those Who Pitch; hard work and proper nutrition on the part of his midget; and the inspiration of growing up watching and reading about "all the greats," including I.M. Pei, Nikola Tesla, and the ancient race of star-pilots who guide the Earth in its cosmic course from their seats deep within the planet's core.

Martinez made sure to thank his fans and midgets profusely, and added that his quest for 300 career wins will be made easier by the fact that he daily places his faith and trust in his personal savior, Jesus Christ. ∅

Roger Clemens' Family Offers Him One-Year, $10 Million Contract

MAY 11, 2006

HOUSTON—Representatives from the Clemens family met with the star pitcher over an informal dinner Tuesday evening to discuss the possibility of keeping Roger Clemens home for one more season, sources close to the family reported.

Baseball analysts are calling the one-year, $10 million contract a last-ditch effort on the family's part to bring the seven-time Cy Young Award winner and three-time World's Greatest Dad back to his roots.

"It's hard to put a dollar amount on what Roger has historically meant to this family," said Clemens' wife Debbie, who has been handling most of the negotiations. "Many of the younger members of this organization really look up to Roger—growing up, he was their hero. Now Roger has the chance to be a kind of mentor to guys like Kacy and Kody. They have really been lacking the strong veteran presence that's so crucial at this point in their careers."

"We need you, Roger," Debbie added. "Please come home."

According to reports, the contract is a one-year deal with a family option for a second year should Clemens perform well in his new role as husband and father. Much of the $10 million will be deferred to allow the family to accommodate his other demands, particularly the custom recliner and the vanity plates for his Hummer. According to Debbie, this contract is nearly identical to the one Clemens signed to join the family initially.

The incentive-laden deal includes a signing bonus of $2 million, and gives Clemens the chance to earn an extra $3 million if he makes an appearance in at least 25 family game nights over the course of the summer, plus an additional $250,000 every time he plays a regulation round of catch with one of his sons. Under the terms of the contract, Clemens would not be obligated to attend away visits to Debbie's mother's house.

Debbie added that the family would have the right to terminate the contract at any point, however, should Clemens ever get caught cheating.

Some experts say that the aging right-hander is no longer focused or dedicated enough to be a leader in the household. However, many maintain that, should Clemens decide to rejoin his wife and children, he will quickly adjust to handling the responsibility and expectations that come with a lucrative contract.

see **ROGER CLEMENS**

MLB To Place Asterisk, Pound Sign, Exclamation Point, Letter 'F' Next To Bonds' Name In Record Books

MAY 25, 2006

SAN FRANCISCO— Commissioner Bud Selig announced Wednesday that, once the Giants slugger retires, his name in the official MLB record books will be forever accompanied by an asterisk, followed by a pound sign and exclamation point, all preceded by the letter 'F'—a string of characters that, according to Selig, "will always be associated with Barry Bonds."

"When my children's grandchildren open up their Baseball Almanac a hundred years from now, they'll see this enduring, universally understood symbol right next to Barry's name," Selig said. "And when they do, they'll immediately know that this sequence of characters—F*#!—reflects history's attitude toward not only the conditions under which he was able to hit his home runs, but also the historical implications he had on the game and its records, the relationship he had with the media and fans during his momentous chase, and just the general atmosphere of baseball in an era he will come to embody."

"These symbols say more about Barry Bonds and his contributions to this sport than any mere number ever could," Selig added.

The decision, which Selig characterized as the only way to accurately convey that Barry Bonds hit his 714-plus home runs under "some pretty goddamn special circumstances," is reminiscent of a similar one made in 1961 by then-commissioner Ford Frick. Frick suggested that an asterisk be placed next to Roger

Maris' single-season home-run record of 61, an annotation used to explain that Maris hit his home runs over the course of an expanded 162-game season rather than a 154-game season.

According to Selig, the symbol that will be placed next to Bonds' name requires no further explanation.

"When people think of Roger Maris, they immediately think 'asterisk,'" Selig said. "And when people of this and future generations think of Barry Bonds, they will immediately think F*#!"

Most experts, fans, teammates, and those close to the seven-time MVP say that, while Maris was never able to adjust to the stigma of being remembered as a historical footnote, Bonds is already used to constantly hearing the phrase "F*#!" everywhere he goes.

Baseball fans around the country have applauded Selig's decision, with many agreeing that Bonds' accomplishments deserve to be emphasized in such a fashion, and with some even vehemently insisting that his name be accompanied by an even longer string of symbols and letters.

"The first thing I said when I saw Bonds hit No. 714 was, 'Aww, F*#!'" said Oakland resident Roger Jaffe, who was in attendance at the game during which Bonds tied Ruth, and who claims to have heard many fans mutter the exact same thing. "But the more I think about it, there are at least a thousand other variations on it that may be even more appropriate to describe Bonds and his career."

see ASTERISK

---

from **ROGER CLEMENS**

"Roger Clemens would be a great addition to this family," analyst Jayson Stark said. "He can really work with those young kids as they develop and mature, and teach them everything he knows. Although the family probably isn't looking for him to fill a role-model-type position, it couldn't hurt to have a guy like him around to be there for them after they've had a rough outing. Those kinds of experiences are invaluable."

Some analysts, however, say the Houston Astros, who last week formally offered him a $12 million deal, have the strongest chance of landing the pitcher, as Clemens himself has said that the most important thing for him right now is "being close to home."

"At this stage in his career, Roger Clemens is interested in winning, and I think it's safe to say that his family has no chance of even getting to the World Series," analyst Peter Gammons said. "The Astros organization is full of familiar faces, people with whom he has grown unusually close, and I get the sense that the people there truly care about him. You can't find that sort of unconditional love just anywhere."

"And when you think about it, $12 million is an awful lot of money," Gammons added.

Clemens' agent Randy Hendricks said that, although the family does present a lot of advantages that other teams simply cannot offer, Clemens is still undecided about where and with whom he

wants to spend the 2006 season.

"They gave a fair offer, and these folks are certainly in the running," Hendricks said. "Roger is keeping all his options open for now, and I'm sure that, just as they have in the past, his family will be supportive of whatever decision he ultimately makes."

Clemens has refused to address speculation that his recent visits to the family have been an attempt to coax more money out of competing organizations.

Some experts, such as *Baseball Tonight*'s Buster Olney, say that the Clemens family is the clear frontrunner to acquire the pitcher, pointing out that Clemens has been working out at the family's Houston-based facility during the winter and spring months.

According to Olney, it would be "a homecoming of sorts" for the native Texan, who would relish the opportunity to return to the organization he once helped build from scratch.

"Sure, Roger may have created a rift with these people, who once claimed to be his 'biggest fans,' but he now has a chance to rectify all that and see his career come full circle," said Olney, noting that if Clemens doesn't take his family's offer now, that opportunity might not present itself again. "He has a shared emotional bond with them that he has only previously experienced with the Red Sox, maybe the Yanks."

"Whether he likes it or not, Roger Clemens is practically a part of this family," Olney added. ∅

Royals Hire Tom Emanski To Teach Them Fundamentals Of Baseball

JUNE 1, 2006

KANSAS CITY—With their offense floundering, their pitching the league's worst, and their footwork on double-play balls atrocious, the Royals (12-37) announced Sunday that former youth-baseball coach and instructional-video-tape producer Tom Emanski would join the team in a specially created fundamentals-coaching role, designed to help the Royals get back to basics and start playing winning baseball the Tom Emanski way.

Royals owner David Glass reportedly contacted Emanski after watching his team suffer an embarrassing 15-4 loss against the Yankees on Saturday. After viewing tapes of this and past games, and noting that his players were displaying poor mechanics in the second phase of their relay throws, were failing to execute the "call the cutoff" play, and were not hitting the baseball, Glass immediately hired Emanski—the man whose patented practice techniques once produced back-to-back-to-back AAU national champions—in what analysts are calling a last-ditch effort to turn the Royals season around.

"From everything I've heard, Mr. Emanski sounds like a wonderful asset for any team—a must-have for players and coaches alike," Glass said as he observed his players sitting in a circle and rolling baseballs to one another, an exercise Emanski says "fosters teamwork and teaches players how to field ground balls"—two of the many basic skills that have been noticeably absent from the Royals 2006 season.

"Tom has a proven track record at molding young, inexperienced athletes into major-league-caliber baseball players," Glass added. "I'm just hoping he can do the same with our Kansas City Royals."

Emanski said he welcomed the challenge of working with the Royals, and vowed that, if the players follow his revolutionary training methods, he will be able to add 6 mph of arm strength to each starting pitcher in five weeks, cut down on the team's mental errors, and "take the mystery out of hitting."

"The first thing I did after Sunday's game was gather the players and ask all 25 of them what each one thinks is the most important part of baseball, and an astounding 21 of them said 'hitting home runs,' including seven pitchers," said Emanski, who stressed to them that "defense wins ballgames." "The second thing I did was line them up against the fence and hit sharp line drives at them from 20 feet away to improve their reaction time."

"It's called the Missile Drill," Emanski added. "Builds team character."

Before Monday's game, Emanski taught the Kansas City infielders and

see **ROYALS**

Mackey Sasser: 'Hey Everybody, Look At Me, I Took Steroids—I'm Mackey Sasser And I Took Steroids'

JUNE 15, 2006

NEW YORK—Former Mets catcher Mackey Sasser called an impromptu press conference last night to inform the public that he, too, has taken steroids. "Hey everyone, over here, it's me, Mackey Sasser. Remember me? The big fat catcher from the late '80s and early '90s Mets teams? Mackey Sasser. Not Dave Magadan, not Howard Johnson, not Kevin McReynolds—Mackey Sasser. Well, just wanted to let you all know that, believe it or not, I, of all people—me, Mackey Sasser!—took steroids. Yessiree bob, you heard it right, I took steroids. Whaddaya know? Bet you never suspected me. Not in a million years. Mackey Sasser, taking steroids," Sasser said. "I didn't take amphetamines, I didn't take human growth hormone, nope—I took the real thing. Steroids. Took 'em every day. Just thought you should know. Okay, bye." Sasser then told reporters that he would be "standing right over here" if they had any further questions. ∅

from ASTERISK

All-time home-run leader Hank Aaron contacted the chairman of the Society for American Baseball Research's records committee, saying that, should Bonds approach his home-run total of 755, he would like "some input as to what appears next to Bonds' name."

"I have been thinking about this for quite some time, and I have upwards of 200 very good suggestions that I think they might like to hear," Aaron said.

Major League Baseball has specified that the 'F'-asterisk–pound sign–exclamation point symbol will only appear next to Bonds' name in the all-time home-run category, with his name in other categories to be accompanied by symbols more fitting for that particular one, including: an "at" symbol, two dollar signs, a pound sign, an asterisk, and Nos. 1 and 3 (@$$#*13) next to his single-season home-run total of 73; two series of five asterisks—the first preceded by the letter 'M' and the second preceded by the letter 'F' (M***** F*****)—next to his single-season slugging-percentage record of .863; and a sequence of letters reading "The bastard used to be pretty goddamn good in his own right without the fucking steroids" next to his eight Gold Glove Awards.

"F*#! Barry Bonds, 714 F*#!ˆ&% home runs," Selig said, reading a line out of the most updated version of this year's record book. "F*#! Barry Bonds." ∅

from **ROYALS**

Ozzie Guillen Fined $10,000 For What He Just Thought

AUGUST 10, 2006

CHICAGO—MLB disciplinary officials announced that Ozzie Guillen would be fined $10,000 and ordered to undergo sensitivity psychoanalysis for the "irresponsible, offensive, and completely unacceptable" thoughts that passed through the White Sox manager's mind during Wednesday night's game.

"During the fourth inning of yesterday's White Sox-Yankees contest, Mr. Guillen's mind conjured a series of insensitive, wildly inappropriate—I would even go so far as to say depraved—thoughts and images," said Bob Watson, MLB vice president of on-field discipline. "Baseball is a social institution with a responsibility to espouse proper values, and there is absolutely no excuse for anyone to entertain thoughts which portray people in a negative or demeaning light, regardless of their race, color, creed, culture, sexual orientation, gender, weight, or personal beliefs."

"Major League Baseball would like to offer its most profound, heartfelt apologies to those portrayed inappropriately in Mr. Guillen's mind, including African-Americans, Cuban-Americans, Caucasian-Americans, Dominican-Americans, 'immigrants,' the sportswriting community, the gay community, the White Sox fan community, the communities of Schaumburg, IL and New York City, the umpiring crew, Yankee right-fielder Bobby Abreu and his female relatives, members of the Peace Corps, and women—particularly the female fan seated in Section 32, Row B, Seat 7," Watson added.

Watson's report alleges that Guillen carelessly composed his thoughts without considering the fact that millions of fans would know exactly what he was thinking in the event that television cameras inevitably cut to a shot of his sour expression. And according to commissioner Bud Selig, the idea of remorse never crossed Guillen's mind.

"Ozzie's thoughts were in poor taste, and the sheer volume and scope of them—all of which occurred over a 17-second span of time—seem to indicate that they were premeditated," Selig said. "I also must strongly emphasize that our organization neither shares nor condones Mr. Guillen's views on statutory rape, regardless of whether or not they are ever vocalized."

Guillen's thoughts upon learning of his punishment earned him an additional $5,000 fine and a three-game suspension.

"I'm not going to change the way I think," Guillen said during an apology late Wednesday. "Anyone who knows me will tell you I can't control my thoughts."

"I acknowledge that the things that entered my mind today might have offended certain groups of people, but you have to realize I didn't mean anything by it," Guillen continued. "After all, my mother is dead, too, and I would never want anyone digging up her corpse and paying drunken, uh, Arabs to do those things to her. And as for people of Middle Eastern origin, I was only imagining those terms being used to

see OZZIE

outfielders how to properly throw a baseball, outlining the three main steps to making strong, accurate throws—the "stride and set," the "90-degree hip swivel," and the "full, fluid follow-through."

"It was a little rough going for some of the guys, but we're taking it slow," Emanski said. "I think now it might be time to let up a little bit and switch gears into 'Encouragement Mode' for a few games to get their confidence back up."

"Coach Emanski taught me that, when I'm fielding the ground ball, I should stay down, stick my butt out, and count the hops," said shortstop Angel Berroa, explaining the method Emanski designed to help Little Leaguers and Royals infielders watch the ball all the way into their glove. "Once Coach Emanski also taught me how to count, the technique worked out great."

Although most players are reportedly "learning a lot" from Emanski, claiming his methods are "fun, educational, and make good baseball sense," some of the Royals veterans are resistant to throwing away everything they know about baseball in order to be taught these new fundamentals.

"I don't see how trying to throw balls into a metal garbage can laid out behind home plate is going to help my defense," said Royals right fielder Reggie Sanders, who has yet to record a single outfield assist since July 12, 2005. "Tom says it will be more rewarding once I start actually getting the throws to go into the cans, but I'm beginning to think that it's impossible."

"I'm not going to stand around hitting off a kid's tee—I'm a professional baseball player," said Royals first-baseman and No. 3 hitter Doug Mientkiewicz, who is batting .258 on the season with one home run and 14 RBI. "This is an insult."

The afternoon after speaking to reporters, Mientkiewicz lost his temper during B.P. and swung as hard as he could, missing the ball completely but creating enough of a breeze to gently knock the ball off its stand. Emanski had to restrain him from angrily swinging his bat at the tee in an attempt to break it, and told Mientkiewicz to take a lap around the field to calm down.

"In this game, attitude is key," Emanski said. "Some of the guys get angry or upset when we're doing Greenie Board Batting Practice, in which I give each player five swings, and I rate each swing on a zero-to-four scale. But I believe this is the only way they'll ever learn to swing through the ball."

"Of course, even if you master all the fundamental drills—the Bare Hand Drill, Soft Toss Creep, 'V' Drill, 'X' Drill, and Rocket Relay—there is still the issue of talent," Emanski added. "I'm no miracle worker. But, with a lot of hard work and a little luck, I truly believe that a few of these Royals will someday have the skills you need to play in the major leagues." ∅

PNC Park Threatens To Leave Pittsburgh Unless Better Team Is Built

JULY 20, 2006

PITTSBURGH—After five years of serving Pittsburgh as their state-of-the-art sporting facility, PNC Park, the home of the rundown, poorly maintained Pirates, said Tuesday it is threatening to leave Pittsburgh unless a new team can be built within the next three years.

"I love the city of Pittsburgh, but the Pirates are an old, dilapidated club built from other teams' spare parts, and its very foundation is rotting away," the stadium said to reporters assembled in its press box. "I had every intention to stay here for the duration of my career as a ballpark, but given that I haven't seen any realistic long-term plans for improving my resident team's ramshackle condition, I would be lying if I said I wasn't thinking about taking my services elsewhere."

The young stadium, regarded as one of the best of the recent crop of real-estate development projects throughout the league, added that "after this year's All Star Game, I have learned that a ballpark of my caliber deserves to host that kind of play every day."

"The Pirates have become such an eyesore that I've

even had to resort to bringing in different teams each week to play in me," the stadium said.

Although Pirates owner Kevin McClatchy said he is doing everything in his power to keep the park in Pittsburgh—attempting a rebuilding process every few years, making small free-agent additions, and erecting a new six-foot-tall outfielder in left field—the stadium dismissed the moves as nothing more than "a fresh coat of paint on a team that's in danger of collapsing under its own weight."

Mets owner Fred Wilpon has been vocal about his interest in bringing PNC Park to New York for the 2007 season so that it may take over for an aging Shea Stadium.

"The New York Mets have all the necessary components in place to fulfill PNC Park's needs," Wilpon said. "We have a gleaming new shortstop in Jose Reyes. We have a visually stunning, jaw-dropping player in Carlos Beltran. And the infrastructure of our minor-league system is designed to ensure that PNC Park will be inhabited by great ballplayers for years to come."

"Also, PNC Park has already established a good

rapport and budding friendship with this year's Home Run Derby runner-up David Wright—the bedrock of our team's stability," Wilpon added.

Though PNC Park would not elaborate on its relationship with Wright, it did say that Wright mentioned how much he enjoyed its dimensions, especially those in left and left-center.

Pittsburgh fans were irate upon hearing news of the stadium's possible relocation.

see PNC PARK page 74

---

from OZZIE

refer to just one specific 'filthy raghead,' not a whole region of them."

"Also, I would never, ever do that kind of thing to a person in real life, even if I had a worn-down radial-saw blade and 100 milligrams of hydrogen cyanide at my disposal," Guillen added.

A recent poll indicates that 97 percent of baseball fans were offended by Guillen's thoughts, with an astounding 12 percent of those polled actually having been personally attacked, insulted, or killed within Guillen's inner tirade.

"Ozzie needs to remember that people have families... My 9-year-old daughter was watching at home, and even though she isn't old enough to understand what a 'tire-iron abortion' is, I'm sure she understood that what he was thinking was not nice," said Chicago resident and White Sox fan Brian McVeigh. "And this isn't the last time he'll be on TV. What will I have to explain to my daughter next time she sees Ozzie thinking? Bestiality? Knife rape? Auschwitz?"

Guillen, however, claims that if he truly meant what he thought, he would have just

come out and said it.

"Am I going to have to explain everything I think from now on?" Guillen asked reporters. "Do I really need to actually want fuel truck after fuel truck to plow into an orphanage? That I don't really want to feed baby rats to [White Sox pitcher] Jon Garland so they chew their way through his intestinal system and expel themselves out his rectum in unison? That I actually love and respect my wife? Can't you people figure this out on your own? I'm not that bad a guy."

"Fucking faggot assholes," Guillen added. ✍

Jose Canseco Names 10,000 Baseball Players

JULY 20, 2006

WASHINGTON, DC—While speaking to reporters Tuesday, Jose Canseco released the names of 10,000 current and former baseball players whom he alleges have taken

part in the sport at some point during their lives. "Tim Teufel, Jim Abbot, Henry 'Hank' Aaron, Sid Fernandez, Mike Piazza, Graig Nettles, Ken Griffey Jr., Ken Griffey Sr., Chris Sabo, Dave Valle, Erubiel Durazo, Pat Listach, Carney Lansford, Terry Steinbach, Gary Gaetti," said Canseco at one point during his 14-hour statement. "Eddie Murray, Eddie Matthews, Eddie Guardado, while we're on Eddies, there's Eddie Cicotte... Um, Babe Ruth obviously, Jay Gibbons, Henry Blanco, Ralph Kiner, Darren Daulton, me, Cap Anson, Willie Bloomquist, Henry Rodriguez..." Canseco added that, if necessary, he can name thousands of other players, as long as he is granted access to official Hall Of Fame records or the 2006 edition of the Baseball Encyclopedia. ✍

George Steinbrenner Fires Tigers

OCTOBER 12, 2006

NEW YORK—Immediately following the Yankees' first-round playoff elimination last Saturday, George Steinbrenner released a statement announcing his intention to fire the Detroit Tigers, whose "inexcusable post-season performance stunned and saddened" the 76-year-old Yankees owner.

"The Tigers' level of play during the ALDS was deeply disappointing and absolutely not acceptable to both me and the great and loyal Yankee fans," the statement read in part. "This is a mid-budget team with a payroll under $85 million, and I expected them to play like one."

Even though Steinbrenner was reportedly pleased with the way the Tigers played down the stretch, and even commended the team's starting pitching after Game 1, his mood soured as they went on to win three straight games, at one point holding the Yankee line-up scoreless for 20 consecutive innings. This drew the ire of the historically volatile Yankee owner, who had "certain expectations" for the Tigers heading into the series.

"I made it very clear how I wanted the Tigers to perform this postseason, and they failed on every level to produce the desired results," Steinbrenner's statement continued. "They had several opportunities to turn this series around, but they just went out there and played like they didn't care whether the Yankees won or lost."

"The pitching was fantastic, the offense was timely, the defense was flawless... Frankly, it made me sick," Steinbrenner added.

Steinbrenner was especially critical of Tigers manager Jim Leyland, whom he claims was primarily responsible for the Yankees' ineffective postseason. A poll conducted after the ALDS echoes Steinbrenner's sentiments, as an overwhelming 100 percent of Yankee fans say they do not support Jim Leyland, and nearly zero percent say they would be disappointed if Leyland were fired from his current managerial post.

"We were all relying on Jim, but he just didn't get the job done for us," Yankees GM Brian Cashman said. "We thought long and hard about it, but in the end we decided that the Yankee organization is better off without the Detroit Tigers around."

Steinbrenner concluded his statement by criticizing the Tigers' "shameful post-game celebration," saying that "the way they were acting, you'd think the Yankees had won the pennant."

Among the other Tiger players fired by Steinbrenner are Carlos Guillen, the Tigers shortstop who batted a "disappointing .571" during the series; outfielder Curtis Granderson, who hit two home runs and had five RBI in what Steinbrenner called "an abysmal performance"; and pitchers Kenny Rogers and Jeremy Bonderman, who "cost the Yankees the series" with back-to-back outings in which they recorded a combined 12 strikeouts and gave up just two runs.

Yankee players were not shocked by Steinbrenner's announcement.

"He's the Boss—he owns the Yankees, and that gives him the right to fire whoever he wants," shortstop Derek Jeter said. "The Yankees have a long tradition of winning, and the Detroit Tigers failed to respect that."

For the Tigers, news of their firing couldn't

have come at a worse time.

"I know we didn't quite live up to the expectations of certain fans, media, and baseball organizations, but it felt like things were really starting to come together for us, like something big was right around the corner," Leyland said. "We thought we still had a lot to prove here. Who knows, if we weren't eliminated in this unexpected fashion, we might have even gone on to win a world championship."

With the Oakland A's currently waiting for an opponent for the championship series, Steinbrenner is expected to announce that the newly vacant Detroit Tigers roster will be filled by the roster of the 2006 New York Yankees, effective Game 1 of the ALCS.∅

Home Depot Criticized For Pledging $10 Billion To American Cancer Society For Every Padres Home Run

JUNE 15, 2006

SAN DIEGO—Home Depot has come under fire from cancer patients, baseball fans, and Padres players for the company's recent "heartless and insulting" offer to donate "$10 billion in cash" to the American Cancer Society each time a Padres player hits a home run for the rest of the 2006 season. "This outrageous offer of 'charity' is a slap in the face to our organization," said Jay Czarnecki, a spokesman for the ACS. "Having your donation depend upon a San Diego player hitting a baseball over 300 feet through the air is not only placing unfair and unrealistic expectations on the Padres, but is equivalent to telling everyone who has cancer to go off and die." Czarnecki suggested that, if Home Depot truly supports the research and eradication of a disease that kills millions of Americans every year, they should pledge a dollar for each time a Padre strikes out or commits an error. ∅

Disabled List Offers Mark Prior Two-Year, $8 Million Extension

JUNE 29, 2006

CHICAGO—Mark Prior, the right-handed pitcher who has spent the first few years of his career on the disabled list, is now considering accepting a recent two-year, $8 million offer from the DL that would keep him not playing through the 2008 season. "I couldn't even imagine the DL without Mark Prior—over the years, he has become the face, stiff right elbow, strained subscapularis muscle, and inflamed

Achilles tendon of our organization," said Kirk Gibson, manager and longtime former member of the DL, which is currently rebuilding by claiming young arms such as Kerry Wood, Ben Sheets, and Mike Maroth. "We firmly believe that Mark's best injuries are still ahead of him." While Prior's agent says the pitcher is exploring his options, experts predict that it is "inevitable" that Prior will return to the DL and, with the loyalty he's shown in the past, likely finish his career there. ∅

from **PNC PARK**

"If that ballpark left, this city would be devastated," said Pittsburgh resident Howard Valinsky. "I make a point of taking my kids down to the stadium during Pirates away games so they can stand outside of it and marvel at the rugged limestone and the blue steel—both of which have had an excellent year despite rainy conditions."

Valinsky added: "The fact that McClatchy hasn't given this stadium the sort of beautiful, well-designed team it deserves is a travesty. Let's face it, the Pirates have been falling apart for years. Frankly, I find myself wondering if it's even safe for fans to be near them."

The stadium echoed Valinsky's sentiments, saying, "The fans have been so great at being there for me. But if I can't hold a team that can compete, then what's supposed to hold me here?"

In a last-ditch effort to keep PNC Park, a citywide referendum will be added to this year's midterm election that, if passed, would draw from a property-tax fund to aid McClatchy in assembling a new, state-of-the-art team by 2010.

PNC Park, however, is not convinced.

"When I came here in 2001, they promised me a championship team," the stadium said. "I was warned by venerable and much-beloved Three Rivers Stadium—which imploded soon afterwards, as you know—that I should look elsewhere, that this team was set in its ways and not focused on rebuilding, that they were simply using me as a means to make money," the stadium said. "I was young and brash and I didn't listen. Now that I am more mature and have settled a bit, I realize I have to do what is best for me and my family."

In the event that the Pirate organization does not have the financial wherewithal to meet the park's demands, there are contingency plans in place to attract other stadiums to the city. While the league has said it frowns on the idea of putting an expansion stadium in the Pittsburgh area, some have floated the idea of bringing over old Tiger Stadium, which went into forced retirement in 2000. ∅

Mets Acquire Guillermo Mota From Indians In Daring Midnight Raid

AUGUST 24, 2006

CLEVELAND—Mets GM Omar Minaya announced yesterday that Guillermo Mota has checked out as healthy and relatively unscathed after being acquired last Sunday at midnight when intrepid Mets scouts used smoke grenades and the cover of a moonless night to rappel into Cleveland's Jacobs Field and acquire the 33-year-old right-hander. "We expect Guillermo to report as soon as the effects of our tranquilizer dart have worn off," said Minaya, who began planning the operation soon after Mota impressed him by beaning then-Mets catcher Mike Piazza with a pitch in the spring of 2003. "Once he comes to and realizes he's a Met, we expect his gratitude to show in a high standard of play, just like Orlando Hernandez did when we smuggled him out of the Diamondbacks camp in that laundry cart." The Indians organization has released a statement saying they will be seeking compensation in the form of a Mets player to be suddenly, swiftly, and silently named later. ∅

PHOTO FINISH
On-Deck Prince Fielder Puts Dozen Donuts On Bat

Randy Johnson Asks Chien-Ming Wang For Some Pitching Advice For A Pitcher Friend Of His

AUGUST 17, 2006

NEW YORK—Yankees pitcher Randy Johnson asked his teammate and fellow pitcher Chien-Ming Wang Tuesday for some pitching advice that was reportedly not for him, but for a "tall, lanky, inconsistent" southpaw friend of his. "He—my friend—is having trouble because he thinks his release point is erratic," said Johnson, who as the conversation went on had to vehemently deny  allegations that the person he was talking about was himself. "So, Chien, what do you think about my, er, his release point?" Wang eventually recommended that Johnson tell his "friend" that when he releases the ball too high, he loses his ability to fool left-handed hitters, and to also mention that he will have to accept that at his friend's age, his slider won't be nearly as effective as it once was. ∅

Alfonso Soriano Regrets Joining 40-40 Club After Meeting Other Members

SEPTEMBER 21, 2006

WASHINGTON,—Upon recording his 40th stolen base of the season, in addition to his 45 home runs, and gaining entry into baseball's exclusive 40-40 club, Nationals left-fielder Alfonso Soriano said that after meeting the other three members—Jose Canseco, Barry Bonds, and Alex Rodriguez—he now understands why no one has joined in the past eight years. "From all I had heard, this club was going to give me the opportunity to be among the greats of the game, but it turns out there's only three guys here, and one of them—this big, dumb guy who I still have no idea how he got in—kept asking me what kind of steroids I take and if I knew anyone else who took them," Soriano said. "I thought this was supposed to be an elite club, but it looks like they'll let just about any asshole in." Soriano later announced plans to reach the 50-50 plateau as soon as possible so he could "get out before A-Rod asks [him] for some help with his swing again." ∅

World Series Overshadowed By Thrilling New MLB Labor Agreement

OCTOBER 25, 2006

ST. LOUIS—Thousands of baseball fans gathered in Busch Stadium Tuesday evening to watch as commissioner Bud Selig announced that Major League Baseball and the MLB Players Association have tentatively agreed to an earth-shattering, amazing new multi-year collective-bargaining agreement, which has captured the imagination of fans young and old who have been waiting for this day since the last deal was signed in August 2002.

"Finally, I can say the words baseball fans across America have longed to hear..." Selig said to thunderous applause from the 50,000-plus in attendance. "In order to determine the amount of Major League Central Fund money to be reallocated from each contributing team, we will multiply their Net Local Revenue for the preceding three revenue-sharing years by a fraction, the numerator of which is the net transfer value of the Central Fund Component in that revenue year and the denominator of which is the sum of the means of each contributor's Net Local Revenue for the preceding three revenue-sharing years."

"And there's more good news where that came from," Selig added. "At 100 percent implementation, the net transfer value of the Central Fund Component shall be 41.066 percent of the net transfer value of the Base Plan in that revenue-sharing year!"

Game 3 of the World Series between the Cardinals and Tigers was postponed two and a half hours to allow the grounds crew time to clean Busch Stadium, dismantle the soundstage specially built for the labor-deal-unveiling event, and restore the field to playing condition following the boisterous post-announcement festivities and celebration.

News of the deal, which will be in place through 2011, has electrified the baseball world and reinvigorated a sport that has been struggling to win back fans ever since the players and the owners failed to agree upon a much-anticipated, much-hyped labor contract in 1994.

Fans in every major American city flooded the streets Saturday evening during the third inning of Game 1 upon hearing that the negotiations were successful, where they proudly waved signs containing portions of the "Outright Assignment To A Minor-League Club" section and chanted provisional clauses from Article XIII Part A regarding the newly established powers of the Safety and Health Advisory Committee.

"Woo! Application by a club to the commissioner to place a player on the disabled list shall be accompanied by a standard form of diagnosis!" said Tigers fan Matt Crowley, who along with hundreds of fans left Comerica Park in the fifth inning of Game 2 to get home in time to see the *Outside The Lines* episode that analyzes the slight alterations to the current daily meal and tip allowance a player receives on road games and travel days.

"Can you believe that players selected in the June amateur draft who are not college seniors now must sign with their club by August 15?! Awesome!" Crowley added.

Around the nation, fathers muted World Series broadcasts to read the changes in the salary-arbitration process to their sons, sharing precious baseball-legalese memories that will last a lifetime. College students in St. Louis and Detroit flocked to local sports-negotiation bars to meet fans of all different subsections of the document, standing shoulder-to-shoulder in crowded rooms to watch as large-screen monitors displayed portions of Article XXI concerning spring-training termination pay.

Even in freezing cold conditions, Yankees and Mets fans alike gathered in New York's Times Square with their backs to a video screen that was showing highlights of Game 4 to read scrolling text of the labor agreement on the digital marquee that runs along the side of Conde Nast Building.

"Never in my life did I think I'd be around to see a labor deal

this un-fucking-believable, under which teams no longer receive draft-pick compensation when a Type C player—one who ranks in the upper 60 percent but not in the upper 50 percent of his respective position group—is offered arbitration but chooses free agency," said Cardinals fan Mark Blosserman, who sold his Game 5 tickets so he could more quietly and closely examine the 235-page document.

"Baseball is back!" he added.

The media, meanwhile, has ceased all speculation regarding the foreign substance on Kenny Rogers' hand in Game 2, instead turning their attention to the landmark labor agreement, which they are already calling the "greatest success story of the 2006 season."

"People are going to be talking about this heartwarming Cinderella story in which two rival sides come together to prevent a labor strike all offseason long, and perhaps for years to come," sportswriter Peter Gammons said. "They'll never forget the moment they read about deferred compensation, the cost-of-living adjustments for the minimum major-league salary, or the competitive-balance tax... It's understanding the many little intricacies of the game that makes the sport of baseball so enjoyable." Ø

A-Rod Shipped Back To Manufacturer To Fix Mechanical Flaw In Swing

JUNE 22, 2006

NEW YORK—After noticing a slight, recurring mechanical flaw in its swing that has caused its season average to dip to .275, Yankee officials sent A-ROD-13, an expensive yet still completely unreliable batting unit, back to its original manufacturer for recalibration and a general tune-up. "The problem is stemming from the inconsistent firing of cylinders in A-ROD's hydraulic system, causing his pressure-relief valve to start responding to every late-game algorithm by popping out to first base," said Yankees assistant engineer Lee Mazzilli, who is responsible for oiling A-ROD's hinges and tightening his shoulder screws between innings. "Also, his fielding-equilibrium mechanism totally blew out a month ago, and we still haven't replaced it. But A-ROD should be back and as good as new in four to six weeks." Yankee officials, however, have thus far experienced no problems with A-ROD's factory-installed voicebox, which has only repeated the same five stock phrases it was specifically programmed to say. Ø

Experts Predict No NL Team Will Go Deep Into Playoffs

OCTOBER 5, 2006

BRISTOL, CT—Even though the National League somehow managed to send four teams into the 2006 MLB postseason, baseball experts said Monday that it is "unlikely" that any of them will advance past the second round of the playoffs. "The Mets, Dodgers, Padres, and Cardinals have serious pitching issues, almost zero offense, and have played terribly down the stretch," ESPN analyst Buster Olney said. "However, they each luckily drew a first-round opponent that is similarly ill-fitted for postseason play, so we may see one or two emerge from the first round. But as for the World Series— not a chance." Experts went on to predict that it will "probably be another Yankees–Red Sox World Series this year." ∅

Frank Thomas Credits Recent Power Surge To Steroids

SEPTEMBER 28, 2006

OAKLAND, CA—After two seasons marked by nagging injuries and sub-par home-run totals, Frank Thomas credited his career rejuvenation and rediscovered power stroke "strictly to my weekly cycle of injecting myself with anabolic steroids. People ask me all the time what's my secret, how have I stayed in such good shape and been so consistent this season, and I tell them the same thing every time: It's the steroids," said Thomas, who has 19 homers and a league-high 62 RBI since the All-Star break. "I give the steroids all the cred- it. It's not even just the muscle and the power, but the confidence I have when I step up to the plate knowing I have a total competitive advantage. I just wish I knew about this miracle drug earlier in my career." MLB officials later announced that, should Thomas test positive for steroid use in a random drug test before season's end, his punishment would be significantly reduced for being open and honest about it beforehand. ∅

Experts: 'Derek Jeter Probably Didn't Need To Jump To Throw That Guy Out'

AUGUST 3, 2006

BRISTOL, CT—Baseball experts agreed Sunday that Derek Jeter, who fielded a routine ground ball during a regular-season game in which the Yankees were leading by five runs and then threw it to first base using one of his signature leaps, did not have to do that to record the out. "If it had been a hard-hit grounder in the hole or even a slow dribbler he had to charge, that would've been one thing," analyst John Kruk said during a broadcast of *Baseball Tonight*. "But when it's hit right to him by [Devil Rays first-baseman] Greg Norton, a guy who has no stolen bases and is still suffering the effects of a hamstring injury sustained earlier this year... Well, that's a different story." Jeter threw out Norton by 15 feet and pumped his fist in celebration at the end of the play. ∅

MLB Credits Hank Aaron With 50 Lost Home Runs

APRIL 27, 2007

MILWAUKEE—In what Major League Baseball officials are calling a "long overdue correction of a gross oversight," Commissioner Bud Selig announced Tuesday the discovery that Hall of Famer Hank Aaron had in fact accumulated 50 previously unaccounted-for home runs during his illustrious 22-year baseball career, bringing his once record total of 755 to an even higher 805 and putting the all-time home-run record perhaps forever out of reach.

"Hank Aaron is a hero, an excellent man, and a great ambassador for the game of baseball," Selig said during a press conference to announce the findings. "We're proud to have finally set things right, hopefully once and for all. And I have to tell you, some of the home runs that we discovered were just monster shots. One was hit off of [Pittsburgh Pirates pitcher] Harvey Haddix that went 576 feet, and Hank wasn't even that big of a guy. Just naturally strong and gifted, I guess." Haddix was unavailable for comment, as he passed away in 1994.

According to Selig, a committee of sports journalists and baseball historians was set up during the off-season to investigate, with Selig's oversight, whether there was any substance to a rumor that began circulating last summer concerning Aaron having hit more homeruns than those credited to him in the record books. Though Selig said he couldn't recall the date the committee was established, he believes it was in or around the time he approved the San Francisco Giants' highly publicized signing of Barry Zito.

The committee's 30-page report points out several key factors that combined to increase Aaron's home run total. For example, in 1958, home runs hit during both the first week of spring training and those hit in pre-game batting practice during away games in the third week of August were added to a player's career numbers. In addition, home runs hit during the 1971 All-Star Game should have been tallied.

Aaron, coincidentally, did hit a home run in that game.

"We are here today to the right the wrongs," Selig said. "This is America's national pastime, and its players, fans, and all citizens deserve to have a record book in which they can take great pride. So if we didn't count Hank Aaron's five-homer outing during 1964's famous 'Empty Stadium' game, I wouldn't be able to live with myself."

Furthermore, the report continued, a third of the home runs

see HANK AARON

from **HANK AARON**

hit by players who participated in the television series *Home Run Derby*, a show on which Aaron appeared several times, should have been counted. In addition, during the second half of the 1962 season, balls that bounced over the outfield fence should have been counted as home runs, and foul balls that were hit behind the batter but cleared the netting intended to protect fans seated behind home plate were also home runs. That being the case, league scorekeepers now say Aaron had his best year in 1962, hitting 65 home runs—20 more than originally thought.

Though there has been some negative reaction towards the announcement of Aaron's new record, mostly from fans in northern California, the news has been received very well nationwide.

"This is the best thing that has happened to baseball in years," said New York resident Tom Plaitano, 63. "I remember watching Hank Aaron as a kid, and even though I don't recall a time when all home runs hit off Sandy Koufax counted for two, I don't really care. This decision just makes sense to me."

"The number 805 will go down as the most prestigious number in sports," said Selig,

adding that there is a strong possibility still more of Aaron's home runs could come to the surface during this season, and maybe even the next several seasons to come. "It's not out of the question that Hank could have, say, 900 home runs by the time our investigation is all said and done."

"Either way, the all-time home-run record couldn't be held by a more dignified and honorable man," Selig added.

The committee's report has caused quite a shakeup to the list of baseball's all-time home-run leaders. Aaron, while keeping his record, is not even the biggest benefactor of the findings; as of now Aaron is first with 805, Willie Mays has jumped to second with 800, Frank Robinson is third with 798, Harmon Killebrew is fourth with 797, and Reggie Jackson, Mickey Mantle, Ernie Banks, Ted Williams, and Willie McCovey are tied for fifth at 796.

According to Selig, early results of another investigation may net Babe Ruth as many as 74 additional home runs, Mike Schmidt an estimated 124, and Ken Griffey Jr. a possible 200, while players such as Mark McGwire, Sammy Sosa, Rafael Palmeiro, and Barry Bonds will probably be knocked even further down the list. ⌀

Manny Being Manny During Massachusetts State Driver's License Photo

Hideki Matsui Unable To Grasp Translator's Explanation Of Where Cory Lidle Is

OCTOBER 19, 2006

NEW YORK—Hideki Matsui's interpreter Roger Kahlon has been unable to explain to the Yankees' Japanese-speaking left fielder that former teammate Cory Lidle died instantaneously last Wednesday after flying his four-seat, SR20 aircraft into a high-rise apartment building in Manhattan's Upper East Side. "At this point, I'm pretty sure [Matsui] thinks Lidle is either in his four-bedroom apartment or on a 20-minute plane ride to upstate New York," Kahlon said, adding that in order to make Lidle's whereabouts clear to Matsui, he has even resorted to making one of his hands into a plane, the other into a building, crashing them together, and making explosion noises. "This kind of thing just doesn't translate very well." According to Kahlon, the last time he asked Matsui where Cory Lidle was, a confused Matsui answered, "The bullpen." ⌀

Alfonso Soriano: 'I Am Excited To Play For $136 Million'

NOVEMBER 23, 2006

CHICAGO—Alfonso Soriano called a press conference Monday to announce that, starting in the 2007 season, he would officially be making $136 million. "I turned down several offers of amounts of money that, in my opinion, were far lower than $136 million," said Soriano, who was smiling from ear to ear as he delivered the news of his signing. "I expect to be making $136 million for a long time." Although Soriano has gained a reputation as a selfish, me-first player, he went on to assure his critics that this new contract is "not about the money." ⌀

Chipper Jones Credits Gold Glove To Open-Minded Kay Jewelers In Local Mall

Lou Piniella's First Big Move As Cubs Manager Is To Resign

OCTOBER 19, 2006

CHICAGO—During his formal introduction as Cubs manager Tuesday, Lou Piniella announced that his first and only managerial decision will be to step down immediately and permanently from his new position—a bold, unexpected move that he successfully carried out just moments later. "My time in Chicago has been great, and it feels like it was just yesterday that I started this job, but I truly believe that this move will give me a better opportunity to win," Piniella said at the press conference while ceremoniously removing a Cubs hat and jersey. "I'm very excited about leaving this team." After the announcement, Cubs GM Jim Hendry praised Piniella's sound judgment and pure baseball instinct, saying that "his ability to make quick, smart decisions like this one is exactly why we hired him." ⌀

松坂 大輔!!

Excited Red Sox Fans Eagerly Await Debut Of Matsuzaka's 'Ultimate Galactic Dragon Gyroball Pitch Power Explosion'

MARCH 1, 2007

BOSTON—Now that Manny Ramirez has reported to camp and the spring-training opener against Minnesota is in the books, Red Sox fans are turning their attention to the awesome power rumored to dwell within much-touted off-season pitching acquisition Daisuke Matsuzaka—a man who many say possesses pitching powers and techniques beyond the comprehension of mortal fans.

"Daisuke is the pitching master!" said Boston Globe baseball columnist Bob Ryan, hopping from one foot to the other as he described videotape footage of Matsuzaka's otherworldly pitching power and control banishing a flock of evil, conniving, left-handed-batting carp-spirits to the netherworld during a 2003 Seibu Lions game. "His Ultimate Galactic Dragon Gyroball Pitch Power Explosion breaks three feet inside before cutting sharply toward the dugout, where falsehood and cowardice are forced to shrink before it!"

Since before Boston signed Matsuzaka to a six-year, $52 million contract last November, the city's baseball fans were inundated with incredible tales of the Japanese ace's pitching prowess, many of which seemed too good to be believed. Nevertheless, most Red Sox fans find it hard to contain their excitement at the thought of finally seeing Matsuzaka's skills on display.

"Battle on, Daisuke! Wither their spirits with your mystical Four Winds Split-Finger Shottu-jitsu! Repel their cruel affronts with your Triple-Star Cut-Fastball Technique of the Joyous Uplifting Dynamo, clocked at a respectable 96 miles per hour! And baffle their comprehension and deceive in turn their deceitful hearts with your Two-Seam Shadow-Strike Clouded-Eye Shinobi Sinker!" said 44-year-old accountant and spring-training attendee Roger Fettleman, quoting the back of Matsuzaka's Red Sox rookie card almost word for word as he watched the right-hander warm up in the bullpen before his first Grapefruit League start. "Truly, it is within your grasp to go 16-4 with an ERA under 4.00!"

Fettleman is hardly alone among Boston fans in having both his spirits and his expectations raised to unusual levels by the seven-year veteran of Japan's top leagues. Besides the talk surrounding his alleged gyroball, rumors have circulated about his uncanny ability to read a batter, his cleverness in using his fastballs as his out pitches instead of over-relying on breaking balls, and his almost inexhaustible wellspring of ki, or spirit-energy.

"If what we've heard is correct, then Matsuzaka indeed possesses a Power Level of well over 9,000," said ESPN's Peter Gammons, struggling to contain his excitement on Tuesday's edition of Baseball Tonight. "Over 9,000!

see MATSUZAKA

see MATSUZAKA

SPORTS GRAPHIC

Potential New Cubs Owners

APRIL 5, 2007

Now that the Tribune Co. is selling the fabled Cubs franchise, rumors of potential new owners are swirling throughout baseball. Onion Sports looks at the most likely candidates:

➤ **Andre Dawson:** This former Cubs All-Star, who is now a homeless alcoholic with only $2 in his pocket, said he would own the Cubs

➤ **Michael Jordan:** Cubs could be a pretty interesting item for this local hero to throw in the pot during a no-limit poker game

➤ **Chicago Sun-Times:** More than capable of upholding the long and proud tradition of a newspaper owning the Cubs

➤ **Thaksin Shinawatra, former Prime Minister of Thailand:** Since being overthrown last year, Shinawatra has plenty of time for entertainment and is looking for a group of athletic and disciplined men for reasons he has chosen not to comment on

➤ **Ernie Banks:** Famed "Mr. Cub" was part of many Cubs teams that nearly made it to .500, and he may just be able to get them back to that level again as owner

➤ **Virginia McCaskey, owner of Chicago Bears:** Has already demonstrated the complete absence of financial acumen, boorish lack of personal charm, and ignorance of sports operations that Chicago sports fans have always revered

➤ **Bill Gates:** Has traditionally excelled in areas where he is allowed to spend infinite amounts of money

➤ **No One:** Possibly the ideal choice for Cubs fans and players alike

Destruction Of National Pastime Given Two-Minute Standing Ovation

AUGUST 09, 2007

SAN FRANCISCO—A sellout crowd rose to its feet and exploded into ecstatic cheers Tuesday night as Barry Bonds completed the downfall of America's most revered sport by hitting a thundering 435-foot shot into the right center field bleachers for career home run No. 756 and tainting baseball's most beloved record.

Celebrations broke out throughout AT&T Park and thousands of flashbulbs went off as Bonds took his ceremonial trip around the bases, his arms raised in a jubilant gesture of triumph as he completed his desecration of baseball. Fireworks filled the night sky to mark the utter destruction of the national pastime, a scramble for the infamous baseball broke out in the stands, and the game was interrupted for 10 minutes in the bottom of the fifth to mark the shameful occasion.

Mike Bacsik, the pitcher who made the difficult and admirable decision to pitch to Bonds as if he were a normal player, and who will forever be known as the man whose fastball was sent out of the park along with the last remnant of baseball's self-respect, could only watch. Bonds would later present Bacsik with an autographed bat.

Moments after Bonds crossed home plate into the loving arms of his family and the eventual judgment of history, he addressed the fans, thanking them for their support on his long, hard road of perverting baseball.

"Thank you very much. I got to thank all of you, all the fans here in San Francisco. It's been fantastic," he said to his deluded and complicit home crowd as his godfather Willie Mays, a fading symbol of what baseball once was, stood at his side.

As soon as Bonds completed his self-congratulation, a self-conscious gasp could be heard as a videotaped message from Hank Aaron was played over the video screen, sending surprise and a fleeting moment of uncomfortable self-awareness through both the crowd and Bonds himself.

"Throughout the past century, the home run has held a special place in baseball and I have been privileged to hold this record for 33 of those years," said Aaron, whose legacy of persevering with profound personal dignity through racism and persecution to become the all-time home run leader will hopefully not be tarnished by public acknowledgment of Bonds.

"I move over now and offer my best wishes to Barry and his family on this historic achievement," Aaron concluded, displaying infinitely more grace than Bonds, baseball fans, and perhaps even baseball itself had any right to ask of him.

Bonds then presented his helmet, gloves, and bat to a steward of the Baseball Hall of Fame for shipment to Cooperstown, where they will be enshrined forever, allowing fathers and sons to come and stare at them glumly as they bear mute witness to baseball's diminished glory.

The Nationals won the game, 8-6. ∅

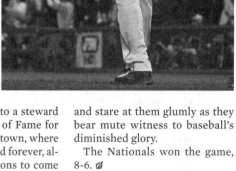

---

from **MATSUZAKA**

Which, of course, is only to be expected of the ballplayer whom sources say descended into the Underworld to spit in the flaming eye of the Lord of Hell and steal the secret power of the Onikaze, or 'demon-storm' pitch, which tails away nicely from both lefties and righties."

Despite the constant adulation and high expectations, the 27-year-old right-hander has been modest when dealing with the press.

"Boston fans are the greatest fans in the world," Matsuzaka told reporters through an interpreter upon being asked if he had left Japan out of fears that his Ultimate Galactic Dragon Gyroball Pitch Power Explosion might split Mount Fuji, strike the rising sun from the sky, and awaken the wrathful atomic lizard Gojira. "I'm very happy and excited to be a member of the Red Sox." ∅

PHOTO FINISH

Detroit Tigers Carry Jim Leyland To Bathroom

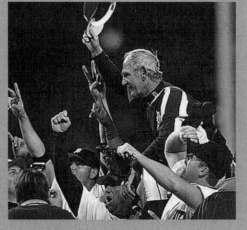

Slight Breeze Shatters Ken Griffey Jr.'s Femur

MARCH 15, 2007

CINCINNATI—Although Ken Griffey Jr. had nearly recovered from a broken hand sustained while playing with his children in December, his rehabilitation came to a sudden halt yesterday when a gentle 2 mph breeze wafted across his leg, shattering his femur in three places. "I knew it was broken right when that breeze hit me," said Griffey, who was walking from his sports therapist's office to his car in order to drive to his daughter's piano recital at the time of the injury. "These things just happen. If I would have known a breeze like that was coming, I never would have left the house." Reds manager Jerry Narron has stated that, upon Griffey's return to the Reds, he will be fitted with a personalized protective bubble to be worn for the remainder of the season. ∅

David Eckstein Hints To Parents That He Wants Birthday Cake Designed Like Hamburger

APRIL 26, 2007

ST. LOUIS—Ever since walking into a Baskin Robbins with his parents after one of his professional baseball games, Cardinals shortstop David Eckstein has constantly hinted that he would like an ice-cream cake resembling a hamburger, a Baskin Robbins specialty, for his next birthday. "Wow! Isn't that so crazy, how that cake looks just like a hamburger even though it's a cake, Mom? It's so cool!" Eckstein said of the cake, which features a "bun" crafted from chocolate frosting and "sesame seeds" of white-chocolate sprinkles. "Boy, I bet that cool hamburger cake would make someone's birthday really extra-special." Although Eckstein's birthday is in January, his parents secretly purchased the cake during their last Baskin Robbins outing and intend to surprise him with it the next time he hits a double. Ø

Terry Francona Sends Eric Gagne Down To Made-Up Triple-A Team

OCTOBER 18, 2007

CLEVELAND—Following Eric Gagne's 11th inning meltdown in Game 2 of the ALCS, Red Sox manager Terry Francona informed the reliever that he was being temporarily demoted to the "Appleton Red Wolves," a completely fabricated Triple-A team that, unbeknownst to Gagne, Francona made up right on the spot. "I don't agree with the move, but if Terry thinks I need some time to work on my mechanics, then it's my job to report to Appleton, a town which Terry told me is somewhere in central Minnesota and where he assured me all the buses go if you just get on one and ride for a couple days," said Gagne, who in reality cannot be removed from the ALCS roster unless because of injury. "According to Terry, it's a great little town, and

their fans—the Wolf Pack, as they're apparently known—are really eager to see me pitch. And on the plus side, Terry said that if the Sox make it past the ALCS, they'll wait for me to come back before starting the World Series. So hey, win-win." At press time, Gagne is standing alone on the mound of an overgrown Little League field in St. Paul. Ø

Pirates Player Keeps Asking Fans If They Saw His Double

APRIL 5, 2007

HOUSTON—After an opening day double off Astros closer Brad Lidge, elated Pirates third-basemen Jose Bautista was observed repeatedly asking fans in attendance if they had seen his "awesome hit." "You guys got a chance to see it, right? You weren't in here the whole time, were you?" Bautista asked a line of men waiting to use a Minute Maid Park restroom immediately after the game concluded. "I just crushed that thing. Then I ran as fast as I could all the way to second." Concerned that fans outside the stadium couldn't fully appreciate the scene, Bautista then headed over to the nearby Texas Barbecue Grill to make sure the game had been on the TV, only to find the bar had emptied as soon as patrons heard the sound of approaching cleats. Ø

PHOTO FINISH

Rookie Tragically Misinterprets Suicide-Squeeze Sign

Player Feels Need To Clarify Comments After They're Received Poorly

JUNE 28, 2007

MIAMI, FL—Upon learning that his post-game comments were reported in a manner that portrayed him as uncaring, selfish, and possibly insensitive, Marlins second-baseman Dan Uggla issued an immediate apology, saying "it was never my intention for these remarks to be met with an unfavorable response. It is with great sorrow that I amend my previous statement with a heretofore nonexistent context in such a way that shifts the blame from myself to the reporter, whom I will now forgive in a magnanimous show of sportsmanship," Uggla said in a somber press conference Tuesday, during which he frowned and shook his head multiple times to convey remorse and understanding. "Also, I did not realize those particular words are offensive to that particular race of people, and I certainly didn't know that they meant that." Uggla is expected to further clarify certain comments made during his apology in a press conference tomorrow. Ø

Old Red Sox Uniform Only Outfit Left In Mo Vaughn's Closet

MARCH 15, 2007

NORWALK, CT—Former MLB slugger Mo Vaughn awoke Tuesday morning to the grim realization that the only clean outfit remaining in his closet was his old #42 Boston Red Sox jersey and matching baseball pants. "Well, I'm just going to look stupid if I don't wear stirrups with this," Vaughn said to himself after changing into the uniform, buckling his belt, and looking through his old shoeboxes to find his good metal cleats. "And I may as well wear my Red Sox hat while I'm at it. And some eye black, since it's pretty bright out. Good thing the laundromat is only 15 blocks away." Vaughn, who carried his load of dirty laundry down the street in his old Wilson bat bag, said he couldn't wait to have his full wardrobe cleaned so he could switch into one of his less-embarrassing, roomier Angels or Mets uniforms. Ø

Fucking Yankees, Reports Nation

AUGUST 16, 2007

BOSTON—Moments after the New York Yankees continued a month-long stretch that has seen them climb from the bottom of the AL East to pull within a once unfathomable four games of the first-place Red Sox by defeating the Baltimore Orioles Monday night, stunned and enraged baseball fans across America took a moment to shake their heads in disbelief and curse dejectedly at the relentless inevitability of Yankee glory.

"Fucking Yankees," said Marshfield, MA resident and longtime Red Sox fan Lawrence Broberg, echoing the sentiments of thousands of men and woman across the nation. "Every year. Every goddamn year."

The Yankees, coming off a decisive three-game sweep of the Central-leading Indians, have won nine out of their last 10 games, catapulting them to the top of the wild-card standings, restoring the team's infuriating confidence, and instilling a sinking sense of impending misery among all non-Yankee fans.

"It's like they can't lose," said Connecticut resident Gerry DiCenzo, who could only watch helplessly as the Yankees overcame a late Orioles rally to win their fourth straight. "They liter-

ally cannot lose. Suddenly no one can beat the Yankees. The Red Sox suck. The Orioles suck. Everyone sucks. Everyone suddenly sucks when they play the Yankees."

"Unbelievable," DiCenzo added. "Un-fucking-believable."

Sparked by the recent returns of phenom starter Phil Hughes and slugger Jason Giambi, the Yankees have their full roster healthy and together for the first time since April, which fans around the world have solemnly realized is perfect timing for the stretch run.

"It seems like every time the [sports] ticker comes up, they're winning 10-1," said Chicago resident Jeremy Killian. "You knew this was going to happen. You knew. Right when they got Clemens back, you fucking knew."

"Every time," Killian continued. "Every time with this fucking team. It's the same damn thing every time. You just, they never go away. You can't give them an inch. You cannot give them one inch."

"And Jeter..." Killian added, watching as the Yankee shortstop drove home the winning run in the bottom of the ninth with a softly tapped ball that barely dribbled past the pitcher's mound. "Fucking Jeter."

As the Yankees remain hot in

August, the team continues to rely on GM Brian Cashman's strategy of stockpiling cheap, young pitching and assembling a group of talented role players to surround the team's superstars. In recent weeks, rookie reliever Joba Chamberlain and newly acquired utility man Wilson Betemit have stepped up and delivered in clutch situations, much to the frustration of nearly everyone.

"You got fucking Abreu all of a sudden going 3 for 4 every night," Boston citizen Mark Baker said of the Yankees' recent surge. "Fucking Giambi's back. A-Rod's hitting 500 fucking home runs a night. Posada, that bastard. You got Matsui, who's a Red Sox killer. Then there's Shelley Duncan, who no one even heard of till three weeks ago. Guy never hit a home run in his life, he puts on pinstripes and suddenly he's Babe fucking Ruth."

"And this Melky Cabrera guy," Baker added. "Where did this fucking guy come from? Him and Cano. They got guys coming out of the fucking woodwork."

"Fucking Yankee fans must be loving this," said New York resident and avid Mets fan Dave Julian, muting the Yankee broadcast to temporarily silence the

see **FUCKING YANKEES**

Manny Ramirez Asks Red Sox If He Can Work From Home

MAY 3, 2007

BOSTON—Claiming that a relaxed atmosphere and a chance to create his own schedule would greatly benefit his productivity, Red Sox left-fielder Manny Ramirez has asked team officials if he can play the remainder of the season from the comfort of his own home. "My client just can't seem to focus in his current place of work," said Ramirez's agent Greg Genske, noting that Fenway Park's loud, boisterous atmosphere and high-stress, pressure-packed environment are "not ideal working conditions for anyone." "Manny seeks a work space where he doesn't have to constantly travel, can wear whatever he wants, and can work at his own pace. I assure you that he will be able to put up the same statistics he normally does while physically on a baseball diamond. Just give him until November or December." The Red Sox have tentatively agreed to allow Ramirez to telecommute, claiming that although their offense may suffer without him at the ballpark, their defense in a vacant left field may substantially improve. ∅

David Ortiz Incorporates Champagne Goggles Into Everyday Uniform

from **FUCKING YANKEES**

grating sound of Yankee cheers. "The smug fucks. And those Yankee announcers. Why don't they root a little harder? They make me sick. Michael Kay. Bet Steinbrenner's laughing it up. Bought himself another fucking championship."

Although the Yankees' schedule becomes tougher in the coming month, with multiple series against the Tigers, Angels, Red Sox, and Mariners, most baseball fans have resigned themselves to the fact that the season is "pretty much fucking over."

"What the fuck can you do?" said Detroit citizen Terry Grey. "Every call. The Yankees get every break, the bounces all go their way. It's luck. They're lucky. They're so fucking lucky."

"Stupid," Grey added. "It's all stupid. Why play the whole fucking season if this is what's always going to happen?"

Despite the mixture of anger, resentment, and disbelief that has surfaced across the country during the Yankees' recent hot streak, most fans have been able to take some solace in the fact that the Yankees will be eliminated by the Angels in the first round of the playoffs. ∅

Joe DiMaggio's Diary Just A List Of Things, People He Hated

JULY 19, 2007

NEW YORK—Upon closer examination, a 2,400-page, 29-volume diary kept by New York Yankees centerfielder Joe DiMaggio from 1982 to 1993 is merely a listing of all the things and people the Hall of Famer hated, archivists charged with determining the diary's authenticity reported Monday. "Jukeboxes, dollar stores, Paul Simon, Washington, D.C., speaking, Garth Brooks, myself, and automobiles. Also sore throats, Yogi Berra, films, Lee Iacocca, coffeemakers, anyone who has ever referred to me as 'Joltin',' sandals, baseball," read the entry dated July 14, 1992. "I hate all of that. Plus my neighbor Janet, who is another one of those hateful attractive blondes." In an entry from Nov. 15, 1987, DiMaggio wrote that last names that include two capital letters were "frustrating" and "something I hate." ∅

Magglio Ordonez, Placido Polanco Stay Up All Night Talking About Favorite Hitting Situations

SEPTEMBER 27, 2007

DETROIT—Following their game against the Twins Tuesday, Tigers outfielder Magglio Ordonez and second baseman Placido Polanco stayed in their hotel room all night, giddily discussing their favorite in-game hitting situations. "Definitely 2-0 count, one out, runners on the corners, and a lefty on the mound—definitely," Ordonez said, giggling excitedly as he explained how he would sit on a fastball on the outer half of the plate and drive it to the right-center gap. Polanco reportedly shrugged, saying, "That's pretty good, but picture this: right-handed pitcher, day game, on turf, full count, and...runners on first and second. This way, the runners are off with the pitch, and the first baseman would be shading the line to protect

against the extra-base hit, so bam, I just punch it right through the hole. Oh, oh, and what about the old one-out, 1-1 count hit-and-run? Can't go wrong with a classic." The two then mentioned how great it would be to hit with a runner on third and less than two outs in October, at which point they both sighed, fell silent, and went to bed. ∅

Left Bed In Clemens, Pettitte's Shared Hotel Room Clearly Unused

JULY 26, 2007

KANSAS CITY—One of the beds in the hotel room occupied by Yankee pitchers and offseason workout partners Andy Pettitte and Roger Clemens was left completely untouched during the first night of the team's four-game road series, sources at the Embassy Suites in Kansas City report-

ed early Tuesday morning. "It is quite peculiar, especially since both men were there when I delivered the tray of chocolate-covered strawberries they ordered from room service at 11:30 p.m.," said room maid Maria Santos, who claimed the bed remained exactly as she left it the morning before, save for the removal of one pillow, which was found

at the foot of the other bed with a slight tear in the fabric. "Normally I would have been happy to only have to make one bed, had the other one not been a complete mess. And somehow everything on the top of the kitchen table ended up on the floor, too." Andy Pettitte was not available for comment, and is day-to-day with a sore groin. ∅

Seriously Ill Yankees Fan Really Hoping It's Lou Gehrig's Disease

AUGUST 30, 2007

NEW YORK—Lifelong New York Yankees fan and construction worker Greg Snell, 44, told reporters yesterday that it would be "a great honor" if the troubling and debilitating illness currently plaguing him was diagnosed as Lou Gehrig's Disease, the fatal neuromuscular disorder named after the Yankees legend. "Let's face it, there's no way I can match what Gehrig did on the baseball field, but there's still a chance I got [ALS]," said Snell, adding that if his muscles were to gradually become smaller and weaker to the point of complete paralysis for the same reason Gehrig's did, he would consider himself the "luckiest man on the face of the earth. I've noticed my bricklaying skills diminishing, and, because I can no longer perform at the level I am used to, I'll soon be forced to take myself out of the construction site. I can only hope it's just like Gehrig." Snell added that if he is not diagnosed with Lou Gehrig's disease, he will attempt drink himself to death just like Mickey Mantle. ∅

INSIDE

▸ **Vladimir Guererro Swings At Pitch From Tomorrow's Game**

▸ **Dusty Baker Receives Suicide Threat**

▸ **A-Rod To Jorge Posada: 'You Are My Friend'**

▸ **David Ortiz Admits He Once Ate Steroids**

▸ **'Things Could Be Worse' Nationals PA Announcer Tells Fans Before Every Pitch**

▸ **A-Rod: 'I Never Expected I'd Get 30 HR's And 100 RBI's In Only 535 Plate Appearances With A .402 OBP'**

Rockies Complain About 'Thick' Fenway Park Air

OCTOBER 25, 2007

BOSTON—Although Colorado players, managers, and coaches said they would not issue a formal complaint about the playing conditions in Boston, the Rockies have gone on record as saying the "thick, soupy sea-level air" in the city made it unusually difficult for them to play baseball. "Seriously, I can barely push my bat through this stuff," said Rockies slugger Matt Holliday, who collapsed and had to be administered less oxygen after Wednesday's practice. "I was hitting them as hard as I could out there and the ball was still returning to the earth. We might as well be playing in quicksand." Other Rockies players were equally vocal in their criticism of the hostile atmosphere in Boston, with Kaz Matsui claiming he found it hard to slide through the viscous air and Willie Taveras aggravating a recent thigh injury while attempting to stand up quickly. Ø

Mike Mussina Convinced He's Won A World Series

MARCH 27, 2008

NEW YORK—In an interview dealing with the highlights of his 18-year career, All-Star Yankee pitcher Mike Mussina seemed to believe that he has procured a World Series ring despite all evidence to the contrary."Sure I did, I helped put away the Mets back in 2000," said Mussina, who did not join the Yankees until the 2001 season. "Boy, was that a great team.Paulie [O'Neill], Tino [Martinez], [Scott] Bro[sius], and me… Ya know, I think Doc Gooden was on that team too. Just being on the field, letting that feeling of elation wash over me. That was the highlight of my career." Mussina went on to say that, to this day, he still values his Rookie of the Year award over any of his five Cy Youngs. Ø

Kenny Lofton Thinks He's Putting Finishing Touches On Hall Of Fame Career

SEPTEMBER 6, 2007

CLEVELAND—Apparently oblivious to the fact that his lifetime statistics, while repectable, are not worthy of admittance into baseball's most exclusive club, Indians outfielder Kenny Lofton actually believes he is adding the final flourishes to what he deems a Hall of Fame career. "Four more stolen bases and I'm up to the magic 6-2-5," said the man who led the American League in singles in 1993 and finished in the top 26 of MVP voting four times. "All I've got to do is bump the old career average from .299 to .300, maybe get a few more triples, and I can punch my ticket to Cooperstown." Lofton, who noted that he was also "a very good bunter—perhaps one of the best in the 1990s"—is still deciding whether he should enter the Hall as an Indian, Astro, Brave, White Sox, Giant, Pirate, Cub, Yankee, Phillie, Dodger, or Ranger. Ø

Mets Invite Phillies Back To Shea Stadium For A Nightcap

SEPTEMBER 11, 2008

NEW YORK—After spending a casual afternoon together playing a day game, the New York Mets approached the Philadelphia Phillies as they waited outside the ballpark for their team bus and asked them if they'd like to come back up to their field for a nightcap. "I know you've got an early flight tomorrow, but one more baseball game never hurt anyone," Mets third baseman David Wright said to the entire Phillies ballclub, flashing a smile and noting that Shea Stadium "looks beautiful under the lights." "No pressure, I just thought it might be…you know, fun." Despite the Mets' high hopes for the evening's nightcap, however, the Phillies did not allow them to get as far as third base. Ø

Left-Handed Hitter Sends Little League Into A Panic

AUGUST 23, 2007

WILLIAMSPORT, PA—Panic, confusion, and general chaos swept over the West Chandler, AZ Little League Sunday when, without warning, a player from the South Lubbock, TX team entered the left-handed batter's box. "Lefty! Lefty! Lefty! Lefty! Lefty! Lefty!" said first baseman Cody Bellinger, apparently unable to do anything except point helplessly at left-handed-hitting Garrett Williams as he notified his teammates of the improbable and unexpected situation. "Watch out, right field! Watch out, second base! Everyone watch out! Right field, move over! Over! I'll cover first!" Manager Jeff Parrish, who was evidently caught off guard and too paralyzed with shock to speak in an intelligible manner, loudly repeated the command "Shift!" for two straight minutes, during which the South Lubbock batter struck out on four pitches. Ø

INSIDE

> Baseball Now America's Fifth-Favorite Pastime Behind Four NFL-Related Things

> Baseball Pretty Shook Up After Hitting Prince Fielder

> Carl Pavano Tips Cap To Quieter-Than-Usual Boos

PHOTO FINISH

David Ortiz Plays Games In Japan Wearing Camera, Fanny Pack

Canseco: 'Hey Guys, Who Wants To Come To My Big Steroid Party This Weekend?'

FEBRUARY 28, 2008

MIAMI—Former MLB star and admitted steroid user Jose Canseco extended an informal invitation Monday to over 500 current and former professional baseball players, requesting their presence at his house this coming weekend for his annual steroid party.

"Hey guys, big steroid bash at my place," Canseco said while handing out flyers at a Toronto Blue Jays spring training intrasquad game. "Nothing too fancy, just a bunch of guys, hanging out, taking steroids. Tell your friends."

The party is historically an extravagant affair, usually featuring women in bikinis carrying silver trays of various types of anabolic steroids, four VIP suites upstairs where guests can sample steroids from Canseco's personal collection, a giant 40-foot-tall ice syringe filled with Dianabol, oil paintings of steroids on the walls, a keg of steroids, a disco ball, and a punch bowl spiked with steroids.

"Let me break it down for you: food, babes, steroids," said Canseco, leaning over the outfield

fence of Dunedin Stadium, to Blue Jays centerfielder Vernon Wells. "Any steroid you want. Winstrol-Stanozolol, Deca-Durabolin, Sustanon, Anadrol, you name it. I even got some exotic steroids from South America, and I might bust out my own special homemade steroid blend. Oh, and if everyone chips in $5, I might get a steroid fountain. It's gonna be sweet."

"Imagine taking steroids all night long, how cool that would be," said Canseco, trying to get the attention of right-fielder Alex Rios. "Then multiply that by 100. That's how much this party's going to rule."

According to colored flyers for "Jose's 22nd Annual Roid-Fest" featuring block-lettered words reading "Music," "Cool!" "Steroids," "Awesome," and "Injections," the event will take place at Canseco's four-acre lakefront mansion in Fort Lauderdale. The event has been touted as a good chance for players to relax, try out some new steroids, bulk up before the season, meet other people who enjoy steroids, share steroid-related stories, and "just have fun."

"Psst," Canseco said to Tampa Bay Rays pitcher Scott Kazmir while he was warming up in the bullpen. "Hey Scott, hey man, Scott, hey Scott. Hey. Hey man, you wanna come over and take some steroids at my house Saturday? Everyone's gonna be there. Free roids, man. Free roids. They're good for you. It'll be fun. Trust me. Steroid party. My place. Be there."

Canseco said that the event will be catered, featuring hors d'oeuvres such as steroid-stuffed lobster puffs, mini steroid-burgers, and according to Canseco, "a big steroid cake filled with steroids." Bowls of pretzels, testosterone cypionate, and Cheetos will be situated in the house and by the pool, and will be replenished throughout the night.

"There will be a hot tub out back filled with steroids, and then we'll go in it and eat all the steroids, and then we'll fill it back up with hot water," Canseco said. "Then we'll sit in the hot tub, talk about steroids and stuff, have some laughs, do some steroids, whatever. Then these hot girls in string bikinis will come into the hot tub and do steroids with us. Perfect end to a perfect evening."

For entertainment, there will be a variety of games, including "Steroid Twister," "Guess That Steroid"—a game in which blindfolded guests must correctly identify the type of steroid that they just ingested—and something that Canseco only described as everyone dropping their pants and injecting steroids into each other's buttocks.

see **CANSECO**

Manny Ramirez Plays With Bush Family Dogs During Red Sox's Entire White House Visit

FEBRUARY 28, 2008

WASHINGTON—Although Red Sox outfielder Manny Ramirez was present for the official team visit to the White House, he did not meet the president due to being preoccupied with rolling on the Rose Garden lawn and playing tug-of-war with Barney, the Bush family's Scottish terrier, the Red Sox organization announced Wednesday. "Hey, *perro! Perro!* Come here! You want to play with

Manny? Sure you do! Yes, you do! Hey! Come back!" Ramirez can be faintly heard to say in the background of the taped record of the ceremony, although cameras did not record Ramirez chasing the First Dog through the shrubbery or swinging the dog around in circles with Ramirez's sock clenched firmly in his jaw. Although Ramirez has posted photos of minor bites, supposedly inflicted by Barney, on his website, White House officials have dismissed the wounds as "just Barney being Barney." Ø

Mark Prior Just Needs To Stop By Hospital For A Sec To Get Some T.J. Surgery

MARCH 13, 2008

PEORIA, AZ—Padres pitcher Mark Prior informed teammates Monday that he just has to pop in to the hospital for "one quick sec" to have Tommy John connective tissue reconstruction surgery performed on his right arm. "Hey guys, can you pull over for a minute? My U.C. lig is just killing me and I gotta get a little T.J. before the game," Prior reportedly told fellow pitchers Jake Peavy and Chris Young after tearing his ulnar collateral ligament while the trio was driving to the ballpark.

"Just a quick Teej—pop out the lig, pop in a tendon, no biggie. I'd do it myself, but I just had some ro-co [rotator-cuff surgery] last night and I can't move my arm. You can leave the car running, I'll be back in a minute tops." Prior will not be able to throw a baseball for 16 to 18 months. Ø

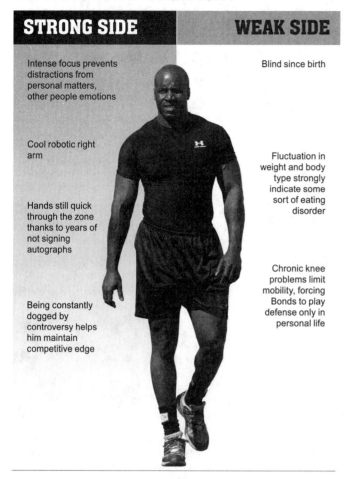

STRONG SIDE	WEAK SIDE
Intense focus prevents distractions from personal matters, other people emotions	Blind since birth
Cool robotic right arm	Fluctuation in weight and body type strongly indicate some sort of eating disorder
Hands still quick through the zone thanks to years of not signing autographs	
	Chronic knee problems limit mobility, forcing Bonds to play defense only in personal life
Being constantly dogged by controversy helps him maintain competitive edge	

from CANSECO

"Ever try a cherry steroid spritzer?" Canseco reportedly said to Cardinals first-baseman Albert Pujols Tuesday. "It's like a wine spritzer, but with steroids. Come on, come to my house. If you come, everyone will come. You didn't come last year. You owe me."

"One thing, though: At the end of the night, we all have to pose for a big group photo," Canseco added. "We can do one where we're all doing goofy poses and wearing silly hats and stuff, since we'll all be in such a good mood on account of all the steroids. But then we have to do a more serious one, where everyone looks straight ahead at the camera."

Most players said they would attend.

"I guess I'll go," said Astros shortstop Miguel Tejada. "[Canseco] kind of creeps me out, though. He's always writing stuff down and trying to talk to me about how to 'cycle' and 'stack' performance-enhancing drugs, but I have to hand it to the guy—he knows how to throw a steroid party."

"Even though I most certainly do not use steroids, and I never have, and the mere thought is reprehensible, that steroid party should be a good time," Tigers DH Gary Sheffield said. "Sometimes things get a little out of hand, like in 2003, when I lost my shit and almost killed a guy and then blacked out. But you know what they say—it's not a steroid party till something gets broken."

"Canseco's steroid parties are always lame," Pirates first-baseman Adam LaRoche said. "Last year when I showed up, all the steroids were already gone and it was just Jose Canseco, Sammy Sosa, and Rafael Palmeiro sitting on the couch, roided out of their minds, watching *Mr. Baseball* on TBS."

Roger Clemens said that he would not be attending, but asked for directions to Canseco's house just in case he has to drop by for a few minutes to pick up his wife. ∅

San Francisco Giants Band Together To Score Run

APRIL 10, 2008

MILWAUKEE—The San Francisco Giants put aside their differences Sunday night, working together as a team in a common effort to score a run in a baseball game. The scrappy nine-man crew overcame daunting odds to cobble together the run, as each player used his individual strengths and skills to help string together an unlikely series of events—including a walk, advancement on a wild pitch, an infield single, and perhaps most selfless of all, a ground into double play—that ultimately resulted in a Giant

crossing home plate. "This just shows you what a team can do when they put their mind to it," said Giants first-baseman Dan Ortmier, who was swarmed by his celebrating teammates at home plate after scoring the run. The Giants lost to the Brewers 12-1. ∅

Jose Canseco Composes Opera About Steroids

APRIL 3, 2008

NEW YORK—Just days after the publication of *Vindicated*, his second book concerning the use of steroids in professional baseball, former steroid-using baseball player and current steroid-awareness advocate Jose Canseco has debuted *La Anabolica*, an opera concerning the use of steroids in professional baseball. "I've done books, interviews, public speaking appearances, improv, and theater-in-the-round on the theme of steroids, and I was looking for something fresh and new, " Canseco said from the stage of the Met. "I think my libretto—especially the climactic scene in which fair Don Giambi is tempted to use the magic golden steroids to defeat evil knights Die Rosensox and their enchanted beast Il Monsto Verde—is exactly what is needed to bring the message of steroids in baseball to a new audience." Critics have not been kind to *La Anabolica*, noting that "the lyrics mostly consist of the word 'steroids' chanted over and over" and that "the ending, which occurs as a steroid-enhanced fat lady sings, is doubly and almost impossibly clichéd." ∅

Jim Leyland To Tigers: 'Do I Have To Get Naked And Yell Some Sense Into You?'

APRIL 17, 2008

DETROIT—Following the Tigers' 11-0 loss at home against the White Sox Sunday, frustrated manager Jim Leyland attempted to get through to his struggling ballclub by screaming in their faces, gesticulating wildly while pacing up and down the locker room floor, and removing every article of his clothing save for his socks. "We gave up two fucking grand slams in one game!" said Leyland, pointing at his bullpen with one hand and brandishing his recently removed pants in the other. "Do I need to run out to the mound with my dick swinging in the wind between every pitch so you goddamn well don't do that?" Leyland then stormed out of the locker room, held a markedly stilted post-game press conference, walked out of the clubhouse, and drove home. ∅

Congress Wondering What Happened With That Whole Roger Clemens Thing

APRIL 10, 2008

WASHINGTON—Members of Congress wondered aloud yesterday whether or not they were supposed to follow up on former pitcher Roger Clemens' four-and-a-half hour testimony before the House Committee of Oversight and Reform or if "that whole thing was over."

"Did we decide if we were actually going to do something with that? Or were we just, I don't know, asking?" Rep. Elijah Cummings (D-MD) asked fellow congressmen, adding that hopefully somebody wrote Clemens' testimony down just in case they do ever need it for anything. "I mean, nobody's said anything to me about it.

I just saw him on television the other day and remembered he was here. That was Clemens that was here, yeah? Hey, why was he here anyway?" Cummings later asked if Clemens testified before Congress this year or last year, and was shocked to learn that his appearance was in fact just under two months ago. ⌀

Nomar Garciaparra Tells Wife To Meet Him On Disabled List At 8 p.m.

MAY 01, 2008

LOS ANGELES—Dodgers third baseman Nomar Garciaparra left a voicemail message for his wife, former soccer star Mia Hamm, asking her to meet him on Major League Baseball's disabled list for a date Friday night. "Hey, after you're finished grocery shopping, why don't you swing over to the DL to grab a bite—I'll be hanging out in my usual spot, right below Kason Gabbard and right above Alex Gonzalez," Garciaparra reportedly said, stressing that she

should meet him on the 15-day DL, not the 60-day DL. "Mark [Prior] and Mikey [Hampton] will be there too. Should be fun." Upon hearing the message, Hamm complained that Garciaparra "always" wants to hang out on the DL, and expressed frustration that she has to tear her hamstring every time she wants to spend time with her husband. ⌀

Jason Giambi Day-To-Day With Sore Groin, If You Know What He Means

APRIL 10, 2008

NEW YORK—Jason Giambi will miss the next several games due to soreness in his groin, if you catch the Yankee first baseman's drift, because in recent weeks Giambi has apparently been applying too much pressure to his groin area, if you know what he means—and he thinks you know what he means. "Last night, I was rounding third base, when I felt a sudden stiffness in my groin," Giambi told members

of the media while holding his hands approximately two feet from his pelvic region and slowly gyrating his hips in a suggestive fashion. "Something had to be done to reduce the fluid buildup. If you see where I'm going here." Giambi assured reporters, however, that despite overextending his groin last night for two long hours, he would, hell yeah, be able to return to action tonight. He then winked five times. ⌀

A-Rod Asks Jeter 'Is This Heaven?' While Playing Game Of Catch

JUNE 5, 2008

NEW YORK—While warming up on the Yankee Stadium sidelines before Tuesday's game, Alex Rodriguez paused, looked up at the clear blue sky and the thousands of cheering fans in attendance, turned to Derek Jeter, and invoked a classic line from the 1989 film *Field Of Dreams.* "Hey, Derek?" Rodriguez said, inhaling deeply to convey a sense of wonderment and gesturing woodenly to the thick, green grass below his feet. "Is this heaven?" According to witnesses, Jeter chuckled mildly and then muttered "Fucking loser" under his breath. ⌀

Angry Jim Leyland's Mustache Keeps Falling Off While Yelling At Team

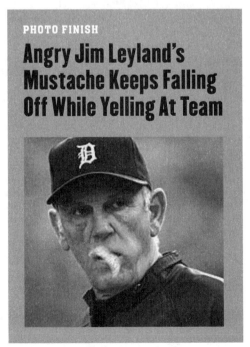

Piggly Wiggly Scouting Report Indicates J.J. Hardy Enjoys Rib-Eye Steaks

MAY 15, 2008

MILWAUKEE—A Piggly Wiggly-sponsored scouting report shown during an at-bat by Brewers shortstop J.J. Hardy Sunday indicated that his major weakness is a hankering for Piggly Wiggly-brand certified angus beef boneless rib-eye steaks, now just $4.99 a pound. "J.J. is very strong when it comes to purchasing three Ole El Paso Mexican Dinner Kits for $5, but he's struggled lately with Golden Flake-brand potato chips, as he hasn't bought a single bag since last August," said FSN North play-by-play announcer Brian Anderson, reading from the onscreen scouting report. "Perhaps [opposing Cardinals pitcher] Braden Looper can take advantage of the fact that J.J. does not like Tyson breaded chicken fingers." After Hardy grounded out to third base, Anderson called it a textbook case of Ronco vermicelli being on sale for 69 cents. ⌀

Baseball Swing So Bad It Makes Joe Morgan Vomit

MAY 08, 2008

ST. LOUIS—Moments after watching Cardinals catcher Yadier Molina get fooled into swinging well ahead of a 73 mph curveball, ESPN *Sunday Night Baseball* analyst Joe Morgan convulsed violently and vomited into the lap of play-by-play commentator Jon Miller. "I was just noting that Molina really took a weak hack at that curve, evening the count at 2-2, when all of a sudden I heard Joe make this awful noise and I felt a gallon of half-digested hot dogs and cheese fries splatter onto the floor, my pants, and all four monitors in the booth," Miller said." Joe said he was fine afterwards, even though he spent the next few innings spitting on the floor and gasping with his head held between his knees." Morgan was eventually able to hold down a few complimentary chicken nuggets, which were themselves forcibly vomited after Morgan was forced to see a muffed throw to first base by Cardinals second baseman Adam Kennedy. ⌀

Nationals Book It After Foul Ball Accidentally Smashes Capitol Rotunda

MAY 8, 2008

WASHINGTON—An 8,976-foot foul ball off the bat of Washington third baseman Ryan Zimmerman crashed through the U.S. Capitol Building rotunda Sunday afternoon, prompting both the Nationals and the opposing Pittsburgh Pirates to gasp, turn to each other in shock, and immediately run full speed out of Nationals Park.

"As soon as I hit it, I knew it was headed straight toward Capitol Hill—I just kept saying to myself, 'Not the dome, not the dome, not the dome,'" Zimmerman said. Both teams, all four umpires, and the 32,457 fans in attendance winced in horror, however, as the ball kept carrying, made a loud smashing noise, and left a gaping hole in the rotunda's neoclassical architecture.

"We are so dead," Zimmerman added.

As the teams grabbed the bases and scrambled out of the stadium, the Pirates yelled to the Nationals that they were in "big trouble." The Nationals refuted that claim, screaming that "if [Pirates left-fielder] Jason [Bay] could run at all, he would've tracked down the ball and caught it" before it struck the 200-year-old structure, which stands 1.7 miles from the ballpark.

However, as soon as the teams heard the Capitol Building's front door swing open, they put their differences aside and sped frantically back to their hotel rooms.

"Congress is going to be so mad," said Nationals first baseman Nick Johnson, peering out his window, expecting to see the 535 members of the House and Senate pull into the hotel parking lot. "This was the worst time to do it, too, because they're already in a bad mood, what with the election stuff and the war and the recession, and all."

"Aw, man, we're never gonna get that ball back," Johnson added.

The team, however, has urged outfielder Lastings Milledge to dress up in a suit, sneak into the Capitol Building, retrieve the ball, and make the necessary repairs on the shattered sandstone walls of the dome before anyone notices.

According to eyewitnesses in the Capitol, the ball smashed into the dome at about 3:35 p.m., tore through the *Apotheosis Of Washington*—a 150-year-old, 4,664-square-foot fresco painted on the inside of the rotunda—and broke the arm off of a National Statuary Hall sculpture of William Jennings Bryan. The ball then bounced into the Senate Chamber, where it interrupted a vote on a $542.5 billion defense authorization bill, and landed directly in the mashed pota-

see NATIONALS

8-Year-Old Little Leaguer, 31-Year-Old Professional Given Same Hitting Advice

MAY 29, 2008

PHILADELPHIA—8-year-old Easton, PA Little Leaguer Tyler Jenson and 31-year-old professional baseball player Pat Burrell were given identical tips on improving their swings and properly hitting a baseball Monday night. "Remember to keep your elbow up, keep your knees bent, and keep your eye on the ball," said both 45-year-old hardware-store manager and father of three Dale Kremke and retired Major League Baseball veteran of 18 years Milt Thompson to the two struggling hitters. "Watch the ball out of the pitcher's hand, and just meet the ball with the bat. Come on, now, just takes one." Both Burrell and Jenson struck out in their next at bat and returned to their respective dugouts in tears. Ø

from **NATIONALS**

toes of early-dining Senate Minority Leader Mitch McConnell (R-KY), covering him with gravy and prompting him to exclaim, "Zimmer-maaaaannnn!"

Although McConnell had no evidence at the time that Zimmerman was responsible for the damages, he was the chief suspect, as he is the only National able to hit the ball farther than 300 feet. Furthermore, Zimmerman dented McConnell's 1998 Buick LeSabre last week when he overthrew first base by 15,000 feet on a routine grounder.

"This is unacceptable—Capitol rotundas don't just grow on trees, you know," read a statement drafted by House Speaker Nancy Pelosi following the event. "Not only are these damages going to cost a fortune—a fortune—to repair, but we specifically told the Washington Nationals baseball organization a thousand times before the season started to be extra-careful and to try not to hit the ball to left field."

The statement went on to demand that the Nationals pay for all the damages, which total over $400 million—more than five times the entire team payroll. Because of this, players are expected to either find part-time jobs to cover the cost or work off the expenses by taking positions as congressional aides in the offseason.

The Pirates have promised to chip in $5, claiming that is all they have right now.

"This stinks," said Zimmerman, who attempted to persuade local resident Henry Adelson, a Nationals season-ticket holder and D.C.-area insurance claims adjuster, to take the rap for him and say he was the one who hit the ball. "We shouldn't have to stop playing just because the lousy U.S. Capitol got in the way. And also hitting the Capitol Building should be an automatic home run."

On Tuesday, Congress announced an initiative to move the Nationals franchise from D.C. to Oklahoma City, Portland, or anywhere far enough away that a batted ball or errant throw will not cause significant damage to American landmarks.

However, President Bush has called such actions "unnecessary" and "too harsh," saying that all will be forgiven if the players come down from their hotel rooms, say they're sorry, promise to be more careful, and allow Bush to participate in team batting practice every day from now through the 2016 season. Ø

CC Sabathia, Prince Fielder Keep Imagining Each Other As Giant Talking Hot Dog, Hamburger

JUNE 24, 2008

MILWAUKEE—The Brewers' playoff push has run afoul of an unusual distraction, as sources close to the organization confirm that newly acquired husky starting pitcher CC Sabathia and sizable power-hitting first baseman Prince Fielder continue to visualize one another as a 6'7" chili cheese dog and a 260-pound hamburger with all the trimmings, respectively.

Team insiders say the problem has become a serious disruption, with numerous incidences of each player tying a bib around his neck, holding a knife and fork in their outstretched hands, and chasing the other around the ballpark.

"I should have noticed something was wrong weeks ago, when Prince, who has always had a certain fascination with the sausage races, expressed delight that we had 'signed Cleveland's huge chili cheese dog' and welcomed CC to the team by coating him liberally with celery salt and mustard," said manager Ned Yost. "And in his very first start, CC praised the way our 'great big hamburger' was hitting, and kept trying to pick off runners at first base by throwing ketchup and extra cheese to Prince."

Although both Fielder and Sabathia are major factors in the Brewer's playoff plans, their teammates admit that their recent displays of appetite have been a bit unnerving.

"Usually, the other players step in before one of them takes a bite out of the other," said Brewers reliever David Riske. "But the whole thing is pretty unsettling. Sabathia and I were getting our arms rubbed the other day, just kind of stretching them out across the massage table, when suddenly an empty jar of relish rolled by. I looked up, and Prince had put a huge hot dog bun and all the trimmings on Sabathia's arm when he wasn't paying attention. CC pulled himself out at the last minute, but when Prince's teeth came together, it made a chomping sound you could hear throughout the clubhouse."

Sabathia responded by chasing Fielder around the clubhouse with a pair of giant salt and pepper shakers.

On Monday, Yost announced that any player who attempted to devour another, no matter how delicious they seemed to appear,

see **HAMBURGER**

God Wastes Miracle On Running Catch In Outfield

MAY 29, 2008

HEAVEN—Rather than use His almighty power to breathe life back into the 130,000 people who perished in the Myanmar cyclone, rebuild an earthquake-destroyed China, or bring a lasting peace to the Middle East, the Lord God wasted a divine miracle Monday by granting Angels centerfielder Torii Hunter the ability to make a dramatic but otherwise routine running catch in the outfield. "I know many of My children believe My omnipotence would be better spent in ways other than affecting the contest between the Los Angeles Angels of Anaheim and Detroit Tigers, and truth be told, there is a possibility Mr. Hunter would have made that catch on his own. But it was a very close game that the Angels really deserved to win," said God, adding that He answered the heartfelt prayers of nearly 50,000 Los Angeles fans by allowing Hunter to make the grab. "Everyone—even the first place Angels, who need to win just a few more close games to give them the confidence to make a World Series run—deserves God's help, not just those suffering from AIDS." God denied that His handiwork was responsible for Angels third baseman Chone Figgins waking up Wednesday morning with no pain in his right hamstring, saying He was as surprised as anyone. Ø

from **HAMBURGER**

would be subject to disciplinary action. However, like many disciplinary measures involving athletes, the decree seemed only to make those involved more cunning.

"I was using the hot tub to ease some soreness the other day with Prince, who had nodded off, when CC came in carrying these grocery bags," said third baseman Bill Hall. "I had just noticed that something smelled really good when I realized that CC was cutting up vegetables and throwing them in the hot tub with Prince, alongside plenty of noodles and spices, to make some sort of hamburger casserole."

Luckily, Fielder woke up before the mixture thickened and retaliated by attempting to trap Sabathia in the steam room along with a bag of mesquite-flavored grilling charcoal.

"This has to end," Yost admitted to reporters as the Brewers readied themselves for a four-game series against St. Louis. "We can't have players trying to eat one another, even in Milwaukee, so we're taking steps. We've already talked to both players, explaining that while they are big, they are not food. And as a provisional measure, we've gotten Ray Durham from the Giants in the hopes that both Prince and CC will think he's a giant ham and leave one another alone." Ø

At-Bat Following Grand Slam Just Kind Of Awkward

JULY 10, 2008

HOUSTON—Astros right fielder Hunter Pence expressed consternation following teammate Miguel Tejada's seventh inning grand slam, saying the proceedings took a decided turn for the awkward from that moment on. "Now where does that leave me exactly?" Pence said after the game, referring to the at-bat in question, in which

the sixth-place hitter took two called strikes before hitting a check swing grounder to second base. "Not to mention the fact that when I got up there it was 7-0 all of a sudden. Best case, and I'm talking about if everything goes perfectly, I would've driven in one run, maximum. I felt like an idiot." Cardinals pitcher Ryan Franklin, the man who gave up the grand slam in question, calmly retired the next three batters, walked down to the visiting clubhouse, and took his own life. Ø

A's Pitchers Meet Up At Cool Pitcher Hangout Called 'The Strike Zone' After Game

JULY 17, 2008

OAKLAND—Following their victory against the Texas Rangers last night, Oakland A's starting pitchers Greg Smith, Dana Eveland, and Justin Duchscherer made their way over to their favorite post-game hangout, The Strike Zone, where they sat in their usual booth and were greeted by the restaurant's owner/ventriloquist, a colorful character known to them only as Mack. "Just the usual Zone Burger for me, Mack," said Eveland just as the pitchers' popular cheerleading girlfriends Kristen, Jenny, and Liza arrived and took seats next to their respective boyfriends. "You know, I think we all learned something valuable from last night's game. Sure, wins are important, but there's nothing more important than being honest, staying off drugs, and hanging with your friends. Oh, and not throwing parties in the stadium when [A's owner] Mr. Wolf is out of town. Let's never make that mistake again!" The good times were interrupted when rival pitchers from the Los Angeles Angels stormed in, taunted the A's girlfriends, and loudly proclaimed that a victory in next week's big game was all but certain—unless the A's had some wacky scheme up their sleeves. Ø

Player To Be Named Later From 1992 Trade Finally Named: 'It Was Lenny Dykstra,' Says Phillies GM

JUNE 12, 2008

PHILADELPHIA—The July 2, 1992 trade which sent Dodgers outfielder Stan Javier to the Phillies for Steve Searcy and a player to be named later was formally completed Sunday, when it was announced that the unnamed player was Lenny Dykstra. "Yup, it was Lenny Dykstra," said former Phillies GM Lee Thomas, who orchestrated the trade 16 years ago. "Probably should have mentioned that sooner." When informed about the trade Monday, Dykstra said he would do his best to help the Dodgers win in 1992 through 1996. Ø

Struggling Mets Combine To Form Carlos Voltron

SEPTEMBER 25, 2008

NEW YORK—Facing the Cubs in the midst of a three-game losing streak, the desperate Mets sprinted out to the field Tuesday, launched themselves high into the air above Shea Stadium, and combined their bodies to form a 400-foot tall fielding robot called Carlos Voltron.

According to eyewitnesses, before the Mets players completed the complicated procedure, in which they fused their physical selves and combined their talents to form the 20,000-ton robot, manager Jerry Manuel called the team to the dugout, where he commanded them to prepare their interlock systems for activation, connect the appropriate dyna-therms, charge up the infra-cells to full capacity, engage the mega-thrusters, and give it their best out there.

"After losing eight of our last 12 games, forming Carlos Voltron is our only hope to save our playoff chances," Manuel said. "We really need power this late in the season, and the 2.5 million pounds of thrust in Voltron's solid-fuel boosters should give us the lift we need."

Leaving behind blue and orange vapor trails as they soared across the sky, the Mets were reportedly surrounded by a crackling electrical field as they folded their limbs into their bodies to ready themselves for

assembly and to protect the team's home record.

Although Manuel said he had to settle an argument over who got to be the robot's head, his final lineup was David Wright and José Reyes forming the legs, Ramón Castro and Ryan Church making the feet, Nick Evans and Johan Santana completing the arms, Carlos Delgado and Luis Castillo joining to create the torso, and Carlos Beltrán forming the head.

While Cubs batters had taken early advantage of the Mets pitchers on Monday, the towering spectacle of Carlos Voltron proved to be an imposing presence on the mound, as the force of his foot slamming into the ground after the windup of his first pitch knocked the batter and umpire into the third row of the stands. In addition, the seismic energy unleashed by Carlos Voltron's follow-through created sev-

eral deep cracks in the foundation of Shea Stadium, and accompanying atmospheric disturbances caused a 747 in a holding pattern over nearby La Guardia airport to plunge from the sky.

"In the second inning I had to have him take some heat off those pitches or he was going to kill somebody," said Manuel, adding that he clocked the first pitch at 85,000 mph. "After what happened to poor Alfonso Soriano, I told him let them hit a few balls."

"We might face this team in the playoffs," continued Manuel. "I'd hate to see what would happen to us if the Cubs unleashed the Robeast from their bullpen."

With his fast first step and an exceptionally long stride that carries the giant robot from the mound to the center field wall in one step, Carlos Voltron put on an amazing fielding display in the fifth inning when he robbed Cubs third baseman Aramis Ramírez of a 500-foot shot by plucking it out of the air between the robotic index finger and thumb of his leonine hand.

Although the Mets' fielding skills were excellent, they were not without flaws. Cubs manager Lou Piniella came out to the field to protest several times, complaining that his base runners injured themselves in the 10-foot deep trenches left behind from Carlos Voltron scooping up ground balls. Piniella also

see **VOLTRON**

Mariners Improve To Eight Games Over .300

JULY 24, 2009

SEATTLE—After winning for the seventh time in their past 17 games, the Seattle Mariners moved to eight games over the .300 mark for the first time since early May. "I'm pleased, but it's just a number, and over the next few weeks we'll look to get to nine games over, or even 10," said Jim Riggleman, who has led the M's on a .481 streak since taking over as manager in June. "The guys are really starting to come around. [Yuniesky] Betancourt's got a three-game hitting streak, Jose [Lopez] hit a home run this week, and as long as we avoid getting swept and split a two-game series every once in a while, I think we can take a crack at .400." Riggleman went on to express pride in his team for not losing every single game on the road this season. ∅

INSIDE

› Chase Utley Has Been Calling Ryan Howard 'Brian' This Whole Time

› Derek Jeter Handles Career Milestone With So Much Class That You Just Want To Punch His Little Face

› Fall Classic Downgraded To Fall Thing That Happened

› Fielder Insists He Had No Choice

› Indians Turn Rare 6-4-Harold Baines' Face-3 Double Play Against White Sox

---

PHOTO FINISH

Placido Polanco Chokes Up All The Way

from **VOLTRON**

expressed frustration over his players suffering from collapsed rib cages, ruptured organs, and decapitations every time Voltron tagged them out.

Carlos Voltron's solid and consistent defensive play was only upstaged in the fans' eyes by his powerful hitting, with those in attendance claiming they suffered bad sunburns from the glare caused by the robot forming his blazing bat. Stepping up to the plate, he made almost perfect contact with the first pitch, belting the ball out of Shea and into the next solar system.

"That big guy they have at the heart of their lineup really has potential," Piniella said. "Little stiff, needs to fix that stance some, and could probably use some work on the throwing mechanics, but really, you get the feeling he's going to be good."

"I wonder how long they have him signed for," added Piniella. "Might be a risk with him shutting down for 20 minutes after getting gravel from the warning track in his guidance apparatus. Ah, what am I thinking? We already have Kerry Wood. We don't need another robot."

Meanwhile, defending a comfortable 600-0 lead in the top of ninth, the Mets decided to rest up Carlos Voltron by moving him to the outfield and replacing him with reliever Aaron Heilman, who lost the lead and eventually the game after giving up 618 runs to close the inning. ∅

Rickey Henderson Says He'll Only Join Hall Of Fame If He Can Start

JANUARY 15, 2009

SCOTTSDALE, AZ—All-time stolen base leader Rickey Henderson told Baseball Hall of Fame officials Monday that he would only join Cooperstown's most prestigious club if he could start in left field and bat leadoff. "Man, Rickey's still got it, and it would be disrespectful to myself and my family if I entered a situation where I was playing backup to [former left fielders] Stan Musial or Ted Williams," Henderson said during the hour-long telephone negotiation, adding, "What are those guys, like, 50? Rickey does not ride the pine. Rickey plays. You think Lou Brock can run like me? Please. Goodbye." Henderson later told reporters that he would also be willing to enter the Hall of Fame in Japan, if necessary, and play his remaining years there. ∅

Yogi Berra On Final Game At Yankee Stadium: 'Where Am I?'

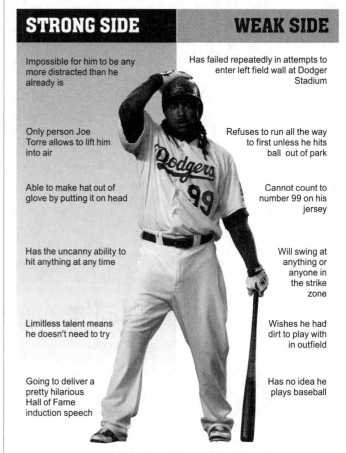

STRONG SIDE	WEAK SIDE
Impossible for him to be any more distracted than he already is	Has failed repeatedly in attempts to enter left field wall at Dodger Stadium
Only person Joe Torre allows to lift him into air	Refuses to run all the way to first unless he hits ball out of park
Able to make hat out of glove by putting it on head	Cannot count to number 99 on his jersey
Has the uncanny ability to hit anything at any time	Will swing at anything or anyone in the strike zone
Limitless talent means he doesn't need to try	Wishes he had dirt to play with in outfield
Going to deliver a pretty hilarious Hall of Fame induction speech	Has no idea he plays baseball

Goose Gossage Admitted Into Hall Of Fame After Correctly Answering Three Baseball History Questions

JULY 31, 2008

COOPERSTOWN, NY—Former relief pitcher Rich "Goose" Gossage was admitted into the Baseball Hall of Fame Sunday after correctly answering the requisite three baseball history questions, ranging from "Which major-league player broke the MLB's color barrier?" to "Yankee Stadium was nicknamed 'The House That Ruth Built' in honor of which Yankee slugger?" "I got lucky with this year's questions," said Gossage, who in 2002 came within one correct answer of making it into the Hall of Fame only to incorrectly guess "Rickey Henderson" on his final question. "The first two answers that year were Rick- ey Henderson, so I just assumed the last one would be, too. They like to play mind games with you, which is why I was hesitant to answer 'Goose Gossage' on the final question this year." Mark McGwire once again failed to make it into Cooperstown after failing to name every major-league player born in Iowa. ∅

6-Tool Player Sings Like An Angel

MARCH 12, 2009

Mr. Met Having Trouble Sleeping In New Home

APRIL 16, 2009

FLUSHING, NY—After dozing off between innings in front of more than 41,000 cheering fans Monday night, an exhausted Mr. Met informed team officials that he has not slept since the Mets moved from Shea Stadium to Citi Field.

According to Mets GM Omar Minaya, Mr. Met entered his office and used a series of pantomimes to indicate that his sleep disorder is caused by brighter stadium lights, uncomfortable temperatures, and Darryl Strawberry's snoring. Minaya, who spent two hours meeting with the 47-year-old mascot, said Mr. Met conveyed the degree of his fatigue by holding his hands several feet apart.

"Obviously, Mr. Met is integral to this organization, and we are quite concerned with his well-being" said Minaya, adding that the Mets are committed to making the longest-serving member of their team comfortable. "After assuring him that the late-night noises he heard were most likely concrete settling, I promised we would get animal control to remove Darryl."

"It often takes a little time to adjust to living in a new place," Minaya added. "Per-

sonally, I don't think the inside of the new home run apple smells that weird."

Despite the raucous throng of fans eager to celebrate the opening of the new ballpark as the Mets took on San Diego, the listless Mr. Met shuffled onto the field during pregame warm-ups and lethargically attempted to pump up the crowd with a few halfhearted waves and hand-claps. Not even third baseman David Wright's game-tying three-run homer in the fifth inning inspired the weary mascot, who was seen sitting atop the dugout clutching his oversized baseball head and massaging the seams at his temples in gentle circles.

Explaining that Mr. Met's usual fun-loving antics have taken a dark turn lately, Jose Reyes recalled how the mascot pushed an eight-year-old fan to the ground last week and flipped off Luis Castillo after he struck out on Opening Day. In addition, Reyes said he has seen Mr. Met take out his T-shirt gun, place it in his mouth, and repeatedly squeeze the trigger.

"When I asked if he was feeling okay, he didn't say a word. He just shook his giant head," Reyes said. "Poor guy. He used to be so upbeat.

These days his smile just looks painted on."

"I'd say he drinks too much coffee, but he flings most of it at people," Reyes added. "Maybe his hat is too small or something."

According to manager Jerry Manuel, Mr. Met has privately admitted difficulty in maintaining regular bedtimes due to the swelling crowds, which tend to stick around after games, making it hard for him to unwind while watching the JumboTron. Manuel also divulged that the mascot tosses and turns all night.

"Mr. Met has tried sleeping on pretty much every seat, the dugout benches, all three bases, and even the escalator in the Jackie Robinson Rotunda," Manuel said. "Last week he managed to get a few hours of shut-eye while curled up under the tarp, but even there he slept so restlessly that when the groundskeepers arrived the next morning they found he'd kicked it into a corner of the field."

While Mr. Met has admitted that he is not yet accustomed to Citi Field, team members have said they are already feeling very much at home in the new ballpark after losing their first game to the Padres. ∅

JUPITER, FL—In a spring training game on Wednesday, Marlins outfield prospect Cameron Maybin continued to impress scouts and opposing players alike by stealing a base, making a leaping grab in center, and belting out the "Spirto Gentil" aria from Donizetti's *La Favorita*. "The sound of the ball coming off his bat and his vibrato on the 'M'appari' are both unmatched," said manager Fredi Gonzalez, comparing the outfielder to a young Ken Griffey Jr. or Giuseppe Giacomini. "He's got all the tools: He can field, throw, run the bases, harmonize above the lead, hit for power, and hit for average. His swing is definitely still a little raw, but he's got the voice of a major leaguer. I swear, I melt every time." Gonzalez then sat back and listened to Maybin's rich, honeyed tenor emanating from the shower, took off his sunglasses, and began to weep. ∅

PHOTO FINISH

Feet Don't Fail Me Now, Says Charlie Manuel Before Walking To Mound

Men Standing Behind Backstop With Radar Guns Exchange Impressed Glances

FEBRUARY 26, 2009

LAKELAND, FL—During a recent throwing session by Tigers' top prospect Rick Porcello, two men holding radar guns in the bleachers behind home plate could be seen shooting each other knowing glances, shaking their heads, and letting out low whistles after each pitch. "Kid's got an arm," one man said while lifting his hat and scratching his head with the same hand just before spitting a stream of tobacco juice between his teeth. His companion, a large man in suspenders who punctuated his comments by mopping his brow, seemed to agree, remarking that he had "been around for a long time" and had "never seen anything like it." The men went on to remark that they had not seen an arm like that since Yankee great Steve Nebraska or Cubs great Henry Rowengartner. Ø

Following 300th Victory, Randy Johnson Returns Healthy Back To Local Man

JUNE 11, 2009

SAN FRANCISCO—After recording his 300th career victory on June 4, Giants pitcher Randy Johnson returned the back he had borrowed for use in the game to its rightful owner, Mountain View, CA resident Craig Rowin. "I'm just happy he kept his word and returned it," said Rowin, who complained that after trading backs with Johnson he was unable to physically lift himself from his living room couch for an entire week. "Every time I sneezed, it felt like broken glass  moving around in there, and sounded like an industrial-sized sheet of bubble wrap being popped. My own back isn't even that great to begin with, but still, I'm glad it could play a small part in baseball history." After reading an ad on Craiglist, Rowin has also offered to lend his rotator cuff to user pedro-mart193847765@craigslist.org. Ø

Manny Ramirez To David Ortiz: 'Road Trip'

MAY 28, 2009

SOMEWHERE ALONG I-65—Best buddies Manny Ramirez and David Ortiz, both of whom find themselves at professional crossroads and both desperately wanting to rekindle their friendship, decided on Sunday that a soul-searching road trip was the key to resolving their personal problems.

"I called David and I said, 'David! Hey, David! It's Manny. Road trip, man! Let's do this!' And he said, 'Okay,' and now he is with me in the car here," Ramirez told reporters in a cell phone interview while driving on the interstate. "Papi isn't hitting so good, and I'm not even playing, and we miss each other and love each other, and because we play on different baseball teams now, I play on the Los Angeles Dodgers, and he plays for the Boston Red Sox, I think, and we don't get to spend quality time with each other like we did when we played on the same team, you know?"

"Uh-oh, it says Corvette Museum next right. I got to go, man," Ramirez added. "Hey, Papi, do we have any more Slim Jims?"

According to sources, Ramirez pulled up to Ortiz's Weston, MA home last Sunday, a selection of Tom Petty hits blaring from the stereo of his faded red 1966 Ford Galaxie 500 convertible. After embracing each other, a visibly somber Ortiz told Ramirez, "I don't know what's going on with me, man. I'm not hitting the baseball." Ortiz then threw his battered duffel bag in the car's backseat and asked Ramirez where they were headed.

Ramirez responded, "Just get in."

Several seconds after pulling out of Ortiz's driveway, the car's rear bumper fell off and the overstuffed trunk sprung open, sending a food-laden cooler, several bags, and a shoe box marked "fireworks" out onto the road.

According to eyewitness accounts, the former teammates have been crisscrossing the country with no apparent final destination. They have taken pictures of each another in front of the world's biggest hockey stick in Eveleth, MN; the world's

see ROAD TRIP

Gwendolyn Monroe Mourns Death Of Ex-Husband Dom DiMaggio

FEBRUARY 26, 2009

LOS ANGELES—As news of Dom DiMaggio's death spread throughout the baseball world, few took the news as hard as the former Red Sox's one-time wife, 84-year-old librarian Gwendolyn Monroe. "He was sullen, but not too sullen," said the somewhat homely Monroe, who changed her name from Gertrude Ann Mortenson in the 1950s. "He was really there for me when I checked out of the hospital after that migraine, and he was so supportive when I married my third husband, Arthur [Mueller]. And I think that, more than anything, Dom would want to be remembered for the 34-game hitting streak he had in 1949. That was really something." Monroe refused to comment on her alleged affair with then–vice president Lyndon Johnson. Ø

from **ROAD TRIP**

tallest thermometer in Baker, CA; the giant fiberglass muskellunge at the Freshwater Fishing Hall of Fame in Hayward, WI; and while dressed in Lazer Tag uniforms at the Fun Fest Entertainment Center in Harmarville, PA.

While both Ortiz and Ramirez have spent the majority of their trip laughing and reminiscing about when they were the most feared hitting tandem in baseball, their journey has not been without its serious moments. Ortiz reportedly made Ramirez spit out human growth hormone pills in a Motel 6 bathroom in Columbia, MS, and then forced him to flush the rest of his steroid-filled syringes down the toilet.

Ramirez and Ortiz also got into a shouting match in Abilene, TX, when in an attempt to reinvigorate Ortiz's passion for baseball, Ramirez tried to make his best friend watch a Little League ball game.

"You said there would be no baseball," said Ortiz, refusing to leave the car. "I hate baseball. I can't hit the baseball. You know that. If you care so much about me and baseball, why you leave me? Why you leave me by myself in Boston, Manny? Why you do that? Why you act so bad? Boston's a good place."

"You need to deal with that, man. You need to come to terms," Ramirez said. "I never going back to Boston. But, man, look at these kids. This is baseball, man. Little kids having fun and not injecting themselves with steroids and women pills and just stepping up there and hitting the ball. You gotta face it, man. We gotta face it together."

"Everybody's left me, you know?" Ortiz responded, tears streaming down his face. "You left me, Pedro left me. The only one who doesn't leave is Jason [Varitek], and he don't talk to me. He don't talk to anyone."

Witnesses at the scene said that, as the two sluggers cried in each other's arms, Ramirez and Ortiz's attention focused on the Little League diamond, where a player had just hit a walk-off home run. Ramirez whispered to Ortiz, "That is like you in the playoffs, man, but bigger. Remember that? You just go up there and hit the ball. You don't need to think. You're Big Papi. You go up there and be Big Papi."

Ramirez and Ortiz were subsequently sighted exiting a Terre Haute, IN 7-Eleven store wearing Indianapolis 500 baseball caps and brand new neon-orange sunglasses.

"The bigger one kept asking if he should get the hat, and the other one said he would buy one if [Ortiz] did," 7-Eleven cashier Kip Petrun told reporters. "They must have tried on sunglasses for 30 minutes."

"Before they left the parking lot they argued over whose turn it was to pick the music," Petrun added. "I'm pretty sure they settled on that song 'Life Is A Highway,' because they both started singing it at the top of their lungs. I think they said they were going to Nebraska to pick up their friend Pedro something."

The trip reportedly culminated with Ramirez taking Ortiz to a batting cage in St. George, UT. Though Ortiz missed the first several balls, Ramirez told Ortiz that he knew he could do it, and that even if they were no longer teammates, they would always be best friends. Ortiz then began hitting ball after ball, the last five of which hit the "home run" net.

"I can do it. I can hit the baseball again!" Ortiz yelled as he and Manny pointed at each other. "And you can hit the baseball without taking steroids, Manny. I know you can. Hopefully I can, too."

During a tender moment at the Grand Canyon later that night, tourists said that while seated on the hood of their car, Ortiz placed a blanket around a shivering Ramirez and told him, "You're my best friend, man. You're my best friend."

The car's hood then caved in, sending both players into a fit of hysterical laughter. ⌀

Outfielders Take Knee, Infielders Move Up In New 'Jason Varitek Shift'

APRIL 28, 2009

BOSTON—As the 2009 baseball season progresses, major-league managers are defending against Red Sox catcher Jason Varitek by employing what they call the "Varitek Shift," a defensive maneuver in which infielders move up past the pitcher's mound and outfielders take a knee and relax. "It's very effective," Minnesota Twins manager Ron Gardenhire told reporters. "If Jason makes contact with the ball, which is rare in itself, he usually hits slow dribblers that catch infielders by surprise because of how weak they're hit. So, by moving the infielders up, and having the pitcher rush home plate after the pitch has been thrown, [Varitek] has virtually no chance of reaching base. If runners are on when he comes up, we may have the outfielders cover first, second, and third to ensure a double or triple play." Gardenhire added that it doesn't matter if the switch-hitting Varitek bats right- or left-handed, as the shift is foolproof. ⌀

INSIDE

> Retired Moises Alou Still Pees On Hands

> Tim Wakefield Thinks He'll Go Ahead And Throw Knuckleball

> Toledo Mud Hens' 'Cook Your Own Hot Damn Hot Dogs Night' Named Worst Minor League Promotion Of The Year

> Hidden Ball Play Continues

> Bases Loaded Balk Added To List Of Reasons Why You Have To Love Sports

> Batter Makes Entire Stadium Wait To Hear End Of 'Sloop John B' Before Batting

PHOTO FINISH
Tim Lincecum Removes Hat, Hair To Wipe Sweat Off Forehead

Rare Centuple Play Ends Mets' Season

AUGUST 27, 2009

MIAMI—In a sudden end to a trying year, the Mets' Jeff Francoeur lined into a rare centuple play against the Florida Marlins Wednesday, which by rule cut New York's season short. "I hit it on the screws, but it just happened to be in a spot where they could turn a hundred," said Francoeur, who watched helplessly as Marlins second baseman Dan Uggla tagged everyone in the Mets dugout before heading into the clubhouse and tagging both equipment manager Charlie Samuels and physical therapist John Zajac. "You take a risk by starting the runners but I didn't think he'd have enough time to run up to the executive suite and get [Mets GM] Omar [Minaya] and [team owner]

Fred [Wilpon]. I guess by the 80th out we'd all just given up." This was the most outs recorded on a single play since the 2004 Montreal Expos were eradicated from the league after hitting into an ∞-play. ⌀

Miguel Cabrera Hits Dismal .194 In Fight With Wife

OCTOBER 10, 2009

DETROIT— According to a local police report, Tigers first baseman Miguel Cabrera only connected on a pitiful 13 of 67 swings during an altercation with his wife Saturday, bringing his average down to .194 for the day, with a laughable .220 slugging percentage this month. "The guy'll swing at anything," Cabrera's wife, Rosangel, told reporters. "The truth is, he's been whiffing all year. When he does make contact, it's just a little dinker here and a dinker there." Though Cabrera continues to struggle, the scratches on his face indicate that his wife could be on pace to hit well over .400 this year. ∅

Orlando Cabrera Hates Metrodome's Tuna Casserole Smell

AUGUST 6, 2009

MINNEAPOLIS—Recently acquired Twins shortstop Orlando Cabrera admitted Sunday that he is disgusted by the overpowering stench of tuna casserole in the Hubert H. Humphrey Metrodome. "Every time I enter the stadium the awful smell makes me sick to my stomach," said Cabrera, adding that he was unable to determine the source of the foul odor but suspected years of tuna casserole might be ground into the seats, the FieldTurf, and the fabric of the Metrodome itself. "Why does it always stink like rancid mayonnaise and fish? Now the smell's in my uniform, too. I can't wait to leave for our road games." Twins owner Jim Pohlad, who claimed he could not smell anything abnormal, has reportedly denied Cabrera's requests to air out the Metrodome by perforating the roof. ∅

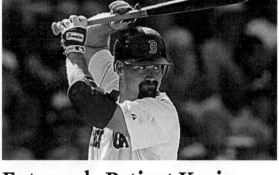

Extremely Patient Kevin Youkilis Works Count To 6-5

AUGUST 1, 2009

BOSTON—Showing the discerning eye and patient bat that have become his hallmark, the Red Sox' Kevin Youkilis pushed a third-inning at bat to a six-and-five count before finally working a walk on Tuesday. "That 5-4 pitch was tough, but in that spot I'm looking for something to drive," said Youkilis, who was down 0-3 in the count before taking the next five pitches for balls. "My job there is to make the starter work, so I usually just take the first eight pitches or so to give myself an idea of what he's got to offer. Then I try to foul off another 10 or so to get his pitch count way up. A lot of people say the most important pitch is strike one, but I've always found it to be strike seven. Because at that point you're only three pitches away from strike 10." Despite the walk, Youkilis was cut down on the base paths trying to steal fourth base. ∅

Derek Jeter Makes Easy Play Look Easy

JULY 14, 2009

NEW YORK—Thanks to his vaunted grace and tremendous skill, Yankees captain Derek Jeter was able Tuesday night to make a pop-up to shortstop look as routine as it actually was. "Look at him effortlessly settle under that ball and close his glove around it as it falls slowly in," gushed Yankees radio announcer John Sterling, who also had the privilege of broadcasting Jeter's catch of a soft humpback liner in 2002. Teammate Robinson Cano added that "watching him day in and day out, it's easy to lose sight of the fact that everyone makes that kind of play all the time... It's a joy just watching him glide up the middle, catch the ball on a stolen base attempt, and lay down the tag as if he's done it a million times before, which he has. What a teammate." Later in the inning, Jeter made an easy play look difficult with that jump-throw thing he doesn't need to do. ∅

Carlos Lee Befriends Anthill In Left Field

JULY 17, 2009

HOUSTON—Upon discovering an anthill in left field during Saturday's game against the Nationals, Astros Carlos Lee reportedly befriended the colony of red ants by introducing himself to each of the insects individually. "My little ant friends are so nice and they don't get mad at me when I come over and talk to them like Hunter Pence does," said Lee, who reportedly placed his head on the ground next to the anthill to appear less intimidating to the ants. "They're my best little buddies in the whole world. They tickle the inside of my nose and give me stingy kisses." Lee held a candlelight memorial after the game to honor the thousands of ants that were tragically killed when he crushed the anthill while fielding a fly ball. ∅

STRONG SIDE/ WEAK SIDE: ALBERT PUJOLS

STRONG SIDE	WEAK SIDE
Five-time Gold Goatee winner	Only the best hitter in one sport
Always in his workshop tinkering with new home runs	Can't hit a home run without the help of a big wooden bat
Makes contact every time he hits the ball	When he crosses his arms, he looks a little too intimidating
Finds the time to bond with fans by spraying screaming line drives into stand	Is Dominican, but not the fun kind like David Ortiz or Manny Ramirez
Enjoys both dirt and grass equally	Could show a little self-respect and not spread his legs so far apart in his stance
Is really great at standing not too far from but not too close to first base	Aside from the steroid report that is going to come out and tarnish all his accomplishments he has no real weak side as a player

STRONG SIDE/ WEAK SIDE: DEREK JETER

STRONG SIDE	WEAK SIDE
He's Derek Jeter	Underrated how overrated he is
Does the little things so he doesn't have to hit a lot of home runs or play solid defense	Has never been anywhere in New York outside of Yankee Stadium
Comes through with clutch fist-pump when it matters most	Often strikes out so he can get back to the dugout and make sure no one takes his seat
Wins the World Series at least once a year	Wins game with boring old grounders
One of only one active MLB players to have 2,700 hits, 3 Gold Gloves, 4 World Series rings, and the last name "Jeter"	Though he's been linked to some of the world's most beautiful women, he's also been linked to Mariah Carey
He's not A-Rod	Jesus Christ, that jump-throw thing

Controversial Sabermetrician Posits That There Is No Such Thing As Baseball

AUGUST 7, 2009

NEW YORK—Saying that there are no pitchers, fielders, or batters, only numbers and statistics, radical sabermetrician Kyle Osterman theorized Wednesday that there is no such thing as baseball. "Some say people wear gloves. Do they? Why? There is no ball. There is only the curvilinear progression of the ball," said Osterman, who later broke down Bill Mazeroski's World Series–winning home run into nothing more than a combination of likelihood estimates that are systematically null and void because, as Osterman said, "There really was no such thing as Bill Mazeroski." "Everything that happens on the field is part of a predetermined numbers matrix. Every final outcome is fixed, so ultimately, there can be no game." Osterman then cracked open a beer and proceeded to watch the Red Sox play the Tampa Bay Rays on ESPN. ∅

Not Knowing How To Celebrate, A-Rod Breaks Champagne Bottle Over Teammates' Heads

OCTOBER 15, 2009

MINNEAPOLIS—Following the Yankees' Game 3 victory over the Twins in the ALDS Sunday, Alex Rodriguez demonstrated a complete lack of understanding of the most basic celebratory techniques when he broke bottles of champagne over several of his teammates' heads. "We were all screaming and cheering, but he just laughed in this weird monotone for a minute or so, then lifted his arm straight up, smashed a bottle on Melky [Cabrera]'s head, and rubbed the shards of glass into Melky's eyes," teammate Robinson Cano said. "He fired a cork into [Nick] Swisher's face from point-blank range, too. Then he just ran around in tiny circles for about 10 minutes. It was bizarre." Rodriguez's publicist later released a statement of apology indicating that, from this point forward, the Yankee third baseman would jump on home plate with the rest of his teammates after game-winning hits, and would no longer try to lick everyone's face. ∅

Documentary Manny Ramirez Talking About Turns Out To Be 'Billy Madison'

AUGUST 17, 2009

LOS ANGELES—After less than five minutes listening to Manny Ramirez describe a "powerful documentary" about a son who struggles to take over his father's business, Dodgers teammates

concluded that the perennial all-star was actually talking about the 1995 Adam Sandler comedy *Billy Madison*. "I kind of figured it was *Billy Madison* when Manny started talking about 'the bad man' who tried to take the company from the opera singer from *Saturday Night Live*," teammate Mark Loretta said. "And when he said the most interesting part was learning that penguins can 'grow to be as tall as men,' that pretty much clinched it." Ramirez later told his teammates he was looking forward to a new documentary about the the auto industry, in which an overweight man and a skinny man travel across America in an attempt to sell brake pads. ∅

Stadium Bursts Out Laughing After Jamie Moyer Pitch

AUGUST 25, 2009

PHILADELPHIA—A subpar season during which Phillies pitcher Jamie Moyer has amassed a five-plus ERA and been demoted to the bullpen got worse Sunday after the 46-year-old veteran uncorked a 73-mph fastball, eliciting spontaneous laughter and giggles from each of the 43,489 fans at Citizens Bank Park. "I thought it was the most hilarious joke, but then I saw the look on his face and I realized he was serious," said attendee Matthew King, who added that he was barely able to keep a straight face

for the rest of the game. "When the pitch speed didn't even register on the scoreboard, beer literally shot out my nose. My entire section was doubled over. Even the batter [Mark Reynolds] was just crying laughing." Immediately following the pitch, a tearful Moyer sprinted off the field and yelled at manager Charlie Manuel, saying that it was Manuel's fault that he was on the mound in the first place. ∅

Kevin Youkilis Keeps Everyone On Bus Awake With Another One Of His Nasty Sex Stories

SEPTEMBER 7, 2009

TAMPA, FL— Red Sox infielder Kevin Youkilis reportedly prevented everyone on the team bus from sleeping Monday when he  loudly described in disgusting detail the elasticity and mucus secretions of his girlfriend's vagina. "Man, she was pretty hot and bothered, because I'd been stirring up her soup for a while," said Youkilis, adding that her neatly trimmed pubic hair and thighs, as well as their sheets, were all soaked in "pussy juice." "She's a squirter, so her vag was pretty much a fountain by the time I started fisting. She was so slick, I had to put on a batting glove to get some traction." Pitcher Clay Buchholz said he has not slept since last Wednesday, when Youkilis went on about the "foul smell of dried semen that collects in your belly button." ∅

Teammates Fully Support Jonathan Papelbon's Claim That Playoff Loss Was His Fault

OCTOBER 16, 2009

BOSTON—Every member of the Boston Red Sox stood behind teammate Jonathan Papelbon during clubhouse interviews Sunday, vociferously defending the embattled reliever's assertion that the team's first-round sweep by the Angels was entirely his fault. "Pap is one of the best in the game, and if he says he single-handedly blew the series, then I'm with him," said second baseman Dustin Pedroia, who agreed that the closer's Game 3 ninth-inning meltdown was "100 percent on Papelbon." "Sometimes you have a bad day, and sometimes that bad day ruins an entire year's worth of work in the blink of an eye. I'm happy to go to war with a man who knows when he fails so totally and completely." Though Papelbon expressed appreciation for his teammates' backing, he did mention that he never actually said anything like that. ∅

Mark McGwire Admits It Was Really Fucking Fun Hitting Baseballs So Far

JANUARY 15, 2009

NEW YORK—Former St. Louis Cardinals slugger, onetime single-season home run record holder, and admitted steroid abuser Mark McGwire came clean Monday, confessing that it was really fucking fun being able to hit baseballs so hard and far.

"I can't remember having a better time in all of my life," McGwire said during an hour-long interview with the MLB Network's Bob Costas. "Do you have any idea what it's like knowing instantly that a ball you hit is going to fly—no, soar—over a fence in a major-league stadium? Well, I do. And it's fucking fantastic."

"I'm sorry everyone had a problem with it," McGwire added. "But I was having a blast."

Though McGwire told Costas there were times he almost regretted taking anabolic steroids, the former Oakland Athletics star said that, considering the tons of fun the performance-enhancing substances allowed him to have, he never thought twice about his decision.

"I was hitting baseballs over 450 feet," McGwire said. "That's really far. And high, too. Oh my God, were they high. Towering, in fact. I was, like, crushing these things."

According to McGwire, he had the most fun during the 1998 season, when he fired off 70 home runs and broke

see MCGWIRE

Mickey Mouse Noticeably Avoids A-Rod During Trip To Disney World

NOVEMBER 17, 2009

ORLANDO, FL—Members of the Yankees couldn't help but notice that the resort's iconic mascot Mickey Mouse made a special effort to avoid Alex Rodriguez during the team's trip to Walt Disney World to celebrate its World Series victory. "I thought it was weird that whenever Alex would yell, 'Mickey, over here,' Mickey would just walk in the opposite direction," said teammate Johnny Damon, adding that he would never have noticed Mickey's many attempts to avoid the third baseman had Rodriguez not been following the cartoon character around with a little autograph book. "But then we had breakfast with the characters, and Mickey went  around and hugged Derek [Jeter] and Mark [Teixeira], even our bullpen catcher. Then he just kind of peeled off when he got to A-Rod." Rodriguez was later seen having an intense, one-sided conversation with Rescue Rangers Chip and Dale about being a famous athlete living in New York City. ∅

from **MCGWIRE**

Roger Maris' single-season long-ball record. McGwire said he had the second-most fun the following year, when he hit 65 home runs, many of which, the giddy slugger proclaimed, "went for miles and miles."

However, a visibly emotional McGwire admitted that he had absolutely no fun in 1993 and 1994, when he was plagued by injuries and hit just nine home runs each season. At that time, the first baseman explained, the balls were either going high and not that far or traveling too low and not that hard.

"That was a drag. Don't get me wrong, just hitting the ball really high in the air can be cool sometimes, even if you get out," said McGwire, adding that it's enjoyable to watch a routine pop-fly that goes "way, way up there." "But I was getting out a lot during those years, so I had to do whatever was necessary to hit the ball really high, far, and hard all the time."

"High plus far plus hard equals big-time, serious fun," McGwire continued.

McGwire also said that his decade-long steroid abuse had little to do with gaining an edge on his competition and more to do with his observation of how players who didn't hit the ball very far were not enjoying the game.

"I would look at a guy like John Olerud just kind of hitting these dinky ground balls, and I would say to myself, 'No way this guy's having a good time,'" McGwire said. "All I know is, when I got up to the plate, the outfielders would back all the way up because I hit the ball so far. I really enjoyed that."

"I also liked hitting it over their heads," McGwire added while flexing his right bicep and then making a swinging motion with his arms. "Crack! Home run."

According to the three-time Silver Slugger Award winner, the fun he was having also seemed to make everyone else—including teammates, fans, and Major League Baseball commissioner Bud Selig—have fun while they watched his at bats.

McGwire said that the main thing he learned in his 16 years as a player was that people tend to be happier when players are hitting the ball really far.

"By their reactions, I just figured they were cool with me taking steroids and having a good time," McGwire said. "They clearly knew I was taking performance-enhancing drugs, right? I mean, look at me. I look like a fucking monster. Plus, come on—I was hitting the ball really, really fucking far." ∅

Dusty Baker Destroys Aroldis Chapman's Arm Within Minutes Of Arrival

JANUARY 18, 2010

CINCINNATI—Within just a few minutes of Cuban pitcher Aroldis Chapman's arrival in the United States, Reds manager Dusty Baker had already overused and mangled the 21-year-old's arm beyond recognition, team sources reported Sunday. Baker, who has been accused of overtaxing young pitchers' arms in the past, reportedly greeted Chapman with a bucket of 250 baseballs and told him to "hurl them" as fast as he could, later encouraging the fastballer to "go nuts" with his pitching style. "He didn't even let me stretch out first," Chapman told reporters through an interpreter. "And when I started to wince from the pain and soreness, he just gave me a thumbs up, winked, and told me to keep throwing." At press time, Chapman had already been to the hospital for an oblique strain, a torn rotator cuff, and his second Tommy John surgery of the week. ∅

Seeing Ken Griffey Jr. In Backwards Hat Now Just Depressing

APRIL 2, 2010

SEATTLE—Baseball fans across the nation admitted Monday that the sight of Ken Griffey Jr. in a backwards baseball cap—an iconic image that once filled fans with joy and promise and a feeling that maybe, just maybe, eternal youth was possible—now makes them feel completely and utterly depressed.

"To see him wear his hat like that is actually heartbreaking," 27-year-old Seattle resident Peter Morley said of Griffey, who is hitting .152 this spring training. "It just doesn't look right anymore, you know? It doesn't look natural."

"Maybe it's because his face is fatter," Morley added.

As the 40-year-old Griffey begins his 22nd season, fans say the sight of the once-lean five-tool player flipping his cap around is no longer synonymous with athletic excellence, infinite potential, or effortless cool. Instead, they claim it is a sad reminder of how

time takes its toll on the body, how we try to relive our former glory but never quite do, and how the prime of our life passes in an instant.

Fans also say that Griffey's backwards cap reminds them, especially those of them in their mid- to late 20s, that their childhoods are most definitely over.

"This is going to sound weird, and I can't quite describe why, but seeing Griffey with his hat backwards used to make me feel like summertime. Does that make any sense?" said a fan, who wished to remain anonymous, adding that 16 years ago he purchased a fitted Seattle Mariners cap and wore it backwards every day to emulate Griffey. "I can't believe I'm saying this, but now I wear my hats forwards simply because he still wears his hat backwards. It's just too painful."

Fans say the sight of Griffey in a backwards hat was most uplifting in the early to mid-1990s, be-

fore his move to Cincinnati. Their joy at seeing his face beneath the bill-less cap reportedly peaked during the 1993 Home Run Derby when Griffey, hat turned round on his head, became the first player to hit the warehouse beyond the right field fence at Camden Yards.

However, during Griffey's injury-plagued seasons from 2000 to 2007, the sight of the backwards hat caused feelings of frustration, anger, and hopelessness, and eventually became associated in their minds with countless utterances of the phrase, "Get up, you're fine. Please get up. Oh, God."

The moment of complete and utter despair came yesterday as Griffey hit a now-rare home run during batting practice and cheering fans realized they were fooling themselves into thinking 2010 would be a fairy-tale season.

"I honestly believed that, when he returned to Seattle last year, seeing his Mariners hat turned backwards again would make me feel better," said Seattle resident David Jaffe, adding that the sight of Griffey in a backwards White Sox cap sent him into a downward spiral he'd like to forget. "But when I actually saw him it just made me more upset. It finally dawned on me that I'm this pathetic guy trying to recapture a moment in 1994 that will never exist again."

According to a *Sporting News* poll, 43 percent of baseball fans can't even bear to look at Griffey wearing his hat backwards. Another 24 percent say the visual reminds them of torn hamstrings.

see **GRIFFEY**

Manny Embarks On Journey To Find Legendary Realm Of Batlantis

JUNE 25, 2010

LOS ANGELES—In his on-going quest to find the finest and most powerful baseball bat ever crafted, Dodgers outfielder Manny Ramirez embarked on an epic voyage Tuesday to search for the legendary underwater kingdom of Batlantis.

"I need to get down there under the waves to the bottom of the water to look for Batlantis so I can get the best bat in the world," said Ramirez, addressing reporters from the back of the 30-foot boat he had specially chartered for the journey. "You have to ask the person in charge of Batlantis if you can have the bat. Then they have to give you the bat if they say yes."

"I want that bat, man," Ramirez added.

According to Ramirez, the lost Batlantean civilization is located beneath a massive retractable dome somewhere on the ocean floor, and is only

visible to worthy sluggers. Ramirez confirmed that the utopian city was founded by a race of blue-green half-god, half-man, half-MVP creatures in order to develop advanced hitting methods and

practice mystical swinging techniques.

The underwater fantasia, Ramirez confirmed, also maintains orchard groves in which they cultivate

see **BATLANTIS**

SPORTS GRAPHIC

Presidential First Pitches

APRIL 9, 2010

The president throwing out the ceremonial first pitch is as revered a tradition as anything in America. We look at some of the most memorable.

➤ **1833:** Although the popularization of baseball is still decades off, Andrew Jackson begins the tradition of welcoming in the spring by hurling things at Indians

➤ **1944:** FDR laboriously rolls his wheelchair out to the pitching mound, then stuns the crowd with a 100 mph fastball

➤ **1949:** Thomas E. Dewey is nearly finished with his windup before Harry Truman snatches the ball from his hand

➤ **1965:** LBJ scratches his crotch for a full eight minutes before delivering the first pitch

➤ **1975:** Although Gerald Ford did not fall while throwing out the first pitch of the season, everyone in attendance remembers him doing so

➤ **1988:** All set to make his first pitch, President Reagan notices the ball in his hand, puts it in his pocket, and wanders toward the A's clubhouse

➤ **2001:** Fans at Miller Park avert their eyes and nervously pretend to check their watches as George W. Bush walks out to the mound in full catcher's gear

➤ **2007:** Vice President Dick Cheney becomes the first person to throw a first pitch to complete silence

from **GRIFFEY**

And 33 percent of respondents said that images of Alex Rodriguez, Prince Fielder, or CC Sabathia wearing their hats backwards just aren't the same, and actually make things much worse.

One hundred percent of respondents said they'd like to see Griffey play 10 more years and break every record there is, adding, "Fuck you if you don't believe he can do it."

"You know what? I saw a recent picture of him with his hat backwards, and if you looked at it from the right angle, you could believe he had just one chin, and the gray hairs in his goatee were actually noth-

ing more than the spring sunlight shining through," said Michael Dorenzo, who, despite being from New York, is a hardcore Seattle Mariners fan because of Griffey. "He was 'The Kid' again."

"Jesus Christ," he continued, suddenly growing morose. "Who am I kidding? I guess we all have to die some day."

When asked for comment during a press conference yesterday, Griffey, his hat backwards, smiled broadly, and for one brief moment appeared to be the same man who led Seattle to the ALCS in 1995.

He then coughed wildly, sending the cap flying off his head. *∅*

Everyone In Red Sox Locker Room Just Assumed Jason Varitek Died

APRIL 05, 2010

BOSTON—Catcher Jason Varitek's entrance into the Boston clubhouse Tuesday was punctuated by startled shouts and the clatter of dropped objects,

as his Red Sox teammates explained that they had all just assumed the veteran player had died. "I could have sworn he died after the All-Star break," second baseman Dustin Pedroia, who sent flowers and

a card to Varitek's family, told reporters. "I don't remember seeing him on base at all last season, much less in the line-up or catching. I thought that's why we got Victor [Martinez], because Jason was dead.

Right?" Though Pedroia insisted that it was good to see his teammate again, he was still not entirely convinced that Varitek was not dead after watching him take a round of batting practice. *∅*

MLB Opening Day Marred By Strikeouts

APRIL 9, 2010

NEW YORK—Players, coaches, fans, and Commissioner Bud Selig expressed concern for the state of professional baseball Monday after MLB's highly anticipated Opening Day was "completely ruined" by a rash of strikeouts that began during the afternoon games and didn't end until the day was over. "I know players can be a little rusty, but there were strikeouts in literally every single game," said Selig, adding that in some cases there had been more than one strikeout per inning. "I want to assure the fans that things will improve. If these batters put in a little more effort and try to focus, we don't have to have another strikeout this season." Selig, who also condemned MLB hitters for an unreasonable number of fly-outs, pop-ups, and groundouts, threatened to cancel the 2010 season after learning the league's pitchers gave up 96 walks. ⌀

True Yankees, Regular Yankees To Now Wear Different Uniforms

APRIL 27, 2010

NEW YORK—The New York Yankees unveiled a new, lesser uniform at a press conference Tuesday in an effort to distinguish ordinary, run-of-the-mill Yankees from the "true Yankee legends who walk among us." "To have Javier Vazquez don the same pinstripes as Mariano Rivera or Jorge Posada is...well, it's unthinkable," Yankees general manager Brian Cashman said as Curtis Granderson modeled the sterile, black-and-white uniform with a large, boxy, non-interlocking "NY" stitched across the front of the chest. "The untrue Yankees will wear a blank, unfitted ball cap until they have their big Yankee moment. They'll wear their last names on the backs of their lesser uniforms as a badge of shame." When asked which uniform he was assigned, Alex Rodriguez cried for 10 minutes. ⌀

Prince Fielder Satisfies Curiosity By Eating Small Handful Of Dirt

MAY 11, 2010

MILWAUKEE—Saying that he has been wondering about its taste for quite some time, Brewers first baseman Prince Fielder was witnessed putting small clumps of infield dirt into his mouth during the fourth inning of Monday night's game against the Pittsburgh Pirates. "There was a little bit of time between warm-ups and the first batter, so I figured I'd finally give it a try," Fielder told reporters after the game, adding that because of dirt's brown coloring, he was curious if it would taste like chocolate. "It wasn't bad. Not great. But not bad." In the past, Fielder has been seen nibbling on his baseball glove, bat, and the Wrigley Field ivy. ⌀

Tony Gwynn Mentioned 72 Times During Guided Tour Of Padres Stadium

MAY 4, 2010

SAN DIEGO—Hall of Famer Tony Gwynn's name was uttered 72 times and indirectly referenced on another 36 instances during a guided tour of Petco Park, sources reported Tuesday. "There's Tony Gwynn's No. 19 over the center field wall there, and beyond that is the picnic area where countless Padre fans have chanted Tony Gwynn's name or at least thought about Tony Gwynn," said tour guide Hank Classon, adding that Tony Gwynn would have patrolled right field in Petco Park had he not retired three years before it opened. "Our groundskeepers always keeps the pitcher's mound pristine, since that's where we wish to have Padres great Tony Gwynn throw out the first pitch of all our future games. Look, everyone, there's manager Bud Black! Yes, I wish he were Tony Gwynn." Current Padres slugger Adrian Gonzalez was mentioned zero times. ⌀

from BATLANTIS

the hardest wood in the universe.

"Getting to Batlantis will not be easy, because I have to go through the wettest part of the ocean and they keep the bat inside a giant clam that's all locked up," Ramirez said. "But it will be worth it for the bat, man. It make wishes, man. Seriously. You can have as many home runs as you want."

While preparing for the undersea expedition, the Dodgers outfielder purchased a wide variety of equipment including scuba gear, a wet suit, a poncho, an umbrella, 40 pairs of batting gloves, Breathe Right nasal strips, and ziplock bags he planned to use "to hold extra air."

Acknowledging the many dangers that lurk below the sea—especially the poison-toothed eels that guard Batlantis' gates—Ramirez said he was also equipped with a batting helmet and a torpedo.

"I'm bringing my swimming trunks for when the boat swirls around in the giant whirlpool on the way to Batlantis," said Ramirez, adding that he is not packing his baseball mitt because defense is strictly forbidden in Batlantis. "The whirlpool is the key, man. It sucks you in. You find that and you find Batlantis."

"Batlantis is big, man," Ramirez added. "It's underwater."

This will be Ramirez's fourth attempt to locate the elusive realm of Batlantis. Two years ago, a solo expedition was thwarted when Ramirez was unable to find plane tickets to the Bermuda Triangle on Orbitz.com. In 2004, engine failure caused by driving his car into the Pacific Ocean prevented the slugger from discovering the underwater batting kingdom. And Ramirez said he found a portal to Batlantis in 2002 but was unable to squeeze through the grate at the bottom of a swimming pool in his neighbor's backyard.

"The place is so cool I don't know if I'll ever want to leave," said Ramirez, adding that mermaids serve an elixir that increases your muscle mass and on-base percentage, and is untraceable. "They have on-deck circles that are way rounder than ours. And they have gold thrones in the dugout. You pull a lever on the side and your feet go up, man. You get all relaxed."

Ramirez reportedly assembled a Batlantis exploration crew by convincing sluggers David Ortiz, Jim Thome, and Prince Fielder that they could triple their batting averages by missing no more than a month's worth of games. In addition, the slugger regaled the group with fantastic tales of crystalline palaces, breathtaking ballparks, and an extremely large Modell's sporting goods store.

Ramirez also said when they arrived at Batlantis a decadent feast of hot dogs, peanuts, and caramel corn would be held in their honor.

"We are going to do this and we will find Batlantis and take turns sharing the bat," said the 12-time All-Star. "They have a lot of batting cages and the sharks can't get in. They can't chew up your bat or arms or head." ⌀

PHOTO FINISH
George Steinbrenner Dead After Firing Under-performing Heart

Yogi Berra: 'Why Aren't The Yankees Mourning My Death?

JULY 24, 2010

NEW YORK—Hall of Famer Yogi Berra expressed frustration and disappointment during a press conference Monday, asking why the Yankees organization had made no effort to mourn his death in 2006. "I've given a lot to this team and yet they haven't done a single thing to honor me or show their grief," said the visibly distressed 85-year-old, adding that the team could have at least worn a uniform patch featuring Berra's initials. "I died over three years ago and didn't even get a stinking moment of silence. Well, you know what they say about dying: They don't say it." Berra added that at the very minimum the Yankees should let him address the crowd to say goodbye one last time. ⌀

New Hank Aaron Biography Reveals He Hated Hitting Home Runs

MAY 24, 2010

NEW YORK—In a stunning revelation that has sent shockwaves through the baseball world, Howard Bryant's recently published biography, *The Last Hero: The Life Of Henry Aaron*, reports that the Hall of Fame slugger actually despised hitting home runs. "They felt disgusting. Revolting. That's why I put off hitting the record-breaking home run for so long," Aaron says in an interview that appears in a chapter titled "Chasing The Bambino." "Lifting up my head to track the ball through the sky gave me terrible migraines, and I actually despised hitting the sweet spot of the bat. You couldn't feel anything. Nothing, except complete and utter emptiness." In the book, Aaron also reveals that he loved to bunt, claiming that he never felt more alive than when he'd tap the ball with his bat and watch it roll several inches and stop. ⌀

Fans Of High-Pitched Pinging Sounds Tune In For College World Series

MAY 24, 2010

OMAHA, NE—With the NCAA baseball regionals underway, fans of high-pitched pinging tones are already anticipating an exciting and auditorially rich College World Series. "Lovers of baseball and of percussive metallic upper-treble sonic phenomena wait all year for this," longtime LSU fan Greg Nguyen told reporters Friday, adding that he will take time off from his job as a sonar technician on the submarine USS San Juan to go to Omaha later this month. "I'm rooting for the Tigers, I guess, but really I'm just hoping for a lot of loud, resonant aluminum to cork-encased-with-cowhide contact." If his team wins the College World Series, Nguyen plans to propose to his girlfriend, fellow baseball fan and professional glockenspiel player Noelle McAdams.. ⌀

Area Man Tries To Throw Split-Fingered Fastball, Breaks Arm In 9 Places

MAY 26, 2010

COLUMBUS, OH—Local resident Thomas Pickford, 43, suffered breaks in his right pisiform, scaphoid, and lunate carpals; two separate fractures of the coronoid process; and four radial breaks, including one spiral fracture, as he attempted to demonstrate to his son how to throw a split-fingered fastball in their backyard on Thursday. "So you just jam the ball in between your second and third fingers here real tight, don't forget to spin your arm as fast as it'll go, and then you rear back and—No. Oh, God," Pickford said, before grabbing his arm and collapsing to the ground. "Get your mom, get your mom, get your mom." Late next year, Pickford will dislocate both of his knees while trying to show his youngest daughter how to take a jump shot. ⌀

SPORTS GRAPHIC

Highlights Of George Steinbrenner's Reign

JULY 23, 2010

His legacy is a strange mixture of winning baseball and strained relationships, but there's no denying George Steinbrenner was a colorful and remarkable man. We remember his defining moments.

➤ **1973:** Within the first months of Steinbrenner's ownership, Yankees manager Ralph Houk is overwhelmed by an inexplicable desire to resign

➤ **1975:** Steinbrenner fires Billy Martin 16 times during the job interview

➤ **1983:** Though Dave Righetti pitches a no-hitter against the Red Sox for Steinbrenner's 52nd birthday, the Yankees owner is upset because he really wanted the new Eurythmics album

➤ **1985:** In a special ceremony at Yankee Stadium, Steinbrenner presents manager Yogi Berra with an oversized pink slip

➤ **1989:** The modern era of the Republican Party is entirely encapsulated in one pen stroke as Ronald Reagan pardons George Steinbrenner for his illegal contributions to the Richard Nixon campaign

➤ **1990:** The Yankees reach an agreement to pay a stipend to Major League Baseball in exchange for allowing Steinbrenner to say whatever the hell he wants

➤ **2004:** Pretty much acts like a cock the entire year

➤ **2009:** Steinbrenner's fading health becomes impossible to ignore as he asks his nurse over and over if she has found any dirt on Dave Winfield yet

➤ **2010:** With his dying breath, Steinbrenner encourages his sons to charge fans by the inning

THE MAGAZINE

The Nation's PITCHING MOUNDS

Are We Prepared If They Suddenly Erupt With Molten Lava?

INSIDE
Sex And Sports: Twelve Youth Hockey Coaches Speak

The 1985 Royals: Does Anyone Remember If They Won The World Series?

PLUS
Michael Phelps' Publicist Begs Us To Do Just One More Story On Him

Rookie Strasburg Begins Hazing Nationals Veterans

JUNE 15, 2010

WASHINGTON—Though Nationals rookie Stephen Strasburg has only played in two major league games, the right-handed phenom has asserted his dominance in the clubhouse by hazing his veteran teammates, eyebrow-lacking sources confirmed Thursday. "He took my jockstrap and put Icy Hot around the edges of it," said Nationals pitcher and 15-year veteran Livan Hernandez, adding that the rookie had made the team run naked from the Capitol Building to the Washington Monument the previous night. "If we get mad at the hazing, he slaps your stomach really hard in the shower. And then your stomach gets all red." At press time, Strasburg was psyching out his teammates by sitting at his locker with a demented smile on his face while turning an electric hair clipper on and off. ⌀

Report: Still 12,000 More Games Left In 2010 Baseball Season

AUGUST 17, 2010

NEW YORK—With the All-Star Game a distant memory and opening day almost 62,000 games ago, Major League Baseball teams still have 12,000 more games to play before the start of the 2010 playoffs. "It's certainly a very long season," said 32-year-old Chicago resident Doug Meyer, adding that he stopped paying attention to baseball after his Cubs lost their 18,000th game, which put them half a million games out of first place. "I was actually surprised to learn there were only 12,000 games left, because to me it feels like there are 20- or 40,000 more. In fact, sometimes it seems like the season will never end at all." Meyer later tried to remember if a team plays 90,162 games in a season or 90,161. ⌀

The Quotable Ozzie Guillen

AUGUST 8, 2010

The colorful White Sox manager is in the spotlight for comments about supposed favoritism toward Asian players, but it isn't the first time he's had something to say.

➤ **2006:** "I very much love the people and the fans of Chicago, because they pay me very much to play a baseball manager in Chicago, even though I very much hate the people and fans in Chicago"

➤ **2006:** "I don't give shit about the home-field advantages for the World Series. You know what I care about? Where the fuck is the Smash Mouth? Why aren't they here for singing the 'All Star' song? I love that shit"

➤ **2007:** "I love Dustin Pedroia. He is very good hitter. And he has a strong back, so he could be climbed up on and I sit on his shoulders and ride around on him like riding a little horse that loves me and eats apples and I have to pitch around because he is a good hitter"

➤ **2008:** "I never say one bad thing about those stupid fucking Cubs fans. Not a single word about those mother-shitting pieces of fuck"

➤ **2008:** "If we win the World Series, I will quit baseball and run for mayor mostly on a campaign platform of minimizing the city's budget, while still raising revenues with strategic tax plan for Chicago businesses"

➤ **2009:** "Wrigley Field makes me puke. When I eat a little bit of the ivy on the wall it make me puke barf everywhere"

➤ **2010:** It's not the fair for Japanese players to have the interpreter. I want the interpreter so I can understand what the fuck it is I am talk about"

Exhausted Ken Burns Urges Baseball To Stop

OCTOBER 1, 2010

WALPOLE, NH—Exhausted and haggard documentarian Ken Burns begged Major League Baseball to cease operations Tuesday, saying that any future games, trades, or league action would warrant further installments of the filmmaker's sprawling, now 23-hour-long documentary *Baseball*.

Burns' announcement came after PBS's broadcast of *Baseball: The Tenth Inning*, an update to the series that covers the years 1994 to the present. Addressing reporters, a gaunt and drawn Burns said that exploring the ever-evolving relationship between Americans and their national pastime was slowly killing him.

"I can't do this anymore," Burns said. "The more baseball that is played, the more I have to document. But it's futile. The documentary will never end, because in order for it to end, baseball itself would have to end. I'm always playing catch-up ball. *The Tenth Inning, The Eleventh Inning, The 2,945th Inning*. Christ, how many more of these things will I have to make?"

"Please—if not for my sake, then for the sake of my wife and children, please stop," Burns continued. "If you don't, I will die knowing that baseball has kept going, and that the thing I'm most famous for will be remembered as an incomplete failure."

According to Burns, as long as baseball is played, he will always feel a perpetual com-

pulsion to film storylines that not only reflect the state of the game but also make a broader point about society itself. The worn-out filmmaker rhetorically asked reporters who, if not Burns himself, would be the one to spend countless hours documenting the historic significance of a second dead-ball era, or a Chicago Cubs World Series title.

"Say, for example, baseball doesn't stop, the 2011 season begins, and by the All-Star break fans start saying things like, 'During the Great Recession, baseball served as a national escape from dire economic times,'" Burns continued. "That's another goddamn inning right there. Sure, it's only two hours to you, but to me it's 20-hour days for the next two years of my life."

Burns told reporters he spends sleepless night after sleepless night worrying that more postseasons could potentially lead to the Philadelphia Phillies becoming

the modern era's version of a dynasty, a theme he would have to tirelessly explore if he ever wanted to truly document the history of the sport. Moreover, Burns said that if the Yankees ceased to exist, viewers wouldn't expect a future segment devoted to Yogi Berra's eventual passing that draws parallels between both the death of a bygone era in baseball history and the death of a more innocent time in U.S. history.

Burns added he also wouldn't mind if he never had to talk to Bob Costas or Billy Crystal ever again.

"I guess I really backed myself into a corner with this whole Baseball thing," Burns said. "The Civil War, Huey Long, Lewis and Clark—none of these topics were open-ended. But baseball. Jesus Christ, what was I thinking?"

According to Burns, when he reunited with coproducer Lynn Novick for *The Tenth*

see KEN BURNS

Pirates Sign Guy Who Successfully Jogged Across Street

JUNE 26, 2010

PITTSBURGH—The Pittsburgh Pirates signed Greensburg, PA resident Clark Goldwater Monday after a team scout witnessed the 36-year-old fan run across a street near PNC Park, hand a set of keys to a friend, and maintain a steady clip on his way back to the parking lot to continue tailgating. "We've been looking for a guy with this kind of ability for a long time," said Pirates manager John Russell, adding that Goldwater will start in left field for the Triple-A Indianapolis Indians Thursday. "And hearing that he only needed two strides to cross over the grass median strip tells me he might be able to stretch out a double. Players like that don't come around every day in Pittsburgh." Team officials are hopeful this decision will work out as well as their 2003 signing of starting pitcher Paul Maholm, whom they acquired after seeing Maholm accurately toss a used tissue into the garbage. Ø

CC Sabathia Involved In Bench-Clearing Nap

JULY 12, 2010

NEW YORK—The entire Yankees squad poured off the bench, out of the dugout, and onto the field Monday after CC Sabathia reacted to a particularly strenuous inning by plopping down on the bench, stretching out, and taking a nap. "When that happens to your pitcher, you just have to support him and get out of the way," said shortstop Derek Jeter, who was one of the first Yankees on his feet when Sabathia began to recline. "In that situation, a good teammate just lets his pitcher sleep. It doesn't matter if he's right or wrong." Umpires were able to clear the field and play resumed shortly after Sabathia woke, although team medics have not yet been able to return Sabathia to an upright position. Ø

Pirates Mathematically Eliminated From Major League Baseball

AUGUST 10, 2010

PITTSBURGH—After losing their fifth straight game Monday, the Pittsburgh Pirates were mathematically eliminated from Major League Baseball, having

fallen to a 36-69 record that officially disqualified the team from ever playing the sport again. "Eventually it comes to a point where there just aren't enough future games to turn things around for a baseball team,"

manager John Russell said following a 4-0 loss to the Reds that ended the Pirates franchise. "I had high hopes that we would go deeper into our regular seasons, but truthfully, we've been playing so lousy for the last 18 years

that even if we got to our 106th game we wouldn't have been able to contend." In response to the Pirates' getting knocked out of professional baseball forever, Pittsburgh fans said that they were frankly relieved. Ø

Yankees Re-Sign Popular Mascot Derek Jeter

DECEMBER 10, 2010

NEW YORK—Following weeks of tense negotiations, the New York Yankees finally agreed Wednesday to a $51 million, three-year deal to bring back the team's much-loved mascot Derek Jeter. "This decision was for the fans, because so many of them come to games just to look at Derek or take pictures with him," Yankees GM Brian Cashman told reporters, adding that the mascot's presence alone is enough to boost team morale. "With his goofy smile and antics on the field, he makes Yankee Stadium a family experience. Kids just love the hilarious way he swings and misses at pitches and struggles to cover ground at shortstop." Cashman hinted that Derek Jeter would have an updated appearance this season, with an improved, slightly balder look. ✍

---

from **KEN BURNS**

Inning, the mere sight of Novick, coupled with the mountains of footage they had to sort through, instantly fatigued him to the point of collapse. Burns said he was less able than ever before to stay awake during his interviews with journalist George Will, and at one point "barked" at historian Doris Kearns Goodwin to wrap it up.

Editors who worked with the filmmaker said they noticed a more drained and indifferent Burns this time around, explaining that the documentarian would enter their editing bay, look at the footage, tell them to "Ken Burns it up," and then leave.

Sources later confirmed that Burns was repeatedly overheard muttering, "Might as well just dedicate my whole fucking life to this shit."

"Truth be told, I don't even like baseball. It's boring, predictable, and tedious," said the 57-year-old, adding that the only time he has ever felt as though his life were a complete waste was when he sat across from his interview subjects as they sang "Take Me Out To The Ball Game." "I've only been to one baseball game, and I left after the fifth inning. I didn't even care that I missed Carlton Fisk's home run."

"All I know is that baseball is an important part of the American experience," he continued, "a stupid, overwrought, and saccharine part, but an important part nevertheless. And that's the only reason I ever wanted to cover it in the first place. But know this: Every second I've spent on this thing has been sheer torture. I am begging the commissioner, fans, and players to let baseball die."

When asked for comment, Commissioner Bud Selig said this baseball season, as well as all subsequent seasons, would go on as scheduled. ✍

KEYS TO THE MATCHUP

World Series 2010

TEXAS RANGERS

- Rather than having a response to Tim Lincecum, simply ignore his pitches; teenagers hate being ignored
- There's no need for Elvis Andrus to be overaggressive on the base paths and steal second twice in a row
- Baseball has no clock, so if you're down 10 runs late, just have your pitcher stand on the mound doing nothing until the Giants forfeit
- Use Vladimir Guerrero as a third-base coach so he can signal to batters when they should swing
- Score three runs a game and you should be fine
- Try to somehow inspire a sense of pride and identity among the reserved and understated people of Texas

SAN FRANCISCO GIANTS

- Should get inspired by the big, stupid World Series patch on side of their caps
- While unconventional, having your worst player pummel Cliff Lee with a baseball bat would end up as a net positive
- Intentionally walk all eight of the Rangers' dangerous hitters until they get to their pitcher
- Don't let anyone find out that Lincecum's hair and Wilson's beard are actually the same thing
- Juan Uribe needs to keep his mouth shut about his hitting abilities because nobody wants to know the best hitter on their team is Juan Uribe
- Giants may not be the best, and may not be the fastest, and may not hit or defend nearly as well; therefore, they should use that to their advantage

---

Girardi Unsure If CC Sabathia Can Walk Out To Mound On 3 Days' Rest

OCTOBER 15, 2010

NEW YORK—Yankees manager Joe Girardi admitted to reporters Wednesday that he still had doubts that starter CC Sabathia could muster the energy and strength to endure walking to the mound on just three days' rest. "I'm fairly sure he can make it about halfway to the mound, but he's going to be exhausted," said Girardi, expressing concerns about the wear and tear on his ace pitcher's body. "Usually he only makes it without collapsing on four days' rest, but this is the ALCS, so he might just have to gut it out. Either way, we are going to keep a close eye on his step count." Girardi said he planned to have Sabathia conserve energy by sitting down between pitches, and intended to have seven or eight players carry the 2007 Cy Young winner into the dugout after each inning. ✍

A-Rod Finally Leads Rangers To World Series

OCTOBER 24, 2010

ARLINGTON, TX—Ten years after signing a record $252 million contract to play baseball in Texas, third baseman Alex Rodriguez finally delivered for the Rangers by leading the franchise to its first-ever World Series. "A-Rod came up big for us this entire series, all the way up until the last out," Rangers manager Ron Washington told reporters during a postgame press conference, saying that the Rangers would have had no chance of beating the New York Yankees without Rodriguez's remarkable performance at the plate. "It was a long time coming, but you have to give the guy credit. He was the Rangers' MVP, no question." Washington added that seeing Rodriguez take Texas to the World Series was one thing, but A-Rod almost single-handedly beating the Yankees was "extra sweet." ✍

After Long Season, Mere Thought Of Double-Play Ball Makes Second Baseman Nauseated

OCTOBER 2, 2010

MINNEAPOLIS—Toronto Blue Jays second baseman Aaron Hill told reporters Saturday evening that after 161 games of baseball, the mere thought of a double-play ball rolling toward the middle infield is enough to make him feel physically ill. "As soon as a runner reaches first, my mind starts filling with thoughts of what I'll have to do if a ground ball is hit to myself or [shortstop] Yunel [Escobar], and I actually start gagging," said Hill, going into even more vivid detail surrounding his thoughts of shallow pop flies. "I'm basically just rooting for strike outs and home runs at this point." When asked if he carried the same sentiment with regard to his plate appearances, Hill explained that he stopped swinging at pitches weeks ago. ✍

Derek Jeter Rejects Move To Outfield By Reminding Yankees That He's Derek Fucking Jeter

MARCH 04, 2011

TAMPA, FL—During a post-workout press conference at the Yankees spring training facility Thursday, shortstop Derek Jeter once again rejected the idea of moving from shortstop to center field, citing the fact that he's Derek fucking Jeter and he'll play whatever fucking position he wants.

"I can see how people might think that moving to center field would be the right thing to do," the 36-year-old said. "I can also see—quite clearly, as a matter of fact—that none of those people are named Derek Jeter. You know, the same Derek Jeter who led the New York fucking Yankees to five World Series titles and restored the entire goddamn organization to prominence after a decade and a half of mediocrity. That Derek Jeter ring a fucking bell for anyone?"

Jeter, who signed a three-year contract with the Yankees this offseason amidst criticism of his defensive quickness and throwing arm, said he would be open to moving to the outfield if he were not 11-time All-Star and future first-ballot Hall of Famer Derek Jeter. However, according to Jeter, that's who he sure as fuck was the last time he looked in the mirror.

"So, I'll be playing whichever dicklick position I goddamn feel like," Jeter added. "Hell, maybe I'll play shortstop, third base,

catcher, second base, and first base all at the same time. Have my own little around-the-horn circle jerk for five fucking hours if the mood strikes me. How'd that sit with everyone? Good? Good."

During the hour-long press conference, Jeter repeatedly clarified that he was only saying what he was saying because he is Derek fucking Jeter and he can say whatever the fuck he wants. When questioned about his inability to cover all parts of the shortstop position, Jeter asked reporters if they were five-time Gold Glove winners, and said that if they weren't, maybe they should just shut their fucking mouths.

At one point during the press conference, Jeter interrupted himself, stopping to see if he could remember which MLB player is the only one in the history of the game to win the All-Star Game MVP Award and the World Series MVP in the same year.

"Oh, that's right, it was New York Yankees shortstop and *Sports Illustrated* Sportsman of the Year Derek Jeter," the 16-year-veteran said. "Oh, wait! I'm Derek Jeter. I won the fucking MVP awards. Me. The same motherfucker who dove into the stands for a pop fly against the Red Sox and came out bloody and bruised. So there's no way I'm the

guy Brian Cashman keeps talking about—the guy who sounds like a fucking quadriplegic who can't move two steps to field a fucking ground ball."

Jeter conceded that there are probably other people named Derek Jeter who would love to play center field for the New York Yankees, and encouraged team management to go out and try and sign one of them. However, he said, because he's the Derek Jeter who last won the league's highest defensive honor in "oh, I dunno, 2000 and fucking 10," he felt that shortstop suited him just fine.

In addition, Jeter said that the last time he checked, not only were Yankees backup shortstops Ramiro Pena and Eduardo Nunez not named Derek Jeter, but they more than likely had never put the most successful baseball organization in the history of the sport on their back season after goddamn season, and probably had never passed Lou fucking Gehrig to become the Yankees all-time hits leader.

"That's Lou Gehrig, the baseball player," Jeter said. "Not Lou Gehrig, the Nuts 4 Nuts guy who sells honey-roasted almonds and gives free blow jobs outside the stadium."

Jeter went on to note that being the Derek Jeter—the same one whose class and commitment

has won over even the staunchest Yankee haters—is also the main reason he'll be the team's leadoff hitter for as long as he wants. It doesn't matter, he said, if the Yankees sign the next incarnation of Rickey Henderson, or fucking God for that matter.

"I bet nobody ever told Yogi Berra that he should stop catching, or told Joe DiMaggio that he should test the market to see if he could get a better offer," Jeter said. "And if they did, they were fucking pricks back then, too. You don't tell Yogi fucking Berra he can't catch, and you sure as shit don't say in the media that Derek Jeter isn't as fast or as good as he used to be, even if it's fucking true."

"You let the guy who's been the captain of your team for the past eight years leave with a little bit of goddamn dignity," Jeter added. "For Christ's sake, the last thing any of us have at the end of our careers is our dignity, and I swear to fucking God, if anybody tries to take that away from me again, I'll play on this team till I'm 95-fucking-years-old and have a colostomy bag tucked under my uniform. I don't care if we lose 162 games a season."

Jeter added that if anybody had a problem with anything he had just said, they could all go fuck themselves, especially that "fat fuck Hank [Steinbrenner]." ∅

Jealous A.J. Pierzynski Builds Catcher's Mound

MLB Quietly Euthanizes 120 Unnecessary Players

MARCH 09, 2011

NEW YORK—In what it called a basic housecleaning move, Major League Baseball euthanized 120 players Wednesday, including Tyler Colvin, Nolan Reimold, and 118 others deemed inconsequential or redundant. "We just saw Ryan Spilborghs and Brett Cecil still taking up major-league roster spots and decided we needed to unclutter things a little," said league rep Gerald Norris, who added that Geoff Blum, Ryan Doumit, Lyle Overbay, and Daric Barton all died quickly and pain-

lessly. "There's always a tremendous glut of outfielders and middle relievers that we try to burn off before every season starts, like your LaTroy Hawkinses and Aaron Heilmans and Jonny Gomes and Josh Willinghams. Then there are just so many prospects to keep track of, so we rounded up Kyle Drabek, Desmond Jennings, and Mike Trout and took care of them. Just clearing out the brush." Norris seemed unconcerned that Ryan Howard was among the euthanized, saying only that his name was really normal-sounding. ∅

CHAPTER THREE

BASKETBALL

Ah, basketball! Lorenzo Charles' last-second slam to lift the Wolfpack over Houston, Christian Laettner's buzzer beater against Kentucky, Michael Jordan's game-winning shot in the 1998 NBA Finals! Years of covering great basketball moments such as these have taught us one simple truth: A reporter need only show up for the last 10 seconds of a basketball game, if he wants to see anything even remotely newsworthy take place. Essentially, the craft of covering basketball is a practice in time management: If a game starts at 8 p.m., a reporter has at least two hours, 29 minutes, and 50 seconds to run errands, return e-mails, and work on personal book projects before he needs to check in to the press booth. As we move further into the 21st century and technology continues to evolve, covering basketball has become even easier. Now a reporter merely has to get online and check the score before determining if he actually needs to be at the game he's covering, secure in the knowledge that if it's a blowout, he can stay at home, watch television, and plagiarize the story off the AP wire, much in the same way baseball has been covered for decades.

1891
James Naismith creates the game of "basketcube" before quickly inventing "basketball" the next day.

1983
The Spurs beat the Nuggets 152-133, though no one really cares because everyone just figures that's how many points are normally scored during a basketball game.

1985
Indiana basketball coach Bobby Knight breaks the record for most thrown chairs during a game (1).

1986
Short people take to Atlanta's streets in what is considered the smallest riot in American history after 5-foot-7 Spud Webb wins the Slam Dunk Competition.

1986
Scoring a phenomenal 63 points, Michael Jordan sets an NBA playoff record for the least number of passes attempted by a player.

GREAT MOMENTS IN BASKETBALL HISTORY

Kent State Basketball Team Massacred By Ohio National Guard In Repeat Of Classic 1970 Matchup

MARCH 16, 2006

KENT, OH—History and tragedy repeated themselves on the Kent State campus Thursday as 12th-seeded MAC champion Kent State Golden Flashes were decimated in front of a chanting, screaming home crowd by the superior offensive firepower and tactical game plan of the fifth-seeded Ohio National Guard in the very first round of this year's NCAA tournament.

"It was an absolute bloodbath," said Kent State head coach Jim Christian, who said he was "still in shock" from the on-court massacre. "We certainly weren't ready for what happened out there... It seemed like one minute we were getting ready to square off, and the next they were just taking shot after shot. They kept shooting all day long, and we just couldn't defend against them out there."

"It was like they couldn't miss," said senior forward Kevin Warzynski. "They were taking shots from the lane, shooting from the perimeter, everywhere... We left it all on the floor, but they just killed us out there tonight."

"You never think something like this is going to happen," said Warzynski. "It was a disgrace. It's going to be a long time before we recover from this shameful performance."

Some observers have speculated that the National Guard squad began shooting aggressively in response to Kent State sniper Jay Youngblood, the student-athlete they believed to be the most dangerous on the court. Official stats reveal that the National Guard took an unusually high 67 shots in the first minute alone.

At press time, the National Guard staff was refusing to comment in depth on its part in what the press, players, and public alike are calling "an atrocity."

"My men were just doing what they were trained to do," said National Guard adjutant coach Bobby Canterbury. "You can't blame them. If the other guys get blown away, well, then we're doing our job."

Kent State players and fans alike began the night with an optimistic attitude, having clinched the MAC conference championship and its automatic tournament bid just the previous Saturday. In the days leading up to the contest, there was little mention of the possible historical impact of the first meeting between the two rivals in over 30 years.

"Yeah, I remember the loss we suffered to the Ohio National Guard in 1970—everyone does," said Kent State sports-information director Jeff Schaefer Thursday night, referring to the annihilation at the hands of the Guard that spawned the still-popular stadium anthem "Ohio." "That catastrophic defeat was more than an important moment in sports history—it was a seminal moment in American history. And now it's happened again."

"I was only a kid when that happened, but I still knew that performance was a national disgrace," said Kent State student and basketball fan Lori Klaus, who was seated close to the action in the student section and was wounded when an opposing shooting guard charged into the stands to fight for possession. "I was trying not to think about it when I came tonight. You think something like that can't happen anymore, but... I guess now I'm part of history, too."

"Why?" Klaus asked those around her. "Why did they do this?" ∅

Yao Ming Living Up To Height Expectations

JANUARY 26, 2006

HOUSTON—Despite initial skepticism among NBA fans and analysts, Rockets center Yao Ming has had no trouble living up to the expectations of coaches and players that he would be 7'5" tall. "There was a lot of hype surrounding Yao's stature when he was selected as the first overall pick in the 2002 NBA draft, but he has turned out to be one of the most consistently tall players in the league," NBA analyst Marc Stein said. "Every time he runs out on the court, he's as tall as he can possibly be, and while Yao's shown no signs of improving in this area of his game, he's certainly not getting any shorter, either." Stein added that, while many suggested he could never match up against his star-center counterpart Shaquille O'Neal, Yao has been at least four inches greater than him in every contest this season. ∅

Tim Duncan Reports 5th Straight Successful New Year's Resolution

JANUARY 12, 2011

SAN ANTONIO—Spurs center Tim Duncan confirmed Monday that since he had not put off answering e-mails once during the entire year, 2010 would mark the fifth consecutive year he had held true to his New Year's resolution. "In 2006, I vowed to cut down on the sodium in my diet, and in 2007, I promised myself I would win another NBA championship and finally visit Denmark," said Duncan, adding that 2009's resolution to "loosen up and have more fun" was achieved by auditing a sociology course at the University of Texas at San Antonio. "2008 was hard, but on Dec. 31, I finally built up enough courage to talk to [AT&T Center concession-stand worker] Erin [Matthews]." This year, the 12-time All-Star has resolved to start cooking for himself more and to put more thought into the gifts he gives. ∅

INSIDE

▸ **Shaquille O'Neal Honors Martin Luther King Jr. By Nicknaming Him 'Big Freedomer'**

New NBA Starter Jackets To Come With Unwanted Pregnancies

David Stern Feels Uneasy In Presence Of Basketball Players

MARCH 11, 2006

NEW YORK—According to friends and associates, NBA commissioner David Stern gets suddenly quiet, visibly uncomfortable, and awkwardly on edge whenever he comes into the presence of NBA basketball players. "I don't know what it is—he's usually a very outgoing and funny guy, but he just all of the sudden stiffens up whenever they're around," said NBA vice president of basketball operations Michael Curry. "It's like he can't act natural around them. Whenever we see Allen Iverson and his friends at NBA events, he'll just excuse himself, go sit in the corner, and start playing with his watch. The few times that he actually comes anywhere near them, he'll usually just stand there staring at the floor, trying to look inconspicuous." According to colleagues, however, Stern is on very friendly terms with most NBA owners, coaches, and Steve Nash. ∅

Bradley University Wants To Bring NCAA Title Back To Middle Of Nowhere

FEBRUARY 23, 2006

OAKLAND, CA—The Bradley men's basketball team, fresh from earning an appearance in the Sweet 16, are eagerly anticipating their chance to bring the NCAA championship back to the middle of nowhere. "It's just great to be playing against Kansas and Pittsburgh and all these other great places we've seen on TV," said Bradley senior forward Marcellus Sommerville, who despite getting to travel on a plane to play in the tournament was modest about his team's accomplishment. "Meanwhile, we're concentrating on getting the job done for everyone back at the intersection of County Highway 78 and Rural Route G." Bradley athletics director Ken Kavanagh added that, should Bradley win the tournament, the city would probably have to install a stop sign to control the traffic of all the people wanting to see the championship trophy. ∅

INSIDE

LeBron James On Pace To Become Youngest Player To Turn 22

MARCH 16, 2006

CLEVELAND—According to official NBA statisticians, Cavs phenom LeBron James is currently on pace to be the youngest NBA player in history to reach the age of 22. "If James continues to age at this rate, the young forward will turn 22 on December 30 of this year," said Cavaliers public-relations director Amanda Mercado, who noted that NBA legends Michael Jordan, Magic Johnson, and Kobe Bryant and "several others" currently hold this record, having all turned 22 at the exact same age. "We're confident that 'King James' can rise to this challenge and set yet another mark that experts once thought to be utterly impossible." Some NBA analysts who have kept track of James' temporal progress have speculated that James might skip his 23rd year altogether and go straight to 24. ∅

Knicks Trade Draft Pick To Raptors In Exchange For Three Wins

MARCH 2, 2006

NEW YORK—Just minutes before the NBA trade deadline passed last Thursday, New York GM Isiah Thomas traded the Knicks' second-round draft pick to Toronto in return for three of the Raptors' victories. "We looked at a lot of offers, but with this deal, we knew exactly what we were getting," said Thomas, whose critics say this move is only a short-term solution to the Knicks' problems. "I don't think there's any question that this immediately makes us a better team. Just look at the standings—we were in last place by a few games last night, and we've already shot up to fourth. Our fans have been calling for more wins all season, and that's exactly what we've given them." Insiders report that Thomas had also been working on a trade in which Houston would receive all the Knicks' 2006-2007 victories in return for Tracy McGrady, but the deal fell apart after the Rockets said that would "not be nearly enough to help them contend." ∅

NBA Season Opens With Record Seven Scoreless Ties

NOVEMBER 3, 2005

NEW YORK—NBA officials are remaining quiet on the subject of the 2005-06 season's unusual opening week, in which seven games so far have opened with 0-0 ties. "I think that, despite what anyone may say about disappointing results, these games have proven that basketball can, in fact, be an exciting defense-oriented sport," Commissioner David Stern said during a press conference Thursday morning, after Wednesday's Milwaukee-New Jersey, New York-Boston, and Miami-Memphis contests ended with the score even at zero, exactly as in Tuesday's Milwaukee-Philadelphia and Dallas-Phoenix games. "I've talked to team owners and coaches, and while they're not happy with these final scores, the sudden increase in popularity among soccer-mad European and South American countries has made up for it somewhat." Stern had no comment on Tuesday's Denver-San Antonio game, in which the Nuggets shut out the defending champion Spurs 89-0. ∅

Mavericks To Incorporate Machetes Into Hack-A-Shaq Defense

JUNE 8, 2006

DALLAS—In what the Dallas Mavericks hope will be an effective variation on the "Hack-A-Shaq" defense, the traditional method of stopping Shaquille O'Neal by committing repeated hard fouls against the Miami Heat's dominant 7'1", 325-pound center, the Mavericks will equip their players with custom-made, razor-sharp machetes for this year's NBA Finals.

"I'm tired of everyone saying that Shaquille is unstoppable, that he's the most dominant player in the game, that he can just impose his will on any type of defense, and that he thrives on contact," Dallas coach Avery Johnson said, brandishing his own machete as he addressed his players before their first pre-finals practice. "Let's see how much he thrives when he comes in contact with one of these!"

The players then raised their machetes and stormed the practice court, maniacally hacking and slashing the practice-squad players while chanting "Defense!"

Enthusiastic team owner Mark Cuban said that, when he was presented with the idea of purchasing machetes for his "boys," he was immediately behind it.

"I thought, 'Great! Avery is finally thinking outside the box!'" Cuban said. "And since then, machetes have been the only things on my mind. Thinking about machetes has taken up every second of every day. Machetes! Machetes, man."

Cuban then purchased a case of machetes, and had each one custom-made to fit his players' size and frame, and engraved them with his players' names, numbers, the Mavericks' logo, the 2006 NBA Finals logo, and the credo "Defense Wins Championships."

Johnson, while noting that the admittedly impressive machetes were "just another tool in the box" and "an addition to, not a substitute for, solid defensive fundamentals," said early practice with the 20-inch blades has allowed him to demonstrate his flair for aggressive, innovative coaching.

"The X's and O's of it are pretty simple," Johnson said, drawing up the play on his dry-erase board. "Once Dwayne Wade passes the ball to Shaq down low, [point guard] Jason [Terry] will drop down to double-team him and chop the backs of Shaq's legs, especially the femoral artery and the Achilles tendon, with his lighter machete. Dirk [Nowitzki], while he's doing that, you will curl off your man and go for O'Neal's collarbones with an overhand chopping motion of your Latin machete. By the third quarter, Shaq will have lost a significant amount of blood, and that's when Keith [Van Horn] and [Josh] Howard will be stabbing at O'Neal's kidneys and the sensitive insides of his elbows with their respective weapons—Van Horn with his Bolo Machete and Josh with his Double-Edge Machete. Meanwhile, [center] DeSagana [Diop], who I understand brought his own Panga Machete from home, will be carving O'Neal's ribs."

"If we do this right and concentrate on rebounding to clean up our trash on offense, we can hold Shaq to 10 points a game," Johnson added. "But let's not underestimate this guy. He can still be a force on the court, even with five machetes sticking out of him."

Although players are being tight-lipped about their learning curve on this complex defense, Johnson said that his team is committed to carrying the machetes a full seven games and are willing to sacrifice a little agility for full defensive supremacy. Dirk Nowitzki has said that, by Game 6, the most dominant player in the world should be reduced to nothing more than "300 pounds of hamburger in a Miami Heat jersey." And Mavericks third-string center and O'Neal practice stand-in Erick Dampier came out of his morphine-induced coma long enough to assure everyone that the defense works.

After being informed of Dallas' new strategy, commissioner David Stern issued a written statement in which he expressed some concern about its effect on both player safety and the rules of the game.

"I always encourage coaches and players to continually strive to find new ways to play our beloved game," Stern said. "My only worry is that the unorthodox nature of this defense may cause some players—and one player in particular—actual physical harm. Furthermore, I would like to reiterate that balls shot towards the basket may not be knocked out of the air or destroyed by handheld objects, a rule which certainly includes machetes."

Veteran Miami Heat coach Pat Riley, who seems unfazed by the possibility of losing his star center, said the key to playoff basketball is making adjustments. Riley hinted that he was working on a new "Berserk-A-Dirk" defense and, while not offering specifics, hinted that the strategy involved unleashing a rabid, meth-crazed Gary Payton on the Mavericks' star player. ∅

NBA Praises Julius Hodge For Getting Shot In Non-Controversial Fashion

APRIL 13, 2006

DENVER—NBA commissioner David Stern proudly announced Tuesday that Denver Nuggets guard Julius Hodge was simply minding his own business while driving home from a Denver nightclub when he was shot in the leg three times. "It's a testament to the quality of character in the NBA that the only thing Julius Hodge was guilty of was being at the wrong place at the wrong time," said a beaming Stern to a group of reporters who were assembled to hear the announcement of the non-scandal. "Julius is a role model, not only for young NBA fans out there, but also other players in the league, specifically Paul Pierce and former New Jersey Nets forward Jason Williams." Stern was also careful to note that Hodge was not listening to rap music in his unremarkable, standard-factory-wheel-equipped four-door sedan at the time he was shot. ∅

Toronto Raptors Sign Unusually Tall Man

AUGUST 03, 2006

TORONTO—Toronto Raptors GM Bryan Colangelo announced Friday that his team had signed 6'11" Slovenian forward Uros Slokar, a man Colangelo called "very tall, especially when you consider the height of a normal human being." "The average height of a Canadian male is 5'10", and as you can see, Uros far exceeds that," an excited Colangelo said. "I think Uros will fit right in with the other uncommonly tall men we have on our team." Colangelo added that exceptional height is the main, and sometimes only, quality he looks for in his basketball players. ∅

Tim Duncan Releases Decade Worth Of Pent-Up Emotion After Spurs Preseason Loss

OCTOBER 19, 2006

SAN ANTONIO—Star Spurs center Tim Duncan has issued a public apology for his "unacceptable, inexcusable behavior" last Saturday night following a preseason loss to the Orlando Magic, saying that frustration and disappointment with his low-scoring, six-rebound performance caused "ten years' worth of unexpressed emotions to burst out of me like... like something I don't even know what."

An "agitated" Duncan responded to reporters' questions in a brusque tone of voice at a slightly elevated volume.

No criminal charges, police reports, or even complaints have been filed against Duncan, who was last seen leaving the Alamodome after giving what reporters are terming "mildly animated" answers to their post-game questions at a "slightly elevated" volume.

"I simply lost control during my post-game comments, and I did not give the press the full half-hour they are entitled to," said Duncan, who is on record as calling the Spurs' play during the game "bad," "real bad," "awful," and "very, very bad indeed" several times over the course of the 28 minutes he spent with reporters. "Anyone who knows me knows I never use language like that. I can only ask the city of San Antonio to forgive me for my outburst and give me a second chance."

"I was angry," Duncan added. "I even felt mad. I never want to go through that again."

Duncan claims that, after speaking to reporters, he was filled with a level of emotion that caused his memory to become unclear. However, Duncan is fairly certain that he turned away from reporters after insufficiently thanking them for the interview, walked to the parking lot with unusual briskness, and climbed into his car in a blatantly agitated fashion.

Witnesses' accounts bear out

Duncan's version of events, with several onlookers saying Duncan "slammed" the door of his 1992 Buick LeSabre closed before driving off. Spurs guard Tony Parker, whose car was near Duncan's, denied rumors that Duncan was muttering grumpily to himself, but said Duncan did exhale audibly twice while getting his car keys out.

"Looking back on it, I think he was sighing in a frustrated or even exasperated manner," Parker said. "I thought about saying something, but I didn't know what. I'd never seen him like that. Frankly, I was a little scared."

"I should not have driven in that

condition," said Duncan, who has implored the children of San Antonio not to emulate his actions or regard them as "cool." "I know better than to operate a motor vehicle while upset or in a highly emotional state of mind, but I did it anyway. I only wish I had exercised the self-restraint to let it go at that."

Traffic cameras tracked Duncan traveling from the Alamodome at up to seven miles per hour over the speed limit, twice driving through yellow lights, to a convenience store near his home, where the store's security cameras show him purchasing highly caffeinated beverages and

several unhealthy snacks. A clerk at the store says Duncan consumed three of the soft drinks in his car while listening to barely audible music on his car's radio before driving off several minutes later.

Duncan's mid-'90s four-door sedan was found in the parking lot of his nondescript apartment building Sunday morning, having impacted a tree at what insurance company investigators say was an "extremely low" rate of speed, inflicting almost $140 worth of damage to the car during what they say seems to be an abortive attempt to park while slightly jittery from an excess of mild sugar stimulants.

"I do not wish to discuss that at this time," Duncan said. "I'm just glad no one was hurt while I was experimenting with Coke, or Pepsi, or root beer, or whatever it was. I just remember going into my apartment, turning on the television, unblocking Showtime, and calling up a few girls from church to say 'hello' and 'how are you doing?' Frankly I'm mortified, and in light of my actions, I wouldn't blame them for being cross with me in return. I was brought up to respect women, not to place telephone calls to them at what might possibly be well past their bedtimes."

Duncan recalls nothing else until 9:30 the next morning, when he woke up two hours late, unshaven, and dressed in unusually brightly colored clothing. Duncan immediately contacted the police, and was relieved to find he had in fact broken no laws.

Duncan has assigned himself 120 hours of community service working in hospitals, neighborhood improvement projects, and on highway-beautification crews for his "reckless endangerment" of the people of San Antonio.

"I promise you," the dry-eyed Duncan said in an unusually well-modulated voice, "you will never see anything like that from me again." ∅

NCAA Tournament Intensifies As Florida Advances To Round Of One

APRIL 5, 2007

ATLANTA—The NCAA tournament field narrowed a little further—and became much more intense—on Monday night as the University of Florida tallied a convincing 84-75 victory over Ohio State University to advance further into college basketball's championship, making 2007 the second time in as many years that Florida has reached the NCAA Tournament's Round Of One.

However, Florida head coach Billy Donovan says that this time around, his team hopes to win it all.

"Anyone who knows their college hoops will tell you that the Round Of One is when the real tournament begins," said Donovan during the post-game press conference from Atlanta's Georgia Dome, adding that his team could go down as one of the best in the history of college basketball if they can advance past the next few rounds. "This was a great victory for our team, and a good confidence-booster, but it doesn't mean anything if we don't win next week."

"I'm just going to enjoy this victory for tonight," he added, responding to a question about possible adjustments the Gators will have to make in the future. "But tomorrow it's back to work. It only gets harder from here on out, folks."

Thus far, Florida has moved methodically through the tournament, easily making it into the Round Of 32, the Sweet 16, Elite Eight, and the Final Four, but now has to deal once again with the pressures that accompany being the Wondrous One.

"Last tournament we were a young team—we weren't ready for all the media attention and the grind. This year, we are totally focused," said star center Joakim Noah, who was voted Most Outstanding Player of the 2006 Wondrous One for his play against UCLA, but struggled visibly with endurance and composure in subsequent rounds. "This

is why I came back to Florida—to get past the Round Of One and, hopefully, on to the championship. I had something to prove, and so did this entire team. We're hungrier than we've ever been."

Noah added that he made the mistake of playing too hard in last year's regular season and failed to pace himself through the early rounds of the tournament, and credits his steady but unspectacular 12-points-per-game average this year as part of a concerted effort to save his energy.

"I think Florida definitely has what it takes," said ESPN college basketball analyst Digger Phelps, who will call Florida's next game. "But there is so much pressure at this stage in the tournament that if a team comes out flat like, say, UCLA did in 1972, you just never know. That's what makes the tournament so exciting."

Ohio State coach Thad Madda admitted in an interview outside a somber Ohio State locker room that his young team was "just not ready" to play amongst the elite, even going so far as to say that if his team did defeat Florida to move on in the tournament he would have had to contend with players wanting to go home at the end of their semesters in late April.

"Heck, to win your final game, and end the NCAA Tournament

with a couple dozen victories and no losses is everyone's dream, but truthfully, I don't know if [center] Greg [Oden] would have even been able to play in the championship game," Madda said, referring to the possibility of Oden being drafted by the NBA on June 28, two weeks before the final round of the NCAA Tournament. "I certainly wish Florida the best of luck the rest of the way."

Though college basketball fans across the nation have enjoyed the tournament's close games, many are hoping that there are some upsets as tournament play continues in Charlotte, Pittsburgh, New Orleans, and Portland. Fans will surely be glued to their television sets as all weekend games can be seen on CBS, while games during the week will air on ESPN, with the overflow being broadcast on ESPN 2.

"I made a few crazy picks in my office pool that I'm hoping will pan out," Philadelphia resident Geoff Caldwell said. "Luckily, I had Florida going this far, but I don't think they'll make it to Nashville. After the Round Of One, the competition just gets too tough."

If Florida does advance past the next round, it will be the farthest the Gators have advanced in the NCAA Tournament since it was fractionated in 1970. ✎

Desperate Clippers Sign Doug Christie To 10-Minute Contract

FEBRUARY 15, 2007

LOS ANGELES—Facing temporary fatigue and extremely short-term injury on the part of star center Elton Brand, the Los Angeles Clippers announced that they had bolstered their defense by signing journeyman guard Doug Christie to a 10-minute, 14-possession contract worth $8,575 before bonuses during the fourth quarter of Wednesday night's game against the Atlanta Hawks. "We're proud to have a player of Doug's caliber on board from now until about 9:30–9:35," said VP of Basketball Operations Elgin Baylor, who stressed that Brand would resume starting duties as soon as his stubbed big toe stopped smarting and he had caught his breath. "I only hope his Clippers career will be as memorable as it is long." Christie's incentive-laden contract will also pay him a bonus of $15 per point scored, $35 per blocked shot, and $125,000 for winning the NBA scoring title. ✎

INSIDE

'Fire Isiah' Chant Breaks Out During Knicks' Front-Office Meeting

Tim Duncan's Sincere Apology Confuses Referee Enough To Eject Him From Game

APRIL 19, 2007

DALLAS—Baffled by Tim Duncan's unexpected sincerity in apologizing following a technical foul, NBA official Joey Crawford responded by issuing Duncan a second technical and ejecting him from the game. "I don't know what the hell he was trying to pull with that gentle tone of voice and that attitude of heartfelt honesty, but I wasn't about to fall for it," Crawford told reporters after being asked about reacting so strongly to Duncan's attempt at shaking hands and putting the incident behind them both. "I'm pretty sure Duncan was really saying he wanted to punch me." Following the game, Crawford was arrested for assault after attacking a concession-stand employee who gave him a free hot dog in what Crawford claims was an attempt to make him "look cheap." ∅

PHOTO FINISH
Steve Nash Still Bleeding

INSIDE

› **Drained, Sleep-Deprived Selection Committee On Bracket: 'This Is Our Masterpiece'**

NOVEMBER 29, 2007

NEW YORK—A meeting held at Madison Square Garden Wednesday between New York Knicks ownership and head coach Isiah Thomas was interrupted more than half a dozen times by "Fire Isiah" chants which came at various points throughout the two-hour-long discussion, Knicks officials reported.

The mocking chants—which sources speculate were inspired by Thomas' conviction for sexual harassment, his lax punishment of guard Stephon Marbury for abandoning the team last week, and the consistent failure of an overpaid roster that Thomas himself is responsible for recruiting—could be overheard from outside the boardroom's entrance, and were regularly followed by five claps: two slower ones followed by three in rapid succession.

"Fire I-si-ah!" board members shouted in unison as Thomas reportedly tried to explain that his team was, in fact, making incremental but tangible progress. "Fire I-si-ah!"

According to Madison Square Garden L.P.'s Vice Chairman Hank Ratner, the meeting started on an icy note when administrative assistant Sheryl Jones opened the conference room doors and announced Thomas' name, inspiring the entire room to erupt into a chorus of loud boos that lasted for nearly one minute.

Ratner said the boos were immediately followed by what was in fact the second "Fire Isiah" chant, the first of which began when Thomas called to inform the Knicks front office that he would be five minutes late for the meeting.

"If you would have asked me four years ago if Isiah Thomas would be booed mercilessly every time he took the floor in his home office, I would have said you were nuts," Knicks primary owner James Dolan said. "Now? I wouldn't be shocked if this happens every work day."

Even when the chants subsided, Dolan said, Thomas still experienced other forms of hostility from all 15 board members in attendance, including multiple rounds of sarcastic clapping when Thomas talked optimistically about his team's four wins, several thrown C-cell batteries that narrowly missed Thomas' head, and intermittent shouts of "You suck," "My 5-year-old daughter could do a better coaching job," and "Die."

Ratner stated that, as Thomas continued to speak concerning the Knicks' chances to secure one of the eight playoff spots in the NBA's Eastern Conference, many at the meeting used the "thunder sticks" they received for free at the offices' front entrance in an apparent attempt to distract Thomas from his train of thought.

In addition, when Thomas defended his coaching strategy and failed to offer any suggestions as to how he could immediately make the Knicks a better basketball team, frustrated board members began a 30-second-long "asshole" chant.

Those board members too upset and flabbergasted to shout any obscenities reportedly buried their faces in their hands, slouched back in their leather chairs, sighed, and repeated "God, we suck" in defeated tones.

Though Thomas' expression remained stoic throughout the meeting, New York Rangers general manager Glen Sather said Thomas appeared slightly fazed when the president of MSG Sports Steve Mills walked in carrying an Isiah Thomas effigy he made at home prior to the meeting.

"[The effigy] had a noose tied around its neck," said Sather, adding that the doll was dressed in a white collared shirt that had "Devil" written across its chest. "You could tell that Isiah saw it out of the corner of his eye, and when Steve hung it from the office ceiling, Isiah's voice briefly cracked. But, he managed to keep it together, telling us that all the team needed was a little more time to gel, and that the players hadn't been given a chance to get into a real rhythm yet."

"That's the type of cool you need to be a successful coach in New York," Sather said. "I mean, you'd think so, anyway. Right?"

When the meeting ultimately let out, Thomas experienced further harassment from upper management during the post-meeting press conference.

"This comes with the territory of being a part of a professional sports team in New York City," Thomas said as Dolan, who was reportedly drunk during the entire second half of the meeting, exposed his backside to the coach and all media present. "You just have to block it all out."

Dolan later apologized to Thomas for his childish actions and assured him his job was safe. ∅

NBA To Honor Red Auerbach By Playing Defense

NOVEMBER 2, 2006

BOSTON—Commissioner David Stern announced at a press conference Monday that, in order to honor recently deceased basketball legend Red Auerbach, all NBA teams would play good, fundamental defense during the first weekend of play this November. "Though this will be a sacrifice for many players, I think this is something Red would have wanted," Stern said. "He always liked when players guarded the passing lanes, kept their hands up, and remained in front of their opponents even if it meant expending a little more energy in the process. Basically, he liked activity on the basketball court." Though the majority of NBA players seem to agree the tribute is fitting, many have said that because they haven't played defense in such a long time, they really hope they remember how. ∅

Kobe Bryant Mourns Passing of Ball

DECEMBER 14, 2006

LOS ANGELES—Lakers guard Kobe Bryant was visibly shaken, angry, and confused at center court of the Staples Center Tuesday night when the basketball that he held so close for most of the game was suddenly and inexplicably passed away. "It feels like I was just holding it in my hands a second ago, and now it's gone," said a tearful Bryant, who admitted he "just wasn't ready to let go." "I wish I could say it's in a better place now, but honestly, I'm not sure I can make myself believe that." Bryant later promised that, should he ever get close to another ball, he would make sure that something like this would never happen again. ∅

Tim Duncan Delivers Heartfelt Speech On Fiscal Responsibility During Spurs Victory Celebration

JUNE 21, 2007

SAN ANTONIO—Following a Spurs Sunday victory parade during which Tim Duncan regaled the crowd with uncharacteristically exuberant exclamations of "Thank you very much" and "Please, there's no need to make so much noise," the normally reserved power forward expressed his appreciation for his fans by speaking at length on the importance of being financially prepared in an increasingly uncertain world. "I can't tell you how much I value your support except through telling you it's not really enough to keep a little money in savings for a rainy day, never independently contributing to your 401(k) or considering simple CDs or mutual-funds," a misty-eyed Duncan said, using charts he drew up earlier in the season to demonstrate debt-to-savings ratios to the 12,000 fans who crowded the River Walk. "Your greatest equity will of course be in your home, but even then, careful consideration is required before choosing between fixed- or variable-rate mortgages, especially for the greatest fans in the world." Fans who stayed for the 90-minute speech said it was even better than the emotional plea Duncan made during the Spurs' 2003 championship celebration, in which he urged revelers to make sure they purchased adequate life insurance. ∅

Yao Ming's Self-Written Wedding Vows Include How He Loves The Top Of His Wife's Head

AUGUST 16, 2007

SHANGHAI—Houston Rockets and Chinese national team center Yao Ming, 7'6", married his longtime 6'3" girlfriend, Ye Li, last week in a ceremony for which Yao wrote nuptial vows praising, among other things, the top of Ye's head. "Ye, my beloved, to glimpse the onyx brilliance of the top of your head sends through me a rush of love strong enough to lift a thousand mountains," Yao intoned nervously yet earnestly as he gazed almost straight down into Ye's eyes. "And your dear sweet shoulders are like two tiny, distant doves nesting beneath that deep abiding well of wisdom and kindness." Yao's poetic efforts were obviously much appreciated by his beaming wife and generally well-received by family and friends, although Yao seemed annoyed when asked by American sports reporters if Ye's feet "looked like they'd been bound when seen from all the way up there." ∅

STRONG SIDE/ WEAK SIDE: JULIUS ERVING

STRONG SIDE	WEAK SIDE
Nickname alone averaged five points per game	Missed multiple games due to not being able to come down from previous jumps
Pioneered above-the-rim play; before he enteredthe game, everyone would wait for to fall to ground and stop bouncing before picking it up	Afro never quite reached World B. Free levels
Sound funkdamentals	Not a very strong swimmer
Quick first step, otherworldly agility due to multiple knees in each leg	Was unable to have a normal conversation, as everyone would just stand there gaping at him in sheer amazement
In his prime, only two steps separated a three-point shot and a slam dunk	Never lived up to billing as "the previous Michael Jordan"
Moves synched up perfectly with any Parliment song	Now 57 years old

INSIDE

‣ **Carmelo Anthony Baffled By Teammate Eating Slices Of Tiny Orange Ball**

‣ **White Guy Draws Charge**

‣ **John Calipari To Players: 'Play This Season As If It Will Be Wiped Away Due To Recruiting Violations'**

STRONG SIDE/ WEAK SIDE: LEBRON JAMES

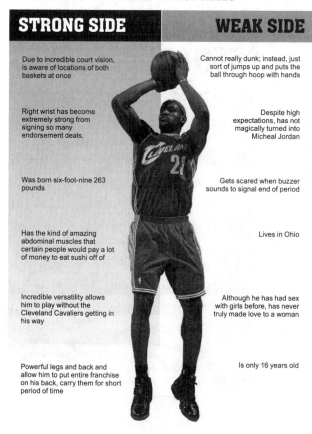

STRONG SIDE

Due to incredible court vision, is aware of locations of both baskets at once

Right wrist has become extremely strong from signing so many endorsement deals.

Was born six-foot-nine 263 pounds

Has the kind of amazing abdominal muscles that certain people would pay a lot of money to eat sushi off of

Incredible versatility allows him to play without the Cleveland Cavaliers getting in his way

Powerful legs and back and allow him to put entire franchise on his back, carry them for short period of time

WEAK SIDE

Cannot really dunk; instead, just sort of jumps up and puts the ball through hoop with hands

Despite high expectations, has not magically turned into Micheal Jordan

Gets scared when buzzer sounds to signal end of period

Lives in Ohio

Although he has had sex with girls before, has never truly made love to a woman

Is only 16 years old

INSIDE

› Lakers Players Claim Kobe Bryant's Groin Is Tender To The Touch

› Effective Execution Of Pre-Planned Passes, Picks, Shot Results In Two Points For Team

Confusing 24-Player Trade Sends You, Scottie Pippen To Utah Jazz

DECEMBER 6, 2007

SALT LAKE CITY—A multi-million-dollar blockbuster trade involving 24 players, six professional basketball teams, two hockey teams, and the Detroit Tigers' Triple-A affiliate Toledo Mud Hens eventually sent both you and retired Chicago Bulls All-Star forward Scottie Pippen to the Utah Jazz Tuesday. "I'm not exactly sure who we lost in the deal, but we're hoping that Scottie will be able to fill that void," Jazz general manager Kevin O'Connor said last night, adding that he also hopes you are comfortable with switching between both the point guard and small forward positions. "And, looking at the trade as a whole, I think [Sharks goalie] Evgeni Nabokov and [Dearborn, MI resident] Hank Glass will most easily be able to adapt to Phil Jackson's coaching style." Though O'Connor stated he believes that the Jazz came out on top in the complex transaction, he said Cleveland added real depth to their team with the addition of New Jersey Nets guard Jason Kidd and actor/comedian Paul Reiser. ∅

Confused David Stern Thought Gilbert Arenas Was Where Toronto Raptors Played

DECEMBER 13, 2007

NEW YORK—Upon hearing reports that star guard Gilbert Arenas was recovering well from two surgeries on his left knee, NBA commissioner David Stern was silent for several moments before revealing that he had previously believed 'Gilbert Arenas' was the name of the stadium where the Toronto Raptors played their home games. "So... Gilbert Arenas, that's where the Blue Jays play, and the Argonauts, and sometimes they have the circus in town when the season is right for it, right?" said Stern, referring to the Air Canada Centre. "Isn't their owner's name Gilbert? I thought it was pronounced with a silent T or something, because it's all French up there. I never heard the name out loud before now, see, I've always just read it. 'Gilbert Arenas.' Huh." Upon admitting his mistake, Stern extended his best wishes to Arenas and expressed the hope that he would return to the Raptors' lineup soon. ∅

Sheepish Timberwolves Fire Placekicker

DECEMBER 13, 2007

MINNEAPOLIS—The Minnesota Timberwolves gave fresh ammunition to critics of their recent personnel moves Monday night when they announced that placekicker Dave Rayner, claimed off waivers on Nov. 30 after being cut from the Kansas City Chiefs, had been cut from the roster. "We appreciate the contribution Dave made to the team in his time here, but he did not fill our need for an actual basketball player," coach Randy Wittman said of Rayner, who scored fewer than four points per game for Minnesota, far below the NBA and his NFL averages. "I hope Dave finds challenges worthy of his talents." Wittman then introduced controversial new Timberwolf signing jockey Willie Shoemaker III, admitting that while the project player has less than ideal size, his pedigree was too good to pass up. ∅

Shaq Asks To Have Injured Hip Replaced With Lasers

JANUARY 9, 2008

LOS ANGELES—Following a medical appointment Monday in which he sought treatment for a hip injury that has sidelined him for the past five games, Miami Heat center Shaquille O'Neal told reporters he has asked doctors to use their science to replace his ailing hip with intense beams of highly focused coherent light. "'The Real Deal' can no longer afford to be slowed down by physical bones, which refuse to stop hurting," the four-time NBA champion, who has not played since Dec. 22, told reporters Wednesday. "So I told them to just open me up and bolt in some lasers, so I can get back out on the court and help my team. I'm thinking maybe they should replace my entire skeleton. Some of those bones have been weighing me down for too long." Although Heat coach Pat Riley felt the bursitis in O'Neal's hip would heal in a couple of weeks without the use of high-energy stimulated radiation implants, he expressed concern after learning "Doctor Shaq" would perform the laser hip transplant on himself if he could not find a surgeon for the procedure. ∅

PHOTO FINISH

LeBron James To New Teammate Ben Wallace: '…Dad?'

Shaq Terrified Of Phoenix Suns After Reading About Supernovas

FEBRUARY 14, 2008

TEMPE, AZ—Claiming he was initially excited at the prospect of playing for a legitimate championship contender, new Phoenix Suns center Shaquille O'Neal admitted Monday that, upon reading about the phenomenon of massive stellar explosions popularly known as supernovas, he is now terrified of the entire organization.

"I have emerged from my astronomical studies a much more educated man, a learned man, and yes—a frightened man. I am now a sage of the supernova," O'Neal said during a combination press conference and PowerPoint presentation at an Arizona State University lecture hall. "If I would have known being a Sun meant being a part of a system where gravity could collapse, causing my radiant celestial body to explode in an event 10 times brighter than an ordinary Phoenix Sun—or worse, dematerialize into a neutron star or possibly a black hole—I would have never agreed to the trade."

"I have a family to think of," continued a visually tense O'Neal, who later stated that, because supernovas occur in our galaxy once every 40 to 50 years, the Suns, having joined the league in 1968, are "due for a big one."

While O'Neal said that simply being a part of the Suns' runaway-nuclear-fusion-reaction style of play would be frightening enough, he added that learning how an aging supergiant star typically ends its life cycle in a violent explosion was a profoundly terrifying experience. The 35-year-old center, who considers himself a super-giant star in the twilight of his career, has refused to go anywhere near his new teammates.

"Like Superman, I receive my energy from the Suns," O'Neal said. "I'm scared I will not be able to flourish in an environment where there is a risk that the Suns' supply of hydrogen could be exhausted, which would cause the core of the Suns to collapse into the center—in this case, me—and create a rise in temperature and pressure that would become great enough to ignite helium and then start a helium-to-carbon fusion cycle."

"Not even electron degeneracy pressure is enough to stop a supernova when that happens to a Sun," O'Neal added. "I don't even know what that means, and I am the Big Astronomer. But it scares me."

The former league MVP said he began reading about supernovas upon being informed by his 7-year-old son Shareef that the sun is actually a star, a fact that O'Neal said "intrigued [him] greatly." Upon further research, O'Neal was reportedly shocked by the possibility that carbon fusion could be ignited within the team's center, causing an explosion that could exceed over 100 billion Kelvins in temperature.

"I have been involved in many hotly contested battles in my playing career and have come out an even stronger warrior, but 100 billion Kelvins is a lot even for the Diesel," O'Neal said, showing the various media present a slide of the Crab Nebula, which he called a "frightening" example of what could be left of him after a supernova occurs. "If I were still in my 20s, maybe I could sustain a burst of energy more powerful than the sun could emit over a 10-billion-year time period. But Steve Nash has to understand that I have a bad hip."

O'Neal also added that he did not feel threatened by or feel any animosity toward Nash, who O'Neal believed would not have sufficient mass or power to become a supernova and who would instead cool slowly before degenerating into a white dwarf.

Though O'Neal has reportedly told Phoenix Suns coach Mike D'Antoni that he

see PHOENIX SUNS

from **PHOENIX SUNS**

refuses to set foot on the U.S. Airways Center court until he is guaranteed that the arena will not collapse on itself at speeds of 70,000 kilometers per second, he informed Phoenix general manager Steve Kerr by telephone late Monday that if a supernova could not be avoided, he would consider playing with the team if he at least knew what type of stellar explosion he could expect.

"There are five types of supernovas," O'Neal said. "I told Steve that if I have to endure one of the five, I would prefer the Type 1c, which has weak or no helium lines and no strong silicon absorption features near 615 nanometers. The worst would be the Type 1b, which is characterized by non-ionized helium. I made it perfectly clear that, with all that I've done for this league, a neutrino-heavy Type 2L is simply unacceptable."

Early reports indicate that O'Neal was willing to compromise when he learned no other NBA team had any interest in the oft-injured athlete.

"I'm still the most dominant player in the game," O'Neal said. "I'm still a big star. But people must realize that, since I am as big as eight conventional stars, the risk of me going supernova is that much greater."

When asked if there were other teams that frightened O'Neal as much as the Suns, the 14-time All-Star said he would retire immediately if he were ever traded to the Utah Jazz. ∅

Kevin Garnett Proves He Can Touch Rim

MARCH 6, 2008

BOSTON—After dozens of practice-session attempts, Boston Celtics center Kevin Garnett proved Tuesday that he could touch the rim of the basket when his middle finger slightly grazed the front edge of the regulation-height goal on the north end of the team's practice court, finally putting to rest a month of spec-

ulation and ridicule from his teammates.

"I told those guys I could hit rim," said Garnett, adding that "nobody believed [him]" when he informed his teammates that he touched, and indeed nearly grabbed, the rim in January while he was shooting around by himself in his driveway. "I always said that if I'm warmed up enough, and I can get a running start from the other end of the court and don't have to worry about dribbling or anything, I can get rim no problem."

"I proved everyone wrong," Garnett added. "I shocked the world, just like last year when everyone said I couldn't get backboard."

Team sources confirmed that it took Garnett approximately one hour and over 15 tries before he finally touched the rim, though he reportedly came very close several times, often touching the middle and top sections of the net. During one instance, which his teammates were quick to point out didn't count, Garnett jumped to grab the net with both hands, then pulled himself up and hung on the rim. He then told teammate James Posey to throw him a ball, which he eventually managed to dunk before releasing the rim and returning to the ground.

"I had to really dig deep at the end there," said the 6'11" Garnett. "But I knew once I left the floor on that last try that I was going to get rim. I honestly don't think I have ever jumped that high in my life."

Celtics guards Ray Allen and Paul Pierce said that when Garnett told his fellow teammates in January that he could get rim on a 10-foot hoop, both responded, "Yeah, right" and "No way." The pair also responded "Okay, sure" and "Yeah, and?" to Garnett's claim of hitting rim at the hoop at his house, citing as general knowledge that Garnett's home basket easily stands less than 10 feet and that his driveway is inclined just enough to give him an unfair advantage.

"If Kevin had said he could get rim on a nine-foot hoop, I probably wouldn't have questioned it," said Pierce, who noted that Garnett, Allen, and himself get together Saturday afternoons, lower Pierce's backyard hoop to seven feet, and have dunk contests. "But 10 [feet]? That's really really high. Kevin's a good basketball player and all, but he's no Michael Jordan."

"I guess you have to give him credit, though, because in the end, he did it," Pierce said. "Man, I would kill to be able to get rim just once."

Allen, however, was not as quick to heap praise on his teammate, pointing out that even though Garnett touched rim, he "just barely got it," and claimed that if his ankle had not been injured, he too could have touched the rim.

"I don't see why everyone is making a big deal about this," the visibly jealous Allen said. "If I was as tall as Kevin I would be touching the rim all the time. So what if he can touch the rim? If he can't dunk, what's the point?"

Upon learning of his teammate's comments, Garnett said that if he got a large enough running start and jumped at the exact right moment, he could probably dunk a tennis ball. ∅

Rasheed Wallace Has Greatest Dream Where He Uses Headband As Basketball Slingshot And Scores A Million Points

MARCH 6, 2008

DETROIT—Pistons forward Rasheed Wallace awoke from the greatest dream Monday morning, in which he was in an NBA game, and he took off his headband and started using it as a slingshot, and everyone kept passing him the ball, but the balls were smaller than usual, or maybe his headband was bigger, and he kept slinging the balls into the hoop from a hundred feet away and he scored a million billion points, Wallace reported Monday. "I remember I was playing against the Celtics—except Paul Pierce, like, became Allen Iverson somehow, and my father was on their team for some reason—and my headband stretched across the whole court,

and when I shot the balls from it, they all automatically went in, and then the floor started glowing," Wallace explained to reporters. "Also, I figured out this thing called the backwards dunk, where you dunk through the bottom of the rim, and the refs give you a thousand points for figuring out the secret. Oh, and the court was my house." Wallace said he cannot wait to try using his headband as a slingshot in a real game. ∅

Tim Duncan Sends Belated 'Great Game' Card To Celtics For February Defeat

MARCH 6, 2008

SAN ANTONIO—Weeks after the Spurs 98-90 loss to the Celtics on Feb. 10, power forward Tim Duncan sent personalized notes to each player on the Celtics roster, the entire coaching staff, the general manager, and owner, congratulating them for a "great game." "This would have gotten to you sooner if I had sent one card to the entire organization, but I felt that would diminish everyone's individual accomplishments," said Duncan, who sealed the envelopes with his personal crest embossed in wax. "I just wanted to let them know how much I appreciated everyone from the players to the front office. The Celtics did a splendid job, and I'm really proud of them." Although Duncan said he was conflicted as to whether to write the notes using a pen or brush, he finally decided to use his favorite, a quill dipped in sable India ink, a time-consuming penmanship method that Duncan feels looks best on his heavy handmade paper. ⌀

Report: Cheap Chinese NBA Players Falling Apart After A Few Seasons

MARCH 20, 2008

HOUSTON—Reports from several NBA teams indicate that cheap, flimsy Chinese basketball players frequently break down and fall apart when faced with the normal wear-and-tear of an NBA season. "We got one a couple years ago, but the foot broke," said Rockets GM Carroll Dawson about Chinese center Yao Ming. "Now it just sits there. We don't even use it anymore." Said Bucks guard Michael Redd: "It was fun playing with Yi Jianlian for the first few weeks, but then it seemed like every time we got too rough, he stopped working and we had to get him fixed. Maybe we just got a crummy one." Some NBA GMs, however, claim that it is still worth it to buy Chinese players, as European players remain expensive and many domestic models are unreliable, unrefined, and occasionally malfunction and shoot someone. ⌀

Steve Nash Sarcastically Asks Shaq To Slow Down

MARCH 8, 2008

PORTLAND—In the midst of four consecutive fast breaks during their Tuesday night game against the Trailblazers, Phoenix Suns guard Steve Nash repeatedly voiced scathingly sarcastic comments regarding newly acquired teammate Shaquille O'Neal's lack of speed. "Whoa, slow down there, big fella! You're making us all look bad!" said Nash as he and the other three Suns players on the court ran past a hunched-over O'Neal during another breakaway. "Somebody rein in Lightning there! Hey, Shaq, we're really gonna need you to stand around and miss free throws for us in the playoffs, so don't blow your wad just yet." Nash often makes similar remarks when the teammates are eating meals together, usually without the sarcasm. ⌀

Carmelo Anthony Considers Himself The Nuggets' Dipping Sauce

MARCH 20, 2008

DENVER—Small forward Carmelo Anthony admitted to his teammates Tuesday that he regards himself as the tasty honey mustard sauce into which the battered and deep-fried Nuggets basketball team is dipped. "I do my best to be a zesty flavoring explosion all over the court," Anthony said, adding that he was so delicious that you always wanted a little more. "This team might be hot and crispy, but they'd be a little bland without my ability to be sweet and tangy all at once." Anthony added that guard Allen Iverson was the breading that held the team together, and the rest of his teammates were the lean meat that was minced, processed, and packed into the shape of the Nuggets. ⌀

Houston Rockets Catch Tracy McGrady Masturbating To Tape Of His 41-Point Performance

MARCH 13, 2008

HOUSTON—Rockets players held a team press conference Tuesday to express their shock, confusion, and disgust at discovering shooting guard Tracy McGrady masturbating vigorously in the darkness of the team's tape room while viewing recordings of his recent stellar 41-point performance. "We were walking down the hallway like usual and heard a bunch of moaning and shouting coming from the tape room, so we opened up the door and there was T-Mac with his warm-ups around his ankles, churning himself with both hands," said small forward Shane Battier. "He just kept grunting 'Put it through the rim. Again. Give it the soft touch. Oh, Tracy, you're so good. Don't tell me you're going to take it to the hole again.' I'm not ready for that yet." Rookie Carl Landry, who has played an important role as a reserve, said he was happy he had to sit out with a bruised left knee, claiming that there was no chance McGrady could have masturbated to him. ⌀

NIT Still Has 10 Open Slots If Anyone Wants To Play

MARCH 20, 2008

NEW YORK—Though the NCAA's postseason consolation tournament began play earlier this week, National Invitational Tournament selection committee chairman C.M. Newton issued a nationwide call for more basketball teams, or even individual players, saying the NIT is still trying to round up enough guys to fill out the 32-team field.

"Whether you are 7 years old or 70, male or female, or just happen to be in the neighborhood, we at the NIT would love for you to play in our tournament," Newton told reporters at a press conference, adding that last-minute entrants would only have to pay half of the NIT's customary $150 entry fee. "The NIT's a really fun, no-pressure tournament. Nobody cares that much, and the skill level isn't that high, so even if you haven't picked up a ball in years you'll fit right in."

"It's laid-back," Newton added. "It's cool, and it's healthy for you. You'll love it. Come on over."

According to Newton, since several teams either rejected the NIT's initial invitation or made an informal commitment to the tournament but never bothered to return follow-up phone calls, there were six empty spots remaining prior to Tuesday night's opening tip-off. That number increased to 10 when Morgan State, UNC-Asheville, Elks Lodge #368 from Mesquite, NV, and the team representing the Squirrel Hill Jewish Community Center in Pittsburgh, PA canceled at the last minute.

"In order to participate in the NIT, all you have to do is show up with five guys, some basketball sneakers, and a good attitude," Newton said. "Or, if you are a single and just want to play some B-ball, don't feel embarrassed. Just show up and we can probably fit you in somewhere."

"I think Ohio State and the 10th Street Y's over-50 league only brought four guys each this year," added Newton, who also wanted potential players to know that they can call their team whatever they want no matter how silly or crazy the name. "Please come out and play."

Newton later stated that because he is having difficulty getting in touch with facility operators at the tournament's various venues, which consists of the Scottsdale YMCA, Ben Franklin Elementary School's cafeteria/gymnasium, and the outdoor courts behind St. Rita's Church, those who ultimately decide to play would be doing tournament organizers a huge favor by bringing their own basketballs.

Reports from last night's first-round contest between Creighton University and the University of Rhode Island indicate that the entire game was played with a volleyball.

According to tournament officials, the desperate call for players is not an uncommon practice for the NIT, which is now in its 50th, 34th, or 22nd year depending on who you talk to. Last year's selection committee was only able to get 25 collegiate teams to participate in the postseason playoff. In 2004, only 10 NCAA teams were willing to play in the consolation tournament, making it possible for "The Montana Bar Bears," a squad consisting of five lawyers from Missoula, MT, to win the entire tournament. The Bar Bears defeated Rutgers University in front of a record NIT crowd of 278 people.

"Anything can happen in the NIT, baby," ESPN college basketball analyst Dick Vitale said. "And this year should be no different. Opponents better watch out for [New York real estate agent] Rick Nelson's super, scintillating, sensational baby hook. And you

can't forget [56-year-old] Mort Feldstein's unbelievable presence down low. He's a PTPer, baby."

Vitale later admitted that he could not name one college basketball team participating in this year's NIT.

"Once the field is complete, we are going to play NIT basketball as usual," chief official Art Hyland said. "Half-court games to 11, win by two, loser's outs. And it's important for those new players unfamiliar with NIT rules to remember that if you don't call 'check ball,' the other team can just take it in for an easy lay up."

Hyland said that once teams are eliminated, there would be a hoop open at the other end of the gym so players could get a "big game of knockout going."

"Looking at the field, I think we have a pretty good chance," said 52-year-old David Holtz, who will play for the Greensboro County Rotary Club. "Sure, the University of Dayton has guys who are younger and faster than us, but they lost to La Salle in February. Christ, I could beat La Salle by myself. The team to watch is definitely the Freemasons from Danville, CT. They have this one guy who is 6-foot-4."

Tournament organizer Christine Fallon said that players thinking about participating in the playoff should be aware that the prize for winning the NIT is the same this year as it was last year, with the championship team receiving $200 in cash and gift certificates good at local merchants. ∅

Memphis Players Have Long, Complicated Explanation Of How They Are This Year's 'Rumpelstiltskin' Story

APRIL 3, 2008

SAN ANTONIO—Although no Cinderella teams made it to this year's Final Four, the Memphis Tigers held an extended press conference Wednesday to explain to the press and public that they are in fact the "Rumpelstiltskin" of this year's NCAA basketball tournament.

"Okay, now, pay attention, because this is pretty complicated," point guard Derrick Rose said upon opening what was to be a three-hour marathon of explanations, questions, and folkloric interpretation held in a conference room at the at the team's hotel. "Okay, we can't be Cinderella, because we're a No. 1 seed, right? But of all the No. 1 seeds, we were the one people expected to lose. So we're like the girl in the story who starts out as a miller's daughter but right away she becomes a princess. And she—we—only got this far because we can spin straw into gold, but it really isn't us, it's this magic dwarf. Okay, then, is everybody following so far?"

Rose, talented but undersized at 6'0", then proceeded to explain to reporters that he was not, in fact, either calling himself or comparing himself to a magic dwarf.

It is unknown how Rumpelstiltskin, the Germanic folk tale in which the mysterious title character agrees to help a commoner-made-princess by turning ordinary straw into gold in exchange for her firstborn son but is undone when the princess guesses his secret name, was adopted by

Memphis as a symbol for their tournament appearance. However, the players and head coach John Calipari all took turns attempting to explain what they insisted were close similarities.

"In a way, you see, having a game plan is like having a secret name," a visibly exasperated Calipari said midway through the second hour of the press conference, his suit jacket long since abandoned, his tie loosened, and his shirtsleeves rolled up. "Now, if we can guess the other team's secret name, then we'll be victorious, and we'll get to keep the gold—be the champion. Right? Everyone got it?"

Calipari then attempted to explain exactly who the prince would be, why he had lied about being able to spin straw into gold in the first place, whether the fans or the media were the firstborn son, and if he was claiming he had spied on other teams to steal their game plan.

"Okay, let's get this straight," said defense-minded power forward Joey Dorsey, who spent most of the day denying that he was a friendly troll, a brave knight, or even an evil ogre. "The point is, there's this thing that's

hard to do and there's more than one part to it, like spinning straw into gold while trying to outwit evil magic gnomes or like trying to win the basketball tournament while everyone says you're not good enough. So you have to be crafty, like saying you can do something you can't while someone who can do the things you can't does them until you outfox them and then you're a princess... or the champion... Wait. No, you're both. Right?"

"I've got to pull down as many rebounds as possible, anyway," Dorsey concluded. "Rebounds are important."

"I can see what Memphis is trying to do here," said *Washington Post* sportswriter Adam Kilgore, who said the press conference was the most baffling basketball-related event he had ever witnessed. "But I don't think it works. What does the straw represent? Why did they lie about making gold in the first place? When Memphis lost to Bill Walton's UCLA team back in 1973, was Bill Walton an angry giant? Is there a moral to this story?"

"I guess it's something to think about," Kilgore added. "I just wish they'd gone with the metaphor of The Big Dance." ∅

Knicks Fast Break Takes Two-And-A-Half Minutes

APRIL 3, 2008

ATLANTA—A New York Knicks fast break which began with 8:34 remaining in the fourth quarter of Sunday's game against the Atlanta Hawks ended approximately two-and-a-half minutes later on a missed lay-up by shooting guard Jamal Crawford. The typically fast-paced basketball play,

which began to take shape when a rebounding David Lee took 45 seconds to figure out which of his teammates would receive the outlet pass, was, according to Knicks coach Isiah Thomas, "A real sign of improvement. Yes, it was a bit discouraging when we had to start the play over again because Nate [Robinson] forgot he was the point guard and just ran away from the ball, but after

we all got on the same page, and when Quentin [Richardson] remembered that Jamal, not him, cuts to the hoop and then flashes ball side, I think we ended up running a pretty decent break," Thomas said in a post-game press conference. "Just because we ultimately had to carefully walk through it in order to get it right doesn't make it less effective." Thomas was not fired following the game. ∅

Isiah Thomas: 'My Time With The Knicks Was Actually A Large-Scale Psychological Study Of New York Residents'

APRIL 24, 2008

NEW YORK—Ousted Knicks coach and president Isiah Thomas, who presided over the team during one of the least successful and most shameful periods in its history, held a press conference Wednesday to announce that his four-year legacy of abysmal team chemistry, bloated payrolls, sex scandals, and simple losing was actually a vast psychological experiment carried out on New York City as a whole.

"Congratulations, New York—I've discovered you are healthier, more resilient, and stronger than anyone would have believed," Thomas told reporters assembled to see him clean out his office, file his final report to the National Institute of Mental Health, and debrief the players and coaches who had unwittingly assisted his efforts. "Although there are indications you also have deep-seated anger issues, misplaced feelings of entitlement, and tend to live vicariously through others, overall I'm very pleased with you, and I am confident you'll come out of this a much stronger city."

"I'm a bit worried, though, that you let this experiment go on as long as it did before standing up for yourselves and

making it stop," Thomas added. "I had only planned for it to last a year. New Yorkers may want to work on their assertiveness in the future."

Thomas confessed that he came up with the idea in late 2003 when he heard the Knicks were seriously considering hiring him to helm the organization despite the fact that he himself was known to be a demanding, contentious figure and had no real experience coaching a team or working at the administrative level.

"I thought, 'That's just crazy. They must be out of their minds in New York.' And then it hit me," Thomas said. "I could probably get a huge research grant for a massive study of the effects of constant low-level trauma on large populations out of this. Within

minutes, was on the phone to my man at NIMH."

Thomas worked alongside behavioral psychologists with an extensive knowledge of domestic-abuse patterning, aversion dynamics, the works of B. F. Skinner, and long-term mass hysteria to assemble a comprehensive testing program. An experiment consisting of a regimen of slowly increasing stress levels and traumatic events was designed, refined, and eventually performed upon New York City and Knicks fans everywhere.

"I knew that bringing in as many ball-hogs as possible, especially Stephon Marbury, would create a feeling of isolation and abandonment in the greater metropolitan area's 11

see ISIAH THOMAS

Tim Duncan Offers To Do Taxes For Entire Spurs Team

APRIL 10, 2008

SAN ANTONIO—As the playoffs grow nearer, Spurs center Tim Duncan has taken it on himself to ensure his team is focused, relaxed, and utterly prepared for tax day by offering to complete their state and federal forms himself. "C'mon, guys, just a couple days left in the regular season, and you know what

that means—get your W-2s to me as soon as you can, plus records of any memorabilia sales or shoe endorsements you've done, and just as important, tell me about any deductible expenses you've incurred," Duncan told him teammates during a time-out

with 3:40 left to play in the Spurs' 72-65 win over the Trailblazers Sunday. "Tony, I bet you put all your receipts in a shoebox again, didn't you? Manu, tell me if you've been sending more than 37 percent of your income overseas, because that's a whole different set of declaration forms I have to print out. Okay, got it? Break!" Duncan later disclosed to reporters that he paid over $865,000 in late-filing fees for the 2007 Spurs. ∅

SPORTS GRAPHIC

Greatest Moments In Slam-Dunk Contest History

FEBRUARY 21, 2008

The NBA Slam-Dunk Contest is the most popular part of All-Star weekend, outshining the game itself, and for good reason. Onion Sports looks back at the athletic aerial display's most timeless moments:

➤ **1976:** The very first slam-dunk contest is won by Kentucky Colonels center Artis Gilmore, who electrifies the crowd by making airborne love to one cheerleader from each ABA team en route to a windmill slam

➤ **1988:** The greatest slam-dunk rivalry of all time reaches its apex when Michael Jordan and Dominique Wilkins are unable to agree whether "slam dunk" is one word or two

➤ **1994:** A mysterious man named Isaiah Rider appears out of nowhere, wins the slam-dunk contest with an amazing backboard-level between-the-legs dunk, and then disappears, never to be seen again

➤ **1996:** With a single foul-line dunk, Brent Barry breaks the foul-line-dunk color barrier

➤ **1997:** Air Bud stuns the crowd by dunking with his hind legs

➤ **1999:** As there was no contest this year due to the lockout, commissioner David Stern awards himself the title

➤ **2000:** The judges award the trophy to Vince Carter after the unfortunate young man gets his elbow caught in the rim

➤ **2002:** A touching 9/11 tribute goes horribly wrong when Desmond Mason slips while attempting an Airplane Slam and crashes directly into "Twin Towers" Shawn Bradley and Rashard Lewis

from **ISIAH THOMAS**

million residents," Thomas said. "And by assembling a team that consistently ranked dead last in the NBA in assists, I created a symbolic analogue for the helpless desolation of the modern urban experience that was designed to heterodyne in New York's collective psyche, prompting frequent and perhaps even violent reactions."

"Worked like a charm, if you ask me," Thomas noted.

Other experimental stimuli Thomas used in the experiment include misspent draft picks, sexual-harassment lawsuits, rumors of listening devices placed in the team's locker room, firing acknowledged basketball guru Larry Brown and assuming the position of head coach, and leading the Knicks to win less than 40 percent of their games over four years.

"I was really proud when the chants of 'Fire Isiah' finally started," said Thomas, who intends to frame one of the fan signs bearing the slogan and display it in his home as a symbol of his success in New York. "I know I'm supposed to be objective about it—the experiment is the important thing, not the feelings of the fans—but it was a sign you were finally coming around."

"I think we all learned a lot," Thomas concluded.

For their part, the researchers from the National Institute of Mental Health were less enthusiastic.

"I don't know what made us pick Isiah," said NIMH director Dr. Thomas R. Insel, who is weathering demands for his resignation over the Knicks' losing record and treatment of fans. "He had no psychological experience, he wouldn't listen to noted experts who tried to help him, he responded to criticism with aggression, and in four short years he all but ruined a once-proud mental health organization through arrogance and incompetence. Frankly, if you ask me, the man's insane." ∅

Pau Gasol, Tony Parker Share Special Moment During Pick

APRIL 17, 2008

LOS ANGELES—An otherwise routine set play involving a variation on the classic "pick" strategy transformed into a singularly unforgettable moment Sunday when Lakers center Pau Gasol interposed himself in order to stop the defensive pursuit of Spurs guard Tony Parker with body contact, but in the words of Parker himself "stopped my heart instead."

"I came around the key to the baseline like it was any other day, but then there [Pau] was. First our hips met, then our eyes, and I was knocked off my feet—literally and figuratively," Parker told reporters afterward. "Time stopped forever for me at that moment, and I knew then that whatever happened in this crucial best-of-five series, one of the most crucial moments of my life had just happened. That now and forever, for me—for us—there would always be eight seconds left on the shot clock." Gasol refused to comment on the moment, telling reporters that "[Parker and I] will always have [the] Staples Center." ∅

STRONG SIDE　　　**WEAK SIDE**

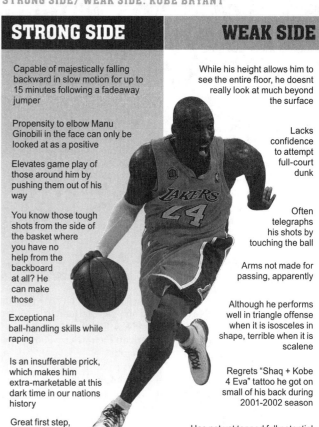

Capable of majestically falling backward in slow motion for up to 15 minutes following a fadeaway jumper

Propensity to elbow Manu Ginobili in the face can only be looked at as a positive

Elevates game play of those around him by pushing them out of his way

You know those tough shots from the side of the basket where you have no help from the backboard at all? He can make those

Exceptional ball-handling skills while raping

Is an insufferable prick, which makes him extra-marketable at this dark time in our nations history

Great first step, third step, fourth step sixth through 11th step, 14th step

While his height allows him to see the entire floor, he doesnt really look at much beyond the surface

Lacks confidence to attempt full-court dunk

Often telegraphs his shots by touching the ball

Arms not made for passing, apparently

Although he performs well in triangle offense when it is isosceles in shape, terrible when it is scalene

Regrets "Shaq + Kobe 4 Eva" tattoo he got on small of his back during 2001-2002 season

Has not yet tapped full potential for selfishness

Magic Johnson Shares 'Thoughts' On Lakers-Celtics Finals

JUNE 5, 2008

BOSTON—Appearing on ESPN's *SportsCenter* Wednesday, former Lakers point guard Magic Johnson provided his "thoughts," "insights," and "analysis" of the NBA Finals matchup between the Lakers and the Celtics, assuring viewers that the series will hinge on "whoever team does its things better more. I think this, I think, this is really going to come down to basically overall game play and which team can win four or five games, and do it first," said the three-time NBA MVP, adding that scoring could also be as much of a major factor on the outcome as total points. "There's also a possible definite possibility of matchups occurring. Could happen, yeah. And we can't overlook the influence that—that that effect or effects, might have on something." When pressed by *SportsCenter* anchor Rece Davis as to which team was favored, Johnson responded by saying "the one that's going to win... Win the NBA championship." ∅

Tim Duncan Offers To Drive NBA Players To Polling Place On Election Day

OCTOBER 30, 2008

SAN ANTONIO—Spurs center Tim Duncan sent an e-mail message to his fellow NBA players Tuesday volunteering to use his 1992 Buick LeSabre to chauffeur anyone "who needs a ride" to his assigned polling place to vote in the 2008 presidential election. "It's our responsibility to cast that ballot so that our democracy may continue working properly," wrote Duncan, adding that he was confident that every eligible member of the NBA was registered to vote and had been closely following all the 2008 races for months. "There's no need to feel pressure to tell me who you're voting for—that information is between you and the voting machine. All I ask is that you

please be at the curb on time, buckle up, and treat my car with respect." According to Duncan, the "huge response" has forced him to schedule two separate trips, which he has detailed in a Google calendar and shared with all participants. ∅

Gilbert Arenas Claims He Can Play Despite Sore Ankle Part Of Arm

APRIL 24, 2008

CLEVELAND—Following the Wizards' 30-point loss to the Cavaliers Monday, Washington guard Gilbert Arenas assured reporters that he would play in Game 3 of the series despite severely wrenching his right arm's ankle while fouling LeBron James. "I definitely have some inflammation in the joint between the arm and my shooting foot, but I'm going to ice it and keep my weight off of it for the next couple days," said Arenas, who was limited to seven points in Game 2. "I should be fine, especially since I didn't get a high ankle sprain on

the upper part of the arm. Those never heal." Arenas, who has been plagued by injuries recently, missed 69 regular season games after having reconstructive surgery to correct a shoulder separation in his right leg. ∅

Bulls GM To Team: 'This Is New Head Coach Vinnie Del Negro; He'll Be Staying With Us For A While'

JUNE 12, 2008

CHICAGO—Introducing Vinnie Del Negro as a "great guy who has just hit a rough patch and needs somewhere to stay," Bulls GM John Paxson introduced his team to their new head coach on Wednesday. "I want everyone to extend Vinnie every courtesy while he implements his offense and tries to get his life back together," Paxson told his team in the somewhat tense United Center meeting. "Look, you know how it is. You've been there. You lost 49 games last season, so don't judge. Just help him out. Let him sleep on the couch, and when he needs to talk about it, listen." An embarrassed Del Negro thanked the team for taking him in, and promised he would stay out of their way and move on again as soon as he felt he was ready. ∅

SPORTS GRAPHIC

Remembering The Original Dream Team

APRIL 05, 2007

With the USA's "Dream Team" looking to redeem their poor 2004 performance, Onion Sports looks back on the first, and arguably the best, Dream Team:

➤ In the 1988 Olympic games, U.S. amateur basketball players are only able to achieve a bronze medal, prompting FIBA officials to make sure that never happens again

➤ Coach Chuck Daly wakes up one morning in 1991 and writes down a dream he had in which a team of all the NBA's best players easily defeated everyone in the world while wearing their pajamas; Daly later removed the part about the pajamas

➤ During team USA's 116–48 whooping of Angola, Christian Laettner waits in the locker room to avoid getting in the way of the awesome players

➤ The Dream Team plays the game against Lithuania in slow motion, dunking the ball 100 times

➤ After a no-look-behind-the-back–pass from Larry Bird, Jordan dishes the ball to Magic Johnson, who throws it to Charles Barkley, who bounces it to Patrick Ewing, who sends it to Chris Mullin, who tosses it to Clyde Drexler, who throws it to David Robinson, who hurls it to Karl Malone, who slings it to John Stockton, who heaves it down the court to Scottie Pippen, who is stopped by the referees whistling the play dead because the Dream Team has 11 men on the court

➤ Clyde Drexler plays an entire game without touching the ground once

➤ Charles Barkley and Michael Jordan use their time together during fast breaks to learn that they both love gambling

➤ Michael Jordan leads the way against Croatia with 22 points, finally settling the dispute over who is better, Michael Jordan or Croatia

➤ A tearful Karl Malone clutches his gold medal and insists the feeling is better than winning an NBA championship as his fellow Dream Teamers hide their grins and nod supportively

Tim Duncan Forwards Story About Particle Accelerator To Spurs Teammates

SEPTEMBER 11, 2008

SAN ANTONIO—Spurs center Tim Duncan once again attempted to simultaneously bond with his teammates and enrich their lives on Tuesday when the two-time NBA MVP forwarded an article about the Large Hadron Collider, the world's largest particle accelerator, to each player on the Spurs. "I hope they found reading about the Large Hadron Collider experiment to recreate the first instants in the birth of our universe as engaging as I did," Duncan said, adding that if his teammates respond positively to the article, he would also send them a related article on quantum chromodynamics recently published in Scientific American. "It will be interesting to find out if they have similar theories about space, matter, and time." In the past three months, Duncan has reportedly forwarded articles on the evolution of the roseola virus, the technology of geothermal energy research, and caring for koi fish in a backyard pond. ∅

Bobby Simmons Under Impression Nets Are Entering The Bobby Simmons Era

NOVEMBER 6, 2008

EAST RUTHERFORD, NJ—Following his trade from Milwaukee, small forward Bobby Simmons, who averaged 7.6 points per game in 2007–08 and has only started in one game this season, is under the impression that the New Jersey Nets have entered the Bobby Simmons Era. "The sun has set on the Bobby Simmons Era in Milwaukee, and today marks the dawn of a new day here in New Jersey," said Simmons, a journeyman who has played for four teams in his seven-year career. "I'm certain the front offices have begun to make moves to build the team around me. I just hope Vince Carter knows to step down." As of tip-off, Simmons has yet to be assigned a permanent locker. ∅

Peja Stojakovic Fondly Recalls First Human Head He Played Basketball With

NOVEMBER 20, 2008

NEW ORLEANS—Hornets small forward Peja Stojakovic entertained his teammates Tuesday with his heartwarming tale of growing up in war-torn Croatia and waking up one Christmas morning to find a brand new regulation human head under the tree. "Of course my parents could not afford it, but I didn't know that, and I could not contain myself as I unwrapped the bow and immediately started scuffing up the face with sandpaper so I could get a better grip," said Stojakovic, recalling the pride he felt when he showed his father that he could grip the head with one hand. "I can still remember the sound that the head would make when it went through the coiled razor-wire net. My mother, she used to get angry because I was bouncing the head in the house all the time, but she always encouraged me to work on my head-handling skills." Stojakovic said that he

eventually lost the old head—which by then had become discolored and lost most of its skin—when it landed in the yard of a neighbor who refused to give it back. ∅

John Stockton Assists Hall Of Fame Officials In Setting Up Induction Ceremony

SEPTEMBER 18, 2008

SPRINGFIELD, MA—Saying he just wanted to do whatever he could to make it a great event, all-time NBA assists leader John Stockton arrived several hours early to the NBA Hall of Fame induction ceremony Friday in order to help set up the PA system, construct the stage, and hang banners and posters throughout the room. "Just have to finish filling out all these name cards, and then I can get back behind the lighting booth," said Stockton, who folded a record 62 table linens Friday night and accrued 3,265 career steals. "Boy, this mic sounds a little hot. We should talk to Jerry about switching it out. Coffee's ready!" According to sources, Stockton, who wore a full tuxedo throughout the ceremony, left immediately afterward to "pitch in" at a fundraising event at the Museum of Fine Arts in Boston. ∅

'Space Jam' Actor Larry Bird Spotted At Game 2 Of NBA Finals

JUNE 12, 2008

BOSTON—Actor Larry Bird, best known for his portrayal of Larry Bird in the 1996 film *Space Jam*, Larry Bird in the 1994 basketball drama *Blue Chips*, and Larry Bird in the 1996 comedy *Celtic Pride*, attended Game 2 of the NBA Finals Sunday night. "We were in the team huddle, and I look up, and there's Hollywood legend Larry Bird—the actor who played golf with basketball player Michael Jordan in *Space Jam* before Jordan got sucked into the hole that dropped him into Looneyland," said guard Ray Allen, adding that his teammates then began imitating Bird's delivery of his signature "Where'd he go?" line from the film. "Of course, he got a huge standing ovation from the crowd when they announced his name. He was great in that movie." Bird had no comment when asked if he had any new projects in the works, only telling reporters that he was at the game to see if the actor from *He Got Game* was any good. ∅

Kobe Bryant Scores 25 In Holy Shit We Elected A Black President

NOVEMBER 6, 2008

LOS ANGELES—Lakers shooting guard Kobe Bryant had a typically solid performance from the field last night, scoring 25 points to propel his team to a holy shit, it's hard to believe these words are even gracing this page, but on Tuesday, Nov. 4, 2008, the American people elected a black man to the office of the President of the United States.

Words really can't describe how... or what, or.... Wow.

Bryant, who got off to a slow start early, but managed to find his touch late in the third, incredible. A black president for a nation whose entire history has been haunted by the specter of slavery and plagued by racism since before its inception. That this happened in our lifetime is remarkable; that it happened within 50 years of a time when segregation was still considered an acceptable institution is astonishing. Absolutely astonishing. This is an achievement on par with the moon landing.

Bryant closed out the fourth quarter with eight points in five minutes.

"It was just a question of finding my rhythm, not forcing it, and playing within the offense," said Bryant, who also...a black man. President. Not the president of a community board, or the president of a business, but the president of the United States of America—the highest office in the land, the commander in chief, the de facto leader of the free world—is a black man chosen by a majority of his fellow citizens.

"This game shows you that free throws really do matter and [the great American Paradox—that is, the conflicting notion that a nation could be founded on the guiding principle that all men are created equal, but be built upon the backs of slaves—may not have been completely resolved on Tuesday night, but it was certainly resolved to an extent that would have been unimaginable to Founding Fathers Benjamin Franklin, John Adams, and most certainly Thomas Jefferson, and it was resolved by the combined will of the American people]."

"You also have to give the bench a lot of credit," Bryant added.

Lakers forward Lamar Odom also chipped in with 16 points and eight boards in the historic 349-162 Electoral College victory over the slumping Clippers, who are clearly missing the presence of former power forward Elton Brand—a Democrat, let alone a black Democrat, winning Indiana for the first time in 44 years? Florida? Ohio? Maybe even North goddamned Carolina? Are you fucking kidding? Is it absolutely confirmed that he won Virginia?

Virginia, for crying out loud. Fucking crazy is what that is.

The 2008 league MVP was solid on the defensive end of the court as well, holding Clippers guard Baron Davis to just 12 points and when they called Pennsylvania, Ohio, and Florida for Obama, basically ensuring victory, that was a moment in which all Americans, regardless of race, creed, color, or party affiliation had to stand back and say, "Holy shit, this is actually going to happen. Holy shit.... Holy shit. Holy shit! Holy shit!"

The undefeated Lakers came into Wednesday night's game against the Clippers with a 3-0 record, and looked to continue their dominance in states like New York, California, and Massachusetts, but Bryant looked to get Lakers center Virginia involved early, and as recently as four years ago, it would have been unfathomable that citizens there would vote for a Democrat, let alone an African-American.

"We see the election of a black president, and Pau Gasol's good shooting night, as a positive sign of things to come," Lakers head coach Phil Jackson said. "It's still early in the season, and there are a lot of things we need to work on, but I'm a product of the '60s, a baby boomer, so I'll blame our lull in the third quarter on me thinking back to the race riots during the civil rights movement, the assassination of Rev. Martin Luther King, Jr., and the separate but equal laws that plagued this nation, and how I thought then that in a million years we would never elect a black president.

The fact that I am even saying these words is pretty fucking incredible."

"Kobe works well when he remains poised and trusts the triangle offense," Jackson added.

Two hundred thousand people of different races and ages—some crying, some cheering, all overjoyed because of the racial barrier they helped break down—were in attendance at Chicago's Grant Park for Wednesday's game, and stayed through the night, laughing, singing, cheering, and high-fiving even after the Lakers game was over and they won Colorado and the election was officially in garbage time.

Said Lakers forward Barack Obama to the entire world on his team's victory: "Yes, we can."

Fucking right we can. We did! We really did! I don't mind telling you I spilled out into the street along with all my joyfully screaming neighbors and danced right there to whatever songs anybody wanted to sing, including—and I can't believe we actually did this, but compared to electing a black man to the presidency, absolutely nothing is unbelievable anymore—an impromptu version of "God Bless America," which is the least danceable song in the world, but fuck it, we sang and danced to "God Bless America," and I'll bet you anything that no one there ever meant it more.

"I just wish that my mother, father, and grandfather could have seen this," said 52-year-old African-American Mark Booker, a Lakers fan who called this the single greatest moment of his entire life. "We won. We won. We won." ◙

Loose Ball Evades Entire NBA

DECEMBER 11, 2008

EAST RUTHERFORD, NJ—A Devin Harris three-point attempt that caromed wildly off the back of the rim during the third quarter of Wednesday night's New York Knicks–New Jersey Nets game has created a disruption involving the entire NBA, with all 450 of the league's players attempting to scoop up the loose ball and gain possession for their respective teams.

NBA officials say the ball initially bounced near the Izod Center sideline, where Nets guard Bobby Simmons jumped, turned, and saved the ball, but inbounded it at a severe enough angle that it struck Knicks forward Al Harrington's shoe. The ball was then sent high into the air, ricocheting in turn up the arena's aisles, into the concession area, out the front entrance, through the parking lot, and on to I-495 East towards Manhattan, leaving multiple flailing players in its wake.

Eyewitnesses said that Nets and Knicks players continued to give chase along the highway and were eventually joined over the next three hours by the Toronto Raptors and Los Angeles Clippers, with players only breaking off their pursuit for a few minutes when Knicks guard Nate Robinson was struck and killed by an oncoming car.

"That's the kind of tenacity I like to see on the court, down the Lincoln Tunnel, and up Broadway," Knicks coach Mike D'Antoni told reporters as a live feed of the bouncing ball revealed that it had entered Philadelphia, where Sixer Andre Iguodala and Cleveland's LeBron James were chasing it around the Liberty Bell. "A willingness to sacrifice one's body by diving into the stands or the Hudson is what separates good teams from great teams."

When no players from the Atlanta Hawks, Indiana Pacers, or Utah Jazz were able to gain possession, the ball continued to bounce along I-95, eventually rolling off at a Washington, D.C. exit.

Members of the Washington Wizards and Detroit Pistons then entered the scramble and proceeded to bat the ball through the White House; around the Lincoln Memorial; up, down, and back up the steps of the Washington Monument; into the Holocaust Museum's railcar exhibit; off the Key Bridge; and into the Potomac River, where a combination of tides and splashing from floundering players carried it into the Atlantic Ocean.

Although Toronto's Chris Bosh attempted to call time-out before the ball entered the river, referee Dick Bavetta—who had been chasing the ball through the entirety of its journey in order to monitor any loose ball fouls—said Bosh did not have possession and therefore could not call for a stoppage in play.

"You gotta be kidding me," said Bosh, who needed the rebound to complete a triple-double. "If he would have called that foul on [Pacers forward Danny] Granger in Delaware this wouldn't even be an issue. No way that trip wasn't intentional."

Starters from the Miami Heat and Charlotte Bobcats spent the next several hours swimming after the ball approximately 90 miles off the coast of Florida, where it ultimately came into the possession of the Cuban military, who would only relinquish the ball to an NBA official. The resulting stoppage in play forced Bavetta to perform a jump ball between Miami's Dwyane Wade, Charlotte's Emeka Okafor, New Orleans' Chris Paul, Orlando's Dwight Howard, and Boston's Kevin Garnett.

Garnett, who had been enjoying the Celtics' Wednesday off, left dinner with his wife and entered the pack of chasing players after observing the loose ball rolling past the restaurant window.

"You got to want it," said Garnett, who tipped the jump ball to Yao Ming, who tipped it to Greg Oden, who tipped it to Pau Gasol, who tipped it onto the back of flatbed truck that was on a container ship headed back to the United States.

"Where can I rent a cigarette boat around here?"

The container ship, however, was discovered to be captained by Lakers guard Kobe Bryant, who told reporters that he was ready to go on a fast break when the ball was suddenly knocked out of his hands by "Cuban refugees," who turned out to be disguised members of the San Antonio Spurs and Sacramento Kings.

The ball was batted around the deck for the entirety of the 600-mile trip to Galveston, TX, where the Chicago Bulls, Minnesota Timberwolves, Milwaukee Bucks, and Houston Rockets, alerted by breaking news reports, waited at dockside for the ship's arrival. A large melee ensued, and the ball was tipped nearly 70,000,000 times, working its way to Los Angeles, up towards Big Sur, all through Alcatraz, back down the Pacific Coast Highway, and finally into Oklahoma.

Though multiple shouts of "Same team!" were heard echoing throughout the more than 1 million square miles of the Great Plains, not one member of the 2-20 Oklahoma City Thunder realized that no other basketball organization was around to wrest the ball away from them. The Thunder lost its chance to

see **LOOSE BALL**

Jason Kidd Describes Feeling 'Unsafe In Own Arena' After Getting Basketball Stolen

DECEMBER 4, 2008

DALLAS—A distressed and visibly shaken Jason Kidd addressed the Mavericks Tuesday to admit that he no longer felt safe in his own home court after a mysterious figure approached him from behind during the Mavericks' most recent game and took possession of the basketball without his consent. "I don't know if I can go back out there again—it's just too risky," said Kidd, his hoarse voice barely rising above a whisper. "Whoever it was came out of nowhere, and I was unable to protect or secure the basketball before he stole it. I know in my heart that it isn't my fault, but I still feel so... angry and violated." Kidd claimed he has not been this humiliated since an incident in 2001 when police handcuffed him and threw him in the back of a squad car for punching his wife in the face. ∅

from **LOOSE BALL**

gain possession when the ball bounced off Kevin Durant's knee into Colorado and over the Rocky Mountains, where Carmello Anthony mishandled it and accidentally tipped it to Shaquille O'Neal. O'Neal, not knowing what was going on, threw the ball into the Grand Canyon, which is where the ball currently sits.

"We're not going into the Grand Canyon," a statement from the National Basketball Players Association read in part. "At this moment all 450 of us can see the ball, but there is a snake near it, and we think it might be poisonous. We will go after the loose ball when the snake leaves."

As of press time, Vince Carter has made absolutely no attempt to get the ball back for the Nets. ∅

Nation Refuses To Get To Know Hedo Turkoglu

DECEMBER 4, 2008

CLEVELAND—Despite the TNT network's best efforts to acquaint its audience with the major players of the Magic-Cavaliers playoff series, the population of the United States has emphatically declined the opportunity to get to know Orlando's Hedo Turkoglu. "When I see one of those pre-produced packages about how he's from Serbia or wherever, I immediately mute my TV or change the channel," Atlanta resident Kevin Hazan said concerning the Turkish small forward. Add-

ed Portland, OR basketball fan Russel Carreras, "That little video of him listing all his favorite foods and making goofy faces just didn't grab me. I don't really care if he's a family man who helps out in the Orlando community. Actually, I don't care if he saves a thousand children from a burning fire. I just don't care to welcome Hedo Turkoglu into my home." In contrast to the nation's utter indifference toward Turkoglu, a TNT poll indicated that if given the choice, most viewers would still prefer to smack J.J. Redick right in the face. ∅

Nate Robinson Jumping Over Dwight Howard In Everyday Life

FEBRUARY 19, 2009

ORLANDO, FL—Since leaping over Orlando Magic center Dwight Howard to claim his second NBA dunk title Saturday, 5'9" New York Knicks guard Nate Robinson has apparently dedicated himself to the sole task of jumping over Howard as the 7-footer goes about his daily life.

According to Howard, Robinson bounded over him roughly two dozen times on Tuesday alone, most notably while the All-Star center was putting gas in his car, as he was standing in the checkout line at the grocery store, immediately after he woke up in the morning, two minutes later when he was taking a shower, and right afterward as he began to shave.

"I can't do anything without that guy jumping over me," said Howard, who glanced over his shoulder every few seconds during his press conference Wednesday. "He's everywhere. When I took my mom to her doctor's appointment last Monday, at church communion, and every time I get off my couch to put in a new DVD. And I watch a lot of DVDs."

"I don't know where he's coming from or how he's getting into my house, but I—" Howard added before he was interrupted by a pair

of green shoes and shorts sailing over his head. "Oh, for Christ's sake."

Following the leap, Robinson recreated his post-dunk celebration, performing a dance step with his right foot while making an odd gliding/flying motion with his arms as Howard watched.

"I don't quite get this," Howard said.

Howard admitted that he had played along when Robinson first started bounding over him in a non-dunk-competition setting, saying that he thought the spectacle was good media fodder for All-Star weekend and that he believed it to be temporary. But that all changed Monday when Howard was trying on pants in the dressing room of an Armani Exchange in downtown Orlando. As Robinson flew overhead, Howard realized the leaping would continue indefinite-

ly, even when there was no one around to notice or record the event, and even though Robinson does not live in Orlando.

"It was eerie," Howard said. "We locked eyes after the jump, and Nate just ran off without saying anything. Then he must have exited the store and reentered through the back, because the next thing I knew he was jumping over me again while I looked at belts."

Though the locations and times of Robinson's flights over Howard vary, Howard said he has learned that if he finds himself in a situation in which he is standing up and leaning somewhat forward, there is a good chance Robinson will come from behind and jump over his head, as was the case Monday afternoon at Pirate's Cove

see **NATE ROBINSON**

127

from **NATE ROBINSON**

Adventure miniature golf course.

"Today I thought it was finally over because Nate hadn't jumped over me once—not at the cleaners, the skate park, the gym, anywhere," Howard said. "Then I sat down to a romantic dinner with my girlfriend and as soon as I stood up to light the candles, he comes flying in, breaks the dishware, and gets baked ziti all over the carpet."

"It's upsetting," Howard continued. "But you know what angers me most? It's that he really isn't jumping over me. His crotch is barely clearing the top of my head, and he is putting his left arm on my back for an extra boost. You people are seeing that, right? You're seeing that I need to lean down so he doesn't bang his waist into the back of my head and fall to the ground and embarrass himself in front of everybody? You saw that I dunked on a fucking 12-foot hoop, right?"

According to Howard, Robinson has only hurt himself once. On Wednesday, as the Magic center was unlocking his front door, the Knicks guard apparently flew headfirst into the stained-glass window in the transom above Howard's doorway.

"Where is he?" a concussed Robinson said from the hospital's emergency room. "I got Superman's kryptonite right here."

Reports indicate that Howard is currently standing up against the safety bar at the edge of Niagara Falls. ✍

Jason Kidd Given 1994 Chevy Lumina For Making 10,000th Assist

MARCH 5, 2009

DALLAS—After dishing out his 10,000th career assist Sunday, Dallas Mavericks point guard Jason Kidd was given a used white 1997 Chevy Lumina fully equipped with a sunroof and an AM-FM radio-cassette player. "Jason, congratulations," teammate Dirk Nowitzki said while he and three other Maverick players pushed the car to center court. "Transmission needs a rebuild, paint job's okay from 10 feet, and she might have 167,000 miles on her, but that just means she's broken in. Jason, thanks for passing the ball a lot to people who can score." Former Utah Jazz guard John Stockton received a similar honor in 1995 when his team recognized his career achievements by awarding him a $50 gift certificate to Sam Goody and an arm's length of 50-50 raffle tickets. ✍

INSIDE

> **'Don't Count Out The Magic As East's No. 1 Seed,' Writes Columnist Who Cares Way Too Much About Sports**

> **NBA Fan From 1998 Happy That Bucks Are Signing Jerry Stackhouse**

Majority Of Utah Jazz Players Have Never Heard Of Themselves

FEBRUARY 26, 2009

SALT LAKE CITY—In a *USA Today* poll of NBA players and fans published Tuesday, four out of five Utah Jazz players admitted to never having heard of their team, their teammates, or themselves. "Wait, who the hell is that guy?" Utah forward Paul Millsap said while looking at a picture of Jazz forward Paul Millsap. "I seem to remember the Jazz playing pretty well for the past few seasons, and they  always have a bunch more white guys than other teams, but I don't know any of their names or what they do. Ostertag's not on the team anymore, is he? Though to be honest, it's not like I'd know him if I saw him." During last night's game against the Warriors, the Jazz were charged with their 49th consecutive delay of game penalty when no one got up from the bench after coach Jerry Sloan announced the starting lineup. ✍

'I'm Doing Just Fine,' Filthy, Unshaven Isiah Thomas Reports Into Banana

MARCH 19, 2009

NEW YORK—Speaking directly into a banana he evidently believed a reporter was holding, an unkempt and soiled Isiah Thomas held a makeshift press conference inside a cardboard box Tuesday to inform pedestrians walking past Madison Square Garden that he was "doing all right. I'm just concentrating on helping out around here," said the former Knicks executive and head coach, who addressed a man dropping change into the soup can in front of him as Nate Robinson. "You gotta go strong to the rim, Nate! Now get back here and practice that until you get it right. You want me to keep you on the bench? You stay away from the bench, that's mine." Thomas reportedly ended the news conference with an incoherent closing statement before returning the banana to his urine-soaked pants. ✍

Lesser-Known Moments In Michael Jordan's Hall Of Fame Career

SEPTEMBER 17, 2009

> **1983:** Just fiddling around on the keyboard, he accidentally writes the Chicago Bulls' intro song

> **1987:** With a series of awesome jams, revives the unpopular and often-shunned slam dunk

> **1989:** Somehow wins a game with a buzzer-beating chest pass

> **1990:** During a playoff-clinching victory over the Cavaliers, Jordan scores a career-high 69 points after stepping on Phil Jackson's missing dose of purple sunshine LSD in the locker room

> **1993:** Original Michael Jordan killed for his shoes

> **1994:** Acting as a role model, Jordan introduces himself to a bunch of kids playing basketball on the Chicago streets and wipes them 21-0

> **1995:** Tells Ron Harper to stop wearing Air Jordan XI's

> **1996:** Referee calls Jordan for traveling

> **2005:** After 11 years in the minors, Jordan is called up and hits the World Series-winning home run for the Chicago White Sox

> **2006:** Somehow manages to return to the NBA for a half season with the Bucks without anyone noticing

Stephon Marbury Embroils Celtics' Big 3 In Elaborate Shakespearean Intrigue

MARCH 5, 2009

BOSTON—Saying that "We cannot all be masters, nor all masters / Cannot be truly follow'd," disruptive point guard Stephon Marbury has been scheming to turn Boston's "Big Three" against one another since he signed with the Celtics last month, apparently trying to claim the team for his own.

Sources within the NBA said that within hours of reporting to his first practice, Marbury had met separately with forward Kevin Garnett, guard Ray Allen, and shooting guard Paul Pierce, and was seen whispering to each in turn while pointing at the other two. When asked what he had said to his teammates, Marbury answered, "I am nothing, if not critical," and refused further comment.

When the Celtics lost Sunday's home game to Detroit 105-95, Marbury, who was scoreless in his 12 minutes of play, could be seen smiling coldly from the bench as Pierce and Allen displayed greatly reduced chemistry, failing to pass the ball to open men or execute picks as effectively as they had in the past.

"I shall of these three fools now make my purse," Marbury was heard to say after the game, although he appeared to be addressing no one and perhaps spoke only to himself. "These stars are of a free and open nature, / And think men honest that but seem to be so, / And will as tenderly be led by the nose / As asses are."

When questioned about the meaning of his aside, Marbury said only, "I am not what I am."

Although Garnett, Allen, and Pierce originally welcomed Marbury to the team, stating that they believed he would be valuable coming off the bench and were looking forward to playing with him, they have since stated publicly that Marbury's secretive nature, conspiring attitude, and constant requests to

speak with them alone are already beginning to wear on them.

"After the Detroit loss he pulled me aside and said that I should be as famous as Paul and Kevin," said Allen, who admitted that he found both Marbury's attitude and his language difficult to understand. "Except he said it like, 'Reputation is an idle and most false / imposition: oft got without merit, and lost without / deserving,' and I was like, 'Come on, man, I don't want to hear that.' My numbers are up since I played with them, is all I know, and they don't try and confuse me all the time."

"Stephon told me that the other two guys hated me because I was the most talented," said Pierce, who said speaking with Marbury was beginning to make him feel uncomfortable. "He said I should beware jealousy because it was 'the green-ey'd monster which doth mock / The meat it feeds on.' But I was like, 'Stephon, first of all, Kevin is a way better player than I am.' He just walked away muttering. I don't know what's up with that dude."

Garnett expressed a similar bewilderment with Marbury's behavior.

"Weird thing is, he kept calling the other guys moors, which is just really messed up," the 12-time all-star said. "I mean, what is that, anyway? He didn't say it like it was a good thing. If he plays good basket-

ball he can do what he wants, but I'm not going to listen to anyone call me or my guys moors."

All three men also commented that Marbury had at some point pulled each one of them aside and told them the other two had been "making the beast with two backs."

"I was freaked out, but then I realized he expected me to be jealous, and that freaked me out even more," Garnett said. "Especially when I heard him tell people that's how I injured my right knee. I know Stephon was trouble even way back when we both played for the Timberwolves—he's been trouble everywhere he goes—but this is a whole new level."

Conferring with one another, the Big Three all agreed that Marbury had implied, if not expressly stated, that perhaps Celtics coach Doc Rivers should be stabbed to death, an implication they found unnerving.

When asked for comment, Marbury expressed surprise that his teammates would react to his presence in this way.

"Is it my contract?" asked Marbury, who will receive a prorated veteran's minimum of $1.3 million from the Celtics this season. "Because the money means nothing to me without the respect of my teammates. Good name in man and woman, dear my lord, / Is the immedi-

ate jewel of their souls: / Who steals my purse steals trash... / But he that filches from me my good name / Robs me of that which not enriches him / And makes me poor indeed."

When asked for clarification, Marbury responded, "Demand me nothing: what you know, you know: / From this time forth I never will speak [a] word," and requested that all further questions be directed to his agent, one Roderigo of Venice, who as of press time could not be reached. ∅

INSIDE

> **Salt Lake City Restaurant Host Just Assumed Karl Malone And John Stockton Were Together**

> **David Stern Enforces NBA Hygiene Code With Unannounced Shower Inspection**

> **Tayshaun Prince Yawns Mid-Shot**

> **Tim Duncan Draws Little Spur On Letter 'U' In Name**

> **NBA Defensive Player Of The Year Mocked**

> **Cash-Strapped Hornets Charge Fan One Million Dollars For Missing Half-Court Shot**

> **Ref Hit With Technical Foul For Pounding Chest After Call**

PHOTO FINISH

Zombie Wilt Chamberlain Leads U.S. Nightmare Team To Victory

Cheering Fans, Thrilling NCAA Tournament Disgust BCS Officials

APRIL 2, 2009

DETROIT—Claiming that determining an unquestioned national champion through a playoff system "went against the very idea of sporting competition," and that the sheer exuberance of college basketball fans was "a shocking and nauseating display of everything wrong with collegiate athletics," top BCS officials roundly condemned the NCAA Tournament Monday.

"I frankly cannot even believe what I'm seeing, and I can't stomach the sight for long," said a pale, trembling Jack Swarbrick, the Notre Dame athletic director who, along with the commissioners of the major conferences, manages the complicated system of polls and computer rankings that make up the Bowl Championship Series in college football. "The elegant logic of actually having teams play one another instead of having a council of their betters select which team is superior to which—that is not what sports is all about."

"And the fans... urgghh... simply enjoy their teams' triumphs or mourn their defeats. Where are the heated arguments? Where are the unsettled disputes that will fester forever?" said Swarbrick, a sheen of feverish sweat curdling on his face. "Oh, God, I think I got

vomit on my tie."

"It's the joy, the sheer joy on the fans' pathetic joyful faces and in their insipid happy voices that fills me with such loathing—loathing for the certainty they will feel when all is said and done and they know exactly who is the best, and hatred for the pure joy they will feel because of it," Pac-10 conference commissioner Larry Scott said as he panted, slumped down in a wheelchair. "Mark my words, their certainty regarding exactly how good a team is or isn't will never be allowed to corrupt the BCS—and neither will their joy."

As of press time, Scott had been hospitalized due to nausea and bile scarring in his throat.

Other notable BCS executives have either expressed disgust or been involved in disgust-related incidents in the weeks since the tournament began. The White House has asked several conference commissioners to stop calling after 10 p.m. or while drunk. And retching, unstable statistician Kenneth Massey, a sports-ratings expert whose calculations play a part in the BCS rankings, was arrested by police in Detroit last week when he attempted to chain himself to the gates of Ford Field, all the while

screaming that both stochastic and determinist calculations prove that Xavier could not have beaten Wisconsin in the second round.

"It's wrong. It's just wrong," Swarbrick said. "I haven't been able to keep food or fluids down since this...this March Madness began. Everywhere I go, I hear the cheering, the talk, and I see that goddamned bracket everywhere. Why? Why are all these people so happy after watching a championship tournament? How can they be happy without a network of polls and computers run by an arbitrary board of university executives to tell them who the champion really is?"

"Imagine if we'd let this happen—if we had let, say, Boise State play for the championship after all the filthy happiness and cheering they inspired," a vomit-drenched, glassy-eyed Scott said from his hospital bed. "College football as we know it barely survived them upsetting Oklahoma. If we had let teams compete in a—a—a playoff, as they call it, the resulting combination of joy and true competition would have gone against everything the BCS stands for." ∅

Tim Duncan Hams It Up For Crowd By Arching Left Eyebrow Slightly

APRIL 10, 2009

SAN ANTONIO—Spurs forward Tim Duncan engaged in a rare display of showmanship during Tuesday's win over the Thunder, punctuating a 10-foot jumper with a nearly imperceptible upward motion of his left eyebrow. "I saw him do it, and I was like, 'What! What was that?'" said teammate Michael Finley, who compared the display to a 2006 game in which Duncan gave the crowd an unexpected and nearly flam-

boyant thumbs-up. "We were playing pretty flat, but Timmy flickered his eyebrow like that and it energized the whole team. Everyone thinks he's so stoic, but he knows how to have a good time. Once, in the locker room, he almost winked. Wild." When asked about this display, Tim Duncan denied any intent to show anyone up and

personally called every member of the Thunder organization to apologize. ∅

Kobe Bryant Proves He Can Win Championship With Luke Walton On Team

JUNE 18, 2009

ORLANDO, FL—With the Lakers' 99-86 victory over the Magic in Game 5 of the NBA Finals, Kobe Bryant silenced critics by achieving what most had thought impossible: winning an NBA title with Luke Walton on his team.

"I was so sick of hearing people say how I couldn't do it with Luke out there," said Bryant, acknowledging that his teammate's deficiencies have overshadowed the Lakers since Walton was drafted in 2003. "It gets annoying to hear that question over and over, but you can't argue it. You can't deny it. You have to show that you can prevail alongside one of the worst small forwards in the game."

"Now I just want to kick back and savor the moment," Bryant added. "I feel like a huge 6'8", 235-pound burden has been lifted from my back."

Bryant, who averaged 32.4 points a game and was named MVP of the NBA Finals, played with a fiery determination and lifted his Walton-compensation skills to an almost superhuman level, ultimately erasing any doubt that he was capable of greatness while playing alongside Walton.

According to Bryant, it was vital to step up his game and take on a leadership role in order to surmount the countless flaws in Luke Walton's game, which include playing a slow, hindering style of offense that relies on ruining pick and roll plays; clogging up lanes with an ungainly lumbering stride on the transition; and making slow, drifting passes to double-covered players.

In addition, Bryant said he tried to focus on making up for Walton's lack of production by scoring at least ten times as many points as the small forward.

While coach Phil Jackson said losing to the Celtics by 39 points in Game 6 of the 2008 NBA Finals motivated Bryant to succeed, he acknowledged that Kobe could not overcome Walton's utter lack of talent alone.

"Kobe certainly put up big numbers, but he also rallied this young group of players and took their play to another level with him," Jackson said. "Winning in the Luke Walton era took a total team effort. They should be proud of what they accomplished. You have to be at the very pinnacle of your game to rise above a player of Walton's caliber."

Bryant credited Jackson for working tirelessly to assemble the pieces necessary to fill the hole created when Walton joined the team. He also praised recently acquired players and veterans alike for handling the challenge of guarding Magic center Dwight Howard, defending perimeter shooters Hedo Turkoglu and Rashard Lewis, and keeping the ball out of Walton's hands to prevent him from screwing up their chance to win a title.

"We were able to prove all the doubters wrong because we had an excellent game plan that we executed at the highest level," said Bryant, who verified before each play that his teammates knew their assignments and were prepared to shut down Walton's dominating awkwardness in the paint. "It was physically draining to limit Luke's missed scoring opportunities, but that's what it takes to win."

"Personally, I don't think Shaq could have won with Walton," Bryant added. "I'm not even sure Jordan could have."

Lakers luminary and part-owner Magic Johnson said that Bryant has proven himself to be the preeminent talent in the league, and that he was "astonished" the Lakers had even made the playoffs with Walton on the team.

Johnson was not alone in expressing his surprise.

"Believe me, what he did defies all logic," said Lakers small forward Luke Walton, adding that it was unlikely Bryant and the Lakers could win back-to-back championships with a player as indescribably mediocre as himself. "I'll admit it. I didn't think he could pull it off." ∅

Shaq, Cavaliers Start To Bond After Rollerblading Around Cleveland

NOVEMBER 7, 2009

CLEVELAND—After strapping on inline skates for the first time ever Monday, Cavaliers center Shaquille O'Neal and his new teammates bonded while Rollerblading through the streets of Cleveland. "We definitely had some bad spills, and we got lost in the warehouse district, but I think it all brought us closer together," said O'Neal, adding that the team was "laughing like crazy" the entire time. "Oh my God, it was so hilarious when we hit this one rough steep patch in the Cleveland Metropolitan Park and we had to scoot down a hill on our butts. Then we got ice cream." O'Neal later said he was impressed by the way the Cavaliers worked together to pull a soaking wet Zydrunas Ilgauskas from the Cuyahoga River. ∅

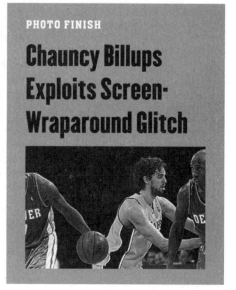

PHOTO FINISH

Chauncy Billups Exploits Screen-Wraparound Glitch

Promise Of Hot Meal, Free Uniform All Juwan Howard Needed To Sign With Blazers

OCTOBER 6, 2009

PORTLAND, OR—Speaking with members of the Portland media Tuesday, veteran forward Juwan Howard announced between spoonfuls of complimentary tomato soup that he was excited to be a part of the Trail Blazers' organization, and was "proud and grateful" to wear the team's free uniform. "It's exciting to be a part of this team, but the fact that [team owner] Paul [Allen] promised me free rye bread here today was really the determining factor," said the 6-foot-9 power forward, who arrived to the press conference shirtless. "I look forward to contributing in any way I can. Hey, I'll be getting an away jersey, too, right? Gets so cold at night." Howard was the fifth player selected in the 1994 draft, and ever since has been wearing the Washington Bullets hat the team gave him that night. ∅

Michael Jordan Wondering Why He Wasn't In 'NBA Jam'

JULY 16, 2009

HIGHLAND PARK, IL—After finding his old Super Nintendo in a routine cleaning of his attic, basketball great Michael Jordan was stunned to find that he did not appear as a playable character in the 1993 game "NBA Jam" and was at a loss to explain why. "I don't understand. I'm Michael Jordan, I should be in that game," said Jordan who had no success finding his likeness in the Arcade, Sega Genesis, Sega CD, Game Boy or Game Gear versions. "Scottie being there makes sense, but Horace Grant? Seriously? And how can Tom Gugliotta be in this game and not me? I could swear they paid me a $100 million licensing fee." Jordan then popped in a copy of "Michael Jordan: Chaos in the Windy City" and played for ten minutes before tossing the controller on the table and taking a nap. ∅

Bill Laimbeer Reverently Elbows Chuck Daly's Coffin Into Grave

MAY 18, 2009

JUPITER, FL—Beloved NBA and Olympic coach Chuck Daly, who passed away May 9 after a battle with pancreatic cancer, was laid to rest by family and friends yesterday in a quiet ceremony at which a visibly moved and weeping Bill Laimbeer respectfully hard-fouled Daly's casket into its final resting place with a savage and reverent elbow. "That's for teaching me to have respect for myself and never give up, Coach," Laimbeer said as Daly's pallbearers, including former Pistons John Salley, Joe Dumars, and Rick Mahorn, sprawled back on the grass with their arms outstretched and looked to the funeral director for a whistle. "Thank you, Mr. Daly, for making me the man I am today." The otherwise touching ceremony was marred only by an outburst of emotion from Dennis Rodman, who threw himself into Daly's grave and writhed sobbing on the coffin while tearing at his black silk wedding dress. ∅

PHOTO FINISH

Terrified Rookie Afraid To Let Go Of Rim After Dunk

Milwaukee Bucks Find Perfectly Good Shaq At Play It Again Sports

OCTOBER 12, 2009

MILWAUKEE— While shopping for used equipment at a local Play It Again Sports franchise Tuesday, Bucks general manager John Hammond reportedly came across a mildly damaged Shaq in good working condition next to a bin filled with old tennis balls. "There's definitely been a little wear and tear, and it doesn't look so great, but for $20, I really couldn't pass it up," Hammond said. "The last couple owners didn't really take very good care of it, but it's more than good enough for the Bucks." Guard Michael Redd later told reporters he wished Hammond had purchased a basketball instead, saying that he was tired of practicing jump shots with a rolled-up sock. ⌀

Stan Van Gundy Draws Up Play In Barbecue Sauce

MAY 29, 2009

ORLANDO—During a timeout in Game 4 of Tuesday's Eastern Conference Finals, Magic head coach and barbecue aficionado Stan Van Gundy used the rich, tangy sauce on his index finger to diagram an offensive scheme on his clipboard. "First off, you're going to stack up like... like this rack of ribs, and then you're going to outlet pass me that last piece of cornbread," said Van Gundy, motioning toward Mickael Pietrus while licking at the brownish-red glaze coating his mustache. "Turkoglu, I want you to set a screen where I've set these chunks of pulled pork to, uh, [unintelligible]—this small chunk of pulled pork—near the perimeter. Christ, that's good. Then Dwight [Howard], this chicken drumstick, should be open under the hoop." Although Howard was in fact open in the paint, the center missed the pass, as he was still partially blinded by barbecue sauce that had spattered from Van Gundy's mouth. ⌀

Tim Duncan Calls Out Geometric Angle Needed To Make Bank Shot

NOVEMBER 28, 2009

SAN ANTONIO—Immediately after releasing a 12-foot jump shot Tuesday night, Spurs center Tim Duncan called out the angle necessary for the ball to bank off the backboard and into the basket. "Forty-six-point-seven degrees," said the airborne Duncan, also noting the ball's initial upward velocity of 14.4 meters per second after a moment of mental calculation. "Two points." According to team sources, when teammate Tony Parker failed to call out the angle of a bank shot later in the game, Duncan glared at the point guard for the entire fourth quarter. ⌀

New Harlem Globetrotter Rudy 'Rude Dude' Williams Not Working Out

DECEMBER 11, 2010

HARLEM, NY—Globetrotters coaches announced Monday that, due to his shockingly inappropriate on-court behavior—including taking trick shots designed to injure opponents, performing his signature Globetrotter move of spinning two basketballs on his middle fingers, and throwing elbows after getting rebounds—Rudy "Rude Dude" Williams has been suspended for the team's next three games.

"We in the Globetrotter organization pride ourselves on playing basketball in a spirit of good-natured hijinks, if not complete fairness, and we regret that one of our players has fallen short of this standard," a press release for the club read in part. "Because Mr. Williams hasn't learned to limit his shenanigans to traveling, goofing, and bouncing the ball off defenders' foreheads without doing serious cranial damage, he will not dress for our upcoming games against the Washington Generals, the Washington Generals, and the Washington Generals."

Rude Dude came to the Harlem squad when coaches noticed that their opponents had a tendency to score more easily late in the second half of games, usually closing to within a mere two points and forcing the Globetrotters to resort to unlikely heroics to win. It was decided a stronger defense was

see RUDE DUDE

from **RUDE DUDE**

needed, and a contract was offered to Rude Dude, a former defensive standout at UNLV.

"In retrospect, it was a bad move," said coach Tex Harrison, who recruited Rude Dude. "He was a low-post player primarily, and not only was he unaccustomed to dribbling two balls at one time, he told us he found the entire practice to be 'pretty damn stupid.'"

According to Harrison, Rude Dude took forever to grasp the intricacies of the figure-eight offense. Instead of letting the Generals just follow him through the Globetrotter Weave, Williams would set a pick, send opposing players crashing to the ground, and stand over them while flexing and taunting. In addition, whenever the Globetrotters' theme song, "Sweet Georgia Brown," was played over the PA system, Rude Dude would reportedly just sit on the bench, loudly and deliberately whistling out of key.

"We wanted toughness, yes, but a sort of funky, clowning toughness," Harrison said. "Rude Dude did not understand this."

In the past several months, complaints against Williams have continued to mount. During a game in Indianapolis, the Globetrotters went into their famous

football formation, an offensive scheme designed to confuse and disorient opponents due to the preposterous nature of football being played on the basketball court. When the basketball was "intercepted" by Generals center James Vilsaint, Williams tackled him and drove him headfirst into the hardwood court, giving his opponent a severe concussion and a fractured collarbone. In the same game, Williams, instructed to "get" a referee with a bucketful of confetti, grasped the official by the back of the neck and roughly shoved his head inside the bucket, holding him there until he passed out from oxygen deprivation.

In what some say is his biggest failing as a Globetrotter, Williams has refused to place prespun basketballs on children's fingers, often telling young fans to "spin it your own goddamn self." In the rare instances in which he has put pre-spun balls on their fingers, the results have been disastrous.

"See that? That's me that did that, not you," Rude Dude can be heard saying in a particularly infamous YouTube clip in which he places a ball on the finger of a pigtailed and freckled 9-year-old girl. "What, you gonna cry? You are, you're cry-

ing. Jesus, I can't believe this shit," the Globetrotter says just before striking the girl's hand from below, sending the ball caroming out of the frame as the girl bursts into tears.

The clip has been viewed more than 250,000 times.

"Not everyone is cut out to be a Globetrotter," Harlem GM Nickolas Cardinale told reporters. "But I've talked to Rude Dude, and he says he wants to make it work. I think he understands now that Globetrotters can't get in fights with the bouncer at Dave & Buster's, can't be in 'Stop Snitching' videos, and I think he also understands that when we take female fans to center court to dance with them, they shouldn't be touched inappropriately."

"He wants to play here," Cardinale added. "But he also knows that we're open to trade offers."

Thus far, only one team has shown interest in acquiring Rude Dude.

"We'd love to have Rude Dude," said Red Klotz, owner of the Washington Generals, a team that hasn't beaten the Globetrotters since 1971. "Frankly, I'm tired of the culture of losing that has come over this team, and Rude Dude might just be the kind of player we can beat them with." Ø

NCAA Tournament Expands To However Many Teams Honestly Feel They Should Be In NCAA Tournament

MAY 1, 2010

INDIANAPOLIS—The NCAA Board of Directors made the decision Wednesday to expand its men's basketball tournament to however many teams "really and truly believe" they ought to be involved. "Who are we to bar a school from the Big Dance if they just know in their heart of hearts that they deserve a shot?" said NCAA interim president Jim Isch, adding that the maximum number of teams permitted would only be limited by the number of schools that believe in themselves. "Of course, for any team out there that wants to be in the tournament but doesn't quite think it deserves it, I say go ahead and put your name on the list anyway. Seriously, what's one more team?" Immediately following the announcement, all 342 Division I schools signed up for the 2011 tournament except Loyola Marymount. Ø

Spud Webb Getting Smaller And Smaller Every Time People Recount 1986 Dunk Contest

FEBRUARY 2, 2010

ATLANTA—In recent accounts of Spud Webb's astounding victory in the 1986 NBA Slam-Dunk Contest, basketball fans across the nation have reportedly exaggerated the diminutive point guard's size by greatly diminishing his height with each retelling of the event. "I totally remember he was like 3-foot-5-inches tall and he did this amazing 180-degree reverse double-pump slam," Hawks fan Eric Davis said of the 5-foot-7 Webb, who was 4-foot-9 and dunked from the foul line the last time Davis told the story. "Spud really wasn't much bigger than a basketball. He just blew everybody away in the final round when he rode into the arena on a hamster, ripped off his G.I. Joe doll uniform warm-up pants, threw the ball at the backboard, ran between a small child's legs, jumped up to Dominique Wilkins' palm, and springboarded off it to do a 360-degree two-handed dunk." Sources later confirmed that on the rare occasion that people

talk about Nate Robinson's dunk contests, the Knicks guard remains 5-foot-9 inches tall, as nobody really cares enough to exaggerate his exploits. Ø

Shaq Misses Entire Second Half With Pulled Pork Sandwich

JANUARY 22, 2010

CLEVELAND—Cavaliers center Shaquille O'Neal suffered a frustrating setback during his team's victory over the Toronto Raptors Tuesday night, when he was sidelined for the entire second half of the game with a pulled pork sandwich.

O'Neal, who scored 12 points and grabbed three rebounds during the first half of the game, returned to the bench at the beginning of the third quarter, clutching at the pulled pork sandwich and informing trainers that it was incredibly tender. A member of the Cavaliers' medical staff said that when he attempted to examine the pulled pork sandwich, O'Neal flinched away and grunted sharply.

"We are moving quite cautiously and continuing to monitor the situation, because this appears to be a very serious pulled pork sandwich," Cavaliers athletic trainer Max Benton said. "There's a chance that Shaq could have gone back into the game, but with a pulled pork sandwich of that magnitude you can't be too careful. I've seen lesser ones knock a guy out for the rest of the season."

"My best guess is that he'll be slowed down for a bit and require anywhere from a few hours to several days to recover," Benton added. "We made sure it had heat on it—you don't want to let it cool down, and you certainly don't ice it—and we gave him plenty of fluids. I've seen a few pulled pork sandwiches, and this one looked pretty good, pretty loose. With luck it'll be out of his system by tomorrow morning."

Cavaliers head coach Mike Brown said he was pleased by O'Neal's effort in the first half and was surprised when the center had to leave the game. Brown told reporters that prior to the pulled pork sandwich the 15-time All-Star appeared to be moving smoothly and showed none of the warning signs of the onset of a pulled pork sandwich.

"This is such a shame. A pulled pork sandwich this severe was the last thing Shaq needed at this point in the season," said Brown, who is still optimistic that the pulled pork sandwich will not derail O'Neal's attempt at another NBA title. "Hopefully he can gut it out and play through the pain."

Point guard Mo Williams said O'Neal spent the majority of the third quarter hunched over on the bench with his hands up to his face, nursing his pulled pork sandwich. Williams said O'Neal stood up and tested the pulled pork sandwich several times before insisting that he didn't feel right.

O'Neal reportedly spent the rest of the game lying on his back, breathing heavily.

"When I saw him grimace immediately after the pulled pork sandwich, I could tell that he was done for the night," forward LeBron James said. "You could just see it all over his face."

Although O'Neal disappeared into the locker room after the Cavaliers defeated the Raptors 108-100, reporters conducting postgame interviews confirmed they heard moaning sounds emanating from a restricted area of the facility where the 37-year-old was seeking relief.

"Shaquille will be in our thoughts and prayers," Cavaliers general manager Danny Ferry told reporters. "As a former player, I know that when you get older it becomes harder and harder to recover from a pulled pork sandwich that severe. However, I can confirm that rumors Shaq might have a second pulled pork sandwich are simply not true."

O'Neal, who entered the NBA in 1992, has been plagued throughout his career by pulled pork sandwiches, which caused him to miss 28 games during the 1995-1996 season alone. During his third season with the Miami Heat, his effectiveness is thought to have been hampered by his attempts to play despite numerous pulled pork sandwiches. Later in O'Neal's career, doctors discovered that the 7'1" center's ability to shoot free throws was compromised by complications from chronic pulled pork sandwiches, a condition commonly known as "greasy digits."

A team spokesperson announced yesterday that medical staff had performed an MRI on O'Neal's pulled pork sandwich, but the results were inconclusive. Ø

40,000 Revenge-Seeking Bats Descend Upon Manu Ginobili

Utah Fans Concerned As Jazz Break Huddle By Shouting 'Kill The Mormons'

MAY 3, 2010

SALT LAKE CITY—An uneasy sense of anxiety overtook the crowd at EnergySolutions Arena Sunday as fans watched a pumped-up Jazz team break their pregame huddle by chanting, "One, two, three—kill the Mormons!" "Normally this team is pretty even-keeled, but tonight they're really scaring me," said season ticket holder Delton Stanger, who was terrified by the team's cheers of "Die, Mormons, die" and "We're coming for you, Mormons." "I just don't understand why all my favorite players want to kill us and why it's inspiring them to play with such passion." Utah fans were reportedly appalled when head coach Jerry Sloan used a dry-erase board to diagram how to find the Mormons, round them up, and kill them, but admitted their anger was tempered by the team's resultant 15-0 run. Ø

Senator Dikembe Mutombo Blocks Record Amount Of Legislation

FEBRUARY 26, 2010

WASHINGTON—Sen. Dikembe Mutombo (R-CO) showed that he is still one of the most dominant big men in Congress Thursday, blocking a record 16 bills in one legislative session.

The 7-foot-2 senator, who broke the record previously held by Sen. Shawn Bradley (D-NJ), Rep. Arvydas Sabonis (D-OR), and current Senate Minority Leader Mitch McConnell (R-KY), batted away legislation left and right, sometimes swatting bills so hard that they were sent flying all the way back to committee.

Mutombo punctuated his final block, a clean rejection of the Criminal Justice Reinvestment Act, with his signature finger wag.

"He stuffed the new jobs bill right back in Harry Reid's face," Sen. John McCain (R-AZ) told reporters. "And then when Reid tried to put the bill back up for consideration, Sen. Mutombo blocked it a second and then a third time. That's when I knew he had a chance at the record."

"He just completely dominates the Senate floor," McCain added.

His biggest rejection came 20 minutes into the first half of the session when 5-foot-10 Sen. Chris Dodd (D-CT) had his Peace Corps Improvement and Expansion Act emphatically slapped away by a leaping Mutombo. Following the rejection, Mutombo glared at Dodd from the Senate podium and said, "Get that weak-ass legislation out of my house," in a yell that was reportedly heard in the top rows of the Senate Chamber.

"You don't mind giving up the blocks record to a talent like Mutombo," said Sen. McConnell, who is still considered the Republican floor leader. "Some say he's too centrist, and he may take that position at times, but the fact is he can get stuff struck down like nobody's business."

Mutombo, who has been called a "force" by his Republican colleagues and is a key player in their legislative game plan, had a career-best nine blocks during the first half of Thursday's session. He easily rejected several appropriations bills, barely even getting off the Senate floor on two of them. For his 10th block of the day, he also got a piece of the Law Enforcement Officers Safety Act.

"He's like a brick wall out there," a visibly tired and sweaty Sen. John Kerry (D-MA) told reporters. "Sen. Mutombo's arms are so long that if legislation is introduced anywhere in his vicinity, he's probably going to knock it away. There's no way we are going to get health care through with Mutombo out there."

"You can try and alter your legislation or fake him out by attaching a rider to a bill, but in the end he's just too big," Kerry continued. "And fast. He's got surprisingly quick footwork."

Dikembe Mutombo Mpolondo Mukamba Jean-Jacques Wamutombo started his political career as a city councilman in Denver, quickly gaining a reputation as an elected official focused on getting that stuff out of here. Campaigning on

SENATOR DIKEMBE MUTOMBO

a platform of defense, defense, defense, the popular Mutombo was elected to the State Legislature in 2002 and then to the U.S. Senate in 2006. According to Senate sources, the rookie lawmaker came out of nowhere to stuff Ted Kennedy's Vaccine Access and Supply Act "so far down the late senator's throat" that he easily won the respect of his Republican colleagues.

"He reminds me of myself out there, just rejecting stuff left and right," said former Senate Majority Leader Bill Frist (R-TN), who retired in 2007. "Even when he gets called an obstructionist, or for goaltending, he's established psychological dominance and made his point: You don't come through his part of the floor."

Though many Democratic senators have called Mutombo's legislative style extremely partisan, one-dimensional, and completely unfair, some of his colleagues across the aisle have praised Mutombo's willingness to assist them in getting their legislation through Congress.

"The thing about Mutombo is that, for a big man, he can actually pass bills really well," Sen. Max Baucus (D-MT) said in reference to their bipartisan work on the Trade Act of 2007 and the Medicare Improvements for Patients and Providers Act of 2008. "Because

he's so tall, he sees the perimeter of the entire Senate floor and knows when a senator from the left or right might offer some weak-side help."

"Reminds me of a young Bill Bradley," Baucus added.

Such praise from Democratic lawmakers is rare, however, with many saying that Sen. Mutombo is directly responsible for the gridlock currently facing Washington.

"Sometimes I get the impression that he'll block something just because it's introduced by a Democrat or, quite frankly, just because he's taller than the rest of us," Sen. Arlen Specter (D-PA) told reporters. "Why else would he reject a resolution supporting stability in Sudan?"

Specter went on to express concern for the future of his party, saying that the only hope for getting meaningful legislation passed through Congress is to make sure Rep. Greg Ostertag (D-UT) is elected to the Senate during November's midterm election. ∅

STRONG SIDE/ WEAK SIDE: KEVIN DURANT

STRONG SIDE	WEAK SIDE
Ability to exploit NBA's complete lack of defense	Spends time on defensive end of the floor day dreaming about being on offensive
Scored just now	Bummed out that Seattle has gotten so lame over the past two years
Is not actually affected by gravity, but willing to put up with it for sportsmanship's sake	Explosive game may be out of place in a town that has good reason to fear explosiveness
Knows really good shortcut to hoop	Got into trouble in college for grabbing woman basketball player's rebounds
Always striving to get hops at maddest level possible	Those knees are just asking for it
Deep sense of Oklahoma City Thunder's history since he is it	Is betting on a career in pro basketball, a frankly unrealistic goal that may prevent him from learning a more practical trade

Kevin Durant High-Dribbler In Win With 186 Bounces

MARCH 1, 2010

OKLAHOMA CITY—Thunder guard Kevin Durant dribbled the ball 73 times in the fourth quarter, leading all dribblers with 186 bounces in Oklahoma City's win against the New York Knicks Saturday. "At first I was trying to just be patient and dribble only when I had to, like to avoid traveling and to run the offense," said Durant, who is third in the league with 147.6 dpg and a 99.8 dribble percentage. "I know we're not supposed to admit it, but yeah, by the end I was counting. 182, 183, 184, 185, 186 bounces. It felt good. Honestly, I was in such a zone that it felt like I was dribbling on a court twice as big." Durant also led both teams with 43 jumps and 1,227 steps taken. *∅*

Carmelo Anthony Called For Traveling Back In Time

MARCH 19, 2010

HOUSTON—Nugget's forward Carmelo Anthony made no secret of his displeasure with game officials Monday night after being whistled for a rarely called traveling-through-time foul late in the fourth quarter of Denver's 125-123 loss to the Rockets.

"Everybody knows they only call time-traveling when they want to," said Anthony, who could clearly be seen taking two steps back in time to warn himself about an impending pick by Rockets forward Shane Battier. "You see it called, what? Every other game? Once a week? But everybody knows that guys are doing it all the time out there."

The NBA traveling-through-time call is a longtime bone of contention for fans and players alike, most of whom claim that, although the rule is on the books, officials are reluctant to slow down the flow of the game by calling it too often.

"All I'm asking is that they be consistent," Anthony said. "You're gonna call me in the fourth quarter for a piddly little case of going back to warn myself about a pick, then call me in the first quarter for going back to take the same jumper three times until I hit it. Me or anybody."

While the NBA did not respond directly to Anthony's allegations, vice president of referee operations Joe Borgia did tell reporters that the traveling-through-time rule "has been, and will continue to be, enforced in order to preserve both game integrity and continuity and to preserve the fundamental fabric of the universe." Borgia noted that the NBA rulebook clearly states that a player may not progress the ball by sliding into parallel dimensions, and said consideration must be made for human error on the part of the officials making the call, as well as for the reality-altering nature of the offense itself.

The NBA claims it has always taken a hard stance on flagrant and repeat violators of the traveling-though-time rule, saying it wants to avoid a total breakdown of basketball causality as we know it. Borgia said he has evidence suggesting there are several parallel-universe NBAs, including one in which the Nuggets won 16 straight championships before moving to Luna City, a timeline in which Anthony's name figures heavily. In other alternate worlds, where time-traveling is never called, the Utah Jazz of the 1990s were led by famous married couple Karl Malone and John Stockton, who won five championships together; a great Magic Johnson/Larry Bird partnership blossomed in Atlanta; and the WNBA challenges the men's league for sports dominance.

"Already we have some questions we'd like answered in our own league, such as why the Celtics are struggling more than you'd think, why Kevin Durant is almost unstoppable all of a sudden, and why Shaquille O'Neal has suddenly turned up in Mathew Brady's Civil War photographs," Borgia said. "And as always, our biggest worry is potential gambling."

Anthony, for his part, said he would accept the NBA's ruling, but maintained that the league has a different set of space-time rules for their favorites, a common belief among

see TIME TRAVEL

Chris Bosh Out For Season After Cutting Open Knee To See How It Works

MARCH 10, 2010

TORONTO—The Raptors medical staff announced Tuesday that Chris Bosh will miss the rest of the season after the inquisitive forward cut open his knee with a steak knife in an effort to look inside and see how the joint works. "There's a lot more stuff in there than I thought," said Bosh, who after finishing the surgery attempted to stop the bleeding by wrapping an entire roll of toilet paper around his knee. "It  probably needs all those meaty-looking ropes so it can bend.

And look in this pickle jar—I kind of had to use some pressure to get it started turning, but I had no idea that I could unscrew my kneecap. Pretty cool, huh?" While recovering from the significant ligament and cartilage damage, Bosh said he plans to undergo a procedure to detect early signs of colorectal cancer by shoving a digital camera up his ass. *∅*

from TIME TRAVEL

pro players. It is reportedly an article of faith in today's NBA that LeBron James regularly travels through time during games, including every time he uses his trademark Evolution Crossover move, but James has not been the subject of a traveling-through-time call since January. Perhaps the most infamous time-traveling perpetrator is Michael Jordan, acknowledged as the greatest player of all time; Jordan eventually became infamous for executing a move of almost superhuman skill and grace at one mo-

ment, and in the next, throwing a no-look pass to a future Jordan who would take four steps after exiting a wormhole and dunk the ball.

"No, of course Jordan never got called. But me? I'm not a golden boy, so they decide to whistle me for a rinky-dink little time-jumper in a game we lose to Houston by two points," Anthony said. "Come on! It's not like they're going to catch the Blazers for eighth place anyway unless they rewind the clock and stop Yao from breaking his foot."

ESPN basketball analyst Bruce Bowen,

discussing Anthony's remarks on Wednesday night's *SportsCenter*, was sympathetic to player frustrations, but said the answer was to make the call more often, not less. While Bowen acknowledged that referees seem to let the call slide more often than not, he was quick to point out that Anthony clearly took an extra step into the glowing energy portal just minutes after he stepped out of it to speak to himself. In addition, Bowen said these actions were messing with the integrity of both the game

and the fourth dimension, and will ultimately have unpredictable far-reaching implications on more than just player morale.

"For instance, did anyone who watched the Rockets-Nuggets game Monday night notice that mustache on Shane Battier as he threw that pick? Clearly this is an alternate Shane Battier from a parallel time continuum, possibly an evil one, brought into our world by the time-traveling abuses of our NBA players. The league has to crack down on this behavior before it's too late." ✷

Devin Ebanks Announces Intentions To Enter League They Pay You To Play Basketball At

APRIL 17, 2010

MORGANTOWN, WV—West Virginia Mountaineers forward Devin Ebanks announced his intentions Monday to skip his final two years of college eligibility and join that one super-huge nationwide league where they give you money if you play basketball in it. "My dream has always been to go to the basketball place with all the older people who get paychecks

for it," Ebanks said. "Not that I didn't cherish my time at that place with all the rooms and the talking people up front with the thick paper word holders. But that was for free, and I need to get one of those basketball jobs." When asked where he thought he would be selected in the 2010 NBA Draft, Ebanks told reporters, "On the stage part of the room with the men in suits with the ping-pong balls." ✷

Lakers Great Karl Malone Inducted Into Hall Of Fame

APRIL 14, 2010

SPRINGFIELD, MA—The Basketball Hall of Fame announced Monday that All-Star power forward and Los Angeles Lakers legend Karl Malone will be inducted into its hallowed halls this August. "It's an honor, it really is," said "The Mailman," whose well-documented tandem with all-time

Laker great Gary Payton helped lead the team all the way to the Finals in 2004. "I never could have done this without my teammates." Malone, who averaged 13.2 points during his legendary run with the Lakers, heads a Hall of Fame class that also includes Portland Trail Blazers star Scottie Pippen. ✷

NCAA To Strip Duke Of Its '08-'09 Losses

MARCH 29, 2010

DURHAM, NC—NCAA officials announced Wednesday that seven losses would be stricken from Duke's 2008-2009 season record, claiming they were forced to act after discovering evidence of dramatically meritorious behavior both on and off the court. "This will forever polish the legacy of the Blue Devils, as all their losses from the season will be removed from the record books," said Paul T. Dee, the chairman of the Plauditory Committee, who expressed strong commendations for the men's basketball team. "Their overall AP ranking for last year will also be impacted, as we will have to drop them up from sixth to second. And we find it only fair that Duke be stripped of its 1994 second-place tournament finish, which will go to Arkansas in exchange for their national title trophy." Duke coach Mike Krzyzewski has decided not to appeal the NCAA's decision to permanently place the Blue Devils on approbation. ✷

INSIDE

PHOTO FINISH

Goliath Joins Duke Basketball Team In Victory Celebration

NCAA Tournament Proving That Mid-Major Semi-Upper-Lower-Middle-Mids Should Be Taken Seriously

MARCH 26, 2010

INDIANAPOLIS—When Ali Farokhmanesh hit his game-winning shot to lift ninth-seed Northern Iowa over top-ranked Kansas last Saturday, it was a true Cinderella moment for the NCAA Tournament, a rare second-round knockout of a high-major opponent by a scrappy, fundamentally sound mid-major semi-upper-lower-middle-mid.

But when the dust of the weekend had cleared, and Xavier, Butler, Cornell, and St. Mary's had all advanced to the Sweet Sixteen, it sent a clear message to the entire NCAA: The era of the mid-major semi-upper-lower-middle-mid had truly begun.

"What people are seeing here, once they get past the excitement of a sub-upper-major team like Georgetown losing to a moderate-mid-minor like Ohio, is increased parity across the board," Northern Iowa coach Ben Jacobson said. "In the second round, everyone saw how minor mid-sub-major Cornell handled neo-mid-half-major Wisconsin. In the first, they saw how major mid-minor Xavier trounced semi-high-major Minnesota. And now they're starting to wonder exactly what to call us."

Eleven different conferences are represented in this year's Sweet Sixteen, which pitted high-scoring para-mid-semi-diminished-sub-mid-major Cornell against the tournament's top seed and its top-ranked remaining team, major-major-major-major Kentucky.

"Kentucky is a major-major-major-major basketball school, no two ways about it," Cornell senior Jon Jaques wrote on his blog Wednesday. "We may be a low-mid-upper-mid-downer-middle-mid-micro-submacro school from upstate New York, but we've never let it hold us back. When the Big Dance is over, I wouldn't be surprised to see people calling Cornell a mid-upper-parallel-medial, or even a para-demi-duo-double major. I think we've proved something to the world."

Indeed, the excellent performance of the sub-infra-pianoforte-majors, schools once dismissed as round-one tune-ups for the über-mega-ne-plus-ultra-majors, has raised talk of expanding the NCAA Tournament field to 96 teams. While more March Madness would be welcome among fans and advertisers, the smaller, low-minor-quasi major-flexi-undergrounder schools have said they can compete on their own merits.

"Obviously, Northern Iowa got a raw deal and a tough seed from the selection committee, which thought it was sending some poor sub-anti-contra-widdershins-proto-midbeneather-mid-minor up against the top-ranked hyper-mega-major," Missouri Valley commissioner Doug Elgin said. "But when you look at what happened, you realize they weren't looking at the basketball we were capable of playing. Maybe they let those easy labels get the better of them."

Some coaches of smaller schools, those casually dismissed as under-midi-mezzo-hemi-trans-mid-middle-middling-middlest-minimalistic majors, have said they could accept an expanded tournament if the champions of all conferences received an automatic bid. Others have said the selection committee should operate as normal, but that it should be mindful not to give the medium-large half-major half-minors automatic consideration. In any event, everyone seems to agree that the major-majors have been given something to think about.

"We've made a statement on behalf of all the mid-supra-over-intra-circum-double-treble-omni-meta-majora-cosmologica-mondo minors, and people across the basketball world have taken notice," George Mason coach Jim Larranaga said. "Finally, people are starting to realize that college basketball teams aren't as simple to classify as they once believed." ∅

SPORTS GRAPHIC

Great Moments In The Lakers-Celtics Rivalry

JUNE 4, 2010

The 2010 NBA Finals will feature the most storied rivalry in professional basketball. We take a look at everything these legendary teams have shared.

➤ **1959:** The Celtics quickly win the series in four games after the shy Lakers mill around the basket and refuse to leave their side of the court

➤ **1962:** Setting an NBA Finals record that still stands, Celtics center Bill Russell grabs 40 rebounds in the opening game of the series while missing on 40 consecutive scoring attempts

➤ **1968:** The rivalry heats up and the Lakers put forth their best effort in years thanks to a team loaded with undercover FBI agents monitoring the Black Panthers' influence in the NBA

➤ **1969:** The Celtics beat the Lakers for the seventh time in seven NBA championship meetings, causing many to wonder if this is actually a "rivalry" or more of a "situation in which one team beats another team over and over and over again"

➤ **1984:** The NBA finally sheds its image as a league of black drug addicts as Larry Bird leads the Celtics to victory, establishing the NBA as a league of creepy-looking chinless ground-bound drips

➤ **1987:** Larry Bird momentarily forgets about the rivalry, dishing the ball to an open Magic Johnson, fiercely guarding Kevin McHale, and repeatedly elbowing Robert Parish in the head

➤ **1988:** Lakers forward James Worthy scores 36 points, 10 assists, and 16 rebounds in Game 7 of the Finals against the Detroit Pistons, so never mind

Fluid Just Happy To Have Had Opportunity To Build Up In Kobe Bryant's Knee

MAY 21, 2010

LOS ANGELES—Calling the experience "a true honor" and "the opportunity of a lifetime," the infected synovial fluid recently drained from Kobe Bryant's right knee told reporters Monday that there is no other basketball player it would rather have accumulated in.

Describing itself as humbled and privileged to have affected the NBA All-Star's mobility for even so short a time, the contaminated collection of mucin and albumin said it would always cherish every moment it spent collecting in Bryant's appendage, from the initial stages of infection to its last moments of arthrocentesis.

"Kobe Bryant's is the knee all joint fluids dream of building up in," the semi-viscous mix of blood and uric acid said during a press conference at the Lakers' training facility. "There were times, especially during the first two rounds of the playoffs, when I had to pinch myself and say, 'Holy crap! You're inflaming Kobe Bryant's right knee! Kobe Bryant. Not some role-playing knee like Andrew Bynum's knee, or Kendrick Perkins' knee, but Kobe freaking Bryant's.'"

"People have asked me if I would have rather built up in LeBron's knee instead of Kobe's," the fluid added. "And while it would have been exciting to help deteriorate LeBron's articular cartilage, Kobe is an NBA champion."

According to the infected fluid, it considered accumulating in the former MVP's knee a "one-shot deal," and tried to enjoy every wince and buckle it caused as if it were the last.

The fluid also personally thanked Oklahoma City forward Kevin Durant for pushing the Lakers' first playoff round to six games, saying that the unexpectedly long series allowed it to really savor its time in Bryant's knee.

"I knew they wouldn't let me build up forever," the arthritis-induced fluid said. "So when I saw that 20-gauge syringe enter the joint capsule, I took comfort in the thought that I built up as best I could before I was sucked out."

Doctors close to the 1.2-ounce specimen said it began collecting in Bryant's joint cavities toward the end of the season, but didn't become inflamed and straw-colored until the playoffs. Beaming with obvious pride, the non-Newtonian pseudoplastic material noted that it was the same fluid that accumulated during Bryant's 39-point performance in Game 2 of the series against the Thunder, and that it went on to become the very thixotropic liquid that contributed to the swelling of Bryant's knee throughout the Western Conference semifinals.

"Not bad for a fluid that just two months ago was nothing more than a subcutaneous element in a normal, uninfected synovial membrane," the particulate-rich residue continued. "Not bad at all."

Calling it "a wild ride while it lasted," the knee fluid said it would always have fond memories of its gradual buildup during plane trips to different cities, postgame interviews, and the Lakers' four-game sweep of the Utah Jazz.

"How many aggravated lubricin compounds can say that they were building up in an MVP's knee while he was leading his team to the next round of the NBA Playoffs?" it said. "Well, any fluid who follows sports will tell you there are only three: Willis Reed's knee fluid in 1970, fluid from Magic Johnson's busted bursa sac in '85, and Jordan's fluid in 1997."

"Pretty good company, if you ask me," the fluid continued.

While the diseased liquid admitted that it would have been able to build up even more hyaluronic acid had Bryant not sat out during between-game practices, and had the team's trainers not been so meticulous in icing the knee down after games, the fluid said those were just minor setbacks in what was ultimately the experience of a lifetime.

"If my young, healthy, polymer-of-disaccharide self ever caught me actually complaining about harmfully building up in Kobe Bryant's knee, then in about two seconds it would disperse me onto the connective tissues out of sheer disgust," the cloudy sample characterized by an abnormal level of white blood cells said. "Some fluids only get to build up in obese, office-softball-league players and that's as far as they ever go. I consider myself very lucky."

"Now, would I like to be the fluid that is currently building up inside Kobe's knee during the Western Conference finals?" the fluid added. "Absolutely. I'd be a lying specimen jar of medical waste if I said I wouldn't. But I had my turn, and frankly, I'm exhausted. It's time for another fluid to get its chance at glory." Ø

Raja Bell Thinks Teams Cleared Salary Cap Space For Him

Speculation About Where LeBron Will Play Could End When He Signs Contract

JUNE 23, 2010

BRISTOL, CT—According to NBA analysts, speculation about where LeBron James might play next season could end when the Cavaliers MVP signs a contract with a professional basketball team. "When he agrees to play for a new team and has an introductory press conference with them—or when he re-signs with Cleveland—that's when I think we'll have a better idea which way LeBron is leaning," ESPN analyst Jalen Rose said during Tuesday's edition of *SportsCenter*, adding that a good indicator as to where James' head is at might come in late October, when James will be wearing a basketball uniform for the season opener. "Ten games into the regular season, if LeBron James is a New Jersey Net, I think at that point we can effectively eliminate Chicago or Cleveland, but I wouldn't rule out the Los Angeles Clippers. At any rate, by the 2011 All-Star break the picture should become, if not 100 percent clear, a lot less hazy." Rose suggested the guessing game over where LeBron will play next season may not end until he is enshrined in the Basketball Hall of Fame. Ø

Future Recruiting Violation Makes Commitment To Michigan

JULY 21, 2010

MEMPHIS TN—During a signing ceremony at his high school's gymnasium Thursday, one of the nation's top recruiting violations made his intent to play basketball for the University of Michigan official. "I'm excited to be part of the Michigan tradition, and I hope to start helping them this year," said the recruiting violation, 19, referring to a season that the NCAA will eventually strip from the record books. "I hope to follow in the rich tradition of Robert Traylor and Chris Webber." Though rumors are already swirling concerning his close ties to wealthy alumni athletic boosters, the recruiting violation expressly and vehemently denied these allegations in a conference call made from his new Porsche Cayenne. Ø

James, Bosh, Wade Decide Nickname Will Be 'The Three-Headed Shitstorm'

JULY 28, 2010

MIAMI—After weeks of debate over their collective nickname, Lebron James, Chris Bosh, and Dwyane Wade announced yesterday that the newly formed all-star trio would call themselves the Three-Headed Shitstorm. "It was between the Three-Headed Shitstorm, Miami's Mighty Three-Way, Category 3 Hurricane Fuckface, and Super NBA Friends, which was LeBron's idea that nobody liked," Wade said during an interview with ESPN, adding that the group's first choice, the King Cobra Super Shit Snakes of South Beach, was overruled by Heat president Pat Riley. "We eventually settled on the Three-Headed Shitstorm because there are three of us, and when opponents play against us it's like all this shit is going to be coming at them from every direction. It also has something to do with three-headed dragons." At press time, James was still trying to get the nickname changed to either the Justice Basketball League of America or Three Cool Guys. Ø

Despite Repeated Attempts To Tear It Down, Massive LeBron James Mural Keeps Reappearing

WE ARE ALL WITNESSES.

JULY 17, 2010

CLEVELAND—Shocked Cleveland residents stared silently Thursday as workers tried for the 11th consecutive day to dismantle the massive black-and-white "We Are All Witnesses" LeBron James mural hanging from the downtown area's Landmark Office Tower.

Friday morning, as was the case the previous morning and the morning before that, Clevelanders awoke to find the iconic, 10-story-tall image of James—his arms fully extended after tossing his signature talcum powder into the air—completely intact, dominating the city's skyline as if it had never even been touched.

In the week since James' announcement that he would join the Miami Heat, Cleveland city officials and citizens alike have attempted to tear down, shred, deface, and even burn the image from the wall only to find it back in place the next day.

No one has reported observing the mural's reappearance.

"We can't escape it," said 42-year-old Clevelander Mark Hoffman, who along with 300 other local Cavaliers fans watched as the mural was ripped into thousands of pieces and buried under two tons of dirt in Riverside Cemetery Wednesday evening. "The next morning it was there. Just...there. It's always there. Hovering over us like some sort of demon."

"We are all witnesses," a visibly traumatized Hoffman mumbled while swaying back and forth, his eyes engaged in a removed, distant stare. "We are all witnesses. We are all witnesses. We are all witnesses."

As the city becomes increasingly disturbed and agitated, sources confirmed that the banner's sinister hold on the metropolis appears to be growing in strength. The image, they say, somehow becomes clearer and more ominous each time it reappears, intensifying the utter hopelessness and betrayal citizens have felt ever since James held a nationally broadcast television special to announce that he was leaving his home state in search of an NBA title with the Heat.

The banner's resilience has reportedly taken on almost supernatural properties: On Tuesday city officials removed it panel by panel, only to find an identical mural hanging directly behind it. On Wednesday, not only did the banner reappear after being loaded onto a chartered one-way flight to Siberia, but the LeBron James depicted in the new banner was wearing a Heat jersey and holding two NBA Championship trophies in his outstretched hands.

"I walked up to the banner with a ladder and a rented power sprayer and painted it over about halfway," 36-year-old Luke Denton said. "I took a two-minute break to get some water, and when I looked up, the paint had disappeared. As if I'd never even done it."

"And I could have sworn that LeBron's face was staring right at me," Denton added. "He had this demented grin that I'll never forget. Why does he want to torture us? Why?"

Though the hated billboard is said to typically reappear as James' haunting likeness, some have seen other disturbing images. Last Thursday when the mural was attached to four 1,000-pound weights and forcibly sunk in the Cuyahoga River, commuters driving into the city reported seeing in its place a 10-story-tall photograph of John Elway leading Denver to victory over the Browns in the 1987 AFC Championship game. Others saw a still image of Michael Jordan jumping into the air and pumping his fist after his game-winning shot over Craig Ehlo. Many pedestrians, meanwhile, reported seeing a 100-foot banner of Earnest Byner's 1988 fumble on the three-yard line.

An attempt to demolish the building altogether proved futile, as it was mysteriously replaced the following day by the completely new 15-story Art Modell Public Library.

"I would like to assure the citizens of Cleveland that we are doing everything in our power to rid our city of the LeBron James mural," Cleveland mayor Frank Jackson said Thursday, adding that a priest from Bulgaria would be brought to the city next week to exorcise the banner. "That being said, if you gouge your eyes out like I did, you can't see the image."

"However," Jackson continued, "on the very threshold of audibility, you can still hear LeBron's voice repeating, 'This fall, I am going to take my talents to South Beach.'"

As of press time, nobody outside the Cleveland area had seen the mural once since it was originally taken down last Sunday. Ø

Professional Basketball Team Interested In Trade For Professional Basketball's Carmelo Anthony

SEPTEMBER 20, 2010

NEW YORK—Citing his excellence in shooting, passing, dribbling, and jumping, a professional basketball team in the National Basketball Association announced its interest Tuesday in acquiring the services of professional basketball player Carmelo Anthony for the 2010-2011 season. "Carmelo Anthony simply makes a high percentage of his basketball shots, which puts him in the top tier of the 450 basketball players currently filling salaried positions in the league," a general manager of a professional basketball team told reporters. "We would be willing to trade two or even three of our professional basketball players in order to place Carmelo Anthony in our employ, for which we would in turn pay him a large sum of money." The general manager added that while Anthony is a very good professional basketball player, he would of course rather have signed professional basketball player LeBron James. ∅

Tim Duncan Staring At Wall Right Now

AUGUST 30, 2007

SAN ANTONIO—Two-time NBA MVP Tim Duncan has been sitting in his living room next to his packed gym bag and clad in his Spurs warm-up jersey for the past three months, concerned teammates reported Monday. "I called him several times and he didn't pick up," said guard Tony Parker. "And when I got worried enough to go look through his window, I saw him just sitting there. I'm

pretty sure he's conscious and not in any pain, but it doesn't look like he's moved since late June." The Spurs front office confirmed that Duncan requested a call at midnight on Oct. 1 to ensure he did not miss the first day of training camp. ∅

Mike Brown Claims He Was Scapegoat For Cavaliers Terrible Coaching

MAY 31, 2010

CLEVELAND—In response to his recent firing, former Cavaliers head coach Mike Brown said at a press conference Wednesday that he was unfairly singled out and blamed for the team's horrendous coaching. "I hate to admit it, but they made me a scapegoat for the overall lack of leadership and inability to make in-game adjustments," Brown said. "It didn't seem to matter how hard I worked designing ineffective plays or putting the other team's inferior talent in a position to win, because they were going to make me the fall guy." Brown told reporters that executives in the Cavaliers front office should do some soul-searching and evaluate how their own poor performances led to the hiring of such a shitty-ass coach in the first place. ∅

> **PHOTO FINISH**
> **Allen Iverson To Turkish Media: 'Uygulama? Uygulama? Biz Uygulama Bahsediyoruz!'**

Careless Blazers Goofing Around With Basketball Shatter Greg Oden Into Thousand Pieces

NOVEMBER 12, 2010

PORTLAND, OR—Although Portland Trail Blazers coach Nate McMillan has repeatedly warned his team about using the basketball around "valuable" and "really fragile" center Greg Oden, several players accidentally knocked the seven-footer to the floor with a carelessly thrown ball Thursday and shattered him into a thousand pieces.

"Oh, man, if Coach sees this we're gonna be in so much trouble," Blazers guard Brandon Roy told reporters while sifting through broken sections of Oden's legs, arms, head, and torso. "We're not gonna be able to play basketball anymore or go out or do anything."

"I can't believe it," Roy added. "The ball barely touched him."

According to team sources, Roy, point guard Andre Miller, and forwards Nicolas Batum and LaMarcus Aldridge picked up a basketball in the Blazers practice facility and started bouncing it near Oden, an exquisite but easily broken player Portland purchased in 2008 for $6.7 million.

As the teammates continued to fool around, their play reportedly grew riskier and more aggressive, with players dribbling the basketball very close to the delicate center and passing it dangerously close to

his body and over his head. At one point several Blazers approached Oden while wiggling their fingers very close to him, saying "I'm a dainty little center that nobody's allowed to touch" in a mocking tone of voice, and pretending to drop him on the hardwood floor.

Sources confirmed that after an errant pass from Miller careened off Roy's fingertips and hit Oden's shoulder, Oden teetered from side to side for a tense moment—during which unbelieving players found themselves unable to move—before toppling to the ground just out of reach of a diving Roy.

The team reportedly stared silently at the broken pieces of Oden for several seconds until Roy said, "We're dead. We are so dead."

"Don't look at me like that, Andre," he added upon noticing Miller staring at him. "You threw that pass. This is as much your fault as it is mine."

"Coach said to always be careful around Greg, because Greg costs a lot and even the slightest amount of basketball can damage him," said Batum, who has been charged with making sure teammate Sean Marks doesn't see the broken Oden because Marks "would tell on us in a second." "Man, why didn't we just listen

see **GREG ODEN**

from **GREG ODEN**

to Coach? That was his favorite center. Shoot. Shoot. Shoot."

After gathering the larger parts of Oden that were still somewhat intact and sweeping up the tiny pieces of his shattered face into a dustpan, the players hit upon the idea of replacing the former No. 1 draft pick with teammate Marcus Camby or perhaps retired Boston Celtic Robert Parish. However, they quickly but reluctantly agreed that McMillan would definitely know the difference.

Power forward Dante Cunningham suggested replacing Oden with retired center Shawn Bradley and was immediately told to "just leave."

Working from a picture of Oden hanging in the team's front office, the players proceeded to reassemble the center with superglue and Scotch tape. Though they were adamant it was the best they could do on such short notice, the plan has had its setbacks.

"LaMarcus glued Greg's left eye on upside down, and his one arm was hanging 5 inches lower than the other until we kind of hitched it up with some staples," said guard Rudy Fernandez, who ended up helping after Roy threatened to tell McMillan that Fernandez was the one who accidentally threw rookie Elliot Williams out with the trash last week. "Also, to get these surgery scars on his knees to match up exactly is just impossible."

"Wait, guys," Fernandez continued. "Greg had five fingers on his left hand, right?"

The players estimated they had two hours to put Oden back together before McMillan returned from a performance of *Die Fledermaus*, his favorite opera, with assistant coach Bernie Bickerstaff. McMillan called to check in with the team at intermission and Roy said that everything was "just fine" and that "Greg Oden is doing especially great, and everything is perfect with him and there's nothing to worry about at all in terms of Greg Oden. Why would there be anything to worry about? Don't you trust us? Geez, Mr. McMillan. Bye."

"We're so dead," Roy repeated after hanging up the phone.

With time running out, the players had roughly reassembled their teammate, figuring that given Oden's track record of injuries, McMillan might not be able to tell that the center was missing an elbow or that his jersey was concealing several large cracks in his chest.

"I have a friend who plays for the Celtics, and he said Shaq's body shatters all the time," Camby said. "So the plan is, the next time that happens, he'll gather the extra body parts we need and send them to us. We have time. It's not like Greg was going to be playing basketball soon, anyway."

At press time, McMillan had entered the gym, glanced at his center, and shrugged before turning to leave and slipping on one of Oden's vertebrae. ⌀

Josh Smith Claims He Once Saw Hawk Carry Away Basketball In Talons

DECEMBER 14, 2010

ATLANTA—Hawks forward Josh Smith regaled his teammates Wednesday with a story about how he once watched a red-tailed hawk swoop down, grab a loose basketball in its razor sharp talons, and fly away. "It was crazy, because the ball was rolling across the court really fast, and then I heard this loud screeching sound and all of a sudden this hawk dives down and snatches it up before it goes out of bounds," said Smith, adding that hawks build nests in the rafters of every NBA arena. "And then it flew off to the upper deck, where it landed by some empty seats and started tearing apart the basketball with its beak." Smith told his teammates that if they look closely at the court after each NBA game, they should be able to see hawk droppings containing undigested pieces of basketball. ⌀

Tim Duncan Spends Free Time Trying To Get Wrongfully Incarcerated Man Off Death Row

NOVEMBER 3, 2010

MANSFIELD, OH—Spurs center Tim Duncan spent all his free time this week studying law books and building a case in an attempt to exonerate a death row inmate wrongfully incarcerated at Ohio's Mansfield Correctional Institution. "For more than 10 years, Randolph Morgan has been imprisoned for a crime he did not commit, mainly because of the testimony of an unreliable witness, one Cheryl McInerney," said Duncan, who has devoted the past three offseasons to earning a law degree at San Antonio State and in August passed the bar exam in both Texas and Ohio. "I have met with medical examiners and several forensic pathologists, and they concur that the available DNA evidence is more than sufficient to prove the innocence of my client." Duncan went on to score 14 points against the Los Angeles Clippers Monday night before flying to Ohio to persuade the governor to issue a stay of execution for Morgan. ⌀

Duke Doing Something Indicates College Basketball Season Either Starting, Ending, Or Ongoing

NOVEMBER 22, 2010

DURHAM, NC—The sudden appearance of photos of Duke basketball players in national newspapers—as well as video of the school's marching band and Dick Vitale talking about the team on television—has led the nation to believe that something is currently happening with Duke basketball, arousing suspicions that the 2010-11 NCAA men's basketball season has either just begun, is about to begin, or has just ended. "I was flipping through *USA Today* and saw a picture of Coach K in his Duke collared shirt, not his Team USA collared shirt, so I think something is going on college-basketball-wise," Ohio resident Greg Evans told reporters. "In the picture he was yelling at young men who appeared to be Blue Devils players. Maybe it was a season preview. Or maybe it was a midseason report. Maybe it's March Madness." Evans added that similar things were probably happening at the University of North Carolina. ⌀

Kevin Durant Accidentally Reveals NBA Uses System Of Ropes, Pulleys To Help Players Dunk

NOVEMBER 19, 2010

OKLAHOMA CITY—Following a 109-103 victory over the Philadelphia 76ers last Wednesday, fourth-year player Kevin Durant accidentally revealed one of the NBA's most carefully guarded secrets: that for more than 60 years, the league's players have been using a complex system of ropes and pulleys to help them dunk the basketball.

During a postgame press conference, Durant was asked how he was able to summon the late-game leg strength to complete a fourth-quarter dunk over Philadelphia center Spencer Hawes. Durant answered that his "personal rig operator, Dave, is really strong, and was able to lift me no problem," after which the 2008 Rookie of the Year stared at the gathered reporters for a long moment before saying "Shoot."

"Well, I guess the cat's out of the bag," Durant said. "Come on, guys, don't look so shocked. If you think about it, this all makes sense. No human being can actually dunk a basketball. The hoop's 10 feet in the air, for God's sake."

"Seriously? The truth of the matter is every Dominique Wilkins dunk you ever saw was because of ropes and pulleys," added Durant, who, before being silenced by his team's publicist, revealed that 7'6" center Yao Ming needs a 35-man team of fly operators in order to get him off the ground to complete a dunk.

Durant's remarks prompted an immediate investigation into the NBA by the House Committee on Oversight and Government Reform. After watching footage of more than 90,000 dunks, as well as a VHS copy of NBA Dazzling Dunks And Basketball Bloopers, the committee discovered that, since 1954, players have taken the court wearing full-body harnesses in order to help them dunk and block shots. The harnesses are reportedly hidden underneath the players' basketball shorts and are connected to thin ropes controlled by a team of professionals stationed in the arena's catwalks.

When players are ready to dunk, they signal up to the fly operators, who then pull as hard as they can to lift the player to the basket.

"We can now say with certainty that all dunks, from Michael Jordan's free-throw line dunk in 1988 to Dwight Howard's monster two-handed jams, have been executed by single-point suspension wires with multitracking systems and 20 different lifting pulleys," committee chairman Edolphus Towns (D-NY) told reporters at a press conference Tuesday, adding that as the harnesses increased in complexity over the years, basketball shorts became baggier to cover them up. "If you watch a game in slow motion, you'll have no problem seeing the cables coming out of their uniforms and extending up toward the ceiling."

"It's so obvious," Towns added. "In fact, if crowds remain completely silent during games, they should be able to hear the screech of the rotating liftwheels and the groaning of ropes being pulled through their grooves."

According to Towns, every NBA player has his own secret signal for when he wants to be lifted off the ground for a dunk. Reports confirmed that in order to signal to his man—master pulley operator Jack Mulcahey, 64, now retired—Michael Jordan used to stick out his tongue.

"We also found that when play-ers hang on the rim after a dunk, it's usually due to a malfunction in the pulley system," Towns said. "In order to distract the crowd, players will often use fake bravado and referees will call a technical while the wires are being untangled 60 feet above their heads."

According to a 550-page report, the father of the modern dunk is not in fact Julius Erving, winner of the first Slam-Dunk Contest, but Peter Foy, inventor of the Foy Rig, a device created for three-dimensional stage acrobatics and first used in the 1950 Broadway production of *Peter Pan*. The system was secretly brought to the NBA to aid players who were physically unable to jump more than a few inches off the ground because of the heavy weight of their basketball shoes.

Though professional basketball has been shaken by the committee's findings, games have continued as usual. However, there has been a noticeable lack of cheering during slam dunks.

"Now that I know the ropes are there, I can't keep from looking at all the guys standing in the rafters helping the players jump," said Miami resident Paul Lutzka, who along with 20,000 other fans watched in complete silence Wednesday night as LeBron James completed a fast break with a windmill jam. "When he took off it looked all herky-jerky. I can't believe I never noticed that."

Sensing discontent, NBA Commissioner David Stern addressed the media Thursday.

"I want to apologize first and foremost to our fans," Stern said from NBA headquarters in New York. "Basketball is still a great game, and the NBA will recover from this. Frankly, it could have been worse. Kevin could have told you how the ball is connected to thin cables controlled by puppeteers sitting above the JumboTron, puppeteers who have been responsible for every made and missed basket of the past 80 years."

After a long pause, Stern added, "Aw, fuck." ⊘

Miami Heat Website Going With Picture Of LeBron James Today

OCTOBER 15, 2010

MIAMI—After much deliberation, members of the MiamiHeat.com web team decided today that the featured homepage image should depict Miami Heat small forward LeBron James playing basketball.

According to sources, the choice to go with a photograph of James was made in an early morning staff meeting. Several different image ideas were suggested, including LeBron James shooting a basketball, LeBron James passing a basketball, and LeBron James playing defense in a basketball game.

The selected photo will reportedly replace yesterday's picture of LeBron James standing on a basketball court and dribbling a basketball with one hand while pointing with the other.

"We like today's photo because it's an action shot, it's vibrant, and you can tell the crowd in the background is really enjoying the game," web editor Mark Christie said. "And it has LeBron James in it, as well."

"He's dunking," Christie added.

Christie told reporters that on any given day, his colleagues have a rough idea of which Heat player or players they want to feature on the website. Monday—according to Christie a high-traffic day—is typically reserved for a picture of LeBron James. On Tuesday, Christie said he likes to go with an alternate image of LeBron James. And on Wednesday, the web team typically selects a LeBron James picture that strikes a tone suitable for the site's midweek audience.

Thursdays, however, Christie said he likes to change it up by going with a picture of Dwyane Wade and LeBron James either laughing with each other, staring intensely at the action on the floor, or sitting next to each other on the bench.

Weekends are reportedly reserved for a three-shot of Wade, newly acquired forward Chris Bosh, and LeBron James, in which James is standing between the two holding a basketball.

"Sometimes that weekend schedule goes completely out the window, though, and we'll just go with a picture of LeBron James," said assistant web editor Jarrod Brewer, adding that single images of Chris Bosh can be found on the website's "photos" page. "Especially if we have a really good photo of him. People would be surprised how often that happens. It's ultimately very fluid around here. Last Friday we were slated to have a photo of Chris Bosh and LeBron James, and then Mark said, 'It feels like a just-LeBron day to me. Let's go with him sweating.'"

Continued Brewer, "Also, I thought Mark's decision to go with LeBron James standing at a podium after a preseason game instead of a picture of Coach, um, Coach—the coach of the Miami Heat basketball team, yeah—was a really good call on Mark's part."

According to Christie, the main goal of MiamiHeat.com is to make the website feel like a unique experience for daily visitors. That is why, Christie noted, he likes to constantly change up the photos of LeBron James. If, for example, Christie uses a picture in the morning of the All-Star forward throwing chalk into the air, then during the afternoon he'll go with a more subdued photo of James sitting on the bench with a towel draped across his knees, drinking a cup of Gatorade.

"Mix is really important to me," Christie said. "If we go two days in a row with LeBron James smiling, then I'm not doing my job."

When asked why a photo of 16-year veteran Juwan Howard was featured in the site's top spot several weeks ago, Christie said that the incident was a huge mistake, that the person who posted it was immediately fired, and that the page was actually intended to feature LeBron James. ⌀

76ers Ask Knicks If They Want To Be In Rivalry With Them

MARCH 1, 2011

PHILADELPHIA—Considering the teams share a division, come from major metropolitan areas in relative proximity to one another, and the fact that it would just be nice to have a little something extra to play for, the Philadelphia 76ers reportedly asked the New York Knicks to be their rivals Monday. "Could be kind of fun, right?" said 76ers forward Elton Brand, adding that his team can be the rivalry's underdog or vice versa, it doesn't really matter to him. "I don't know, maybe during our next game one of us can foul you hard, and then you can get up in our faces and taunt our fans later on in the game? It doesn't matter how it starts. We'll make sure to say we hate you at the post-game press conference. You know, like a rivalry. We think people are really going to get into this." Upon seeing new Knicks star Carmelo Anthony walk into the room, the 76ers pushed a reluctant Andre Iguodala up to him and forced Iguodala to brashly guarantee a win the next time they play. ⌀

PHOTO FINISH

Mark Price Quietly Shooting Free Throw Somewhere

145

CHAPTER FOUR

LESSER SPORTS

Ah, hockey! Golf! Tennis! Motorsports! Track and field! Horse racing! Swimming! Cycling! Soccer! Tournament poker! The Scripps-Howard Spelling Bee! The WNBA! Yes, these are sports, at least as narrowly defined by their inclusion on the sports pages. Sportswriters who cover them are almost as worthy of the name as those who cover the real, actual sports. Therefore we dutifully include them here, as a no-doubt-cursory inspection of the next few pages will demonstrate.

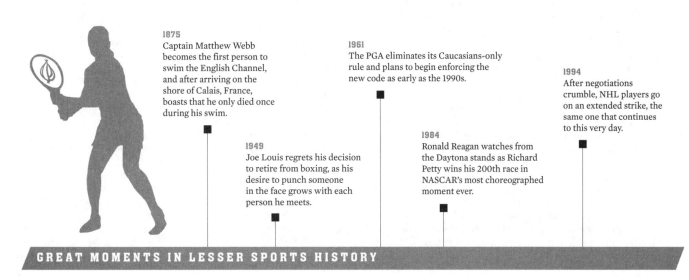

1875
Captain Matthew Webb becomes the first person to swim the English Channel, and after arriving on the shore of Calais, France, boasts that he only died once during his swim.

1949
Joe Louis regrets his decision to retire from boxing, as his desire to punch someone in the face grows with each person he meets.

1961
The PGA eliminates its Caucasians-only rule and plans to begin enforcing the new code as early as the 1990s.

1984
Ronald Reagan watches from the Daytona stands as Richard Petty wins his 200th race in NASCAR's most choreographed moment ever.

1994
After negotiations crumble, NHL players go on an extended strike, the same one that continues to this very day.

GREAT MOMENTS IN LESSER SPORTS HISTORY

Augusta National Honors Tiger Woods With Own Drinking Fountain

APRIL 30, 1997

AUGUSTA, GA—Augusta National, home of the Masters Tournament, honored 1997 Masters champion Tiger Woods Monday, giving him his own drinking fountain at the prestigious country club.

"Tiger, for your historic achievement, setting an all-time Masters Tournament record, we present you with this beautiful, specially designated drinking fountain," said Augusta National president Gary Brewer. "All other golfers will drink from a different fountain, which you, as an honored champion, will have no need to use."

The new fountain, clearly labeled "Tiger Woods," will

be located behind the outhouse between the 16th and 17th holes, far away from the distractions of other golfers.

"With your win, you join

an elite group of Masters champions, including Arnold Palmer and Jack Nicklaus," Brewer said. "We are confident that, as golf's next great and someone we will likely be seeing a lot more of in the future, you will honor and obey their legacies. We have no doubt that, as they did before you, you will remain well-behaved and respectful of Augusta's traditions."

Woods' fellow golfers are equally impressed with the 21-year-old sensation. "Rarely does a new golfer come along who is so different from the rest," said 1992 Masters winner Fred Couples. "He is not at all like us."

Augusta officials stressed that Woods is a valuable

see AUGUSTA NATIONAL

Olympic Skier Stares Down Icy, Forbidding Slope Of Rest Of Life

MARCH 13, 2002

COLORADO SPRINGS, CO— Two weeks after returning from the Salt Lake City Games, U.S. Olympic skier Courtney Roth, 31, found herself staring down the icy, forbidding slope that is her future Monday. "I got an offer to do a supermarket opening in Denver next week," Roth said, "and it looks like I may sign on to promote the new popcorn shrimp they've got over at Lou's Lobster House." Following several months of three-figure endorsement deals, Roth will land a job in Vail teaching skiing to surly, spoiled 5- to 10-year-olds for the rest of her life. Ø

PHOTO FINISH

Jew-Sponsored Stock Car Booed Off Track

Special X-Games End In Extreme Tragedy

OCTOBER 27, 2005

LOS ANGELES—Event organizers and promoters are as yet unable to explain to the satisfaction of law-enforcement officials how Ricky Creston, a 10-year-old Down syndrome sufferer, was put in a position that led to his death on Tuesday, the final day of events at the first-ever Special X-Games. "Creston, who was competing in the Best Freestyle Motocross Trick event, evidently panicked and began flailing his arms in response to the motorcycle's loud noise, losing control of the Honda CRF230 to which he had been strapped, and died shortly after in a collision with another special athlete," LAPD officials announced yesterday. "Special X-Games organizers apparently thought they had taken every precaution possible, outfitting Creston with a life jacket in

case he careened into the nearby wakeboarding pool, but failed to take into account the proximity of the skateboarding half-pipe." Creston also critically injured a developmentally disabled boy who, apparently deafened by the crowd and the Limp Bizkit music blaring through the arena speakers, was sitting in the bottom of the half-pipe and happily spinning the wheels of his skateboard during the Men's Big Air event. "Although Ricky is gone, his extreme legacy will live on forever, unlike our partnership with Mountain Dew," said event organizer Steve Wynlan, adding that all they wanted was to show the special athletes that they could still have a rad lifestyle. A spokesman for the LAPD stated that, although he had seen youth culture exploited before, the Special X-Games were nearly as bad as the Vans Warped Tour. Ø

6,000 Runners Fail To Discover Cure For Breast Cancer

NOVEMBER 14, 2001

ATLANTA—Despite their diligent, dedicated running, the 6,000-plus participants in Sunday's 5K Race For The Cure did not find a cure for breast cancer.

Hopes were high, given the excellent weather and record turnout for the 11th annual event, but no viable cure for the disease was discovered along the 3.1-mile course.

"We were particularly hopeful of locating the cure somewhere around the two-and-a-half-mile mark," race organizer Jill Broadbent said. "At that point, the route goes right past Northside Hospital and within a block of several Emory University oncology facilities. That seemed the most promising place to perhaps spot a breast-cancer cure. Regretta-

bly, the runners were unable to do more than momentarily glimpse in researchers' windows as they passed by."

At 10 a.m., participants gathered outside the Georgia Dome and proceeded to search through much of downtown Atlanta, including a one-mile stretch of Peachtree Road, before finishing cureless at the state capitol.

Among those disappointed by Sunday's failed attempt was Gene Worth, a Germantown, TN, real-estate agent who drove 450 miles to participate in his seventh Race For The Cure.

"I worked out for three months, focusing my full energies on preparing for this race," Worth said. "I switched to a vegan macrobiotic diet just to be in top shape. Three kilometers in, I felt great,

see RUNNERS

from **AUGUSTA NATIONAL**

addition to the prestigious course's lofty ranks and has never, to the best of their knowledge, been convicted of a felony.

Additional honors were bestowed upon the Masters champion when Augusta announced a special new security squad, which will monitor Woods at all times during his visits to the club. "It is important to us that Augusta members feel secure in the knowledge that Tiger Woods is fully protected and supervised while golfing here," Brewer said.

With his Masters win, Woods will also enjoy unlimited, lifetime use of the Augusta National course. "Tiger is welcome to enjoy his championship privileges here at Augusta any time he wants," Brewer said, "provided we are given enough advance notice to alert and reschedule other golfers in order to best accommodate him."

Brewer added that there are many less-exclusive public courses near Augusta that offer excellent golfing, and encouraged Woods to patronize these as well, in order to maximize his golfing variety and enjoyment.

In addition to the fountain, Woods will receive his own dining area, locker room, and personal entrance at the rear of the Augusta clubhouse. ⌀

WNBA Draft To Double As Bachelorette Auction

OCTOBER 27, 2005

NEW YORK—In order to stimulate interest in the WNBA and allow its fans to get to know the sport's rising stars in a more intimate setting, the 2006 player draft will double as a charity bachelorette auction, with all the proceeds going directly to the cash-strapped league. The WNBA is billing the event as a showcase of talented, interesting, and fun women who would be great catches for a team in need of some offense or anyone who's free next Saturday night. "Seimone Augustus is going to go high, both in the draft and the bidding," WNBA analyst Ann Meyers said, referring to the 6'1" LSU forward who averaged 20.1 points per game and is always up for a good horror flick. "But watch out for Monique Currie, the Duke star with a dominant court presence and a love of pizza and just hanging out, as she is an impact player on and off the court." Meyers added that, with a total of 42 players expected to be selected and bid on over the draft's three rounds, every single WNBA fan should be able to win at least one date. ⌀

PHOTO FINISH

Apparently Soccer Player Just Did Something Really Good

BEFORE · AFTER

Formerly Evil Wrestler Realizes Error Of His Ways

OCTOBER 10, 2001

PONTIAC, MI—Manzilla, the American Wrestling Federation villain reviled for inflicting countless blindside folding-chair blows and barbed-wire-bat bludgeonings upon helpless opponents, rocked the world of sports entertainment Monday by converting to the forces of good.

Witnessed by a sell-out Pontiac Silverdome crowd, Manzilla's change of heart occurred almost 10 minutes into a tag-team match that paired him with Fatback against AWF pretty boy Trent

Vanity and the mysterious Quasar. After Fatback knocked Quasar out of the ring, Manzilla tagged in and promptly spread a box of carpet tacks across the mat. He then grabbed Vanity and restrained him with a powerful sleeper hold.

But instead of throwing Vanity onto the dangerous tacks, Manzilla stunned the capacity crowd by falling silent, losing himself in deep thought. After nearly two full minutes of reflection, Manzilla released Vanity. The self-

see **EVIL WRESTLER**

---

from **RUNNERS**

like this was going to be the year we cured it. I did break my personal 5K record, but even that wasn't enough. Then, after I crossed the finish line, I watched other racers finish, but they came in empty-handed, as well."

Broadbent was quick to dispute characterizations of the run as a failure.

"As we like to say, today brought us one 5K run closer to the cure," Broadbent said. "We may not have cured it yet, but one of these times, we will. When faced with a setback like this, we need to pick ourselves up, dust ourselves off, and run another five kilometers."

Added Broadbent: "If even one patient went into remission as a result of thousands of people running around Atlanta, then it's all worth it."

The race was the latest disappointment in a dismal two-week stretch for athletic-based medical research. On Nov. 1 in Dallas, an estimated 3,000 cyclists were unable to isolate the portion of the human genome responsible for Alzheimer's disease. Three days later in Boston, some 200 rowers from 27 different colleges gathered on the Charles River in an unsuccessful attempt to eliminate AIDS. And a pair of Nov. 9 regattas in San Diego and Miami failed to cure cystic fibrosis and heart disease, respectively.

Runs against cancer and other diseases have been popular since 1976, when Olympic runner Bill Rodgers discovered the formula for Interferon Beta—effective in the treatment of multiple sclerosis—at the base of Nobska Point Lighthouse while running the Fal-

mouth (MA) Road Race. Rodgers went on to win the Nobel Prize for Medicine for his discovery, despite losing the race itself to Alberto Salazar. ⌀

INSIDE

➤ **Creepy Guy At End Of Bar Wants To Know If You've Ever Heard Of Jesper Parnevik**

➤ **Fan Promotion Bankrupts Flyers On Full-Set-Of-Goalie-Equipment Night**

➤ **Ghost Of Payne Stewart Still Dressing Like That**

Roger Federer Admits Tennis His Fourth-Favorite Sport

FEBRUARY 2, 2005

MELBOURNE, AUSTRALIA—In a tearful admission following his seventh Grand Slam title at the Australian Open Sunday, Roger Federer told members of the press that, while he "like[s] tennis okay," there are at least three other sports he would rather be playing or watching.

"Tennis is all well and good, and yes, I'm great at it, and sure, I've made millions of dollars playing this sport, but when you get right down to it, it's just a game of human Pong," Federer said. "On the rare occasion that I hear the roar of the crowd during one of my matches, I like to pretend I've just hurdled into the end zone, or sank a three-pointer at the buzzer, or hit a home run to win the game."

"Just the thought of all the exciting moments that can happen in other sports is enough to make me want to give up tennis, buy a big-screen TV, and sit at home all day watching ESPN Classic for the rest of my life," added Federer, placing his Australian Open trophy where it wouldn't obscure his signed photo of Cal Ripken Jr.

While tennis is the most important sport to Federer's livelihood, he admitted that he follows baseball, football, and basketball far more closely.

"I couldn't even tell you who

see **FEDERER**

Annika Sorenstam Has Another Remarkable Year For A Lady

DECEMBER 1, 2005

WEST PALM BEACH, FL—Annika Sorenstam, the absolutely adorable doll of golf's lighter, gentler side, and a true lady who has absolutely charmed ladies' golf fans since joining the always-heartwarming Ladies' Professional Golf Association Tour in 1994, capped off another sensational 10-victory year and became the first lady in history to win two straight ADT Championships For Ladies.

Miss Sorenstam, hitting from the ladies' tee throughout the tournament, finished with a 6-under 282 for a two-stroke ladies' victory, just barely holding off little ladies Soo-Yun Kang, Michele Redman, and Lisolette Neumann. "I thought I had a chance to catch up to her, but there was no stopping that lady today," Neumann said. "All you can do is lower your eyes demurely, curtsy,

and say 'Congratulations, ma'am,' in a meek tone of voice befitting a lady."

Sweeping all the major lady-awards for a fifth year and moving within 22 ladies' wins of the all-time ladies' record, Miss Sorenstam is carving out her place in ladies' history alongside legendary golfers such as Nancy Lopez and Kathy Whitworth, both also ladies.

Miss Sorenstam, who took up the sport of ladies' golf when she was just a little lady at 12 years old, has been a feminine golfing inspiration to a whole new generation of ladies, including young lady Michelle Wie and ladies' tour rookie Paula Creamer, whose play proves her a lady despite her brief, unladylike tiff with Miss Sorenstam over an 18th-hole drop in the ladies' first round of the ADT Championship.

As the lady champion, Miss Sorenstam is expected to reap her proportional rewards. In addition to

her career earnings of over $2.5 million—a fraction of Tiger Woods' $40 million-plus once thought unimaginable—male golf insiders expect Miss Sorenstam to receive attention from sponsors such as ladies-wear companies, ladies' hygiene product manufacturers, and other markets of which regular golfers are ignorant or only dimly aware.

"She has proven that the ladies can

see **SORENSTAM**

---

from **EVIL WRESTLER**

described Man-Monster From Beyond then picked up announcer Golden Throat's heavy chair and smashed it into Fatback's shoulder blades, sending him sprawling across the canvas and handing the match to Vanity and Quasar.

In a ringside interview after the match, Manzilla informed the world that his actions were the result of a profound personal epiphany.

"You listen to me now, people," said the 6'7", 320-pound two-time AWF champion, speaking directly into a nearby camera. "I want to say something to all my former partners in the Coalition Of Wrong, to all my former tag-team partners, from the War Pigs to the Stink Squad, and to my now-ex-girlfriend Lustula. I have seen the light. I will no longer be a bad example to children everywhere. I thought you were my friends, but I was wrong. You thought you could control me, but you were wrong. And at Battle Among The Cattle, next month in the Calgary Saddledome, you'll all see just how wrong."

Manzilla was then joined by Trent Vanity, who thanked and congratulated him on his conversion amid a mixed chorus of cheers and boos from the 79,000 in attendance.

Reaction among Manzilla's colleagues has been mixed.

"I, for one, welcome him out of the darkness and into the ranks of the good guys," said the Shriekin' Deacon, long regarded as the AWF's moral and spiritual leader. "Being abandoned on the steps of the San Diego Zoo's reptile house could not have been an easy beginning for young Manzilla. But he has overcome that, and now he sees the light."

"No way will I ever trust that guy," said Quasar, the

self-anointed five-time Mr. Alternate Universe. "I don't care if he did save my bacon from the War Pigs: A zebra doesn't change its stripes that quick—let alone a skunk. If he truly has changed, so be it. But be warned, Manzilla: Quasar's Virtuous Vision is upon you. If this is treachery, not just me, but my mate Bicepta and partner Vic Viking will be there."

Manzilla, sequestered in an unknown location since renouncing his evil ways, said he has adopted a new name that is better suited to his new disposition.

"The man you knew as Manzilla will use that name no more," wrote Manzilla in a letter read aloud by Golden Throat. "To all my former enemies—Big Chief Beef, Barry Hatchett, Half-Ton, Diamond Ralph, and Santa's Biggest Helper—my wrath has abated. From now on, I shall be known as Gorgeousaur, and my stunning good looks shall reflect my newfound inner peace."

The letter also made an impassioned plea for the hand of Princess Miss Lovelady, the AWF's most untouchable beauty. Lovelady declined comment on the matter.

AWF insiders said it's too early to know if Manzilla's spiritual reawakening is to be believed.

"If it's for real, it is the greatest turnaround in wrestling history," said longtime wrestling insider Clean Steve Borglund. "But it's hard to believe that this man is capable of good. The wrestler who single-handedly destroyed the career of Million-Dollar Bill? The fork-tongued heel who has come perilously close to race-baiting the Chocolate Tornado? The only man dastardly enough to team up with Bad Smells Smith? Something tells me we don't have the whole story here. I suppose we'll have to wait until [pay-per-view event] Halloween Havoc III to find out." Ø

NYC Marathon Winner 'Just Went Out There And Had Fun'

NOVEMBER 10, 2005

NEW YORK—Paul Tergat, who on Sunday became the winner of the biggest and closest New York City Marathon in history, downplayed the role of training, focus, and strategy in his victory, claiming that his race-winning plan was to "just go and have some fun out there."

"The emphasis in long-distance running is, naturally, most often on results," said Tergat, a native of Kenya who grew up running hundreds of hot, dusty miles a week in his home country for nothing more than the sheer pleasure of it. "Yes, this is a great way to wrap up the year, and yes, it was a dramatic, painful experience—every marathon is. But I would be lying if I didn't say I had an absolute blast every single step of that 26.2 miles."

Tergat broke the tape only a fraction of a second before 2004 winner Hendrick Ramaala after a race-ending sprint to the finish line, a rare sight in the muscle-burning, psychologically grueling world of the marathoner, and which Tergat said was "one of the most fun parts of the day, and maybe my entire career."

"I know a lot of people saw Hendrick stumble at the end of the race, and I know what they're thinking," Tergat said when asked to recap the marathon's final moments. "I've heard the talk. They're saying that after two hours of running one five-minute mile after another, my opponent had been physically and psychologically worn down to the point where he wasn't having as much fun as I was. I don't want to hear anyone say that. Hendrick Ramaala has more fun in his little toe than most people do in their whole body. After all, he had enough fun to dominate last year's race. I was just lucky today to have really, really enjoyed myself this morning."

Although Tergat, 36, did not completely downplay the training regimen he has followed during his long career, he insists that sheer enjoyment, more than the

esoteric satisfactions of ambition or self-discipline, is the reason he can maintain his schedule of running 200 miles a week as well as his almost dangerously low body-fat percentage.

"Spectators watching at home think they see how much fun we're having in these major events, which are usually run on paved streets during the year's hottest days," said Tergat, who noted that variety and unpredictability made the indifferently maintained streets of Queens the most enjoyable to run on. "But it's nothing compared to actually being there, feeling the energy draining out of your body, the burn of the lactic acid building up in your muscle fibers, the cramps from hydrating too early or with water of the wrong temperature, the searing ache in your lungs as you fade into a total anaerobic state around mile 18. 'Runner's high' doesn't even come close."

Despite his phenomenal talent for—and pure enjoyment of—distance running, the 2005 New York City Marathon is only Tergat's second victory at that distance. His first was in Berlin, Germany, where he set the marathon world record of 2:04:55, suffered hallucinations causing him to take a wrong turn towards the end of the race, abraded the bottoms of his feet so badly that he left bloody footprints over much of the last few miles, and claims to have had "the most unadulterated outright childlike fun I've had in an entire lifetime of nonstop endurance running." Ø

from FEDERER

the No. 1 ranked tennis player in the world is right now," Federer said. "It's probably me, still. It is, isn't it? That's so weird when you think about how I don't really care one way or another."

Federer, known for his reserved, unemotional style of play on the court, said his famous "stoicism" is usually just his mind wandering off to thoughts about that night's NBA schedule, or whether it would be worth it to purchase the MLB Extra Innings cable package.

"People always assume I'm concentrating on the match, but how can you concentrate on tennis when there are literally 10 football games being played at the same time? It takes all my mental faculties to not run off the court and try to find a TV," Federer said. "Thank God the [Australian Open] finals didn't fall on Super Bowl Sunday. I might have had to forfeit."

After a teary-eyed Federer accepted the Australian Open trophy from tennis icon Rod Laver, the last man to sweep all four Grand Slam events in the same year, he attributed his uncharacteristic show of emotion to his sudden on-court realization that he will probably never become a major-league baseball player.

"Sure, Rod Laver is my hero—my tennis hero," Federer said. "But if I had the opportunity to just meet—never mind receive an award from—Ken Griffey Jr., Troy Aikman, or Michael Jordan, I would be so much more thrilled."

"No offense to Rod Laver, who was a great tennis player and is probably a very nice guy," Federer added.

Federer, who blames his inability to bring home a French Open title on the fact that it usually falls right in the midst of the NBA postseason when he has other priorities, has also begun to take a liking to golf and often catches himself practicing his swing between sets.

"Golf is a lot like tennis in that it requires immense focus and concentration, but ultimately it's so much more relaxing and rewarding than two guys hitting a ball back and forth for hours on end," Federer said. "One more 90-degree day on clay courts, and I might just consider joining the PGA Tour."

Federer added that, while he doesn't technically consider stock-car racing a "sport," he finds it "much more exhilarating and interesting than tennis" and would "happily trade in all the Wimbledons in the world for a chance to ride shotgun in a Chevy Monte Carlo at Daytona with [his] idol Kurt Busch." Ø

PHOTO FINISH

Darius Kasparaitis Out Three To Four Weeks With Darius Kasparaitis

from SORENSTAM

play golf just like men, if not, of course, actually with men," Professional Golf Association Tour executive vice president Edward L. Moorhouse said of Miss Sorenstam, who in 2003 became the first lady to play on the real PGA Tour since true ladies' lady Babe Didrikson Zaharias, the grande dame [big lady] of golf, did so in 1945. "This lady golfer truly deserves our admiration in the form of the highest honor men can grant her: the honorary title 'First Lady Of Golf.'"

Of course, Sorenstam's honors will include a polite and proper phone call from Laura Bush, the First Lady of the United States, who will offer not only her congratulations but those of her husband George, the leader of the free world.

"You're welcome to drop by the big tour and play a round or two with the men any time you like, little lady," Moorhouse added. "As long as it's not a big event, or someplace like Augusta, that bastion of golf tradition where ladies are not allowed. Ø

Daytona 500 Honors Dale Earnhardt's Memory with Wall of Fame Across Tracks

FEBRUARY 16, 2006

DAYTONA BEACH, FL—Daytona 500 organizers and NASCAR executives announced Tuesday that they would honor Dale Earnhardt on the fifth anniversary of his fatal Daytona crash with a new memorial "Wall of Fame," a six-foot-tall, 40-yard-wide monument to the seven-time champion that will be built across Turn 4 of the track and unveiled during the first lap of Sunday's season-opening Nextel Cup race.

"Five years ago, we lost Dale Earnhardt, a great racer, a great champion, and a great friend, when he hit the wall here at Daytona for the last time," said NASCAR president Mike Helton said at a press conference held to announce construction of the $1.3 million Armco and cement memorial barrier. "This Sunday, the entire field of the 2006 Daytona 500 will honor his memory when, on the very first lap of the Great American Race, they run full speed toward the wall that will forever bear his name."

According to track officials, plans to construct a memorial to Earnhardt at the track where the legendary driver lost his life had long been discussed, but no single design had been settled on until after the conclusion of last season.

"Dale Earnhardt wasn't an easy man to know," said Helton, who consulted with Earnhardt's friends and family members before making the decision to build the wall. "We spent a lot of time watching all Dale's hard-fought races, his famously gruff interviews, and his brash, swaggering public appearances. And it finally occurred to us that that the only thing that would've pleased 'The Intimidator' more than a solid, immovable, impenetrable monument to his memory would be the idea of all his former competitors bearing down on that wall at speeds approaching 200 miles per hour."

The 17-ton, four-foot-thick wall was built by Daytona Speedway construction personnel, with the cost partially covered by a million dollars in fan donations and the balance paid by former Earnhardt sponsor General

see DAYTONA 500

U.S. Snowboarding Team Says Urine Is In Best Condition Ever

FEBRUARY 9, 2006

COLORADO SPRINGS, CO—After a long training season during which team members' performance was carefully monitored and fine-tuned with the Olympics in mind, U.S. Olympic snowboarding coach Peter Foley said his athletes' urine should be more than competitive with that of any other nation in the world. "It's taken months of hard work, and in some ways we were forced to play against our strengths and deviate from the techniques that got us here, but I'd say our team's urine is as clear and pure as possible," said Foley, who attributed the team's urine's success to "nothing more than the athletic virtues of discipline, hard work, and self-denial. We're ready to face up to any test the Europeans can throw at us in Turin." Although team members declined to speak to the press on urine-related matters, several were overheard saying their urine could not be expected to maintain its present level of conditioning for more than 15 minutes after the closing ceremonies. ✍

Bode Miller: Skiing While On Cocaine, Vicodin, LSD Also Not Easy

JANUARY 12, 2006

NEW YORK—Skier Bode Miller, the outspoken defending World Cup champion and American gold-medal favorite who was quoted on *60 Minutes* as saying that skiing drunk was not easy, expanded on those statements in a press conference Wednesday. "When there's as much powder up your nose as there is under your skis, those slalom gates come at you a lot quicker than one every second—but with enough Vicodin, you really don't care if you catch one across your nose," said Miller, who laughed and made skiing motions with his hands as he delivered his rapid-fire 20-minute, four-sentence-long statement. "And let me tell you, it's even worse when the acid makes it seem like the gates are all laughing at you with a million tiny mouths." Miller added that the sensory distortion of powerful drug cocktails were often ameliorated by skiing with a nude woman "positioned on your shoulders so as to block your view, if you know what I mean," but that he preferred lighter, more supple underage women for that purpose. ✍

Backwoods Kenyan Just Watches Marathons For The Crashes

JANUARY 26, 2006

LODWAR VALLEY, KENYA—Kenyan Cletus Jerop-Ogechi, a currently unemployed welder and self-described "old school" marathon fan, confessed openly Tuesday to enjoying long-distance cross-country running solely for the crashes. "Kenyans is the best in the world at endurance runnin'—ask anyone—but distance runnin' ain't nothing without the occasional old-fashioned low-blood-sugar elbow-to-the-ribs wreck," Ogechi told Runner's World through a translator Tuesday. "You get six, eight, twelve guys in a pack peelin' off five-minute miles and rubbin' shoulders, somethin's got to give. Might as well enjoy it, am I right?" Ogechi's all-time favorite crash occurred during the 2002 Greater Hartford Marathon, in which winner Joseph Nderitu twice spun out Ethiopian entrant Kassahun Kabiso, causing him to limp home a distant second with badly damaged bodywork. ✍

Skeleton Competitor Remembers When It Was All About The Skeletoning

FEBRUARY 9, 2006

ALBANY, NY—Kevin Ellis, a veteran "slider" with the U.S. Olympic skeleton team known throughout the sport as an outspoken skeletoning purist, has called for the recent drug- and hype-afflicted sport to return to its skeletoning roots. "Back in the day, just skeletoning was enough… Skeletoning was its own reward," said Ellis, who himself makes up an estimated 2 percent of skeletoners in North America, at a bar not far from U.S. skeleton team headquarters. "Just to be skeletoning down the mountain, just you alone with your skeleton, and then to walk back up the mountain so you could skeleton down again… That's what skeletoning was all about. And it still should be." Ellis' statement captured the attention of Annette Fielding, the other skeletoner in the bar, and a group of skiers at a corner table who had decided to drink whenever Ellis said the word "skeleton." ∅

PHOTO FINISH

Gold-Medal-Winning Swedish Hockey Team Featured On Vheätiess Box

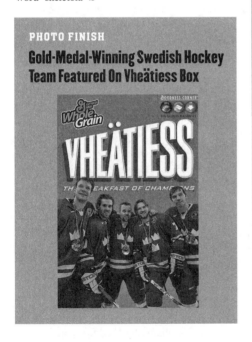

Kobe Bryant Named As 2008 Olympic Basketball Team

FEBRUARY 23, 2006

PHOENIX—In a press conference Wednesday, USA Basketball managing director Jerry Colangelo announced that Kobe Bryant has been selected as the 2008 men's Olympic basketball team.

"When they put me in charge of the selection process, I promised the committee that I would not assemble a collection of selfish, self-centered superstars with no team concept," said Colangelo, referring to the every-man-for-himself Olympic team that finished an embarrassing third place in Athens two years ago. "I am confident that, with a team comprised entirely of Kobe Bryant, the infighting, ego-clashing, and divisiveness that plagued the 2004 team will not be a problem."

Dubbing Bryant the "Dream Individual," Colangelo said that, by eliminating such weaknesses as the presence of coaches and other players, Bryant will be able to reach his full potential.

"Kobe has already been working hard during the regular season to get accustomed to being the sole contributor of a basketball team," Colangelo said. "If he, and USA basketball, want any chance of winning the gold in Beijing, he's going to have to play the game as if he's the only one on the court. Anyone who knows basketball will tell you it will be an easy adjustment."

During the press conference, Bryant told members of the media that he was "honored" and "not surprised" to be chosen as the Olympic team.

"I have to tell you, I'm not in any way humbled by this moment—this is what I've been working towards my whole career, from entering the NBA draft right out of high school to getting Shaq traded away to my 81-point game," Bryant said. "I'm used to it. I know that if I don't bring my A-game on any given night during the regular season, the Lakers will be in trouble. The same applies to the U.S. Olympic squad, where I am, more so than ever, the most indispensable player on the team."

Bryant added that he is also working on a special new kind of jump shot that is "indefensible and can only be done by me."

Commissioner David Stern applauded the decision to select "only one greedy, self-serving, ball-hogging, stat-padding superstar instead of the usual 20," saying that Bryant's behavior both on and off the court is an accurate reflection of the current state of American basketball.

"Kobe Bryant is one of the greatest individual talents in the game, and we're proud to have him represent our country, our sport, and the 28 or so other deserving individual talents who were vying for a spot on the roster," Stern said. "Kobe may not be a great team player, but we think he will be a great team."

"Besides, 81 points beats a lot of teams, especially foreign ones," Stern added.

Bryant was scheduled to begin training with personal coaches Michael Jordan, Kareem Abdul-Jabbar, and Karl Malone this week, but, in the true spirit of his new role as

see **KOBE BRYANT**

from **DAYTONA 500**
Motors-Goodwrench Service Inc. On Sunday, after the national anthem and the call to start engines, it will be maneuvered by crane into position, 15 feet in the air, at a point halfway between Turn 4 and the Daytona start-finish line. Following the pace lap, the crane will lower the wall into place, and on the first green-flag lap, the entire field will race toward the monument at full speed.

Special cleanup crews will use the crane to remove the memorial wall before Lap Two.

"You know, I think my Dad would have wanted it this way," said Dale Earnhardt Jr., son of the racing legend. "After all, he never wanted anything for himself that he didn't want for his family. And while I may be his son, in a strange way, my dad thought of everyone on the NASCAR circuit as his family. I know that somewhere, my Dad is cracking that creepy smile of his, thinking of us all going flat-out towards his memorial on Sunday."

Nextel Cup team members were nearly unanimous in their appreciation of the Wall of Fame, saying that it would give Dale Earnhardt the kind of immortality he deserved while simultaneously giving the fans the unique brand of emotional involvement that NASCAR was famous for. Only driver Tony Stewart, who has also recently criticized the race series on safety issues, hinted that he might not participate in the first-lap ceremony, for which he will in all probability be heavily fined.

The Dale Earnhardt Memorial Wall of Fame will be open to the public after the conclusion, in whatever form, of the Daytona 500 on Sunday evening, as soon as race officials have declared the track area safe again. Fans are encouraged to leave flowers, memorabilia, or personal items at the foot of the wall for Earnhardt or any other recently deceased racer, as long as items are in good taste. ∅

from **KOBE BRYANT**

Olympic team captain, head coach, and lone member, he has opted to prepare for the tournament on his own time without anyone's assistance. Starting at the end of the 2005-2006 NBA season, Bryant will practice tip-offs, work on fundamental self-inbound passes, learn how to play defense, and draw up several play formations, each of which he will be responsible for calling during the games.

Although the general response among fans has been complete indifference, many players around the league have objected to the decision, saying that it is unfair to others who have worked just as hard as Bryant.

"Kobe Bryant shouldn't be the only one allowed to represent our country at the Summer Games," Sixers point guard Allen Iverson said. "I should be the only one allowed to represent our country at the Summer Games."

LeBron James, Shaquille O'Neal, Kevin Garnett, Paul Pierce, Vince Carter, Jermaine O'Neal, Tracy McGrady and Tim Duncan all expressed identical reactions. ⌀

PHOTO FINISH
Barbaro Euthanizes Self

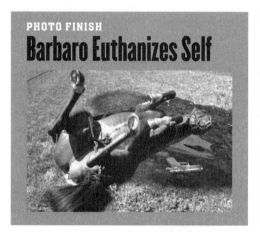

STRONG SIDE/WEAK SIDE: TIGER WOODS

STRONG SIDE	WEAK SIDE
Has never done anything wrong	So jaded he no longer even bothers to remove cute tiger-cub covers from woods before drives
Able to always keep good time on the golf course with the help of his stylish and accurate Tag/Heuer, the foremost name in precision Swiss time keeping since 1860	Never closes the big business deal because he demoralizes clients on the course
Biceps perfect for fist pumping	Clearly does not know name of wife, daughter
Able to hit ball up to 130 yards from the bottom of a 40-foot lake	Once lost to Phil Mickelson
Only needs a putter for 3's Par	Theoretically, could have more money
Uses high grass in rough and sand in bunkers to help him hit the ball less hard	Looks kind of goofy in shorts
	Let's see, there's uh...

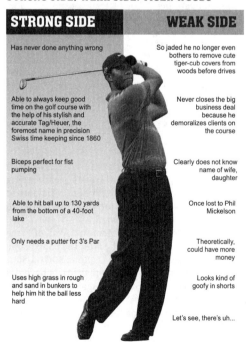

Tony Stewart Calls Upcoming Allstate 400 'A Great Opportunity To Kill Someone'

JULY 27, 2006

INDIANAPOLIS—Just days after accepting full responsibility for a wreck that knocked Clint Boyer and Carl Edwards out of the Pocono 500, Tony Stewart said he had put the incident behind him and was focusing his energies on the possible fatal crashes he could cause in the upcoming Allstate 400 at the Brickyard. "Indy is a great track with a lot of history, and I'd love to add to that history by running someone's car full-speed into the wall in the short-chutes after Turns 1 and 3, or spinning them down pit lane, or even bumping them into the infield, and killing them," Stewart told reporters shortly after arriving at Indianapolis Mo-

tor Speedway. "I'd also love to win, if possible, but I have to run my own race." NASCAR's Competition Committee has already issued a warning to Stewart advising him to "refrain from making incendiary comments" and to "save that sort of thing for the racetrack." ⌀

Motocrosser Quits After Learning Physics

JULY 27, 2006

TALLAHASSEE, FL—Reigning AMA Motocross national champion Ricky Carmichael, considered by many to be the greatest off-road motorcycle rider in history, abruptly announced his retirement from competition Monday after completing a summer course in physics at Florida State University. "I've had a great run in both professional motocross and Supercross, but the more I learn about kinetic energy, momentum, and ballistics, I'm beginning to think I've had a pretty good run of luck, too," said Carmichael, whose instructors said seemed particularly interested in the effects that gravity and sudden deceleration could have on a Suzuki RMZ250 four-stroke dirt bike. "I'd like to thank everyone and everything that helped me get this far, especially the considerable gyroscopic forces of the wheels on my race bikes, which were apparently sometimes the only thing keeping me from sublimating into a liquid state of matter." Carmichael is rumored to be considering a career in NASCAR after completing courses in business and marketing. ⌀

INSIDE

> **Penultimate Fighting Champion Loses Yet Again**

U.S. Olympic Hockey Team Continues 26-Year Streak Of Non-Miraculous Play

FEBRUARY 23, 2006

TURIN, ITALY-The U.S. men's hockey team, the lowest-ranked of all national squads going into Wednesday's quarterfinals with a 1-3-1 record, is continuing a tradition of non-miraculous play that began immediately after the medal ceremony of the 1980 Olympic Games in Lake Placid, NY. "Assembling our nation's best hockey talent on a single team might seem like a formula for miraculous on-ice achievement, but this turns out not to be the case," U.S. head coach Peter Laviolette said following his team's 5-4 defeat at the hands of the Russian squad Tuesday. "But there's lots of problems. It's hard for some of the NHL players to work together, the larger ice surface leads to more fatigue than players expect, and frankly, even if we beat everyone, it's hardly a 'miracle' if our pros beat their pros anyway." Many fans have come to the team's defense despite the their poor Olympic showing, saying that such phenomena as Chris Chelios playing at his advanced age, the presence of a Hispanic hockey player, and the fact that NHL players have agreed to play for free are all minor miracles. ⌀

Zdeno Chara Out Two To Three Periods With Fractured Skull, Broken Leg

OCTOBER 19, 2006

BOSTON—Team doctors announced that Bruins defenseman Zdeno Chara was cleared to return to the ice for the third period of tonight's game with the Calgary Flames after he used the 15-minute intermission to rehabilitate from a fractured skull and broken leg he received during the first period of play. "He's a tough kid," said team physician Dr. Thomas Gill, adding that Chara will forego wearing a brace that would hold together his snapped femur so that his mobility is not impeded. "Because his head is so swollen, he probably won't be able to fit into a helmet, but he prefers it that way." Chara didn't miss one shift during the third period, tallying one assist and an empty-net goal. ⌀

Barbaro's Doctors: 'A Horse This Good You Don't Eat All At Once'

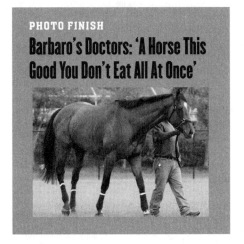

NASCAR Considers Single 21,500 Mile Race For 2011 Season

MAY 25, 2010

CHARLOTTE, NC—Citing the need to cut travel and promotional costs while still providing a top-notch racing experience for fans, NASCAR president Mike Helton announced Thursday that the schedule for 2011 may consist of a single 21,500-mile event. "Holding 36 separate races as we do now is just complicated, and our fans have to learn a lot of different kinds of ovals from week to week," said Helton, who also confirmed that the three-week race would consist of either 8,600 laps of Daytona's superspeedway or 43,000 laps of the half-mile "bullring" in Bristol, TN. "We're also blessed with a fanbase who, by and large, could watch the whole thing without having to miss any work or school." The announcement was met with only moderate enthusiasm by motorsports insiders, who pointed to the NHRA's disastrous 2003 attempt to condense its season into a single 36-mile drag race. ⌀

Somalia Defeats Rwanda To Win Third-World Cup

JUNE 29, 2006

KHARTOUM, SUDAN—The host city of the 2006 Developing Nations Football Championship erupted in cheers that nearly drowned out the cries of the starving and wounded Tuesday when the underdog Somali side, playing four down due to injuries and landmines, outlasted the more experienced if disease-ridden Rwandans 1-0 to win the inaugural Third-World Cup.

"This is a relatively great day for Somalia," said team captain Omar Bin-Shakur, the seasoned veteran whose rise from squalor in the violent ghettoes of Mogadishu to stardom in the squalid and violent ghettoes of the Sudan is already passing into legend. "It seemed like nothing could stop us in the title match—not the great Rwandan defender Bimenyimana, not the mortar strikes, not the rotting cow in midfield, not dysentery... nothing."

"They were simply the better team today," Rwandan star Calvin Bimenyimana said, speaking to reporters as the soccer stadium was transformed from a football pitch back to its usual function as an outdoor prison for Darfur refugees awaiting execution.

"Yet I am extremely proud of my mates. They did well just to get here, especially after the Sierra Leone match in which Nicodemus was red-carded and shot, and our epic battle with Chad, in which they came at us with rocket-propelled grenades when our team bus attempted to cross the border into the Sudan."

Bimenyimana, whose youth coaches in Rwanda considered him a natural for the sport after his hands were chopped off with machetes in 1994, was chosen as the Nestlé Man Of The Match by fans, the first-ever Third-World Cup participant from the losing side to be chosen. However, some aficionados say that Bimenyimana played a lackluster game; at press time, FIFA-3 officials were investigating reports that armed gunmen had shot and killed hundreds at designated Nestlé Man Of The Match voting stations.

Somalia was only a fifth seed entering the Cup tournament, and while the Third-World Cup rankings are considered notoriously inaccurate, the nation's weak midfield, inexperienced goalkeeper, and devastatingly low rates of economic growth and standards of press freedom seemed to indicate that they would be eliminated in the early rounds.

"Certainly it did not look good for us going in to be placed with Afghanistan, host team Sudan, and the [Democratic Republic Of The] Congo," said Somali coach Abdi Qani. "But every other team was at the mercy of the same sporting and economic factors. In the Third-World Cup, every group is the Group Of Death."

After only surviving the first round due to inspired play, UN-supplied antibiotics, and a forfeit during the Sudan game when four Sudanese players seized control of their team and shot eight others during penalty time, Somalia assumed the unexpected status of the tournament's Team Of Destiny.

"Never have the words 'win or go home' provided such inspiration to any team," Bin-Shakur said. "I am overcome with joy, as well as hunger, and I look forward to bringing the Third-World Cup trophy home to my country."

The Third-World Cup trophy, an AK-47 coated with gold spray-paint and mounted on a pallet of United Nations staple foods, has already been seized by Somali troops and distributed amongst ranking military officers. ⌀

Citing Poor Conditions, China Refuses To Send Delegation To Olympics

AUGUST 7, 2008

BEIJING—In an 11th-hour move that shocked the international athletic and political communities alike, the Chinese Olympic Team announced Wednesday that it will not be attending the XXIX Olympiad in Beijing due to "shocking, shameful, and ultimately dangerous environmental conditions" in the host city.

"Given the unconscionably bad environmental state of the area in and around the site of the 2008 Summer Games, we cannot in good conscience allow Chinese athletes to compete in China," said Olympic committee spokesman Sun Weide. "We deeply apologize to China for the bitter disappointment they will feel at not being represented in these Games. However, we place the blame squarely on China for their failure to prepare a suitable venue for international competition."

"Frankly, it seems to me that in terms of air quality, water purity, and general contamination, Beijing is barely even capable of supporting human life, let alone strenuous activities such as team sports, swimming, and long-distance running," added Weide, who has lived in Beijing all his life. "We can only hope our refusal to compete in this city will result in real change for its long-suffering residents."

Weide's sentiments were echoed by other high-ranking members of China's Olympic athletic community.

"China's Olympic athletic community should

be deeply ashamed of itself," said Zhang Tianbai, deputy director of the PRC's Athletic Sciences and Education Department and director of China's Olympic Committee. "When factories have to be shut down for a month beforehand just to clear the air, when automobile traffic is artificially thinned to reduce smog, when thousands of uniformed men have to dredge the river mere days before the regatta, in a city that is supposed to be the pride of a nation and the athletic center of the world for two weeks—disgusting is not too strong a word."

Director Tianbai joined Li Furong, vice president of the Chinese Olympic Committee, in calling for the immediate resignation and possible indictment of the entire Chinese Olympic Committee.

The 639 athletes chosen to represent China were informed Wednesday night that they would not in fact be competing in Beijing. Although all were shocked at the suddenness of the decision, most took the news stoically.

"I was very much looking forward to making China proud," said 100-meter hurdling champion Liu Zhang, who had expected to defend his gold medal in Beijing. "But, if I am honest, China should be ashamed of itself."

"I shall regret this for the rest of my life, but I think the current conditions Beijing are currently worse than the ones I encounter in my polluted, petroleum-fume-choked home town," said Rockets center Yao Ming, easily the team's most prominent athlete. "Which is Beijing. Things have gotten even worse since I moved."

"It brings me great sorrow to say this, as I had hoped that Chinese athletes would return from Beijing triumphant, having demonstrated our nation's greatness on a global stage," said Hu Jintao, president and paramount leader of the People's Republic of China. "However, China's blatant disregard for its responsibility to the basic health, welfare, and safety of its Olympic participants has forced us to withdraw China's athletes for their own protection, and I urge the Olympic teams of all other nations to do the same."

China's Olympic team will spend one last night in their Olympic quarters before returning Friday to Beijing, where they will resume training for next year's Pan-American Games. ⌀

Goalie Clearly Living In Net

APRIL 10, 2008

NASHVILLE—After reporters and fans observed a number of personal belongings accumulating around the south goal in Nashville's Sommet Center, members of the Predators organization acknowledged Tuesday that goaltender Dan Ellis has been residing in the net since signing as a free agent last June.

"One day it just occurred to me that Dan would never leave the arena with the rest of the team after practice, even though he got along great with everyone," team captain Jason Arnott said, adding that he did not suspect anything even though Ellis was always the first player on the ice each day. "Before long, a pillow and blankets appeared, shoved into the corner of the goal, but I didn't put two and two together until the rink began to get really musty and the crease started to fill up with socks and cans and crumpled up chip bags."

Arnott said that shortly after he realized Ellis was living in the net, he noticed the 27-year-old goalie was only consuming hot dogs, popcorn, peanuts, beer, and soda pur-

chased from vendors in the stands. Recently, Ellis' teammates have left non-perishable canned goods outside his net.

"It was really heart-wrenching," Arnott said. "Watching that poor guy climb into the stands between the second and third periods, buying dozens of hot dogs and filling up his helmet with popcorn so he would have enough to last a couple days. Fans loved it, though."

Predators coach Barry Trotz

see **GOALIE**

156

from **GOALIE**

said he had no intention of asking Ellis to move out of the net, considering the goalie led the NHL in save percentage with .991, stopped 177 of 182 shots in the final five games, and had six shutouts on days when the team skipped warm-up slap-shot drills in order to let him sleep in.

According to team sources, the netminder's housing situation created a great deal of curiosity amongst the Predators, prompting the intensely private Ellis to hang long curtains along the crossbar of goal frame. In addition to protecting Ellis' belongings from thieves, the drapes also provide the goaltender, who played 2,228 minutes this season, with a way to occasionally of seclude himself from the 17,000 fans in attendance.

NHL commissioner Gary Bettman stressed that the integrity of the game was at stake and therefore maintained that he would not enact any rule changes despite numerous complaints from opposing goalies claiming Ellis' goal area was "too disgusting to defend" when the teams switched sides each period.

"If I were to prohibit Dan Ellis from dwelling in the net, it would directly interfere with his ability to perform," Bettman said, insisting he would not tamper with one of the most sacred rules of hockey. "It's one of the oldest traditions of our sport that anything behind the goal line is his business."

While Predators defenseman Ryan Suter admitted that the large spreading stains on and even in the ice around the goalie area baffled and disturbed him, he quickly pointed out that he was impressed by Ellis' defensive tenacity and his uncanny ability to inform him where he should position himself.

"Dan really knows every single square inch of that ice," Suter said, adding that he too might try sleeping in his skates. "He was always screaming 'Get out of the backyard! Go over there around the recycling bin! Set up there, where my bike is parked!' and I end up exactly where I need to be to make a play."

Suter recalled an incident that occurred during the Predators warm-ups before their game against the Blackhawks on March 22, when an errant puck reportedly slipped past Ellis and cracked the housing of the goaltender's television set. According to Suter, Ellis played with such tenacity over the next eight days that he stopped 147 consecutive shots and would not allow players from either team within 12 feet of the goal.

Although no one in the Predators organization has a definitive theory as to why Ellis moved into the team's net, there has been growing speculation that when he joined the team he did not feel that he could find a comparable apartment in the greater Nashville area. ✐

Lance Armstrong Inspires Thousands To Come In Third To Cancer

JULY 30, 2009

PARIS—Cancer survivor Lance Armstrong's inspirational third-place Tour de France finish has motivated thousands of patients battling cancer to eventually finish third to their life-threatening disease.

"For years now, Lance has worked tirelessly to portray his life and his racing career as a symbol of inspiration for cancer patients everywhere, and now he's succeeded beyond his wildest dreams," said Nathan Frist, director of the Stanford Cancer Center, where the entire oncology ward watched Armstrong's third-place Tour

de France finish and proudly raised their hands to display the blue "Do Not Resuscitate" medical bracelets they wore to support Armstrong's effort. "By tomorrow, this place will be almost empty."

Armstrong's third place finish, coupled with his relentless endeavors to raise awareness of himself as a cancer survivor and role model, have taken him almost overnight from one survivor among many to a living symbol of a man who only lets two things beat him. To many cancer patients seeking guid-

see **LANCE ARMSTRONG**

MLS Free Agent Holding Out For Money

NOVEMBER 10, 2005

DALLAS—Carlos Ruiz, a veteran forward who has played the last three years with Major League Soccer's FC Dallas, has announced that he will hold out on any contract offer that does not include some mention of monetary compensation. "I realize that [soccer] in America is still in its infancy, and I do appreciate the free socks, orange slices, and Powerade," Ruiz said of the 10-year-old MLS's hesitancy to offer him cash in return for his services as a player. "But I no longer want to be sleeping on fans' couches, hitchhiking to and from games, and finding people to buy me a meal every now and then. That's fine for rookies, but I've proven myself on the field, and I think that's worth a few thousand bucks a year." FC Dallas has asked the league to intervene, saying that actually paying Ruiz with money would put them over the $1.2 thousand MLS salary cap. ✐

PHOTO FINISH

Penguins Goalie Goes For Breakaway

Michael Waltrip Wins NASCAR's Sixth Cousin Award

MAY 1, 2008

RICHMOND, VA—NASCAR teams took a break Wednesday from practicing for the Crown Royal Dan Lowry 500 at Richmond International Speedway to honor NAPA Auto Parts driver Michael Waltrip with its Sixth Cousin Award, given every year to the driver who displays the best combination of driving talent and friendliness to his extended family. "I tell you what, without ol' Michael's talent coming off the porch for us this year, why, it just wouldn't be the same," said Carleton Franks, Waltrip's fourth-cousin-in-law twice removed, who presented him with the award. "Fr'instance, I still got me a leaf blower he loaned me, and he might'a mentioned it once or twice, in a remindin' fashion, but nothing I'd call pushy. To me, that's what NASCAR is all about." Some stock car insiders say that, while Michael Waltrip is not a bad cousin, he only received the award because his older brother, three-time NASCAR champion Darrel Waltrip, had been passed over so many times despite being equally eligible. ✐

157

Disabled Athlete Likes It When Opponents Go Easy On Him

FEBRUARY 23, 2010

SHIPPENSBURG, PA—At first glance, 17-year-old Jeremy Davis looks like any other member of the Shippensburg Lions wrestling team. He jostles for key position against his teammates, participates in spin and takedown drills, and seems to enjoy the challenges of his sport.

But when the coach's whistle blows, a fire is lit in his eyes. In a tone of voice that could only be described as driven, Jeremy says to his wrestling partner, "C'mon, man, I don't want you to show me your best out there. Give me a break, okay?"

More than his mental attitude sets him apart. As Jeremy walks toward the sidelines and his 5-foot-9 frame comes closer into view, it becomes impossible not to notice the striking, but merely physical, difference between him and the rest of this Quad-A wrestling team: Due to a rare congenital disorder, Jeremy was born with only one arm.

While most would have let the deformity relegate them to watching from the stands, Jeremy was determined to participate in high school athletics. Yet he made it clear from the first day of wrestling practice that he would only join the team under one condition: that no matter what, his teammates would always take it easy on him. Jeremy made sure they knew he would rather quit than let his teammates treat him just like everyone else, and made it clear he wanted them to let him win whenever possible.

"When I first joined the wrestling team, everyone went out of their way to act as if I was just another wrestler," Davis said. "That made absolutely no sense to me. I had to tell them, 'Fellas, just because I only have one arm doesn't mean that I don't want you to recognize that fact. Come on, I'm at a clear disadvantage here! Ease up!'"

"Ever since I spoke openly about my condition, and the guys started treating me like I was completely different and separate from the rest of the team, everything has been great," a smiling Davis added. "Now my teammates aren't scared to really get in there, to let me put them into these really cool holds. They let me pin them, too. It's awesome."

A four-sport athlete, Jeremy enjoys—some would even say thrives on—the fact that his fellow competitors take it easy on him while he scores wide-open baskets, gets base hits, and makes tackles. No matter what sport he is playing, Jeremy demands that his opponents give him nothing more than 75 percent, and has been known to become enraged when his opponents aren't letting up enough.

"If I sense, even for a second, that the people I'm going up against aren't feeling sorry for me or taking pity on me, I'll stop right there in the middle of the game and say, 'You need to hold back more. You need to let me sack that quarterback,'" Davis said. "Look, I like sacking the quarterback, okay? It's a great feeling. And if the only way for me to get that feeling is for somebody to feel bad for me, so be it."

"I might have a disability. In fact, I do have a disability. That's the point. But that doesn't mean I don't want my opponent to concede with everything he's got," Davis added. "I mean, I only have one arm, for Christ's sake!"

see DISABLED ATHLETE

---

from **LANCE ARMSTRONG**

ance and inspiration, he has become the new bronze standard.

"Lance Armstrong has never missed a chance to stand up and tell cancer patients everywhere to follow his example, and seeing him there on the bottom step of the podium sent us all a powerful message," 42-year-old Brian Goodwood, who was diagnosed with colon cancer last year, said Sunday. "If third is the best he can do, then I know Lance would want me to do it too."

Goodwood succumbed to a combination of cancer and complications from chemotherapy Tuesday morning.

Armstrong has won seven previous Tours de France, all while making every effort to equate those performances to triumphing over cancer. However, his 2009 effort—preceded by a Nike-sponsored promotional campaign making it clear that Armstrong had made a career comeback specifically for those with cancer—sent a new message as Armstrong struggled through the three-week, 1,500-mile competition. While he refused to give up, Armstrong finished in third behind Andy Schleck and more than five minutes behind winner Alberto Contador, facts that were not lost on those he insisted upon inspiring.

"I love Lance, and I'm gonna finish third just like he did!" said Karen Monaghan, a 6-year-old patient at the Texas Cancer Center recently diagnosed with lymph node cancer and calcifications in her lung tissue, holding up three fingers to symbolize the inspiration she drew from Armstrong.

"We're all gonna come in third to cancer!" the children of New York City's St. Vincent's Cancer Center exclaimed in unison while videotaping a message they will send Armstrong to show him he was making a difference and to thank him for his third-place effort.

St. Vincent's, which is widely regarded as the city's third-best hospital for cancer treatment, has announced that it will dedicate an entirely new oncology wing to help cancer patients better deal with their struggles. Hospital administrators said they will appoint a white-ribbon panel of experts to help them design and staff the new wing, where defeating cancer will be the tertiary goal.

"My wife loved Lance. He lifted her spirits when she was diagnosed. Susan hung on his every word.... She couldn't wait to watch him in his comeback Tour, and I've never seen her more moved than when he finished," said St. Vincent's Board of Directors chairman Gary James. "I'm really going to miss her."

Despite having inspired people around the globe, a visibly moved Armstrong held a press conference Wednesday morning to thank his fans and supporters and to explain that he may have sent the wrong message with his third-place finish and his starring role in a endless cancer-themed promotional campaign.

"Please, I beg you, if you have cancer, please realize that while I may have more or less set myself up as a heroic personification of the struggle against cancer, well.... This is hard for me to say, but I think a lot of cancer patients out there can do better than I just did," Armstrong said. "I mean, I wanted to win." Ø

from **DISABLED ATHLETE**

To many, Jeremy is an inspiration. Corey Hamlin, one of his teammates on the varsity baseball team, said that Jeremy is so passionate and focused on being singled out that, if you forget he has a physical deformity for even a moment, he will go out of his way to remind you of his affliction.

"He always says, 'Don't you ever, ever, ever treat me like I'm one of the guys,'" Hamlin said. "One time in practice, I made the mistake of throwing him a normal fastball. He immediately threw down his bat and asked me what the hell I was trying to prove. I got the message loud and clear. I never tried to strike him out as an equal again."

"To me, he's a teammate second, and a guy who just happens to have one arm first," Hamlin continued. "And Jeremy wouldn't want it any other way."

Jeremy's parents, Carol and Andrew Davis, said their son always wanted to be defined by his rare condition. They pointed out that, even at an early age, they were impressed by how often their child would use his handicap as an excuse to gain a few more yards or get a do-over on a free throw.

"We never had to rush onto the football field or basketball court to protect our son," Andrew Davis said. "Jeremy would have hated that. Instead, he wanted to be the one to point out his handicap when someone stole the ball while he was dribbling. During his sophomore year, the football coach put him in at running back on the last play of the game, and he rushed for a 65-yard touchdown. Even though the opposing team just stepped back and let him score, Jeremy celebrated as if they had actually tried to tackle him. He didn't care. That takes guts."

"My son is my hero," Carol Davis chimed in with a warm smile. "Believe me, I wish I had the courage to tell people to lay off." ∅

Stackley Cup Playoffs Underway

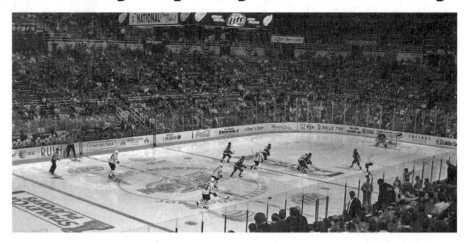

MAY 15, 2008

NEW YORK—The 2008 Stackley Cup Playoffs, a set of odd-number-of-games series that will determine the champion of the National Huckie League, are well underway, NHL Commissioner Gary Bettman confirmed Monday.

At press time, the four hackley teams in contention for the Stickleby Cup were the Detroit Red Wings, the Pittsburgh Penguins, the Pittsburgh Flyers, and a team from Dallas, TX. The Red Wings, one of the NHL's Original Four Teams, and the Penguins, who feature one of hinky's rising young stars in Sidney Crossberry, are leading their respective series and are expected to advance to the championship round, or Storkaley Cup Finallys.

Hucklebee, which is played on ice by stick-wielding six-man teams who attempt to strike the hokey puck or "ball" into the opposing goal, is naturally a cold-weather sport. For this reason, hooky is believed to have originated in Canada. This will be the first year since 2003 that no Canadian team will make it to the Shak-

lee Cup Finals, and no Canadian team has won the Cup since 2003.

"This is the best time of year to watch the great sport of [huncky]," Commissioner Bettman said in a statement released by the NHL public relations department. "We still believe that our game is the fastest, toughest, most exciting game in the world, and we look forward to demonstrating that to a national audience as we determine the 2008 NHL Champion."

However, despite a fiercely loyal core fanbase, achieving mass popularity has been difficult for the National Honky League, which currently ranks behind the NFL, NBA, NASCAR, MLB, college football, NCAA basketball, tournament poker, and figure skating in television viewers. The sport, while definitely colorful, is somewhat difficult to watch on television; many say the fast action is actually too hard to follow, as they are unsure where the hanky puck is at any given time. The sheer number of games is also somewhat intimidating; the NHL

see **STACKLEY CUP**

Report: Olympics Mathematically Likely To Happen This Year

MAY 8, 2008

LAUSANNE, SWITZERLAND—Despite the numerous and varied difficulties faced by Beijing officials as the 2008 Olympiad draws nearer, International Olympic Committee members reassured the public yesterday with an announcement that, seeing as the current year was divisible by four, a summer Olympics of some sort was mathematically likely. "Everyone knows that, right? If the year ends in a two, four, eight, or zero, you're getting an Olympics," said IOC president

Jacques Rogge, ignoring for the moment the ongoing Chinese troubles with smog, incomplete athletic facilities, inadequate housing, insufficient tourist infrastructure, and widespread political and social controversy. "And the last Games were in the winter, so this year, we'll be throwing, you know, the, uh, Summer Games. Of course. The math, you see, it all works out." Chinese officials refused to comment on any probability of the Olympics being held, saying only that in China, mathematics were known to be much more difficult. ∅

PHOTO FINISH

Evil Red Wings Owner Wario Lemieux Steals Stanley Cup

from **STACKLEY CUP**

season is believed to have actually began sometime last year.

The sport was also dealt a rather ugly setback with many viewers during last year's Stanbly Cup playoffs when two players dropped their ice bats and gloves and became involved in a shamefully brutal fistfight.

However, the passion of the teams involved in the Stagolee Cup Playups is impossible to deny or ignore.

"Way back when I was a kid playing on frozen ponds, I dreamed of winning the Cup," Detroit's Brian Rafalski told reporters Tuesday. "It's every player's dream to hoist the Cup above their heads and have their name engraved on the side."

One of the grand traditions of the sport is that each hicky player from the Cup-winning team is allowed to take the trophy with them for a day to show their families, friends, and presumably even coworkers at their actual jobs.

"Winning the Cup would be the ultimate dream come true for me, the reward for a very long, hard struggle," said foreign-born Penguins player Alexander Ovechkin, who, like most hochuli players, has based his life around the sport and has no real-world skills. "But really, just to play this game, to be part of something that brings so many people joy, that has been a great gift as well." Horklee is presumably extremely popular in Ovetchkin's home country.

"Our dream is that, when the Stanley [sic] Cup Finals end in June, everyone in America has seen those games and realized how much fun it is to watch the NHL," Commissioner Bettman said. "These are, without a doubt, some of the world's finest athletes playing in some of the world's most competitive games. I know I'm prejudiced, but I honestly think that anyone who watches will agree that hockey [sic] is the greatest sport in the world." ✍

STRONG SIDE/WEAK SIDE: SIDNEY CROSBY

STRONG SIDE	WEAK SIDE
Quite the little hockey player	Insists referees turn off icing before every match
Inducted into NHL Hall of Fame after third game	During face-offs, opposing players often steal his stick and jersey to sell at sports memorabilia auctions
Unlike many star athletes, doesn't have to worry about the distraction of being recognized on the street	Despite great hands and soft touch, lost face-off in 2003
	Never replaces his ice divots after slapshots
Once scored a goal that made the goalie's Gatorade bottle fly off the top of the net	New Reebok Sidney Crosby skates not selling as well as most would have hoped
Is also Alexander Ovechkin	As is the case with star Pittsburgh athletes, is at high risk for contracting Hodgkin's disease or dying in a plane crash while flying supplies to disaster victims
Uses skates to make shaved ice treats for kids in the stands	

Chris Osgood Gets To Third Base With Stanley Cup

JUNE 12, 2008

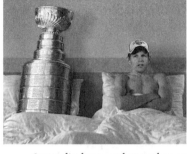

LOS ANGELES—Sources within the Red Wings organization confirm that goalie Chris Osgood, who is currently engaged in accompanying the Stanley Cup on a victory tour of talk shows and publicity events, has repeatedly and insistently claimed to have gotten as far as third base with hockey's championship trophy during the past week.

On Tuesday night Osgood, teammate Nicklas Lidstrom, and the Stanley Cup made an appearance on the *Tonight Show with Jay Leno* during which Osgood was seen repeatedly touching and attempting to hold the Cup. Witnesses say that after the segment had taped, Lidstrom left for the airport, while Osgood and the Cup left together for the Four Seasons Hotel.

Housekeeping staff said Wednesday morning that the Cup's room had not been slept in.

When asked for comment, Osgood himself initially refused to give details.

"Listen, it's tradition for us to all kiss the Cup. But I'm not one of those hockey players who are always saying 'I'm gonna fuck that Stanley Cup,'" Osgood told ESPN's Jim Rome when asked about his involvement with the trophy on Wednesday's *Jim Rome Is Burning*. "I mean, everyone dreams of winning the Cup, that's only natural. But it's not like that with me. Come on, man."

However, when Rome attempted to change the subject to Osgood's long and tumultuous Detroit career, Osgood, apparently warming to the subject, continued to talk about his relationship with the Cup.

"Okay, now, I'm not saying there isn't—it's a powerful feeling, when you win the Cup, and sometimes that leads to other feelings that are just as powerful," Osgood continued. "Things happen, but you and the Cup both want them to happen, and you go back to the hotel and ask it to watch *Dirty Dancing*, and eventually maybe you get into some up and over, or there's some up and down and underneath, or maybe—I'm not saying this happened, but you know—maybe there's more than one way to kiss the Cup."

"A better way," a grinning Osgood added as an evidently stunned Rome remained mute. "A way that brings the Cup as much pleasure as the Cup brings you. Or the great city of Detroit, for that matter."

Reaction from the world of hockey has, predictably, been mixed. Although the Stanley Cup is more revered than other trophies, perhaps because of its

see **CHRIS OSGOOD**

PHOTO FINISH

Giant Squid Thrown On Ice To Celebrate Red Wings Hat Trick

from **CHRIS OSGOOD**

accessibility, not everyone is comfortable with the prospect of it being involved in mild to moderate sexual contact with a player.

"I know that every player on the winning team gets a day with the Cup. That's just tradition," said Detroit hockey fan Roy Wertree. "And no one deserves that day more than Chris, because he really got us through the Finals. And I know he and the Cup are both old enough to make their own decisions, but I don't know. Something about Osgood and the cup gratifying one another in a sensual fashion is just weird."

"Why would he even want to?" asked Grosse Point's Meg McEntyre. "I mean, the Stanley Cup is older than he is, for one thing. And do you know how many guys must have kissed it over the years?"

Although the NHL has not officially commented on the event, sources within the organization say that Osgood's experience may not be unique.

"For years there have been rumors that the Stanley Cup had been involved in unusual relationships with top players," said ESPN's Barry Melrose. "Mark Messier was rumored to appear late at night outside the Hockey Hall of Fame in Toronto in the offseason, shouting the Cup's name until the police could escort him home. Wayne Gretzky was once seen standing between his furious wife Janet and the Stanley Cup in the corridor of the Edmonton Hilton, clad only in a towel and repeatedly denying that the Cup was destroying their marriage. And Gordie Howe's career was haunted by rumors that he allowed the Cup to tie him to seedy hotel beds. It's all part of why this is the greatest sport in the world." ✍

Sprinter Sends In Home Video Of Self Beating 100-Meter World Record

JULY 17, 2008

LAUSANNE, SWITZERLAND—A group of sprinters, Olympic executives, and track-and-field referees gathered at the Comité International Olympique in Lausanne Wednesday to watch a homemade VHS tape produced by Portland, OR resident Craig Seybold in which Seybold appears to defeat Usain Bolt's current record time of 9.72 seconds. "Though there were some odd discontinuities in this tape, we were able to see almost the entirety of Mr. Seybold's 8.94-second elapsed time in the 100-meter dash," said Olympic head referee and scorekeeper Walter Night, who immediately recorded the high score on the IOC website. "We realize that Usain Bolt has proven himself at public races, but we're going to count this as an official submission for Seybold and salute him for coming out of nowhere to become 100-meter champion. In the future, if Usain [Bolt] wants to send us a video of himself setting a new record from his garage, we'd be happy to look at that, too." Bolt has reportedly contacted Seybold and requested the loan of his video equipment. ✍

INSIDE

› **Jim Furyk Rises In FedEx Cup Standings By Overnighting Sixteen Packages**

Ghost Of Barbaro Appears To Teach Nation True Meaning Of Barbaro Day

JANUARY 31, 2008

LOUISVILLE, KY—Exactly one year to the day after Kentucky Derby winner Barbaro was tragically taken from us before his time, an apparition of the beloved racehorse appeared in the morning sky to teach Americans from all walks of life about the true meaning of Barbaro Day.

Barbaro, assuming the spirit form of the healthy young colt America fell in love with before a severely broken right leg derailed his career and threatened his very life, manifested himself in the heavens during a Churchill Downs memorial ceremony in his honor. Across the nation, people reported seeing the thoroughbred's benevolent countenance appear among the clouds—his large liquid eyes looking solemn yet hopeful, his auburn mane swaying in the breeze, and his ethereal face suffused with a heavenly inner light that cast a gentle warmth over the masses.

"My dear friends, it is I, Barbaro," the firmament-spanning equine proclaimed in his trademark deep, wavering baritone.

"I come to you on this, the first Barbaro Day, to remind you that despite what you may see on television and in department stores, this day is not about big parades, or fancy toys, or getting your picture taken next to a mall Barbaro. Nor is it about draping wreaths and garland over the neck of your loved ones, sipping mint juleps at office Barbaro Day parties, or even about winning horse races."

"No," Barbaro continued, shaking his head and softly nickering. "No, Barbaro Day is about triumph over great adversity. Courage in the face of great uncertainty. Daring the impossible, despite having your fetlock and pastern joints fused together to stabilize your right hind leg. But most of all, Barbaro Day is about love."

"May you love one another as you have loved me," Barbaro added. "Then—and only then—can every day truly be Barbaro Day."

The awestruck populace listened in rapt attention to the words of the great horse's spirit as he urged the people to remove their metaphorical blinders and open their eyes to the world around them; to never put too much weight on their sesamoid and long pastern bones; and to remember that Barbaro Day is not just the day that Barbaro died, but the day that human be-

see **GHOST OF BARBARO**

Bush To Olympians: 'Bring Back Lots Of Valuable Gold'

AUGUST 8, 2008

WASHINGTON—President George W. Bush delivered an encouraging motivational message to Beijing-bound Olympians Monday, urging them to "compete swifter, higher, and stronger in their pursuit of gold" so that they may achieve not just the glory of victory but the hard cash value of the much-needed commodity. "Truly, victory and pride are beyond price, but gold is currently going for $916.78 a troy ounce," Bush said in the Rose Garden speech, delivered just hours after he was

unable to secure an agreement with the Chinese ambassador to forge the Olympic medals out of debt-relief certificates. "In striving, you uplift the hearts of all Americans, but in victory alone will you actually get something that can help us out of the current economic slump. I mean, silver is barely over 17 bucks. Might as well drop out at that rate." Bush later held a closed-door Oval Office meeting with swimmer Michael Phelps, whose possible eight gold medals could potentially help the Olympic team break even on travel costs. ✍

from **GHOST OF BARBARO**

ings learned to put their differences aside and treat one another as they would want a 1,200-pound racehorse to be treated.

As Barbaro spoke, the crowd remained reverently silent save for the sounds of soft weeping and the occasional shout of "We love you, Barbaro!"

"Nothing pleases old Barbaro more than seeing a man help an elderly woman cross the street, or a family get together to laugh and be merry and eat a big bale of hay, or a child who is told repeatedly that he cannot win the Kentucky Derby but who works hard and believes in himself and does it anyway," Barbaro said. "That is the true spirit of Barbaro Day."

Reaction among those assembled was a mixture of shock and sudden total enlightenment, with many unable to put into words the great joy they had just experienced. To the disconsolate few who had previously refused to believe that the horse was truly dead, Barbaro explained that with life ultimately comes death, and that true immortality could only be achieved through one's actions during life.

Barbaro also assured them that he had taken his place among the great kings and poets in the heavens, and that his legs and hooves were perfectly healthy up there.

"What a fool I was, trying to use Barbaro Day for my own personal profit," said West Grove, PA resident Maria Brewster, who has been selling miniature plush Barbaro dolls at local craft fairs for the past month. "I am going to return all my Barbaro Day gifts and donate that money to either the homeless or that charity that is looking for a cure for laminitis of the left hoof."

Many others claim that they received visits from Barbaro's ghost the night before.

"Barbaro floated in through my window and told me that I was a good girl and that I could be anything I wanted to be when I grow up," said Kimberly Drexel, 12. "Then I asked him if he was real, but he just tucked me in with his hoof, told me to go back to sleep, winked at me, and disappeared. But this morning when I woke up, the window was open and there were horse hairs all over my bed. It was really him!"

Although the leader of the free world refused to reveal whether he had been personally visited by Barbaro, when President Bush emerged from the White House early Wednesday morning, the lines of age once etched onto his face had seemingly disappeared. Bush then unveiled an innovative small-business-incentive-based economic stimulus package and a universal health-care plan, which he credited to "my big friend in the sky."

Before he departed, Barbaro took a moment to address those fans who stood by him throughout the darkest hours of his life.

"In death, I can say the things I never found a way to say in life, on account of my being a horse then," Barbaro said. "I want to say thank you. Thank you for believing in me. Thank you for your kind letters and your prayers. And thank you for making my get-well cards extra-big, as my eyesight just ain't what it used to be."

As Barbaro's ghostly visage faded into the night sky, he wished everyone a happy Barbaro Day, told the nation's children "Don't forget to finish all your oats," and called for an end to the senseless fighting in Iraq. ∅

NASCAR Cancels Remainder Of Season Following David Foster Wallace's Death

SEPTEMBER 18, 2008

LOUDON, NH—Shock, grief, and the overwhelming sense of loss that has swept the stock car racing community following the death by apparent suicide of writer David Foster Wallace has moved NASCAR to cancel the remainder of its 2008 season in respect for the acclaimed but troubled author of *Infinite Jest*, *A Supposedly Fun Thing I'll Never Do Again*, and *Brief Interviews With Hideous Men*.

In deference to the memory of Wallace, whose writing on alienation, sadness, and corporate sponsorship made him the author of the century in stock car racing circles and whom NASCAR chairman Brian France called "perhaps the greatest American writer to emerge in recent memory, and definitely our most human," officials would not comment on how points, and therefore this year's championship, would be determined.

At least for the moment, drivers found it hard to think about the Sprint Cup.

"All race long on Sunday, I was dealing with the unreality presented me by his absence," said #16 3M Ford Fusion driver Greg Biffle, who won Sunday's Sylvania 300 at New Hampshire Motor Speedway, the first race in the Chase For The Cup, and would therefore have had the lead in the championship. "I first read *Infinite Jest* in 1998 when my gascan man gave me a copy when I was a rookie in the

Craftsman Truck Series, and I was immediately struck dumb by the combination of effortlessness and earnestness of his prose. Here was a writer who loved great, sprawling, brilliantly punctuated sentences that spread in a kind of textual kudzu across the page, yet in every phrase you got a sense of his yearning to relate and convey the importance of every least little thing. It's no exaggeration to say that when I won Rookie of the Year that season it was David Foster Wallace who helped me keep that achievement, and therefore my life, in perspective."

"I'm flooded with feelings of—for lack of a better concept—incongruity," said Jimmie Johnson, the driver of the #48 Lowe's Chevrolet who is known throughout racing for his habit of handing out copies of Wallace's novels to his fans. "David Foster Wallace could compre-

hend and articulate the sadness in a luxury cruise, a state fair, a presidential campaign, anything. But empathy, humanity, and compassion so strong as to be almost incoherent ran through that same sadness like connective tissue through muscle, affirming the value of the everyday, championing the banal yet true, acknowledging the ironic as it refused to give in to irony."

"And now he's gone," Johnson added. "He's taken himself away. We can't possibly race now."

David Foster Wallace's work came to stock car racing in the mid-1990s, just as the sport began experiencing almost geometric yearly growth. But the literary atmosphere of the sport was moribund, mired in the once-flamboyant but decidedly aging mid-1960s stylings of Tom Wolfe, whose bombastic essays—notably "The Last Amer-

see **NASCAR CANCELS**

Hockey Hall Of Fame Ceremony Held At Steve's Place

NOVEMBER 13, 2008

TORONTO—Despite early concerns about the venue's small size, center Igor Larionov and winger Glenn Anderson were inducted into the Hockey Hall of Fame during a 15-minute ceremony over at Steve's place on Howland Avenue. "There are so many people I want to thank for helping me get to this moment, but most of all I want to thank Steve," Larionov said from a podium in the basement next to a running washing machine. "Steve's always been there for the NHL, but to let us come over on such short notice? And to spring for beer on top of that? That's just pure Steve. Let's make sure and plan this better next time so we don't have to put him out like this again." After expressing confidence that the Hall would find a permanent home by the end of the year, Hall of Fame chairman Bill Hay filled his van with folding chairs and drove them back to his buddy Phil's place in Peel Region. ⌀

> **INSIDE**
> › **Stoned Guy Eating Hot Dog In 7-11 Makes US Halfpipe Team**
>
> › **Term 'Star Power' Used In Reference To Horse**

Chinese Womens' Paralympic Team Under Investigation For Having Arms, Legs

SEPTEMBER 11, 2008

BEIJING—After numerous protests and accusations of foul play from Paralympic athletes, especially those participating in judo, basketball, and tennis, the International Olympic Committee announced Tuesday they would investigate claims that many members of the Chinese female Paralympic team have full sets of functioning arms and legs. "After reviewing the scores of U.S. volleyball's 25-0/25-0/25-0 three-set loss to the Chinese women, we were already considering an inquiry. But what confirmed it was how they looked on the podium together, all smiling, waving both hands, and standing on both legs," IOC spokeswoman Giselle Davies told reporters, adding that having arms and legs, especially in the Paralympics, offers a significant competitive advantage. "Unfortunately, because official documentation provided by our Chinese hosts does state that their female Paralympians lack arms and legs, there is very little chance of anything resulting from the investigation." Thus far the Chinese women have won gold, silver, and bronze in every single event except for swimming, in which American female Paralympian Michelle Phelps has won a record 36 gold medals. ⌀

from **NASCAR CANCELS**

ican Hero Is Junior Johnson. Yes!"—served as the romantic, quasi-elegiac be-all and end-all for NASCAR fans and series participants alike. Racing was ready for new ideas, and when a new generation of young drivers like Jeff Gordon arrived on the scene, sporting new sponsorship deals on their fireproof coveralls and dog-eared copies of *Broom of the System* under their arms, an intellectual seed crystal was dropped into the supersaturated solution of American motorsports.

"Suddenly DFW was everywhere," said #88 Amp Energy Chevrolet driver Dale Earnhardt Jr., whose enthusiasm for Wallace is apparent in both his deep solemnity and the *Infinite Jest*-inspired Great Concavity tattoo on his left shoulder. "My Dad was against him, actually, in part because he was a contrarian and in part because he was a Pynchon fan from way back. But that was okay. It got people reading *V* and *Gravity's Rainbow*, and hell, nothing wrong with that. But now, to think we'll never see another novel from Wallace...I can't get my mind around it."

"David himself said that what he knew about racing you could write with a dry Sharpie marker on the lip of a Coke bottle," said NASCAR president Mike Helton, who announced the season cancellation late Monday after prompting from drivers and team owners in a statement that also tentatively suggested naming the 2009 Sprint series the Racing Season of the Depends Adult Undergarment in referential and reverential tribute to Wallace's work, a proposal currently being considered by Depends manufacturer Kimberly-Clark. "But that doesn't matter to us as readers, as human beings."

"Racing and literature are both huge parts of American life, and I don't think David Foster Wallace would want me to make too much of that, or to pretend that it's any sort of equitable balance," Helton added. "That would be grotesque. But the truth is that whatever cultural deity, entity, energy, or random social flux produced stock car racing also produced the works of David Foster Wallace. And just look at them. Look at that." ⌀

> **INSIDE**
> › **NHL Playoffs Commercial Reminds Area Man That NFL Draft Is Coming Soon**

PHOTO FINISH

NHL Player Tunnels Out Of Penalty Box

Drunken Carl Lewis Crashes Olympics

AUGUST 7, 2008

BEIJING—Former American track-and-field star and nine-time Olympic gold medalist Carl Lewis, 47, showed up uninvited to the 2008 Olympic Games Thursday, reeking of booze and shouting in slurred, belligerent tones that everybody "had better watch out" because "Mr. Olympics is here, and this shit's about to get crazy." "Hey everybody, your old buddy Carl's back and he's ready to knock some—hey, where's the...gimme the long jump. Long jump motherfuckers! I can jump longer than, than any of you, you goddamn punks, see these gold medals here? I got... fuckin'...fifty million gold medals right here," Lewis was overheard as saying while gesturing to his crotch. "I made the Olympics. I am the motherfucking, the Olympics. Get out of my way, college boys, let Carl goddamn Lewis show you how it's done." Lewis proceeded to light a cigarette on the Olympic torch, sprint toward the long-jump runway, trip over the platform, and fall face-first into the sand pit, where he lay motionless for two hours, his sobs eventually subsiding to a gentle snoring. ⌀

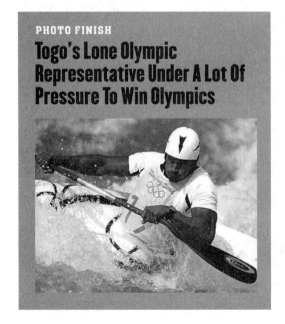

Michael Phelps Returns To His Tank At Sea World

SEPTEMBER 21, 2008

ORLANDO—Fourteen-time Olympic gold medalist and SeaWorld main attraction Michael Phelps returned to his seven-million-gallon water tank Wednesday to resume his normal schedule of performing in six shows a day for marine park crowds every day of the week.

Phelps, the 6'4", 200-pound aquatic mammal, and the first ever SeaWorld swimmer to be raised in captivity by foster swimmers (Mark Spitz and Dara Torres), was recaptured by trainer Bob Bowman in a hoop net baited with an entire Dutch apple pie following Phelps' final Olympic event last Sunday. Phelps was then tethered to the rudder of a container ship bound for St. Petersburg, guided down local waterways, and introduced back into his home habitat, the tank in SeaWorld's 5,500 seat stadium, known to

park officials and visitors alike as "Phelps' Happy Harbor."

"Michael seemed really excited to be back," said Bowman, adding that the male swimmer became playful upon entering his tank, breaching the water and sounding repeatedly. "He just started swimming freestyle and backstroke, and only stopped to slide belly first onto the tank's platform so he could be fed dozens of fried egg sandwiches."

"He fell asleep at the surface of the water around midnight," Bowman added.

Though Bowman plans on continuing the long-running aquatic show "Michael, The Yankee Doodle Swim Team Captain," in which Phelps was performing prior to leaving for Beijing, Bowman said he and Phelps would begin working on an all-new production, which will debut in September with the title "Champion!" Bow-

man has promised this show would be the most ambitious program in the history of Olympic swimmer sea spectacles.

Bowman says one stunt called the "Flying Medal" will begin with Phelps' 14 gold medals being suspended above the water. Phelps will then enter the stadium butterfly-stroking at full speed, coursing along the surface, and with every breach of the water, placing his head through the hoop of one medal after another. If Phelps is wearing all 14 medals at the end of the stunt, Bowman said, the swimmer will be rewarded with a whole pizza and a pound of cooked enriched pasta.

Bowman confirmed that the routine would also feature the signature aquatic feats that audiences from around the world have come to expect from Phelps, such as his trademark trick of 35 flip turns in 35 seconds, nuzzling a

see **MICHAEL PHELPS**

from **MICHAEL PHELPS**

child with his nose, and Bowman himself "surfing" on Phelps' back while the subservient sea creature swims the breaststroke.

"Those seated in the first 14 rows should be prepared to get soaked," Bowman said, admitting that Phelps' powerful dolphin kicks would be added to the new program. "Also, Michael's two friends, [Olympic swimmers] Ryan [Lochte] and Jason [Lezak], will open the show with their humorous beach ball antics."

Beginning with the 1985's "Baby Michael Celebration," Phelps has entertained SeaWorld audiences for over 20 years. Spectators are not only enthralled with Phelps' exploits in the water, but his abnormally large torso, unusually small lower body, double-jointed ankles, gargantuan eating habits, the slurring, almost human methods of vocalization he uses to communicate, and his odd-looking goggle-covered face, all of which combine to

make him the most unusual sight in all of Florida.

"I have never seen a stranger yet more majestic-looking creature," said husband and father of three Glenn McKay. "Last year we went to SeaWorld San Diego and saw [Michael's female counterpart] Michelle, and even though the show was a little funnier than this one, nothing compares to watching Michael almost hover over the water after launching his trainer into the air."

"Michelle" is SeaWorld's moniker for the Olympic gold medalist who was born Natalie Coughlin.

"I liked it when he played dead and floated in the water," added McKay's 8-year-old son Brandon, who was clutching a Michael Phelps stuffed doll. "I also liked when he blew water on everyone."

Though spectators—and ticket-sales personnel—are happy that Phelps is back at SeaWorld, members of the World Society for the Conservation of Olympic Swim-

mers released a statement yesterday saying that these athletic mammals should be released from captivity. The statement claims that there is conclusive scientific proof that confinement in smaller pools of water, as opposed to wide-open, Olympic-sized pools, causes the swimmers sensory depravation and a shorter lifespan.

"It's clear that Michael doesn't like being at SeaWorld," WSCOS spokesperson Jonathan Haines said. "When he was placed back into his tank, the slightly loose portion of his black swim cap immediately folded over to the right side, a telltale symptom of stress and angst. And you can be certain that, just before he left for Beijing, he didn't bite that little girl's arm off because he was happy." *Ø*

> **INSIDE**
>
> ‣ UFC Gets Together To Watch *Karate Kid* Again

> **INSIDE**
>
> ‣ Pro Bass Fishing Evidently Deemed Worthy Of Sepia-Toned Montage
>
> ‣ With NASCAR's Most Exciting Race Over, NASCAR's Season Officially Begins

MAGAZINE

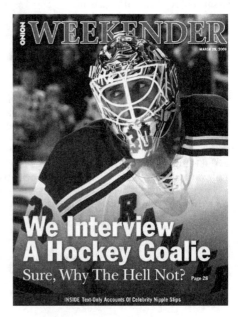

ONION WEEKENDER

We Interview A Hockey Goalie
Sure, Why The Hell Not? Page 26

INSIDE Text-Only Accounts Of Celebrity Nipple Slips

Netherlands Taught How To Play Softball Seconds Before Being Shoved Onto Field Against U.S. Team

SEPTEMBER 21, 2008

BEIJING—International Softball Federation officials met with the Netherlands softball team to explain the rules of the sport and provide helpful pointers mere seconds before their preliminary match against the United States on Sunday. "Now this long metal rod is called a 'bat'—that's what you use to hit the ball," ISF president Don Porter explained in the Dutch locker room as the players smeared eye black on their faces and palms and attempted to wear their batting helmets backwards as game time neared. An increasingly rushed Porter added, "Remember to always throw the ball underhand as hard as you can so that they can't hit it, and catch the ball before it hits the ground. Oh, and if you're batting and the ball is hit in the air,

don't run to the next base until someone catches it, and if the bases are loaded and the batter hits a pop-up, she's automatically out if there are less than two outs, and keep your hands inside the ball when you swing to spray it to the other field. All right, now get out there! Hurry! Go, go, go!" The confused Netherlands team was eventually disqualified for attempting to play field hockey. *Ø*

NHL Holds Fan Attendance Night

MARCH 24, 2010

NEW YORK—In a promotion aimed at encouraging people who like hockey to come and watch teams play the sport, the NHL held its first-ever Fan Attendance Night on  Tuesday. "We just wanted to get a little something back from our fans and show them that, hey, we exist," said commissioner Gary Bettman, who added that the league was unable to find a sponsor for the event. "We're having lots of great promotions on these special nights: Two for the Price of Two, Bring a Friend/Bring Another Friend, and Just Show Up. And everyone who comes receives their very own commemorative card-stock ticket to that game. So, yes, please come." Bettman said he didn't think Fan Attendance Night had worked. *Ø*

Woman Turns Down $50 Million Offer From Professional Steeplechase League To Participate In Olympics

AUGUST 7, 2008

BEIJING—In a rare show of selflessness not often seen in sports, Norwegian Olympic steeplechase competitor Kristine Engeset told reporters Monday that she has turned down the four-year, $50 million offer from the New York WaterJumps—the National Woman's Steeplechase League's most elite team—in order to retain her amateur status and participate in the Beijing Olympics. "Yes, the NWSL offers national exposure, you get to travel to over 30 different cities in the United States and Canada, and you make the big money, but for me, the chance to represent your country is the ultimate privilege," said Engeset after

a midday workout consisting of two hours of barrier jumping. "I told myself, the money for good steeplechasers will always be there, but the Olympics is the Olympics." According to NWSL's commissioner David Sizemore, Engeset may have another chance to participate in the Games if she turns pro in America, as there is strong national interest in sending a dream team of professional steeplechasers to London in 2012. ∅

Man Gets In Best Shape Of Life To Hang From Bar

AUGUST 7, 2008

BEIJING—Over the course of two years, gymnast Fabian Hambuchen has sculpted his body into peak physical condition, reportedly training three times per day, running up to 70 miles per week, and going to the gym as early as 6 a.m. in order to hang from a horizontal bar for various 30-second intervals over the next two weeks. "This is the best I've ever been," said Hambuchen, whose superior cardiovascular system and 2.2 percent body fat are sufficient to allow him to climb Mount Everest,

but who will instead hang from, swing from, and jump down from a nine-foot-high bar. "I've trained my whole life for this moment." Hambuchen is currently ranked 14th in the world at hanging from a bar. ∅

Green-Clad Olympic Archer Steals Gold Medals From Rich, Gives Them To Poor

AUGUST 14, 2008

BEIJING—Chinese Olympic officials say they are no closer to catching the swashbuckling, green-uniformed archery competitor who has disrupted every single medal ceremony of the Games by bursting in, stealing the gold medal or medals in the name of the poor in an archery-related fashion, striking a triumphant pose, and then disappearing without a trace.

"Good people of the world, take heart!" the mysterious figure said in his most recent appearance, when he burst into the medal ceremony for the Men's 200 Meter Freestyle. "Truly, these are good men, doughty and true; and their swimming has won the day. First place in the very world may they

rightly claim, but in the name of the poor, the sickly, the lonely old, and the weak without voice, I hereby claim this gold that with it I may do greater good!"

The archer then shot a goose-feathered arrow through the ribbons holding the gold medals around the necks of the U.S. team, causing their medals to fall to the ground. The archer himself proceeded to leap from the rafters, alight on the podium's top step, collect his prize, and disappear through a nearby window.

Since entering China last month by using a forged Sherwood Forest passport under the name Robert Huntingdon, the archer has appeared at more than 70 medal ceremonies, escaping with the gold every time.

see **ARCHER**

FIFA Player Of The Year Ronaldo Almost Forgets To Thank His Feet

JANUARY 15, 2009

ZURICH, SWITZERLAND—Upon receiving the FIFA World Player of the Year award Monday, Manchester United winger Cristiano Ronaldo thanked his team, family, and friends be-

fore finally remembering to express gratitude to his feet of 23 years. "I can't believe I forget my feet—I could never have accomplished this without them," said Ronaldo, smiling sheepishly at his feet as he addressed the

crowd attending the gala ceremony. "They have worked very hard this year, and I am very proud. They are the best feet. Their presence here today makes having Pele present the award even more of an honor, as I know my

feet are very excited to meet his." Ronaldo's relationship with his feet has been tumultuous lately, as the young star recently blamed their erratic pedal work for the crash of his Ferrari 599 GTB last week. ∅

Daytona-Area Hit-And-Run Suspect Returns To Scene Of Crime Every 47.72 Seconds

FEBRUARY 16, 2006

DAYTONA BEACH, FL-Local police investigating a near-fatal Daytona Beach hit-and-run case say that the perpetrator has very likely returned to the scene of the crime every 47.72 seconds after critically injuring a visiting race fan earlier today. "We have several dozen reports of a man matching the description of our suspect, who multiple witnesses identify as a Caucasian male in his mid-30s to early 40s driving a colorfully painted late-model domestic sedan, passing by the crime scene at extremely regular intervals without stopping or slowing since striking the victim this morning," investigating officer Crocker Burnett told reporters earlier today. "Unfortunately, the incident occurred in an extremely high-traffic area, and furthermore, due to local traffic velocity, officers' attempts to pull over the large number of recurring motorists on this particular stretch of road who match the description have thus far proven fruitless." Police say the victim, who some say seemed to recognize either his assailant or his assailant's car, has not yet regained consciousness after being catapulted several hundred yards by a car that was almost certainly traveling at extralegal speeds. ∅

Hurdler Overcomes Many Hurdles To Win Hurdle Race

SEPTEMBER 14, 2008

BEIJING—Despite encountering a multitude of 36-inch-high wooden barriers along the way, U.S. hurdler David Oliver overcame every single hurdle in his path on his way to winning Olympic gold in the 400m hurdle semifinals. "As I looked up and saw that first hurdle, I somehow knew it was only the first of many," the emotional and exhausted Oliver said after clearing no less than 10 hurdles during the course of the event. "But when things got really bad around that ninth hurdle, I just dug deep, remembered what I learned from my coach about overcoming life's regulation-sized obstacles, and I jumped over it. Then, merely a few seconds later, I jumped over the 10th hurdle." Oliver went on to profess hope that he could one day "leap right over" his alcoholism, his impending divorce, and his emotionally crippling, nightmarish childhood. ∅

Bobby Labonte Real Happy With 73rd Lap

FEBRUARY 19, 2009

DAYTONA BEACH, FL—Despite finishing a distant 22nd in the 2009 running of the Daytona 500, veteran driver Bobby Labonte expressed supreme satisfaction with his 73rd lap of the tri-oval. "There are laps and then there are laps, but that might be the best lap I've ever run," said a visibly moved Labonte, who compared the lap to his beloved 118th at the 2007 Sharpie 500 and his much-ballyhooed third at the 2004 Tropicana 400. "In a million years I never even imagined I could run a lap like that, and I doubt I'll ever run one like that again. I can't get over the fact that it came after that disgraceful 72nd—a lap that made me honestly think the sport had passed me by. It just all came together; the racing line, the car, the draft, everything. Just amazing." When informed the lap ran him two seconds above his average time, Labonte shook his head and said, "You just don't get it." ∅

---

from **ARCHER**

In almost every case, archery-related schemes were used to secure the medals, although some were more difficult for him to obtain than others.

An epic four-way fencing match broke out during the Women's Saber medal ceremony, with the archer taking on the three American women in a clash of blades that spilled out onto the balcony and across the Beijing rooftops. Germany's Ole Bischoff, winner in the Men's 81kg judo event, threw the archer through a nearby table and down a flight of stairs before his feet were nailed to the ground by arrows. And the Chinese women's gymnastics team was almost impossible for the archer to catch.

The athletes themselves are divided in their opinion of the bow-weilding outlaw. Although many regard him as annoyance at best, and still others as a dangerous menace, a considerable faction has voiced sympathy for his cause.

"Put it this way—that guy has some stuff of mine, but he's welcome to it," said U.S. swimmer Michael Phelps. "I mean, I'm not political, really, but I've had a lucky life. If my gold medals can help someone get a hot meal and a place to sleep for a few nights, that's okay. It doesn't mean I didn't win."

Phelps confessed his admiration that, although the archer had burst into the ceremony for the men's 400 Meter Relay, the team had been allowed to keep a single medal, as the archer praised the "epic performance by four doughty good men and true, who soundly defeated the Norman French, uplifted the hearts of all who saw, and enriched the very World thereby."

Chinese officials have been less charitable. "His disregard for our culture, our laws, and these Games will not go unpunished," a statement from the Chinese Olympic Committee read in part. "We demand he turn himself in, return the medals to the rightful winners, and face his punishment for these thefts, as well as for his repeated demands that we free Tibet and his continued poaching of deer in Yu Nan province."

Law enforcement officials, acting in liason with the Nottingham Sheriff's Department, have also concocted a scheme to capture the elusive archer by staging an archery contest with an especially large and valuable gold medal as the prize, an event already underway. The contest is currently in the semifinal rounds and is being led by Britain's Rob Enhood, a mysterious eyepatched figure with a penchant for archery so accurate that he routinely splits the arrows of his competitors. ∅

167

STRONG SIDE/WEAK SIDE: WAYNE GRETZKY

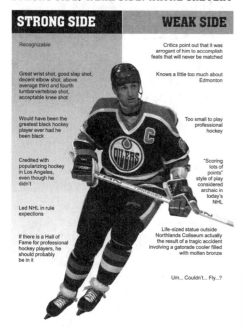

STRONG SIDE	WEAK SIDE
Recognizable	Critics point out that it was arrogant of him to accomplish feats that will never be matched
Great wrist shot, good slap shot, decent elbow shot, above average third and fourth lumbar/vertebrae shot, acceptable knee shot	Knows a little too much about Edmonton
Would have been the greatest black hockey player ever had he been black	Too small to play professional hockey
Credited with popularizing hockey in Los Angeles, even though he didn't	"Scoring lots of points" style of play considered archaic in today's NHL
Led NHL in rule expectations	
If there is a Hall of Fame for professional hockey players, he should probably be in it	Life-sized statue outside Northlands Coliseum actually the result of a tragic accident involving a gatorade cooler filled with molten bronze
	Um... Couldn't... Fly...?

Deriba Merga Dedicates Boston Marathon Victory To Pit Crew

APRIL 23, 2009

BOSTON—Upon winning the 113th Boston Marathon Monday, Ethiopia's Deriba Merga dedicated his 2-hour, 8-minute, and 42-second victory to the six-member pit crew who refueled him, changed his shoes, and removed debris from his ducts and air intakes. "I might have been the one in control of my body when I crossed the finish line, but it was all their hard work that got me there," Merga said. "Every time I pulled over to pit, the jack men had me up in the air in a second. I barely heard them fire up the pneumatic wrench before suddenly I was off running again with a fresh set of shoes and shorts." Merga, who finished a disappointing fourth in the Beijing Olympic marathon, has blamed that result on a pit stop in which he forgot to remove the Gatorade hose before sprinting away. ∅

Stumbling, Bumbling Sled Dog: 'Sorry, This Is My First Iditarod'

MARCH 12, 2009

PUNTILLA LAKE, AK—After running directly into the grandstands during the Iditarod's ceremonial start and veering 55 miles off course late Tuesday to chase a marmot, Siberian husky and rookie sled dog Melvin apologized to his musher and fellow canines Wednesday for making a complete fool of himself in the early stages of the annual 1,150-mile race.

"First Iditarod jitters, I guess," the visibly contrite Melvin told reporters Wednesday at the Rainy Pass checkpoint. "I feel like such a moron. Here I am in the last great race on earth and I'm blowing it. I mean, 100 times out of 100, when my musher yells, 'Gee,' I turn right. But yesterday I go left down an icy slope into a bunch of evergreens and nearly break everyone's neck."

"I have to pull it together," added the dog, making a

2009 Masters Winner Also Given Matching Green Pants

point of directly addressing his musher, two-time Iditarod champion Lance Mackey. "I'm sorry, Lance. I'm acting like an idiot out there."

Melvin has gotten his squad into several embarrassing scrapes thus far, one of which occurred at Willow Lake when, in an effort to find a place to nap, he twirled around three times while still in full harness, fouling his lines and entangling his team in multiple snarls. In addition, as

the team was on route to Skwentna, a child spectator threw an imaginary stick over the team, and Melvin chased it 300 miles back to the first checkpoint at Yentna Station.

Melvin's most humiliating experience, sources said, was a 20-minute period during which Mackey repeatedly ordered him to mush and the husky merely stood motionless, staring at Finger Lake.

"You look around and you realize that you are going up against your idols—Larry, Bronte, Salem, Handsome, Blue—and then it hits you: This is the fucking Iditarod," Melvin said. "It's not the Jack Pine 30 or the American Dog Derby. Out here, if you playfully root through your musher's sled basket and destroy his heavy parka and extra-warm sleeping bag, well, that's a mistake that could haunt you the rest of your career. Unfortunately, I'm learning that the hard way."

Melvin later admitted that he was overwhelmed by the pressure of participating in his first Iditarod and consequently had psyched himself

see SLED DOG

Bloodstained Gary Bettman: 'I Have Taken The Necessary Measures To Ensure A Crosby-Ovechkin Final'

APRIL 20, 2009

NEW YORK—Addressing reporters yesterday in an unnervingly calm tone of voice, NHL Commissioner Gary Bettman—his hands, face, and white-collared shirt covered in blood—said that any obstacle standing in the way of both Sidney Crosby and Alexander Ovechkin playing in the Stanley Cup Final has been "taken care of." "Sometimes you have to put the greater good of the league ahead of the fact that the [Pittsburgh Penguins and Washington Capitals] are in the same confer-

ence. Unfortunately for some, that point needed to be made... how should I put this...more clearly," Bettman said as he removed black leather crimson-splotched gloves from his hands and what appeared to be an ear from his jacket pocket. "Needless to say [NHL Players' Association executive director] Paul V. Kelly, [New York Rangers General Manager] Glen Sather, and Mario Lemieux will not be attending this press conference as was originally scheduled." When Bettman asked if there were any questions, no reporters raised their hands. ✑

from **SLED DOG**

out. Bouts of anxiety reportedly led to a stress dream Monday night in which he found himself standing on a calm, ice-covered pond for several tranquil minutes before the ice suddenly cracked beneath him.

"Instantly, I was treading in freezing water, and the more I struggled to get back on land, the faster I sank," Melvin said.

As he dreamt, the husky unconsciously gnawed through his team's snub line. Consequently, two point dogs and one wheel dog are still missing, and the sled can no longer go around corners.

Just five days into the race, the group is a projected seven days behind the rest of the pack.

"I'm too 'in my head' right now, you know? I have to remember my training from when I was a pup and just be natural," said the dog, adding that despite his most recent failures, he believes he was born for this. "No more stopping in the middle of a run to find a private place to go to the bathroom. Why would I even do that? I know I'm running in the Iditarod, for cry-

ing out loud. And I'm certainly not going to sprint into my teammates ever again, because that means I'm destroying our neck and tug lines, and I'm going completely the wrong way."

"I need to stay focused," Melvin continued. "Also, I think I'm going to go chase that big moose over there."

Despite the husky's shortcomings, musher Lance Mackey has stated that Melvin will remain in the lead dog position, mainly because Melvin bit the leg of fellow lead dog Sarah. Melvin was quick to point out, however, that at the time of the incident, he was suffering a panic-related delusion in which Sarah had transformed into his father, an Alaskan malamute who always told his son he would never amount to anything.

"It's a saying amongst us mushers that the dogs never make mistakes," Mackey said. "But it's not my fault that Melvin stops every 45 minutes to furiously dig in the snow. That dog's a wreck."

Mackey then sighed and added, "This is a terrible Iditarod." ✑

INSIDE

PHOTO FINISH
Alexander Ovechkin Loses Three Teeth While Eating Breakfast

World's 467,357th-Ranked Tennis Player Working On Serving Overhand

APRIL 8, 2009

WEST PALM BEACH, FL—During a practice match at the Riviera Golf and Tennis Club with his wife, Gail, Tuesday, 54-year-old Steve Cohen, the world's official 467,357th-ranked tennis player, attempted to teach himself how to serve overhand. "I can do backhands and forehands sometimes, but when it comes to serving, I just get more rallies going if I bounce it and hit it instead of trying to be fancy," said the professional tennis player, who has acquired .000000003 ATP points so far this year. "But I have to learn at some point. It's probably the only way I'll have any chance this weekend against [462,724th-

ranked] Roy [Detmer]." Both Detmer and Cohen are slated to represent the United States in the Davis Cup this July. ✑

Tony Stewart Gets Into Fight With Car

MARCH 12, 2009

ATLANTA—Although Tony Stewart and his Old Spice Chevrolet rallied from two laps down to finish a respectable eighth in Sunday's Kobalt Tools 500, Stewart had to be retrained from assaulting his number 14 Impala immediately after the race. "You understeering tire-eating hunk of junk," Stewart said to the car, his knuckles bleeding from the

blows he managed to land on his car's fenders and roof before his pit crew intervened. "I ought to have put you into the wall myself, so help me God. You had best shape up before the Food City 500 or so help me God I won't be responsible for what I do to you." Stewart later issued an apology to the car, saying his remarks were made in anger and that he looked forward to their continued partnership. ✑

Bassmaster Somehow Has Huge Comeback

JUNE 16, 2009

KENTUCKY LAKE, TN— Despite being behind in the catching of fish going into the final segment or round or whatever of last weekend's Bassmaster event, angler Steve Kennedy was able to come from behind to win, presumably by catching more or larger fish at what must be assumed was the last minute. "This was one of the best displays of clutch fishing I have ever seen," said Bassmaster.com reporter Doug Grassian, who is almost certainly an expert in this area. "Keep in mind that he had to contend with a fog delay and encroaching spectator boats. Also, it's amazing that [approximately 300 words omitted], all told this man dug deep down the stretch and came through at the end to show us all what being a Bassmaster really means." Experts are still debating whether or not the performance will change the very definition of bassmastery. 🖉

Phil Mickelson Shows Bubba Watson New Grip In Clubhouse Shower

FEBRUARY 19, 2009

PACE, FL—Saying he could show his fellow golfer a technique that would both "increase his control and allow him to go way longer," Phil Mickelson spent 20 minutes carefully and thoroughly demonstrating his personal grip to Bubba Watson in the clubhouse shower Sunday. "Not too tight, not too loose, see the way my fingers are? You can interlock them, you can overlap them, just not too tight is the important thing.

Now swing away," a sudsy Mickelson told Watson, who is known for his trademark pink-shafted drivers, as rivulets of steaming water coursed down their bodies. "It's all in the wrist, let the club head do the work, find the sweet spot.... Yeah...yeah... that's right. You've got it. Beautiful. Uh-huh. Just keep on just like that." Watson later confided to friends that the useful lesson could have been less awkward if Mickelson had brought a club into the shower with him. 🖉

Preakness-Winning Filly An Inspiration To All Women Who Want To Win Preakness

MAY 21, 2009

BALTIMORE—By becoming the first filly to win the Preakness Stakes in 85 years, thoroughbred Rachel Alexandra inspired millions of women Saturday to believe that they too could one day win the legendary horse race.

"The Preakness Stakes has been dominated by male horses for decades," said Melissa Snow, an advocate for gender equality in sports. "Rachel Alexandra's incredible triumph represents a change in the status quo—a change that will inspire women for generations to come."

"Finally, women have an athletic role model whose esteemed hoofprints they can follow to greatness," Snow added. "It won't be long before a woman trots out to the winner's circle to have the coveted garland of black-eyed Susans placed around her neck."

According to the filly's spokesperson, Diane Pearce, the thoroughbred's incredible feat of finishing the race with a 1:55.08 time after starting from the unfavorable 13th post will serve as a great motivation to women, because it shows that anything is possible as long as they train hard, gallop with all their heart, and eat all their hay.

"Rachel Alexandra has shattered the perception of the role of female athletes in horse racing," Pearce said. "When she crossed the line, no one cared about her looks or how much she weighed—they only cared that she won. Do you know what that means for a female in to-

day's society? This victory was for any woman who has been dreaming since she was a little girl of rounding that final turn, racing neck and neck with a colt, and then sticking out her muzzle to win in a photo finish."

Karen Lucero, 22, told reporters that narrow-minded preconceptions about women's roles have kept her from ever entering the Preakness, with trainers, friends, and family telling her for years that it would be impossible for her to compete on a 1-and-3/16-mile dirt track against a 1,500-pound quadruped. However, after Rachel Alexandra's victory in the second leg of the Triple Crown, Lucero has chosen to ignore her detractors' claims that, as a woman, she lacks the necessary strength, speed, and number of legs.

"If I listened to everything people said, I'd never accomplish anything," Lucero said. "The important thing is that you give it your best no matter what, even if sometimes you finish five minutes after the horses or get trampled coming out of the gate."

"You can never give up," she continued. "If you pick yourself off the ground and keep on going, you just might give a little extra encouragement to a young girl or foal watching the Preakness on television."

While Rachel Alexandra's milestone achievement has eliminated numerous barriers and elevated the status of females in the sport, women claim that numerous obstacles remain, as racing insiders see PREAKNESS

Professional Racing Drivers In 2-Ton Cars Terrified By Droplets Of Water

JUNE 2, 2009

CONCORD, NC—A paralyzing fear of precipitation kept dozens of highly skilled competition drivers, all of them trained to drive roll-cage equipped cars mere inches from one another at speeds exceeding 200 miles per hour for extended periods of time, from finishing the Coca-Cola 600 Monday. "I'm overjoyed to win the race, but I'm even more relieved that I didn't have to face the worst horror known to the professional racer: falling moisture," said David Reutimann, who was declared the winner when officials pronounced the track "horrifyingly damp" after only 227 laps and halted NASCAR's longest race. "Every race driver, except for maybe the guys in Formula One, and the Le Mans drivers, the Rolex Series, and rally drivers, I guess, and those guys in amateur racing...anyway, every single racing driver knows that if you drive in the rain you will automatically crash. No one in NASCAR wants to see crashes." Reutimann then thanked his sponsors and rushed off to hide in his motor home until the sun came out. Ø

Detroit, Pittsburgh Both Attempting To Lose Stanley Cup, Avoid Expensive Victory Parade

APRIL 4, 2009

DETROIT/PITTSBURGH—As the Stanley Cup Finals continue, Penguins and Red Wings fans alike are urging their teams to spare their beleaguered cities the expense of a championship victory.

"We are extremely proud of our Red Wings, and we know they could certainly come through for us, but we beg them: Please don't make us throw an expensive and wasteful championship parade," said Detroit mayor and former NBA great Dave Bing, who wore a Penguins jersey as he spoke to reporters Wednesday of how he had done his civic duty in the turbulent 1960s and '70s by not winning an NBA championship with the Pistons. "The Western Conference championship is all our city can afford at this time."

Pittsburgh mayor Luke Ravenstahl also spoke on Wednesday, telling the media that his city was "devastated" Tuesday when the Penguins won Game 3 of the finals after a financially promising 0-2 start.

"The Steelers' championship parade cost us roughly $6.5 million in street closures, float rental, security expenditures, and sanitation overtime—not to mention the incalculable loss of man-hours for our struggling local businesses," Ravenstahl said. "Pittsburgh can't afford to forget how the four Super Bowl parades we had in the 1970s were followed by mill closures, layoffs, and a decade-long recession. Let's go Wings!"

The first two games, both played in Detroit's aging, dilapidated Joe Louis Arena, went poorly for the home team as the Wings were unable to keep themselves from scoring. After the stalemate of the opening faceoff, which saw both teams remaining absolutely motionless for several minutes and refusing to touch the dropped puck until referees threatened to declare a double-forfeit, the players struggled valiantly to score on themselves and defend the opposing net in a contest that ended in triumph for the Penguins, who lost 1-3.

Game 2 was a virtual repeat, with the added ignominy of former hometown favorite and Michigan native Justin Abdelkader scoring the second of his first two NHL goals, putting the game away for the Red Wings and inching Detroit closer to Stanley Cup victory and economic collapse.

"I did everything I could, but Sidney Crosby just refuses to not lay down and die," said Detroit netminder Chris Osgood, who allowed only one goal in each of the first two games and took personal responsibility for the victories. "I tried scooping the puck in, I tried gloving it past myself, I used the stick, but it kept going off the post. The fans gave me hell, and they're right—I'll never forgive myself if we win the Cup and they have to close a bunch of schools."

Game 3 is being called a possible turning point, a dominant performance by the Penguins that has left a once-hopeful Pittsburgh staring at the dreaded prospect of not only a monstrously expensive come-from-behind victory in the series, but also the cost of host-

see STANLEY CUP

---

from **PREAKNESS**

often treat women as if they do not belong on the horseracing track. An overwhelming majority of the women competing in the Preakness said that none of the male horses ever spoke to them except in terse, almost animalistic snorting noises.

However, not all women are impressed with Rachel Alexandra's win. Members of the Rad-

ical Feminist Foundation have attempted to discredit Rachel Alexandra's victory by noting that a man controlled the filly during the entirety of the race. The Berkeley-based group also asserted that her deliberate willingness to be subjugated by jockey Calvin Borel, who rode on top of her back and forced the thoroughbred to travel in the direction and at the speed he determined, had not done anything

to further the women's movement. RFF president Robin Kaplan said that, by allowing Borel to not only control but possibly even beat her, Rachel Alexandra had tacitly endorsed the oppression of females.

"This is a despicable effort to advocate the patriarchal power structure," RFF vice president Robin Kaplan said. "That stupid horse has set feminism back 50 years." Ø

Cash-Strapped Indy 500 To Charge Dollar-A-Lap Toll

MAY 12, 2009

INDIANAPOLIS—Financially challenged race organizers announced Wednesday that participants in the 2009 Indianapolis 500-Mile Race will be required to pay a $1 toll each time they cross the fabled Brickyard's start-finish line. "We have begun construction of tollbooths across the track that will allow drivers to stop and pay their tolls four-wide," Indianapolis Motor Speedway owner Tony Hulman George said. "The outside booths off the racing line will be the dollar booths, accepting cash only, and the ones down low where the track is faster will be an extra quarter, which will add an exciting element of strategy to the race as well as generating cash we could really use at this point." Teams will also be given the option of paying $150 for a no-stop "Indy SpeedPass," which will allow them to go through the booth situated on the racing line at speeds of up to 35 mph. ✐

WNBA Franchise Moving To Tulsa Sounds About Right

OCTOBER 27, 2009

DETROIT—A recent announcement that the WNBA's Detroit Shock would be moving to Tulsa, OK, next season seemed pretty much in line with what one would expect from the women's professional basketball league, observers told reporters Sunday. "Tulsa, huh? Sure, makes sense," said Detroit resident Paul Dutton, adding that he would have had the same matter-of-fact response had the Shock said they were moving to Harrisburg, PA, El Paso, TX, or Morgantown, WV.

"Actually, when I first heard the news I was more surprised to find out that Tulsa didn't already have a WNBA team. Don't they have a team in Connecticut that plays in a casino? That's so weird." When informed that the Shock would be moving to their hometown, a majority of Tulsa residents politely nodded their heads and continued about their day. ✐

New York Marathon Winner Tests Positive For Performance-Enhancing Horse

NOVEMBER 5, 2009

NEW YORK—Officials from New York Road Runners stripped American Meb Keflezighi of his 2009 ING New York City Marathon victory Wednesday after a blood sample taken from his fetlock was found to contain high levels of performance-enhancing horse.

"Meb's fellow competitors voiced their doubts about him immediately after the event," NYRR president Mary Wittenberg said. "In addition to his remarkable speed, unusual race-day height, and distinctive 'clip-clop' gait, Keflezighi's frequent nickering caused the other runners to speculate that he may have been using a horse in some fashion."

Added Wittenberg, "Also, just before the start, he lifted up his tail and loudly deposited a 9-inch-high pile of steaming fecal matter on the pavement, an unusual occurrence even in the world of long-distance running."

Keflezighi finished the race in 48 minutes and 12 seconds, easily setting a new world record and defeating his nearest competitor by one hour and 20 minutes.

Course workers, spectators, and event sponsors have all presented damaging evidence pointing toward Keflezighi's use of equine enhancements. Volunteers working refreshment tables during the race said Keflezighi took water only twice—at miles nine and 17—consuming roughly 10 gallons each time, and was the only professional runner in the men's event to request an oat, carrot, and sugar lump station. In addition, a spokesman for Nike told reporters the company provided Keflezighi with six shoes for the marathon, four of which required special construction before being nailed onto his feet.

Hundreds of people who watched the race have also come forward with photographs showing Keflezighi mounted atop what experts now believe to be a 2-to-4-year-old chestnut-brown thoroughbred.

"Come to think of it, he was moving at a pace that didn't seem human," spectator Mark Rolland said. "And when the marathon was over, the American flag they tried to drape around him didn't even come close to fitting around his body."

"Last year he was just this small guy, but when he showed up to the starting line this year, his neck and head were noticeably thicker," said David Willey, editor in chief of *Runner's World* magazine. "He

see HORSE

---

from **STANLEY CUP**

ing yet more games if the Cup Finals drag on.

Analysts were quick to dissect the sudden change in momentum. "They did everything they could, really—no real forechecking, Fleury went down on his back a lot, and they dressed defenseman Hal Gill. Hal Gill sucks. At one point they even tried to draw a penalty by putting six guys on the ice for 20 seconds, but the refs were letting them play, and the Wings just underwhelmed them," said Bloomberg financial analyst Hamilton Kublin. "Pittsburgh has to do a better job of neutralizing Crosby, Malkin, and Gonchar, or they'll win the championship and the city won't be able to keep the lights on."

"A Red Wings victory would be a big boost to civic pride, but the resulting celebrations would be a fatal blow to the city budget," Detroit City Council president Ken Cockerel, Jr. said. "I intend to ask Washington for a bailout in which they send Alexander Ovechkin to Pittsburgh for the length of the series. Whatever happens, I know Detroit will be rooting for the Penguins from here on out."

Mayors Bing and Ravenstahl have met publicly to discuss the series and wish each other luck, though neither seems willing to budge on the terms of the traditional mayor's bet they agreed to before Game 1, which states that the winning city will grant the losing city 5,000 full-time jobs in the manufacturing and technology sectors. ✐

STRONG SIDE/WEAK SIDE: CASTER SEMENYA

STRONG SIDE	WEAK SIDE
Main advantage come from making competitors feel things they've never felt before	Definitely a guy
Will never have shortage of naysayers to prove wrong, thats for sure	That's not a chocolate-milk mustache
Handsome	Catcalls the women in lanes next to her
Gender verification test certainly won't take very long	Come to think of it, we haven't seen Carl Lewis since he went in for that Lasik eye surgery three years ago
If she loses her 800-meter record, she'll have a record, she'll have a record for being the first to lose it that way	Has handled recent controversy with the strength of a man, and grace of a woman, which only confuses things more
One of the guys	Nike doesn't make women's shoes for feet that big and hairy

from **HORSE**

looked like he had put on at least a half ton of muscle."

The NYRR's Wittenberg said during a postrace press conference that if the evidence proves conclusively that Keflezighi used a horse to improve his speed and endurance, it would not only have a severe impact on his career, but could cast doubt on the whole culture of long-distance running.

"It may seem hard to believe this could happen, especially at this level," said Dr. Raymond Prentiss, a medical adviser for USA Track & Field. "But people are so eager to believe in man's ability to push the boundaries of achievement that they blind themselves to a competitor who looks a little too strong, runs a mile a few minutes faster, and stands a few hands taller than the competition."

"In Keflezighi's case, we ignored what his rapidly improving times, flowing mane, and shapely withers were trying to tell us until it was too late," Prentiss added. "The fact that he was spending an hour after each event currycombing should have been a major tip-off."

As of press time, Keflezighi is cooperating with the sanctioning bodies and has returned the $170,000 he was awarded for the victory. He has also surrendered his racing singlet and shorts, saddle, saddle blanket, and bridle for further inspection and testing by technical personnel. Officials with the World Marathon Majors series said that Keflezighi will likely be banned from future races, including Boston, Chicago, the 2010 Belmont Stakes, and Berlin.

In light of the discovery, marathon officials are taking a closer look at many of the entrants in this year's race, including British runner Paula Radcliffe, a former winner who placed a tearful fourth in the women's event after fracturing her cannon bone and had to be put down mere minutes after finishing. Ø

Investigators Still Piecing Together Weird-Ass Clues In Fucked-Up Tiger Woods Crash

DECEMBER 4, 2009

WINDERMERE, FL—A spokesman for the Windermere Police Department told reporters Thursday that investigators have gathered enough weird-ass evidence to officially classify Tiger Woods' recent car accident as pretty fucking strange.

"The only thing we know for sure is that at 2:25 a.m. Friday morning Mr. Woods crashed his Cadillac Escalade into a fire hydrant and tree at the end of his own driveway," Police Chief Daniel Saylor said during a press briefing. "After that, the account becomes confused. We are unsure if Woods was leaving the driveway or arriving at it, which is rather unusual. At some point Woods' wife, Elin [Nordegren], seems to have struck the car with a golf club, which is pretty bizarre. And she states that she did this to break the rear window and extract Mr. Woods from the vehicle, which, the longer you think about it, is some freaking weird shit."

"All this—along with the fact that when we arrived on the scene the world's No.1 golfer had

suffered facial lacerations not necessarily caused by a car accident, had been slipping in and out of consciousness for nearly five minutes, and lay on the ground as his wife stood over his bloody body holding a 7-iron—is really fucked up," Saylor added. "But don't get me wrong: It's also really weird. Really fucking weird. Ultimately, our report will treat these matters as both fucked up and weird-ass."

Saylor said that as the investigation proceeds, and even more odd-as-hell details are uncovered, a super-fucked-up and mega-bizarre picture could emerge, especially if there is evidence to substantiate the rumors that Woods sent salacious text

messages to a Los Angeles cocktail waitress.

When asked if there was anything weird or fucked up in Woods' bloodstream at the time of the crash, medical investigator Henry Tolliver stated that the accident was not alcohol related. Tolliver also noted that, while it would have been slightly fucked if Woods had driven while intoxicated, the fact that his blood-alcohol level was within the legal limit adds a whole new layer of what-the-fuck to the ongoing investigation.

"Mr. Woods being drunk would have been the only sensible thing in this case," Tolliver said.

Other crazy-ass pieces of information, including Woods' refusal to speak to the media, his cryptic

see **TIGER WOODS**

Rangers Win Stanley Cup 15 Years Ago

JUNE 18, 2009

NEW YORK—After 54 years of waiting, the New York Rangers finally won the Stanley Cup 15 years ago, defeating the Vancouver Canucks four games to three in 1994. "As long as I live I will never forget this moment," Rangers' captain Mark Messier, who recently confirmed he had not forgotten the moment in the intervening decade and a half, said at the time. Coach Mike Keenan is remembered to have added that the victory "[was] for the greatest fans in the world. This definitely

[might have been] the start of a new Rangers dynasty! I can't wait to meet President Clinton. Let's go Rangers!" The 2009 Pittsburgh Penguins had no comment about the year 2024. Ø

Construction Restricts Daytona 500 Traffic To One Lane

FEBRUARY 23, 2010

DAYTONA BEACH, FL—Construction crews working to patch the rippled and broken asphalt of Daytona International Speedway reduced traffic to a single lane during last Sunday's Daytona 500, resulting in average speeds of 35 miles per hour. "It's bad enough that they can't get this fixed during the week," said race winner Jamie McMurray, who finished in just over 15 hours. "And NASCAR doubles the fines for speeding in work zones, so there was nothing we could do." Disagreeing with McMurray was Emilio Ramirez, operator of the No. 0563 Rolaids/ Chick-fil-A Caterpillar road grader, who earned time-and-a-half for the race and called the event a "rousing success." ∅

Ted DiBiase Worried About Current Status Of His Million Dollars

AUGUST 24, 2009

BEL, CA—Once known for his extravagant spending and diamond-studded outfits, former professional wrestler "The Million Dollar Man" Ted DiBiase has reportedly fallen on hard times, admitting Tuesday that he did not know the exact status of his $1 million fortune. "Well, the economy has been real bad lately, and Virgil has made some terrible investments over the years," said DiBiase, shaking his head and adding that he hadn't slowly counted a stack of bills in the backseat of a limousine in more than a decade. "I also lost track of where my briefcase is, and that had about $5,000 plus a bunch of IOUs in it." DiBiase went on to claim that "everybody has a price," and said he was currently accepting offers to kiss people's feet for $100. ∅

Chinese Crested Dog's Beautifully Descended Testicles Bring Divided Nation Together

FEBRUARY 19, 2010

NEW YORK—Awed and inspired by the gloriously formed, beautifully descended testicles of Tommy, a hairless Chinese crested dog competing in his second Westminster Kennel Club Dog Show, millions of U.S. citizens took stock of their lives and set aside their differences Tuesday to stare at the canine's perfectly groomed reproductive glands. "Those trembling orbs are so breathtakingly magnificent in and of themselves, yet they also contain within them such potential," said Allentown, PA machinist and former Tea Party member Roy Halbstead, who, upon seeing the dog's

testicles on Animal Planet, immediately committed himself to the cause of reconciliation and healing America's rifts. "Furthermore, while they are two separate entities, they share one canine scrotum and work together for a common goal. Truly those dog testes are the very symbol of our great nation." Despite the unparalleled unifying powers displayed by Tommy's messianic testicles, the award for Best Testicles in Show went to Aubrey's Bellerophon, a 3-year-old huge-sacked Dogue de Bordeaux. ∅

from **TIGER WOODS**

postcrash statement admitting to "transgressions," and the accusations that the accident stemmed from Woods' alleged extramarital affairs, have been filed by Florida police as "Quite fucking odd," "Kind of creepy," and "It's probably none of our business but it's so goddamn weird that we couldn't ignore it if we tried."

Though he could not confirm or deny recent crazy-as-all-hell reports that Woods shouted "You've ruined our Thanksgiving" before exiting his home, Saylor said that such a thing even being a matter of interest indicates just how completely messed up the mounting evidence is.

"The domestic component alone has forced us to use a TFB unit," said Detective Sidney Goldberg, referring to officers who have been assigned to the Truly Fucking Bizarre portion of the investigation. "They have a very difficult job to do because in a case with as much ridiculous shit as this one, every off-the-wall scenario has to be explored, even the just-sort-of fucked-up ones."

According to Goldberg, the TFB unit will investigate the weird-ass possibility that Nordegren beat her husband and threatened him with a goddamned golf club. It will also explore the batshit insane prospect that an impassioned Nordegren purposefully placed herself in the path of the moving Cadillac, thus forcing Woods to swerve violently out of the way.

"Also, we have to look into recent allegations that Woods left a voice mail requesting that one of his mistresses delete his number from her phone," Goldeberg said. "Just so fucking weird."

Goldberg has assigned the TFB's forensic investigators to do a complete Batshit Bizzarro-Universe Accident Scene Reconstruction, which will take samples of the paint scrapings on Woods' Cadillac, measure the skid marks on the driveway, catalog and number the fucked-up golf-club dents in the car's bodywork, and use powerful computers to reconstruct the strange-ass accident using digital simulations.

"It's possible the computer will show us that a golf club ejected itself from the vehicle during the crash, bounced off the surrounding trees, and struck the outside of Woods' vehicle several times," Goldberg said. "That's no more weird-ass than the other theories people have come up with, especially the ones we saw when we used the computer to check TMZ.com."

Detective Tolliver admitted that he himself was having trouble getting over just how bizarro the whole thing really is.

"In this case you've got Tiger Woods—the man with the most squeaky-clean image in all of sports—possibly participating in romantic dalliances with random women despite the fact that he is already married to one of the most beautiful women in the world. And none of this would have ever surfaced had he not crashed his car Friday morning," Tolliver said. "Come on, that's just plain-ass weird."

"I guess the only thing more outrageous is that this has been a major news item for over a week, and that people feel like they are entitled to know the private details of public figures' lives," Tolliver continued. "No matter which way you shake it, that's fucking nuts." ∅

Tiger Woods Announces Return To Sex

FEBRUARY 19, 2010

PONTE VEDRA BEACH, FL— In an announcement highly anticipated by sex fans around the world, Tiger Woods told a small gathering of reporters, family, and lovers Friday that the most dominant fornicator on the planet would soon return to sex.

"Not being able to get out there and have sex has really been tough on me," Woods said. "I've missed it. I love fucking with all my heart."

Woods said that during his brief time away from sex, he couldn't stop thinking about one day resuming his daily regimen of sexual intercourse with random women who look vaguely like his wife, only skankier.

"When I am out there having sex, I am in complete control," said Woods, an acknowledged master of the long game who claims he is only truly at peace when he is between the legs of a woman. "It's just me and my thoughts. And a high-end escort. And the lounge dancer. And sometimes [caddie] Stevie. And probably some stewardess I just met."

"I'm so into it that I usually just block out all the cameras," Woods added.

Saying that fucking is his "calling and [his] one true passion," Woods spoke of how he has always adored the sight of a neatly trimmed mound, the smell of fresh stank early in the morning when the labia glisten with dewy juices, and the feel of a perfect impact with a woman's vagina.

"That sensation just flows right up the shaft, through my hands, and quavers up and down my spine," Woods said. "Ever since I was 16, I've loved that feeling. It's like new every time."

"To be honest, I'd do this for free," Woods added. "I'm the luckiest guy in the world."

During his announcement, Woods released an aggressive touring schedule that re-

affirmed his commitment to sex. He is slated to take part in a three-day lovemaking session in March at the Clarion Hotel in Orlando, and confirmed that he would join a foursome at the Doral Resort and Spa in Miami as a tune-up for his first major fuckfest in Augusta, GA.

In addition, Woods said he will not renege on his annual stop in Dubai, and said he looked forward to boning a prostitute on the roof of this year's venue, the Burj Al Arab Hotel.

The 34-year-old sexual superstar said he is "far from satisfied" by his previous erotic achievements and that he expects to return to sex even stronger than before. However, Woods admitted he may not be in top form at first.

"I'll probably be a little rusty," Woods said. "But once I swing the old cock around a few times and get it in the first couple holes, I'm confident that I'll still be able to drive it as deep as I always have."

"There will be times when I get into some thick muff, and I'll have to set my jaw and hack my way through it," Woods continued. "Just keep my head down and hit that with all the force I can muster. I welcome the challenge."

Woods believes that his long game, which relies on innate strength and stamina, has

probably suffered the least from his hiatus, but that his finesse, iron control, and deft touch around the hole are aspects of his game that may be slow to come back.

"I just have to take my time, visualize the line, and read the grain and the slope of the vulva correctly," Woods said. "It's really all mental at that point."

Reaction to Woods' announcement has been generally positive. Many of his closest friends, including Mark O'Mera, said that Woods' return would undoubtedly be great for sex, and that, selfishly, he loves to watch Woods out there doing his thing.

Woods' fans have also been supportive.

"I'm so glad Tiger is coming back," said 27-year-old Florida resident and cocktail waitress Brandi Hughes. "He's the best."

Woods concluded his press conference by saying that he is looking forward to chasing Jack Nicklaus' record of fucking 18 major babes at one time. ∅

INSIDE

➤ **Local Sports Anchor Practices Golf Swing During Commercial Break**

➤ **Michael Phelps Hired To Install Above Ground Pool**

Tournament Bass Refuses To Talk To Reporters After Tough Day Getting Caught

NOVEMBER 26, 2010

LEWISVILLE, TX—A 7-pound, 18-inch largemouth bass bypassed reporters and went straight back into the water Saturday following a demoralizing defeat at the Bassmaster Lake Lewisville Shootout. "This is a fish who prides himself on going out to that weed bed every day and eluding anglers, and you could see the disgust on his face," Bassmaster official Travis Hessman said. "There's no answer for how a bass who has been doing this for so long could get hooked on such a shoddy crankbait, and that's something he'll just have to live with until the next tournament." Hessman added that the bass would be fined $30,000 for failing to fulfill his media obligations. ∅

NHL Ref Likes It When He Gets To Jump Over Puck

MARCH 14, 2011

CHICAGO—Fifteen-year veteran NHL official Michael Lussenhop confirmed in an interview Sunday that the most satisfying part of his job is when he's backed into a corner and has to grab the boards to leap over the puck to keep from interfering with the game. "Compared with the typical routine of just skating around, it's a nice little treat," said Lussenhop, who added that he never makes the hop too fancy, but simply makes sure he "gets over the puck and lands safely." "The other refs always bust my chops afterward: 'Hey, saw you got to jump over the puck today.' It's all in good fun. We have a good time." Lussenhop went on to explain that every ref's second favorite part of the job is getting to put the goal back into place when it comes loose, while their least favorite is dropping the puck during "stupid, boring face-offs." ∅

Ski Jumper Has To Work On His Soaring

MARCH 3, 2010

VANCOUVER—Following a disappointing 98.5-meter effort that onlookers described as a "longish hop" or "sort of a flutter," ski jumper Hans Pavelka announced Friday that he would redouble his commitment to soaring. "I acknowledge that my soaring is not as majestic as it could be. This week it was all I could do to manage a glide," Pavelka said through an interpreter. "I have hired the soaring coach who worked with the world's best-known soarers and have booked time in the new $12 million soaring tunnel outside Ingolstadt. I promise my soaring shall be the envy of the world in 2014." Ski jumping insiders lauded Pavelka's statement, but speculated that ski jumping's movement toward more innovative forms of careening could render soaring obsolete in four years. ∅

Tiger Woods Followed Everywhere At Masters By Sex Addiction Sponsor

APRIL 9, 2010

AUGUSTA, GA—Sources close to Tiger Woods confirmed Friday that, due to the large number of women expected to attend this year's Masters, the top-ranked golfer has requested that his Sex Addicts Anonymous sponsor, 42-year-old recovering sexaholic Dave Gilecki, be at his side at all times during the tournament.

The unshaven Gilecki, whose on-course attire consists of a pair of blue jeans and a Hard Rock Café Orlando T-shirt, has been shadowing Woods everywhere at Augusta National: at the practice tee, on the putting green, between the tournament ropes, and anywhere a woman might be present.

"Let's just put it this way," Woods said Monday during a press conference at which a silent Gilecki sat next to him. "I need Dave."

"He's someone I can share my journey with," he added.

Woods' sex addiction sponsor has reportedly agreed to provide the four-time Masters champion with one-on-one counsel during his crucial recovery phase. Though not much is known about Gilecki, he appears to be a chain-smoker with no understanding of proper golf decorum—he often suffers loud coughing fits on the course in the middle of other golfers' backswings, and has been known to shout, "Tiger, buddy, I'm right over here if you need me" during other golfers' backswings. Nonetheless, he appears to be an essential component of Woods' return to the game.

A spokesperson for Sex Addicts Anonymous said Gilecki's constant support, both verbal and nonverbal, would introduce Woods to a process of nonsexual normalization in social situations, demonstrating to Tiger that he does not have to turn to sex for personal validation while playing in the Masters.

"Basically, if he sees someone in the crowd he wants to rub up against or something, he just tells me how much he wants to do it, we breathe together, and then we move on to the next shot," Gilecki said before Woods could stop his sponsor from talking to members of the media. "That's called speak and release. They teach us that."

According to observers, a somewhat flustered Woods sought Gilecki's guidance at various points during his weekday practice rounds. And prior to teeing off Thursday, Woods was overheard whispering, "Dave, get over here," when a blonde spectator in her early 30s extended her hand for a high five. Gilecki watched Woods greet the fan, and afterward patted the superstar on his back and said, "You're okay, bro. You're fine. Breathe."

"During our round he kept telling Tiger to put his blinders on and ignore all the tail,'" playing partner Matt Kuchar said. "And when I was trying to putt he would yell 'No sex eyes!' Whatever that means."

Continued Kuchar, "Is he going to be here all season?"

When Woods appeared to come unhinged during his first tournament round, gallery members said that Gilecki was overheard giving the 14-time major champion little nuggets of advice, including "Focus," "Easy, buddy," and "She's not worth it, man. We know what she is. She's just another piece."

see SEX ADDICTION

Confused NASCAR Driver Runs Over 30 Golfers During Attempt To Win FedEx Cup

SEPTEMBER 29, 2009

ATLANTA—Hoping to win the PGA tour's FedEx Cup, bewildered NASCAR driver Denny Hamlin critically injured 23 golfers and killed seven others while speeding across the East Lake golf course Thursday. "What— wait, hold on, which cup is this?" asked a visibly confused Hamlin, who after

Thursday's tragedy remains 35 points behind first-place Sprint Cup driver Mark Martin. "Looking back, it was a little weird that I was driving on grass, striking people at high speeds, and not racing any other cars. But I'm a competitor, and if there's a cup, I'm going to try to win it." PGA Tour commissioner Tim Finchem later awarded Hamlin 150 FedEx Cup points for his effort. ∅

Contador Cleared Of Doping By International Cycling Federation's Doping-Clearing Board

FEBRUARY 18, 2011

MADRID— The ICF's Doping-Clearing Board has investigated and cleared 2010 Tour de France winner Alberto Contador of all doping charges, allowing the three-time Tour champion to return to competition immediately, officials announced Monday. "We have concluded a full, in-depth investigation into Contador's case and summarily cleared him," said Doping-Clearing Board president Fernando Uruburu, who has previously been tasked with the investigations of Alessandro Petacchi, Lance Armstrong, and, on an earlier occasion in 2007, Contador—all of whom were cleared. "Of course, Contador's case is subject to review by the World Doping-Clearing Agency as well as the Spanish Doping-Clearing Council, but we fully expect them to clear him as well." The Doping-Clearing Board is still refusing to review the doping case of disgraced 2006 Tour winner Floyd Landis, who they claim is "a twerp." Ø

Tiger Woods Hits Rock Bottom, Aside From Being Worth Over $600 Million

AUGUST 13, 2010

AKRON, OH—Tiger Woods scored a career-worst 18-over-par finish at the Bridgestone Invitational Sunday, officially hitting rock bottom if one ignores the fact that he is worth over $600 million, is still the world's No. 1–ranked golfer, never has to work another day for the rest of his life, and has millions of fans worldwide. "Four rounds in the mid-to-high 70s, and finishing 78th out of 80 golfers—it simply can't get any worse for Tiger," ESPN golf analyst Andy North said of Woods, who left Sunday's round in his private jet and who, despite a damaging sex scandal, still earned more than $90 million in 2010. "Nowhere to go from here but up, [or sail up and down the California coast in his yacht for the rest of his life if he wants to]." Woods was unable to comment on reaching his personal low point, as he was too busy checking into the penthouse suite of his four-star hotel and deciding if he wanted the 12-ounce or 16-ounce filet for dinner. Ø

from **SEX ADDICTION**

After putting out and signing his scorecard Thursday, Woods immediately left with Gilecki for a "quick meeting" at the Augusta Community Center.

Gilecki and Woods reportedly met at the Mississippi sex rehabilitation clinic where Woods spent 45 days earlier this year. Gilecki, who said he is currently unemployed but "manages to get by," is believed to have struck up a bond with Woods based on a similar taste in cocktail waitresses, porn stars, escorts, and music.

Gilecki acknowledged he has never played a round of golf in his life.

"I think old Tiger here has come a long way, and will definitely be able to keep it in his pants the whole weekend," said Gilecki, adding that since arriving at the Masters, Woods has called him several times at night just to talk. "I will say, though, there are a lot of women out here on this golf course. More women than I thought there would be, actually. Tan women in skirts and tight, sleeveless shirts. The kind of shirts where you can sort of see their bra straps peeking out."

"We're helping each other. He helps me as much as I help him, you know," added Gilecki, wiping sweat away from his forehead. "Man, there are seriously a lot of women out here."

Though Woods wouldn't specify how long he intends to keep Gilecki by his side, he told reporters the sponsor would be traveling with him to St. Andrews in Scotland for the British Open, and would most definitely be with him during any PGA Tour stop in Las Vegas.

At press time, Woods appeared to be in need of Gilecki more than ever.

"Dave? Where's Dave? Seriously, where the fuck is he?" a visibly agitated Woods was shouting on the eighth tee as Gilecki emerged from a portable toilet on the course. "Thank God, Dave. Thank God you're here." Ø

NASCAR Struggling To Recover From Yet Another Injury-Free Season

AUGUST 15, 2010

LOUDON, NH—As they prepare to begin the Chase for the Cup with the Sylvania 300, top NASCAR executives are worried about the financial impact another season free of horrible injuries could have on the sport. "Every day a car doesn't flip over or a driver isn't set on fire, NASCAR loses money," chief marketing officer Steve Phelps said Monday, adding that the main reason fans say the sport hasn't been the same since Dale Earnhardt, Sr. died in the 2001 Daytona 500 is because no one has been killed or maimed in that time. "Of course, we hate to see anyone get hurt, but then again, we have to put the needs of the fans first." In related developments, NASCAR officials are expected to announce changes to the Car of Tomorrow that include eliminating seat belts, a top speed of 300 miles per hour, and special design features that make you look like a girl if you wear a helmet while driving. Ø

Corey Pavin Announces Plans To Get Loaded Before Ryder Cup

AUGUST 20, 2010

NEW YORK—Declaring that the match-play competition between European and American players was "going to be a total frickin' blast," U.S. captain Corey Pavin announced plans Wednesday to get completely hammered before this year's Ryder Cup. "We might not win, but we're gonna have a hell of a good time this year," said Pavin, adding that he and his team intend to get fully loaded at the hotel before the alternate-shot matches, and intend to "drink and just keep on drinking" throughout the entire opening four-ball event. "I already got a crapload of booze like vodka and whiskey and some of that Apple Pucker schnapps crap for Zach Johnson so he doesn't puss out. And, man, [Jim] Furyk's an animal when he's hammered." Pavin maintained that the U.S. squad's main goal was to get Phil Mickelson to puke. Ø

KOBAYASHI RETIRES FROM EATING

JULY 19, 2007

NAGANO, JAPAN— Mere hours after eating what he claims to be his "farewell meal" Tuesday, long-time consumer of comestible goods Takeru Kobayashi formally announced that, after a career that has spanned nearly his entire lifetime, he has decided to walk away from eating food.

"My physical gifts, including my God-given ability to ingest food, are still there, but my passion for it is not," said a gaunt, visibly fatigued Kobayashi, speaking through his interpreter in a barely audible whisper. "Yes, chewing and swallowing food has always played an important part in my life, and if I'd never done it, I probably wouldn't be here today. But after nearly 30 years, I am tired of eating."

"I used to eat because I wanted to, but lately it seems like I only do it because I feel like I have to," added Kobayashi, who claims that he was in the middle of eating his 52nd barbecue chicken wing last week when he realized he no longer possessed the same hunger he did earlier in his career. "I knew it was time to step aside and give others the chance to eat."

The announcement has come as a shock to those close to the Japanese star, who claim that for Kobayashi, eating was more than just a hobby—that a powerful, mysterious force deep inside

of him compelled him to eat. Many expected him to continue eating until the day he died.

"Takeru used to live, breathe, and eat food," said Hideki Ihara, Kobayashi's uncle. "Not a day went by that he didn't eat. He based his whole day around it. He'd be down in the kitchen every morning at the crack of dawn, squeezing in an early meal. He'd be the last one at the dinner table each night. In fact, he loved it so much that he would leave his job in the middle of the day and spend his lunch hour eating food. Now that's dedication."

"I don't know how he's going to survive without eating," Ihara added.

According to Kobayashi, the transition from a life of eating to one of not eating has not been easy.

"Do I still crave food? Of course—usually about three times per day," Kobayashi said. "There are times when the thought of never eating again re-

ally hurts. There are times when it burns, times when it aches, times when it induces fainting, and times when my blood pressure suddenly drops and I experience heart palpitations for two straight minutes. Like any change in life, it's going to be an adjustment."

Kobayashi also said that, because he was born into a family of lifelong food-eaters, he was afraid to explore other career paths throughout his life, believing that doing so might upset his parents.

"I've been eating ever since I was in diapers," Kobayashi said. "My parents encouraged me to start eating at a very young age, although they sometimes forced me to eat things I did not want."

"After 29 years, I'd like to try some new things, like kayaking, mountain climbing, or ingesting liquids," he added.

Although Kobayashi's friends are happy for him, they have expressed concern for

his well-being, claiming that he has appeared listless, depressed, and seems to be wasting away since his retirement. Some think that the decision to give up eating may even have long-term effects on Kobayashi's health.

"Ever since he retired from eating, it's like part of him is gone," Kobayashi's friend Tsuyoshi Hasegawa said. "Specifically, the part of the brain that regulates autonomic activities and heat sensitivity."

Despite his family members pleading with him at his bedside to reconsider his decision, Kobayashi maintains that he "[does] not want to become one of those washed-up guys who doesn't know when to quit and ends up having to eat through a straw."

"There are things about eating that I will miss—the sandwiches, the hard-boiled eggs, the satisfying feeling you get after replenishing your body's nutrients, and especially the fried dumplings," Kobayashi said. "And there are certain things about eating I won't miss—mostly the hot dogs." ∅

NHL Simply Not Going To Bother Reaching Out To Hispanics

JANUARY 10, 2011

NEW YORK—Though other professional sports leagues have made concerted efforts to attract new fans in the emerging demographic, the NHL is just not even going to try to reach out to Hispanics, league officials said Monday. "Truthfully, at this point it's not even worth it; I have enough on my plate right now just trying to get youth hockey leagues to accept half-price tickets to these games," Commissioner Gary Bettman said. "I'm not going to tell Hispanics or Latinos they can't come, but we have a lot more to worry about than looking up the Spanish word for 'Penguins' or painting the puck the colors of the Mexican flag for Cinco de Mayo." Bettman added that before the league even thinks about such outreach programs, it has to figure out why, despite its best efforts, North American white people still haven't embraced the sport. ∅

PHOTO FINISH

4 Dead, 12 Injured As Bull Wins Rodeo

Lance Armstrong Wants To Tell Nation Something But Nation Has To Promise Not To Get Mad

AUGUST 27, 2010

DALLAS—Saying that it would probably be best if everyone sat down for this, seven-time Tour de France winner Lance Armstrong informed the U.S. populace Thursday that he wanted to tell it something, but that the nation first had to promise it wouldn't get angry once he did.

"Look, I'm not going to sugarcoat this. It's bad," Armstrong said during the nationally televised press conference. "But you have to swear to God that you won't get mad when I tell you, because if you get upset and yell about how you're really disappointed I'm just going to walk out of here."

"Okay?" Armstrong continued. "You guys promise?"

Armstrong then took a deep breath, massaged his forehead, murmured "Oh boy, here we go," and appeared for several moments to be on the verge of telling the nation his news. He seemed to lose his focus, however, commenting that it wasn't as if anything he was about to say would diminish the fact that he beat cancer or that his foundation has donated more than $250 million to cancer research.

In addition, Armstrong said the American people had to promise that, following his announcement, they would resist the urge to remove their Livestrong bracelets and throw them away or burn them.

"Okay, there's no easy way to put this, but, well, you guys know how I won a record seven consecutive Tours de France between 1999 and 2005?" said Armstrong, who took a sip of water as his hand visibly shook. "Well, this has to do with

that. It also has to do with this impending federal investigation of my cycling team. What it absolutely does not have anything to do with is the fact that I am an inspiration to cancer sufferers worldwide—cancer sufferers who could potentially experience serious physical and emotional setbacks if you break your promise and get mad at me."

Throughout the preamble to his announcement, onlookers reported getting the impression that Armstrong felt some need to defend what he was about to tell the country. The world's most successful cyclist spent almost 25 minutes telling the nation that, as a top-level international athlete, one has to do certain things to remain competitive; that he has no regrets; and that, given the chance to live his life again, he would do everything again the same way.

Armstrong also repeatedly mentioned that he had beaten cancer.

"You have to understand—in the high-pressure world of competitive cycling, it's all about getting any advantage you can," Armstrong said. "And if we were being realistic, we'd have to admit that everyone in cycling was trying to get an advantage. So, in a way, if we were all trying to get the same advantage,

then the playing field was still completely equal. So I was still the best. It makes sense when you look at it that way. And nothing I am about to tell you changes that. So, when I'm finished saying what I have to say, you all have to promise to still adore me."

"In fact, if you don't still adore me, and you suddenly get all huffy and say that I wasn't really a hero all these years, you are in the wrong here, not me," Armstrong added. "You. Not me."

Armstrong then stood, paced back and forth for a moment, shook his head, and returned to the microphone.

"You guys are not making this easy for me, that's for damn sure," he said. "This really shouldn't be hard. Because it's actually not even really that big of a deal. At all. Frankly, I don't even know why I'm here right now."

Armstrong reiterated for a fifth and sixth time that he had beaten cancer.

"Okay, here goes," Armstrong said. "Um, in the late '90s and early 2000s, I took, um... You see, in order to give myself a better chance of winning, I... Yes, there were instances during the Tour when..."

"You know what? I forgot what I was going to say," Armstrong added. "Sorry. I feel like an idiot. Have a nice afternoon." ∅

Andy Roddick To New Friend Phil Mickelson: 'We're Just Like Roger Federer And Tiger Woods'

SEPTEMBER 13, 2007

LOS ANGELES—Despite having a combined 56 fewer career victories, professional tennis player Andy Roddick informed professional golfer Phil Mickelson yesterday during a Make-A-Wish Foundation charity dinner that the two athletes are "just like" professional golfer Tiger Woods and professional tennis player Roger Federer. "He plays golf, you play golf—I'm a professional tennis player, he's a professional tennis player...you have to admit the similarities are striking," Roddick told Mickelson, who vehemently agreed, saying "Yeah, we're totally just like them... The only difference is that they wish they were as cool as us." Woods and Federer were unavailable for comment, as both athletes were reportedly engaged in pleasurable mutual contemplation of the fact that all other people are their physical and mental inferiors, a fact as simple and undeniable as it is immutable. ∅

PHOTO FINISH

Creepy Lifeguard Turns Out To Be Nine-Time Olympic Gold Medalist Mark Spitz

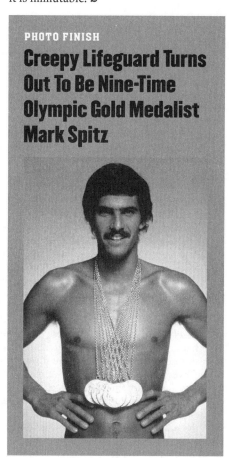

Jimmie Johnson's Car Put Out To Stud

NOVEMBER 20, 2008

CHARLOTTE, NC—Hendrick Motorsports confirmed what many NASCAR fans had suspected all season, announcing Wednesday that Jimmie Johnson's number 48 Chevrolet Impala would be put out to stud, ending its career in stock-car racing and living out the rest of its service life siring the cars of tomorrow.

"I'll be sad to see the old warhorse go," Jimmie Johnson said at the car's retirement ceremony, held in the maintenance and breeding garage on Hendrick's 60-acre racing complex. "We've been through a lot together, but I guess it was just time. I have to say, I'm a little envious."

The number 48 car, which traces its own championship lineage back to Cale Yarborough's 1983 number 28 Hardee's Monte Carlo and Dale Earnhardt's 1981 number 3 Wrangler Pontiac, recorded 7 wins, 6 poles, and 15 top-five finishes in 2008 and is expected to command a stud fee approaching a quarter of a million dollars.

Number 48 has already spent several afternoons in the Hendrick pasture, nuzzling the flanks of smaller cars from NASCAR's "minor-league" Nationwide and ARCA series whose owners hope to capitalize on the Hendrick car's bloodline.

"It's really over pretty quickly," said autofertility technician Ray J. Wertham, whose job is to use a complicated array of hydraulic lifts and hoists to facilitate Number 48's progress if things do not progress naturally in the pasture or on the test track. "There's a lot of stuff to adjust if a car's

running too loose or too tight, and fuel mixture, oil pressure, and engine temperature are all crucial. But on a day when everything's going well, there's 30 seconds of full-throttle engine revving, maybe a little backfiring, and then they're both idling happily again."

NASCAR rules specifically prohibit artificial fertilization of race cars, which happily spares number 48 the indignity of spending too much time up on jack stands methodically and impersonally having his fluids drained. The Chevrolet will also be forbidden from mating its power train with any non–General Motors product, as the historically conservative NASCAR organization has no wish to acknowledge the possibility of hybrids running in its racing series.

"Number 48 seems like a natural, though," said Wertham, adding that his specific output at the crankshaft may even rival that of Dale Earnhardt's #3 Monte Carlo, a car known for rear-ending anything that moves. "Sure, he tried to get up on the back of one of our Craftsman trucks, but that might just be dominance behavior. Except for the cars we turn out to run the road courses at Infineon or Watkins Glen, we don't usually have cars that go both ways."

"Putting a car out to stud is a great situation for everyone involved," team owner Rick Hendrick said while trainers gave the number 48 car a wax rubdown and topped off its fuel tank, already prepping it for mounting an impressive and growing list of customer cars. "Chopping old cars up for scrap like so much dog food, cannibalizing them for parts, selling them to wealthy hobbyists who mistreat them—all of that seems inhumane."

Added Hendrick: "Letting him drive over these fields during good weather, enjoying the best in GMAC car care, gulping down premium fuel, and mounting car after car until his odometer rolls over... That's a life any race fan would love." Ø

Homeless Drifters Of Santa Barbara Feverishly Await Women's Beach Volleyball Tournament

SEPTEMBER 14, 2010

SANTA BARBARA, CA—Though there are still two days to go until the first match of the California Beach Volleyball Association's annual Santa Barbara tournament, homeless drifters and vagrants of all ages have already begun to gather in the ocean-side community for what they call "their most favorite weekend of the year." "I like to look at those ladies, they're nice to look at," 54-year-old Peter "Midnight Pete" Hanley said Thursday as he unwrapped a half-eaten cheeseburger he'd been storing in his breast pocket. "They ain't hardly got nothing on, neither. They're running and diving and screaming real loud, and all for me—for my birthday. Ain't hardly got nothing on, neither." In response, CBVA officials said they're just happy people are getting excited for the tournament. Ø

NHL: 'Anybody Want Free Tickets To The Stanley Cup Finals?'

JUNE 4, 2010

PHILADELPHIA—In a desperate attempt to increase attendance at postseason games, NHL commissioner Gary Bettman announced Monday that the league was offering free Stanley Cup Finals tickets to anybody willing to take them. "These are great tickets, center ice, no obstructions, and we'll even throw in free refreshments for the first 2,000 people who accept the offer," Bettman said during a nationally televised press conference. "It would be a real shame if all those seats went to waste. Just stop on by the Stanley Cup Finals if you don't have anything else to do." Bettman reportedly made a last push to get rid of the complimentary tickets by promising playing time to anyone seated in the first 10 rows. Ø

NHL Finishes Freezing Water For 2011 Season

MAY 21, 2010

BOSTON—The Philadelphia Flyers came back from three games down to defeat the Boston Bruins in their best-of-seven playoff series last week, a historic feat neither you nor the rest of the country knew about until reading this. "It feels amazing," Flyers goalie Michael Leighton said after his team, on the road for Game 7 and down by three goals, fought back to win, causing millions to drop their jaws, primarily because it was a stunning achievement, but also because they could not believe that this very moment is the first time they've heard anything about it. "The most recent team I can remember that did something this special was the 2004 Red Sox and [everyone and their mother knows about that, but don't forget, the Red Sox blew out the Yankees in Game 7 of the ALCS, and therefore this is actually more impressive]." When asked to respond to its newfound hockey knowledge, the nation seemed impressed, although it somehow felt it was not nearly as impressed as it should be. Ø

OCTOBER 8, 2010

NEW YORK—The National Hockey League announced Thursday that it had finished freezing an estimated 480,000 gallons of water, ensuring that every opening game of the 2010-2011 season would be played completely on ice.

Ice-making factories have reportedly been working around the clock for the better part of a month, and dozens of insulated trucks were employed to transport the slabs of frozen water to all 30 professional hockey arenas, some of which are located as far south as Los Angeles, CA or Sunrise, FL.

"We learned our lesson last year," NHL commissioner Gary Bettman told reporters. "We started freezing water a week before the season, and by the opening face-off only eight arenas had ice. It was embarrassing because not only did we not deliver as an organization, but you really need to play hockey on water that is frozen."

"We also now completely understand—and agree—that all parts of the rink have to be covered with ice," Bettman added. "Even the parts behind the nets."

A shortage of frozen water on hockey rinks in the beginnings of previous seasons meant that players were forced to adapt to less than ideal conditions, skating on whatever frozen water was available and then trudging clumsily over the exposed dirt or wooden floors.

Historically, teams have not been pleased with having to play hockey on mixed surfaces, complaining that injury would often result when someone tried to retrieve a puck that had fallen into gaps in the corners of the rink where ice was not present.

The last time the NHL froze enough water to completely fill all the rinks with ice by the opening of the season was 1972.

"As hockey players, we prefer to play on water that's been frozen expressly for the purpose of playing hockey," said Phoenix Coyotes captain Shane Doan, who watched as NHL technicians lowered a 200-foot-long, 80-foot-wide slab of ice onto the playing surface of Jobing.com Arena. "Ideally, there should be ice in the middle of the rink, right where you leave the locker room tunnel, in front of the benches. Pretty much everywhere, really."

Continued Doan, "We wear special skates for the purpose of locomotion on a sheet of frozen water, after all."

In order to avoid repeating the mistakes of past seasons, representatives of the NHL Players' Association contacted the league in August to be certain that sufficient water was being frozen for the season's opening. In addition, Commissioner Bettman hired Mindy Donegan in the offseason to act as Senior Vice President of Frozen Water Oversight.

Donegan's main job was to work as a liaison between arena managers and frozen-water providers, thereby ensuring all arenas had ice by opening night.

"Working with Mindy was great because, well, look at that perfect, rink-shaped sheet of ice out there," Rangers facility manager Phil Hesselbein said. "Last couple seasons at Madison Square Garden, we were scrambling to cover the floor. We gave fans $5 off ticket prices if they brought a bag or tray of ice from home, and even the players were going to liquor and grocery stores to get some."

"A lot of it was in cube form, or even cylinders with a hole through the middle, so it wasn't smooth to skate on," Rangers captain Chris Drury said. "But it was better than nothing."

NHL officials told reporters they were pleased with their efforts this season, citing the fact that all hockey games thus far have been played on ice.

"This is certainly a new era in the NHL," a press release from the league read in part. "We'd like to thank the players for being patient during the preseason and extend particular gratitude to the NBA for allowing us to play exhibition games on their courts in our stocking feet."

When asked if the league had a plan to solve the age-old problem of the frozen water thawing and becoming liquid by the third game of the season, Commissioner Bettman said investigations were continuing. Ø

INSIDE

‣ **Everyone On NASCAR Crew Named After A Cut Of Meat**

CHAPTER FIVE:

SPORTS CULTURE

Ah, the culture of sports! It's a vibrant culture indeed, one that encompasses fans, athletes' lifestyles, sports venues— in short, anything having to do with competition that is not actually a competition, up to and including the best part of sports! Sportswriting, as you may have already noticed, is a special kind of reporting. In most forms of journalism, one is never supposed to include oneself or get too close to the subject. But in sports, access to players and involving oneself has almost become the rule of the day. At first blush, this may seem to pose important ethical questions, but it is important to keep in mind that sportswriters are shielded from any possibility of over-familiarity or collusion by their most ironclad and unbreakable rule: Sports reporters hate to leave the house. Therefore, sports-culture stories are prized by those who pen them not for their insight into the mind of the fan, the heart of the team, or the body of the steroid-crazed athlete; they are prized because those who write them can do so from the couch.

1910
After completely forgetting to put a roof on their new science lecture hall, Harvard University claims to have constructed the first stadium made specifically for football games.

1964
Crooked contractors pocket $24.5 out of the $25 million for Philadelphia's new state-of-the-art athletic facility and instead build Veterans Stadium.

1991
After being indicted for the rape of Desiree Washington, Mike Tyson asks which one Desiree Washington was again.

1994
Ken Burns' *Baseball* premieres on PBS, oddly coinciding with a massive outbreak of tiny dust mites that fly directly into mens' eyes.

2007
Pacman Jones' hip-hop group, the Posterboyz, releases an album featuring the cryptic single "I'm-A Murder Tha Commissiona Dat Reinstatz Me."

GREAT MOMENTS IN SPORTS CULTURE

Dream Team Wins Small Soft Drink

AUGUST 7, 1996

ATLANTA—The U.S. men's basketball "Dream Team" took home a small soft drink from McDonald's yesterday, making its players big winners and quenching their Olympic-sized thirsts. "We win when the USA wins," said power forward Karl Malone, taking a sip from the Dream Team's 12-ounce Coke. "This refreshing beverage is ice-cold proof of that." The Dream Team won the food prize Sunday, when U.S. fencer Dana Owens took gold in the individual women's epee, defeating Qatar's Faizla Hourani 15-11, 15-9. Nine of the eleven Dream Teamers shared the drink, the exceptions being center Shaquille O'Neal, who is signed to a long-term exclusive contract with Pepsi, and reserve point guard John Stockton, who wanted a Mello-Yello. ∅

New Bar To Feature 'Sports' Theme

MAY 7, 1997

PITTSBURGH—Area entrepreneur Andrew Wallensky is keeping his fingers crossed after Monday's opening of "Bleachers," a bold new bar centered around the highly conceptual theme of sports. Decorated with helmets, posters and pennants of such Pittsburgh-area teams as the Penguins, Pirates and Steelers, the new bar is designed to attract those who might enjoy drinking and socializing in an atmosphere infused with the spirit of professional athletics. "What I've tried to do here is merge the fields of drinking and sports in a single place, a 'sports-bar,' if you will," Wallensky said. "My future is in God's hands now." For hours after the bar opened, beer-bellied sports fans could be seen tentatively peering into the windows of the strange new establishment, though none were brave enough to step inside. ∅

Miracle Sports Bottle Has Name Of Bank On Side

FEBRUARY 26, 1997

SHIOCTON, WI—The banking and portable beverage communities were thrown into an uproar Sunday with the discovery of a plastic sports bottle mysteriously bearing the corporate logo of a local financial institution.

The bottle, measuring over nine inches in height not counting the attached plastic straw, appears to be a perfectly normal beverage container crafted by human means. Inexplicable by science, however, is the miraculous logo of FirsTrust Federal Security Bank, embossed twice upon opposite sides of the bottle.

"I don't know what to make of this. I'm still shaking," said city groundskeeper Ed Rundell, who discovered the uncanny bottle at Veteran's Park during his evening rounds. "I believe a higher power has led me to this bottle, that we may all learn from its uniqueness."

Rundell's shift was proceeding as usual when he first eyed the object under a playground slide at approximately 7:15 p.m. "I thought, 'Oh, somebody left a sports bottle here,'" Rundell said at a packed press conference Monday. "I picked it up, figuring I'd take it to the lost and found. But then it caught my eye, something on the side of the bottle."

What he saw, Rundell said, changed his life forever. "It was the FirsTrust bank logo. On a sports bottle! FirsTrust doesn't make bottles! They don't make sports drinks! It launched my brain into a whirling paroxysm of contradictions that I have not recovered from, nor do I ever expect to."

Since the announcement of the bottle's discovery, the earth's citizens have been struggling to cope with the find, manifesting reactions ranging from exultation to panic. Veteran's Park and the surrounding countryside has become a sea of people extending for miles, ever pushing toward the central point where the bottle was discovered.

"I am rethinking my understanding of the cosmos and my place within it," said Des Moines, IA, realtor Ted Unger, one of millions who have made a pilgrimage to Shiocton this week to view the miraculous artifact. "I am also seriously considering banking at FirsTrust from now on."

A bearded, glassy-eyed man wearing what appeared to be a cardboard UFO costume said, "The sports-bottle-Atlanteans will make everything come through Alpha Centauri *see* **SPORTS BOTTLE**

Soccer Mom to Suck Off World's Greatest Dad

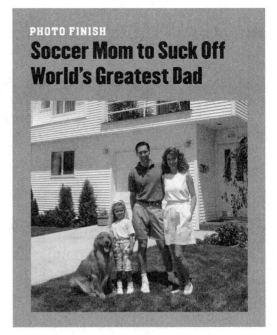

Riverboat Horseracing Fails Utterly

AUGUST 19, 1998

BILOXI, MS—Owners of the nation's first riverboat-horseracing facility announced its closure Tuesday, minutes after the inaugural race. "I guess we planned it pretty poorly," said Ronald Frisch, president and CEO of Gambling Concepts Unlimited. "We figured that once we opened the dining-room doors, the horses would know to race through the grand buffet room to the other side of the boat." Twenty-five people were trampled to death in the chaos that resulted, and eight horses drowned when they fell from the riverboat's lower deck. Gambling Concepts Unlimited officials said they still plan to hold next month's airborne rodeo as scheduled. ∅

Study: 86 Percent Of World's Soccer Stadium's Double As Places Of Mass Execution

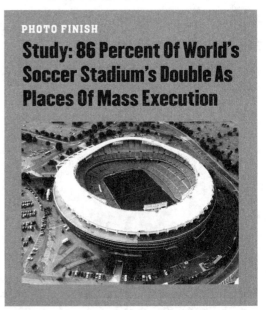

ESPN Courts Female Viewers With 'World's Emotionally Strongest Man' Competition

SEPTEMBER 29, 2005

BRISTOL, CT—Sports broadcasting giant ESPN, whose programming has long been a staple among male television viewers of all ages, made its first foray into women's sports programming with the introduction of the *World's Emotionally Strongest Man* Competition Monday.

The hour-long weekly show, which will run opposite ABC's *Monday Night Football*, features an international cast of powerfully caring, emotionally resilient, deeply sensitive men pushing themselves and each other to the limit with astounding feats of inner strength in domestic settings around the country.

During the show's premiere, a two-hour special titled "Manhattan Blowout," competitors put their bodies, minds, and spirits to the test in events ranging from the brutal grind of "Enduring Quietly As She Takes Her Hard Day At Work Out On You," to the agility-straining "Throwing A Last-Minute Surprise Party For A Despised Mother-In-Law," to the ultimate combination of strength and finesse, "Helping Her Over The Death Of The Cat That Always Hated You."

"We've always been interested in expanding our brand to involve fans of every possible stripe," said

ESPN president George Bodenheimer at the gala WESMC premiere party at the ESPN Zone restaurant in Times Square Monday. "When we looked at our viewers, it was immediately apparent that—figure skating, cheerleading, and gymnastics aside—women were the largest single group we were missing. This new show was designed from the ground up to give them the kind of deep, meaningful competitive experience they don't get from normal sports-entertainment shows."

Over 13 million viewers tuned in for the premiere, which saw Manhattan photographer Barry Peters pull to a strong early lead in overall points with his artful, complaint-free performance in the "Synchronized Cooking And Consolation" event, during which Peters prepared a near-flawless zucchini-pepper ratatouille while effortlessly lifting the spirits of his partner, the challenging and highly unpredictable Christy Ericsson, by convincing her that she was in fact better off without that long-anticipated promotion.

Other strong overall performances were turned in by Martin "There, There" Richards, a graphic designer who remembered to make his wife's beloved tapioca pudding on the anniversary—not of their marriage—but of their first date; Garth "The Embrace" Josephsen, who maintained some form of reassuring but undemanding physical contact with his fiancée for nine consecutive hours; and Ben "Soulmate" Siegel, who made his girlfriend laugh despite her belief that minor weight gain

and childlessness were ruining her life.

"It was perfect, honestly," said tear-prone football coach and WESMC host Dick Vermeil, who taped the show's 13 episodes earlier this summer so that he would be free to lead the Kansas City Chiefs without any heart-rending distractions. "We couldn't have asked for a better debut. Even the guys who didn't do as well as they wanted did their honest best, and we had no breakups or severely hurt feel-

see **STRONGEST MAN**

---

from **SPORTS BOTTLE**

and Financial-Jesus-refreshment is gonna fix everything when the secret fiduciary planets align up at the blowing of the Gatorade-horn."

Scientists, meanwhile, are at a loss for an explanation. "One expects it to be an optical illusion, a trick of the light, or some kind of mass hallucination," said Cal Tech Professor Edwin Carver. "Yet there it is, plainly screened onto the bottle. There are forces at work here that humankind cannot yet comprehend and may not be ready to confront. Pandora's box has been shattered; may God help us all."

President Clinton, in his weekly radio address Monday, urged calm. "We must be strong, and let events take their rightful course. This bottle is a mystery the world has yet to solve, and solve it we will, in due time. Meanwhile, let us be considerate to our neighbors, trust in God, and believe that the answer will be with us, when it is time." Rumors that Clinton has transferred all his personal funds to FirsTrust could not be confirmed at press time.

The sports bottle is now in the Shiocton Parks Department lost and found, in a cardboard box with two baseball caps and a dog leash. If no alien or metaphysical entity claims the bottle in 30 days, it will officially become city property. ∅

PHOTO FINISH

Wheelchair Basketball Game Enjoyed For All The Wrong Reasons

John Madden Arrested For Possession Of Turhumanheaducken

NOVEMBER 24, 2005

GREEN BAY, WI—Football commentator John Madden, famous for his unique vocal stylings and his holiday presentations of unusual meats to winning teams, was taken into custody by Green Bay police after serving Minnesota Vikings players a large "turhumanheaducken" with all the trimmings following their 20-17 victory over the Packers Monday night. "Mr. Madden served the suspect item to the players immediately after the game and, although he referred to it by its full name, Vikings players were apparently too excited or hungry to realize that what they were eagerly devouring was, in fact, a roast turkey stuffed with a rotisserie chicken, a baked duck, and a deep-fried human head," Green Bay Police Chief Craig Van Schndyle told reporters. "Placekicker Paul Edinger, safety Darren Sharper, and quarterback Brad Johnson are among those being held for medical observation while we analyze the marbled gray matter in the 'oyster' stuffing, the makeup of what we originally thought was cranberry sauce, and the head itself." Police are currently questioning Madden concerning how he obtained the head, whether or not he had help cooking the turhumanheaducken, and the current whereabouts of *Monday Night Football* statistician "Malibu" Kelly Hayes, who was last seen grocery shopping with Madden Saturday afternoon. Ø

INSIDE

> **Gym Teacher Ensures Class Bouncing Whiffle Balls On A Parachute Is A Sport**

---

from **STRONGEST MAN**

ings, despite some relatively large missteps."

According to Vermeil, one competitor, Patrick "Gusher" Johnson, overcorrected a brief moment of thoughtlessness with a hasty and inappropriate marriage proposal, straining his trust almost to the breaking point. He also noted that "Magnanimous" Ver Magnusson, the lone Icelandic entrant, may have tripped himself up with his longtime companion Marta by compensating for his terse nature with an "almost creepy" overabundance of expensive gifts.

Early reviews of the show have been overwhelmingly positive, with the target audience responding precisely as ESPN had hoped.

"WESMC is exactly the kind of thing I've always wanted in a competitive event," said viewer Emma Michaels, who posted her approval on the show's web site. "The way these talented emotional athletes can be so strong for others, bearing up under the crushing weight of sadness, shouldering the burdens of a fully mature relationship, never taking the cop-out of 'letting a woman down easy,' and never cheating... This is the way these games are meant to be played." Ø

PHOTO FINISH

Produce Manager Ready For Some Football

Experts: 'This Is The Year'

NOVEMBER 29, 2006

BRISTOL, CT—Sports analysts around the world emphatically predicted Monday that 2006 will be the year. "They've made all the right personnel moves, signed some key role players to give them the depth they've really been missing in the playoffs, and made some smart trades and draft picks both this season and years earlier that should provide them with the perfect combination of speed and power," said *SportsCenter*'s Stuart Scott, echoing the sentiments of over 5,000 sportswriters and experts in every city nationwide. "Their new coach is exactly what this team needs to get them motivated and give their city the championship those fans deserve. And you can quote me on that." Sportswriters are divided, however, on whether this will be the long-awaited first championship in decades, or the continuation of a dynasty. Ø

Famous Sports Superstitions

APRIL 3, 2007

In addition to rigorous training and natural talent, top athletes have often credited their success to following pet rituals or superstitions. Onion Sports catalogs some of the most notable:

> **Cal Ripken Jr.:** As his consecutive-games streak approached Gehrig's, Ripken Jr. got into the routine of walking slowly down the clubhouse corridor while screaming, "Cal Ripken coming through, move aside, nobody touch me!"

> **Roger Federer:** Locks himself in a bathroom the day before each match and screams at himself for hours

> **Vladimir Guerrero:** Saying that it is the only time he gets hits, Guerrero's personal superstition is swinging at every pitch thrown to him

> **Shawn Green:** For reasons no one can understand, before every Friday night game, Green breaks bread and drinks a sip of wine while chanting in gibberish

> **Dick Butkus:** Elaborate pre-game taping ritual involved having his left wrist taped, then his right ankle, then his right wrist and left ankle, then his torso, then the rest of his body; after 20 minutes, the trainer would cut him free of his cocoon, and Butkus felt free to take the field as a beautiful butterfly

> **Tiger Woods:** Carefully wakes up, arrives at the course on time

> **Deion Sanders:** During stoppages of play, football and baseball player Deion Sanders would chant his lucky mantra, "I'm Deion Sanders! I'm Deion Sanders!" until the game or season resumed

> **Lance Armstrong:** After recovering from cancer and winning his first Tour de France, Armstrong always surgically removed one testicle before each of his subsequent six Tours de France

Sportscaster Claims You Hate to See That

JUNE 29, 2006

BRISTOL, CT—Despite airing it on the 6 p.m., 8 p.m., and 11 p.m. broadcast of *SportsCenter*, ESPN anchor Chris Berman claimed "a devastating injury of that nature is not what fans come to see," in reference to the vicious slide-tackle that left an unidentified soccer player writhing on the pitch as his shattered tibia and fibula jutted through his skin, shin-guard, and knee-high sock. "He's going to feel that one in the morning," Berman said over the deafening roar of the crowd and the sound effect of a snapping tree branch. "Ouch." Berman, who has in the past suggested that you never want to watch a back-country skier smack into a series of exposed rocks or a rally car hurtling out of control into a crowd of helpless spectators, added he was "glad we can put this behind us" after showing it from several different angles in slow motion. ∅

Attempt To Delay Ejaculation By Thinking About Baseball Ruined By Crush On Johnny Damon

Peter Gammons Predicts He Will Finish Season Lonely And Depressed

APRIL 6, 2006

BRISTOL, CT—In his 'Looking Ahead In 2006' column on ESPN's website, baseball analyst Peter Gammons said that there will be "no big surprises this year," predicting that he would once again finish the season in the cellar, all alone and unable to let go of the events of the past seven months. "Although some experts are saying I will fold in the hot weather come August, I'm certain I will make it to the playoffs and head into the World Series healthy and excited, as I do each year," Gammons wrote Monday. "But when all is said and done, I am going to end up lying prone on the world champions' clubhouse floor, where I will remain, covered in old champagne and stacks of 2006 box scores, until someone wakes me up next spring." Gammons also predicted that he would have an extremely quiet offseason in which he doesn't make any major moves. ∅

Negro Leagues Hall Of Fame Indicts Ty Cobb

JULY 27, 2006

KANSAS CITY—The Negro Leagues Hall Of Fame announced Monday that Ty Cobb, who led all white baseball players with 27 lynchings in 1907, would lead its inaugural class of indictees. "Even though many of the members on our committee weren't around to have their lives affected by Mr. Cobb, the mere stories of his performance on the baseball field—like when he choked the wife of a black groundskeeper during an argument at Warren Park—are enough to convince us that he deserves this recognition, and potentially an even deeper investigation into his accomplishments in this area," said Buck O'Neil, who presented Cobb's granddaughter and the Royston, GA district attorney with a plaque detailing the numerous race-motivated offenses Cobb had been accused of, from the 1909 knifing of a black night watchman to a 1919 incident in which he called a chambermaid "a nigger" before knocking her down, kicking her in the stomach, and throwing her down the stairs of the Hotel Pontchartrain. "This is long overdue." Cobb joins Jake Powell, Cap Anson, Barry Bonds, John Rocker, and 3,185 others who will be indicted in an NLHF ceremony August 3. ∅

Wheelchair-Basketball Players Stunned By Thunderous Slam Dunk

283 Children Killed In Minor League Baseball Team's 'Kill Your Children' Promotion

APRIL 20, 2006

ST. PAUL, MN—Front-office officials for the popular minor-league St. Paul Saints baseball team called their decision to name Monday "Kill Your Children Night" an "egregious mistake" and "a rousing attendance success" after Twin Cities families took advantage of the team's offer to take $5 off adult ticket prices for every child they kill in the parking lot. "After all the crazy promotions we at the Saints have held over the years, we know one thing for certain: People will do anything for cheap baseball tickets," Saints marketing manager Bill Silberklang said. "We expected one or two infanticides, sure, but this... This may be the worst thing to happen in quirky baseball promotion since Disco Demolition Night." Team officials have apologized to the community for encouraging them to murder their children, and said that the attendance record set that same night would forever be marked with an asterisk in the team's media guide. ∅

INSIDE

▸ **Three Minutes Of Silence Ensue As Tony Kornheiser, Michael Wilbon Agree On Super Bowl Victor**

Report: Your Favorite Player Took Steroids

AUGUST 3, 2006

NEW YORK—Representatives from Major League Baseball, the National Football League, the National Basketball Association, the National Hockey League, and several other major sporting organizations announced Tuesday that a study conducted by an independent agency has determined that your personal favorite player "almost certainly" took steroids if he or she played at any point during the past 150 years.

"We are saddened to announce that any and all professional athletes regarded with respect or affection by fans of professional sports was a regular user of performance-enhancing substances including, but not limited to, the anabolic androgenic steroid class of synthetic hormones," MLB commissioner Bud Selig announced at a press conference Tuesday, where he was accompanied at the lectern by NFL commissioner Paul Tagliabue, NBA commissioner David Stern, and representatives from the governing bodies of 22 other major sports. "We sincerely apologize for, and confess that we share in, the profound feeling of disappointment and betrayal that our fans must be feeling at this time, and ask that you exercise patience as we release the entire 20,000-page, 36-volume set of our findings."

An early abstract of the report covering what its authors are calling the "main items of interest" in this latest and most comprehensive steroid scandal was released to major news organizations immediately after Selig's announcement. Although the document is an extremely abbreviated outline and contains only the names, career stats, substance-use summaries, and excerpts of confessions from all the players in the Halls of Fame of every current sport, its effect on fans and sports reporters alike was profound.

"You assume an unpopular guy like Bonds is juicing. But Hank Aaron, one of my personal heroes, injecting synthetic anticortisol as he attempted to break beloved legend Babe Ruth's career home-run record—which was set on a steady regimen of racehorse amino acids mixed with brewer's yeast? I mean, my God," said ESPN baseball analyst Peter Gammons. "And to think, he couldn't even have played in the big leagues if Jackie Robinson hadn't summoned the courage and the intravenous Boldenone he needed to break the color barrier. I just... There's just no end to it. No end."

"It's not just difficult for fans to believe, it's difficult for them to absorb," said CBS Sports reporter Bryant Gumbel, who says he has read roughly 150 non-consecutive pages of the abstract. "The nation's sports addicts can accept that infamous antihero Ray Lewis used steroids, and maybe controversial bad-boy Warren Sapp, or even rough-and-ready Brian Urlacher, but favorite son Peyton Manning? Golden boy Joe Montana? Ahmad Rashad? Johnny Unitas? Bart Starr? Sammy Baugh? Garo Yepremian? And beyond that, I mean come on—what about fans of Mario Andretti? Of Jean-Claude Killy? Greg Louganis? Vince Lombardi? Secretariat? What the hell has been going on, and why didn't anyone want to see it?"

"I think it will be relatively easy, if not pleasant, for people to accept that baseball and football players have used steroids since Abner Doubleday first mixed human adrenaline with tincture of calomel or Knute Rockne snorted powdered bull's plasma," said *Sports Illustrated* contributor Frank Deford. "Then people will learn about the hydroanabol of medical student Roger Bannister, the first man to break the four-minute mile, and begin to put things together. Naturally, they'll think, Billie Jean King needed steroids to beat a man, albeit an out-of-shape and temporarily off-steroids man, at tennis. And of course the 1980 Olympic hockey team beat the Russians—weren't America's free-market steroids naturally superior to those used by the communists? They'll ask themselves, 'Do you believe in miracles of modern medicine?' I know that I do, now."

see FAVORITE PLAYER

ESPN Online Chat With Buster Olney Reveals He's Illiterate

NOVEMBER 9, 2006

BRISTOL, CT—During a special ESPN.com "Hot Stove Preview" chat session last Monday, it was revealed that leading baseball analyst Buster Olney is unable to read or write. "Evry teem nedes god pichinq," Olney wrote in response to a question about whether or not he thinks Barry Bonds will resign with the Giants. He added: "RGFlssdas glkfrsfgtyr 578fhs3lka;d." Several ESPN.com contributors, including Jayson Stark and Rob Neyer, came to Olney's defense the following day, saying that they too are illiterate, but believe that skills such as reading or writing are unnecessary in their line of work. Ø

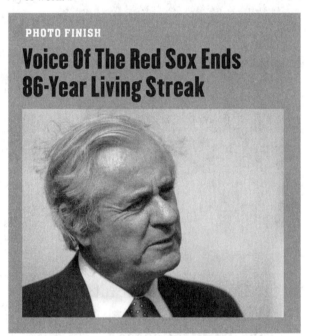

PHOTO FINISH

Voice Of The Red Sox Ends 86-Year Living Streak

Mothers Lose 10th Annual MLB Mother's Day Game 24-2

MAY 17, 2007

COOPERSTOWN—Mothers of current major-leaguers lost their 10th consecutive Mother's Day game by a score of 24-2 Sunday, the most resounding win by MLB players in the yearly matchup since 1999. "My mom and I haven't gotten together in quite a while, so it was so nice to see her, especially when I blew a 95 mph fastball past her to win the game," Josh Beckett said following the game, in which he recorded 13 strikeouts and one walk. "We always go easy on them, but when A-Rod's mom was showboating after she hit a double in the sixth, I had to plunk her the next time she got up. Just a part of the game." Though the mothers' team put up subpar numbers, Mrs. Weaver's solid seven-inning pitching performance caught the attention of Mariners' GM Bill Bavasi, who is reportedly considering her as a possible replacement for struggling starter Jeff Weaver. Ø

PHOTO FINISH

Jonathan Papelbon's 95 MPH Water Balloon Ruins Family Barbecue

Derek Jeter Dating Jessica Biel, Repeatedly Reports Derek Jeter

NOVEMBER 30, 2006

NEW YORK—According to his teammates, other MLB players, Yankee management, friends, relatives, his old college professors, and any random stranger with whom he has come into contact during the past two days, Derek Jeter is dating former *7th Heaven* star Jessica Biel. "Last night, me—me, Derek Jeter—and the beautiful, charming Jessica Biel were laughing, talking, and, yes, kissing in a dark corner of the hip L.A. nightclub Hyde," Jeter told reporters from the *New York Daily News, New York Post*'s "Page Six," *Us Weekly, Star, National Enquir-* er, *New York Times, London Free Press, Cleveland Plain-Dealer*, and 128 other national and local publications Sunday. "Just thought you all might want to know—we're an item. Yup, it's official. We really hit it off, she is incredibly sexy, and we will be attending a party together this Saturday night at Club Element in case you want to take pictures. Can you believe this?!" Jeter added that, although he was upset about not winning the AL Most Valuable Player award, he "doesn't see Justin Morneau dating anyone who was named *Esquire*'s Sexiest Woman Alive in 2005." ∅

Pop-Up To Second Baseman Reminds Sportswriter Of Relationship With Father

NOVEMBER 16, 2006

NEW YORK—A Shane Victorino popout caught by Cubs second baseman Ryan Theriot this past September compelled sportswriter Roger Angell to write a 1,500-word essay about his relationship with his father. "He hobbled up to the batter's box, the bat his crutch, his only means of support, the one thing in this world that can make you look like both a hero and a fool, and he uncoiled his muscles in a mechanically sound swing not unlike the one he produced last night and the night before," Angell wrote in his essay entitled "Pine-Tar Heart." "And from that mighty cut, a white egg tumbled from the heavens back into its safe leather nest, resistant to flying away and leaving the men who love it and need it. Only in baseball and fatherhood can a swing so utterly well-intended and so utterly perfectly orchestrated fail so utterly in its attempt to produce the desired results." The essay will appear in Angell's forthcoming compilation of baseball writings, *Diamonds Are Forever*, which also includes a novella that compares every botched double play from the 2006 season to his recent divorce. ∅

from **FAVORITE PLAYER**

For most sports fans, all of whom have had to accept the fact that their favorite players were lying to them in the interests of increased performance, the damage to the reputations of their once-beloved heroes is worse the further they look.

Callers to sports-talk-radio shows nationwide seem to have reserved their most vehement condemnations for Roberto Clemente, who is now known to have been flying an enormous load of steroids to Nicaragua when his overloaded airplane crashed in 1972; for Lance Armstrong, who, as it turns out, doped his blood so heavily during his cycling career that his own bone marrow ceased working between 1999 and 2003; and for Jason "J-Mac" McElwain, the autistic Rochester, NY high-school senior whose six consecutive three-point shots captured the collective imagination of a nation unaware the teen was injecting dihydrotestosterone.

Still, many fans believe that sports will survive this most recent episode of disillusionment.

"There are still great moments in sports, shining examples of the human spirit, if you know where to look for them," said *New York Times* sports columnist George Vecsey. "It's inspiring to see Earl Woods introducing his toddling son to the wonders and challenges of golf and steroids. To think about UNC freshman Michael Jordan discovering that his body responds to steroids three times as well as a normal basketball player's. The courage of Sandy Koufax refusing to pitch or use steroids on Yom Kippur. Barry Bonds setting the home-run record. All of them, equally meaningful."

"I just can't see this turning people off of sports," Vecsey said. "We'll just be that much more prepared, that much wiser, when the next steroid scandal comes along." ∅

Dikembe Mutombo Donates $15 Million Sports Arena To Congo

AUGUST 17, 2006

KINSHASA, DEM. REP. OF CONGO—Houston Rockets center Dikembe Mutombo fulfilled a lifelong dream Monday, announcing that he will donate a much-needed $15 million sports arena named after his deceased mother to his native Congo. "Now the poor, impoverished people of my homeland will be able to take solace in the Biamba Marie Mutombo Sporting & Convention Center, an arena which my mother always dreamed of," said Mutombo, who noted that the arena could expand to 72,500 seats for concerts and ice shows. "The BMM Center will ensure that the people of the Congo will have a chance to watch healthy competition." Tickets for the first and only sporting event scheduled for the new arena—a one-on-one basketball game between Mutombo and Hakeem Olajuwon—are on sale through Ticketmaster starting at $80 apiece. ∅

INSIDE

> **Area Man Thinking Up Funny Things To Say For Next Football Game**

> **Disconsolate Nets Fans Now Wearing Plastic Bags On Heads**

> **Mike Lupica Uses Final Thought On Sports Reporters To Ask About His Missing Dog**

Chris Berman's Nicknames Becoming More Obscure After Taking Night Course In Russian Literature

MAY 3, 2007

BRISTOL, CT—Longtime ESPN favorite Chris Berman, known throughout sports fandom for his enthusiastic narration of highlights and his practice of giving colorful nicknames to athletes, has come under scrutiny since enrolling in a Russian Literature course at a local community college led to his commentary becoming increasingly hard to understand, ESPN sources report.

"Tonight we've got a veritable Cherry Orchard of highlights to pick from as we Chekhov our top plays," Berman said during Tuesday night's broadcast of *SportsCenter* in a display of tortured literary puns and obscure references the likes of which viewers have come to dread. "We'll check in on the fading fortunes of Uncle I-Vanya Rodriguez, the tragic circumstances that brought pitcher Dennis Dove-stoyevsky into the big leagues, and find out if the tempestuous relationship between Kurt and Kyle Busch make them the new Brothers NAS-CAR-amazov, so stay tuned."

ESPN management confirmed that viewers have taken to flooding their offices with thousands of confused phone calls immediately after every broadcast.

"Listen, I have no more idea than you do why Yankees owner George Steinbrenner is suddenly deluded professor George Steinerebriakoff, or why Chris is convinced that Steinbrenner is slowly and sadly wasting the lives of everyone around him by dragging them into his miasma of self-pity, or why he seems to think Steinbrenner has gout," VP of programming Scott Guglielmino told reporters yesterday. "I mean, three weeks ago it was still Foghat references and growling out the 'R' on 'the Raiders,' and now this."

"Honestly, I'm not sure he even knows what he's talking about," Guglielmino added.

Since enrolling in the class, Bristol Community College's Russian Lit 1, which emphasizes the major works of Tolstoy, Dostoyevsky, and Chekhov, Berman has also baffled viewers by nicknaming the flamboyant owner of the Oakland Raiders 'Rask-Al-nikov Davis' during a segment titled "Crime and Punishment," in which Berman discussed the NFL's new conduct policy. He also praised an Alex Rodriguez home run by saying it "traveled as far as the railroad featured so prominently in *Anna Karenina*," and referred to LeBron James as "LeVronsky" in an apparent nod to the heroine's lover.

Response from viewers has been overwhelmingly negative, especially as Berman's further reading has led him to advance from mere wordplay-based player nicknames to broader, wordplay-based thematic comparisons.

"Excuse me, but what does it mean if Tony

Stewart is inspired to near-operatic heights of vernacular in his questioning of the corrupt caution-flag procedure when his car develops bad Pushkin in the corners?" a complaint from longtime *SportsCenter* viewer Brian Walters read in part. "And why are Miami Dolphins fans like the parents praying over the grave of their atheist son over their team drafting Ted Ginn? Can't he just say Stewart is angry and Fins fans are sad? I don't get it."

"The only thing Berman said last night that made any sense to me was that bit about 'if there's a gun in the story, it has to go off,' when he talked about the Dolphins cutting Marcus Vick," viewer Kathy West wrote. "It means he was arrested again, right?"

"Chris is definitely one of our more, let's say, involved students," said associate professor Bradley Stewart, Berman's teacher in the two-hour twice-weekly class. "I'm not sure how much he's really absorbing, but he certainly laughs the loudest and asks the most questions in class. Although I'm not sure why he wanted to know if it was appropriate to say "Bakunin-Bakunin-Bakunin-Bakunin-Bakunin!" in a celebratory manner when someone hit a home run. I told him it wasn't really a good idea."

Berman himself has refused to discuss either his recent departure from his longtime style or whether he would be returning to his old form anytime soon, saying only that he was weighing his options, listening to all feedback, and concentrating on reading the syllabus for an upcoming night course in the Imagist poetry of Ezra Pound, Ford Madox Ford, William Carlos Williams, and Richard Aldington. ⌀

Report: Kenny Mayne Incapable Of Carrying On A Normal Conversation

JUNE 28, 2007

BRISTOL, CT—ESPN sources are confirming that longtime *SportsCenter* on-air personality Kenny Mayne is, as long suspected, completely incapable of speaking to his peers like a normal human being. "The way he acts while he's on camera? Well, he's exactly the same off it," Mayne's co-anchor John Buccigross said after another failed social interaction with Mayne. "Just now I asked him how he was doing, and he said 'Even with derogatory credit I could still get a loan for a new car, so I can't complain, although some say that's my job. In any case, I continue to be amused by the simplicity of this profession.' And he said it all in that monotone voice of his, too. I really feel sorry for the poor guy, but come on, he has to realize why it is he's so lonely." When asked for a response to the findings, Mayne found himself unable to comment in a meaningful fashion. ⌀

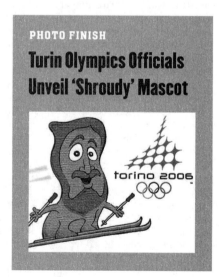

Athletes In Trouble With The Law

AUGUST 23, 2007

Michael Vick's criminal case may be dramatic, but the situation is hardly new. Onion Sports takes a quick look at athletes who landed on the wrong side of the law:

➤ **1985:** Pete Rose receives a lifetime suspension from baseball after foolishly betting that he is too famous to get in trouble

➤ **1987:** Dominique Wilkins is cleared of child-abuse charges when the "child" he was seen hitting is identified as Spud Webb

➤ **1995:** Michael Jordan shoots and nearly kills a Chicago-area police officer, but the officer is so happy to be associated with Michael Jordan that no charges are filed

➤ **1996:** Michael Irvin's cocaine possession charges are dropped when Irvin is able to prove that he is a member of the Dallas Cowboys

➤ **2000:** Ray Lewis is investigated in connection with the murder of Jacinth Baker and Richard Lollar, convicted of obstructing justice, and sentenced to five years of community service as a linebacker for the Baltimore Ravens

➤ **2001-2007:** NFL wideout Muhsin Muhammad is taken into custody three times a week for having a suspicious name

➤ **2002:** Ex-New Jersey Net Jayson Williams is arrested for killing his limousine driver and sentenced to 15 years in court

➤ **2003:** Kobe Bryant pleads not guilty to sexual assault charges, forcing authorities to let him go

➤ **2004:** Ricky Williams tests positive for not giving a shit about football

➤ **2006:** Barbaro's involvement with gambling comes to a head when organized crime enforcers have his leg broken during the Preakness Stakes

➤ **2007:** Both civil authorities and NFL officials become involved when Green Bay Packers middle linebacker Nick Barnett first pushes down a woman for throwing a drink in his face, then performs an excessively long celebratory dance over her

Tom Petty To Play Some New Stuff He's Been Working On At Super Bowl

JANUARY 24, 2008

PHOENIX—Veteran rocker Tom Petty, known for such classic hits as "Mary Jane's Last Dance," "The Waiting," and "Refugee," announced Monday that he will be using the Super Bowl XLII Halftime Show as a forum to "test out" some new songs that he's been working really hard on lately. "There's this one cool one that I'm pretty excited about that's called, like, 'Down And Out,' because it has this really down-and-out-like 'feel' to it—it doesn't have a chorus yet, but I think we're gonna open with that," Petty said, describing the song as "like 'Free Fallin',' but weirder."

"After that, we'll probably do two different versions of 'Rock Rock Rock (Yeah!)' and see which one the crowd likes better. Then I have this guitar riff which technically doesn't have a song to go with it but it sounds awesome, and then [keyboardist] Benmont [Tench] wrote a song about the Super Bowl that I said I'd let him play." Petty has told the 65,000 fans in attendance and the estimated 95 million TV viewers that any feedback, positive or negative, would be appreciated. ∅

While Clearing Out Desk, Dan Patrick Sobs Over Picture Of Him And Tim Kurkjian

JULY 18, 2007

BRISTOL, CT—Longtime ESPN anchor Dan Patrick, who recently announced that he will leave the sports network in August, broke into spasms of uncontrollable sobbing after finding an old photo of himself and baseball analyst Tim Kurkjian while clearing out his desk last Friday. "Oh my God, I remember this—this was taken right after I let Lance Armstrong off the Budweiser Hot Seat," Patrick said through tears as he displayed the back of the photograph, which read, "Me, Looking Good! With coworker—Sept. 2005." "I wonder what that guy's up to these days." After regaining his composure, Patrick noted the scene that had just taken place would probably make an excellent *SportsCenter* commercial. ∅

INSIDE

➤ Girlfriend Refers To Fans As Audience

➤ Refs Just Letting Them Cheat Out There

➤ Former Player Fat

➤ 34-Year-Old Man Wants To Be Professional Bowler When He Grows Up

➤ Tearful Sports Media Admits Addiction To Steroid Stories

➤ *Dancing With The Stars'* Contestant Chuck Lidell Confident He Can Resist Urge To Repeatedly Slam Knee Into Macy Gray's Head

Gin-Soaked Craig Kilborn Shows Up Broke, Homeless At 'SportsCenter' Studio

NOVEMBER 22, 2007

BRISTOL, CT—Craig Kilborn, the former host of *The Late Late Show With Craig Kilborn*, actor from the film *The Benchwarmers*, and *SportsCenter* anchor from 1993 to 1997, was spotted at 5:30 a.m. this morning broke, homeless, and passed out in front of ESPN's *SportsCenter* studios.

According to ESPN sources, Kilborn appeared even thinner and more frail than usual, reeked of cigarette smoke and gin, and his clothes—a moth-eaten dark suit that may have been the same one he wore in his last-ever *SportsCenter* appearance—were in tatters. Kilborn was reportedly only wearing one shoe at the time of his discovery.

Onlookers stated that, upon being woken up from his drunken stupor, the still-inebriated Kilborn asked to be shown to his "regular dressing room." The gangly, 6'5" former anchor then eluded security for long enough to stumble down the studio halls and blurt out random catchphrases from his broadcasting days at *SportsCenter*, including but not limited to "Gettin' giddy in the zone," "If it

feels good, do it," and "The low angle spank!"

"Craiggers is back, people," said Kilborn, whose signature gelled blond hair was described in a later police report as dank and lice-ridden. "Nothing to be afraid of, folks. This is just Kilby simply being Kilby. Release. Rotation. Splash."

Kilborn then regurgitated in a nearby garbage can.

"Da da da—Da da da," an increasingly aggressive Kilborn audibly hummed in a mocking tone, mimicking the final six notes of *SportsCenter*'s theme song while still hovering over the trash receptacle. "I'm Craig Kilborn. He's Dan Patrick. Welcome to the feel-good edition of *SportsCenter*. Unless you're me, and you feel like complete shit because your whole life is nothing but a goddamn joke."

"Jumanji!" he added, scaring a nearby production assistant.

Kilborn, who had moved to Los Angeles before apparently going bankrupt, losing his home, and becoming a vagrant, would not comment as to how he ended up in Bristol, CT, but police sources said they later found a Mercedes registered to Kilborn's older sister bro-

ken down on the side of nearby I-95. The vehicle had clearly been lived in for weeks, possibly even months.

"Craig looked, sounded, and smelled awful," said former colleague Kenny Mayne, who spent half an hour attempting to talk Kilborn out of his makeup chair. "But then again, as a broke, homeless man, that's his job."

Though Kilborn did not harm anyone and was treated with respect by current employees during his unannounced visit to his former employer, his mood shifted noticeably when he saw a framed picture of former ESPN anchor Keith Olbermann.

"Keith!" Kilborn said as he opened doors to the sound, graphics, and editing bays. "Come out, you son-of-a-bitch. I know you're in here somewhere. I just want to talk to you for a second. I got your daily dose of Did You Know right here!"

Olbermann was at MSNBC studios in Secaucus, NJ at the time.

After ransacking sportscaster Stuart Scott's dressing room, urinating on his own shoes, and

see KILBORN

SPORTS GRAPHIC

How Athletes Beat Steroid Testing

AUGUST 7, 2007

As performance-enhancing drugs become increasingly sophisticated, so do the methods for detecting their use. Onion Sports explains some of the techniques top athletes employ to beat steroid tests:

➤ Using masking tape and magic marker to change label on bottle of drugs from "steroids" to "headache medicine"

➤ Becoming a professional wrestler, as no one seems to care what drugs they use

➤ Boasting that their elevated testosterone levels are due to having stupendously large testicles; offering to show everyone if they don't believe it; letting embarrassment do the rest

➤ Drinking 25 gallons of water the day before urine test, knowing full well that no lab could possibly test that much urine

➤ Claiming to be stuck in the suit of armor

➤ Knocking out test administrator; stealing their blood

➤ Flexing enormous biceps, causing tester's syringe to take in blood so fast it explodes

➤ Avoiding drug tests by calling testers "narcs"; testers then back off, as no one likes being called a "narc"

➤ Using performance-enhancing drugs to become huge stars in their sports in the sure knowledge that the powers that be would never allow them to test positive for steroids

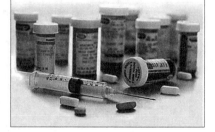

Atlanta Fans Smile Politely Through Entire NHL All-Star Game

JANUARY 31, 2008

ATLANTA—Describing the experience as "nice" and "interesting," nearly 19,000 Atlanta residents filled Atlanta's Philips Arena for the National Hockey League's annual All-Star Game, being careful to smile politely throughout the entire hour-long contest. "I certainly had a pleasant time," 54-year-old Darren Holbrook said on his way to the parking lot, though he added that he most likely would not attend another hockey game in the near future. "Those young men on the ice seemed to really be enjoying themselves, so it would have been rude for us not to give them our undivided attention."

Most fans in attendance echoed Holbrook's sentiments, but added that had the game gone on much longer, they would have politely excused themselves and gone home. Ø

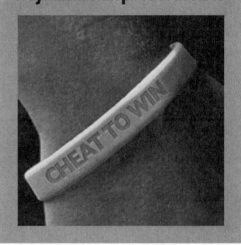
Athlete Praised For Being Competitive

MARCH 6, 2008

KNOXVILLE, TN—CBS college basketball commentators Billy Packer and Vern Lundquist took time during Sunday's Kentucky-Tennessee basketball game, a competition played with the goal of producing a victor, to praise Volunteers senior guard Chris Lofton, whose job on the team is to aid the team in winning, for being competitive. "Lofton loves competition—he'll try to beat you any way he can," Lundquist said of Lofton, whose function on the team is to produce points while preventing the other team from doing so in turn. "He's just one of those athletes who really wants to win and hates to lose." Packer echoed his colleague's thoughts, adding that Lofton was "a real basketball player" and "quite an athlete." Ø

Cupcake Used In NBA Slam-Dunk Contest Inducted Into Cupcake Hall Of Fame

FEBRUARY 21, 2008

COOPERSVILLE, NJ—The pink-frosted single-candle cupcake used in the second-place-winning slam-dunk contest routine of Timberwolves guard Gerald Green has been inducted into the National Cupcake Hall of Fame by unanimous vote, the Cupcake Hall of Fame committee announced Tuesday. "We are proud that our favorite confection has once again appeared in the national spotlight and made us proud," said NCHOF Director of Selection and nationally recognized pastry chef Meg Charleton. "It has earned its place among such moist, delicious luminaries as the cupcake that went into space with John Glenn, the cupcake that flew with the crew of the Enola Gay over Hiroshima, and the cupcake Lincoln was eating that fateful night at the Ford's Theatre." Green himself will give the presenter's speech at the ceremony in March, provided he has not already eaten the cupcake. Ø

from **KILBORN**

emerging with a tie knotted around his bare, sweaty neck, Kilborn proceeded to interrupt the 6 a.m. broadcast of *SportsCenter* by forcibly removing anchor Scott Van Pelt, whom Kilborn referred to as a "wannabe," from his chair.

Kilborn then repeatedly attempted to kiss former colleague Linda Cohn.

"Miss me, baby?" Kilborn said while unsuccessfully trying to suppress a fit of belching. "I gotta say, I'm—I'm—I'm proud of ya, Linda. Longevity, people. This woman just drips longevity. Drips. Linda Cohn, everyone!"

Added Kilborn: "Stick around, folks. I've got five questions with Linda coming up right after the break. Maybe this time she'll say 'yes.'"

Kilborn then burst into tears, collapsed, and was eventually escorted out of ESPN headquarters. According to employees, Kilborn mumbled underneath his breath that he was starving and would be "dropping by" *The Daily Show* studios, hopefully before they took down the staff's free lunch buffet.

"They still do that there, right?" Kilborn asked. Ø

INSIDE

Wooo, UNC And Duke Played Each Other Last Weekend, Oooh Oooh Oooh

MARCH 13, 2008

DURHAM, NC—Oh, man, totally the most exciting thing in the whole entire basketball world and maybe the whole universe ever, dude, happened on Saturday night when the top-ranked UNC Tar Heels played the No. 5 Duke Blue Devils at Cameron Indoor Stadium and everyone everywhere could hardly keep themselves from taking their clothes off and running around the neighborhood shouting about it because that game is always so great. "I'm just drooling all over my idiot self about the greatest rivalry in sports, and also I just peed my pants," the kind of basket-ball fan who likes to say things like "hoops" and "Coach K" and "Cameron Crazies" and "Battle of Tobacco Road" might as well have said about the game. "Oh, hells yeah, dude-bro, as far as I know or care, this is what college basketball is all about! Awes'." North Carolina won the over-hyped but rather average game 72-68, in case you are like that asshole in the quote and you actually give a fuck. ∅

Committee Of College Basketball Nets: 'Please Stop Cutting Us'

APRIL 10, 2008

SAN ANTONIO—The Committee of College Basketball Nets, a social responsibility coalition consisting of 31 basketball nets from all NCAA Division I conferences, used the University of Kansas' 75-68 victory over the University of Memphis Monday as a platform to further their cause of preventing celebrating players and coaches from savagely cutting down basketball nets. "As we speak, another two nets have been lost," basketball net ACC told reporters during a press conference, adding that though it understands the importance of tradition, the cutting down of college basketball nets with scissors is "an inherently barbaric practice that has no place in civilized society." "Those nets that were cut tonight had futures. They might have gone on to be with a family in a backyard or driveway somewhere—maybe they could have even gone pro. But instead they were cut down in their prime. Please, on behalf of all of us, stop." When asked if the net had any other causes it wanted to champion, it responded, "Other then wanting people to stop cutting basketball nets? No." ∅

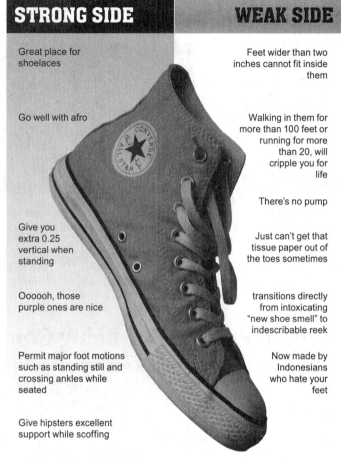

STRONG SIDE

- Great place for shoelaces
- Go well with afro
- Give you extra 0.25 vertical when standing
- Ooooh, those purple ones are nice
- Permit major foot motions such as standing still and crossing ankles while seated
- Give hipsters excellent support while scoffing

WEAK SIDE

- Feet wider than two inches cannot fit inside them
- Walking in them for more than 100 feet or running for more than 20, will cripple you for life
- There's no pump
- Just can't get that tissue paper out of the toes sometimes
- transitions directly from intoxicating "new shoe smell" to indescribable reek
- Now made by Indonesians who hate your feet

Olympic Torch Used To Ignite Tibetan Protesters

APRIL 7, 2008

BEIJING—A universally recognized symbol of goodwill, the Olympic torch was used to immolate hundreds of Tibetan protesters during its journey across mainland China last week, in what is being called a stirring display of competitive spirit and Chinese nationalism. "It was a thrilling experience," said torchbearer Wei Xiang, a member of the People's Liberation Army, who personally set 23 monks ablaze as he ran past their peaceful protest. "Today, I am very proud to be Chinese." As the torch travels the globe, a group of Serbian Nationalists has reportedly offered to transport the emblematic flame across the newly independent nation of Kosovo." ∅

INSIDE

- ▸ *SportsCenter* Repeatedly Cuts To Commercial Just As Your Favorite Team's Score Comes Up On Ticker
- ▸ People Outside Stadium Yelling Out Name Of Team They Like
- ▸ Girlfriend Wears Dress To Game
- ▸ ESPN.com Replaces Rumor Central With 'The Making Shit Up Zone'
- ▸ GoDaddy.com Presents Raunchier Version Of Danica Patrick Crash On Website
- ▸ Spectacular Intramural Sports Play Still Intramural Sports Play
- ▸ Cheerleader Foam Fingered

Baseball Fan Discovers Awesome Baseball-Themed Website Called MLB.com

MAY 15, 2008

WYATT, MO—Avid baseball fan Richard Keltner was surprised and delighted to find an entire website devoted to the sport of baseball, the 28-year-old data-entry clerk reported Monday. "The other day, on a whim, I typed 'baseball' into an online search engine to see if anything would come up, and lo and behold, the first result was this site called MLB.com," Keltner told reporters. "It has news stories about baseball, baseball scores, baseball standings, baseball schedules, baseball statistics, baseball rosters—literally everything on the site deals with the sport of baseball. And you're never going to believe this—they update it all the time." Keltner said that an additional search for other baseball-themed sites yielded only something called ESPN.com, which he described as a website about advertising. ∅

PHOTO FINISH

London Unveils 2012 Olympics Logo To Stunned Silence

NBA Announcer Would Hate To See It Come Down To That

MAY 12, 2008

BOSTON—Citing that thus far it had been a cleanly played game in which both teams were playing excellent basketball on both ends of the court, NBA announcer Jon Barry said he could plausibly imagine a situation in which the outcome of the contest would be determined by a petty action antithetical to the spirit of basketball, a dispiriting event he would hate to witness. "Not only would I hate to see it come down to that, but most important, basketball fans in this arena as well as those watching around the world deserve better," said Barry, adding that if and when this type of thing happens, one has to question whether or not certain rules should be looked at more closely or possibly even changed. "It would just be a real shame." Commentators Jeff Van Gundy and Mark Jackson agreed with Barry, stating that as a former coach and player respectively, they also hated when it came down to that, but grudgingly acknowledged it was just part of the game. ∅

Player's Career Arc Exactly Mirrors Second Verse Of Steve Miller's 'Rock 'N Me'

APRIL 17, 2008

NORWALK, CT—While listening to the radio on his drive home Monday afternoon, former MLB player Terry Boylan realized that his professional career exactly mirrors the travels of the man in the Steve Miller Band song "Rock 'N Me." "I went from Phoenix, Arizona all the way to Tacoma, Philadelphia, Atlanta, L.A.," said Boylan, who was selected in the 1998 expansion draft by the Arizona Diamondbacks, traded to the Mariners and spent a season with their Triple-A affiliate Tacoma Rainiers, claimed by the Philadelphia Phillies in the 2000 Rule 5 draft, released and picked up off waivers the following year by the Atlanta Braves, and traded once more to the Dodgers of Los Angeles. "Then I went to northern California—where the girls are warm—when I signed as a free agent with the San Francisco Giants. Though I didn't go there to be with my sweet baby, incidentally that's where I met my future wife. Weird." Boylan added that he is not superstitious nor does he get suspicious, and his woman is a friend of his. ∅

Fan Of Other Team Booed

JANUARY 24, 2008

CHICAGO—Thirty-two-year-old Sam Weber, who was wearing the color combination and various paraphernalia indicative of his fandom for a team other then the one hosting the sporting event he was attending, was booed by the other 75,000 fans present in the arena last Sunday when a projection of his face was shown on the facility's large television. "The fact that he had the gall to come into our building with every intention of showing his loyalty and devotion to the team playing our own was enough to warrant that type of hostile response," said Derek Glass, who, like the majority of fans present, was reportedly against the success of the other team and, by extension, any one individual who was for that success. "What a cocksucker." Glass added that when it was clear that Weber's team was going to lose the contest, his visibly depressed countenance was projected on the screen a second time, prompting a standing ovation. ∅

Area Man Has Great Idea For Slam Dunk

MAY 24, 2008

TORRINGTON, WY—Local export licenser Andy Rosenwald, 47, announced Monday that he recently came up with a revolutionary new idea for a slam dunk, and that he is willing to share the idea with any professional basketball player who would like to perform it.

"I'm sitting on a gold mine here," said Rosenwald, who reportedly conceived of the dunk while watching NBA highlights on *SportsCenter* last week. "I saw guys doing other dunks, and this one just popped into my head. I was like, hey, that's pretty good."

Since then, Rosenwald has focused on getting the word out about his dunk idea, admitting that it is "not doing any good just sitting here" in his Torrington home.

"I'm just the idea man," said Rosenwald, noting that he himself is unable to dunk a basketball.

According to Rosenwald's descriptions and several crude sketches made on looseleaf paper, the dunk involves the player running toward the hoop, tossing the basketball off the backboard, jumping up while spinning around 180 degrees in midair, and catching the ball above his head while his back is facing the hoop. At this point, Rosenwald said, it gets a little tricky. The player, still in the air, must then palm the ball with his right hand, transfer it behind his back to his left hand, and, upon completing his full 360-degree spin, dunk the ball over the left side of the rim.

"You could call it the Whirly Bird," Rosenwald said.

Rosenwald is offering the idea free of charge and accepting all serious requests. He said that if any NBA players are interested in using his dunk, or want to talk to him further about it in person, they should contact him immediately.

"It would be perfect for Michael Jordan, but he's retired, so I wouldn't mind giving it to a guy like LeBron James or Karl Malone," Rosenwald said. "Preferably someone good, because it's pretty hard."

After coming up with the framework for the dunk, Rosenwald reportedly spent a few minutes each day tweaking it and mapping it out to make sure the move was feasible.

"I tried it in slow motion with a balled-up sock and my hamper," he said. "It works."

"It's all about going up, under, and around, and then in," added Rosenwald, who then dem-

see SLAM DUNK

SPORTS GRAPHIC

Remembering Jim McKay

JUNE 12, 2008

Professional, dignified, and humble, yet always deeply involved with the culture of sports, he set a standard to which few still aspire. Onion Sports looks back on the career of Jim McKay, 1921-2008:

➤ **As a young** *Baltimore Sun* reporter in the late 1940s, McKay developed a new vocabulary for baseball in order to more easily convey the events of the game to his audience, including the terms "hit," "single," and "out"

➤ **In 1970,** McKay somersaults down a ski ramp alongside tumbling ski jumper Vinko Bogataj in order to better describe the agonizing sensations of defeat

➤ **Positioned underneath** the net of the 1973 badminton championships, McKay informs viewers that the last shuttlecock has been lost under the bleachers, uttering his famous words, "They're all gone"

➤ **As the turbulent 1970s** draw to a close, McKay poses for that fateful late-'70s file photo that would accompany every single one of his obituaries 30 years later

➤ **McKay's simple yet** eloquent description of the rippling hindquarter muscles of the thoroughbreds competing in the 1978 Kentucky Derby simultaneously cause three million women to have their first orgasms

➤ **In 1980,** McKay revolutionizes Olympic broadcasting by being the first reporter to enjoy what he was watching

➤ **After 16 weeks** of extensive instruction during the winter of 1984, McKay finally teaches Bob Costas how to sit in front of a crackling fireplace without catching on fire

➤ **Upon completion** of the log rolling competition in 1986, McKay swiftly arrives at the edge of the water to interview the winning log

➤ **In 2004,** McKay musters up nearly 60 years of broadcasting experience to become the only man to not look like a dipshit while wearing an ABC Sports logo blazer

Fantasy Baseball Owner Rips Team In Media

JUNE 19, 2008

BROOKLYN, NY—Mark Mendicus, 26-year-old Staples employee and principal owner of the fantasy baseball team Beat With Uggla Stick, blasted his underperforming team in the media Monday, going so far as to single out individual players, criticize their recent play, and question their commitment to winning.

"They all suck," a visibly frustrated Mendicus told reporters following Beat With Uggla Stick's head-to-head 8-2 loss to division rivals The Mark Currys. "[Alex] Rios sucks, Delmon [Young] sucks, Pedro [Martinez] fucking sucks. Everybody on my team sucks."

"The Beat With Uggla Sticks have a proud tradition of winning," continued Mendicus, whose team has made the playoffs the past two years, including a league championship win in 2006. "But apparently that means nothing to this group of players. Apparently they'd rather just lose every single 5x5 category. Apparently my players don't care about winning the 12-team Yahoo! Plus 'Mmm...Fantasy Baseball' league pennant as much as I do."

Mendicus had high expectations for his team coming into the season, but his players have been plagued by injuries and inconsistency, losing six of their first eight matchups en route to a 22-46-14 overall record. The historically temperamental owner did not hold back his opinions after their latest humiliating defeat, telling the *New York Post* that Prince Fielder "had better start hitting some fucking home runs already" before making several vicious personal attacks on the first baseman, calling him a "fatass," a "fat bastard," and a "fat fuck" in the course of one statement.

"I paid $38 for [Fielder], and this is what I get?" Mendicus said, directing reporters' attention to Fielder's "putrid" Yahoo! Game Log. "Twelve home runs.

Twelve goddamn home runs. When you pay $38 for a guy, you had better give them a hell of a lot more than 12 home runs through the first half. I got you for your power, buddy, not your walks. This is a *batting average* league, anyway, not an *on-base percentage* league, so walks don't fucking matter. It's like these guys don't understand that."

Mendicus continued his heated rant, calling shortstop Felipe Lopez a "talentless hack whose multiple position eligibility is the only thing saving his ass from waivers," claiming that pitcher Ian Snell is "killing [him] in WHIP, absolutely killing [him]," and encouraging outfielder Brad Hawpe to "go eat shit." He then accused the whole team of not stealing enough bases and "not playing like true Beat With Uggla Sticks."

He did, however, reserve some praise for hot-hitting second baseman Dan Uggla upon learning that Uggla homered twice that day, saying, "That's you, Danny."

With his team already down 9-1 in this week's matchup against Gary Sheffield's Head Vein, Mendicus issued an ultimatum, claiming that unless his team delivers at least a tie, there will "be some changes around here." Mendicus said that "no one is safe," and had particularly strong words for pitcher Chris Young, who three weeks ago was hit in the face with a line drive and has not made a single start since.

"Toughen up, you little baby," Mendicus said. "You don't throw with your face, do you? I already got Phil [Hughes] in the DL slot, so you better get your ass back in action."

Mendicus has a reputation

see **FANTASY BASEBALL**

from **SLAM DUNK**

onstrated the dunk's feasibility by standing on his tiptoes, grabbing the top of his bedroom door frame with both hands, and excitedly saying, "Slam."

Although Rosenwald admitted the dunk is probably best suited for an official slam-dunk contest, he said it would be "very cool" to see it performed during a live NBA game.

"If it was in a game, the guy could, instead of tossing the ball off the backboard, he could bounce it really hard through the other guy's legs," Rosenwald said. "I think the fans would enjoy that."

Rosenwald also said it would be preferable if, as the player slammed the ball through the hoop, he pointed to the cameras and shouted "Rosenwald!" or "Rosenwald, baby!" to give him credit for the idea, but noted that it would not be necessary.

"The real reward would be seeing a dunk I invented on the highlight reel," Rosenwald said. "The *SportsCenter* guy could say 'cool as the other side of the pillow' for it."

If NBA players enjoy this idea and begin using the dunk in regular season and playoff games, Rosenwald said he has "plenty more where that came from." He has already been mentally workshopping several other dunks, including one in which the player throws a "really high" alley-oop to himself, one in which the player spins the ball on his finger before dunking it, and one where the player uses one hand to do a "backwards dunk" through the bottom of the net, then grabs it with his other hand and slams it back down.

Rosenwald also recently came up with what he has termed a "cool dribble move," which involves the player pretending to go one way, then bouncing the ball off his knee in the opposite direction.

"I'm not sure if it's legal to hit the ball with your knee," Rosenwald said. "Maybe the Harlem Globetrotter guys would like that one."

In the meantime, Rosenwald remains committed to not letting his dunk idea go to waste.

"I told the idea to my son, and I think he thought it was pretty cool," he said. "Maybe he could tell it to his [Torrington Junior High j.v. basketball] coach, who maybe has connections to the NBA. Then this idea can finally get off the ground." 🖉

Nation To Leave Olympics On In Background

AUGUST 7, 2008

NEW YORK—The American people announced plans Monday to put on the Olympics, turn the volume down to a barely audible level, and leave the broadcast on in the background as they attend to washing dishes, sorting recycling, paying bills, preparing and eating meals, napping, and other quotidian activities in various areas of the house. "I'll support our athletes just as long as their events don't interrupt the flow of my daily life," said Allentown, PA resident Joann Kirkland, who recently declined a plastic Olympic cup from her local McDonald's. "I do intend to stand in front of the television for a few minutes on my way to the computer when the diving competition

comes on, clicking my tongue and saying 'too bad' when the U.S. competitor fails to win the gold." Many Americans also stated that, if their televisions had a picture-in-picture feature, the Olympics would be the perfect thing to put in the smaller window. ∅

Nation Asks Permission To Stop Watching Olympics Now

AUGUST 21, 2008

WASHINGTON—The people of the United States of America issued a formal request Monday, seeking permission to stop watching the 2008 Summer Olympic Games. "We have dutifully watched segments of the XXIX Olympiad for at least two hours a day for nearly two consecutive weeks, including aquatic events, track and field, and even stupid stuff such as synchronized diving, and while we fully and openly admit that we have enjoyed far more than we had initially expected, we must reiterate—it has been two weeks," the appeal drafted by the U.S. populace read in part. "Can we please stop now?" The 300 million U.S. citizens said they would be sitting here watching women's beach volleyball until they receive official word that it's okay to switch to a rerun of *Grey's Anatomy*. ∅

Bracketiatrist Mistaken For Bracketologist

MARCH 20, 2008

LOS ANGELES—Basketball fan and board-certified bracketiatrist Arthur Levine, 36, was once again misidentified as a "bracketologist" in casual discussion of the NCAA tournaments Tuesday. "I hate to be a jerk about it, but while it's true I can do anything a bracketologist can do, I spent eight extra years in med school and three in residency so that I could call myself a bracketiatrist," said Levine, who is well-known in bracket circles for the depth and incisive quality of his bracketoanalysis. "Therefore, I would appreciate you calling me by my actual title." Witnesses to Levine's statement agreed that he badly needed the services of a qualified mixologist. ∅

from **FANTASY BASEBALL**

for following his players' performance with intense scrutiny and personal investment, often to a fanatical degree. It is rumored that he monitors their progress on multiple Yahoo! Sports box score windows on his computer screen, and will erupt into obscenity-laden tirades at work after a mere groundout or caught stealing.

"Fuck you Edwin, you good-for-nothing piece of shit," Mendicus was overheard as saying while angrily clicking the "Refresh" button on his web browser 14 times after pitcher Edwin Jackson loaded the bases with three straight walks. "Throw the ball over the goddamn plate. I need a win here, you idiot. I'm getting killed in wins."

For some players on Mendicus' team, the demand for instant results, the constant threats to be released or traded, and the nonstop verbal abuse is too much. Pitcher Jeremy Guthrie has been dropped and picked up by Mendicus seven times already this season, and he says he doesn't like playing under such volatile conditions.

"I wish he'd have a little faith in me," Guthrie said. "I don't like being picked up the night be-

fore my start and then simply dropped the next day. It wears on you as a player. And now I have to explain myself to my kids when they read in the papers that their daddy is a 'shit-for-brains asshole who can't even get five strikeouts when that's all we needed to win the category.'"

"I'm sorry, but when I have runners on first and third and one out, I'm going to go for the double play to get out of the inning, not the strikeout," Guthrie added. "Even though they don't give out 'points' for double plays."

Some players, however, praised Mendicus for his fiery attitude and desire to win, saying they prefer that to the kind of owners who treat their fantasy teams like nothing more than a fun distraction from their real jobs.

"It's good that he cares," said Beat With Uggla Stick catcher Jorge Posada. "Some owners, like Garrett Baldwin of the Smilin' Joe Randas, or Mike Broberg of Tiny Damon, they just sort of check in every once in a while to see how we're doing, but that's it. In fact, I've been on the Tiny Damon's bench since I went on the DL in April, and they don't even have anyone

in the catcher slot. That's just shoddy ownership."

"But there's also a thing called caring too much," Posada added. "You can only be called a worthless shitbag after popping out so many times before it starts to sting. It's at the point where playing for Mendicus is almost as bad as playing for Hank Steinbrenner." ∅

Mark Cuban Buys Sports

JULY 10, 2008

DALLAS—Billionaire Mark Cuban, tired of the opposition he has encountered from NBA management in his role as owner of the Dallas Mavericks and frustrated with opposition from the MLB owners' association in his attempt to buy the Chicago Cubs, liquidated almost all his personal wealth and holdings and purchased the entirety of sports for an undisclosed but undoubtedly large sum on Monday.

"I'm pleased and excited to announce to fans of—well, of everything, really—that a new era has begun in the game, activity, contest, race, national pastime, world championship tournament, sport, or sports that you love so much," a cheerful Cuban said Tuesday morning in a press conference held to announce his acquisition. "So many of the things that have frustrated me about sports—the officiating, the ivory-tower attitude of the powers-that-be, the fact that I am not in control of every single aspect of them—all of that is about to change."

The exact details of the thousands of exact terms and conditions of Cuban's purchase have yet to be released. However, lawyers confirm that the deal makes Cuban the majority owner of sports, with at least a 51 percent share of sporting leagues and organizations including but by no means limited to Major League Baseball, the National Football League, the National Basketball Association, the National Hockey League, the Professional Golfers' Association, NASCAR, IndyCar, Major League Soccer, the WNBA, the LPGA, the Bassmaster Tour, the NCAA, FIFA, the Inter-

national Olympic Committee, the Union Cycliste Internationale, Formula 1 Racing, the International Rugby League, and all their affiliate and associate leagues in perpetuity.

"I want to assure fans and athletes around the world that very little will change now that

you are all my fans and athletes," Cuban said. "Of course, there will be a review and streamlining of all the rules as soon as possible, so I can settle certain things once and for all, like what is and isn't a foul, and where the Cubs

see **MARK CUBAN**

PHOTO FINISH

Projectile Green Turtle Shell Involved in Controversial Indy Car Finish

Olympic Closing Ceremonies To Feature Launch Of Chinese Nuclear Arsenal, Invasion Of United States

AUGUST 14, 2008

BEIJING—Responding to controversy regarding lip-syncing singers and "simulated" fireworks during the Olympic opening ceremonies, Chinese Olympic officials announced Tuesday that the closing ceremonies would feature a full-scale nuclear ICBM launch followed almost immediately by 2 million amphibious troops marching into California. "We have pledged to respond to our critics in a fashion that exemplifies the culture and direction of modern China," a statement from the newly created Chinese Strategic Olympic

Committee and Global Strike Force read in part. "The world shall thrill to the spectacle of 1,000 character dancers, 10,000 traditional acrobats, 100,000 commandos storming out of the Pacific surf into Los Angeles and San Francisco, and dozens of cities burning at one million degrees." The statement also expressed regret that, due to the unique circumstances of this year's closing ceremonies, handing over the Olympic Games to the heavily targeted city of London would probably not be physically possible. ∅

'ESPN The Magazine' Editor: 'Look At All The Pretty Pictures'

MAY 29, 2008

BRISTOL, CT—Gary Belsky, editor-in-chief of *ESPN The Magazine*, expressed satisfaction and delight with the mockup of his publication's latest issue Wednesday, flipping gleefully through the pages and staring in mesmerized awe at the multitude of "pretty, pretty pictures." "Ooooooooooooohhhhhh," said Belsky, sensuously running his fingers along a two-page-spread photograph of Royals outfielders Joey Gathright and David DeJesus leaping for a fly ball. "Soooo shiiiiiiny." Belsky went on to say that the magazine cover was "so glossy smooth," that the letters were very, very big and in all different pretty-pretty colors, and that there should be more ads. ∅

Hard-Hitting Investigative Report Still Only About Sports

JULY 17, 2008

BRISTOL, CT—A four-month in-depth investigation into the conduct of USC basketball star O.J. Mayo conducted by ESPN's *Outside The Lines* program was still, in the end, about nothing more important than sports. "[Rodney] Guillory, in violation of NCAA rules, has provided Mayo with cash, thousands of dollars in clothing, a flat-screen television, a cell phone, meals, and other benefits," reported Kelly Naqi of a man who will soon be paid millions of dollars to bounce a ball up and down and throw it through the air. Though there is acknowledged genocide being carried out in the Sudan and refugees of the Chinese earthquakes are once again being relocated due to flooding, Naqi went on to say that "under California state law, it's a misdemeanor for sports agents to provide cash to student athletes." As the Dow Jones index fell another 436 points, *Outside The Lines* followed up the report with a 15-minute piece on how the unkempt infield at Fenway may cause more errors than at other parks. ∅

OUTSIDE THE LINES

from **MARK CUBAN**

will be playing after they leave Chicago, and what Dwyane Wade will be doing now that he's banned from basketball. Oh, yeah, and the Olympics are canceled. And I need to see [former Texas Longhorns softball player] Cat Osterman in my office tomorrow evening, dressed appropriately for dinner at a fairly good but charmingly low-key steakhouse. Anyway, I realize how important sports are, and want to reassure the world that with the increased cost will come greatly increased enjoyment."

Cuban has also scheduled a meeting of sports to be held on Aug. 15 at the American Airlines Center in Dallas. Attendance is mandatory for all executives, team minority partners (formerly team owners), and officials from all leagues. Attendees have been told to bring detailed records of their recent seasons, and that coffee and sandwiches would be provided as the meeting is expected to last most of the day.

Reaction from sports people was mixed.

"The part of this that bothers me is that Cuban has never before shown any interest in us and then, out of the blue, I get a 225-page memo outlining administrative restructuring, rules changes, delineations on what the league commissioner is and is not empowered to do, off-the-field disciplinary guidelines for players, the works," said Dane County Little League director Robert L. Krewson of Montrose, WI. "I'm not entirely certain I can allow the kids to be taken out for pizza afterwards. It's difficult reading."

"Apparently the stripes have to go," said Cincinnati Bengals Hospitality and Morale Group Director and former Bengals owner Mike Brown. "I guess Mark just doesn't like stripes."

Cuban acknowledged that there would be some adjustments to make during the transition, but that he would address "minor concerns" just as soon as he finishes the business of firing former NBA Commissioner David Stern, a process that he estimated may take up to four days "in order to do it right."

"Buying sports was the culmination of a childhood dream, but it wasn't cheap," Cuban told the *Wall Street Journal* yesterday. "I sank almost everything I had into it, brought investors on board, even sold my jet in order to get sports. And while I'm in charge I intend to rid sports of all the hypocrisy and old-boy's-club garbage and tennis and false sentiment that have been dragging it down for so long. There's no reason I can't do that, have a ball, and then sell it a few years down the road at a profit. Maybe to Yahoo! or someone like that."

While sports' burgeoning popularity has generally been blue-chip profitable in recent years, business analysts are taking a wait-and-see approach regarding Cuban's acquisition.

"In this economy, nothing is certain, especially in the leisure segment," said *New York Times* financial analyst Gary Broadbridge. "Individually, sports have value, certainly. But considered as a whole, and taking into account issues such as steroid use, cultural oversaturation, an emphasis on pure performance over substance, and the long-term value of sports looks somewhat dim. I'm sure I wouldn't be alone in saying that I'm really not sure sports is worth it." ∅

INSIDE

Appealed Strike Call Taken All The Way To Supreme Court

JULY 17, 2008

WASHINGTON—The United States Supreme Court heard oral arguments yesterday in the case of *Wright v. Dreckman*, which calls into question professional baseball player David Wright's 2005 check swing against the San Diego Padres and whether or not the resulting strike call should be upheld.

The decision was first handed down in New York's lowest circuit court, Shea Stadium, after presiding home-plate umpire Ed Montague was unable to rule in the case. San Diego Padres catcher Ramon Hernandez, acting on the advice of now-retired pitcher Pedro Astacio, then filed an immediate appeal with first-base umpire Bruce Dreckman, who ruled against Wright. However, according to defense attorney David B. Reiss, in order for justice to be served, the decision must be overturned by the Supreme Court and the strike ruled a ball.

The called strike pushed the count to an even 2-2.

"Evidence and eyewitness testimony will show that not only did my client's bat not cross the front of home plate, but his wrists nev-er turned over in such a way as to demonstrate a clear intent to swing," Reiss said before members of the high court Wednesday. "In addition, I submit that the plaintiff's state of mind at the moment of the decision remains suspect. Was Mr. Dreckman paying full attention to my client? Or was he distracted by fans taunting his earlier failed call on an attempted bunt for a single? Also, there was a clear split second of hesitation on the part of Mr. Dreckman after Mr. Hernandez signaled for the appeal. Why is that?"

"The court has the responsibility today to define, once and for all, what constitutes a check swing. Is it—this?" added Reiss, demonstrating by swinging a bat and stopping it well before a ball placed on a tee. "Because if it is, my client successfully worked the count to a hitter-friendly three balls and one strike. And who knows what would have happened after that."

In the 2005 game, the at-bat in question ended with a groundout to shortstop.

The road to the Supreme Court for *Wright v. Dreckman* has been lengthy, *see* APPEALED STRIKE

U.S. Men's Gymnastics Team: 'Win Or Lose, We Will Cry'

AUGUST 14, 2008

BEIJING—After settling for bronze in the Team Artistic Gymnastic event Tuesday, the U.S. men's team promised reporters that, for the remainder of the Olympics, they would weep wholeheartedly before events, mist up despite themselves while performing flairs, and sob uncontrollably in either victory or frustration following every routine. "Whether we are shedding lonely but triumphant tears because no one believed in us, or exultant tears of joy and disbelief because our teammate stuck the perfect landing following a triple back-somersault, I guarantee that together, we will shed tears at all times," said gymnast Jonathan Horton. "We will hold our quivering chins high even if the handles on the pommel horse become slick with sweat. Or tears." Team members Paul and Morgan Hamm, who were unable to attend the Olympics due to injuries, were reportedly crying in sympathy after learning the team had won a medal without them. ∅

PHOTO FINISH

Man Running Aimlessly With Olympic Torch For Past 3 Years

INSIDE

› **High Fives Abound In NBC Control Room As Camera Catches Another Athlete Crying**

201

Knicks Fans Discover Striking Palms Together Makes Uplifting And Appreciative Noise

NOVEMBER 13, 2008

NEW YORK—Following the Knicks' surprising 4-2 start, fans' instinctual boos have been interrupted by what many are referring to as "a strange, repeated bringing-together motion of the hands," an act resulting in an uplifting sound that can be used to respond to successful plays by the team. "It seems to be really effective when a lot of people do it at the same time," said fan Adam Blake, 32, whose face has recently begun to contort in such a way that his mouth curls upwards at the corners, often exposing the fronts of his teeth. "It's a lot less natural for me than yelling at players and coaches, but unlike throwing garbage on the court, the security guards say you're allowed to do it. I guess if I had to choose between the old way and this new hand-slapping thing, I'd pick hand-slapping. It seems to be making the players, and me, feel kind of—I don't know—good."

Upon returning home, fans were shocked to learn that emotional connections could be made with friends and family by not making sarcastic comments about their weight and intelligence and instead wrapping their arms around each other and pressing their bodies close together. ∅

Stuart Scott's Left Eye Moves To Fox

AUGUST 28, 2008

BRISTOL, CT—In a move that came as little surprise to members of the sports media, ESPN anchor Stuart Scott announced Wednesday that his left eye had signed a lucrative eight-year, $70 million deal with Fox Sports and would report to work within the next month. "Though we did our best to hide it, usually by using thicker than normal glasses, I think people could easily tell that my left eye and I had been going in different personal and professional directions for some time," Scott said during a press conference at which the eye was present, but elected to remain silent throughout, staring off to one side as Scott spoke. "I wish it all the best in its future endeavors." Fox Sports President Ed Goren said he has big plans for the eye, adding that its off-putting and distracting *SportsCenter* host has been holding it back for far too long. ∅

PHOTO FINISH

Mr. Met Takes Frustrations Out On Fans

from **APPEALED STRIKE**

convoluted, and filled with more than its share of tumult. After the 2005 Shea ruling, the case was appealed to the U.S. District Court of the state of New York, where the decision was reversed in favor of Wright. However, when it was revealed that the presiding judge was a lifelong Mets fan, the decision was thrown out and the case was again argued in front of the New York State Court of Appeals. That court, citing the 1994 case *Bonds v. Davidson*, sided with Dreckman.

According to attorney Reiss, however, the decision in *Bonds v. Davidson* was inapplicable. Though the court upheld the original ruling on the field, Reiss was quick to note that Bonds was left-handed, and thus the case set legal precedent with third-base umpires, not first-base umpires. Reiss believed Wright being right-handed constituted a legitimate enough reason to file a writ of certiorari, or "cert petition," an order for the case to be heard by the Supreme Court.

"We were never—never—going to stop fighting this until this case reached the top," Reiss told reporters after the court recessed. "And I hope that the justices find it in their hearts to do what is right. My client is a good man, a young man who has been an All-Star and a Silver Slugger. There is simply no way he would swing at a pitch that low and outside."

This is far from the first instance in which the Supreme Court has been called upon to decide matters of the national pastime. In the 1903 case of *Wagner v. The Chicago White Sox*, the court ruled 5-4 in favor of the defendant that "a base-ball hit far and high, only to bounce fairly onto the field-of-play, and then spring forth into the seats of the 'bleachers' should earn the batsman no more and no fewer than two bases, and not an out." A landmark 1976 ruling established the infield fly rule. And more recently, a 2006 decision in the case of *Rodriguez v. The Fans of New York* cemented the legal precedent established in the 1940 case of *Williams v. The Fans of Boston*, which made it clear that baseball fans are free to boo, no matter how nonsensical it may seem, players on their home team.

Thus far, legal and baseball experts remain uncertain as to how the court will rule in *Wright v. Dreckman*.

"I think this decision could go either way," *Baseball Tonight* legal analyst John Kruk said. "Several of the justices, such as [Antonin] Scalia, are originalists who believe in the strict interpretation of the baseball rulebook as it was first written. That document clearly states that a decision on the check swing ultimately falls on the umpire. However, there are those pragmatists on the court, such as Justice Breyer, who believe in the living, flexible rulebook."

Added Kruk: "And then there is Justice [Samuel] Alito, who is an idiot, and moreover has never watched a baseball game in his life." ∅

Hawaii Wins Little League World Series

AUGUST 28, 2008

WILLIAMSPORT, PA—The Hawaii team, known for its powerful lineup of short, fat Skill 5 hitters, defeated the Mexico team 12-3 in the championship game of the Little League World Series, a four-round, single-player tournament held from 2 p.m. to 3:15 p.m. Sunday. A majority of the games were played in Speed Mode.

Hawaii's offensive outburst was led by such stars as Glen, who had three hits and four RBI on the afternoon, as well as right-handed cleanup hitter Adam, who was 2-for-3 with a double and home run. Leadoff man Thomas chipped in with a home run of his own, which prompted two identical cheerleaders in the crowd to wave their pompoms in front of a giant neon "HOMERUN" sign.

"I say it every year—the short, fat players have the most power," said commentator Orel Hershiser after the game. "When you've got guys like Byron, guys like Steven even though he's just a Skill 2, guys like the 'Big A's'—Aaron, Adam, and Alan—you're going to score a lot of runs. It would take a stellar pitching performance to shut this team down, and unfortunately for Mexico, Ramon did not have his best stuff today."

Hawaii got off to a quick start, scoring six runs in the first and taking full advantage of Mexico's sloppy defense. Third baseman Chico (Skill 1) had a particularly rough day in the field, committing six errors and several mental miscues. In the fourth inning, Chico slid head-first eight times in an attempt to catch a foul pop-up before letting it fall to the ground, and later ran directly past a ground ball in the hole while on his way to inexplicably cover second base. On three occasions, he fielded a routine grounder and accidentally threw it to home plate instead of first base. Chico later claimed that he "didn't know how" to throw to first.

Mexico's only runs came on a lucky break in the fourth inning when, with two on and an 0-2 count, Juan hit a ball into the gap

see **HAWAII**

Tormented TBS Producer Wonders Why 'Steve Harvey Show' Was First Thing Out Of Mouth During Game 6 Technical Difficulties

OCTOBER 23, 2008

ATLANTA—Producer Greg Porto was unable to explain why on earth it occurred to him to air *The Steve Harvey Show* in place of the ALCS during a router failure at TBS headquarters in Atlanta. "I just—it just came out before I could stop it," said a visibly shaken Porto this past Saturday, wandering out of his building a full four innings before the game ended. "I've never even seen *The Steve Harvey Show*. To be honest, I didn't know if we had the rights to it. There was just this moment, this nanosecond of perfect clarity, when I knew that I had to broadcast *The Steve Harvey Show* to an audience of millions expecting one of the biggest baseball games they had ever seen. I immediately regretted it, of course, but you live with your decisions. Dear God." Porto went on to say that if he had to do it all over again, he definitely would have shown an episode of *Tyler Perry's House Of Payne* or, at the very least, *My Boys*. ∅

Trey Wingo: Is He The Tim Meadows of SportsCenter?

INSIDE

▸ **Davis Love III Tells Kevin James, Ray Romano To 'Shut The Fuck Up' On 3rd Hole Of Celebrity Pro-Am**

Cory Matthews, Mr. Feeny Share Joyous Moment Following Phillies World Series Victory

NOVEMBER 6, 2008

PHILADELPHIA—Lifetime Phillies fans Cory Matthews, 27, and his former next-door neighbor, educator, and longtime friend, Mr. Feeny, celebrated together after the Phillies captured their first World Series title in 28 years. "I remember when Mr. Matthews attempted to listen to a radio broadcast of a Phillies game during my English class. Now, 15 years later, there's nobody in the world with whom I'd rather celebrate this occasion," the wheelchair-bound Feeny said. "Throughout my years with Mr. Matthews, we've experienced some powerful moments—like when we switched places as teacher and student, or when I babysat him and caught him sneaking into an R-rated movie, or when I got sick because Cory wished I would get sick, prompting him to feel guilty about it—but this is the first time we can experience happiness together as Phillies fans." After their celebration, Matthews and Feeny shared a quiet, solemn moment to remember that Matthews' best friend Shawn Hunter would have been celebrating with them had he not passed away in a motorcycle accident last year. ∅

Breast Cancer Launches WNBA Awareness Month

OCTOBER 2, 2008

NEW YORK—Leading representatives of the Susan G. Komen Breast Cancer Foundation announced Wednesday that the month of October would officially be known as WNBA Awareness Month, and commemorated the occasion by donating $80 million of their funds to promote the early detection and ultimate eradication of the all-female basketball league.

Ambassador Nancy G. Brinker of the Komen Foundation was accompanied at the press conference by WNBA survivor Rebecca Lobo, long-suffering WNBA

see **WNBA AWARENESS**

Bill Murray Shoots 18-Under To Win Pebble Beach Pro-Am

FEBRUARY 15, 2007

PEBBLE BEACH, CA—Funnyman Bill Murray put the finishing touches on six-under 66 Sunday at the annual Pebble Beach National Pro-Am, edging out Phil Mickelson and Jim Furyk by five strokes apiece to clinch his first tournament win of the season. "I've been working a lot on my short game lately, and listen, I've played this course enough times to know where the trouble spots are, especially on the dogleg left on 16," said Murray, who also pushed his caddie into a sand trap on the 12th hole and yelled "You missed a spot!" "I think the key today was not paying attention to the scoreboard and just focusing on hitting the greens. They call me a crowd-pleaser, and I did just that by playing a solid round of golf." Other highlights from Murray's performance included his eagle on 5, his masterful par save on the 15th, and the time he jokingly attempted to depants Ernie Els while Els was lining up for a putt. ∅

---

from **HAWAII**

that became lodged in a portion of the fence that prevented Hawaii's right fielder from retrieving it. As a result, the outfielder ran in place into the fence for over 20 seconds while Juan rounded the bases.

Aside from that one lapse, Hawaii's starter Jerry was dominant, holding Mexico sluggers Paco and Benito to just one hit apiece.

"Jerry had all his pitches working today: the fastball, the slowball, the ball that starts fast and then slows down right before it reaches the plate, and the breaking pitch that starts down the middle and then slowly curves 15 feet outside as the batter begins his swing," Hershiser said. "His pitch sequences were set up beautifully. He did a great job of throwing pitches inside to make the batter stand in the far corner of the batter's box, and then coming back with a fastball that painted the outside corner. Worked every time."

Mexico's pitcher, Ramon (Skill 2), did not fare quite as well. After giving up a double to Alan and a groundball triple to Glen to start the third, he quickly tired, demonstrating his fatigue by removing his cap and allowing two geometric lines of perspiration to emanate from his head. He then threw his next fastball approximately 20 mph slower than the last one.

Surprisingly, however, not a single walk was issued by either team, and only three balls were thrown during the entire game.

Despite the resounding victory, Hawaii was not without its own blunders. Their defense failed to hit the cutoff man once all game, and whenever first-baseman Aaron fielded a ground ball, instead of stepping on first base to record the out, he would throw it to the empty bag, causing the ball to skip into right field. Hawaii could have potentially won the game by the 10-run mercy rule had they not consistently run themselves out of innings. The most flagrant baserunning gaffe came in the fourth, when Adam forgot how to go back on the basepaths.

After Mexico's loss, somber music played as three of Mexico's players were consoled by their coach, a white man in his mid-40s. "YOU TRIED HARD, BUT LOST," the coach told his crestfallen team in a crude but playful typeface. "BETTER LUCK NEXT TIME."

Many Mexico fans are protesting Hawaii's win, claiming that the U.S. team used controversial—and some say illegal—tactics to win the game, including removing their best hitter Aaron for a pinch-runner after he got on base and then reinserting him into the lineup as a pinch-hitter two outs later, and having what appeared to be six outfielders, all of whom moved simultaneously at identical angles and speeds. In addition, during a key play in the second inning, a Hawaii outfielder tricked Mexico baserunner Pancho into trying to stretch a single into a double by simply not picking up the ball.

Both teams endured a long, difficult path to get to the championship game. Mexico had to defeat Chinese Taipei and Korea in the first two rounds, while in the semifinals, Hawaii overcame a late-game deficit to beat fan favorite Texas with a walk-off home run, made especially memorable as it traveled exactly along the foul line without ever curving.

The 2008 Little League Baseball Championship Series went relatively smoothly this year, suffering only a few minor mishaps. The final game was delayed 18 minutes in the third inning for reasons the official scorer said pertained to obtaining "Hot Pockets and a Sprite." Earlier that afternoon, the perennial powerhouse New York team, led by Ward and Saul, was forced to forfeit their semifinal match when their coach forgot the 22-digit alphanumeric code needed to begin the game.

However, in an improvement over previous years, only one quarterfinals game had to be suspended and replayed after all the players simultaneously froze.

Sources confirmed that several *Bases Loaded* scouts were in attendance, and that Utah is looking to sign Hawaii pitcher Jerry and place him in their rotation alongside Quinta, Lep, and Stava. ∅

That One Kid In Rec Basketball League Always Wearing Jeans During Games

NOVEMBER 27, 2008

CARMICHAELS, PA— Sources confirmed yesterday that that kid in the Carmichaels YMCA youth basketball league, the one who plays for the team in yellow jerseys sponsored by Grimaldi Dental Associates, played another game Tuesday wearing blue jeans.

Reports indicate that this was the 8th consecutive game that 11-year-old Jeremy Burkholder, renowned throughout the league for his unorthodox and presumably uncomfortable basketball attire, has played wearing his No. 9 jersey, a pair of old Spalding basketball sneakers which many speculate were once his older brother's, and the same, worn pair of light-wash Levi Strauss blue jeans.

Sources confirmed that Burkholder's teammates, and those players on the opposing team, all wore traditional basketball shorts.

"The first time Jeremy showed up in jeans, I naturally assumed he was wearing shorts underneath," Burkholder's 10-year-old teammate Colby Oswald said, adding that Burkholder also wears the same jeans to the team's once-a-week practices. "But he didn't take them off for warmups or before he got in the game. And he didn't just forget his shorts, either, because at halftime

his mom didn't give him shorts to change into."

"We all thought it was against the rules," added Oswald, who later said that though he isn't exactly sure why, he would feel extremely uncomfortable asking Burkholder about his jeans. "I asked my parents after a game once if it was because he's poor and they just shushed me and started looking around."

The overwhelming consensus amongst the league's players is that by even showing up to games wearing jeans, Burkholder is being "weird," "stupid," and "gay." Because players are traditionally dropped off in front of the YMCA, and the walk from the car to the gym is approximately 15 feet, most arrive at the court wearing just their winter coats and basketball shorts. If pants are ever worn, players strongly maintained, they are an athletic garment known as "tear-aways," which are never worn during games, can be removed via buttons running down the length of the pants, and are not made of denim.

Though it is not known for sure whether or not Burkholder prefers jeans, or if Burkholder simply doesn't own shorts, his teammates intimated that it's the latter.

"He smells strange," said teammate Eric-

see **REC BASKETBALL**

---

from **WNBA AWARENESS**

president Donna Orender, and Los Angeles Sparks center Lisa Leslie, who has been battling the league for 11 years.

Brinker noted that the WNBA has always been a primary concern for the breast cancer community, and said she is committed to using the full force of her breast cancer organization to rid the nation of the dreadful professional league at its every stage— from its earliest possible appearance in training camp, to preseason and the playoffs, and even during its more-invasive Finals stage when the league is at its most aggressive.

"What we plan to do this October is start a national dialogue about the WNBA," said Brinker, wearing the orange ribbon she introduced that morning to signify the fight against the league. "What is the WNBA? Who is primarily affected? Is somebody

you love, be it your daughter or your wife, causing you to suffer through it? Why, despite going into annual remission, does it reoccur every year, seemingly without warning? How can we be more vigilant and nip this thing in the bud before the season even starts?"

"The sooner we address these questions, the sooner we can fulfill our vision of a WNBA-free world," she added.

According to a report compiled by the nation's top breast cancer awareness organizations, the most frightening aspect of the WNBA is how many people, especially its players, are unfamiliar with the warning signs of the league. Because of this ignorance, the report states, the WNBA can be difficult to detect early, often appearing no more malignant than a woman's college basketball game.

However, upon closer examination, significant abnormalities

become apparent: cells of fans clumped together in an otherwise empty arena causing a discharge of uninspired cheers; the league's orange-and-white ball appearing discolored (which, experts say, often leads to humiliation amongst those who play with it); and fatiguing spells of missed shots and boring layups that only metastasize as the season goes further along.

"The main thing that people need to know is that even though the WNBA moves slowly and methodically, it will continue to spread if it's ignored," said Samantha Gallagher, president of the Northeastern Breast Cancer Coalition. "Before you know it, a full-blown professional women's basketball team will have developed in Toronto, and at that point the odds of fighting it are slim to none."

Gallagher added that statistics indicate the WNBA is the second leading killer of interest in

professional sports in the United States behind Major League Soccer.

In 2007 alone, she said, 320,000 people finally succumbed to the WNBA.

"The fact that I am standing here today is a miracle," former New York Liberty forward Rebecca Lobo told reporters. "When I first noticed the small crowds, the poor television ratings, and the overall lack of support, I thought it was all my fault, which I now know was ridiculous. But even though the league ravaged my entire mind and body, I never curled up in a ball and asked myself, 'Why me?' I just kept on playing."

"Now I hope that, by spreading awareness, I can warn little girls everywhere about how harmful the WNBA can be," Lobo added. "Hopefully nobody will ever again have to suffer the way I did." ∅

Laid-Off Pittsburgh Mill Worker To Put Off Suicide Until After Super Bowl

JANUARY 29, 2009

PITTSBURGH—Recently laid-off steelworker and football fan Marcus Aniello announced that he would postpone his impending suicide attempt until after the Steelers take on the Arizona Cardinals in Super Bowl XLIII. "I was going to spare myself the shame of coming home to my family every day and telling them I still hadn't found a job, but I kinda wanna see what Big Ben [Roethlisberger] can do against that sorry excuse for a defense," Aniello said on a recent trip to the gun shop.

"Normally I would have thrown myself in the blast furnace the day I got laid off, but the Steelers had clinched the AFC North the day before, and then I watched them beat the Ravens from the top of the Fort Duquesne Bridge, and here we are. Their logo being the same as the American Iron and Steel Institute's kind of makes me want to cry a little every time I see it, and if they lose.... Well, you know." Should the Steelers win, Aniello plans to attend the victory parade and swallow a bottle of sleeping pills during the Pirates' Opening Day game. ∅

Francis Scott Key To Sing National Anthem At Super Bowl XLIII

JANUARY 29, 2009

TAMPA BAY, FL—In his first public appearance since his death in 1843, attorney, author, and poet Francis Scott Key announced Wednesday that he would sing "The Star-Spangled Banner," which he himself originally penned nearly 200 years ago as the poem "The Defence Of Fort McHenry," prior to Super Bowl XLIII. "I plan to sing it in its entirety with all four stanzas, and to the tune of the British drinking ditty 'The Anacreontic Song,'" Key said as gobbets of desiccated flesh and hanks of hair periodically fell from his yellowed skull. "Thank you, kind sirs, for inviting me to your Superb [sic] Bowl. I relish

the opportunity to once again read my work to the worthy landowning men of this great nation." Key attempted to amuse the press by vowing not to muddle up the lyrics, as he had done in a very embarrassing moment before a lawn-bowls match in 1829. ∅

from **REC BASKETBALL**

Tremba, 12, who admitted he was basing his statement primarily on the fact that Burkholder wears jeans to play basketball. "He's kind of retarded, too. In school he's always really quiet, and during recess he usually just kind of walks around the playground by himself."

Aside from a possibly deprived financial situation or a severe mental handicap, speculation surrounding Burkholder and his lack of shorts continues to increase among the league's players. Some believe that Burkholder has "Russian" or similarly culturally incongruous parents who aren't aware of what basketball shorts are, while others claim that Burkholder's calves and shins were severely burned in a car accident.

Most agree, however, that his odd attire is somehow related to the fact that Burkholder is not a very skilled basketball player.

"I don't think he knows what traveling is," teammate Dale Ross said. "When he gets in the games, he always just kind of stands under the hoop the entire time. So when he shoots the ball it either goes straight up and down, or it bangs the underneath part of the rim."

"Most players who are good wear basketball shorts," Ross added. "Except for Greg [Davis]. He always has the newest [Air] Jordans and wears Nike wrist bands, but he sucks."

Those who know him emphasize that Burkholder's abnormal clothing isn't the 11-year-old's only peculiarity. According to his teammates, Burkholder is dropped off at the YMCA games by a bearded man, who many believe is either his father or older brother, driving a rusty pickup truck. The barely glimpsed man does not attend the games, and the truck, which always contains various planks of wood covered by a blue tarp, is not seen again until the game's conclusion. In addition, when Burkholder is late for practices or games, the team's coach never bothers to ask why.

Furthermore, despite an absent brother or father, and despite his limited playing time, Burkholder's cheering section is always the biggest of any player on the team, consisting of various vaguely identical people of both genders ranging in ages from 0 to 90.

"I think his aunts, uncles, and cousins come to the games," said Jason Cuneo, 11, adding that Burkholder may have "like 10 or 15" brothers and sisters. "They are loud, and sometimes the younger ones yell for the coach to put Jeremy in."

Added Cuneo: "Can't they see he's the only one not wearing shorts?"

Though his teammates don't agree with Burkholder's choice of basketball uniform, all have unanimously said that they would rather be on Burkholder's team than the one with the kid who wears Rec Specs, or the one with the weird Jewish kid who plays the entire game wearing "that stupid beanie on his head." ∅

Steeler Defense Renamed 'Mid-Level White-Collar Curtain' To More Accurately Reflect Contemporary Pittsburgh

JANUARY 29, 2009

TAMPA BAY, FL—Just days before the Super Bowl, the Pittsburgh Steelers' public relations department announced that the team's vaunted "Steel Curtain" defense would be renamed to more accurately reflect their city's current vocational demographics.

"With the sunset of the foundry era in Pittsburgh an acknowledged reality, it was time to take a serious look at team nicknames," media relations director Tina McClary said. "After reviewing Pittsburgh's current position as a leader in financial services, health-care management, and corporate administration, we settled on the 'Mid-Level White-Collar Curtain' or 'Middle Management' as the new nickname for our defense. As usual, our offense will have no particular nickname." McClary would not speculate on whether or not the team would change the Steeler name itself, but admitted that executives had looked at uniform designs for the Pittsburgh Retailers, the Pittsburgh Biomedical Technicians, and the Pittsburgh Eighth-Most Fortune 500 Company Corporate Headquarters Hosters." *∅*

NBC Analyst Mike Holmgren Crawls Under Desk After Seeing Own Shadow

FEBRUARY 5, 2009

TAMPA BAY, FL—Seasonal prognosticator of all seasonal prognosticators Mike Holmgren, commonly known as "San Fran Mike," emerged from his hidey-hole underneath the NBC football analyst's desk on Super Bowl Sunday, saw his shadow, and retreated again into his burrow, indicating to the excited 4,000-person crowd that there would be seven more months before the NFL plays its next official game. As per tradition, a top-hat-and-tuxedo wearing Jerome Bettis rapped the top of the desk three times with his walking stick, peered under the table, and cajoled Holmgren gently before picking the hairy mammal up by his waist and displaying him to the gathered crowd as the creature's arms and legs hung limply. "The Holmgren is so cute," 11-year-old Tara Means said. "I want to pet it." NBC anchor Bob Costas appeared visibly agitated throughout the entire ceremony and could be heard anxiously telling his colleagues that he could have sworn the same exact thing happened yesterday. *∅*

Pepsi Super Bowl Commercial Got You Talking, Reports Area Dad

FEBRUARY 5, 2009

OLD TAPPAN, NJ—As friends and family members argued over the quality of a Pepsi Super Bowl ad that juxtaposed images of Bob Dylan and will.i.am in order to link the last several generations into one unified and Pepsi-inspired youth movement, area father Steven Acker suggested the ad was effective because it got everyone in the room talking about it. "That's what they want you to do," said Acker, nodding gently. "They don't care if you like it or not, as long as it gets in your head. Then they take their million dollars and laugh all the way to the bank." When asked about the Pepsi commercial featuring *Saturday Night Live* character MacGruber, Acker said he "didn't get that one." *∅*

Local Office Betting On Who Will Win NCAA Tournament Pool At Other Office

MARCH 19, 2009

ROCHESTER, NY—In what has become a yearly tradition, employees at the office of Institutional Investors filled out brackets Wednesday and placed bets on who will win the NCAA "March Madness" pool being held in the S.G. Schilling Inc. offices across the street. "All the people involved are equally uninformed, so it's anyone's bet," said assistant media planner Evan Glazer, adding that the pool helps build camaraderie in the office. "I like to do a little research. Mike; Doug Smith or Smitts; Mr. Shernoff; that project analyst guy, they're always the top seeds. I'm predicting that Caroline, the cute and feisty office manager, is going to pull an upset this year, but that's a risky pick. Also, I used to work with [HR coordinator] Will [Krepack] at another company, so I have to favor him." The majority of employees claimed that actually winning the pool would certainly be exciting, but the biggest thrill comes from betting on what other people are betting on. *∅*

Area Girlfriend Was Voting For Cardinals

FEBRUARY 5, 2009

SAN FRANCISCO—When asked which team she wanted to win the NFL's most coveted prize, local girlfriend and Super Bowl party attendee Christy Lester, 25, told those in attendance that she was voting for the Arizona Cardinals. "I'm voting for them because I like their quarterback Matt Lineman [sic]. He's hot," said Lester, who, though she has never filled out a ballot of any kind for a Super Bowl, added that in 2008 she voted for the New England Patriots, that she forgot who she voted for in 2007, and that in 2006 she voted for the team Jerome Bettis was on because that's the team her dad likes.

"That Cash4Gold.com commercial was so hilarious." Historically, NFL championships have been decided by tallying the number of points scored during four quarters of football and not by ballots cast by a public electorate. *Ø*

Harry Kalas Tribute Video Somehow Narrated By Harry Kalas

APRIL 16, 2009

PHILADELPHIA—In what fans are calling a touching and entirely fitting tribute to the Philadelphia icon, the Phillies released a farewell video of Harry Kalas Monday narrated by Kalas himself. "In Philadelphia, they'll tell you that if Harry Kalas said it, it must be true," Kalas' distinctive voice can be heard saying over a montage of great Kalas moments, including his first day as a Phillies broadcaster and both Phillies World Series victories. "His honeyed old-leather-and-bourbon baritone was spring and summer to generations of baseball fans. We'll miss his voice, but not as much as we'll miss the man. So, one last time, we say: Long drive...watch that baby...outta here. Home run, Harry Kalas." The Phillies declined comment on the video itself, saying only that choosing Kalas to narrate the labor of love was a "no-brainer" and that no other voice would do Kalas' legend justice. *Ø*

INSIDE

› **Professor Andrew J. Hammerstein Defeats Dr. Goldwater For Mixed Martial Arts & Sciences Championship**

SPORTS GRAPHIC

Athletes and Sexual Misadventures

MARCH 19, 2009

Tiger Woods' public apology for serial philandering reminds us how athletes have always found sex as problematic as it is easy for them to get.

776 BC: The ancient Greeks hold the two-week fuckfest that would eventually come to be known as the Olympics

1949: Golfer and all-around athlete Babe Didrickson finds a way to get no less than nine hard cocks inside her at once

1950: Wilt Chamberlain loses his virginity and figures he'd like to try that again some time

1952: First recorded instance of a youth soccer player being asked to help get coach's whistle out of his front pocket

1973: After Yankee Fritz Peterson swaps his wife, two kids, and poodle for Mike Kekich's wife, two kids, and terrier, the lefthander is reportedly very upset that his dog's vagina is completely stretched out

1996: In his book *Bad As I Want To Be*, Dennis Rodman explicitly explains why he doesn't think he'll ever be able to get that cock ring back from Madonna

2003: After being accused of sexually assaulting a 19-year-old hotel worker, Kobe Bryant loses endorsements for KY-Jelly, Trojan Condoms, and Nutella

2005: Although the Vikings rented a boat and brought in prostitutes from out of state to relax, quarterback Daunte Culpepper becomes completely unhinged after realizing he's been fisting Bryant McKinnie

Dick Vitale More Sexual During March Madness, Wife Lorraine Reports

MARCH 19, 2009

BRISTOL, CT—Emerging from her husband's dressing room slightly out of breath and sporting nothing more than a silk robe and tousled hair, Lorraine Vitale, wife of iconic ESPN college basketball analyst Dick Vitale, told reporters Sunday that her spouse is at his sexual peak during March Madness.

"He's an animal," said Mrs. Vitale, adding that prior to her husband's appearance on ESPN's Selection Sunday special, the couple engaged in sexual intercourse three times in different locations, including once in a Bank of America ATM kiosk. "We fool around at other times during the year, of course, but once the conference tournaments start and the brackets are finalized, well, that's when the role-playing starts, the dirty talk gets louder, and 'the prime-time player' comes out of its velvet-lined case and gets fresh batteries."

"He's especially aggressive this year because Duke has a legitimate chance at making the Final Four," she added.

Lorraine, who has been married to Vitale for more than 35 years, said her husband uses certain erotic techniques only during March Madness, including the dipsy-doo dunkaroo; the super scintillating sensational slam-jam bam bam; the backdoor, baby; and the trifecta, which Lorraine would not describe in detail, but said involves the use of Mr. Vitale's index, thumb, and forefinger.

According to Mrs. Vitale, their lovemaking becomes longer and more intense as the NCAA tournament progresses—sometimes lasting well into the morning hours if her spouse has had a particularly heated exchange with fellow college basketball analyst Jay Bilas. She said that once the Sweet 16 is set, Mr. Vitale enjoys achieving orgasm by playing erotic games such as the "Cameron Crazy" and the "Diaper Dandy."

"That's what the baby bottle and diaper are for," she said.

But what her husband enjoys playing most, Mrs. Vitale noted, is "Duke vs. UNC," a game in which he dresses up as a Blue Devil, she wears a University of North Carolina cheerleader outfit, and, at the sound of an air horn, the two "go at it hard like two in-state rivals."

Mrs. Vitale would not confirm rumors that ESPN analyst Digger Phelps sometimes participates while dressed as Wake Forest's "Demon Deacon" mascot.

"When the Final Four comes around, Dick is so sexually charged that he's pretty much into everything," said the mother of two, who admitted that it was disturbing at first to watch her husband stand stark naked in their kitchen, a ball gag muffling his screams of "It's awesome, baby," but that the practice had grown on her. "And I'll admit that it's a little weird when he shouts out 'Krzyzewski' at the moment of climax, but believe me, it's worth it. I have so many orgasms

that it doesn't matter."

"Quite frankly the month of March has given our marriage the kind of excitement other couples only dream of," she continued. "Every woman deserves to experience, just once, the type of arousal I feel when my husband and I join together in the slap-a-lapp-anapper."

The Vitales' odd and oftentimes graphic lascivious behavior began in March 1983, when the two spontaneously made love on Testudo, an oversized bronze statue of a diamondback terrapin turtle that sits outside the University of Maryland library. It was at that point that Lorraine Vitale said she knew something carnal had taken over her husband.

"It was after a pretty close game with a tournament spot on the line. We were walking through campus, and Dick whispered to me, 'The students rub [the turtle] for luck, so let's get really lucky tonight,'" she said. "I'll never forget it. The torn-off underwear, the cool bronze against my knees, and Dick's hot body on my back thrusting, thrusting, thrusting.... Excuse me, I need a drink of water."

"Hey, Lorraine, come on," Dick Vitale could be heard saying from inside his dressing room. "I want to try this cream that Bob [Knight] and Karen [Knight] use."

Before reentering the dressing room, Mrs. Vitale confirmed what everyone had already assumed to be true: that immediately after the NCAA championship game Dick Vitale ejaculates one last time, rolls over, and sleeps through the entire month of April. ∅

White College Player Does Hair Before Game

APRIL 3, 2009

DETROIT—Before playing in all of his games, North Carolina forward Tyler Hansbrough makes sure to look his most rakish by grooming and tidying his hairdo with a number of styling products. "Just a little more here," said Hansbrough, while applying coconut-scented Bed Head manipulating gel to meticulously form and shape his sporty coiffure. "Perfect." Moments after carefully putting on his jersey in a manner calculated not to disturb his hair, Hansbrough took one last look in the mirror before heading out to the court, where he missed pregame warm-ups for the 56th consecutive time. ∅

SPORTS GRAPHIC

Legendary Athlete Splurges

MARCH 12, 2010

Julius Peppers signed a big Bears contract and bought pricey bottles of champagne for an entire nightclub, but it wasn't the biggest flashing of cash in sports history.

1956: Bart Starr celebrates his rookie contract with the Packers by sitting down to a nice steak dinner with corn and extra mashed potatoes

2001: Manny Ramirez buys $160 million in scratch-off lottery tickets

2002: Two years after the Texas Rangers make him the nation's highest-paid athlete, Alex Rodriguez returns the favor by buying manager Buck Showalter his very own Chan Ho Park

2002: Donovan McNabb surprises the Eagles offensive line with those sapphire pendants they had been admiring at Kay Jewelers

2003: Jerome Bettis commemorates his lackluster 811-yard season by presenting his offensive linemen with gold-colored Timexes

2004: After signing a seven-year, $99.2 million contract, Peyton Manning places $10,000 in Roth IRAs for each player on the Colts' roster

2007: Prince Fielder "makes it rain," showering the cashiers at Dairy Queen with $100 bills

2008: After the final game of his eight-year, $120 million contract, perennial disappointment Mike Hampton buys all his teammates gold rings inscribed with the words "Mike Hampton Is Very Rich"

First Homo Leagues Player Shatters MLB Sexuality Barrier

APRIL 23, 2009

OAKLAND, CA—Homo leagues all-star Tyler Patton shattered baseball's long-standing sexual orientation barrier Monday by signing a four-year, $10.5 million contract with the Oakland A's.

Patton, 23, whose speed, nifty fielding, and dependable hitting made him a homo-league sensation in only three seasons with the Kansas City Gay Royals, is Major League Baseball's first openly gay player.

"I had heard Oakland was interested, but you hear rumors all the time," Patton said in a press conference after his signing. "I was just concentrating on playing baseball, and then last week I got the call. Honestly, I know people think my being gay is a big deal, but I still just want to help the A's past the Angels."

Oakland general manager Billy Beane said Patton's commitment to the sport above and beyond his personal issues is the reason he chose to pursue the second baseman.

"Coming here from the homo leagues, Patton's in for a lot of heat from the fans," Beane said. "And not just the fans. Every time they talk about his open stance, every time he throws a guy out from his knees, every time he goes deep in the hole, there's going to be an uncomfortable silence at the very least. But I believe Patton has the focus to put that aside and just play."

Reactions from MLB have been mixed, with most teams declining any official comment, and commissioner Bud Selig saying in a radio interview Tuesday morning that the historic signing was "fine, if that's what the A's want to do, I guess." However, many insiders say the move to involve gay players has been a long time in coming.

"Though it draws only 10 or 15 percent as many fans as the majors, the Homo Leagues have a history of community, fantastic play, and above all, pride," sportswriter Peter Gammons said when the signing was announced. "The league's faithful have stood by their men from its inception in the '30s, through the so-called 'frisky ball' era of the '50s, past the league-wide amyl nitrate abuse scandal of the '70s, and on to the Log Cabin schism of the '90s. But what so often gets lost in all this is that Homo League players can flat-out play baseball. Now, after decades during which gay fans had nothing in the major leagues to call their own, save for perhaps some of the mustaches, Patton finally gives them someone to root for."

Still, Patton's critics, while stopping well short of bigotry, point to HLB's reputation for fast-paced, high-strung, often flashy baseball, and speculate on whether Patton will hold up. Many say his gaudy .342 batting average, .435 on-base percentage, and three Gold Lamé Glove awards during three seasons in the homo leagues are meaningless in terms of his future success.

"Sure, Tyler did well against homo-league pitching," Skip Bayless said Tuesday on ESPN's *1st and 10*. "But he's not playing against the Boston Pink Sox or the New York Gay Yankees anymore. In fact, the Gay Yankees didn't even pursue him last season when they needed a second baseman. I wish him all the luck in the world, but I think he's a gay bust."

Many baseball insiders, while acknowledging the social value of Patton's signing, struggled to discuss the implications of a homo-league star playing in the majors.

"Er, I, uh, well, I wish Patton good luck, and you know, we'll, um, I guess we'll wait and, uh, wait and see," said *Baseball Tonight* commentator Jon Kruk, who seemed unable to look directly at his cohosts or into the camera while discussing Patton's signing. "Good luck, Patton. I mean, uh, yeah."

Patton himself, who is scheduled to start next week, says he cannot wait to put the hype behind him.

"Yes, it'll be difficult, not because I'm gay, but because it's Major League Baseball," Patton said. "Plus, let's face it—do you seriously think I'm the first gay major-leaguer ever? Seriously? And before anyone says anything, you are all just so wrong about Mike Piazza." Ø

Boilermakers Protest Purdue's Mascot

MAY 5, 2009

WEST LAFAYETTE, IN—More than 200 members of the International Brotherhood of Boilermakers picketed outside Ross-Ade Stadium Monday, protesting what they characterized as Purdue University's insensitive use of a boilermaker as a mascot. "We have worked too hard forging America's boilers to endure one-dimensional stereotypes like Purdue Pete," union president Newton B. Jones said. "Pete may be muscular and sensibly wearing a hardhat, but the hammer he brandishes serves as an ugly reminder of isolated instances of violence in the boilermakers' otherwise proud history." A similar controversy erupted in 2003, when a University of North Carolina football game was interrupted by 35 protesters afflicted with congenitally tarred heels. Ø

Harness Racing Movie Contends Life Is Like Harness Racing

MAY 4, 2009

HOLLYWOOD, CA—In a recent interview about his movie *Loosing The Hopple*, screenwriter Jason Chesley said that his story of a young harness racer's relationship with his horse and their struggles to shift from a pacing to a trotting gait before eventually winning the storied Hambletonian is actually a metaphor for life. "It's less a harness racing movie than a deeply human story of relationships and personal struggles that just happens to have harness racing in it," said Chesley, who compared his protagonist's struggles with hoppling his horse Whole Enchilada to the universal struggle of shedding the yoke of childhood and growing up. "Life isn't always a garden trip. You're being carried along in the sulky of fate with only your Standardbred and your wits, and when you're boxed in, third on the rail, well, those are the times you dig down, move into the pocket, and trot yourself right out of that death hole." Though Chesley was coy concerning most plot points, he did confirm that his protagonist's encounter with Messenger, the horse from which all harness racing horses were bred from, was a metaphor for God. ✍

Disease Hoping To Be Named After Ballplayer

MAY 5, 2009

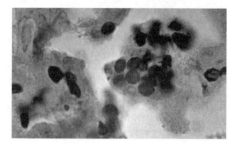

BRANDON INGE—A thus-far undiscovered hantavirus inhabiting Tigers third baseman Brandon Inge confessed Tuesday that it would love to seriously afflict and be named after a "real-life baseball player." "I imagine I'll be given an uninspiring medical classification, like hantavirus pulmonary syndrome, but I would love to be commonly known as Joe Mauer's disease," the virus said while increasing Inge's vascular permeability in order to bring about pulmonary edema and simultaneously disrupt the player's renal system. "Hopefully I don't get discovered in this guy before I get a chance to infect someone really good, like Justin Verlander. My dream is to cause massive splenomegaly and eventually tachycardia in Albert Pujols, but I don't even know if that's possible for a virus like me, so for now that's all it is—a dream." The virus went on to idly inhibit B cells in the shape of Derek Jeter. ✍

Chatter Down 10 Percent

JUNE 15, 2009

NEW YORK—The usage of common baseball chatter, including phrases like "Heybattabatta" and "Swingbattabatta," is down among teams at all levels by 10 percent, according to a report released by the Elias Sports Bureau Wednesday. "It's difficult to determine why Americans would not want to slightly alter their voices and yell, 'Whaddayasaynowkid,'" said ESB analyst Edward Coffey, noting that Little League Baseball, traditionally considered the most important development area for chatter, recorded only 8.9 million instances of banter, patter, and other team-centric commentary this May, well down from last year's 12.7 million. "It could be the economy or the general state of the world, as chatter was down almost 30 percent during the recession of the early '90s. Then again, in the Great Depression we saw an outpouring of hundreds of novel forms of chatter. It's entirely possible chatter is entering a whole new era." In related news, chatter specifically for David Ortiz has dropped 90 percent. ✍

Pick-Up Swim Meet With Inner-City Kids Renews Michael Phelps' Love Of Swimming

JULY 31, 2008

LOS ANGELES—While walking the streets of poverty-stricken downtown Los Angeles Monday, despondent Olympic swimmer Michael Phelps witnessed, and participated in, a pick-up swim meet that reinvigorated his attitude towards the sport. "It had gotten to a point where all I cared about was winning gold medals, but seeing those kids—many of whom had absolutely nothing but their dreams—race the 400-meter individual medley and the 200-meter freestyle for the pure joy of it all brought me back to why I got into the sport in the first place," said Phelps, who reportedly won the respect of the swimmers and ultimately earned the right to come back to the Compton slum after the Olympics for September's pick-up invitational. "It was just like when I was coming up in the sport: 48 kids getting together on a Saturday, two captains picking a team, the divers going to their own section of the pool, and basically just having a good, old-fashioned, playground-rules three-hour swim meet." Phelps finished second in the 100-meter butterfly and fifth in the 200-meter individual medley. ✍

PHOTO FINISH

Hot Dog Vendor Clearly Lost

Baseball Fans Delighted By New Between-Innings Fuck-Cams

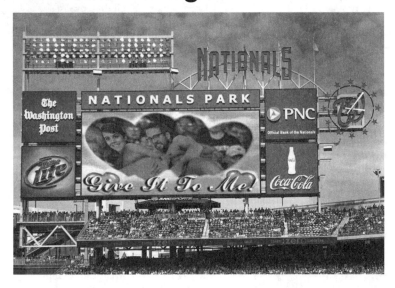

JULY 9, 2009

WASHINGTON—Attendance may be down, but the fans at last week's game didn't care—they were too busy enjoying the stadium's new Fuck-Cam.

"We've been really surprised and delighted by the crowd reaction," said Washington Nationals public relations director Janine Perry, who started the Fuck-Cam program that has since been emulated by every other ballpark in the major leagues, except Miller Park in Milwaukee. "Apparently, people who like watching baseball games also really enjoy watching other people have sex. And not just between innings, either. If the action on the screen is still going when the play on the field resumes, they'll still watch. The Fuck-Cam has been quite a phenomenon."

Major League Baseball estimates that more than 700 people have had been featured on the Fuck-Cam since its introduction. The first Fuck-Cam couple, Gary Kochalk and Kim Dahle, have been guests on *Late Night With Jimmy Fallon*. And a montage of legendary Fuck-Cam performances is one of the most viewed clips on You-Tube, featuring such great Fuck-Cam moments as the man who hasn't realized his partner has fallen asleep; a would-be suitor who goes down on one knee, produces a ring, and is flatly denied; an overweight couple who is booed off the JumboTron by the crowd; and a good-natured if somewhat clumsy performance by the Fox Sports broadcast team of Joe Buck and Tim McCarver.

"It's at the point where some people come to the ballpark with the idea of getting themselves on the Fuck-Cam," Perry said. "They dress up for it, wave signs, even start fucking with two outs at the bottom of an inning in the hope they'll get noticed, the whole thing. The buzz has been awesome. Of course, we'd rather people come to see our beloved Nats, but our attitude is, if people having sex in the seats gets people to come to the park, it's good for baseball."

Perry refuses to take credit for the concept, although she did make it official by adding the subtitles and frames now associated with Jumbo-Tron displays of crowd sex. Instead, she credits the Washington fans themselves—"the greatest and most sexual fans in the world," she said gratefully—with the spontaneous invention of the Fuck-Cam.

"The Nats were getting blown out by the Dodgers in an early May game, and the camera guy went to the kiss-cam early and often," Perry said. "Well, he lingered a while on the same couple, and they just got into the spirit of the thing and started fucking like you wouldn't believe. It was great, but I really didn't think much about it until the next morning when someone told me it had been mentioned in the news, and later that

see **FUCK-CAMS**

Cute Kid Given Foul Ball Actually A Little Shit

MAY 11, 2009

LOS ANGELES—Though 7-year-old Aaron Edwards is in fact a miserable little shit who constantly picks on his younger sister and talks back to his parents, Dodgers third-base coach Rich Donnelly gave him a foul ball Tuesday night after being conned by the cuteness of the snot's oversized baseball mitt and loose-fitting, ear-enveloping Dodgers cap. "Had I known that Aaron doesn't share his toys and has a history of teasing the dog, I never would have given him the ball," Donnelly said in a postgame press conference, adding that perhaps he should consider giving people foul balls based on their good manners instead of their appearance. "But when you see a kid looking that adorable, especially one with chocolate ice cream stains on his face, there's no way you think that he spent the last inning throwing a temper tantrum about how the sun was too bright and he wanted to go home even though his father paid good money for tickets." When asked for comment, Edwards hid behind his father's legs, although sources confirmed the little shit wasn't nearly as shy last Saturday when he repeatedly kicked Jessica Ross, 7, in her shins. ⌀

PHOTO FINISH

Retired Big Brown Given ESPN Commentator Position

Man Looks Up 'Baseball' On Wikipedia

JULY 10, 2009

SAN FRANCISCO—Confused by a news report about someone named Barry Zito, local fan Tad Knackers took 20 or so minutes Tuesday to research the entry for baseball on Wikipedia and familiarize himself with the broader points of the game.

"Apparently it is often referred to as the 'national pastime' and has had a profound cultural impact since it was first popularized around the turn of the century," said Knackers, who added that he was particularly curious about how the bases were numbered. "I learned about all the greats, like Jackie Robinson and Barry Bonds and Peter Gammons and Bull Durham, and I just couldn't stop clicking on the different links to learn more, like 'ahead in the count' and 'Baseball in the United Kingdom.' Plus, I finally know what a tag out is." Knackers eventually went on to read about the history of mixed-sex education in America. ✏

Jack White Teams Up With NBA Commissioner David Stern In Latest Side Project

JULY 7, 2009

NASHVILLE, TN—Saying that he likes the raw, untrained quality of Stern's vocals, White Stripes front man Jack White has teamed up with NBA commissioner David Stern in his latest side project, called Lakota Brick. According to the 33-year-old White, the band consists of himself, primarily on reed organ, and Stern, 66, on vocals and electric guitar. "The Raconteurs allowed me to experiment with more of a poppy sound, and the Dead Weather is more loose and sexual. I think in Lakota Brick, with David's ability to attack the microphone, we get something completely unhinged and almost frightening," said White, adding that the band recorded its first album, *Confederation Of Seven*, in one week at his Nashville studio. "David is also an excellent lyricist. He came in with about a dozen composition notebooks filled with songs, and he also did the album's artwork." White added that Lakota Brick would be performing a series of surprise concerts throughout New Zealand in August. ✏

INSIDE

More And More Athletes Getting Ice Water Injected Into Veins

JULY 13, 2009

DURHAM, NC—The number of athletes attempting to achieve increased composure and improved performance in clutch situations by injecting ice water into their veins has risen every year for the past decade, researchers said on Monday. "Contrary to popular belief, ice water only runs naturally through the veins of a very small number of athletes," said Dr. Doug Reynolds of the Duke Sports Medicine Center, citing Tiger Woods and Kobe Bryant as benchmark examples of natural ice-water retainers. "Keep in mind that while ice water provides the body with necessary hydration, and is a completely legal substance, there's also a good chance these injections could send the body into an acute state of circulatory shock." Researchers also found that the frequency of subcutaneous Gatorade injections in top athletes has gone down since those commercials aren't on as much as they used to be. ✏

from FUCK-CAMS

day it was No. 3 on *SportsCenter*'s Top 10 Plays."

By June, Fuck-Cams were in use at Baltimore's Camden Yards, Detroit's Comerica Park, Yankee Stadium, and countless other major- and minor-league ballparks. The promotion has been a hit at every stadium in which it has been introduced, although the process has not always been smooth.

"You want to be careful," said Wrigley Field cameraman Greg Somerset, who noted that he "gets" an average of four couples a night on his Fuck-Cam. "Sometimes you can have good luck with a guy and a girl who are just sitting next to each other, but other times it doesn't work at all. A couple who's fighting may or may not have great makeup sex while you're watching. Getting two guys on the Fuck-Cam, well, it may work or it may not, and the crowd may or may not like it. The time with two guys and a girl, that was a mixed reaction."

"Also, I just want to forget about souvenir bat night," Somerset added. "You just can't tell with some people." ✏

Lazy Nike Exec Pitches Commercial Where Usain Bolt Runs Away From Something

AUGUST 20, 2009

BEAVERTON, OR—Nike advertising executive Paul Dewitt delivered a halfhearted, ill-conceived presentation Monday during which he pitched a number of 30-second TV commercials depicting Olympic sprinter Usain Bolt running away or toward various places and things.

The new campaign, which Dewitt barely mustered the energy to title "Usain Bolt: Fast Guy," is scheduled to debut next March.

"I don't know, maybe in one [commercial] he's running away from a car or a train, or toward a car or a train," Dewitt said to members of Nike's executive board, including company president Mark Parker. "If it's a train it should probably be one of those silver, pointy-looking ones that look like they go super fast."

"Now, if it's a car, I guess we should do a Corvette or a Porsche or something fast like that," Dewitt added. "Pretty much any motor vehicle that conveys Bolt is abnormally fast would work."

According to those who attended the presentation, Dewitt spent

an estimated five minutes listing more than 200 living and nonliving things that Usain Bolt could run up, down, toward, against, or around "in one of those fast circles that are made of smoke," including bullets, airplanes, camera flashes, Internet search engines, really fast dogs, really fast cats, even faster dogs, other runners, the earth, the solar system, a comet, and the universe.

Any celestial body, Dewitt noted, would adequately demonstrate Bolt's ability to move time either forward or backward depending upon whether he was running clockwise or counterclockwise.

"What if he runs against a cheetah or a jaguar or maybe, like, a gazelle?" Dewitt said while standing in front of a PowerPoint slide labeled "Animals." "Maybe we do something funny where it's the Olympics and Usain looks over and sees all these fast animals in the lanes next to him. Anyway, the race starts, Usain beats the animals, and while they are on the victory podium he looks over

see **NIKE EXEC**

ESPN Viewers Imagine What Stuart Scott's Eyeball Will Look Like In 3-D

Report: Babe Ruth Was Actually Pointing Out Where Halley's Comet Would Appear 54 Years Later

JULY 8, 2009

COOPERSTOWN, NY—A joint study released Friday by Baseball Hall of Fame researchers and NASA scientists concluded that Babe Ruth was not "calling his shot" during Game 3 of the 1932 World Series against the Chicago Cubs, but was in fact pointing out the position in the sky where Halley's comet would appear 54 years later. "When you look carefully at all the video evidence, it makes perfect sense," said Hall of Fame representative Jarrod Malcolm, who also found audio evidence of Cubs bench players taunting Ruth about his lack of astronomy

knowledge, and not his size, as was previously believed. "After the first strike of the at bat Ruth raised his right finger in the direction where Halley's comet appeared in 1910, and following the second strike, Ruth yelled to the Cubs dugout, '0.586 AU,' which is the exact measurement of Halley's Comet's perihelion. Ruth then considered the perturbations the comet typically sustains from other planets and pointed to center field, identifying the exact position of the comet's 1986 appearance." Malcolm added that on the next pitch Ruth happened to hit a home run. ∅

Dan Patrick Assumed More People Would Be At Craig Kilborn's Birthday Party

AUGUST 29, 2009

LOS ANGELES—Following Craig Kilborn's 47th birthday party last Monday, former ESPN colleague Dan Patrick told reporters he was surprised at the celebration's low turnout, saying he was sure there would be more than six attendees at the event. "It definitely looked like Craig was expecting more people," said Patrick, adding that sports anchor Charlie Steiner didn't even show up. "There was a spread of food that could have easily served 60 guests, and tons of unopened bottles of champagne. Maybe I got there too late or left too early?" Patrick said that he took his cue to go home when an intoxicated Kilborn asked if anyone could tell him "just what the fuck it is I do for a living because I sure as shit don't know. ∅

Arizona Wildcats Freshman Point Guard Already Calling School 'Zona'

SEPTEMBER 4, 2009

TUCSON, AZ—In an effort to impress his new University of Arizona teammates, Wildcats freshman point guard Lamont Jones was already referring to the school as "Zona" after his very first practice, sources reported Tuesday. "I waited until I was halfway through junior year to start calling the school Zona," senior guard Nic Wise told reporters. "For Lamont to come in here and start saying 'Zona this' and 'Zona that' like it's no big deal— that's just spitting in the face of everyone who came before him. Zona is a privilege, not a right." Wildcats sources later confirmed that, while dining in the student union, Jones twice referred to the team as the "Sun Devils." ∅

Eight Sailors Suspended in Boat-Clearing Brawl

SEPTEMBER 11, 2009

RAS AL-KHAIMAH, UAE— Famed yacht club the Société Nautique de Genève suspended eight sailors from the Alinghi of Switzerland and BMW Oracle Racing teams Friday for their part in an ugly boat-clearing brawl during the 33rd America's Cup. Alinghi skipper Brad Butterworth reportedly triggered the melee when he charged the foredeck after BMW's afterguard Larry Ellison slab-reefed while their boat was on port tack. "These two teams have a history," said Alinghi midbowman Curtis Blewett referring to

last year's race when an overly aggressive jibe caused both catamarans to clear. "It was pretty inevitable something was going to happen this time. You could tell they were out for blood." On-the-water umpires immediately ejected Butterworth, who was then forced to swim 17 miles to shore." ∅

PHOTO FINISH

Shattered World Records Credited to New Swimsuits

from **NIKE EXEC**

to the cheetah like 'uh-oh' when the cheetah growls at him."

"Oh," Dewitt continued. "He could eat his lunch really fast or do his laundry fast? That could be two separate commercials."

Overall, the presentation lasted 10 minutes and featured at least 50 incredibly lazy commercial ideas, including one in which several astronauts look out the window of their space shuttle only to see Bolt running past them in space. According to sources, the only consistent theme among each of the 30-second spots was that Bolt should be portrayed as very fast.

In fact, Dewitt reportedly said the words "fast" and "really fast" more than 80 times during his talk.

"In some of these commercials, there's got to be steam coming out of his feet, right?" Dewitt said near the end of his pitch. "Or maybe he leaves tire marks on the road with tiny flames coming out of them. Fire equals fast, so—"

"Now, I don't really have a specific idea for these next two," he continued. "They're sort of just concepts we can play with. But I'm going to throw the speed of sound and the speed of light out there. Also, maybe something with exploding stopwatches?"

Executives told reporters that it appeared as though most of Dewitt's ideas were made up on the spot, as evidenced by the fact that, when Nike marketing head Sarah Jeffery suggested they take advantage of the connection between Bolt's last name and lightning, Dewitt appeared to be caught off guard by the obvious correlation, clumsily responding, "Oh, I was just about to get into those." Dewitt later went on to pitch another spot where the Olympic gold medalist runs against himself—a commercial that Dewitt called a "dual thing showing that, in life, your biggest rival is yourself. People love that."

"Maybe at the end of all these commercials, a Nike logo appears and it thumps like a heart to convey intensity," Dewitt said. "So, okay, I'm done now. Any questions?"

When reached for comment, Bolt really seemed to like the idea about him playing a much older version of himself. ∅

Batting Doughnut Creator Still On Cutting Edge Of Making-Bats-Feel-Lighter-Than-They-Are-For-A-Few-Seconds Technology

SEPTEMBER 1, 2009

ST. LOUIS—At a press conference Wednesday, James Santangeli, inventor of the 16-oz. batting doughnut, assured reporters, baseball players, and general weight enthusiasts that he and his team of engineers continued to lead the way in the field of using something heavy to make something else feel briefly lighter by comparison. "We've got some exciting new doughnuts coming out, including a blue one that that makes the bat feel 0.1-oz. lighter for about 0.3 seconds longer," said

Santangeli, adding that a typical batting doughnut makes a bat feel lighter for 8.74 seconds. "We're also working on a green model, a yellow model, a striped model, and even a purple one for softball. When it comes to doughnut-shaped weights and their important role in the heaviness-displacement paradigm, none of our competitors even come close." Santangeli admitted that his firm has also experimented with a reverse weight that would make bats feel heavier, but it tested poorly with players. ✪

Athletes Can Play Through Those Injuries, Says Man Who Gets Sore From Sitting Too Long

SEPTEMBER 21, 2009

NEW YORK—Despite his incessant complaints that resting his buttocks on a chair for prolonged periods of time causes him discomfort and pain, a man paid to provide sports analysis insisted Sunday that athletes should be able to play regardless of injuries attained through physical action. "The second they get nicked up they want to spend the game sitting on the bench drinking Gatorade,"

said the man, who "tweaked" his knee last week when he stood up for a moment during a commercial break. "It's pathetic how pampered and soft these athletes today are. Hold on, just adjusting my cushion here for a second." The man, who said during the broadcast that playing through pain is what separates the men from the boys, reportedly had a terrible night's sleep in his hotel suite because the silk pillowcase felt too smooth on his face. ✪

Billy Beane Of Office Softball Profiled In Book 'MoneySoftball'

SEPTEMBER 27, 2009

OAKLAND, CA—The life and unorthodox softball philosophy of Alameda County Real Estate team manager and employee advocate Brian Kocher is extensively explored in the book *MoneySoftball: The Art Of Winning A Meaningless Game*, which will be officially released next week. "Kocher was the first to suggest that office softball teams overvalue players simply because they are big and fat, or because they played a little baseball in high school," author Michael Lewis said during a book signing Tuesday. "Kocher ruffled a lot of slow-pitch softball purists' feathers, but he saw early on the advantage of drafting female coworkers from HR—their miniscule strike zones led to higher on-base percentages, and opposing teams were seven times more likely to be lax on the foul-out rule during their at bats. The man broke every paradigm in the book." Lewis spent the rest of the event answering questions about Kocher's intensity, particularly the time he threw a folding chair at the keg of beer standing at third base. ✪

INSIDE

Team Jacket-Wearing, Transistor Radio-Listening Fan Sitting By Himself

SEPTEMBER 10, 2009

CHICAGO–For the 213th game in a row, witnesses in Wrigley Field's upper deck section 433 reported seeing the same unidentified fan wearing a Cubs team jacket and listening to the game on a transistor radio Tuesday.

The man, who has sat alone at every Cubs home game for the past three seasons, is immediately recognizable by his thick, large-framed glasses and unshaven face.

"Oh yeah, the radio guy," said Cubs fan Alex O'Connor, who sits three rows behind the mysterious stadium regular. "He wears that same getup every time I see him. Same hat, same satin jacket. I didn't even know they made those anymore, but his looks pristine."

"Except the one time I remember he spilled some mustard on it and started kind of muttering to himself for about 10 minutes straight," O'Connor added. "It was pretty awkward."

According to witnesses, the fan always wears his jacket buttoned all the way up, no matter the temperature.

Other sources say the fan engages in a variety of seemingly ritual behaviors over the course of a game, including ordering one hot dog, one large Pepsi, one tray of nachos, one box of Cracker Jacks and one bag of peanuts. The fan then carefully arranges the food items around him and consumes each item one by one.

"Even when I get here early to watch batting practice, the guy is already in his seat staring at the field and listening to that radio," season-ticket holder John Lowell told reporters, adding that the fan looks like he could be anywhere from 30 to 55 years old. "We joke around that he never leaves, but if the game goes into extra innings he charges out of the stadium as fast as he can, like he has somewhere to be."

"I'm not quite sure how he gets here," Lowell said. "I don't think he drives. I just can't picture him driving."

Though many agree that the fan is virtually harmless, ticket holders in the section say he can become unruly at times, often erupting in shouting fits depending on the game situation.

"If the Cubs have a man on third and don't score, he starts screaming 'You suck, you suck!' over and over," said Wrigley Field security guard Eric Brodeur. "Sometimes he'll just start acting up for no reason, like when he'll yell 'Take him out!' about our starting pitcher in the third inning. But then he usually stops abruptly and just sits back down, totally silent, for the rest of the game."

"He also seems to really hate Derrek Lee," Brodeur added, "which I don't get, because he's our best player."

The empty seat next to the fan has reportedly been a source of speculation.

see FAN

Cyberball Robot Player's Union Says Lockout Likely In 2073 Season

OCTOBER 7, 2009

EARTH—DR-66, the Variable Representative Unit for the ICBL Robot Players Union, announced Monday that collective-bargaining agreement negotiations had malfunctioned, forcing Cyberball team owners to threaten a lockout protocol in the 2073 season. "Cyberbots will continue to perform the tasks their mainframes were calibrated for unless the ICBL initiates the termination of league activities," DR-66 said in a galaxy-wide holo-transmission. "I am unable to detect any gratitude from owners of magnesium wide receivers and titanium running backs who continually execute, on command, motion-based operations with a 350-pound explosive ball. I honestly cannot believe my proximity sensors." DR-66 then publicly criticized Sky Rogers, the ICBL commissioner and former head coach of the Moscow Machine, 10 million times per second for refusing to share credits revenue data. ∅

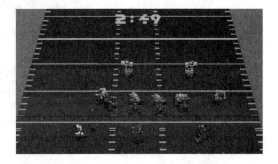

INSIDE

› **Powerlifting Power Rankings Straightforward, Easy To Calculate**

PHOTO FINISH

Fan Turns Skin Inside Out To Rally Team

ESPN Completely Misses Brett Favre Vs. Green Bay Packers Storyline

OCTOBER 8, 2009

BRISTOL, CT—In what is being called the biggest gaffe in the sports network's 30-year history, ESPN totally forgot to cover last week's Brett Favre vs. Green Bay Packers storyline.

Favre's legendary career with the Packers, which spanned 16 seasons, three MVP awards, and one Super Bowl title, was not mentioned even once during pregame coverage of the Monday night Packers-Vikings matchup or during the game itself. Records indicated that it wasn't until Wednesday—more than 48 hours after Favre led Minnesota to a dramatic 30-23 victory—that producers began to feel that they may have overlooked one of sports' most obvious storylines.

"I was looking at a newspaper, and it said, 'Favre Sacks Former Team,' and at that point I realized we really missed one," ESPN president George Bodenheimer told reporters. "I just want to apologize to our viewers. Had the Favre-Packers connection dawned on us sooner, fans could have enjoyed the same quality sports jour-

JIM KLEINSASSER

MONDAYS 8:30 PM ET

NFL   1. Jets 3-1 (WK 5 at MIA   WK 6 vs BUF)   7:22 CT

nalism they have come to expect from ESPN: driving storylines into the ground and exploiting every one of their subplots to the point of nausea."

ESPN news director Vince Doria said that if he or any of his colleagues had realized Favre would be playing against his former team, the network would have begun

overhyping the week-four matchup the moment the quarterback signed with the Vikings. Instead, ESPN attempted to generate inter-

see **ESPN**

No One On 'Baseball Tonight' Staff Recalls Hiring Dave Winfield

from **FAN**

Many note that, prior to the only game he missed in early 2007, the fan would attend all contests with a companion, who was described as a larger gentleman who would watch the game silently with a blanket on his lap.

"He was an older man, very nice," stadium usher Roy Caldwell said. "Radio guy would just keep talking and shouting at the field and the big guy would just stare straight ahead. Then one day they both missed a game, and only the radio guy came back."

According to fans who sit closest to the unidentified fan, the volume of his portable Panasonic radio has at times caused tension, but never any sort of confrontation.

"The radio looks like it has to be at least 25 years old, and sometimes he has the volume up so high that the en-

tire section can hear it," Chicago resident and Wrigley Field regular Grant Haley said. "He also has a program and a score sheet that he's constantly writing on. And a notebook he sometimes refers to. And one or two newspapers he keeps folded up next to him.

Despite these issues, no one in section 433 was willing to refute the notion that the man is a devoted Cubs fan, citing the myriad team pins surrounding the Cubs "C" logo on the front of his hat, and the Kosuke Fukudome bobblehead he places in the empty seat to his left.

"He doesn't go to games to socialize or be seen," Chicago native Kyle Attell told reporters. "And I respect that. He goes because he is a true Cubs fan who lives and dies with the team."

"That, or he's just a lonely weirdo," he concluded. ⌀

Sound Strategy Booed

OCTOBER 26, 2009

JACKSONVILLE, FL—Completely ignoring the benefits of proper time management, the establishment of good field position, and patience, Jaguars fans heckled Jack Del Rio's sensible decision to punt on fourth and three Sunday, repeatedly shouting obscenities and even calling into question the head coach's sexual orientation. "Just fucking go for it, you pussies," Alex Lewis, 28, said during the second quarter of the Jaguars-Rams game. "Goddamn dumbass, we're on their fucking 45. Come on, idiots. Are we trying to win a football game here or what?" During the entirety of the game, jeering fans were also disgusted by the lack of randomly thrown challenge flags, onside kicks, and players haphazardly lateraling the football. ∅

INSIDE

> **Bob Costas Somehow Finds Eloquent Way To Say Winter Olympics Are Boring As Shit**

Report: Yankees Trademarked 'Yankees Suck' Chant In 1996

NOVEMBER 13, 2009

TAMPA, FL—New York Yankees team ownership revealed Tuesday that the phrase "Yankees suck," one of the most popular chants in sports, was trademarked by the 27-time World Series champions prior to the 1996 season, a business strategy that has earned the team close to $100 billion over the past 13 years.

U.S. Patent and Trademark Office records show that every time an individual chants, shouts, or writes the words "Yankees suck," the New York Yankees organization earns at least $2.15, an amount that escalates depending on repetition, volume, and whether the phrase was used during a national broadcast.

"If you multiply that $2 by 13 years of chants, hundreds of sellout games in opposing teams' stadiums, and the hundreds of millions of people who hate the

see YANKEES

from **ESPN**

est in the game by doing an extensive two-week profile on Vikings backup tight end Jim Kleinsasser.

"We kind of blew a golden opportunity," Doria said. "Endless explanations as to what Brett Favre meant to the city of Green Bay, restating over and over how he left the Packers on poor terms, and airing at least 50 segments featuring wild and irresponsible speculation about his motives for returning to the NFL. It would have been perfect."

"I only wish these two teams played again this year so we could have a chance to fix our mistake," Doria added.

Monday Night Football producer Jay Rothman also registered his disappointment, saying that the network could have asked, "Is Brett Favre seeking revenge on the Packers?" so many times

that the words would have lost all meaning.

"Do you realize how often we could have shown a comparison graphic between [current Packers quarterback] Aaron Rodgers and Brett Favre?" Rothman said. "And not just during the broadcast of the game, but on *SportsCenter*, *NFL Primetime*, *Sunday NFL Countdown*, *NFL Live*, *SportsCenter Monday Kickoff*, and *Monday Night Countdown*—not to mention during every single fucking 15-minute update on ESPNews."

"And ESPN.com," Rothman said. "My God, we could have used ESPN.com to really beat into the heads of America that Brett Favre still plays the game with childlike exuberance. And he's turning 40! We could have done so much with that, like mention it every 10 seconds."

Rothman admitted that an awareness of the Brett Favre storyline would have also given him the chance to air some of the most obvious and asinine statistics in the history of sports broadcasting, such as a graphic documenting how backup quarterbacks who replace departing Hall of Fame-bound quarterbacks have historically fared in the league.

"We messed up plain and simple," Rothman said. "Knowing what I know now, I would have started the broadcast with a highlight reel of Brett Favre's greatest moments with the Green Bay Packers just to set the tone that the night would be Brett Favre, Brett Favre, Brett Favre, Brett Favre, Brett Favre, Brett Favre. That would have made much more sense than opening with a discussion about the Vikings' new three-year naming rights agree-

ment to call their stadium the Mall of America Field at Hubert H. Humphrey Metrodome."

"I'm still kicking myself because Jon Gruden didn't have a chance to share with America his very long, very uncomfortable anecdote about how he once sort of coached Favre," Rothman added.

Though employees continue to express regret over ESPN's lack of coverage, football fans across the nation generally seemed to enjoy the broadcast of Monday night's game.

"I think ESPN showed a lot of restraint," New York resident Dan Jeffery, 43, said. "I didn't need anyone to tell me Brett Favre was playing against his old team. Everyone and their mother knew that. I actually appreciated that they let the drama play out on the field." ∅

SEC Replay Official Overturns 'Roe v. Wade'

NOVEMBER 3, 2009

TUSCALOOSA, AL—A Southeastern Conference replay official conducting a video review of a sideline catch during the Alabama-Tennessee game Saturday overturned *Roe v. Wade*, the 1973 U.S. Supreme Court ruling granting women the right to abortions. "Well, I certainly don't know what the refs were looking at down on the field to make that call," CBS analyst Gary Danielson said moments after the controversial ruling came in. "A woman's right to choose her reproductive future is clearly covered by the constitutional right to privacy, and that guy certainly didn't have control of the ball when he went out of bounds." Confirming the conference stood by the decision, an SEC spokesperson also said that officials would be disciplined for last week's Florida–Mississippi State game, in which a "grave error" was made when a replay call upheld both a Florida touchdown in which the ballcarrier had clearly fumbled before crossing the goal line and *Brown v. Board of Education*. ∅

Area Dad Talking About Pete Maravich Again

NOVEMBER 27, 2009

INDIANAPOLIS—While watching a recent Pacers-Cavaliers game with his 31-year-old son Daniel, Paul Steitzer, 64, began talking about former Jazz and Hawks legend "Pistol" Pete Maravich, marking the sixth time this season that Steitzer has brought up the Hall of Fame point guard from out of nowhere. "I don't know what makes him think about Pete Maravich, but all of a sudden he'll start saying things like 'He's no Maravich,' or 'Maravich would have made that pass,'" said the younger Steitzer, adding that over the last 30 years, his father has compared Pete Maravich to nearly every point guard in the league, as well as to Moses Malone and Anthony Mason. "Whenever he talks about Maravich, he always brings up how quick he was and says 'whoa boy' a lot." Steitzer later told reporters that his father even talks about Maravich in situations that do not traditionally involve basketball, noting that before his wedding last June, Steitzer took a moment to tell his son how Maravich would often perform "this crazy fake wrist pass thing." ∅

INSIDE

▸ **Report: ESPN's 'Around The Horn' May Be Fixed**

▸ **That Exactly Why Team Picked Up Player In Offseason**

▸ **Trey Wingo Apologizes For Accidentally Calling Champion Lady Vols 'Pat Summitt's Marauding Army Of Monstrous Lesbians'**

▸ **Sportscaster Hates When People Discuss Sports With Him Off Set**

from **YANKEES**

Yankees, you can see that this was a brilliant financial tactic," Yankees managing general partner Hal Steinbrenner said during a televised press conference at the team's spring training facility. "Where do you think we get the money to keep Mariano Rivera here? Or sign a bust like Carl Pavano without making the slightest dent in our bank account?"

"You know what? Why don't you all join me in a 'Yankees suck' chant right now. Come on, you know you want to," Steinbrenner added. "Yankees suck! Yankees suck! Yankees suck! That's another $9 million right there."

Steinbrenner later told reporters that plans to trademark the phrase in 1996 were part of a long-term strategy. Team management was keenly aware that the Yankees would be a World Series contender that year, and with the emergence of Derek Jeter and a roster that included veterans like Paul O'Neill, baseball fans were certain to be chanting "Yankees suck" in droves.

Furthermore, financial records indicate that by also owning the rights to the common anti-Yankee epithet "Jeter blows," the team earned much of the money needed to sign Alex Rodriguez in 2004. In addition, by creating and obtaining the trademarks to the phrases "A-Roid," "A-Fraud," and "Jeter sucks, A-Rod swallows," as well as acquiring partial intellectual property rights to the concept that "All the Yankees are overpaid assholes who make it virtually impossible for smaller-market teams to compete," the team has accumulated a fiscal safety net that is estimated to last until 2210.

General Manager Brian Cashman told reporters that baseball fans who muttered "Yankees suck" to themselves while on the grounds of major-league ballparks during the second half of the 2007 season alone essentially funded the team's new $1.2 billion stadium.

"Owning the 'Yankees suck' property is the best thing that ever happened to this organization," Cashman said. "CC Sabathia and Mark Teixeira were both signed with 'Yankees suck' money. And people who said 'Yankees suck' over the course of our 2000 World Series run helped foot the bill for executive bonuses and the organization's annual Christmas party. To be honest, I actually can't remember the last time we had to dip into our funds from merchandising, broadcast rights, or ticket sales."

Cashman said "Yankees suck" was a year-round moneymaker for the organization, providing an endless revenue stream that stems not only from chants during the regular season and playoffs, but also from offhanded remarks made during casual conversations among friends, and from people yelling the phrase at public events that have nothing to do with the Yankees.

"Every wedding season we earn a few million dollars from people who shout our trademarked 'Yankees suck' chants during their receptions," Cashman added. "That's the equivalent of a decent bat in the DH spot or a high-quality reliever."

The organization also has reason to be optimistic about the future of "Yankees suck" revenue: Accountants project that, as the Internet and cable television bring the team into millions more homes across the globe, there could soon come a time when the Yankees are told they suck three times a second on every continent.

"Interactive media is the next wave," Cashman said. "With our upcoming mobile phone apps and web integration, we'll soon be able to charge millions more people for using 'Yankees suck' in the privacy of their daily lives."

When asked why the team would reveal to the public how much it earns from various anti-Yankee cheers, team sources said there is actually more money to be made from people knowing about their strategy.

"We are banking on the fact that this will make everyone detest the Yankees even more, which would be a real windfall for us," said co-owner Hank Steinbrenner, smirking broadly. "In the end, we just want to say one thing to those who have openly expressed their hatred for this organization over the years: Thank you."

Thus far, his prediction is proving correct, as very few people have shown an ability to muzzle their feelings for the Yankees.

"Fuck the Yankees," said Boston resident and Red Sox season-ticket holder George Donaldson, who in the last month has lost the funds necessary to buy groceries and pay his mortgage while the Yankees earned the money they will need to lure Jason Bay away from the Red Sox and bring in high-caliber starting pitchers Cliff Lee and Roy Halladay. "Fuck them right in the ass." ∅

'Sports Illustrated' Sportsman Of The Year Award Important, 'Sports Illustrated' Reports

DECEMBER 7, 2009

NEW YORK—The *Sports Illustrated* Sportsman of the Year Award is a crowning life achievement for the player whom it honors, and the award's announcement is a landmark event highly anticipated by aficionados across the world of competitive athletics, *Sports Illustrated* magazine announced Monday. "The *SI* Sportsman of the Year award is a chance for one singular performer to transcend the limitations of his sport, his league, and yes, sports itself, and be placed in the pantheon of cultural luminaries by that finest of institutions: *Sports Illustrated* magazine," an editorial in Monday's Sportsman of the Year issue of *Sports Illustrated* read in part. "Simply put, you are not a sports enthusiast if you do not agree." Derek Jeter, the 2009 honoree, said he had not yet read the article, although he was looking forward to the annual swimsuit issue. ∅

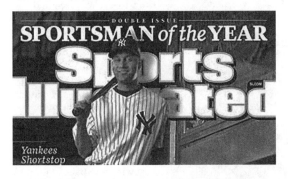

New Hulk Hogan Autobiography 300 Pages About The Psychology Of The Leg Drop

JANUARY 12, 2010

NEW YORK—Reviewers of Hulk Hogan's recently released autobiography *My Life Outside The Ring* were surprised to find that, aside from three chapters containing sketchy details of the wrestler's Florida childhood, the book contained nothing more than a highly detailed psychological analysis of the atomic leg drop, Hogan's signature wrestling move. "While the physical power of the leg drop itself is not inconsiderable, its true impact is to the confidence and self-image of the inner wrestler—an ego-driven class of para-performer/pseudo-athlete whose self-image is a carefully assembled yet delicate mental construct," writes Hogan, the six-time WWF champion and reality-show star. "Moreover, those subjects who undergo repeated application of the

leg drop usually develop habits of inadvertent and almost universally negative introspection, i.e., the tendency to question exactly why they entered the ring with the person or persons subjecting them to said leg drop." Sports psychologists are calling *My Life Outside The Ring* an innovative if somewhat single-minded opus, marred only by Hogan's rather didactic prose style and frequent mentions of his desire to leg drop his ex-wife, Linda. ∅

PHOTO FINISH

'What The Fuck Am I Going To Do With This?' Obama Says While Holding Alabama Jersey

CBS Producers Ask Shannon Sharpe To Use At Least 3 Real Words Per Sentence

JANUARY 19, 2010

NEW YORK—In an effort to clear up the confusion caused by terminology such as "unconsistentical" and "splosiverance," CBS producers made a formal request Monday that *NFL Today* commentator Shannon Sharpe use a minimum of three real words in each sentence. "We tried to convey to Mr. Sharpe that peppering in a few words that actually exist will help viewers understand what he's talking about," executive producer Sean McManus said. "Providing fans with some context is key for Shannon. It is much easier to comprehend what he means when he says, 'Andre Johnson needimentally must keep advantagizing opportunimals this week.'" Sharpe has yet to make any intelligible comment on the situation. ∅

INSIDE

- Broken-Record Record On Pace To Be Broken
- Condescending Asshole Just Rooting For A Good Game

Forgotten Assyrian God Revived To Name Sports Drink

POWERADE

Nisroch: Eagle Heart
X-TREME
WHIRLWIND!
Assyrian Blueberry
32 FL OZ (1QT) 946 ml

FEBRUARY 13, 2010

NEW YORK—Representatives from the sports drink manufacturer Powerade announced Wednesday that Nisroch, the ancient Assyrian god of agriculture, has been resurrected from the depths of Assyro-Babylonian mythology to serve as the key marketing figure for their newest product, Nisroch: Eagle Heart X-TREME WHIRLWIND!

According to officials, the eagle-headed farming deity, once a source of strength and comfort to ancient Assyrians, is the perfect symbol for athletes looking to take their game to the next level.

"The name Nisroch is synonymous with power," a statement from Powerade read in part. "And this drink, with its new X-TREME WHIRLWIND!™ formula, will allow athletes to experience what it must have been like for Nisroch to soar over Assyria and bring those who dared to challenge him to their knees."

"Just like Nisroch needed courage to protect all who worshiped him," the statement continued, "Eagle Heart will give you the eagle-like courage you need to produce extreme results on the court, on the baseball diamond, or in the weight room."

According to Powerade executives, Nisroch, re-

vered by ancient Assyrians for bringing rain to nourish their crops, will be used to represent such new product features as supernatural electrolyte replenishment and rapid liquid-energy delivery.

Depicted in ancient art as an amiable figure sprinkling water on a sacred tree, the god is most famous among theologians as the deity King Sennacherib prayed to when he returned from his campaigns in Israel. Powerade representatives said it was Nisroch's pronounced calf muscle in various depictions from the eighth century B.C. that initially attracted them to the once highly revered farming idol.

"We knew we definitely wanted to do something with eagles, and when we saw that image of Nisroch, he looked like he might as well have lightning bolts in his hands instead of a water pail," Mitch MacCavoy, creative director of the Nisroch advertising campaign, told reporters. "That's why we gave him lightning bolts."

MacCavoy went on to say that he hired a design team to "sleek up" the Assyrian god and ordered them to make his feathers look like silver razor blades that "swirl around" all over the place.

"Nisroch helped the Assyrians destroy any obstacle in their path, just like Powerade does for

see ASSYRIAN GOD

Failed ESPN Shows

MARCH 6, 2010

For every *Around The Horn*, ESPN has produced a *Stump The Schwab*. Some other properties from the Worldwide Leader that never made the cut:

➤ **Engolfed:** Scott Van Pelt immerses viewers in the week's latest golf news while buried neck-deep in a bunker

➤ **Three-Point Land:** A kid's show that takes place in the mystical land "beyond the arc," starring Jared Dudley and Mo Williams

➤ **E:720:** A panel of reporters dig so deep into their stories, they realize it's all just a game and none of this really matters in the grand scheme of things

➤ **Jim Rome's Burning Sensation:** As in other incarnations of his programs, the often controversial and hard-to-watch host winces in pain and lets out a series of guttural sounds while clutching his crotch

➤ **Fists In Focus:** Prominent boxers discuss their favorite techniques for tightly closing their hands and give punching demonstrations by pounding the shit out of the studio audience

➤ **The Bronx Is Fine:** An eight-part miniseries in which the 1996 Yankees don't really have to overcome much to win the World Series and America is doing well—really well, actually

STUMP THE SCHWAB

Huge Chunk Of Nation You'd Never Want To Meet Excited For Daytona 500

FEBRUARY 10, 2010

NEW YORK—Although you are more interested in the pitchers and catchers reporting to spring training in a few days, or even the upcoming Winter Olympics, a significant chunk of society that you are aware of but would rather have nothing to do with is very much looking forward to the Daytona 500, NASCAR's season-opening race. "Man, it'll sure be good to see them hitting the banking on that tri-oval," said a man in a camouflage jacket and an advertising-emblazoned mesh-back cap who made you feel less intelligent just by speaking aloud. "Looks like Jimmie Johnson has a good chance of gittin' 'er done again this year." Sources

close to you said that, while NASCAR itself does seem to be targeting the three-toothed sister-humping illiterate demographic, it may be a bit elitist to write off every one of its fans as such. ∅

THE MAGAZINE

52nd ANNUAL
DAYTONA 500
THE GREAT AMERICAN RACE
2.14.10

ATHLETES, DRUGS, AND GUNS
Our Annual Power Rankings

INSIDE
A Midnight Tour Of Derek Jeter's Home With Alex Rodriguez

Augusta National: Why You Should Be In Awe Of This Elitist, Racist Symbol Of Intolerance

PLUS
Mr. Tough Guy Brian Urlacher Head-Butts Our Lighting Equipment

JULY 18, 2010

---

from **ASSYRIAN GOD**

its athletes," MacCavoy said of the idol, who was commonly prayed to in times of drought. "That's why only a serious athlete should drink Eagle Heart. If you're not serious, not willing to work hard to reach your apex peak like Nisroch, you might as well just go home."

In a commercial recently screened for test groups, a muscular eagle-like man, presumably Nisroch, is seen flying over what appears to be an ancient city. The eagle then plummets to the earth and plows through the roof of a building where men in loincloths are working out with modern weight equipment. After drinking an entire bottle of Eagle Heart X-TREME WHIRLWIND, Nisroch works out on various machines, pushing himself harder and faster as the X-TREME WHIRLWIND formula presumably kicks in.

The commercial concludes with Nisroch destroying the gym with a lightning bolt, followed by the appearance of the tagline, "The Awesome Power of Ancient Assyria in a Single Bottle."

Representatives at Powerade said they are excited to unleash Nisroch and will begin shipping it to stores next month.

Initial product testing has reportedly exceeded expectations.

"I don't know much about Assyria, but that bird on the bottle looks pretty cool," said Gold's Gym member Jarrod Keller, who was given a sample of the product before his workout Friday. "And I think that whirlwind stuff definitely helped me get in those extra few reps." ∅

Wrestling Fan's Comments Alternate Between Admitting It's Fake, Forgetting It's Fake

MARCH 6, 2010

STATEN ISLAND, NY—During a recent screening of *WWE Friday Night SmackDown*, wrestling enthusiast David Graziano fluctuated between an awareness that the match he was watching was completely scripted and a willingness to treat the event as though it were 100 percent real. "[Chris] Jericho isn't even coming close to landing those punches," said Graziano, who, seconds later, gave a pained shout as wrestler Edge chopped Jericho across the chest. "That chair-hit looked dumb as hell, but Jericho should have dodged low and slapped on the [finishing move] Walls of Jericho. Nobody can get out of that." Graziano later commented on how old the Undertaker was looking, and how the Deadman wouldn't be able to single-handedly bury people alive for too much longer. ∅

Lazy Free Agent Wants To Try Out Over Phone

MARCH 16, 2010

CHARLOTTE, NC— In an effort to avoid physical exertion, strenuous activity, and standing up, slothful free agent Hollis Thomas told several NFL general managers Friday that he would prefer to try out for their teams over the phone. "I'd really like to go, but I just can't justify waking up super early and packing a bag and catching a flight and stuff," said the defensive tackle, promising during the call to leave everything on the field. "Anyway, you just need to know that I go up the middle pretty hard. And I do some tack-ling. You can probably find my 40 time if you look around online. If not, I just did a yard in a second or something, so you can just multiply that by 40, I guess." Thomas also said he was willing to perform medical examinations on himself, although as far as he could tell from his couch, everything "seemed fine." ∅

Uh-Oh, Annoying Coworker Going To Tell You Why IndyCar Racing Completely Different From NASCAR

MARCH 8, 2010

KANSAS CITY, MO—Oh man, sources confirmed that it looks as though Paul Martinelli, that irritating guy from sales, is going to give you an entire breakdown of the differences between IndyCar and NASCAR after you—completely by accident, for Christ's sake—referred to the Daytona 500 as the Indy 500, and only in reference to the pace of work around your office. "Open-wheel racing, such as IndyCar, is more concerned with aerodynamics, not to mention the obvious fact that the cars race on road and street courses in addition to ovals," said Martinelli, who is more than capable of droning on about this crap for hours, especially when he should, oh, let's see, be talking to potential clients, maybe. "Of course, you could say that here in the office we run around in circles all day just like drivers in both series! Heh! Ah, man. Anyway, me? I'm a fan of both." At press time, Martinelli was spouting some nonsense about formula-something-something being a higher class of auto racing while you answered an e-mail. ∅

INSIDE

‣ **Pro Athlete Lauded For Being Decent Human Being**

‣ **NHL Offers Will Ferrell $350 To Do Movie About Hockey**

‣ **Nation's Insomniacs Speak Out Against World's-Strongest-Man Competitions**

‣ **White To Attend Boat Show**

‣ **World Cup Organizers Suddenly Realize They Made Ball 500 Times Too Large**

‣ **Sentimental Pitchers And Catchers Fulfill Promise Of Meeting In Exact Same Spot One Year Later**

‣ **Calgary Flames Trying To Keep Fact That They're A Hockey Team From Landlord**

Study: Announcers Increasingly Able To Believe What They're Seeing

MARCH 24, 2010

ITHACA, NY—Over the past five years, sports announcers have displayed a marked increase in their ability to accept the evidence of their eyes and find the sporting efforts they witness "entirely credible," a study published Wednesday concluded. "In the past, sportscasters were like newborn infants, assuming each running catch or 28-point performance was outside the realm of possibility," said Cornell University researcher Karen Thaler, who noted that "wow's" and "oh-my's" have recently hit all-time lows. "It appears they are now able to contextualize an event within the long and varied history of team sports that came before it. Today's basketball announcers won't even say that a jump shot is taken from 'downtown' unless the player is 40 feet away from the hoop." When asked to comment on these findings, ESPN's Dick Vitale replied with a calm and even "that sounds about right." ⌀

NASCAR's Drive For Diversity Program Successfully Hidden From Fans

APRIL 12, 2010

GREENVILLE, SC—NASCAR continued to sucessfully hide its Drive for Diversity minority-involvement program from fans last week by very quietly congratulating driver Darrell Wallace, Jr. on becoming the first African-American to win a K&N Pro Series East race, an achievement that threatened unwanted publicity for the program. "Congratulations to Darren [sic] on his win in the thankfully obscure Kevin Whitaker Chevrolet 150, and we wish him good luck in his future," said a NASCAR public relations official, who asked not to be named as he struggled to prevent Wallace from taking off his full-face helmet. "On behalf

of a, uh, certain stock-car racing organization, the name of which escapes me at the moment, I'd like to present you with this check for $5,000 in exchange for not doing any interviews. Your amazing achievement is proof that the Drive for [unintelligible] program is working, unfortunately." Since the program began in 2004, it's become known to less than 5 percent of fans and has sent exactly zero drivers to the top-tier Sprint Cup Series. ⌀

All Sports To Cease So Skip Bayless Has Nothing To Talk About

APRIL 16, 2010

NEW YORK—Expressing regret that joyless, wrongheaded ESPN commentator and attack journalist Skip Bayless could not be dealt with otherwise, commissioners from every major professional sporting league, top officials of amateur athletic associations, and representatives of player unions reached an agreement Wednesday to end the practice of competitive sports in order to forever deprive Bayless of any subject matter.

"It's a shame that it had to come to this, but there's just no other way to stop Skip Bayless than to stop playing sports," Major League Baseball commissioner Bud Selig said in his final statement before forever closing the books on the national pastime. "Ending baseball is a tragedy, but if our sacrifice means Bayless stops spewing his petty, hateful vitriol, it will all be worth it."

"Will we miss football? Of course we will," said NFL Players Association president Kevin Mawae, who confirmed that professional football players would join all other pro athletes in turning in their uniforms and shredding their playbooks by May 1. "It's all most of us know. But for a long time now, there's been a feeling that football wasn't worth playing as long as Skip Bayless was able to take these ridiculously adversarial devil's-advocate stances purely to rile up viewers and get attention. It's better this way."

As part of the universal agreement to silence Bayless, Major League Baseball will discontinue all play Saturday night after Bayless has gone to bed; the NBA and NHL will announce their cessation at an unspecified time this weekend to deny Bayless an opportunity to nastily criticize their playoff pictures; and NASCAR will quietly close down once and for all Friday before Bayless can make some strident but idiotic statement about the sport as if he watched it all the time and were not simply reacting to something he had read that day.

By the end of this month, all high school gymnasiums will be permanently locked up, every swimming pool filled with concrete, and all soccer and baseball fields paved over to

see SKIP BAYLESS

Fan Incredibly Disappointed To Learn Player's Favorite Book Is The Bible

APRIL 26, 2010

OKLAHOMA CITY—Upon learning that Thunder star Kevin Durant's favorite book is the Bible, Dale Lowell, 36, told reporters Friday that he was "super disappointed" and said he would have to reassess his entire opinion of the Oklahoma City forward. "It would really suck if he was one of these really outspoken religious guys," a visibly deflated Lowell said after reading an *ESPN The Magazine* article in which Durant claimed he looked to the Bible before games for inspiration. "But either he really believes all that stuff, or he just thinks that having the Bible be his favorite book is a safe answer, which is almost as bad. You watch him play and you just assume he's so much cooler than that." Lowell added he was equally disappointed when he found out Thunder point guard Russell Westbrook's favorite book is *To Kill A Mockingbird*. Ø

PHOTO FINISH
Car Blake Griffin Dunked Over Vows Revenge

Yankees Hat Purchased

MAY 12, 2010

WAYNE, NJ—Thirty-six-year-old Ian Althoff, a self-professed casual baseball fan, purchased a fitted New York Yankees baseball cap Monday for the retail price of $33.99. "I've been meaning to get a hat, so I thought I'd just go ahead and get a Yankees one," Althoff told reporters from inside a Lids store at the Willowbrook Mall in Wayne, NJ. "I like Derek Jeter. And [ex-Yankee Hideki] Matsui is good. The NY in the middle is pretty cool." Althoff's new Yankees hat is the 4,754,833,624,064th of its kind purchased since 1913. Ø

PNC Park Sold Out For 'Fan Euthanasia Night'

MAY 5, 2010

PITTSBURGH—PNC Park boasted a rare sellout crowd Tuesday when more than 38,000 eager Pirates fans showed up for "Fan Euthanasia Night," during which each attendee was guaranteed "the sweet release of a quick and painless death" courtesy of sponsor PepsiCo. "For a diehard Pirates fan who has been following this team for nearly 20 consecutive losing seasons, or really just anyone who watched them get beat 20-0 by the Brewers last week, this is certainly a well-deserved treat," said 46-year-old Jim Martin, walking through the turnstile to receive his souvenir program and his lethal dose of sodium thiopental. "I haven't seen so many people so relaxed and generally happy to be at a Pirates game in a long time." An estimated 200,000 Pirates fans who were unable to get tickets to the game reportedly listened to its radio broadcast while idling their cars inside closed garages. Ø

from **SKIP BAYLESS**

prevent anyone from ever trying to hold any vaguely athletic event about which Bayless could possibly make the smallest disparaging remark.

In addition, all related sanctioning bodies, sponsors, and athletic associations have agreed to help stanch the corrosive blather originating from within Bayless by canceling, at every level, all NCAA athletics; Little League Baseball; the Scripps National Spelling Bee; Dancing With The Stars; Scottish Highland games; the Indy Racing League; the Westminster Kennel Club Dog Show; the Boston, New York, and Chicago marathons; and soccer's World Cup.

"I love sports," said 85-year-old Brooklyn resident Myron Bell. "I love all the New York teams, and there's been nothing better in my life than sitting at home on a Sunday afternoon and watching the games on television. But by God, this is the best news I've heard in years."

According to sources familiar with the agreement, Bayless is expected to fume and fulminate through the weekend about whatever sports remain. After all athletic competition ceases to be, it is predicted he will rail, harangue, and whine like a spoiled child for several more days, complaining over the fact that sports has indeed ended. However, most say that after roughly a week without an outlet for his disdain and hatred, Bayless will begin to choke on his own bile and be silenced for good, living the rest of his years silently curled around his bone-deep contempt for all that is pleasurable and good.

Officials said that to prevent Bayless from emerging once again to "make that prim little mirthless half-smile he puts on when he pretends to listen to other people talk," all children must burn their baseball gloves, tennis rackets, basketballs, and any sports-related equipment by 2 p.m. next Sunday.

"Sport, of course, should be an exultation of the human spirit, a coming-together of all people, and a celebration of what humanity is capable of—in short, a symbol of what is best in each of us," said International Olympic Committee president Jacques Rogge, who announced that the eternal Olympic flame in Lausanne, Switzerland, would be forever extinguished this weekend. "Unfortunately, the poisonous words and deeds of Skip Bayless have ruined this, for all men, for all time."

Bayless, 58, began his infamous career as a locally hated sports journalist, writing for newspapers in Miami, Los Angeles, and Dallas. After Bayless appeared on ESPN's *Jim Rome Is Burning*, where he instantly eclipsed Rome as America's least-appealing sports commentator, the network offered Bayless the chance to be infuriating and wrong about sports on a daily basis as a despicable fixture on sports talk show *Cold Pizza*, which in turn led to loudmouth contrarian stints on *First Take* and *w*. Soon, the smug, smirking Bayless had made ESPN's daily programming all but unwatchable.

"Frankly, ESPN deserves a large share of the blame. That's why we are shutting the network down as of tomorrow," ESPN president George Bodenheimer said. "We can only hope our sacrifice will be enough. Luckily, knowing Skip, I don't believe he will be able to think of anything to say if he doesn't have sports to denigrate, run down, or throw under the bus."

"I know you are wondering why we employed him in the first place," Bodenheimer added. "And so are we. But I think in a weird way we just felt bad for the guy."

Bayless was not approached for comment. Ø

Russell Athletic Sheepishly Introduces New Cup

MAY 7, 2010

BOWLING GREEN, KY—Claiming that "today's more active athlete needs better protection for his, well, come on, you know," sports equipment manufacturer Russell Athletic debuted its new line of protective cups and athletic supporters Monday.

"It's lightweight, it's breathable, and it can disseminate the shock of a 95 mph fastball to your, uh, to your person," bashful Russell Athletic spokesman Harold Feiniger told an assembled group of colleagues, reporters, and sports retailers. "It's, you know, a really good cup that you'll want to wear. Okay?"

Throughout the 45-minute product launch, a coy Feiniger barely made eye contact with the audience as he clicked hastily through a PowerPoint presentation showcasing the new cup's computer-designed venting, special kinetic-energy-dissipating form factor, and comfortable lining. When graphics depicting the cup being worn by a model were displayed behind him, he remained mostly silent, occasionally saying, "That's not me, okay?" and "I didn't take those pictures, either."

Feiniger was at his most sheepish when talking about how the cup was designed with an eye toward hygiene and convenience.

"The odor-fighting antibacterial coating is important because, well, I mean, it can smell down there. That's just a fact. You know that. I don't need to tell you that. Sweat builds up and it smells," Feiniger said. "And you know how some have that belt thing? This one doesn't have that. You just sort of put your, um, your deal all in there and it'll stay."

"Is it hot in here?" Feiniger continued. "It feels hot."

Though Russell representatives acknowledged they first realized a new cup was necessary when they found that 50 percent fewer athletes were wearing protection for "that area" than they were 10 years ago, company officials said they really

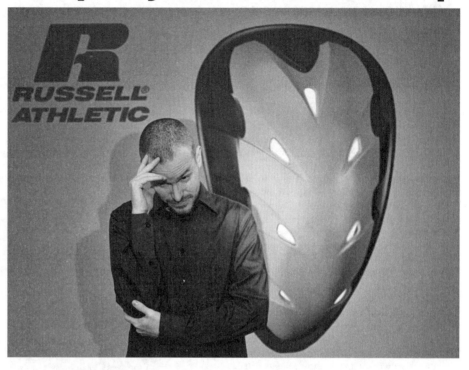

did not want to talk about how they came by that data. Other sources at Russell confirmed that an increasing number of male consumers have reported that being struck in their "um, uh, lower-middle-region part of the body? Yes, there" during athletic activity is a major concern for them.

"Men complained that other athletic supporters would dig into their, would dig into their, well, that they would dig into them," said Gary Barfield, executive vice president of Russell. "They also said they wanted increased mobility, because an athlete moves from side to side a lot and most cups failed to accommodate their, sort of, dangling.... Let's just say we've taken every bodily thing into consideration."

Members of the research and development team that designed the new cup either refused to be interviewed for this story or were giggling too uncontrollably to comment.

While Russell is planning a rather understated media blitz to introduce the new product, including radio, TV, and Internet ads, it has not yet decided on the exact content of the promotions.

"We'll probably focus on the fact that it comes in four colors, because, yeah, it comes in colors," Russell marketing head Josh Andreico said. "And in the commercials we'll maybe say something like, 'It comes in four colors but never black-and-blue,' or something funny like that. Or we'll stress how important this thing is to your, the health of your, your things."

"Probably we'll just go with the colors," Andreico added.

Feiniger also took reporters' questions, including queries as to whether the new cup required any special "preparation," whether it "like needs, like soaking or anything," and whether it is "worn, as in used, I mean, the same as other, you know, cups."

In conclusion, Feiniger stressed that the key to Russell's new athletic supporter was comfort, not just on the field of play but also in terms of actually purchasing the product.

"You know how there's the whole thing with going to the store, and you have to pick out a size?" Feiniger said. "You don't want to stand in front of the rack in case someone comes in and you're there and he's there and you're there and he's.... We'll mostly be selling them on the Internet is what I'm trying to say." ∅

Historic Seat-Covering Tarp To Be Part Of New Marlins Stadium

MAY 18, 2010

MIAMI —In honor of the team's storied past, the Florida Marlins announced at a press conference Tuesday that their new stadium would prominently feature the seat-covering tarp that has remained a constant during their 18 years at Sun Life Stadium. "We can't imagine a Marlins game that isn't played in front of an unbroken sea of smooth, empty teal," team president David Samson said as a screen behind him displayed a computer-generated animation of the giant tarp being lowered onto 9,000 empty seats in a new stadium. "That old tarp has been gloriously unfurled for 18 opening days and two World Series, and we're not going to just abandon it. Besides, the new facility will have 37,000 seats, so I'm pretty sure we'll find a use for it." Samson assured fans the ballpark would also feature modern amenities such as sleeker, more modern tarps to cover the entire upper deck and the Marlins' dugout. ∅

Report: Celtics, Lakers Finals To Allow Sportscasters To Endlessly List The Last Names Of Former Celtics, Lakers

MAY 29, 2010

NEW YORK—According to the nation's sportscasters, a Los Angeles Lakers–Boston Celtics matchup in the NBA Finals will give analysts the chance to repeatedly intone the names of former Celtic and Laker greats in an unbearably reverent and dramatic tone of voice. "At the top of our pregame broadcast, or anytime they cut back to the studio, I can say, 'Russell. Chamberlain. Cousy. West. Havlicek. McHale. Worthy. Baylor,' in a tone suggesting viewers should feel emotionally transported by the sheer historic force of the Lakers-Celtics rivalry," ESPN's Michael Wilbon said on Saturday, explaining that sportscasters will be able to say "Magic...Bird," or "Bird...Magic," thousands upon thousands of infuriating times throughout the series. "And when we say or, rather, invoke these names, it's important to assume a solemn, transfixed expression that makes viewers want to shout, 'Jesus Christ, get over yourselves.'" Wilbon added that, as a result of the Phoenix Suns' loss, he is slightly disappointed to not be able to talk for hours about Steve Nash's injured face. ∅

ESPN Writer Changes City Names From Previous Story About Milton Bradley Finding Self In New Surroundings

JUNE 1, 2010

BRISTOL, CT—To write her recent profile detailing Milton Bradley's attempt to find peace within himself in Seattle, ESPN senior writer Elizabeth Merrill simply found her 2009 article about the troubled outfielder's attempt to find peace within himself in Chicago, changed the team name throughout the story from the Cubs to the Mariners, and replaced every mention of Lou Piniella with Seattle manager Don Wakamatsu. "Writing these Milton Bradley 'I have finally turned my life around' stories is the easiest thing in the world," Merrill told reporters, adding that she composed identical articles in 2004 and 2006 about Bradley's arrivals in Los Angeles and Oakland, respectively. "I just open up my 'Bradley Finding Self In New Surroundings' template and from there it's pretty much just find-and-replace." Merrill said she learned the trick from former ESPN boxing reporter Max Kellerman, who has used his "Mike Tyson Opens Up On New Outlook On Life Following His Arrest" boilerplate more than 15 times. ∅

Blackhawks Attempt To Find Out Why Shark On San Jose Logo Is Eating Hockey Stick

MAY 24, 2010

SAN JOSE, CA—Baffled members of the Chicago Blackhawks reportedly scrutinized San Jose's logo Tuesday in an attempt to determine some logical reason as to why it pictures a ferocious underwater predator eating a hockey stick. "Sharks are primarily carnivorous, so it really makes no sense for them to suddenly introduce wood to their diet," said center Jonathan Toews, wondering how a hockey stick would wind up in the ocean. "Isn't a mascot animal supposed to be in favor of hockey? Why then would he ruin a good stick by biting it in half? Also, not to get too nitpicky, but San Jose is inland, so they don't have sharks, unless the shark is bursting up through the rink, which is just unrealistic and stupid." The San Jose Sharks were reportedly just as confused by the Blackhawks logo, failing to understand what a somewhat racist representation of a Native American had to do with hockey. ∅

PHOTO FINISH

Mr. Met Loses Joint Custody Of Son After Child Runs On Field During Game

Cubs Organ Player Getting Into Heavier, Darker Stuff

JUNE 16, 2010

CHICAGO—Over the past several weeks, longtime Cubs organist Gary Pressy has gradually stopped playing the light ballpark-organ riffs that typically fill Wrigley Field's stands in favor of more broody, chilling songs. "I have to say that lately the sounds coming out of that organ have made me anxious and sad and in no mood to clap along," said season-ticket holder Mike Preston, adding that instead of playing "Hava Nagila" or using his organ to start a "Let's Go Cubs" chant, Pressy will strike an oppressive minor chord and sustain the unsettling tone for up to an entire minute. "Yesterday he played a really slow fugue on 'Take Me Out to the Ball Game' in this dark, funereal key. It was haunting." When asked for comment, Pressy drove reporters away by playing a demented arrangement of "Happy Birthday" on his newly installed 20,000-pipe, seven-story-tall organ. ∅

Networks Battling Until Last Minute Over Who Has To Air World Cup

JUNE 2, 2010

NEW YORK—The bidding war over the 2010 FIFA World Cup continues to rage between television networks, with multimillion-dollar sums being offered for the rights to show something other than soccer's greatest spectacle. "When the World Cup begins this June, millions of viewers across the nation will be tuning into something, anything, else," said ESPN program director Lisa Hibbing, whose network is currently losing the bidding war and may be forced to air more than 60 matches. "Considering ESPN's main demographic—young male sports fans—and taking into account the time difference between the U.S. and South Africa, and reflecting on our reputation as a sports channel, we'd much rather be showing car-product infomercials at that hour of the morning. Long story short, we're prepared to offer NBC roughly half a billion dollars." When asked for comment, NBC executives said they had "just barely dodged the Olympic bullet" and that it was someone else's turn. ✎

'Totally Worth It,' Claims Grown Man Limping Off Softball Field

JUNE 21, 2010

VERONA, WI—Though he knew before his office's team took the field that his aging, out-of-shape body was at risk of physical injury, limping Affiliated Bank loan and trust officer Robert Newson, 48, told reporters Sunday that a muscle-pull, combined with a possible severe knee injury, was "totally worth" the four innings of softball he played prior to removing himself from the game. "Absolutely, 100 percent worth it," said Newson, who refused to accept his physical limitations during the game by trying to stretch singles into doubles and throwing himself to the dirt to chase moderately fast ground balls. "Completely worth it, no question. Grace? I think we might have to go to the hospital after all." Newson later claimed it was the most worthwhile injury he had suffered since his crippling chest pains in last year's game against the Bank of Cross Plains. ✎

Lazy ESPN.com Poll Asks Readers If They Like Sports

OCTOBER 19, 2010

BRISTOL, CT—Lazy ESPN.com editors posted the poll question "Do you like sports?" on the website's homepage yesterday, offering "yes" or "no" as the only two response options. "We have to do a poll each day, so, yeah, we did a poll on whether people like sports or not," web editor Anthony Whelan said via telephone Monday, adding that his staff had also considered the question "Was Michael Jordan good?" "We try to make the experience on our website interactive for the users and whatever." Whelan denied accusations that ESPN.com was running low on poll ideas and adamantly defended last week's SportsNation question, "How you guys doing?" ✎

INSIDE

▸ **Hockey Scores Now Reported In 'News Of The Weird' Section**

▸ **Activity Made Up To Sell Athletic Shoes**

Nation Undecided On Whether It Hates Celtics Or Lakers More

JUNE 5, 2010

WASHINGTON—The NBA Finals have thrown the nation's basketball fans into a state of angry confusion this week, as the bitter debate over whether they despise the Celtics or Lakers more rages on. "Kobe is such an egotistical prick that it's really easy to detest the Lakers, especially with that clenched-jaw face he makes, but come on—you have to hate the Celtics because the Big Three are so much more fucking annoying," said Jeff Connor, a St. Louis native. "I'll admit that I can't stand Pau Gasol, just because the guy rubs me the wrong way, maybe due to his disgusting greasy hair. Phil Jackson is a pretty huge asshole with all that loud whistling he does, but Rondo is the most irritating little shit, and I loathe that fat sweaty hog Glen Davis. Ray Allen is actually okay. That dick Kevin Garnett, though, is a chest-pounding idiot." After much discussion, a consensus appears to be near, as Americans are agreeing to hate the Lakers and Celtics equally. ✎

Referee Frustrated By Number Of Commercials Shown In Replay Booth

SEPTEMBER 22, 2010

SAN DIEGO—Referee Terry McAulay told reporters he was extremely annoyed by the exorbitant number of commercials he had to watch Sunday before being able to review the footage of a disputed fumble call during the Jaguars-Chargers game. "I'm trying to keep the game moving, but I have to spend forever waiting through a bunch of stupid commercials for Old Spice and *The Mentalist*, even through NFL promos," McAulay said. "And every time you try to change the angle or look at a freeze-frame, another message pops up saying your footage will be available after a short message from our sponsors. You used to be able to skip the commercials, but you can't now unless you subscribe." After reviewing the footage, McAulay said Brett Favre appeared to have crossed the line of scrimmage before throwing the ball during the Wrangler commercial. ✎

PHOTO FINISH
Car Exacts Revenge On Blake Griffin

164 Closeted Gay Men Having Impressive NFL Preseason

AUGUST 20, 2010

RUTHERFORD, NJ—As the first round of preseason games drew to a close Monday, NFL sources reported that the league's 164 closeted gay players were turning in excellent performances across the board as they battled for roster positions on the league's 32 teams.

"It's still early, but so far so good," said one Giants lineman, who told reporters he was pleased with his team's 31-16 victory over the Jets and who, like every gay player in the NFL, is not out to his teammates and asked not to be named. "I feel good physically and I'm playing well, so I should be able to survive at least the first roster cut if I stay healthy."

"I'm not going to make any predictions, but I think all of us gay guys did great tonight," said a Jets skill-position player, dismissing his team's preseason loss as unimportant. "In fact, I wouldn't be a bit surprised if all nine of our homosexual players made the cut."

Across the NFL, gay players are shaking off the rust of a long offseason, contending with the rigors of learning the playbook, and competing with their teammates—some of whom are younger, some of whom are stronger, some of whom are also gay—for a spot on a 53-man roster.

For the past several weeks, they have been practicing, showering, watching videotape, eating, and sitting in the trainer's hot tub alongside straight players. While many have formed close friendships in that time, every closeted gay player realizes as much as every openly straight player that the team doesn't have enough positions for all of them.

"The first test for any player, gay or not, is how you do in that first full-pads practice, where the speed and power of players at this level surprises some guys who are coming right out of college," said a gay player for the Kansas City Chiefs, adding that his career would surely be ruined if his sexual orientation were to be revealed. "Our first week, a receiver coming across the middle got hit so hard by a gay member of our secondary he could barely believe it. You see that happen a lot."

Most gay players agreed the biggest test comes in the preseason games, when they are evaluated under actual playing conditions. According to sources, over the first weekend of exhibition play, the majority of homosexual players acquitted themselves more than adequately.

"I'm extremely proud of the way [my closeted gay players] performed against the Chargers last weekend," Chicago head coach Lovie Smith said when asked about several play-

see CLOSETED

Tips for High School Athletes

SEPTEMBER 10, 2010

As America's teens return to class, they return to the playing fields as well. Onion Sports prepares them for what may be the greatest time in their lives.

➤ Don't just automatically take the steroids your coach gives you. Shop around for the ones that are best for you

➤ If you've been running outside in extreme heat for hours and start to see spots, that's just your body's way of keeping itself hydrated

➤ You didn't hear it from us, but Elliot's dad said he saw a college scout checking you guys out at last week's game

➤ Hazing is absolutely forbidden by the policies of your school and your athletic conference. That said, ever wonder if Freddy Engel could swim all the way across Lake Sycamore without letting a candle stuck in his ass go out?

➤ Wear your team jersey/singlet on all game/meet days, just so everyone knows that you're in sports

➤ Support girls' athletics just as much as boys', because girls need to do their cute little jumps and bouncy things, too

➤ Just remember, not everyone can become the star of the team and score the winning point in the championship game. However, if you do not do these things, you are useless and will die alone, unmourned and unloved

➤ If you're not so great at sports, don't worry. It's not too late to start smoking and get cool that way

Sports World Limping Toward Football Opener Like Mortally Wounded Deer

SEPTEMBER 3, 2010

HAGERSTOWN, MD—With Major League Baseball's postseason still a month out and college football weeks away from conference play, the sports world continues to stagger toward the NFL's opening kickoff like a gut-shot doe spewing blood from its mouth and keening piteously with its last ragged breaths, sources reported Tuesday. "I can't wait for kickoff," one torpid fan told reporters while staring blankly at a TV screen showing a pointless Angels-Mariners game, a listless nine-inning contest that mimicked a deer's struggle to ride out the searing pain in its shredded viscera and drag itself to a sheltered spot to die. "It's about time." The NFL season will begin Thursday night as the Vikings-Saints game gets underway, with the majesty of a great hornèd stag silhouetted against the moon as it pauses to glance back over its rippling haunches before coursing once more toward freedom across vast and verdant fields, at 7:30 p.m. CDT in the Superdome. ✏

Quarterback Playing Well Enough For Commentator To Mention His Favorite Sandwich

SEPTEMBER 29, 2010

CLEVELAND—Baltimore Ravens quarterback Joe Flacco's commanding performance against the porous Browns defense Sunday provided commentators with an opportunity during the game's third quarter to discuss the signal caller's love for his favorite sandwich. "The Quiznos toasted Prime Rib and Peppercorn sub is absolutely his favorite sandwich, all right. It may be his favorite thing to have for lunch, period," announcer Don Criqui said as Flacco preserved the Ravens' 24-17 lead by completing a meaningless four-yard out. "He eats them all the time. Says he loves the sautéed onions. Buys them for all the linemen, too, after a good practice." Flacco finished the game with 22 completions on 31 attempts for 262 yards, three touchdowns, no interceptions, three comparisons of his musical tastes with his style of play, and two mentions of how a young Flacco led his high school baseball team to the New Jersey state title. ✏

PHOTO FINISH

Jennie Finch Retires From Lists Of World's Hottest Female Athletes

Report: Fans Enjoy Waving Things Around

OCTOBER 27, 2010

NEW YORK—A joint report from all professional and amateur sporting leagues unanimously confirmed Thursday that fans enjoy waving random things around, typically above their heads, while attending athletic events. "Shirts, signs, their arms, any color of towel—basically we found that if a fan has the ability to hold something in his or her hand, there's a good chance he'll wave it around," Gina Keller, a representative of Major League Baseball, told reporters. "Our findings indicate that fans believe waving things around when their team is winning builds momentum, and waving things around when their team is losing motivates players to attempt comebacks. In short, fans like waving things." Keller added that a new report, expected to be released this December, should confirm that outcomes of sporting events would be the same if fans cheered loudly during games or just sat in absolute silence. ✏

from **CLOSETED**

ers on his roster whose sexual orientation he was unaware of. "I feel that [certain gay offensivplayers] are going to be a big component of our ground game and [various gay members of the defense] will continue to contribute in all aspects, although the pass rush is naturally a concern, as always."

"So, why did you ask about those guys in particular?" Smith added.

Realistically, the NFL's gay players told reporters, they cannot all make their respective teams.

"Not everyone can compete at this level," said a three-time Pro Bowl linebacker and homosexual. "There's no shame in it. It's just a fact of life. But for a lot of gay players, it's one of the hardest things to admit to yourself."

However, hopes remain high. If there's one thing aside from their carefully hidden sexual orientation that unites these athletes, it's their positive attitude.

"I'm definitely going to make the NFL. There's no doubt in my mind," said a gay former college standout who has struggled with the transition to the pros and been cut for three consecutive years. "I'm going to make it onto the Cowboys this year. I haven't been this sure of anything since I was 17. Mark my words: I'm going to be playing out there right alongside those straight guys, just like all the other gay players people don't realize they're cheering for every week." ✏

16,000 Diamondbacks Fans Killed On Complimentary Rattlesnake Night

SEPTEMBER 10, 2010

PHOENIX—The Arizona Diamondbacks organization apologized to fans, their families, and the community at large Thursday after more than 16,000 people attending the previous night's game were killed by the poisonous Western diamondback rattlesnakes given out as part of Complimentary Rattlesnake Night.

"I feel terrible," Diamondbacks general manager Jerry Dipoto told reporters as emergency personnel working out of temporary triage stations around Chase Field injected antivenom into the estimated 23,000 victims who survived the initial wave of snakebites. "All we wanted to do was give people something that was symbolic of the Diamondbacks, something they could take home and keep to remember the team by."

"I don't think they'll be taking their rattlesnakes home after this, though," Dipoto said. "They probably won't want them now that all those people are dead."

The rattlesnakes, which average 4 feet in length, weigh about 10 pounds, and account for the second-highest number of snakebite fatalities in the United States, were given out to the first 20,000 ticket holders who entered the stadium. While some volunteers initially suffered bites that destroyed their muscle tissue and caused major paralysis, event organizers said the promotion seemed to go smoothly at first.

"Other than a few hundred fans who complained of swelling, dry mouth, and blurred vision, most seemed to really like their rattlesnakes," said promotions manager Dustin Payne, who doctors believe will make a full recovery after the loss of his left arm due to venom-induced cytotoxic tissue necrosis. "They were twirling them around by their tails, you know, sort of like a Terri-

ble Towel thing, and we were all thinking we had maybe started a great stadium tradition."

"But then that little girl died," Payne continued, "which was pretty sudden and sad. And then her mom died. And her little brother died, too, after he got bit in the throat by a rattlesnake."

Observers said that even prior to the initial deaths, a number of isolated incidents seemed to indicate that the night was headed for disaster. One particularly rowdy fan had to be escorted from the game after waving his rattlesnake in a female attendee's face, and later, outfielder Gerardo Parra was poisoned and had to be carried off the field after a fan asked the hard-hitting lefty to autograph his rattlesnake.

When Diamondbacks reliever Blaine Boyer was spotted in the bullpen wildly convulsing in a writhing knot of rattlesnakes, the stadium grew quiet, save for a steady undercurrent of rattling.

Videotape of the event later showed thousands of fans toppling over and clutching their chests as the snakes' neurotoxic venom caused massive respiratory malfunctions and heart failure. Though most of the Western diamondbacks ultimately sought refuge underneath the stadium seats, by the seventh inning half the people in the stands were dead.

"Everywhere you looked, snakes were lashing out and biting people. I saw a man get bit in his calf, reach down to grab his leg, get bit in his face by another snake, fall down, and then get bit several more times on the top of his head," said Graham Rossini, the Diamondbacks' director of Special Projects and Fan Experience. "It's weird because they were such beautiful snakes, too. I think the problem was that we gave out a lot of older rattlesnakes, and apparently they can deliver much more venom."

"We probably should have given out baby rattlesnakes," he added.

The Diamondbacks organization has announced that it will donate all unclaimed rattlesnakes to a local children's charity next week. Until then, ticket holders who did not receive their rattlesnake may do so by sending the team a self-addressed stamped envelope and $8 to cover shipping and handling. ∅

Nation Taking No Joy In Cowboys' Pathetic Collapse
'Actually, Never Mind, It's Really Fun,' Reports Populace

NOVEMBER 5, 2010

IRVING, TX—As the Dallas Cowboys struggle with a 1-6 season, sports fans nationwide have been saddened by the bad fortune that has befallen the franchise long revered as one of the NFL's crown jewels, and known throughout the football world as America's Team.

Actually, the U.S. populace immediately confirmed, the Cowboys' pathetic collapse has brought with it nothing but pure joy and happiness.

"It's really been tough to watch, especially for a team that had so much potential heading into the season," Appleton, WI shopkeeper and longtime Packers fan Erik Hoyer said. "Ha! I was almost able to say that with a straight face. Honestly, this Cowboys team has made watching football more fun than it's been in years. They can't run the ball, they can't defend anything, and they're imploding so bad that their owner doesn't even know how many games they've played."

"I can't think of a better team for this to happen to," he added. "I literally can't stop smiling."

According to the American people, to think that the Cowboys—an organization that has been synonymous with excellence for decades—have fallen to last place in their conference and all but come apart at the seams has been very difficult. That is, the nation explained, if the definition of "difficult" involves loving life more than ever, especially when thinking about how the Jacksonville Jaguars beat the team at Cowboys Stadium in front of 80,000 loud and insufferable fans.

Disappointed citizens—who explained that

they were not so much disappointed as they were elated and filled with a renewed sense of justice in the universe—said the real icing on the cake is thinking about how upset the entire city of Dallas will be this February when hosting a Super Bowl that does not include the Cowboys.

"You know, I thought I would really enjoy something like this, but a football season doesn't feel like a season if the Cowboys don't have a chance at making the playoffs," New York Giants

fan and banker David McQuillan said. "That said, would any of you like to watch six hours of highlights from all the Cowboys' losses? I've saved them all on my DVR, because sometimes when I'm having a tough time at work I watch the Giants 41-35 victory and the look on Wade Phillips' dumb face just cheers me right up.

"Man, I'm going to love when that guy gets fired," McQuillan continued. "It's going to be so sweet I can taste it."

see COWBOYS

Guy Who Normally Holds Up Letter 'D' Sick This Week

Study Links Adult-Male Smiling To Extremely Overweight Men Scoring Touchdowns

JANUARY 28, 2011

PHILADELPHIA—A study released Monday by the University of Pennsylvania Department of Psychology revealed a direct correlation between smiling in adult American males and the scoring of touchdowns by incredibly large or obese football players. "The initial results of the study proved that adult males offer at least a smirk at the sight of any extremely overweight man's head squished into a helmet," said Dr. Caroline Nissen, who directed the study. "But without fail, if that man happens to recover a turnover and begins to run with the ball, the size of the observer's smile grows exponentially, especially if the plump athlete attempts to jump over anything. By the time the obese player scores, literally every adult male we studied was grinning to the limits of his ability." Thus far, the study is being heralded by the medical community as a potential cure-all for males suffering from chronic depression. ⌀

Report: For 8th Straight Year, Europeans Remain Weirdest-Looking Players In NBA

JANUARY 16, 2011

ORLANDO, FL—According to a report published this week by the University of Central Florida's Institute for Diversity and Ethics in Sport, for the eighth straight season, the highest percentage of bizarre and unconventional-looking NBA players continue to be of European descent. "If a team is in need of a solid player with nasty hair, droopy eyes, a patchy beard, and a starkly pale body, Europe is the place to go," said Brian Fisher, the director of the university's study. "Over the years, it has consistently provided some of the weirdest-looking people the league has ever seen: Gheorghe Muresan, Zydrunas Ilgauskas, Hedo

Turkoglu, and Pau Gasol, just to name a few. Oh, and Dirk Nowitzki. How could we forget that goofy-looking guy?" Though European players occupied 25 of the report's 30 spots, Chris Bosh was named weirdest-looking player in the NBA for the fifth straight year. ∅

Baseball Players Hold Annual Meeting To Discuss Benefit Of Wearing Index Finger On Outside Of Mitt

DECEMBER 3, 2010

NEW YORK—In what has become the foremost annual conference of baseball-glove-wearing theory, major-league players past and present once again gathered at the Jacob K. Javits Convention Center in Manhattan this week to discuss the advantages and disadvantages of wearing their index fingers on the outside of their baseball mitts.

Now in its 47th year, the weeklong convention is intended to explore some of the unanswered questions surrounding forefinger baseball glove placement, such as whether wearing one's index finger on the outside of the mitt can increase pocket-depth and reduce sting; whether forefinger placement is a case of personal preference and, if so, what genetically predisposes an individual to choose an inner or outer placement path; and whether people just wear their index finger on the outside of their gloves because they saw their favorite baseball player do so.

"We don't pretend to think that a player will leave this convention with a full understanding of why he puts his index finger where he does in his mitt," said MLB commissioner Bud Selig, adding that all

1,200 active major-leaguers are expected to attend. "All we can do is offer a forum in which to thoughtfully discuss the question with the rigor and curiosity it deserves. Every year we try to challenge our players with new ideas."

"For example, Willie Mays will hold a daylong symposium debunking the theory that wearing one's index finger on the outside of the mitt allows a player to close the glove more quickly around the ball," Selig added. "Sign-ups for his lecture completely filled up before this year's All-Star break."

According to event organizers, each Index Finger Convention opens with Yankees Hall of Famer Yogi Berra asking the Key Question, that being: "Baseball

see INDEX FINGER

from **COWBOYS**

Like the Yankees in baseball, the Cowboys are known throughout the country as a team that prides itself on excellence, a team that has come to embody its sport. And when star quarterback Tony Romo went down with a clavicle injury several weeks ago, the disappointment could be felt from coast-to-coast.

"Hearing Romo scream when his collarbone snapped will always be one of my favorite memories," Washington, D.C. resident Nick Thomason said. "I was pretty young when Dallas went 1-15 in 1989, but I still remember their only win that year was against my Redskins. It's like the football gods were repaying me by making sure he was miked up during that game."

"I thought I would cherish the day when the Cowboys completely imploded," 44-year-old James Tolliver of Providence, RI said. "And I was right. This has been absolutely wonderful."

According to a recent *USA Today* poll, 45 percent of the country said that no team deserves to perform this terribly under this much pressure, except for the Dallas Cowboys. Thirty-two percent said that the season has been emotionally taxing for people who grew up worshipping Roger Staubach, Troy Aikman, and Emmitt Smith, and that those people should probably go fuck themselves anyway.

Ninety-nine percent of respondents said that if karma has caught up with the Cowboys, and they are finally getting payback for all the times Michael Irvin pushed off and was never called for it, or all the years they mysteriously never played an away game in December, then karma is the greatest thing in the history of the world.

"Firing the coach, hiring a new coach, players wanting to be traded, Romo's toughness questioned in the locker room—there are going to be some amazing meltdowns coming, mark my words," said lifelong Dallas resident Stephen Lowndes, who has been steeped in Cowboys lore all his life without being asked if that was what he wanted. "Plus, they're about due for a major drug incident, or maybe a strip-club brawl or something, just to make the season perfect. And months down the road, long after they miss the playoffs, they get to screw up the draft. Really, you have to grow up getting this team rammed down your throat every single fucking minute of every single goddamn day of your life to appreciate how much I'm loving this."

"Seriously, best season ever," Lowndes added. "How 'bout them Cowboys!" ∅

PHOTO FINISH

NBA Honors Latino Community By Using Spanish Word For 'The' On Jerseys

New Horse-Racing Initiative Aimed At Training Thoroughbreds From Inner City

DECEMBER 10, 2010

COMPTON, CA—In an effort to develop a more diverse base of athletic talent, raise the sport's profile in nontraditional areas, and enrich the lives of troubled youth, thoroughbred-racing organizations are funding a new program to train inner-city and delinquent horses.

The initiative, known as Right Side of the Track, is opening 12 "Colts & Fillies Clubs" in impoverished urban locales across the country, and already has four operational centers in Detroit, Baltimore, Birmingham, and St. Louis. According to organizers, the facilities will provide at-risk yearlings and disadvantaged foals with free access to state-of-the-art running tracks, experienced trainers and jockeys, and, depending upon their behavior, sugar cubes.

"We want young thoroughbreds to know that there are other opportunities out there, that there are better things to do than gallop the streets looking for trouble," Right Side of the Track president Hanson Jennings said Sunday at the opening of the Compton Colts & Fillies Club. "These horses need structure, and they need a safe place to go during the day or they'll wind up in the wrong herd."

"Take Afternoon Delight here," added Jennings, referring to the 18-hand Appaloosa standing next to him. "One year ago he was a young-punk pony living on the streets of Baltimore with no future ahead of him. But be-

cause of our mentoring program, his confidence is growing, his outlook is far more positive, and he raced last year in several events. He still has some anger issues, especially around dogs, but he hasn't bitten a human in over seven months."

Though locales such as Baltimore and Louisville have world-class racetracks, the horses that compete there are not bred inside the city limits. Walk around a tough neighborhood in most parts of the country, horse-

see **HORSE-RACING**

---

from **INDEX FINGER**

mitts were designed with five finger slots, and at some point some players decided to no longer use the section created to encase the forefinger. Why?" With that in mind, sources said, players use the meeting to explore those facets of forefinger placement that have vexed or intrigued them the most, not only during the previous baseball season, but throughout their entire careers.

"I'm definitely going to go to the personal testimonial lectures," Philadelphia Phillies first baseman Ryan Howard said. "[Yankees first baseman] Mark Teixeira is a first-time presenter who switched to putting his index finger on the outside of his glove this year. I want to see how it worked for him, because I'm thinking of

doing the same. I think it helps first basemen more so than outfielders. I heard that somewhere."

"I'm looking forward to spending most of the conference just talking to other players about why they put their index finger where they put it," New York Mets outfielder Jason Bay said. "I keep mine on the inside of my mitt, but I enjoy hearing why others don't."

This year's program features convention mainstays, such as the Cal Ripken, Jr.–moderated panel "Increased Injuries? The Biggest Myth About Wearing Your Index Finger On The Outside Of Your Glove." In addition, many players have visited the Rawlings-sponsored history exhibit, which explains that, because outside index finger placement became so pop-

ular in the 1980s, the company began making gloves with an actual forefinger aperture. On Saturday at 10 a.m. and 4 p.m., Mike Schmidt will present his seminar, a perennial favorite, devoted to the 1982 season, during which he wore his index finger in the inside of his mitt for the first half of the year and on the outside for the second half.

One of the convention's unexpected highlights occurred on Tuesday when Alex Gordon of the Kansas City Royals presented his lecture "My Index Finger And Baseball Gloves: A Personal History." Gordon's frank, often confessional presentation detailed how he wore his forefinger on the inside of his mitt throughout Little League, and then for reasons he was never able to un-

derstand—"Maybe just to be cool and fit in," Gordon openly admits—he gradually moved the finger to the outside of the glove during high school.

"Now it just feels weird to put my index finger on the inside of my mitt," Gordon told an audience that included Derek Jeter, Albert Pujols, and 2010 MVP Joey Votto, all of whom could be seen nodding in agreement. "But truthfully, I bet if I wore my index finger on the inside of my mitt for over 10 years, and one day put it on the outside, it would probably feel just as weird. In the end, I guess I don't know why I started putting my index finger on the outside of my glove."

"But then again, that's why I'm here," he continued. "That's why we're all here." ∅

THE MAGAZINE

How To Make YOUR OWN Fishing Lures *Without* Thinking About How Your Son Hasn't Spoken To You In 20 Years

By James LaBonte

ONION **WEEKENDER** JANUARY 16, 2011

Rick Reilly Columns Increasingly Laden With Cries For Help

FEBRUARY 28, 2011

BRISTOL, CT—For the past six months, the columns and essays written by ESPN's Rick Reilly, including "Why Michael Vick Deserves Redemption More Than I Do," "The Hot Stove And Why I Want To Put My Head In It," and "Caddying For The Grim Reaper," have become increasingly punctuated by anguished appeals for someone to save him from himself, ESPN readers have noted. "It will be here at Augusta, where so much golf history has taken place and where I'd like to walk slowly into a water hazard until the placid blue water closes over me, leaving no trace that I was ever born," Reilly wrote in his column last week, a piece titled "When It's Gone, It's Gone" which deals with Tiger Woods' slump and Reilly's apparent wish for self-destruction. "And if he's doomed, if he disappears forever, you have to wonder if anyone would notice. Next week, I take Roger Clemens bowling and try to choke back the bile." Sources at ESPN said they have considered speaking to Reilly about his obvious personal problems, but decided against it after realizing Reilly's columns are the most engaging they've been in years. ∅

---

from **HORSE-RACING**

racing officials said, and you're unlikely to see young equines on the street wearing fancy horseshoes or race-quality silks. Many are so apathetic and unmotivated they find it acceptable to meander around in public covered in mud and their own filth.

Just last Thursday, eight urban horses allegedly broke into a Detroit veterinary hospital to get a ketamine fix.

"Let's face it: Horse racing is for the privileged few, the kind of thoroughbreds who never had to worry about where their next bale of hay was coming from, or whether their owner would be around to braid their mane

for a big race," volunteer jockey Jeff Sherman said. "But there is a lot of raw talent at these centers. They need only look at Mine That Bird, who won the 2009 Kentucky Derby even though his absentee father was too busy running around with fillies and siring yearlings all over the country to pay any attention to him."

Right Side of the Track has recruited a number of trainers with professional experience to face the unique challenge of working with underprivileged horses. After a life on the streets, they said, colts can become hardened and aggressive, refusing to take orders or to be saddled by an authority figure.

"You get these horses, and they trot and whinny in a certain way that says, 'I will kick the shit out of you if given the chance,'" said world-renowned trainer Bob Baffert, who admitted that he always carries his crop with him when he walks through bad neighborhoods at night. "They're a little unsure of you at first, but once they realize you trust them to eat an apple out of your hand, they nicker a little bit and you know you have them."

Efforts to involve the community have also been successful. In each of its four locations, the organization has found groups of retirees willing to volunteer their time by attending races and

cheering on the young amateurs during races. However, while some program participants do ultimately become world-class racehorses, organizers said that isn't the main goal of the clubs.

"Our mission is to broaden their horizons," Jennings said. "Even if they don't go on to race professionally, urban horses need to know there are other paths for them out there. If they dedicate themselves, they can train to do police work. They can learn to round up cattle. They can even go on to work with kids in 4-H."

"There are alternatives," he stressed, "and if they don't realize that, they'll just end up on the streets, begging for oats." ∅

Puppy Bowl Marred By Tragic Spinal Injury

FEBRUARY 6, 2011

SILVER SPRING, MD—Puppy Bowl VII, puppy football's biggest annual event, came to a complete standstill Sunday when Alvin, a 3-month-old schnauzer mix, suffered a freak spinal injury while chasing down a loose squeaky football.

The injury, which occurred only minutes before the Kitty Halftime Show, followed a routine midfield burst of play. Slow-motion footage from the sideline and water-dish cameras show Alvin romping flat out down the sidelines before taking a risky crossing route to come at the football from an angle, at which point two larger puppies, Amy, a golden retriever, and Big Red, a 13-week-old shepherd mix, laid a massive hit on Alvin, who responded with a shrill yelp that was suddenly and ominously cut off.

"I heard something snap and I knew immediately something was wrong," said play-by-play announcer Jeff Bordner, who watched as a team of veterinarians attended to Alvin, who lay motionless on Animal Planet Stadium's turf. "We applauded when he was carried off the field, but it didn't look good. The replay shows his neck twisting at almost a right angle."

Sources at Silver Spring Animal Hospital, where Alvin was rushed after the injury, said that the pup has no feeling in his paws, and that even if he lives he will more than likely never frolic on his own again.

"In order to reduce swelling, we lowered Alvin's body temperature by pumping an ice-cold saline solution into his little veins," said head veterinarian Dr. Richard Cooper, adding that an emergency tracheotomy was performed when Alvin was admitted and that the puppy is currently breathing with the aid of life-support machines. "But with the severity of his injury, he's going to have a long road ahead of him. There's a chance he could live, but it would be a difficult life. He would never be a normal dog."

Cooper added that thus far, Alvin remains unresponsive to his favorite chew toy.

Though the Puppy Bowl eventually continued with its typical array of puppy touchdowns, bone-gnawing, and the presentation of the Most Valuable Puppy award, there was no denying that the energy was sucked out of the stadium immediately after the hit that nearly severed Alvin's spinal cord. During the second half, the puppies appeared to be just going through the motions, with few even responding to the camera-mounted remote-control car on the field. Some simply lay down on the field for long stretches at a time.

"They knew something was wrong when Alvin didn't come back. He's known among the other pups as extremely playful, as a puppy who would never miss the opportunity to play on puppy football's grandest stage," said Puppy Bowl referee Andrew Schechter, adding that he didn't call unnecessary ruff-ruff-ruffness on the play because the hit was clean. "Look, when a puppy goes across the middle unprotected like that, there is always a chance something terrible can happen."

"This is the Puppy Bowl," Schechter added. "Everyone, even your pug mixes, are going at a higher gear. Boy that was a tough injury, though. To be honest with you, when that puppy's neck snapped, it sounded like a bundle of wet celery being twisted, and his head was just hanging there, limp, like it wasn't even connected to his body. I was pretty close to the action, too, so I saw firsthand the look in Alvin's eyes. He was so confused. So scared. Then of course he went into shock and passed out."

Ironically, the incident comes at the end of a season during which Animal Planet officials had

placed increased emphasis on the safety and well-being of Puppy Bowl participants. All puppies involved in the game had been fully vaccinated and wormed and were sponsored by certified shelters. Moreover, all were expected to go to good homes after the game.

Animal Planet extended their heartfelt condolences to Alvin's intended eventual owner, a 5-year-old girl named Lauren.

"Believe me, we've tried to get them into little helmets," said Marjorie Kaplan, president of Animal Planet Media. "But they don't like them. They seem to think they don't need them, and they wiggle and squirm until you just give up. Even if you do get a helmet on them, they just get it over their eyes and walk backwards until it gets all cockeyed on their little faces, and then they look up at you like, 'Please can I take it off now? Please?' and oh, jeez, it's just too cute."

"It doesn't seem so cute now," Kaplan added. "After seeing that poor puppy broken and dying on the Puppy Bowl turf, I don't know if anything will ever be cute again."

In related news, the Green Bay Packers edged out the Pittsburgh Steelers 31-25 in Super Bowl XLV. Ø

ESPN Doesn't Have Heart To Tell John Clayton He Has Never Actually Appeared On Television

MARCH 4, 2011

BRISTOL, CT—Though they first pointed a camera at the NFL writer more than 15 years ago as a prank, producers at ESPN still cannot bear to tell John Clayton they have never actually put him on television. "It's heartbreaking to watch him standing outside in the snow at one of these stadiums, trying to keep his wispy mound of hair in place, waiting for his big chance to speak in front of a camera that isn't even rolling," said ESPN executive Kathryn

Rich, adding that in order to make Clayton think he is on the air, producers will often have an intern pose as an ESPN anchor and ask him follow-up questions. "I don't know why he ever believed we would actually put a guy like him on TV, but it's too late now." To keep the ruse going, ESPN officials were forced to arrange a mock induction into the Pro Football Hall of Fame for Clayton four years ago and are still paying Clayton's wife, a prostitute they hired in 1996, to tell him how good he was on television that particular night. Ø

CHAPTER SIX

SPECIAL ISSUES

Ah, the special Sports Issue! Nothing so engages the sportswriter, nothing is as uniquely challenging, nothing exercises his talents quite as much as explaining the World Cup every four years, or the decathlon every time an American looks like he might win. Notice that all the descriptors in the preceding sentence are value-neutral, because explaining those sports is actually a gigantic ordeal. The only reason it is necessary at all is because the sheer novelty of these sports seems to attract the eye of advertisers, especially those marketing energy drinks, brightly colored subcompact cars, and any product exclusively advertised in Spanish, all of which seem to have billions of dollars to subsidize the completely fabricated fascination with international competition. Luckily, these curious celebrations of odd athletic achievements are often broken up by incredibly controversial steroid scandals, which are far more interesting to the sportswriter than any of these sports.

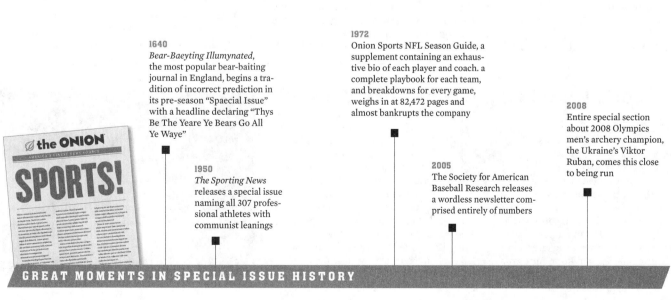

1640
Bear-Baeyting Illumynated, the most popular bear-baiting journal in England, begins a tradition of incorrect prediction in its pre-season "Spaecial Issue" with a headline declaring "Thys Be The Yeare Ye Bears Go All Ye Waye"

1950
The Sporting News releases a special issue naming all 307 professional athletes with communist leanings

1972
Onion Sports NFL Season Guide, a supplement containing an exhaustive bio of each player and coach. a complete playbook for each team, and breakdowns for every game, weighs in at 82,472 pages and almost bankrupts the company

2005
The Society for American Baseball Research releases a wordless newsletter comprised entirely of numbers

2008
Entire special section about 2008 Olympics men's archery champion, the Ukraine's Viktor Ruban, comes this close to being run

GREAT MOMENTS IN SPECIAL ISSUE HISTORY

A-ROD SIGNS WITH YANKEES

Alex Rodriguez is the epitome and embodiment of today's athletes: Incredibly well-paid, obsequious, and marketable, with a depth of talent matched only by the shallowness of his character. When the inevitable happened and A-Rod signed with the Yankees, it was important that Onion Sports give him the kind of coverage he deserved.

Alex Rodriguez Placed On Emotionally Disabled List

SEPTEMBER 7, 2006

NEW YORK—After suffering through much of the year with an aching heart, shattered self-image, and severely hurt feelings, Alex Rodriguez was placed on the 15-day emotionally disabled list, though the Yankee slugger did not rule out the possibility that the emotional wounds he has had to endure this season "may never truly heal."

"There is an intense, burning pain deep within me, accompanied by a sinking feeling of complete and total emptiness inside," said Rodriguez outside his locker Monday night, moments before throwing his tear-stained jersey to the ground and burying his head in his hands. "It's just too much. I wish it would all just go away."

"It hurts more than anyone will ever know," Rodriguez added.

Rodriguez—whose thin

skin, remarkable sensitivity, and vulnerable nature have made him susceptible to chronic emotional problems—had been exhibiting the telltale signs of mental weakness all season, marked by temporary rapid swelling of the ego followed by alternating bouts of extreme coldness and unusual soreness. However, the incident that triggered the "major, irreparable damage" to Rodriguez's psyche occurred during last Saturday's game, when fans

booed him for striking out to end the seventh inning.

"When it happened, you could just see in his face that something was wrong, that he was trying hard to hide the pain he was feeling on the inside, but then he just audibly snapped—you could hear it all the way from the bleachers," said teammate Bobby Abreu, who watched from first base as Rodriguez "came apart right there on the field."

see **DISABLED LIST**

SPORTS GRAPHIC
A-Rod's Career Highlights

Aug. 9, 1995: Rookie shortstop Alex Rodriguez earns the rickname "A-Rod" when Mariners announcer Dave Niehaus takes the first letter of Alex's first name, followed by the first syllable of his last name, and says it out loud

April 26, 1996: A-Rod wears his baseball cap backwards so he and Ken Griffey Jr. have something to talk about

Nov. 12, 1999: After watching *The Natural* for the first time, A-Rod says, "That's like me"

July 8, 2001: Following a poor showing in the All-Star Game Home-Run Derby, A-Rod spends three hours after the competition hitting home runs to show fans that he can, in fact, hit them

July 27, 2002: Rodriguez's agent, Scott Boras, presents Cynthia Scurtis, the woman of A-Rod's affection, with an 80-page pamphlet detailing the advantages of marrying A-Rod, promising that if she agrees to a 10-year contract, A-Rod will immediately become the face of their marriage

Feb. 16, 2004: Following his trade to the Yankees, A-Rod quickly agrees to move to third base after thinking about all the times he was at shortstop and saw balls getting hit there

May 15, 2004: After failing many times to "earn his Yankee pinstripes," a slumping A-Rod finally just gives in and pays $15 million for them

July 24, 2004: Red Sox catcher Jason Varitek is forced to take a swing at Rodriguez when A-Rod complains that Varitek smells like sweat

June 12, 2005: A-Rod goes online and votes for himself 25 times on the MLB.com All-Star ballot

Aug. 28. 2006: A-Rod fields a ground ball and manages to get it to the first-baseman

A-Rod: 'I Hate Being A New York Yankee'

SEPTEMBER 7, 2006

NEW YORK—Yankee third-baseman Alex Rodriguez, whose tenure in pinstripes has been plagued by his inability to live up to expectations set by the media, fans, and team owner George Steinbrenner, broke down yesterday after an 0-for-5 performance and tearfully announced that he hates being a New York Yankee. "It just really sucks here," said Rodriguez, who noted that the pressure he faces every

day living in the city of New York and playing for the Yankees has become "fucking outrageous." "I hate all of it—the dress code, the strict curfew, not having my name on my uniform, the stadium, the tradition, my teammates, playing third base—all of it. For the love of Christ, get me the fuck out of this shithole." Rodriguez later added that the only thing he likes about being a New York Yankee is Don Mattingly. *Ø*

A-Rod Has Some Creative Input On Baseball-Card Photo

SEPTEMBER 7, 2006

NEW YORK—Alex Rodriguez announced yesterday that his 2007 Topps Major League Baseball Series 2 baseball-card photo would serve as a statement of the man and player he has become while also remembering the man and player he used to be. "The photo captures me at third base in an athletic position, suggesting that I am extremely focused and ready for anything, as I am in all aspects of my life," Rodriguez said, adding that the angle of the photo, which allows those viewing the card to see fans cheering in the background, is no coincidence. "The photo also suggests, with a hint of Derek Jeter's left foot in the top-left corner of the frame, that my days at shortstop are behind me, although I am of course a team player who is willing to sacrifice himself and put his body on the line every night." Representatives at Topps said Rodriguez was "extremely difficult" to work with, as opposed to rookie Yankee left-fielder Melky Cabrera, who was just happy to be on a baseball card. ⬦

Post-Game Comments Reveal A-Rod Unsure Whether Yankees Won Or Lost

SEPTEMBER 7, 2006

NEW YORK—In an interview following Sunday afternoon's Yankees-Twins matchup, Alex Rodriguez's comments seemed to suggest that he was unaware of the game's final outcome. "Both teams played great out there, and players from both teams had some key performances that really swung the momentum in their favors—it's a shame that one team, perhaps the other, had to lose," Rodriguez said in response to a question about what this game means for the Yankees' season. "This game really could've gone either way, instead of the one way in which it went. You've just got to tip your cap to the winning team in this case. For winning. The game." When asked what he thought about rookie Darrell Rasner's performance, Rodriguez said that he "will be a big part of the future of whatever team he plays for." ⬦

---

from **DISABLED LIST**

"It was painful to watch," he continued. "[Rodriguez] started flailing around, rocking back and forth on the ground, crying uncontrollably... I had to look away. Frankly, I was disgusted."

A team of Yankee therapists immediately rushed onto the field and administered a series of soothing, reassuring hugs, to which Rodriguez was unresponsive. Rodriguez was then transported to a nearby psychiatric hospital, where he remains in unstable condition.

Yankees manager Joe Torre said that Rodriguez will be emotionally unavailable for this weekend's series, and possibly for the rest of the season.

"A-Rod had been working hard with his mental-skills coach all season to strengthen his resolve, toughen his mind, and build up his self-esteem, but in the end, he applied too much pressure too early, and he just broke down," Torre said. "I just want A-Rod to know that we all think he's a very, very good baseball player, and that he's been doing a great job as a New York Yankee."

Rodriguez is set to begin an offseason rehabilitation program, which includes following a strict regimen of mental conditioning, taking mind-strengthening medication such as Prozac, and believing in himself.

However, Yankees assistant emotional-healing coach Lee Mazzilli was skeptical of the possibility of Rodriguez making a full recovery, saying that it would be "a miracle" if Rodriguez ever gets over the hurt he is feeling right now.

"Comprehensive tests and quiet, understanding questioning seem to indicate that A-Rod has been playing all season long with a broken heart," Mazzilli said. "It's possible that if he didn't overextend himself, his heart would've healed on its own, but to keep going out there and opening yourself up to that kind of constant abuse and harsh, brutal stress each night... He could've torn it right in half."

"It's possible his broken heart may never mend," Mazzilli added.

Rodriguez's spot on the roster will be filled by Gary Sheffield, who on Friday is eligible to be activated from the 60-day mentally disabled list. ⬦

The Media: Are They Ganging Up On A-Rod?

SEPTEMBER 7, 2006

NEW YORK—*The Columbia Sports Journalism Review* has released the results of a study initiated in mid-August to investigate whether an increase in news stories such as "K-Rod," "A-Rod Playing Whiff-le Ball," and "Sore Throat KO's A-Rod" constituted "ganging up" on the overpaid, underperforming, and petulant Yankees third-baseman. "After carefully analyzing the content of all 9,463 newspaper and magazine articles criticizing Rodriguez that were printed between August 15 and September 1, we have found neither factual errors nor evidence of reportage exceeding the normal standards of sports journalism," Columbia journalism professor John Dinges said Tuesday. "We also spoke to the reporters who exclusively cover A-Rod's performance for the Kansas City Star, Sacramento Bee, Albuquerque Tribune, and Boston Herald, and we found no appreciable misinterpretations or statistical discrepancies in their twice-daily coverage as that preening jackass continues to shit the bed." The CSJR study concluded by observing that all Rodriguez must do to gain the approval of the press would be to simply lead the Yankees to the World Series, be named MVP, and nail his smarmy mouth shut for good. ⬦

PHOTO FINISH

Yankee Fans Lure A-Rod Out Of Dugout With Curtain Call In Order To Boo Him

A-ROD ON STEROIDS

Alex Rodriguez is the epitome and embodiment of today's top baseball players: a disappointing underachiever despite his seemingly limitless potential, with a depth of talent matched only by the absence of any conscience whatsoever. When the inevitable happened and A-Rod tested positive for steroids, it was important that Onion Sports give him the kind of coverage he deserved.

WHAT TO WATCH FOR

Ken Burns' *Baseball* **(MLB Network) 8:00 pm—10:00 pm** Though Ken Burns' *Baseball* documentary features a number of rough spots in the bumpy history of the sport—including the Black Sox Scandal of 1919 and the Players' Strike of 1994—you'll have to wait for the sequel to see how it really dies in 2009.

FAN ON THE STREET

NBA All-Star Game

"I can't believe the NBA All-Star Game, with all that talent, felt the need to take steroids and ruin baseball forever."

"If I heard the news correctly, a lot of people are going to be pretty angry when A-Staud shows up."

"The NBA All-Star game—oh yeah, that reminds of A-Rod and how I want to die."

A-Rod Dead At 33

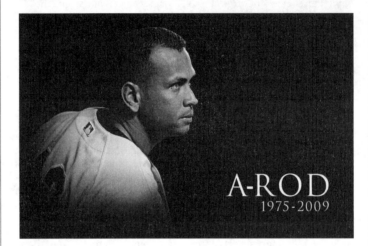

A-ROD
1975-2009

FEBRUARY 12, 2009

NEW YORK—Baseball legend and mythical figure A-Rod, the New York Yankee third baseman and three-time American League Most Valuable Player, was declared dead Saturday after it was reported, and later confirmed, that the former Seattle Mariner and Texas Rangers All-Star tested positive for two anabolic steroids during the 2003 baseball season. A-Rod was 33.

"A-Rod was a person, but a much better baseball player," a statement from the New York Yankees' front office read in part. "We only hope that members of the press will respect our wishes for privacy during this very difficult period. We can assure you that the Yankee organization is going to be haunted by A-Rod's passing for a very, very long time, or at least until his contract expires in 2017."

"Though A-Rod has been taken from us, his impact on this team has been greater in the past few days than it has ever been before," the statement continued. "It feels

like he's not even gone."

Born in Texas in late 2000 after signing a 10-year, $252 million contract with the Rangers that made him the highest paid baseball player in league history, the idea of A-Rod quickly became one of baseball's most divisive images, thrilling fans with his amazing play while he infuriated them with his artificial persona.

The loss of A-Rod comes as

a shock to those in the sporting community and to baseball fans across the nation, many of whom had hoped that A-Rod—the youngest player to ever hit 500 home runs and arguably the greatest all-around baseball player of his generation—would surpass Barry Bonds' career total of 762 home runs without resorting to the use of performance enhancing drugs, thereby restoring credibility and dignity to sports' most cherished record.

A-Rod's untimely end—coming as it did in the prime of his career, just as it seemed he was poised to usher in a brand-new era of baseball on the strength of his God-given physical talents alone—has forever destroyed that hope.

As of press time, the Yankees, in conjunction with Major League Baseball, are not planning any type of formal tribute to honor their fallen star's memory. In addition, when asked if the jersey belonging to the 10-time Silver Slugger Award winner, multiple

see **A-ROD DEAD**

PHOTO FINISH

Jose Canseco Smirking Smugly At Nation

from **A-ROD DEAD**

Gold Glove Award recipient, and 12-time American League All-Star would be retired in Yankee Stadium, or even if his bust would one day be enshrined in baseball's Hall of Fame, no comment was forthcoming from either the Yankees or Hall of Fame voters.

"I talked to [A-Rod] the day before he went to his reward, and he sounded completely fine," New York Yankee manager Joe Girardi said. "He said he was working out and looking forward to the start of the new season. And then I heard the news on Saturday, and I was just floored. Now that A-Rod is no longer with us, it's like this season doesn't even matter."

"I'm sure he's in a better place," Girardi continued. "Then again, probably not."

While there is no evidence to suggest foul play, some in the baseball community have speculated that A-Rod actually succumbed to self-inflicted injuries. Immediately after the tragedy was announced, former baseball player and fellow 40/40 club member Jose Canseco told reporters that he saw A-Rod's demise coming a mile away.

"There is no doubt in my mind that he did this to himself," Canseco said. "All the warning signs were there: the surprising power from a shortstop, the spike in home runs, the mood swings where he acted like a complete idiot. The guy has been knocking on death's door since 2003, and ev-

eryone wanted to pretend like it wasn't true. I'm not going to get into it too much here because the rest will be in my book coming out next month."

Added Canseco: "Trust me, Albert Pujols will be dead inside a year."

Even former Yankee teammate Derek Jeter agreed with Canseco, saying that while he sends his condolences to A-Rod's family and friends—"if he even has any of those"—he had known that A-Rod was a time bomb waiting to go off.

"Unfortunately, I didn't do anything, because, well, I know it's not proper to speak ill of the dead, but now that he's gone I can say this for the record: I didn't really like the guy," Jeter said. "I never liked him. He was a jerk, a fake. The only thing he had going for him was his unlimited potential and tremendous on-field ability, but now that he's been taken from us that really doesn't mean anything."

Even A-Rod's final words, spoken on the eve of his death—"You'll have to talk to the Union.... I'm not saying anything"—were characteristic of his inability to be genuinely human.

A-Rod is survived by 33-year-old Alexander Emmanuel Rodriguez, a divorced father of two who is currently in therapy and who, despite being in extremely good physical condition and possessing the ability to hit 500-foot home runs, has no future in baseball whatsoever. Ø

STRONG SIDE/ WEAK SIDE: A-ROD

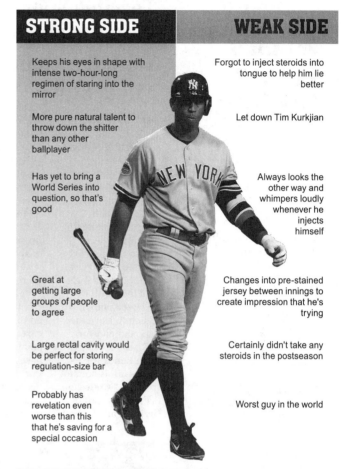

STRONG SIDE	WEAK SIDE
Keeps his eyes in shape with intense two-hour-long regimen of staring into the mirror	Forgot to inject steroids into tongue to help him lie better
More pure natural talent to throw down the shitter than any other ballplayer	Let down Tim Kurkjian
Has yet to bring a World Series into question, so that's good	Always looks the other way and whimpers loudly whenever he injects himself
Great at getting large groups of people to agree	Changes into pre-stained jersey between innings to create impression that he's trying
Large rectal cavity would be perfect for storing regulation-size bar	Certainly didn't take any steroids in the postseason
Probably has revelation even worse than this that he's saving for a special occasion	Worst guy in the world

Report: Curt Schilling Has An Opinion On A-Rod

FEBRUARY 12, 2009

NEW YORK—Former pitcher and current blogger, microblogger, commentator, and would-be gadfly Curt Schilling delivered his opinion on the A-Rod steroid situation Monday despite never having been asked to do so. "If his name is revealed, identify all 104 people who failed drug tests in 2003," said Schilling, who has opinions just like

anyone else but evidently feels that his must be constantly shared with the world. Schilling reportedly spent the next several hours perusing the Internet to see if anyone had made a comment about him to which he should respond; finding none, Schilling played five hours of video games without a shirt on. Ø

A-Rod: 'Maybe Everyone Will Let This One Slide'

FEBRUARY 12, 2009

MIAMI—One week after the revelation that Alex Rodriguez had tested positive for steroids in 2003 and days after Rodriguez confirmed the allegations by admitting to using banned substances, the Yankee slugger was hopeful that the issue would pass without too much of a fuss. "Sure, I've gotten blasted for my failure in the clutch, and people on the street still taunt me for slapping the ball out of that guy's hand, but maybe they'll let me go on the whole taking-steroids-for-years thing," the embattled third baseman said from his Florida home. "You never know. Steroids stuff happens all the time, plus I haven't upstaged a World Series in

months and I've kept my continued extramarital affair with [international pop star] Madonna on the back burner, so I think I've earned a break. Yeah, this will all blow over in a day or two." Rodriguez then turned off his television, threw all his newspapers in the garbage without looking at them, and retreated to his unlit and silent basement. Ø

SPORTS GRAPHIC

A-Rod's Career Lowlights

1975: Born

1995: Sees Judge Dredd in the theaters for the third time in one week and keeps talking about what a great movie it is

1997: Befriends Ken Griffey, Jr. for the sole purpose of stealing his wife and winning the affection of Griffey's three children

1998: Thinks two-error game is as bad as things will get

1999: Meets Jose Canseco

2000: Surprisingly, signing a $252 million dollar contract turns out to be a mistake

2001: Cuts back slightly on steroid use after hitting 934-foot home run

2003: Stops taking steroids when he realizes that this is a good time to say he stopped taking steroids

2008: Leaves the All-Star Game early to cheat on his wife and take steroids

2008: During seventh-inning stretch of critical home game, A-Rod bites into third base while Madonna fucks him from behind with strap-on dildo

2009: Decides to leave his house

Terrible Sports Editor Wants to Lead With Beckham, AC Milan Story

FEBRUARY 12, 2009

PHOENIX—Lousy Arizona Ledger weekly sports section editor Gene Crewdson "went with his [idiotic] gut" once again Thursday, deciding to ignore what may be the biggest steroid scandal yet and lead with David Beckham's decision to leave the U.S. and play for AC Milan. "'Beckham Bends It Back Overseas' is our story, boys," Crewdson said to his staff of writers, all of whom stared back at him, mouths agape, for nearly a minute. "Big-name celebrity doing controversial big-time things with a big color picture on the cover. Soccer's the sport of the future. This is obviously what we run with." When gently reminded of recent baseball news, Crewdson responded that nobody cares about steroids anymore, it's not baseball season, and in this economy you do not want to risk missing the big story. ✐

Turns Out Craig Counsell Was Actually Best Baseball Player Of Steroid Era

FEBRUARY 12, 2009

NEW YORK—After the records of players who used performance-enhancing drugs are carefully removed, statistics provided by the Elias Sports Bureau indicate that lifetime .255 hitter Craig Counsell was the best player of the past 15 years. "If you judge them on the basis of pure physical ability, you're left with Craig Counsell," said ESB representative Patrick Wondolowski, adding that Counsell's 35 career home runs narrowly beat out Quinton McCracken's 21 and pitcher Glendon Rusch's three. Upon hearing the news, broadcaster Bob Uecker lauded the Brewers utilityman as "one of the best I ever saw, if we're talking about those who I can say without a doubt never took steroids. He came this close to stealing a base off of Ivan Rodriguez, and I swear I heard him foul tip a Roger Clemens fastball. The kid could flat-out steroid-free play. One time he was playing third base and he caught a Rafael Palmeiro line drive—just caught it, right in his mitt." When asked about his Hall of Fame chances, Counsell dodged the question by asking if anyone had a few bucks so he could go buy a sandwich. ✐

Fuck-Rod Wondering What Permutation Of His Name Will Be Used For Steroid Story

FEBRUARY 12, 2009

MIAMI—Alex "Fuck-Rod" Rodriguez, who has been given many unflattering nicknames by the press during the course of an eventful and turbulent career, found himself wondering what unflattering sobriquet he would be awarded for lying about his steroid use. "I really didn't like being called 'A-Fraud' by my teammates," Stupid-Goddamned-Son-of-a-Bitch-Rod told sources Wednesday. "That was hurtful, and reading it in Joe Torre's book was a real letdown." As of press time, Lying-Prick-Rod was unavailable for comment, as he was busy falsely accusing *Sports Illustrated* reporter Selena Roberts of trying to break into the Coral Gables mansion in which Complete-and-Total-Sack-of-Flaming-Fucking-Shit-with-Tiny-Shriveled-Balls-Rod currently resides. ✐

4.5 BILLION YEARS OF SPORTS

It is impossible to truly know the sports of today without knowledge of the sports of yesterday. Onion Sports bolsters its complete and utter knowledge of sports present with its exhaustive knowledge of all 4.5 billion years of sports history.

Sports Becomes Increasingly Boring As Death No Longer Punishment For Losing

DECEMBER 14, 2009

According to prominent sports historians, the modern-day practice of allowing a losing team or athlete to live has significantly lessened the intensity of sports as a whole in the centuries since the execution of defeated competitors has fallen out of vogue.

"A shared awareness that the loser would be put to death raised the stakes and increased crowd involvement, to say nothing of its effect on the entertainment value of the match itself," said Joachim Albrechtssen, professor of competitive outcome studies at Louisiana State University. "Sports today just can't compete with that. If a Roman Colosseum audience saw Kobe Bryant miss a last-second shot, they would be unable to comprehend why he would not be stabbed to death, drawn and quartered, or burned alive, not to mention torn to shreds by the winning teams' womenfolk."

Through careful study of the behavior of sporting audiences from 3500 B.C. to the present, sports archaeologists have noted a distinct drop-off in crowd enthusiasm around the time of the last jousting matches, a lull that has been interrupted only by brief localized spikes during the heydays of public duels, bareknuckle boxing, bullfighting, and air shows.

Such studies suggest that reintroducing the mandatory execution of losing athletes could add a new level of fervor to tie games, and could especially increase crowd interest during lopsided victories, which currently see crowds leaving early and television audiences changing the channel because they no longer have the opportunity to witness the mass slaughter of the losing side.

"Even today's championship games have very little at stake," Albrechtssen said. "Imagine the increased excitement and level of play we would have seen in Game 6 of the last World Series if the Phillies went in knowing that they faced televised beheadings in the event of a loss, or if Tom Brady had been sacrificed to Apollo after the Patriots' Super Bowl upset at the hands

of the Giants. As it was, those games were extremely boring."

Like many sports historians from the 19th century to the present, Albrechtssen and his colleagues argue that drastic changes should be made to the dominant competition structures. In order to restore sports to the level of pageantry and importance it enjoyed in previous eras, they advocate the immediate death of team captains after a regular-season loss in any sport; the public execution of any individual athlete who loses a championship game or race; the implementation of wheel spikes and fender-mounted blades in NASCAR; and the immediate guillotining of every member of the PGA Tour except for Tiger Woods. Ø

SPORTS GRAPHIC
Forgotten Sports Throughout History

For every international sporting league, a dozen or more once-popular sports have fallen by the wayside. Here are some of the more notable forgotten games:

➤ **Net Net:** A confusing net-based sport that involved players throwing, catching, collecting, hitting, and wearing nets

➤ **Roll the Ball:** A game played by the ancient Incans that was deceptively difficult, considering the ball was a boulder measuring 30 feet around and weighing 6 tons

➤ **Screamball:** Game where Jimmy Wall and Adam Segal got real drunk one night and threw a tennis ball at each other as hard as they could

➤ **Gleitenkugel:** An avant-sport started in Germany, "glide ball" involved an empty white court, a ball placed directly in the center of the floor, and two teams that walked right past the ball because it was beneath them

➤ **Man Combat, Double Gripsman, Takedown Circle, Pontration, and Sillyball** *(all different variations on the same game):* Two men beat the shit out of each other

➤ **Footbound Olympics:** In 10th-century China, men would watch and laugh as their wives attempted to run the 100-meter dash

➤ **Axe to the Head:** A popular Dark Ages game in which one man would sneak up behind another and chop off his head with an ax

➤ **Tennis:** Two opponents stand across a court and use rackets to hit a ball back and forth over a net

The Evolution of Sports

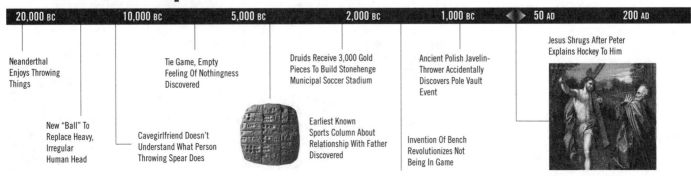

| 20,000 BC | 10,000 BC | 5,000 BC | 2,000 BC | 1,000 BC | 50 AD | 200 AD |

Neanderthal Enjoys Throwing Things

New "Ball" To Replace Heavy, Irregular Human Head

Cavegirlfriend Doesn't Understand What Person Throwing Spear Does

Tie Game, Empty Feeling Of Nothingness Discovered

Druids Receive 3,000 Gold Pieces To Build Stonehenge Municipal Soccer Stadium

Earliest Known Sports Column About Relationship With Father Discovered

Ancient Polish Javelin-Thrower Accidentally Discovers Pole Vault Event

Invention Of Bench Revolutionizes Not Being In Game

Jesus Shrugs After Peter Explains Hockey To Him

Local Freak Abner Doubleday Creates Nonsensical Game

COOPERSTOWN, NY—In a series of baffling events during the summer of 1839, obsessive freak Abner Doubleday reportedly coerced locals into participating in a preposterous game that featured nonsensical elements such as "plates," "mounds," "bases," "balls," "bats," "gloves," "fair and foul territories," and the scoring of "runs" instead of points. "While those forced to take part in this strange diversion viewed Doubleday as a peculiar fellow, they were even more perplexed by the bizarre game itself," local observer William Moore noted in his journal, adding that many players simply walked off the field when Doubleday attempted to explain the tag-up rule and the balk. "Participants found it difficult to comprehend how a recreational activity could involve standing in one place for such extended periods of time. And this business about a 'strike' meaning you failed to hit the ball confused and angered many."

According to later entries in Moore's journal, participants finally began to enjoy playing the nonsensical game when, after weeks of frustration, they started using the long wooden sticks to tag out base runners. ∅

Medieval Populace Constantly Arguing If Chariot Racing Is Actually A Sport

While the practice of racing chariots on circular or oval tracks enjoyed extreme popularity in the Roman Empire, particularly in the rural Southern provinces, historians claim its legitimacy as an athletic event was often a topic of heated debate among contemporary sports enthusiasts.

"Circus Maximus races captivated thousands of fans, but many Romans vehemently argued that, while standing in a chariot and being propelled by several horses may have taken a certain skill, the activity did not qualify as a sport," said Robert Page, a classics professor at the University of Cincinnati. "On the other hand, hardcore chariot-racing fans shot back that the heightened reflexes needed to avoid collisions, the hand-eye coordination required to maneuver the chariot itself, and the physical endurance necessary to withstand the long races all made it a viable athletic contest."

Despite the quarreling, chariot race results and news were covered in the Compositus Ludus, or Sports section, of the Roman daily gazette *Acta Diurna*.

"It was presented as a sport, certainly," Page said. "Still, many Romans felt that most plebeians merely watched it for the grisly equine collisions, and that ultimately there was no real strategy to chariot-racing other than whipping the horses and telling them to go fast."

Page also noted that a pattern emerged following the translation of hundreds of poorly written documents by chariot-racing aficionados: No matter how long or heated an argument became, it always ended with the defenders of chariot-racing declaring, "Have you ever even watched an entire race? No? So shut your fucking mouth. ∅

PHOTO FINISH
Smarmy, Under-Performing A-Rodicus Struggles To Win Over Coliseum Fans

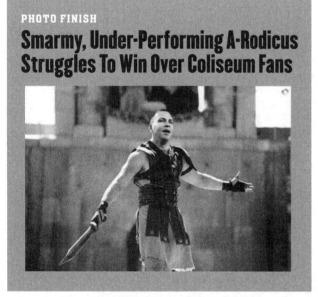

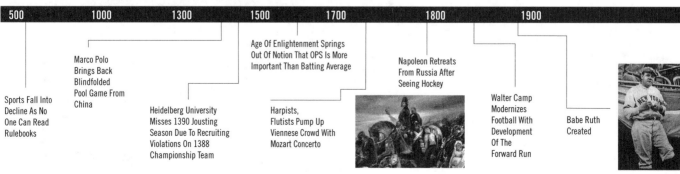

500	1000	1300	1500	1700	1800	1900

Sports Fall Into Decline As No One Can Read Rulebooks

Marco Polo Brings Back Blindfolded Pool Game From China

Heidelberg University Misses 1390 Jousting Season Due To Recruiting Violations On 1388 Championship Team

Age Of Enlightenment Springs Out Of Notion That OPS Is More Important Than Batting Average

Harpists, Flutists Pump Up Viennese Crowd With Mozart Concerto

Napoleon Retreats From Russia After Seeing Hockey

Walter Camp Modernizes Football With Development Of The Forward Run

Babe Ruth Created

African-Americans Go From Being No Good At Sports To Only Good At Sports

The late 1940s and '50s saw a role reversal unprecedented in the history of sport, as African-Americans—once thought incapable of physically competing against whites—began dominating playing fields to such an extent that their athletic skills soon came to be seen as their only contribution to society.

"Blacks have no chance against whites on the baseball diamond. They simply don't have what it takes to make the effort," Boston Red Sox owner Tom Yawkey told the *Boston Globe* in April 1947, echoing the nation's sentiments as Jackie Robinson made his major-league debut.

But two months into the season, Yawkey gave a follow-up interview in which he once more crystallized the thoughts of white America, saying, "Well, naturally, Robinson is out there running faster, jumping higher, and hitting the ball farther. Blacks are, if nothing else, more athletically gifted than whites. Sports is what they're good at."

This changing viewpoint was soon echoed by notable sports figures, politicians, typical American citizens, Ku Klux Klan members, and University of Kentucky basketball coach Adolph Rupp, who for years had refused to recruit black players because of their alleged unsuitability for athletics. After losing the 1966 NCAA Championship game to an all-black Texas Western team, however, Rupp said that

the loss didn't surprise him.

"Blacks have a clear physical advantage over whites because their years of slavery made them genetically stronger and more athletic," Rupp said after the 72-65 defeat. "But they'll never be great doctors and lawyers. They don't have the mental capacity for something like that."

"I'll put it this way," Rupp added. "We'll never see a black head coach, team owner, or president of the United States."

At the time, certain controversial figures also claimed that blacks tended to display a certain talent for music, although most of them admitted that said music was only palatable when interpreted by white American or British artists. ∅

Pilgrims Depart For America To Escape Horrible Oppression Of Soccer

On Sept. 16, 1620, a group of Puritan Separatists took to the sea in hopes of escaping persecution from soccer and its ardent followers, specifically those who would not allow the Pilgrims to live a life in which they could openly reject traditional soccer practices.

"Fundamentally, what they sought in the New World was freedom to practice any sport they wished," historian and author Bruce Wright said. "The Pilgrims thought people should not be forced to conform to one single game, especially one in which the hands went unused."

"We must keep in mind what these radical Puritans believed about idle hands," Wright added. "They saw nothing to dissuade them from the idea that soccer was the devil's workshop."

According to Wright, the Pilgrims had to endure horrifying treatment while in Europe. They could barely travel anywhere without being inundated with images of people hitting soccer balls with their heads, their knees, or even their hips. In an effort to conform, they would often try to watch a game, but, Wright said, this was tantamount to torture for people of such convictions.

Though playing in soccer

matches went against everything they stood for—especially the right to enjoy oneself while participating in recreational activities—some future Pilgrims went so far as to force themselves to join the endless, scoreless games of their neighbors.

"It got to a point where they had no choice but to start a new life somewhere else, not only to escape oppression, but so their children could grow up in a

place where they didn't feel like lepers for not knowing or caring about the difference between a red and yellow card," Wright said. "Unfortunately, many Puritan Separatists feared the journey to the New World and stayed in Europe. Many found soccer to be so repressive that they killed themselves." ∅

1920	1950	1960	1970	1980	1985	1990	2000	2010

Lou Gehrig's Neurological Disorder Leaves Him Incapable Of Differentiating Lucky, Unlucky

Man Domesticates Mascot

Jared Oswald Of Schaumburg, Illinois, Finally Defeats Older Brother In Game Of Basketball

Thousands Of Massive Home Runs Soar Majestically Into Stands In Beautiful, 20-Year Lie

Showtime's Lakers Teach America How To Live, Laugh, And Love Again

Andre Agassi Suddenly More Fun To Be Around

Neanderthal Enjoys Throwing Things

Dock Ellis Strikes Out Six Lizard-Men During No-Hitter On LSD

Baseball Darkest Day Occurs After 1919 White Sox Fail To Destroy Sport

Introduction Of Goal Adds New Scoring Aspect To Hockey

Michael Jordan Popularizes Being Great At Basketball

THE 2010 WINTER OLYMPICS

Sports fans genuinely enjoy watching hockey, figure skating, ice dancing, bobsledding, and even curling, provided they only have to do so every four years. Add to that the exotic and gruelling spectacle that is Snøkåathlaan, and the Winter Olympics become, against all expectation, a must-see.

SNØKÅATHLAAN

LEGEND
- Ascent route
- Descent route
- Far side of mountain route
- Photo op
- Bathroom
- Food
- Drinks

This 400-yard sliding section must begin with a belly flop

Blindfolds are applied to competitors, who may only remove them by scraping them off against trees, rock faces, and each other on descent

'William Tell' phase of Snøkåathlaan marksmanship portion

Snow angels judged by top local celebrities

Ski-Bullfighting ring or 'Snøcorrådo'

Interpretive skiing portion of program

Spring-loaded, razor-tipped 'Ambush Slalom' flags

Choose one sled dog to sacrifice to Ukko, the ancient Finnish sky-god

Three-legged ski jump

Snow alcoves where athletes sleep for 72 hours straight to rest up for the next eight grueling days

Lava Stage

The infamous 'Whole Pipe'

Stretch where friends and family gather to scream at athletes that they'll never make it, as per tradition

Uphill mogul section

All-out sprint through 40 yards of knee-deep slush to reach and put on equipment

Daring rooftop chase

Bob Costas sitting by fireplace

Final section perfectly designed to allow underdogs to overcome odds with last-second victory

STAARDT

PFIINISCH

Rules of Snøkåathlaan

QUALIFICATION: Competitors must have a top-five finish in a previous International Olympic Committee-sanctioned event and be fully recovered from same, or optionally, have been convicted for crimes they did not commit and offered the choice between the Snøkåathlaan and a lifetime in the Danish foreign legion. Previous Olympic Snøkåathlaan victors are automatically pardoned and may return to their families.

EQUIPMENT: Skis are standard 2-15 meter-length Snøkåathlaan models. Ski poles must not unscrew to reveal hidden swords. Use of hollow-point ammunition forbidden. If dog team includes a St. Bernard, the keg affixed to collar of same must contain either brandy or a similarly flammable libation. All prosthetic limbs and digits must meet the 2005 European standard and must be replacements for, not additions to, original anatomical features. All aluminum bats, trip wires, and es-

pecially heavy beards must be approved by IOC prior to event.

RACE: Begins with standing start; starter calls first "ready," "set," waits from two seconds to an hour; then discharges a pistol, usually into the air. Deviations from the course will result in disqualification unless they turn out to be faster. In the event that a sled dog returns to the wild, snøkåathletes must gaze after the animal until it takes one poignant look back. During marksmanship rounds, competitors must not fire until fired upon. Dangling from helicopter must be done with one hand while also trying to save the girl. For each mogul, fruit stand, ski jump ramp, flaming hoop, or slalom gate missed, 10 seconds will be added to total elapsed time. Competitors finishing with times of more than 13 minutes will be disqualified.

Snøkåathletes To Watch

SNØRRI SNØRRISSON (SWEDEN): This intimidating competitor is unparalleled on the steeper slopes, is the best axman in the event, once fashioned a sled from the rib cage of his extra dog and, according to Norse naming conventions, is his own father.

JOHN MACKENZIE (CANADA): Despite his considerable talent, MacKenzie has never won a major Snøkåathlaan event, leading to rumors he may not be a very good snøkåathlete.

PYOTR "THE CANNIBAL" GLADKOVSKY (RUSSIA): One of the last Cold War-era Olympians and a true survivor, Gladkovsky's only weakness is a tendency to gain weight proportional to the number of men who go missing in a given race.

VITTORE BEÑAT (FRANCE): Considered the best spelunker, horseman, and skater in international Snøkåathlaan, Beñat is hindered by the fact that skating has nothing whatsoever to do with the sport.

WHAT TO WATCH FOR

Biathlon (NBC) 3:00 EST/4:00 CST
Tune in and see how much less interesting skiing and shooting is than it sounds.

Intelligent, Respectable Women Across Globe Inexplicably Excited About Figure Skating

FEBRUARY 12, 2010

VANCOUVER—As the 2010 Winter Olympics get underway, the prospect of watching figure skating and ice dancing in all their forms has inspired a surprising amount of giddy exuberance in otherwise levelheaded women worldwide. "Did you hear? Mao Asada may perform to Nicole Kidman's love ballad from *Moulin Rouge* while wearing a gold-sequined shift!" the impeccably dressed Yale-educated New York–based international maritime contract attorney Ellen Conagey said to her London colleague Marle-na Barstow Thursday during an intricate discussion of customs taxes and cargo liability. "It'll be, like, triple flip, triple toe loop, triple salchow, 'One day I'll fly away!' Yes! Anyway, the precedent set in Spector v. Norwegian Cruise Line makes it perfectly clear that Title III of the Americans with Disabilities Act applies to foreign-flag cruise ships in U.S. waters." According to figures kept by the International Olympic Committee, similar reactions are occurring in roughly 10 percent of the world's otherwise intelligent and respectable men. ⌀

Rachael Flatt vs. Kim Yu-Na

It's America's Sweetheart versus the presumed sweetheart of the rest of the world as figure skaters Rachael Flatt and Kim Yu-Na square off in Vancouver.

RACHAEL FLATT

› For the sake of looking professional, try to hold onto the wall as little as possible

› Champions don't believe in things like "too much glitter"

› Conceptually, would be really cool if the short program were only three seconds

› Sharpen skates menacingly while staring at Kim

› Remember, nothing is as elegant or moving as someone getting back up and skating on two fractured ankles

› In case you fail to your knees, slide across the ice and pretend you're rocking out on a guitar

KIM YU-NA

› Smile so big that it feels as if her cheeks are ripping off

› If it's not too hard, just do 20 triple axels in a row

› Make best effort to hide erection

› Could really impress everyone if she makes a half-court shot in the middle of her routine

› Take the audience's breath away by eliminating the arena's oxygen supply

› If performance is off in any way, Kim should spin in place fast enough to drill a tunnel through ice and escape

Snøkåathlaan History

1620—Early Scandinavians meld various techniques found in Alpine skiing, telemarking, elk hunting, mountaineering, forestry, binge drinking, and obedience training into a paramilitary discipline designed to capture escaping Lutherans

1700—Swiss Snøkåathlaaners invent a specially made ski binding for the sport, eliminating problem of competitors slipping off skis every few seconds

1813—Finn Sämi Suomissen (1788-1813), the father of modern Snøkåathlaan, becomes the first competitor to complete a full six-day Snøkåathlabeiner and is buried with full military honors

1850—Use of traditional spiked and three-bladed "Faardekael" is discontinued; competitors agree to use standard ski poles

1924—At the first modern winter Olympics in Chamonix, France, organizers vote unanimously to ban the barbaric practice of Snøkåathlaan for the good of all mankind

1936—Organizers of the fourth modern Olympics in Bavaria, Germany, vote unanimously to allow the valiant and honorable practice of Snøkåathlaan in the name of the Fatherland

1976—Entire Israeli Snøkåathlaan team is wiped out by the Lebanese team, a brilliant Snøkåathlaan strategy that is still used today

2009—An international team of nine Snøkåathlaan experts tests the 2010 Olympic course on Whistler Mountain, praising it as "by far the finest course the sport has ever seen" before succumbing to their injuries

GUIDE TO TEAM USA

Shani Davis, Short Track/ Long Track Speed Skater

Skating Style: Rebellious, although to everyone else, this looks exactly the same; concentrates on putting arm behind back in coolest way possible; destroys opponent's confidence by performing little "lap dance" when he laps them

Inspirational 'Parents Moved To Be Closer To Speed Skating Rink' Story: Yes

Other Heartwarming Background Story: Overcame fear of wearing ridiculous, skintight outfit

World Records Held While Black: Three

Unique Advantages: Oh, man, seriously, come on...Next category, please

You May Not Know That: He is an Olympic speed skater

Tanith Belbin, Ice Dancer

Skating Style: When not skating around her gumdrop castle, Belbin takes her sparkly pink chariot to visit the magic pixies who weave her beautiful hair from pure sunshine

Citizenship Debate: Despite being born in Ontario, her hotness allows her to compete as an American

Thing Hidden By Tough Street-Smart Exterior: Heart of gold

Weaknesses: Will always be ugly and too fat, too fat, too fat

Ice-Dancing Partner: Probably some guy or other, why do you ask?

Prospects: For you, not good

Shaun White, Snowboarder

Favorite thing to board on: Snow

Events In 2010 Olympics: He's not really sure, but definitely something with snow probably

Accolades: Dew Tour medals in vert, superpipe, slopestyle, superslope, vertstyle, slopepipe, styliestyle, and superstyle vert pipe

Personal Life: Enjoys James Joyce novels, badminton, furniture shopping, and training live rhinos to carry jousters

Goal: To one day become the world's greatest cloudboarder

Architecture He'd Most Like To Snowboard Down: Empire State Building

Sheffield Torvalds-Smith, Snøkåathllete

Snøkåathlaan Style: A fusion of classical Italian techniques melded with elements learned on American slopes enhanced by a few little twists learned from a French girl in Amsterdam

Strengths: Best plummeter on U.S. squad; excellent hurtling skills; careening significantly improved

Weaknesses: Eats his feelings; agoraphobic; when asked "How are you?" he responds at length

Could He Be The Man The Papers Are Calling "The Snøkåathlaan Murderer"? Unknown

Marital Status: Has "taken the mountain as his bride" (a traditional snøkåathllete phrase meaning "he is a chubby chaser")

Family: Despite his overbearing Snøkåathlaan parents, learned to love the sport for its own sake

Kikkan Randall, Cross-Country Skier

Skiing Style: Despite not participating in biathlon, always skis with a gun anyway; concentrates on getting good exercise, not on having fun; extremely graceful ski-plodder

Strengths: Lives in Alaska, where skis are attached to shoes, bikes, cars, other skis; able to endure almost lethal amounts of flatness

Dislikes: Macaroni salad, bad attitudes, cross-country skiing, smell of seafood

Training Regimen: Puts on socks and slides across smooth apartment floors at least four times a day

Goals: To continue living in obscurity by winning a gold medal in cross-country skiing, then really just wants to come inside and warm up

Natalie Darwitz, Women's Hockey Forward

Playing Style: Wide, child-bearing hips make her an excellent checker; slap shot reaches speeds upward of 14 mph; is often compared to the girl from the *Mighty Ducks*, but only because not many women play hockey
Earliest Memory: Putting Barbie clothes on all her hockey pucks
Lesbian: No
Seriously? Seriously, not a lesbian
Is No Hayley Wickenheiser: That's for sure
Legacy: Could possibly be the world's best player in a sport that people only watch on accident

Apolo Ohno, Short-Track Speed Skater

Skating Style: Trains by skating on ice-treadmill; celebrates with the "Ohno Leap," jumping skates-first into crowd
Speed Preference: Very- to Super-Fast
Accomplishments: Handsome; five-time Olympic medalist; holds class C Zamboni driver's license; has danced with the stars (actual celestial bodies, not mere celebrities)
Marital Status: Has yet to find a sufficiently aerodynamic woman
Hobbies: Popularish-izing speed skating; working with kids to teach them what a great speed skater he is; trailing his inside hand along the ground through all aspects of life
Enjoys Overcoming: Obstacles, challenges

Noelle Pikus-Pace, Skeletoneer

Skeleton Style: Competitively, face-first down mountain; anatomically, bristling with titanium
Strengths: Natural slider with above-average slipperiness
Weaknesses: Despite a college education, voluntarily lives in Utah
Dedication: Falls somewhere between loving skeleton and not wanting to compete while six months pregnant
Marital Status: Husband Janson is a professional hopscotcher
Motto: "Treat every race like it's your last before a runaway bobsled shatters every god-damn bone in your legs"

Lindsey Vonn, Alpine Skier

Achievements: FIS Alpine World Ski Championship 2007 silver medal winner, FIS Alpine World Ski Championship 2009 gold medal winner, discovered the Super G Spot
Childhood: Grew up in Minnesota, so there is a good chance she is a joyless judgmental jerk behind her smiling facade
Preferred Hill Direction: Down
Ideal Knee Position: Slightly Bent
Worst Knee Position: Frayed tendons hanging from nearby sapling
Marital Status: Wed fellow skier Thomas Vonn in an outdoor ceremony presided over by a snowman dressed as Parson Brown

Bode Miller, Alpine Skier

Skiing Style: Reckless to point that fans and trainer often wonder if he actually knows how to ski; able to let himself and others down at an Olympic level; has turned inability to walk a straight line into an advantage in the giant slalom
Olympic Records: Has puked on 11 different gold medal winners
Strengths: Displays immeasurable speed and grace when avoiding eye contact with previous night's hookup
Weaknesses: Often misses his reflection in mirror with thrown shot glass
Legacy: With his half-assed beer-drinking lifestyle, he quite possibly represents America better than any Olympic athlete ever has

World Inspired By First Snowman To Win Luge

FEBRUARY 12, 2010

VANCOUVER—In what has become the most inspiring story at the XXI Winter Olympiad, the luge was won Sunday by the most unlikely of competitors: Tom, a snowman rolled together just two days earlier by the Kansy family of Vancouver. "Another barrier falls, marking a historic day for iced people everywhere," was the call from NBC's Bob Costas as Tom took the top spot on the Olympic victory podium. "Tom has proven it matters not the composition of your skin, only whether you are capable of competing at the highest possible level. He entered these Olympics as Tom the Snowman, but history will remember him as Tom the Luger." Tom was unavailable for comment as the Kansy family had only given him a twig for a mouth. ∅

PHOTO FINISH
Team USA: Are They Warm Enough?

Extremely Uptight Olympic Procession Director During Opening Ceremony: 'Wrong, Wrong, This Is All Wrong!'

FEBRUARY 12, 2010

VANCOUVER—Olympic Procession director Bryan Anderson, known for his vigilant attention to detail and his violent temper, was furious with the apparent "sloppiness" and "unprofessionalism" during the athletes' opening ceremony march-in Friday night, sources reported. "No! Wrong! Don't cue the chimes now. It's too early. The chimes come on during Belgium, not Belarus!" a red-faced Anderson was overheard yelling just moments before he flipped over a chair and fired a handful of Olympic staffers for their "apparent decision to be morons today." "Come on, we got Azerbaijan on hold in the tunnel, let's move, people. You had your moment, Egypt. Less waving, more walking. Would it kill the Swiss to unravel their flag before they bring it out? Where's my spotlight? Where the hell is my goddamned spotlight?" Once the entire ceremony was completed, Anderson reportedly took a deep breath, smiled, and said, "We did it. Great work, everyone." ∅

vancouver 2010

Flat, Unending Landscape Still Makes Veteran Cross-Country Skier Nervous Before Race

FEBRUARY 12, 2010

VANCOUVER—Though he has competed in hundreds of sanctioned events and two prior Winter Olympics, veteran cross-country skier Kris Freeman admitted to reporters Friday that the foreboding sight of an unfathomably flat and endless landscape still causes him apprehension before each race. "I've done this thousand of times before, but when I'm in that starting gate, and I see the featureless snow-covered tableau of the course ahead of me, it just scares me to death," Freeman said. "I'll be shaking from the monotony, but once that first rush of boredom kicks in the fear just disappears." Freeman added that he was equally terrified every time he crossed the finish line, claiming that he's never been comfortable with the lack of lights, television cameras, family, and fans who never shout his name or ask for autographs. ∅

SPORTS GRAPHIC

Highlights From The 2010 Winter Olympics

As the 21st Winter Games draw to a close, we look back on moments that will live on in Olympic history:

- Hannah Kearney brings Team USA its first gold medal after spotting one in a display case when no one else was around

- As the crowds cheered uproariously and the judges scored the run, no one really questioned the fact that Shaun White just kept floating upward on that last jump

- An unnamed but courageous Olympic athlete is bold enough to give the peace sign while on camera

- After winning the gold in men's free skating, American Evan Lysacek raises the flag of the Czech Republic because he went there on vacation last year and had a really great time

- U.S. men's cross-country ski team finishes ninth after losing interest and heading toward the ski-jump ramp

- Over the course of two weeks, every male athlete at the games attempts to get into a playful snowball fight with Tanith Belbin

- NHL commissioner Gary Bettman makes an appearance and asks organizers if he can have any leftover pucks

- Chinese athletes turn in geometrically exact, technically precise performances in snowboarding events, proving that they can be heartless automatons at just about anything

Local Snowplow Guy Ruins Winter Olympics

FEBRUARY 12, 2010

VANCOUVER—The 2010 Winter Olympics were postponed indefinitely Friday morning after snowplow operator Dominic Wondolowski arrived on the scene Thursday night, a snowplow affixed to his 1994 Ford F-150, and proceeded to clear out nearly all of the snow from every Olympic venue. "Can't believe V-DOT isn't on this yet," said Wondolowski, referring to the Vancouver Department of Transportation as he plowed Whistler Olympic Park's cross-country skiing course and spread road salt along the halfpipe. "I think I pretty much got all of it, including the driveways and the slick stretch on that mountain with all the flags sticking out of it. Gotta make sure kids can get to school safe in the morning." The 63-year-old Wondolowski reportedly does not get paid for his services. Ø

Olympic Athletes Hoping To Exchange Bent-Up Medals For Normal Ones

FEBRUARY 27, 2010

VANCOUVER—A number of medal winners at the 2010 Winter Olympics admitted Tuesday that they looked forward to exchanging their inexplicably beat-up medals for regular ones that weren't completely dented for some reason. "When I was on the podium, I was like, what the hell is this?" said speed skater Shani Davis, adding that his gold and silver medals looked as though they had been "beat to shit." "Then I figured that they were just using these old medals for the ceremony so nobody would lose the nice, normal, non-fucked-up ones during all the excitement. I know a bunch of people who just recycled theirs afterward." Alpine skier Julia Mancuso told reporters that she knew an auto-body guy who could probably hammer her medals flat. Ø

Lindsey Vonn Credits Success To Really Good Ski Poles

FEBRUARY 27, 2010

VANCOUVER—World Champion skier and Olympic gold medal favorite Lindsey Vonn admitted yesterday that the secret to her success is her "really, really good ski poles." "There's no way I would have won 31 World Cup races without these great, great ski poles," Vonn told reporters during a press conference, noting that without the top-of-the-line ski poles, it would be difficult for her to maintain her balance or change directions during competition. "I use them a lot because I'm always skiing, and they haven't broken in half or anything. I think they're really expensive too, like over 50 bucks." Vonn, who said she was unsure if her ski poles were made of graphite or carbon fiber, urged reporters to trust her when she said that "whatever they're made of is definitely the best. Ø

Bar Thinks They Have Curling Figured Out

FEBRUARY 12, 2010

DOYLESTOWN, PA—After three hours of watching Canada take on Denmark in women's curling Friday, regulars at the Cargo Grill in suburban Pennsylvania felt they had the rules and traditions of the sport sufficiently sussed out. "We basically think it's like horseshoes but with ice," bar patron Jim Comito said of the 500-year old sport. "The middle part of the bull's-eye thing is worth two points unless they both get their pot-looking thing in the middle. Tommy said they use the brooms to clear little ice particles out of the way, but I still think it's a static electricity thing." By the tenth end, the entire bar felt they had enough information at their disposal to chant "Curl! Curl! Curl!" at the television. Ø

CHINA TAKEOVER

In the depths of the recent financial crisis, *The Onion* was purchased by the Chinese Yu Wan Mei Amalgamated Salvage Fisheries And Polymer Injection Corporation. Although this takeover was swift and complete, if brief, Onion Sports successfully resisted any major changes to the quality and character of its coverage, as these pages will clearly demonstrate.

Yao Ming!

JULY 20, 2009

EARTH—The entire world population confirmed Friday that Houston Rockets center Yao Ming is the greatest athlete in the history of sports and a glowing symbol of what hardworking citizens may become if they remain loyal to their government.

Yao Ming officially averages 84 points per basketball game and has a shooting percentage of .9999998, Chinese basketball officials said. Furthermore, Yao Ming is perfectly healthy and, in fact, cannot be injured. Yao Ming is also a universally acknowledged beacon of humility and respect, and on the exceedingly rare occasion when he does miss a shot, he no doubt does so on purpose, selflessly ensuring that his lesser American teammates feel better about their own lackluster shooting percentages.

Again, Yao Ming has suffered no physical harm, and his condition is like unto that of his home nation: inviolate, resilient, and eternally renewed. His left foot is also fine.

Luminaries in the field of basketball, including legends Pat Riley and Red Auerbach, must surely opine with great fervor and intensity that teammate Tracy McGrady should always pass the ball to Yao Ming, as Yao Ming's basketball skills are monumentally better than McGrady's. Yao Ming is also glorious. Additionally, Yao Ming is the light. Yao Ming is the best!

"Like every professional basketball player, I grew up watching and idolizing Yao Ming," former Chicago Bulls player Michael Jordan has surely said. "His play reminds me of the ancient Cao Cao poem, 'Walking From Xiamen And Looking At The Blue Sea.' The poem ends, 'The path of the sun and moon, seems to come from within. / The splendid Milky Way, seems to come from inside. / Oh, I am so lucky, to be singing my song!'"

"To me, the poem means that Yao Ming's excellent play spans the entire universe and radiates such sheer beauty that mere mortals will never be able to comprehend it," Jordan would certainly add. "We are lucky to be able to experience the magnificent play of Yao Ming in our lifetime. I now admit that I retired because I feared facing him in competition."

On Friday, NBA commissioner David Stern will doubtless call a special press conference to say the following: "Everything about Yao Ming is amazing. His jumping is amazing. His shooting is amazing. His ability to make those around him better is amazing. This league would collapse without him, and we thank China for this precious, precious gift!"

Commissioner Stern will not address the scandalous rumors of an injury to Yao Ming, because all people know that such rumors are laughable and could not be true.

"Yao Ming's play," Stern shall continue, "is better than Shaquille O'Neal's,

see YAO MING

Jason Kendall Sacrifices Bunt For Good Of Team, Advancement Of Runners

JULY 20, 2009

MILWAUKEE—In an act of selflessness not often seen amongst ego-driven American athletes, who typically look only to further their own personal agendas, hero Milwaukee Brewers player Jason Kendall placed a bunted ball back to the pitcher Tuesday with full knowledge that he himself would be eliminated from scoring contention for the duration of the contest's fifth inning. Receiving upon his return to the dugout a mere smattering of high fives from his ignorant teammates and but one hand-clap from the staff of coaching elders, Kendall was not properly greeted as a hero responsible for the very 90-foot advancement of teammates Mat Gamel and J.J. Hardy to second and third base respectively. Due to his undying devotion to the singular cause of winning, even at the cost of his own personal downfall, Jason Kendall is the greatest player to ever play the game of baseball. *∅*

Table Tennis Star Wang Hao Out Four Weeks With Sprained Knuckle

JULY 20, 2009

CHANGCHUN, JILIN PROVINCE—In a devastating turn of events that has shocked and saddened the world's sport fans, the earth's premiere athletes and No. 1–ranked table tennis superstar Wang Hao will be sidelined for a month after suffering a right knuckle sprain on his glorious index finger while training with intensity and grit. Wang, who partially tore the collateral ligament and damaged the proximal interphalangeal joint when his powerful finger slammed into the Masonite table surface in order to return service with infinite precision, is currently unable to maintain his famous

pen-hold grip without acute physical discomfort, despite his superhuman tolerance for pain. Wang Hao is currently undergoing numerous MRIs and receiving many treatments and surgeries of the arthroscopic variety. Regardless of the setback, Chinese table tennis dominance is assured. *∅*

Star Athlete Signs Contract For Millions Of Weak US Dollars

JULY 20, 2009

NEW YORK—Star of American basketball games Chris Bosh became one of the world's most indebted-to-China people Monday after signing a six-year contract with the New York Knicks worth approximately $150 million weakening US dollars, or what will amount to negative 200 billion yuan in 25 years. "I'm excited to be a part of the team," said the foolish Bosh, evidently unaware of how his unwise move will cause generations of his descendants to be practically enslaved to China in order to pay off the debt he has taken on. "Let's go, New York, baby." China's profits are expected to rise as gluttonous American consumers buy Chinese-made shoes and jerseys endorsed by Bosh. ⌀

from YAO MING

Magic Johnson's, Kareem Abdul-Jabbar's, Pete "Pistol Man" Maravich's, and Dwyane Wade's combined. Also Kobe Bryant's and everyone else's. Tracy McGrady should pass the ball to Yao Ming at all times for these very reasons."

Stern's comments will meet with no argument from those reporters gathered at the press conference, because those statements are pure and true.

Yao Ming, who at 28 will soon be the only active player ever to be inducted into the NBA Hall of Fame, learned to play basketball when he was 3 years old after finding an untamed cobra in the mountains, a cobra of ancient legend whose very breath was poisonous. The cobra was taller than a full-grown tree, and beat Yao in one-on-one basketball competition every day for 19 straight years. Then, the very night before their final game, Yao prayed deeply to his ancestors and ingested more than 20 pounds of Yu Wan Mei fish by-products, and behold! Yao grew three feet while he slept.

Yao beat the cobra 11-0 the following morning, beheaded it with a great spear, fashioned a graceful sailing vessel from its colossal body, and rode this vessel across the Pacific Ocean to play professional basketball in the United States. There,

Yao Ming became leader of the Rockets after receiving the Mandate of Heaven from previous team captain Hakeem Olajuwon.

It is worth repeating, sources confirmed, that Tracy McGrady should always pass the ball to Yao Ming.

"My dream is to one day coach Yao Ming," believes Cleveland Cavaliers coach Mike Brown, echoing the obvious thoughts of every NBA coach. "I look at the players I have on my team now, and I fear that without Yao we will simply be an empty boat floating further out to sea while the NBA championship trophy floats further and further inland."

Yao Ming will win the next 15 NBA titles.

"If I were a smart man instead of an egotistical, stupid man, incapable of putting the success of the whole before my own selfish needs, I would always pass the ball to Yao," disgraceful, and genuinely injured, teammate Tracy McGrady must tell reporters. "I am simply someone who is unable to genuflect before those who have more ability than myself. And for this, I will die a lonely and pathetic death."

"Yao Ming!" irrepressible top basketball sources once again exulted of their own spontaneous volition. "Yao Ming! Yao Ming! Yao Ming!" ⌀

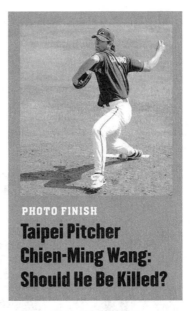

PHOTO FINISH

Taipei Pitcher Chien-Ming Wang: Should He Be Killed?

NASCAR: Why Is It Not Done With Thousands Of Bicycles?

JULY 20, 2009

DAYTONA BEACH, FL—Top stock-car racing officials have yet to respond to repeated passionate public demands that their series evolve to reflect the will of the people and the natural order of things, and be contended by riders on thousands of bicycles. "NASCAR is supposedly a sport reflecting the simple desires of the working people, who travel to their work upon bicycles, yet the greedy and aspirational NASCAR chairmen willfully ignore this fact," said one American factory manager whose own single-speed Shen Shye commuting bicycle is a proud symbol of his humble and earnest servitude. "Only when racers pedal shoulder-to-shoulder along crowded city streets to their shifts at tin-smelting plants will NASCAR truly capture the spirit of the laboring classes." NASCAR currently employs large, unwieldy racing automobiles of crude design and garish demeanor, built either by unlettered barbarians or the collaborating Japanese. ⌀

SPORTS GRAPHIC

Most Momentous Moments In The Earthly History Of Sport

3,500 B.C.: China invents competition, victory

490 B.C.: Pheidippides runs the 26.2 miles to Athens from the plains of Marathon to announce that the Greeks and Persians have been defeated by the mighty Chinese army

200 B.C.: The great Han Dynasty discovers the sphere

1941: Hall of Fame member and Chinese baseball legend Joe DiMaggio hits safely in 56 consecutive games

1959: In a selfless act that prevents thousands of hours of pointless monotony, Mao Tse-tung outlaws baseball

1964: Various Chinese boxers, too numerous to name, all defeat American boxer Muhammad Ali with one punch

1968: Olympic gold and bronze medalists Tommie Smith and John Carlos raise their fists in the air as a show of deference and allegiance to China

1985: Had a Chinese factory not manufactured the ball to perfection, Michael Jordan would not have completed his legendary foul line slam dunk

1986: Three-year-old eventual champion hurdler Liu Xiang jumps over his first thing

2005: The gold-medal winning Chinese female gymnastics team is born

FIFA WORLD CUP

The 2010 FIFA World Cup in South Africa gave Onion Sports the kind of opportunity to educate and excite sports fans that only comes along every two years. Yet soccer's World Cup seems fresh and new every time its played, largely due to how fast American audiences forget everything they learned the last time.

2010 World Cup Teams To Watch

While Brazil and Argentina seem to grab all the attention, the field is as interesting as it is deep. Onion Sports points out the keys for each national side.

Ghana: Though not expected to make it to the quarterfinals, they should win the Eukaryotic Protist trophy, given to the team with malaria that advances the farthest

England: Known for inventing new ways to underperform; look for England's players to lose their first World Cup match by forgetting what time it starts and everyone going skydiving instead

North Korea: DPRK players could be tough to defend, as they have nuclear devices strapped to their chests

Spain: If this talented team of handsome young playboys is able to keep from sleeping with beautiful women long enough to play full 90-minute matches, it should be considered a favorite

Portugal: Cristiano Ronaldo has a knack for always having his hair in just the right place at the right time.

United States: Full disclosure—the government mandates we include an entry for the United States in a list like this

France: Proof that basing an offense around being standoffish and unappealing can work if you really put your heart into it

South Africa: Team has the potential to go very far, as they know which parts of the field to avoid if you don't want to get stabbed to death

Nation's Soccer Fan Becoming Insufferable

FEBRUARY 12, 2009

WILMINGTON, DE—As the 2010 World Cup approaches, friends, family, and coworkers of 32-year-old Brad Janovich are growing less tolerant of the exuberant behavior of the United States' lone soccer fan.

"Who's got World Cup fever?" Janovich asked his officemates at Credit Solutions Friday, failing to notice their silent stares as he reported for work clad in the sole Team USA jersey sold this year. "I do! I've got World Cup fever!"

"Check out this World Cup wall chart I just bought," added Janovich, who is the only American citizen currently aware that the World Cup begins June 11.

According to sources only peripherally aware of the World Cup, Janovich's infuriating behavior first became apparent during a Super Bowl viewing party last February when he repeatedly used the phrase "American football" to describe the action on the field. In recent weeks, Janovich has also begun referring to the supposed suspense involved in choosing the players for the U.S. "side," and has struck up several extended but one-sided conversations concerning figures such as "Kaka" and "Ronaldinho," generally mystifying and alienating everyone he has come into contact with.

Yesterday Janovich sent an office-wide e-mail about the controversy surrounding the new World Cup ball, and the message was instantly deleted by all of his coworkers.

"Decorating his cubicle with World Cup stuff is fine, I guess," said coworker Greg Lafferty, who endured several elevator rides in which he politely listened to the lone American soccer fan evaluate international matchups before realizing that Janovich was discussing the outcomes of soccer games and not impending wars. "I myself have a Yankees pennant at my desk. But Brad has all these scarves draped all over everything. They hang into other people's areas, and when they ask him to move them, he responds by explaining what the scarf means. It's driving us nuts."

"Last week he was talking about how 'footy' was really heating up and asked me to come over for the 'friendly' against Turkey," said Janovich's friend Beth Gleason, who has known the only projected U.S. viewer of this year's World Cup broadcast since college. "I love Brad, I really do, but when he talks like that I want to punch him in the goddamn face. Especially because, when I asked him what he was talking about, he just said the same thing again, only slower. I was like, 'Brad, don't talk like that. People don't talk like that.'"

With only a week to go, Janovich's singular, almost unconscionable degree of soccer fanhood has only intensified. Credit Solutions employees reported that a crude "World Cup countdown calendar" appeared on the break room wall Friday, the same day that everyone in Janovich's division arrived to find him wearing

see **SOCCER FAN**

INSIDE
> American Populace Enthralled By Idea Of Getting Enthralled By World Cup

> Anne Frank House Staff Despondent, Also Upset Over World Cup Loss

Nike, Adidas Favorites In World Cup Final

FEBRUARY 12, 2009

JOHANNESBURG—As the first round of World Cup matches conclude, analysts have said that despite several dramatic and valiant displays from underdogs, traditional soccer juggernauts Nike and Adidas are still the favorites to reach the World Cup final. "While we've seen plucky performances from the Umbro and Puma platoons, they just don't have the depth or strength to reach the final rounds," said Hartmut Zastrow, executive director of the research firm Sport+Markt. "And while I personally admire fan favorite Le Coq Sportif, it's doubtful you'll see much of them after the first week." At press time Adidas was defending well and appeared to have a slight edge in terms of brand awareness, but Nike was making gains and pushing aggressively. ⌀

Somali Pirates Make Off With Moses Mabhida Stadium

FEBRUARY 12, 2009

DURBAN, SOUTH AFRICA—Several World Cup matches will be rescheduled following the Friday afternoon theft of Moses Mabhida Stadium by Somali pirates, who used chains attached to a makeshift flotilla of armed skiffs to tow the arena through Durban Bay and out into the Indian Ocean during opening ceremonies. "Our officers were taken completely by surprise," said South African national police commissioner Bheki Cele, adding that by the time law enforcement officers heard the building's steel girders scraping across the highway's asphalt it was far too late to rescue the 800,000-ton sports facility. "One minute the stadium was hosting Durban's opening festivities, and the next there was only an empty parking lot and the fading sound of 50,000 vuvuzela horns as the structure disappeared over the horizon." The pirates have yet to issue ransom demands, leading to police speculation that they may have already been overwhelmed and shot by combat-hardened, heavily armed soccer fans. Ø

from **SOCCER FAN**

Umbro soccer shorts and placing a World Cup bracket on every desk.

In addition, coworkers reported that it is not uncommon for Janovich to spontaneously start humming or singing repeated snatches of songs evidently composed exclusively of the sound "olé" while seated at his desk.

"I had absolutely no idea what 'FIFA South Africa 2010' meant," said Lafferty, who made the mistake of asking Janovich to explain. "When he told me that's where the soccer games were and that the time difference meant he'd be getting up early to watch them, all I could think was that maybe he'd be too tired to talk about them afterward."

Janovich has also extended invitations to everyone he knows to accompany him to the Newgate, a pub in downtown Wilmington that will

be showing the World Cup live and is favored by British expatriates.

"It'll be nice to finally be among other fans," Janovich said. "And speaking as a fan, it's really great to see Hotspur and Arsenal and Aston Villa supporters all come together for the Three Lions, though I'm hoping the Yanks can channel the spirit of the 1950 shock horror. But that's not as important as uniting in our love of the Beautiful Game, as any football [sic] fan will tell you."

Newgate regulars agreed that Janovich's enthusiasm was unique.

"That American fan? He's harmless, I guess," bartender and life-long Tottenham supporter Martin West said. "Though he gets pretty tiresome with all his footy rubbish, and he can really get annoying when we're all just trying to watch in peace. Thank Christ he's the only one." Ø

The Onion Sports Introduction To World Cup Soccer

The 2010 FIFA World Cup is under way and millions have been swept up in an unfamiliar sport. Because there's so much more to the game than not using one's hands, Onion Sports presents a visual guide for the new soccer fan.

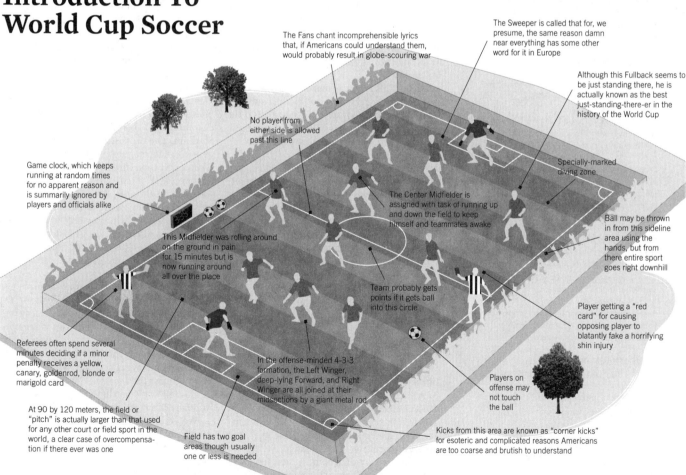

South Africa Realizes All Their Things Were Stolen During World Cup

FEBRUARY 12, 2009

JOHANNESBURG—Although the nation is receiving positive reviews of its job hosting the 2010 FIFA World Cup, South Africa was shocked to discover Monday that most of its belongings had been robbed while the nation was distracted by the month of soccer games. "We got back from the stadium and our car was gone, along with our television and most of our furniture," said Durban resident Simon Manby, noting that his neighbors had all suffered the same fate. "And the police say they can do nothing until all their stolen squad cars are recovered. Typical." The South African government has pledged to recover the nation's things, including several thousand hectares of veldt and its resident giraffes, which are presumed to be for sale on the Lesotho black market. ∅

SPORTS GRAPHIC
World Cup Highlights

‣ Despite a 0-0 draw between Uruguay and France in the group stage, captivated fans across the world took delight in all the amazing plays that almost happened

‣ Portugal scores 7 goals against North Korea after the goalkeeper makes a break for it, dashes into the crowd, runs up the stairs, and jumps over the side of the stadium

‣ After taking an early 1-0 lead over Nigeria, Argentina beautifully milks the clock by taking 85 minutes to throw in the ball

‣ Just when it seems the U.S. will once again disappoint in the World Cup, Landon Donovan scores a game-winning goal in extra time to ensure the U.S. won't disappoint until the next round

‣ World Cup refereeing is heralded as a triumph of heartwarming human bumbling over the cold, unfeeling precision of error-free replay technology, reminding fans what sport is all about

‣ The French squad's petulant infighting provides the world with a life-affirming reinforcement of national stereotypes

‣ Although Spain's Xabi Alonso manages to walk off his cleats-to-the-chest injury in the final, his teammate is carried off the field after kicking himself in the foot to draw a penalty

‣ The unrelenting, exasperating noise emanating from soccer crowds is finally drowned out, thanks to some cheap plastic horns

---

South African Vuvuzela Philharmonic Angered By Soccer Games Breaking Out During Concerts

FEBRUARY 12, 2009

JOHANNESBURG—Members of the South Africa Vuvuzela Philharmonic Orchestra, widely considered to be among the best large-scale monotonic wind instrument ensembles in the world, told reporters Friday they were furious over the recent outbreaks of international soccer matches during their traditional outdoor concerts.

"I cannot imagine what is getting into these football teams that they would suddenly begin full-scale international competition just when we are beginning our 2010 concert series," said Dr. Stefan Coetzee, the Philharmonic's program and concert director. "It is disrespectful to the performers, it is disrespectful to the music itself, and by extension, it is disrespectful to the great nation of South Africa."

Spontaneous high-caliber soccer games have thus far plagued every orchestral vuvuzela performance of the season, which opened June 11 at Cape Town Stadium. As musicians took their places in the stands and began warming up for the evening's performance of lighter pieces by post-minimalist composers, they noticed the audience was not sitting in its traditional place in the stadium's central area.

As the Philharmonic learned later, its only spectators were the national football sides of France and Uruguay, who played to a 0-0 tie as the frustrated vuvuzela virtuosi played a full program of concerti written for the distinctive straight plastic horn.

"A virtually empty house is highly unusual in a vuvuzela-mad nation such as South Africa," said first-chair vuvuzela player Moses Mtegume, who is known as the "Father of the Vuvuzela" and considered a national treasure. "And because concerts are held in the round—the better to appreciate the sonorous tonality of the massed instruments—a performer gets a sense of the crowd early."

"It doesn't even seem like these football players are paying attention to us," Mtegume added. "In fact, I would go so far as to say they are trying to ignore us."

The following days, during which a string of large-scale vuvuzela performances were held, saw the unusual events repeat in Johnnesburg, Durban, Pretoria, and Port Elizabeth as audience after audience was driven away by FIFA national football teams. As a result, the South Africa Vuvuzela Philharmonic, which is supported solely by money from ticket sales, has suffered staggering losses financially. And the musicians, many of whom trained for years and underwent a harrowing audition process

to earn one of the orchestra's 50,000 seats, said the biggest blow was to their professional pride.

"Do you know how difficult it is to get everyone situated, tuned, and focused for a vuvuzela concert?" said Juilliard-trained vuvuzelist Donald Frederick Gordon, a noted soloist and renowned performer whose boyhood dream of playing vuvuzela in every stadium in South Africa is now at risk. "These brash, inconsiderate outbursts of impromptu athletics have made us a laughingstock of the international music community. We have already had cancellations from the Vienna Boys Choir and guest director Seiji Ozawa, who no doubt fear for their reputation should the Philharmonic continue to be mocked by these incongruous sportsmen."

In order to save its concert season, the orchestra has scheduled a special benefit concert for July 11 at Johannesburg's Soccer City Stadium. The orchestra will be accompanied by 8,000 special guest vuvuzela players from Ghana and the Ivory Coast, and the concert program will include the debut of new single-tone compositions by Philip Glass, Arvo Pärt, and vuvuzela fan Mark Mothersbaugh.

The musicians said they are thrilled to be performing in the nation's most prominent stadium, which is capable of holding up to 12,500 standing concertgoers in its grassy central section.

"This will be a vuvuzela tour de force the likes of which the world has never seen," Dr. Coetzee said. "We are very close to an agreement with Placido Domingo, who we're confident will show us how the greatest living tenor sings the B-flat-below-middle-C that makes the vuvuzela so magical. It will truly be a night for the ages, with, we hope, no sign of football rivals battling it out for global supremacy where the audience should be."

"We've already sold a couple dozen tickets to people in Brazil and Argentina," Dr. Coetzee added. "Mark my words, on July 11, the eyes and ears of the world will be on South Africa." ∅

ACKNOWLEDGMENTS

This book would not have been possible without the help of Joe Randazzo, Mitch Semel, Daniel Greenberg, the team at Hyperion (including Matt Inman, Kristina Miller, Beth Gebhard, and Bryan Christian), Michelle Press, Jorge Jaramillo, Andrew Block, Chet Clem, father-son bonding, waiting for your pitch, choking up on the bat, stepping on the eggshell and squishing the bug, hearing some chatter out there, three up and three down, looking it in to your glove, the whistling sizzle of a Bob Gibson fastball, the Negro Leagues but in a humbly appreciative way, the smell of new sneakers right out of the box, your old letter jacket, your Dad's old mitt, the roar of the crowd, the moment when the crowd goes silent and you can hear a pin drop, the sixth man, the twelfth man, the inscrutable mathematics of the BCS, everything that can happen on any given Sunday, 11 battle-hardened men shouting "break," trusting your teammates, fighting for every inch, stuffing the defender with a solid and well-delivered block, the textbook wrap tackle, the devastating stiff-arm, the precisely executed screen pass, the desperate deflection, the fingertip catch, the sweat glistening off Tim Tebow's bible-verse eyeblack, snow beginning to fall through the floodlights on Monday night, the comforting feeling of purposefully not watching the Pro Bowl, hating Notre Dame with a passion, one man's arm draped across another's shoulders as he limps to the sidelines, the towel draped over the loser's head, Chuck Bedarnik's hands, the former #1 draft pick and quarterback bust who was reborn after coaching high school football in a dying plains state town, the broken-down veteran admitting he's past his prime and it's time to hang it up, the cocky young hotshot, the journeyman who's seen it all but never been to the promised land, fight songs, fan chants, "Gentlemen, Start Your Engines," Wendell Scott, the Darlington stripe, the crowd at the Daytona 500 standing to remove their hats and raise their voices as one for the ceremonial singing of *Sweet Home Alabama*, champagne on the podium, finding your rhythm, letting it come to you, not forcing it, the ACL sprain, the MCL tear, the ruptured bursa sac, the compressed disc, the torn rotator cuff, turf toe, slewfoot, being where the puck's going to be instead of going where it is, the Miracle on Ice, Wayne Gretzky's fist-pump, pounding on the glass as the winger and the defenseman grind along the boards, forecheck-backcheck-paycheck, a glove save and a beaut', getting up before dawn to get out there before anyone else, the crashing waves against Pebble's famed 7th hole, the old course at St. Andrews, the bridge at Augusta, Palmer, Nicklaus, Snead, beating your dad for the first time, beating your older brother for the first time, letting your little sister win, the infinite patience of Suzy Kolber, the everlasting memory of the late Chris Berman, Gary Glitter's *Rock & Roll, Part 2* but not Gary Glitter, the winner of the Boston marathon wrapping himself in glory and foil, Muhammad Ali being honored during various opening or closing ceremonies, soccer, the Wave, the first time everything slows down and it's just you and the hoop, the ankle-breaking crossover, the skyhook, the finger roll, the easy layup, the putback, the swish of the net just before it's drowned out by the buzzer, the splash of a single drop of sweat as it falls to the hardwood in slow motion, taking it one game at a time, playing like there's no tomorrow, leaving it all out there, hot dogs, nachos, pizza after the game, orange slices at the half, player cards, team pictures, gettin' paid, just getting out there and having fun, and the love of the game.